ALL · IN · ONE

CompTIA

CySA+™

Cybersecurity Analyst
Certification

EXAM GUIDE

(Exam CS0-003)

ALL·IN·ONE

CompTIA

CySA+™

Cybersecurity Analyst Certification

EXAM GUIDE

Third Edition

(Exam CS0-003)

Mya Heath, Bobby E. Rogers, Brent Chapman, & Fernando J. Maymí

Mc Graw Hill

New York   Chicago   San Francisco
Athens   London   Madrid   Mexico City
Milan   New Delhi   Singapore   Sydney   Toronto

CompTIA CySA+™ Cybersecurity Analyst Certification All-in-One Exam Guide, Third Edition (Exam CS0-003)

1 2 3 4 5 6 7 8 9   LCR   29 28 27 26 25 24 23

Library of Congress Control Number: 2023943838

ISBN   978-1-265-45243-8
MHID   1-265-45243-1

Sponsoring Editor Lisa McClain	**Technical Editor** Rob Shimonski	**Production Supervisor** Thomas Somers
Editorial Supervisor Janet Walden	**Copy Editor** Bart Reed	**Composition** KnowledgeWorks Global Ltd.
Project Manager Tasneem Kauser, KnowledgeWorks Global Ltd.	**Proofreader** Rick Camp	**Illustration** KnowledgeWorks Global Ltd.
Acquisitions Coordinator Caitlin Cromley-Linn	**Indexer** Kevin Broccoli	**Art Director, Cover** Jeff Weeks

Elijah,
You've unlocked within me an abundance of love, ignited joy, and guided me towards an inner peace I hadn't known before. Inspired by you, I strive to be the best mom and person I can be.
My deepest hope is that, one day, you will look back and find in me the same inspiration you spark within my heart each day.
With all my love,

–Mom (Mya)

I'd like to dedicate this book to the cybersecurity professionals who tirelessly, and sometimes thanklessly, protect our information and systems from all who would do them harm. I also dedicate this book to the people who serve in uniform as military personnel, public safety professionals, police, firefighters, and medical professionals, sacrificing sometimes all that they are and have so that we may all live in peace, security, and safety.

–Bobby

ABOUT THE AUTHORS

Mya Heath, CySA+, CISSP, GCFA, is a seasoned detection engineer, threat hunter, and purple teamer with over 20 years of experience in the cybersecurity industry. She has held pivotal roles at prominent organizations, leveraging her expertise to develop advanced detection technologies, improve security architecture, and secure critical systems against advanced persistent threats.

Mya has built a robust career that marries proficiency in Python programming, adversarial simulation, and cloud security with an in-depth understanding of data science and machine learning. Her ability to bridge the gap between these key areas has not only facilitated the creation of next-generation technologies but also improved threat hunting and detection efforts on a global scale.

In every facet of her work, Mya has demonstrated a commitment to diversity, innovation, collaboration, and the advancement of the cybersecurity field.

Bobby E. Rogers, CySA+, CISSP-ISSEP, CRISC, MCSE: Security, is a cybersecurity professional with over 30 years in the information technology and cybersecurity fields. He currently works for a major engineering company in Huntsville, Alabama, as a contractor for commercial, state, and federal agencies, helping to secure their information systems. Bobby's specialties are cybersecurity engineering, security compliance auditing, and cyber risk management, but he has worked in almost every area of cybersecurity, including network defense, computer forensics, incident response, and penetration testing. He is a retired master sergeant from the US Air Force, having served for over 21 years. Bobby has built and secured networks in the United States, Chad, Uganda, South Africa, Germany, Saudi Arabia, Pakistan, Afghanistan, and several other countries all over the world. He has narrated and produced over 30 information security training videos for several training companies and is also the author of *CRISC Certified in Risk and Information Systems Control All-In-One Exam Guide, CompTIA CySA+ Cybersecurity Analyst Certification Passport*, and *CISSP Passport*. He is also the contributing author/technical editor for the popular *CISSP All-In-One Exam Guide, Ninth Edition*, all from McGraw Hill.

Brent Chapman, CySA+, GCIH, GCFA, GCTI, CISSP, is an information security engineer with more than 15 years of experience in information technology and cybersecurity. He is a former cyber operations officer in the United States Army and has held a number of unique assignments, including researcher at the Army Cyber Institute, instructor in the Department of Electrical Engineering and Computer Science at the US Military Academy at West Point, and project manager at the Defense Innovation Unit in Silicon Valley. He is a professional member of the Association of Computing Machinery, FCC Amateur Radio license holder, and contributor to several technical and maker-themed publications.

Fernando J. Maymí, PhD, CISSP, is a consultant, educator, and author with more than 25 years of experience in information security. He currently leads teams of cybersecurity consultants, analysts, and red teamers in providing services around the world. Fernando was the founding deputy director of the Army Cyber Institute, a government think tank he helped create for the secretary of the army to solve future cyberspace operations problems affecting the whole country. He has served as advisor to congressional leaders, corporate executives, and foreign governments on cyberspace issues. Fernando taught computer science and cybersecurity at the US Military Academy at West Point for 12 years. Fernando has written extensively and is the coauthor of the ninth edition of the bestselling *CISSP All-in-One Exam Guide*.

About the Technical Editor

Robert Shimonski, CySA+, CASP+, PenTest+, Security+, is a technology executive specializing in healthcare IT for one of the largest health systems in America. In his current role, Rob is responsible for bringing technical, tactical, and operational support into the future with the help of new technologies such as cloud and artificial intelligence.

His current focus is on deploying to cloud (Azure, AWS, and Google), security solutions like CNAPP, DevOps, DevSecOps, AIOps, digital transformation, machine learning, IoT, and the development of new technologies in healthcare. Rob spent many years in the technology "trenches" doing networking and security architecture, design, engineering, testing, and development. A go-to person for all things security, Rob has been a major force in deploying security-related systems for 25+ years.

Rob has worked for various companies, reviewing and developing curriculum as well as other security-related books, technical articles, and publications based on technology deployment, testing, hacking, pen testing, and many other aspects of security. Rob has written and edited over 100 books on security-related topics. Rob also helped develop CompTIA exams as an SME and has over 20 current CompTIA-based certifications.

CONTENTS AT A GLANCE

CONTENTS

ACKNOWLEDGMENTS

This book wasn't simply written by one person; so many people had key roles in the production of this guide, so we'd like to take this opportunity to acknowledge and thank them. First and foremost, we would like to thank the folks at McGraw Hill, and in particular Lisa McClain and Caitlin Cromley-Linn. Both had the unenviable role of keeping us on track and leading us to see their vision of what this book is supposed to be. They are both awesome people to work with, and we're grateful they had the faith to entrust this project to us! We'd also like to thank the authors of the first two editions of this book, Brent Chapman and Fernando Maymí, for their work; they did a great job of providing the right tone for the book and helping people to learn the material and get CySA+ certified. We owe a debt of thanks to the editorial supervisor, Janet Walden; the project manager, Tasneem Kauser; and Bart Reed, the copy editor. All three were great people to work with and always did a fantastic job of turning our rough attempts to explain critical technical concepts into a smooth-flowing, understandable book. We definitely want to thank and acknowledge the contributions of our technical editor, Robert Shimonski, whose expert advice greatly increased the quality of this book. And last, but certainly not least, we also want to thank our respective families for their patience and understanding as we took time away from them to write this book. We owe them a great deal of time we can never pay back, and we are very grateful for their love and support.

—Bobby and Mya

I'd also like to acknowledge the amazing contributions of my coauthor, Mya Heath. Mya is truly an expert in this field and is far more knowledgeable than I am about some of the more cutting-edge, detailed activities involved with modern cybersecurity analysis, including threat hunting and cybersecurity operations. I know that I could not have written this book without her, and this book is *so* much better for her contributions.

—Bobby

I want to extend my heartfelt gratitude to my coauthor, Bobby, who has been an unwavering guide through this journey. As I embarked on my first book, apprehension was natural, but Bobby, with his innate ability to mentor, assuaged my fears. He has been extremely patient, answering every question and sharing wisdom that has transformed me into a more seasoned author and collaborator. The time we've spent working together is truly cherished, and I look forward to any future projects we may undertake. His contributions have greatly enriched this book, providing our readers with a depth of knowledge that is truly exceptional. My deepest thanks, Bobby.

—Mya

INTRODUCTION

This third edition of the *CompTIA CySA+ Certification All-in-One Exam Guide* represents a major overhaul of the material covered in the previous editions. Fully updated to reflect the new objectives for exam number CS0-003, this book will not only prepare you for your certification but also serve as a desktop reference in your daily job as a cybersecurity analyst. Our ultimate goal, as before, is to ensure that you will be equipped to know and be able to take the right steps to improve the security posture of your organization immediately upon arrival. But how do you convey these skills to a prospective employer within the confines of a one- or two-page resume? Using the title CySA+, like a picture, can be worth a thousand words.

Why Become a CySA+?

To answer that question simply, having CySA+ at the end of your signature will elevate employers' expectations. Hiring officials oftentimes screen resumes by looking for certain key terms, such as *CySA+*, before referring them to technical experts for further review. Attaining this certification improves your odds of making it past the first filters and also sets a baseline for what the experts can expect from you during an interview. It lets them know they can get right to important parts of the conversation without first having to figure out how much you know about the role of a cybersecurity analyst. The certification sets you up for success.

It also sets you up for lifelong self-learning and development. Preparing for and passing this exam will not only elevate your knowledge, but it will also reveal to you how much you still have to learn. Cybersecurity analysts never reach a point where they know enough. Instead, this is a role that requires continuous learning, because both the defenders and attackers are constantly evolving their tools and techniques. The CySA+ domains and objectives provide you a framework of knowledge and skills on which you can plan your own professional development.

The CySA+ Exam

CompTIA indicates the relative importance of each domain with these weightings on the exam:

Domain	Percent of Examination
1.0 Security Operations	33%
2.0 Vulnerability Management	30%
3.0 Incident Response and Management	20%
4.0 Reporting and Communication	17%

The CySA+ exam is administered at authorized testing centers or via remote online proctoring and presently will cost you US$392. It consists of a minimum of 85 questions, which must be answered in no more than 165 minutes. To pass, you must score 750 points out of a maximum possible 900 points. The test is computer based and adaptive, which means different questions will earn you different numbers of points. The bulk of the exam consists of short multiple-choice questions with four or five possible responses. In some cases, you will have to select multiple answers to receive full credit. Most questions are fairly straightforward, so you should not expect a lot of "trick" questions or ambiguity. Still, you should not be surprised to find yourself debating between two responses that both seem correct at some point.

A unique aspect of the exam is its use of scenario questions. You may see only a few of these, but they will require a lot of time to complete. In these questions, you will be given a short scenario and a network map. There will be hotspots in the map that you can click to obtain detailed information about a specific node. For example, you might click a host and see log entries or the output of a command-line tool. You will have to come up with multiple actions that explain an observation, mitigate threats, or handle incidents. Deciding which actions are appropriate will require that you look at the whole picture, so be sure to click every hotspot before attempting to answer any of these questions.

Your exam will be scored on the spot, so you will know whether you passed before you leave the test center. You will be given your total score but not a breakdown by domain. If you fail the exam, you will have to pay the exam fee again, but you may retake the test as soon as you'd like. Unlike other exams, there is no waiting period for your second attempt, though you will have to wait 14 calendar days between your second and third attempts if you fail twice.

What Does This Book Cover?

This book covers everything you need to know to become a CompTIA-certified Cybersecurity Analyst (CySA+). It teaches you how successful organizations manage cybersecurity operations as well as cyber threats to their systems. These threats will attempt to exploit weaknesses in the systems, so the book also covers the myriad of issues that go into effective vulnerability management. As we all know, no matter how well we manage both threats and vulnerabilities, we will eventually have to deal with a security incident. The book next delves into cyber incident response, including forensic analysis.

Though the book gives you all the information you need to pass the test and be a successful CySA+, you will have to supplement this knowledge with hands-on experience on at least some of the more popular tools. It is one thing to read about Wireshark and Snort, but you will need practical experience with these tools to know how best to apply them in the real world. The book guides you in this direction, but you will have to get the tools as well as practice the material covered in these pages.

Tips for Taking the CySA+ Exam

Though the CySA+ exam has some unique aspects, it is not entirely unlike any other computer-based test you may have taken. The following is a list of tips in increasing order of specificity. Some may seem like common sense to you, but we still think they're important enough to highlight.

- Get lots of rest the night before.
- Arrive early at the exam site.
- Read all possible responses before making your selection, even if you are "certain" that you've already read the correct option.
- If the question seems like a trick one, you may be overthinking it.
- Don't second-guess yourself after choosing your responses.
- Take notes on the dry-erase sheet (which will be provided by the proctor) whenever you have to track multiple data points.
- If you are unsure about an answer, give it your best shot, mark it for review, and then go on to the next question; you may find a hint in a later question.
- When dealing with a scenario question, read all available information at least once before you attempt to provide any responses.
- Don't stress if you seem to be taking too long on the scenario questions; you will get only a handful of those.
- Don't expect the exhibits (for example, log files) to look like real ones; they will be missing elements you'd normally expect but contain all the information you need to respond.

How to Use This Book

Much effort has gone into putting all the necessary information into this book. Now it's up to you to study and understand the material and its various concepts. To benefit the most from this book, you may want to use the following study method:

- Study each chapter carefully and make sure you understand each concept presented. Many concepts must be fully understood, and glossing over a couple here and there could be detrimental to you.
- Make sure to study and answer all the questions. If any questions confuse you, go back and study those sections again.
- If you are not familiar with specific topics, such as firewalls, reverse engineering, and protocol functionality, use other sources of information (books, articles, and so on) to attain a more in-depth understanding of those subjects. Don't just rely on what you think you need to know to pass the CySA+ exam.
- If you are not familiar with a specific tool, download the tool (if open source) or a trial version (if commercial) and play with it a bit. Since we cover dozens of tools, you should prioritize them based on how unfamiliar you are with them.

Using the Objective Map

The table in Appendix A has been constructed to help you cross-reference the official exam objectives from CompTIA with the relevant coverage in the book. Each objective is listed along with the corresponding chapter number and heading that provides coverage of that objective.

Online Practice Exams

This book includes access to practice exams that feature the TotalTester Online exam test engine, which enables you to generate a complete practice exam or to generate quizzes by chapter module or by exam domain. See Appendix B for more information and instructions on how to access the exam tool.

PART I

Security Operations

CHAPTER 1

System and Network Architectures

In this chapter you will learn:

- Common network architectures and their security implications
- Operating systems
- Technologies and policies used to identify, authenticate, and authorize users
- Public Key Infrastructure
- Protecting sensitive data

You can't build a great building on a weak foundation.

—Gordon B. Hinckley

In Part I of this book, we will cover a portion of foundational knowledge that a cybersecurity analyst will need to perform their job. This includes information on infrastructure and the architecture, managing security operations, the nature of attacks, tools and techniques used for cybersecurity, security data analysis, and the nature of threat intelligence and threat hunting.

In this first chapter, we will look at the architectural foundations of the systems malicious entities will be attacking and we are defending. We will discuss several foundational but critical concepts, such as infrastructure architecture and concepts, including operating systems. We'll also discuss critical security processes such as logging, identity and access management, encryption, and how to protect sensitive data. Note that this is just the beginning of these discussions, not the end. We will be discussing these topics throughout this book.

It's important to note that a single chapter cannot adequately cover all the technologies you will encounter as a cybersecurity analyst. However, you should at least be familiar with many of the things we will discuss in this chapter. We're not going to make you an expert on networking architectures, applications, cloud environments, or the like. However, you will need some basic knowledge to begin and progress in your career as a cybersecurity analyst—and to be successful on the exam. The CySA+ exam assumes you have basic familiarity with infrastructure concepts, such as the ones we will discuss.

Therefore, we will not be going in depth on any one of these technologies but will instead focus the context on how they relate to your job as a cybersecurity analyst. This first chapter will cover Objective 1.1, "Explain the importance of system and network architecture concepts in security operations."

The Importance of Logging

You may recall that auditing is the process of examining the actions of an entity, such as an individual user, with the goal of conclusively tying the actions taken in a system, or on a resource, to that entity. Auditing directly supports accountability and nonrepudiation, in that individuals and entities can be held accountable for their actions, and they cannot dispute that they took those actions if auditing is properly configured. For example, we audit the use of higher-level privileges so we can conclusively determine that a given user took a specific action that required higher-level privileges. Also, we may audit resources that are accessed and used, such as the editing of a document or the deletion of a folder and its contents. Auditing the actions entities have taken in the infrastructure is highly critical for security processes, such as incident response, forensics investigations, troubleshooting, and so much more.

Auditing would not be possible without the process of logging. Logging is the activity that takes place at the lower level to ensure that we can audit actions. Logging is the process of recording these actions, as well as specific data related to those actions. When we log events or actions, we want to capture information, such as the user or process that took the action; the time, date, and system the action was taken on; the resource that was affected; and so on. There's so many other characteristics of an event that we can capture only through logging, assuming it is configured properly to capture these events.

Logging Levels

The *logging level* refers to how much detail or the extent of information located in a log entry. On the surface, there are likely only a few of several possible data elements that could be contained in a log entry that are of interest, which are more than likely the most often used. The typical log events include information such as the following:

- Source IP address or hostname
- Destination IP address or hostname
- Networking port, protocol, and service
- Username
- Domain name
- Nature of the event (account creation, deletion, file modification, and so on)
- Event ID
- Timestamp of the event indicating when it took place

However, depending on the logging level configured on the system, there could be much more information available for the analyst to comb through. Logging levels can be configured on the host to obtain the bare minimum information to log the event, or to obtain much more detail. Obviously, the more detail provided for each log entry, the more storage space the logs can occupy. Additionally, the more detail provided for the event usually means the more log events are generated. For instance, configuring process tracking as enabled on Windows machines instantaneously generates volumes of log entries, which can quickly consume up all available disk space and also be problematic for the analyst to sort through and examine. Operating systems, applications, and security management tools often have different logging levels that can be configured, based on the needs of the organization.

Log Ingestion

Log ingestion is the means and processes by which logs are collected, stored, analyzed, and managed. Since most infrastructure devices can be configured to generate logs, it can be problematic for analysts to visit each individual device and either review the logs on the device or remove the logs to consolidate them for later review. Figure 1-1 illustrates the ability to review logs through the Event Viewer utility on a single Windows 11 host. This is actually how it was done in the "old days" before the advent of centralized log collection, aggregation, and analysis utilities, such as syslog, and then later, advanced security event information management (SIEM) systems.

Modern logging mechanisms are configured either through an agent installed on the device or via an automated network-based push/pull subscription mechanism to send

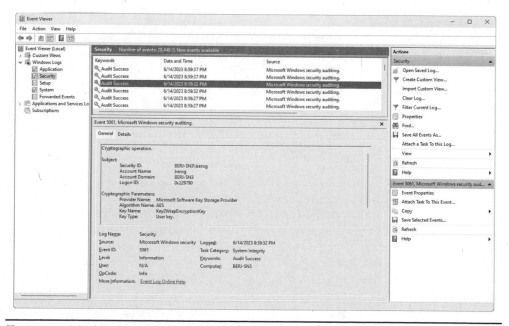

Figure 1-1   Windows 11 Event Viewer

the logs from various hosts to centralized collector machines, where they are integrated and their data aggregated. SIEMs offer the capability of taking all of these log events, in aggregate, and performing some of the heavy-lifting tasks, such as data reduction, de-duplication, and initial analysis, cutting out the noise that comes invariably with massive logging as well as providing more succinct information for the analyst to work with. This entire process is referred to as log ingestion and can greatly facilitate the analysis of massive volumes of logging information where critical, time-sensitive events may be missed by human beings. Note that SIEMs and the use of automation technologies to help reduce the workload and better focus the analyst on critical security events is covered in Chapter 2.

 EXAM TIP The default location for logs in the Linux operating system is the /var/log directory. In the Windows environment, you can use the Event Viewer to view the event logs, which are stored as .evtx files in the %SystemRoot%\System32\Winevt\Logs folder by default. Other operating systems' log file locations may vary.

Time Synchronization

Accountability directly depends on auditing, and auditing, in turn, directly depends on how well the organization logs events. Logging, to continue down this path, depends on accurate network time sources. Without an accurate time source, an event cannot be accurately recorded in a log. Even the difference of a few seconds can call into question exactly who performed an action and when that action was performed. Accurate timestamps for logged events are critical for many security processes, including troubleshooting, and especially incident response and investigating suspicious events.

Most modern networks use network-based time sources, rather than relying on the individual times generated by the host device. While the timestamps generated by a host may start out as accurate, over time even sophisticated clocks can drift, causing discrepancies in the timestamps between devices. A network-based time source maintains a correct, consistent time for all devices. This is not only critical to logging but also to some network services, such as Kerberos authentication. Discrepancies in proper timestamping of logged events may cause issues with comparing audit logs from different devices and the inability to establish a timeline for an incident or other negative event.

Note that network time synchronization uses the Network Time Protocol, or NTP, over UDP port 123. Typically, a network-based time source provides timing to all network devices on the internal network. This network time device, in turn, receives its timing from an external source, such as from NIST. The system uses a hierarchical layered system of time sources to ensure accurate time synchronization. These layers are referred to as a *stratum* and are numbered from the highest level stratum, beginning with 0, which is the most accurate timekeeping devices, such as atomic clocks. Higher-level stratum devices provide time services to lower-level devices, one of which will be the network's designated time source.

Operating System Concepts

As with many of the other infrastructure concepts we will discuss in this chapter, we will not go extremely in depth on operating systems and how they are constructed, as this would be something you would find in entire volumes devoted to the subject. However, there are a few key points of operating system (OS) structure we can discuss here that are relevant to your duties as a cybersecurity analyst.

Although most people are familiar with the four major variations of operating systems, such as Windows, UNIX, Linux, and macOS (these last two are variants and descendants of original UNIX, however, and are thus very similar), there are countless other variations, including embedded and real-time operating systems as well as older operating systems, such as BSD, OS/2 Warp, and so on.

Operating systems are distinguished by several characteristics. First, the operating system is in charge of managing all the hardware and software resources on the system. The OS also provides abstraction layers between the end user and the hardware; users can simply drag and drop objects in a graphical user interface to make hardware changes, for instance, or they can interact with software. The operating system also serves as a mediator for applications installed on the system to interact with both the user and system hardware.

At its basic level, the operating system consists of critical core system files—those that are used to boot the system into operation as well as those that are used to control applications, resources, utilities, functions, and so on. Critical operating system files are typically protected and stored in standardized file locations or directories.

In addition to the core system files, and extensive configuration settings for the host itself, operating systems also provide the ability to execute applications on the system. They also provide the ability for the user to interact with those applications and hardware, either through a command line or graphical interface.

Windows Registry

Every single configuration element for the Windows operating system is contained in its *registry*. The registry is the central repository database for all configurations settings in Windows, whether they are simple desktop color preferences or networking and security configuration items. The registry is the most critical portion of the operating system, other than its core executables. The reason the registry is so important to a cybersecurity analyst is that this is likely one of the first places they will go to look for issues, along with the log files, if Windows is not functioning properly, if its performance is failing, or if the analyst suspects the operating system has been compromised. It would take several books to fill up all the details regarding the Windows registry, but we will include a few details here.

The Windows registry is a hierarchical database, which is highly protected from a security perspective. Only specific programs, processes, and users with high-level permissions can access it. Since this is where Windows stores all of its configuration information, it contains a lot of sensitive data that could be used to gain valuable information about the host, or even the network and the entire organization. If the registry were to become compromised or corrupt, it can completely disable the operating system to the point where the host would not even boot.

This hierarchical database is composed of major entries called *hives*. Each hive relates to a specific set of contexts and functions. For example, there is a hive dedicated to user configuration items, one to the machine configuration itself, and so on. The major registry hives have hundreds of associated entries, called *keys* (which also contain multiple levels of subkeys). Keys have names, data types, and values. The five hives are listed here:

- HKEY_CLASSES_ROOT (HKCR)
- HKEY_CURRENT_USER (HKCU)
- HKEY_LOCAL_MACHINE (HKLM)
- HKEY_USERS (HKU)
- HKEY_CURRENT_CONFIG

 NOTE While the registries between different versions of the Windows operating systems are essentially the same, there can be subtle differences between versions, such as keys, for example. These differences are based on Windows versions, features, applications, or even the security mechanisms installed on the host.

Delving into each one of these hives, their keys, and their values is far beyond the scope of this book. However, as you gain knowledge and experience as a cybersecurity analyst, you should definitely take the time to delve into the registry and discover the information you can glean from it during troubleshooting, incident response, or a security investigation. Note that Chapter 4 provides some extensive coverage of the Windows registry with regard to areas you should more closely examine from a security perspective if you suspect the host has been compromised. Figure 1-2 shows an example of viewing registry settings in Windows.

 EXAM TIP Although the registry stores all configuration details for the Windows operating system and installed applications, configuration changes routinely are not made to the registry itself. They are usually made through other configuration utilities that are part of the operating system and its applications. For instance, you would not make changes to group policy directly in the registry; you would simply use the group policy editor, which would update the registry. For the purposes of the exam, you may see distractors that indicate you should edit the registry directly, but usually these are not the correct answers.

Linux Configuration Settings

Although the CySA+ exam objectives don't specifically list the requirement for knowing how the Linux configuration settings work, it is definitely worth noting here, since you may use this information on an almost daily basis as a cybersecurity analyst. Even though we will not go in depth on Linux configuration files in this book, you should know that

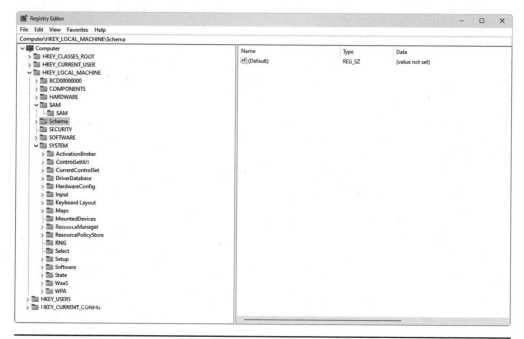

Figure 1-2 The Windows registry

for most Linux distributions (and even other UNIX-based operating systems), configuration settings in Linux are much different than they are in Windows. Rather than storing configuration settings in a proprietary hierarchical database, as Windows does, Linux configuration settings are stored in simple text files. Most of these configuration text files are stored in the /etc directory and its related subdirectories. These text files are not integrated, although you will often see references to other configuration files in them. For instance, the configuration file for the Secure Shell utility is contained under the /etc/ssh directory and has configuration files that relate to both the Secure Shell client and the Secure Shell server daemon. It's important to note that configuration files in Linux are well protected and only certain applications, daemons, and users, such as root, have direct access to them.

 EXAM TIP On the exam, you may be asked to answer questions regarding scenarios that test your understanding on the fundamentals of both Windows and Linux configuration settings. At minimum, you should understand the very basic concepts of configuration settings such as the registry.

System Hardening

When a system is shipped from a vendor, or is even bought from a big box store, it typically comes with default configuration settings. Examples of these default configuration settings include a blank or commonly used password for the administrator account, services configured to be running by default, even if they are not necessarily needed by the organization, and so on. Before a system is put into operation, it should go through a process known as *hardening,* which means that the configuration of the system is made more secure and locked down. Although each organization may have its own hardening procedures provided by vendors, security organizations, or even the government, typical actions taken for system hardening include the following:

- Updates with the most recent operating system and application patches
- Unnecessary services turned off
- Unnecessary open network ports closed
- Password changes for all accounts on the system to more complex passwords
- New accounts created with very restrictive privileges
- Installation of antimalware, host-based intrusion detection, and endpoint detection and response software
- Configuration of security policies, either locally on the machine or inherited from the organization's centralized directories services, such as Active Directory

In addition to these actions, which may be implemented using manual or automated means, typically organizations will also implement security using hardening tools or scripts to change complex configuration settings, such as those found in the Windows registry. Once these configuration changes are made, it's considered a best practice to scan the system, using vulnerability scanning software to determine if there are any outstanding vulnerabilities that remain on the host. The results of this vulnerability scan can be used to further harden the system if needed.

 EXAM TIP You should keep in mind that one of the very first things you should do with a new system is harden it and securely configure it to your organization's standard baseline.

File Structure

The file structure of an operating system dictates how files are stored and accessed on storage media, such as a hard drive. The file structure is operating system dependent; in other words, the type of operating system installed in the system dictates how files are structured, accessed, deleted, and so on. Most modern operating systems organize files into hierarchical logical structures, resembling upside-down trees, where a top level node in the tree is usually a directory and is represented as a folder in a graphical interface. Folders can have files in them, or even subfolders and files. Most often files have individual extensions that are not only somewhat descriptive of their function but also make it easier for the applications that use those files to access them. For example, a file with an extension of .docx can easily be identified as a Microsoft Word document, and the extension enables the Microsoft Word application to identify the file and use it.

This structure is called the *file system*. Each operating system has its own specific type of file system, which is controlled by the core system operating files. For instance, Windows uses the NTFS file system, proprietary to Microsoft, and most modern Linux variants use a file system known as ext4. The differences in these file systems relate to how they prepare media for storing files, such as creating different volume or partition structures, how files are categorized and indexed on the system with relation to their location and storage space, and how those structures are accessed by the core operating system, applications, and users. As we have stated before, it would take volumes of books to examine the intricacies of even one of these file systems, but we will discuss issues related to file systems throughout this book.

Individual files can be classified by their extensions, but also by how they are constructed internally. For example, there are text files, picture files, music files, as well as system files and executables. Files typically have unique signatures that are easily identifiable using file verification utilities. This can help a cybersecurity analyst to determine if a file has been compromised or is the correct file that belongs on a system.

System Processes

Processes are ongoing activities that execute to carry out a multitude of tasks for operating systems and applications. Processes can be created, or *spawned*, by operating system core functions, application executables, utilities, and so on. Hundreds of processes may be running on a system at any given moment carrying out even very minute tasks. As a cybersecurity analyst, you should be familiar with the basic processes for operating systems and applications that you work with on a daily basis. This will help you identify any troublesome processes that may be causing performance and functionality issues, or, more importantly, rogue processes that may be malicious in nature. Windows processes can be viewed using a utility such as Task Manager, as shown in Figure 1-3.

The same concepts regarding processes in Windows apply to Linux and other operating systems. In Linux and other UNIX-based systems, processes are referred to as being spawned by Linux services, or *daemons*. One of the basic tools for viewing processes in Linux is the **ps** command. This command-line tool has multiple switches and options (some of them depending on the Linux variant itself), but simply reviewing the processes running on a host can be accomplished by executing the **ps** command at the shell, as illustrated in Figure 1-4.

Note that processes on either operating system can be paused, stopped, restarted, or otherwise interacted with. There are also utilities available in both operating systems to view the associated executable that spawned the process. This can be useful in incident forensics.

 EXAM TIP You should understand how to view and interact with processes for both Windows and Linux for the exam, using Task Manager and the **ps** command, respectively.

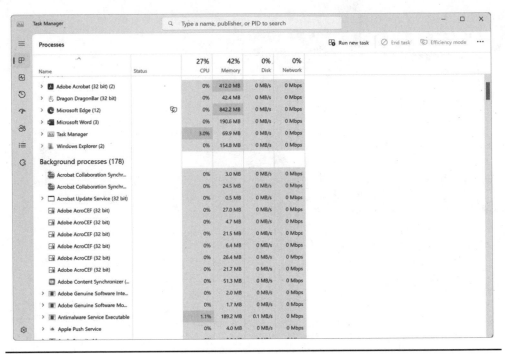

Figure 1-3 Viewing processes in the Windows Task Manager

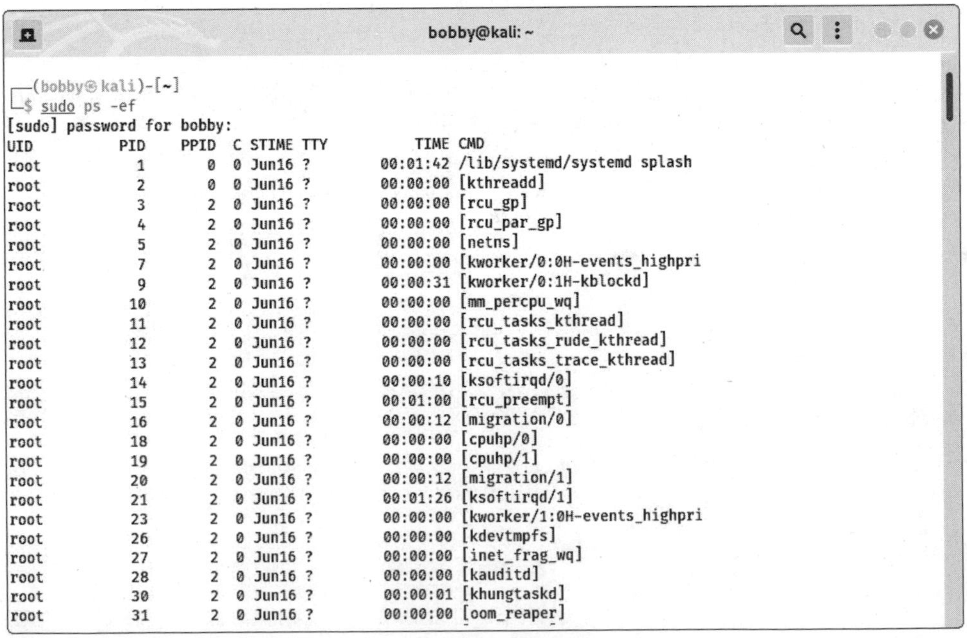

Figure 1-4 Viewing processes in Linux using the **ps** command.

Hardware Architecture

Hardware architecture refers not only to the logical and physical placement of hardware in the network architecture design but also the architecture of how the hardware itself is designed with regard to the CPU, trusted computing base, memory allocation, secure storage, boot verification processes, and so on. Some hardware architectures are better suited from a security perspective than others; many hardware architectures have security mechanisms built in, such as those that use Trusted Platform Modules (TPMs) and secure boot mechanisms, for instance.

Network Architecture

A *network architecture* refers to the nodes on a computer network and the manner in which they are connected to one another. There is no universal way to depict this, but it is common to, at least, draw the various subnetworks and the network devices (such as routers, firewalls) that connect them. It is also better to list the individual devices included in each subnet, at least for valuable resources such as servers, switches, and network appliances. The most mature organizations draw on their asset management systems to provide a rich amount of detail as well as helpful visualizations.

A network architecture should be prescriptive in that it should determine the way things must be. It should not just be an exercise in documenting where things are but in placing them deliberately in certain areas. Think of a network architecture as a military commander arraying their forces in defensive positions in preparation for an enemy assault. The commander wouldn't go to their subordinates and ask where they wanted to be. Instead, the commander would study the best available intelligence about the enemy capabilities and objectives, combine that with an understanding of their own mission and functions, and then place their forces intentionally.

In most cases, network architectures are hybrid constructs incorporating physical, software-defined, virtual, and cloud assets. Figure 1-5 shows a high-level example of a typical hybrid architecture. The following sections describe each of the architectures in use by many organizations.

On-premises Architecture

The most traditional network architecture is a physical one. In a *physical network architecture,* we describe the manner in which physical devices such as workstations, servers, firewalls, and routers relate to one another. Along the way, we decide what traffic is allowed, from where to where, and develop the policies that will control those flows. These policies are then implemented in the devices themselves—for example, as firewall rules or access control lists (ACLs) in routers. Most organizations use a physical network architecture, or perhaps more than one. While physical network architectures are well known to everybody who has ever taken a networking course at any level, they are limited in that they typically require static changes to individual devices to adapt to changing conditions.

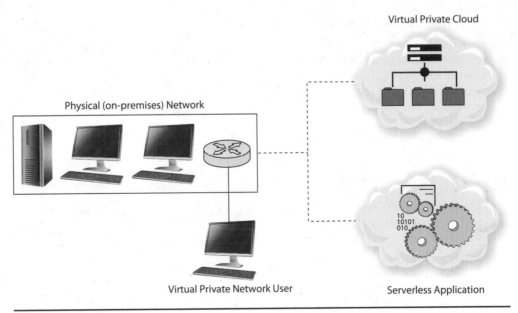

Figure 1-5 Hybrid network architecture

Network Segmentation

Network segmentation is the practice of breaking up networks into smaller subnetworks. The subnetworks are accessible to one another through switches and routers in on-premises networks, or through virtual private connections and security groups in the cloud. Segmentation enables network administrators to implement granular controls over the manner in which traffic is allowed to flow from one subnetwork to another. Some of the goals of network segmentation are to thwart an adversary's efforts, improve traffic management, and prevent spillover of sensitive data. Beginning at the physical layer of the network, segmentation can be implemented all the way up to the application layer.

Network segmentation can be implemented through physical or logical means. Physical network segmentation uses network devices such as switches and routers. Networks are placed on different network interfaces, resulting in physical subnets that are programmed in the network device. Logical segments are implemented through technologies such as virtual local area networking (VLAN), software-defined networking, end-to-end encryption, and so on. In a logical segmentation design, hosts don't have to necessarily be physically separated, but they can be and still be part of the same logical network. Most logical network segmentation takes place at the Internet layer of the TCP/IP protocol stack (equivalent to the Network layer of the OSI model) but can be implemented at other layers.

EXAM TIP   Keep in mind the reason why you might want to segment hosts from others on the network: to protect sensitive data. Also remember that you can segment hosts both physically and logically. Logical segmentation can use methods such as VLANs and encryption.

Zero Trust

Zero trust is a relatively new concept in network architecture. It simply means that hosts, applications, users, and other entities are not trusted by default, but once they are trusted, through strong identification and authentication policies and processes, that trust must be periodically reverified. This process considers the possibility that a host or other entity has been compromised after an initial trust was already established. The reverification process ensures that even if a host has been trusted at one point, it cannot always be trusted to access sensitive resources. The trust process verifies the ongoing identity and authorization of the host. Zero trust can be implemented through many different levels of the infrastructure, using a variety of software tools, strong authentication methods, network access control, and so on.

EXAM TIP   Zero trust requires periodic reverification after the initial trust is established in case the host becomes compromised.

Software-Defined Networking

Software-defined networking (SDN) is a network architecture in which software applications are responsible for deciding how best to route data (the control layer) and then for actually moving those packets around (the data layer). This is in contrast to a physical network architecture, in which each device needs to be configured by remotely connecting to it and giving it a fixed set of rules with which to make routing or switching decisions. Figure 1-6 shows how these two SDN layers enable networked applications to communicate with each other.

One of the most powerful aspects of SDN is that it decouples data forwarding functions (the data plane) from decision-making functions (the control plane), allowing for

Figure 1-6
Overview of a
software-defined
networking
architecture

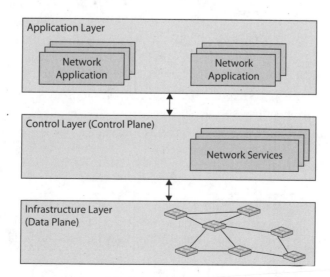

holistic and adaptive control of how data moves around the network. In an SDN architecture, SDN is used to describe how nodes communicate with each other.

Secure Access Secure Edge

Secure Access Secure Edge (SASE) is another basic concept to recently come to maturity. It is a group of hybrid technologies that combine software-defined wide area networking (SD-WAN) with zero trust concepts and delivered via the cloud. This framework is designed to securely connect entities such as users, systems, devices, whether local or remote, to authorized correct applications and resources. SASE is identity based; in other words, access is allowed based on the proper identification and authentication of both users and devices. Another key characteristic is that SASE is entirely cloud-based, with both its infrastructure and security mechanisms delivered through cloud technologies (discussed in upcoming sections). SASE seeks to encompass all aspects of physical, digital, and logical boundaries. Finally, SASE is designed to be globally distributed; secure connections are applied to users and devices no matter where they are in the infrastructure, either logically or physically (geographically).

 EXAM TIP Secure Access Secure Edge (SASE) combines the concepts of software-defined wide area networking and zero trust, and the services are delivered through cloud-based deployments.

Cloud Service Models

Cloud computing enables organizations to access on-demand network, storage, and compute power, usually from a shared pool of resources. Cloud services are characterized by their ease of provisioning, setup, and teardown. There are three primary service models for cloud resources, listed next. All of these services rely on the shared responsibility model of security that identifies the requirements for both the service provider and server user for mutual security.

- **Software as a Service (SaaS)** A service offering in which the tasks for providing and managing software and storage are undertaken completely by the vendor. Google Apps, Office 365, iCloud, and Box are all examples of SaaS.

- **Platform as a Service (PaaS)** A model that offers a platform on which software can be developed and deployed over the Internet.

- **Infrastructure as a Service (IaaS)** A service model that enables organizations to have direct access to their cloud-based servers and storage as they would with traditional hardware.

 EXAM TIP Although there are a wide variety of "something as a service" offerings, the three basic ones you will need to remember for the exam are Software as a Service, Platform as a Service, and Infrastructure as a Service.

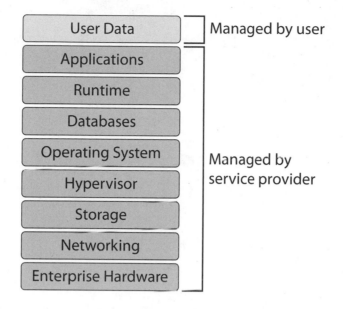

Figure 1-7 Technology stack highlighting areas of responsibility in a SaaS service model

Software as a Service

SaaS is among the most commonly used software delivery models on the market. In the SaaS model, organizations access applications and functionality directly from a service provider with minimal requirements to develop custom code in-house; the vendor takes care of maintaining servers, databases, and application code. To save money on licensing and hardware costs, many companies subscribe to SaaS versions of critical business applications such as graphics design suites, office productivity programs, customer relationship managers, and conferencing solutions. As Figure 1-7 shows, those applications reside at the highest level of the technology stack. The vendor provides the service and all of the supporting technologies beneath it.

SaaS is a cloud subscription service designed to offer a number of technologies associated with hardware provision, all the way up to the user experience. A full understanding of how these services protect your company's data at every level will be a primary concern for your security team. Given the popularity of SaaS solutions, providers such as Microsoft, Amazon, Cisco, and Google often dedicate large teams to securing all aspects of their service infrastructure. Increasingly, any security problems that arise occur at the data-handling level, where these infrastructure companies do not have the responsibility or visibility required to take action. This leaves the burden primarily on the customer to design and enforce protective controls. The most common types of SaaS vulnerabilities exist in one or more of three spaces: visibility, management, and data flow.

Platform as a Service

PaaS shares a similar set of functionalities as SaaS and provides many of the same benefits in that the service provider manages the foundational technologies of the stack in a manner transparent to the end user. PaaS differs primarily from SaaS in that it offers

Figure 1-8
Technology stack highlighting areas of responsibility in a PaaS service model

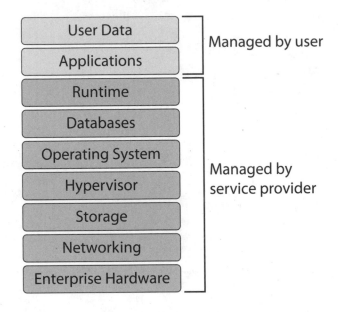

direct access to a development environment to enable organizations to build their own solutions on a cloud-based infrastructure rather than providing their own infrastructures, as shown in Figure 1-8. PaaS solutions are therefore optimized to provide value focused on software development. PaaS, by its very nature, is designed to provide organizations with tools that interact directly with what may be the most important company asset: its source code.

PaaS offers effective and reliable role-based controls to control access to your source code, which is a primary security feature of this model. Auditing and account management tools available in PaaS may also help determine inappropriate exposure. Accordingly, protecting administrative access to the PaaS infrastructure helps organizations avoid loss of control and potential massive impacts to an organization's development process and bottom line.

At the physical infrastructure, in PaaS, service providers assume the responsibility of maintenance and protection and employ a number of methods to deter successful exploits at this level. This often means requiring trusted sources for hardware, using strong physical security for its data centers, and monitoring access to the physical servers and connections to and from them. Additionally, PaaS providers often highlight their protection against DDoS attacks using network-based technologies that require no additional configuration from the user.

Infrastructure as a Service

Moving down the technology stack from the application layer to the hardware later, next we have the cloud service offering of IaaS. As a method of efficiently assigning hardware through a process of constant assignment and reclamation, IaaS offers an

Figure 1-9
Technology stack highlighting areas of responsibility in an IaaS service model

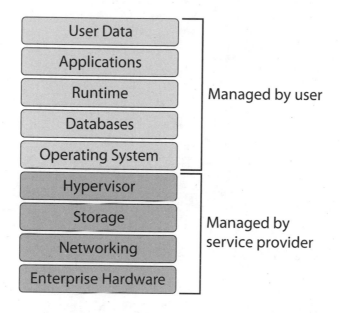

User Data
Applications
Runtime
Databases
Operating System

Managed by user

Hypervisor
Storage
Networking
Enterprise Hardware

Managed by service provider

effective and affordable way for companies to get all of the benefits of managing their own hardware without incurring the massive overhead costs associated with acquisition, physical storage, and disposal of the hardware. In this service model, shown in Figure 1-9, the vendor would provide the hardware, network, and storage resources necessary for the user to install and maintain any operating system, dependencies, and applications they want.

The previously discussed vulnerabilities associated with PaaS and SaaS may exist for IaaS solutions as well, but there are additional opportunities for flaws at this level, because we're now dealing with hardware resource sharing across customers. Any of the vulnerabilities that could take advantage of flaws in hard disks, RAM, CPU caches, and GPUs can affect IaaS platforms. One attack scenario affecting IaaS cloud providers could enable a malicious actor to implant persistent backdoors for data theft into bare-metal cloud servers. A vulnerability in either the hypervisor supporting the visualization of various tenant systems or a flaw in the firmware of the hardware in use could introduce a vector for this attack. This attack would be difficult for the customer to detect because it would be possible for all services to appear unaffected at a higher level of the technology stack.

EXAM TIP Remember that Software as a Service typically only offers applications, Platform as a Service generally offers a configured host with the operating system only, and Infrastructure as a Service usually offers a base server on which the organization installs its own operating system and applications.

Security as a Service

Security as a Service (SECaaS) is a cloud-based model for service delivery by a specialized security service provider. SECaaS providers usually offer services such as authentication, antivirus, intrusion detection, and security assessments. Similar to managed security service providers (MSSPs), SECaaS providers bring value to organizations primarily based on cost savings and access to on-demand specialized expertise. The primary difference between the two models is that SECaaS, like other cloud service models, enables organizations to pay only for what they use. Unlike most MSSP agreements, SECaaS models do not necessarily follow an annual contract-based payment agreement.

Cloud Deployment Models

Although the public cloud is often built on robust security principles to support the integrity of customer data, the possibility of spillage may rise above the risk appetite of an organization, particularly organizations operating with loads of sensitive data. Additionally, concerns about the permanence of data, or the possibility that data might remain after deletion, can push an organization to adopt a cloud deployment model that is not open to all. Before implementing or adopting a cloud solution, your organization should understand what it's trying to protect and what model works best to achieve that goal. We'll discuss three models, their security benefits, and their disadvantages.

Public

In public cloud solutions, the cloud vendor owns the servers, infrastructure, network, and hypervisor used in the provision of service to your company. As tenants to the cloud solution provider, your organization borrows a portion of that shared infrastructure to perform whatever operations are required. Services offered by Google, Amazon, and Microsoft are among the most popular cloud-based services worldwide. So, for example, although the data you provide to Gmail may be yours, the hardware used to store and process it is all owned by Google.

Private

In private cloud solutions, organizations accessing the cloud service own all the hardware and underlying functions to provide services. For a number of regulatory or privacy reasons, many healthcare, government, and financial firms opt to use a private cloud in lieu of shared hardware. Using private cloud storage, for example, enables organizations that operate with sensitive data to ensure that their data is stored, processed, and transmitted by trusted parties, and that these operations meet any criteria defined by regulatory guidelines. In this model, the organization is wholly responsible for the operation and upkeep of the physical network, infrastructure, hypervisors, virtual network, operating systems, security devices, configurations, identity and access management, and, of course, data.

Community

In a community cloud, the infrastructure is shared across organizations with a common interest in how the data is stored and processed. These organizations usually belong to the same larger conglomerate, or all operate under similar regulatory environments. The focus for this model may be the consistency of operation across the various organizations as well as lowered costs of operation for all concerned parties. While the community cloud model helps address common challenges across partnering organizations, including issues related to information security, it adds more complexity to the overall operations process. Many vulnerabilities, therefore, are likely related to processes and policy rather than strictly technical. Security teams across these organizations should have, at a minimum, standard operation procedures that outline how to communicate security events, indicators of compromise, and remediation efforts to other partners participating in the community cloud infrastructure.

Hybrid Models

Hybrid clouds combine on-premises infrastructure with a public cloud, with a significant effort placed in the management of how data and applications leverage each solution to achieve organizational goals. Organizations that use a hybrid model can often see benefits offered by both public and private models while remaining in compliance with any external or internal requirements for data protection. Often organizations will also use a public cloud as a failover to their private cloud, allowing the public cloud to take increased demand on resources if the private cloud is insufficient.

NOTE   More often than not, the hybrid model is typically used in most of the cloud deployments to which an organization subscribes.

Cloud Access Security Broker

Before the emergence of diverse cloud computing solutions, it was a lot simpler for us to control access to our information systems, monitor their performance, and log events in them. Doing this became even more difficult with the shift toward using mobile (and potentially personal) devices to access corporate resources. How do you keep track of what's happening when a dozen different cloud services are in use by your organization? A *cloud access security broker* (CASB) sits between each user and each cloud service, monitoring all activity, enforcing policies, and alerting you when something seems to be wrong.

We generally talk of four pillars to CASBs:

- **Visibility**   This is the ability to see who is doing what and where. Are your users connecting to unauthorized resources (such as cloud storage that is not controlled by your organization)? Are they constrained to services and data that they are authorized to use?

- **Threat protection**   This pillar detects (and, ideally, blocks) malware, insider threats, and compromised accounts. In this regard, features in this pillar look a lot like those of an intrusion detection or protection system but for your cloud services.

- **Compliance**   If you are in a regulated environment (and, let's face it, with data laws like the GDPR, most of us are), you want to ensure that any data in the cloud is monitored for compliance with appropriate regulations concerning who can access it, how, and when.

- **Data security**   Whether or not you are in a regulated environment, you likely have an abundance of data that needs protection in the cloud. This includes intellectual property, customer information, and future product releases.

 EXAM TIP   A cloud access security broker mediates access between internal clients and cloud-based services. It is normally installed and managed jointly by both the client organization and the cloud service provider.

Infrastructure Concepts

The infrastructure of an organization is a multilayered entity. Analysts new to the IT and cybersecurity fields sometimes believe that infrastructure is just the network, and while it does include networking devices, media, protocols, and so on, there is so much more to the infrastructure than that. Infrastructure includes the networking components, certainly, but also the host devices, their operating systems and applications, management structures, processes, architectures, and so on.

The infrastructure can be a very complex entity to understand, and even the most experienced IT and cybersecurity people sometimes must take time to fully understand the entire complete infrastructure of even a small organization. Performance and function issues, as well as cybersecurity issues, can take place on several different levels simultaneously, and it can often be confusing to determine where the root cause of an issue is and how to remediate it. Without going into a lot of depth on infrastructure concepts, the main point you should be aware of is that for your role as a cybersecurity analyst, you should become intimately familiar with your organization's infrastructure. This includes the network and how it is architected, as well as its topology and connected devices. It also includes all the different operating system used on the infrastructure, the line-of-business and enterprise applications used, as well as the small nuances of some of the individual hosts that may be particularly critical or sensitive, or just plain troublesome. You also need to be aware of some of the specific technologies your organization uses, a few of which we will discuss in the upcoming sections. These include serverless architecture, virtualization, containerization, and so on, and how they interact with the infrastructure.

Virtualization

Virtualization is the creation and use of computer and network resources to allow for varied instances of operating systems and applications on an ad hoc basis. Virtualization technologies have revolutionized IT operations because they have vastly reduced the hardware needed to provide a wide array of service and network functions. Virtualization's continued use has enabled large enterprises to achieve a great deal of agility in their IT operations without adding significant overhead. For the average user, virtualization has proven to be a low-cost way to gain exposure to new software and training. Although virtualization has been around since the early days of the Internet, it didn't gain a foothold in enterprise and home computing until the 2000s.

Hypervisors

As previously described, virtualization is achieved by creating large pools of logical storage, CPUs, memory, networking, and applications that reside on a common physical platform. This is most commonly done using software called a *hypervisor,* which manages the physical hardware and performs the functions necessary to share those resources across multiple virtual instances. In short, one physical box can "host" a range of varied computer systems, or *guests,* thanks to clever hardware and software management.

Hypervisors are classified as either Type 1 or Type 2. Type-1 hypervisors are also referred to as *bare-metal* hypervisors because the hypervisor software runs directly on the host computer hardware. Type-1 hypervisors have direct access to all hardware and manage guest operating systems. Today's more popular Type-1 hypervisors include VMware ESXi, Microsoft Hyper-V, and Kernel-based Virtual Machine (KVM). Type-2 hypervisors are run from within an already existing operating system. These hypervisors act just like any other piece of software written for an operating system and enable guest operating systems to share the resources that the hypervisor has access to. Popular Type-2 hypervisors include VMware Workstation, Oracle VM VirtualBox, and Parallels Desktop.

 EXAM TIP You should understand the concepts related to virtualization, as it is critical for understanding concepts such as containerization and serverless architectures.

Containerization

As virtualization software matured, a new branch called *containers* emerged. Whereas operating systems sit on top of hypervisors and share the resources provided by the bare metal, containers sit on top of operating systems and share the resources provided by the host OS. Instead of abstracting the hardware for guest operating systems, container software abstracts the kernel of the operating system for the applications running above it. This allows for low overhead in running many applications and improved speed in deploying instances, because a whole virtual machine doesn't have to be started for every application. Rather, the application, services, processes, libraries, and any other dependencies can be wrapped up into one unit. Additionally, each container operates in a sandbox, with the only means to interact being through the user interface or application programming interface (API) calls. Containers have enabled rapid development operations, because developers can test their code more quickly, changing only the components necessary in the container and then redeploying.

 EXAM TIP Containerization is simply running a particular application in a virtualized space, rather than running the entire guest operating system.

Serverless Architecture

Hosting a service usually means setting up hardware, provisioning and managing servers, defining load management mechanisms, setting up requirements, and running the service. In a serverless architecture, the services offered to end users, such as compute, storage, or messaging, along with their required configuration and management, can be performed without a requirement from the user to set up any server infrastructure. Serverless architecture takes advantage of the technologies we just discussed, such as virtualization and containerization. In this type of application of these technologies, the focus is strictly on functionality. These models are designed primarily for massive scaling and high availability.

How the services are delivered, whether it is through a full hardware server-based setup or through the use of a small piece of containerized application code, is fully transparent to the user. Additionally, from a cost perspective, they are attractive, because billing occurs based on what cycles are actually used versus what is provisioned in advance. Integrating security mechanisms into serverless models, however, is not as simple as ensuring that the underlying technologies are hardened, although that must be considered as well. Because there is limited visibility into hosted infrastructure operations, particularly those belonging to a third-party and provided as a service to the organization, implementing countermeasures for remote code execution or modifying access control lists isn't as straightforward as it would be with traditional server design. In this model, security analysts are usually restricted to applying controls at the application or function level, and implementing other security mechanisms becomes a responsibility of the hosting organization.

 EXAM TIP Serverless architectures rely on the concepts of containerization and virtualization to run small pieces of microcode in a virtualized environment to provide very specific services and functions.

Identity and Access Management

Before users are able to access resources, they must first prove they are who they claim to be and that they have been given the necessary rights or privileges to perform the actions they are requesting. Even after these steps are completed successfully and a user can access and use network resources, that user's activities must be tracked, and accountability must be enforced for whatever actions they take. *Identification* describes a method by which a subject (user, program, or process) claims to have a specific identity (username, account number, or e-mail address). *Authentication* is the process by which a system verifies the identity of the subject, usually by requiring a piece of information that only the claimed identity should have. This piece could be a password, passphrase, cryptographic key, personal identification number (PIN), biological attribute, or token. Together, the identification and authentication information (for example, username and password) make up the subject's *credentials*. Credentials are compared to information that has been previously stored for this subject. If the credentials match the stored information, the subject is authenticated. The system can then perform *authorization,* which is a check against some type of policy to verify that this user has indeed been authorized to access the requested resource and perform the requested actions.

Identity and access management (IAM) is a broad term that encompasses the use of different technologies and policies to identify, authenticate, and authorize users through automated means. It usually includes user account management, access control, credential management, single sign-on (SSO) functionality, rights and permissions management for user accounts, and the auditing and monitoring of all of these items. IAM enables organizations to create and manage digital identities' lifecycles (create, maintain, terminate) in a timely and automated fashion.

Multifactor Authentication

Unfortunately, authentication is still commonly based on credentials consisting of a username and a password. If a password is the only factor used in authenticating the account, this approach is considered *single-factor authentication*. *Multifactor authentication* (MFA) just means that more than one authentication factor is used. *Two-factor authentication* (2FA) is perhaps the most common form of authentication and usually relies on a code that is valid for only a short time, which is provided to the user by another system. For example, when logging in to your bank from a new computer, you may enter your username and password and then be required to provide a six-digit code. This code is provided by a separate application (such as Google Authenticator) and changes every 30 seconds. Some organizations will text a similar verification code to a user's mobile phone (though this approach is no longer considered secure) if, for example, you've forgotten your password and need to create a new one. For even more security, multifactor (two, or more factors used) authentication such as a smart card, PIN, and retinal scan, is used, particularly in government scenarios.

EXAM TIP   Multifactor authentication is the preferred modern authentication method. It requires that more than one factor, such as the knowledge factor, be used. Factors include something you know (knowledge factor), something you are (biometric or inherence factor), and something you possess (possession factor). Other factors can be included with multifactor authentication to further secure the process, including temporal factors (such as time of day) and location (such as logical IP address, hostname, or even geographic location).

Passwordless Authentication

Passwordless authentication works just like it sounds. It's essentially any method of authentication that does not use a password as an authenticator. Authentication methods using more secure means, such as multifactor authentication methods, one-time passwords, preregistered devices such as smartphones, USB security keys, and so on, are considered passwordless authentication methods. These methods can help prevent some of the more common pitfalls with using passwords, such as passwords that are shared between users, passwords that are written down, password cracking methods, and so on. While passwordless authentication methods are definitely more secure, the disadvantage is that they can be more costly; provisioning users with tokens or smart devices is generally more expensive than simply having them remember a password. However, any method that does not use a password as an authenticator is obviously preferred.

Single Sign-On

Employees typically need to access many different computers, communications services, web applications, and other resources throughout the course of a day to complete their tasks. This could require the employees to remember multiple credentials for these different resources. *Single sign-on* (SSO) enables users to authenticate only once and then be able to access all their authorized resources regardless of where they are. Note that all the resources accessed must be able to trust that the user has been properly authenticated.

Using SSO offers benefits both to the user and the administrator alike. Users need to remember only a single password or PIN, which reduces the fatigue associated with managing multiple passwords. Additionally, they'll save time by not having to reenter credentials for every service desired. For the administrator, using SSO means fewer calls from users who forget their passwords. Figure 1-10 shows the flow of an SSO request in Google using the Security Assertion Markup Language (SAML) standard, a widely used method of implementing SSO.

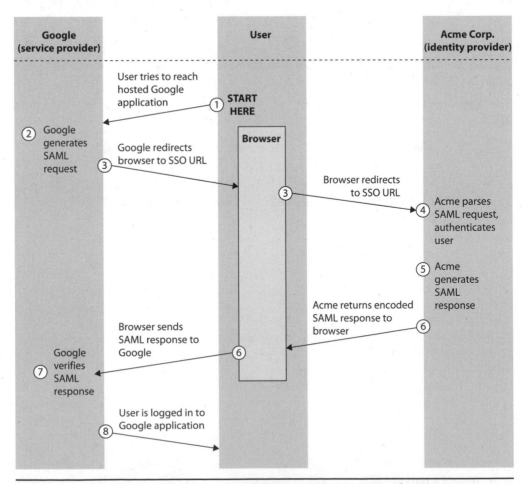

Figure 1-10   Single sign-on flow for a user-initiated request for identity verification

SAML provides access and authorization decisions using a system to exchange information between a user, the identity provider (IDP), such as Acme Corp., and the service provider (SP), such as Google. When a user requests access to a resource on the SP, the SP creates a request for identity verification for the IDP. The IDP will provide feedback about the user, and the SP can make its decision on an access control based on its own internal rules and the positive or negative response from the IDP. If access is granted, a token is generated in lieu of the actual credentials and passed on to the SP.

Although SSO improves the user experience in accessing multiple systems, it does have a significant drawback in the potential increase in impact if the credentials are compromised. Using an SSO platform thus requires a greater focus on the protection of the user credentials. This is where including multiple factors and context-based solutions can provide strong protection against malicious activity. Furthermore, as SSO centralizes the authentication mechanism, that system becomes a critical asset and thus a target for attacks. Compromise of the SSO system, or loss of availability, means loss of access to the entire organization's suite of applications that rely on the SSO system.

EXAM TIP   You will not be required to understand the SAML protocols and processes, but you should understand that they are associated with single sign-on and federated identities.

Federation

Federated identity is the concept of using a person's digital identity credentials to gain access to various services, often across organizations (referred to in this context as a *federation*). Whereas SSO can be implemented either within a single organization or among multiple ones, a federated identity applies only to the latter case. The user's identity credentials are provided by a broker known as the *federated identity manager*. When verifying their identity, the user needs only to authenticate with the identity manager; the application that's requesting the identity information also needs to trust the manager. Many popular platforms, such as Google, Amazon, and Twitter, take advantage of their large memberships to provide federated identity services for third-party websites, saving their users from having to create separate accounts for each site.

OpenID

OpenID is an open standard for user authentication by third parties. It is a lot like SAML, except that a user's credentials are maintained not by the user's company but by a third party. Why is this useful? By relying on a specialized identity provider (IDP) such as Amazon, Google, or Steam, developers of Internet services (such as websites) don't need to develop their own authentication systems. Instead, they are free to use any IDP or group of IDPs that conforms to the OpenID standard. All that is required is that all parties use the same standard and that everyone trusts the IDP(s).

OpenID defines three roles:

- **End user**   The user who wants to be authenticated in order to use a resource
- **Relying party**   The server that owns the resource that the end user is trying to access

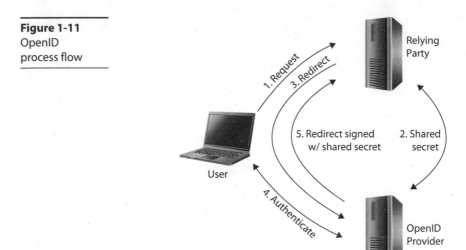

Figure 1-11
OpenID
process flow

- **OpenID provider**   The IDP (such as Google) on which the end user already has an account, and which will authenticate the user to the relying party

You have probably encountered OpenID if you've tried to access a website and were presented with the option to log in using your Google identity credentials. (Oftentimes you see an option for Google and one for Facebook in the same window, but Facebook uses its own protocol, Facebook Connect.) In a typical use case, depicted in Figure 1-11, a user wants to visit a protected website. The user's agent (typically a web browser) requests the protected resource from the relying party. The relying party connects to the OpenID provider and creates a shared secret for this transaction. The server then redirects the user agent to the OpenID provider for authentication. Upon authentication by the provider, the user agent receives a redirect (containing an authentication token, also known as the user's OpenID) to the relying party. The authentication token contains a field signed with the shared secret, so the relying party is assured that the user is authenticated.

Privileged Access Management

Over time, as users change roles or move from one department to another, they often are assigned more and more access rights and permissions. This is commonly referred to as *authorization creep*. This can pose a large risk for a company, because too many users may have too much privileged access to company assets. In immature organizations, it may be considered easier for network administrators to grant users more access than less; then a user would not later ask for authorization changes that would require more work to be done on their profile as their role changed. It can also be difficult to know the exact access levels different individuals require. This is why privileged access management (PAM) is a critical security function that should be regularly performed and audited. Enforcing least privilege on user accounts should be an ongoing job, which means each user's permissions should be reviewed regularly to ensure the company is not putting itself at risk.

This is particularly true of administrator or other privileged accounts because these allow users (legitimate or otherwise) to do things such as create new accounts (even other privileged ones), run processes remotely on other computers, and install or uninstall software. Because of the power privileged accounts have, they are frequently among the first targets for an attacker.

Here are some best practices for managing privileged accounts:

- Minimize the number of privileged accounts.
- Ensure that each administrator has a unique account (that is, no shared accounts).
- Elevate user privileges only when necessary, after which time the user should return to regular account privileges.
- Maintain an accurate, up-to-date account inventory.
- Monitor and log all privileged actions.
- Enforce multifactor authentication.

Sooner or later every account gets deprovisioned. For users, this is usually part of the termination procedures. For system accounts, this could happen because you got rid of a system or because some configuration change rendered an account unnecessary. If this is the case, you must ensure that this is included in your standard change management process. Whatever the type of account or the reason for getting rid of it, it is important that you document the change so that you no longer track that account for reviewing purposes.

Encryption

Encryption is a method of transforming readable data, called *plaintext,* into a form that appears to be random and unreadable, which is called *ciphertext.* Plaintext is in a form that can be understood either by a person (such as a document) or by a computer (such as executable code). Once plaintext is transformed into ciphertext, neither human nor machine can use it until it is *decrypted.* Encryption enables the transmission of confidential information over insecure channels without unauthorized disclosure. The science behind encryption and decryption is called *cryptography,* and a system that encrypts and/ or decrypts data is called a *cryptosystem.*

Although there can be several pieces to a cryptosystem, the two main pieces are the algorithms and the keys. Algorithms used in cryptography are complex mathematical formulas that dictate the rules of how the plaintext will be turned into ciphertext, and vice versa. A key is a string of random bits that will be used by the algorithm to add to the randomness of the encryption process. For two entities to be able to communicate using cryptography, they must use the same algorithm and, depending on the approach, the same or a complementary key. Let's dig into that last bit by exploring the two approaches to cryptography: symmetric and asymmetric.

Symmetric Cryptography

In a cryptosystem that uses *symmetric cryptography,* the sender and receiver use two instances of the same key for encryption and decryption, as shown in Figure 1-12.

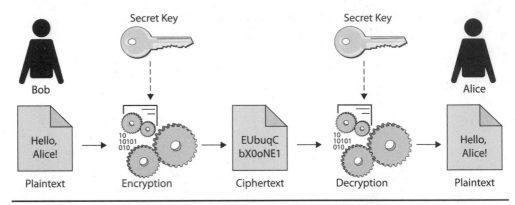

Figure 1-12 When using symmetric algorithms, the sender and receiver use the same key for encryption and decryption functions.

So the key has dual functionality, in that it can carry out both encryption and decryption processes. It turns out this approach is extremely fast and hard to break, even when using relatively small (such as 256-bit) keys. What's the catch? Well, if the secret key is compromised, all messages ever encrypted with that key can be decrypted and read by an intruder. Furthermore, if you want to separately share secret messages with multiple people, you'll need a different secret key for each, and you'll need to figure out a way to get that key to each person with whom you want to communicate securely. This is sometimes referred to as the key distribution problem.

Asymmetric Cryptography

Another approach is to use different keys for encryption and decryption, or *asymmetric cryptography*. The key pairs are mathematically related to each other in a way that enables anything that is encrypted by one to be decrypted by the other. The relationship, however, is complex enough that you can't figure out what the other key is by analyzing the first one. In asymmetric cryptosystems, a user keeps one key (the private key) secret and publishes the complimentary key (the public key). So, if Bob wants to send Alice an encrypted message, he uses her public key and knows that only she can decrypt it. This is shown in Figure 1-13. What happens if someone attempts to use the same asymmetric key to encrypt and decrypt a message? They get gibberish.

So what happens if Alice sends a message encrypted with her private key? Then anyone with her public key can decrypt it. Although this doesn't make much sense in terms of confidentiality, it assures every recipient that it was really Alice who sent it and that it wasn't modified by anyone else in transit. This is the premise behind digital signatures.

 EXAM TIP Symmetric key cryptography uses a single key shared between all entities involved in the communications, while asymmetric cryptography uses two keys, designated as a public and private key. Only the public key is shared with anyone; the private key is maintained securely by its owner.

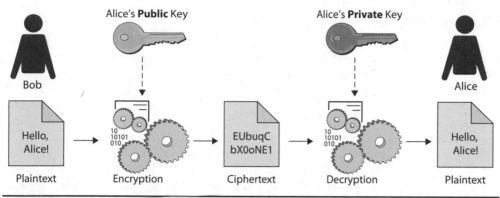

Figure 1-13 When using asymmetric algorithms, the sender encrypts a message with the recipient's public key, and the recipient decrypts it using a private key.

Symmetric vs. Asymmetric Cryptography

The biggest differences between symmetric and asymmetric cryptosystems boil down to key length and encryption/decryption time. Symmetric cryptography relies on keys that are random sequences of characters, and these can be fairly short (256 bits), but it would still require years for an attacker to conduct an effective brute-force attack against them. By contrast, asymmetric key pairs are not random with regard to each other (remember, they are related by a complex math formula), so they are easier to brute-force at a given key size compared to symmetric keys. For this reason, asymmetric keys have to be significantly longer to achieve the same level of security. The current NIST recommendation is that asymmetric key pairs be at least 2048 (and preferably 3072) bits in length.

The other big difference between these two approaches to cryptography is that symmetric cryptosystems (partly because they deal with smaller keys) are significantly faster than asymmetric ones. So, at this point, you may be wondering, why use asymmetric encryption at all if it is slower and requires bigger keys? The answer goes back to the key distribution problem we mentioned earlier. In practice, when transmitting information securely, we almost always use asymmetric cryptography to exchange secret keys between the parties involved, and then switch to symmetric cryptography for the actual transfer of information.

The synergistic use of both symmetric and asymmetric encryption together is what makes Public Key Infrastructure, along with digital certificates and digital signatures, possible. We'll discuss these topics next.

EXAM TIP Symmetric key cryptography is much faster and is very efficient when encrypting and decrypting a lot of data. However, key exchange is a significant problem. On the other hand, asymmetric key cryptography is much slower and cannot easily encrypt bulk data. However, key exchange is simple since the public key can be shared with anyone. This makes both of these different methods of cryptography complimentary and well suited to use together.

Public Key Infrastructure

When we discussed asymmetric key encryption, we talked about publishing one of the keys, but how exactly does that happen? If we allow anyone to push out a public key claiming to be Alice, then how do we know it really is her key and not an impostor's key? There are two ways in which the security community has tackled this problem. The first is through the use of a *web of trust,* which is a network of users who can vouch for each other and for other users wanting to join in. The advantage of this approach is that it is decentralized and free. It is a common approach for those who use Pretty Good Privacy (PGP) encryption.

Most businesses, however, prefer a more formal process for verifying identities associated with public keys, even if it costs more. This formalized process is the basis of what we refer to as Public Key Infrastructure, or PKI. What businesses need are trusted brokers who can vouch for the identity of a party using a particular key. These brokers are known as *certificate authorities* (CAs), and their job is to verify someone's identity and then digitally sign that public key, packaging it into a digital certificate or a public key certificate.

A *digital certificate* is a file that contains information about the certificate owner, the CA who issued it, the public key, its validity timeframe, and the CA's signature of the certificate itself. The de facto standard for digital certificates is X.509 and is defined by the Internet Engineering Task Force (IETF) in RFC 5280.

When a CA issues a digital certificate, it has a specific validity period. When that time elapses, the certificate is no longer valid, and the owner needs to get a new one. It is possible for the certificate to become invalid before it expires, however. For example, we stressed earlier the importance of keeping the private key protected, but what if it is compromised? In that case, the owner would have to invalidate the corresponding digital certificate and get a new one. Meanwhile, the public key in question may still be in use by others, so how do we notify the world to stop using it? A *certificate revocation list* (CRL), which is maintained by a revocation authority (RA), is the authoritative reference for certificates that are no longer trustworthy.

Digital certificate management involves the various actions undertaken by a certificate owner, its CA, and its RA to ensure that valid certificates are available and invalid ones are not used. From an organizational perspective, it is focused on acquiring certificates from a CA, deploying them to the appropriate systems, protecting the private keys, transitioning systems to a new certificate before the old ones expire, and reporting compromised (or otherwise no longer valid) certificates to the RA. It can also entail consulting a CRL to ensure the continued validity of certificates belonging to other entities with whom the organization does business.

 CAUTION   Many organizations disable CRL checks because they can slow down essential business processes. This decision introduces serious risks and should not be taken lightly.

Digital Signatures

Digital signatures are short sequences of data that prove that a larger data sequence (say, an e-mail message or a file) was created by a given person and has not been modified by anyone else after being signed. Suppose Alice wants to digitally sign an e-mail message.

She first takes a hash of it and encrypts that hash with her private key. She then appends the resulting encrypted hash to her (possibly unencrypted) e-mail. If Bob receives the message and wants to ensure that Alice really sent it, he would decrypt the hash using Alice's public key and then compare the decrypted hash with a hash he computes on his own. If the two hashes match, Bob knows that Alice really sent the message and nobody else changed it along the way.

 NOTE In practice, digital signatures are handled by e-mail and other cryptographic-enabled applications, so all the hashing and decryption are done automatically, not by the end user.

Sensitive Data Protection

Although we take measures to protect all kinds of data on our networks, there are some types of data that need special consideration with regard to storage and transmission. Unauthorized disclosure of the following types of data may have serious, adverse effects on the associated business, government, or individual. In this section, we will describe just a few of the sensitive data types you must consider, as a cybersecurity analyst, that must be protected. We will also discuss data loss prevention as a key cybersecurity process as well as a group of technologies.

Personally Identifiable Information

Personally identifiable information (PII) is data that can be used to identify an individual. PII is sometimes referred to as *sensitive personal information*. Often used in a government regulatory context, this type of data may include biometric data, genetic information, sexual orientation, and membership in professional or union groups.

This data requires protection because of the risk of personal harm that could result from its disclosure, alteration, or destruction. This information can be unique, such as a Social Security number or biometric profile, or it may be used with other data to trace back to an individual, as is the case with name and date of birth. This information is often used by criminals to conduct identity theft, fraud, or any other crime that targets an individual. Depending on the regulatory environment in which your organization operates, you may have to meet additional requirements with respect to the handling of PII, in addition to following federal and state laws. The US Privacy Act of 1974, for example, established strict rules regarding the collection, storage, use, and sharing of PII when it is provided to federal entities. In many industries and market segments, documents and media that contain PII are required to have appropriate markings

Personal Health Information

The Health Insurance Portability and Accountability Act of 1996 (HIPAA) is a law that establishes standards to protect individuals' personal health information (PHI). PHI is any data that relates to an individual's past, present, or future physical or mental health conditions. Usually, this information is handled by a healthcare provider, employer, public health authority, or school. HIPAA requires appropriate safeguards to protect the privacy of PHI, and it regulates what can be shared and with whom, with and without patient authorization. HIPAA prescribes specific reporting requirements for violations, with significant penalties for HIPAA violations and the unauthorized disclosure of PHI, including fines and jail sentences for criminally liable parties.

Cardholder Data

Consumer privacy and the protection of financial data has been an increasingly visible topic in recent years. Mandates by the European Union's General Data Protection Regulation (GDPR), for example, have introduced a sweeping number of protections for the handling of personal data, which includes financial information. Although similar modern legislation is being developed in the United States, some existing rules apply to US financial services companies and the way they handle this information. The Gramm-Leach-Bliley Act (GLBA) of 1999, for example, covers all US-regulated financial services corporations. The GLBA applies to banks, securities firms, and most entities handling financial data and requires that these entities take measures to protect their customers' data from threats to its confidentiality and integrity. The Federal Trade Commission's Financial Privacy Rule governs the collection of customers' personal financial information and identifies requirements regarding privacy disclosure on a recurring basis. Penalties for noncompliance include fines for institutions of up to $100,000 for each violation. Individuals found in violation may face fines of up to $10,000 for each violation and imprisonment for up to five years.

This leads to a discussion on the Payment Card Industry Data Security Standard (PCI DSS). PCI DSS is an example of an industry policing itself and was created by the major credit card companies such as Visa, MasterCard, American Express, and so on, to reduce credit card fraud and protect cardholder information. As a global standard for protecting stored, processed, or transmitted data, it prescribes general guidelines based on industry best practices.

PCI DSS does not specifically identify what technologies should be used to achieve its associated goals. Rather, it offers broad requirements that may have multiple options for compliance. Though used globally, PCI DSS is not federally mandated in the United States. However, it's worth noting that if a business fails to adequately protect cardholder data (CHD), they could be banned from processing such data by the companies that make up the Payment Card Industry. Although some US states enact their own laws to prevent unauthorized disclosure and abuse of payment card information, PCI DSS remains the de facto standard for cardholder data protection. Note that some aspects of PCI DSS will be discussed in more detail in Chapter 9.

 EXAM TIP You should implement security mechanisms that meet regulatory requirements for sensitive data protection, such as PII, PHI, and cardholder data. These mechanisms may well be above and beyond what you may implement to protect less-sensitive data.

Data Loss Prevention

Digital communication increases the speed and ease of interaction, particularly across great distances. Combine this with the decreasing cost of storage, and the security risks are apparent. Even in the days before high-capacity, removable storage and high-speed connections, unauthorized removal of data from organizations was the bane of auditors and security professionals. What's more, the increasing trends related to data spillage are not restricted to actors who are knowingly malicious. In fact, many employees don't realize that it may be inappropriate to store the company's sensitive materials on a personal device or in unapproved cloud-based storage. At the core of the challenge is a tension between IT and the security team's responsibility to ensure that data is protected when stored, accessed, and transmitted, while simultaneously allowing the unencumbered flow of data to support business operations.

Data loss prevention (DLP) comprises the actions that organizations take to prevent unauthorized external parties from gaining access to sensitive data. That definition has some key terms you should know. First, the data has to be considered *sensitive*. We can't keep every single piece of data safely locked away inside our systems, so we focus our attention, efforts, and funds on the truly important data. Second, DLP is concerned with *external parties*. If somebody in the accounting department, for example, gains access to internal research and development data, that is a problem, but technically it is not considered a data leak. Finally, the external party gaining access to our sensitive data must be *unauthorized* to do so. If former business partners have some of our sensitive data that they were authorized to get at the time they were employed, that is not considered a data leak. Although this emphasis on semantics may seem excessive, it is necessary to approach this tremendous threat to our organizations properly.

There is no one-size-fits-all approach to DLP, but there are tried-and-true principles that can be helpful. One important principle is the integration of DLP with our risk-management processes. This enables us to balance out the totality of risks we face and favor controls that mitigate those risks in multiple areas simultaneously. Not only is this helpful in making the most of our resources, but it also keeps us from making decisions in one silo with little or no regard to their impact on other silos. In the sections that follow, we will look at key elements of any approach to DLP.

Many DLP solutions work in a similar fashion to IDSs by inspecting the type of traffic moving across the network, attempting to classify it, and making a go or no-go decision based on the aggregate of signals. After all, if you can detect a certain type of traffic coming in, you ought to be able to do the same for outbound traffic. Early iterations of DLP were most effective with predictable patterns such as Social Security and credit card numbers. These techniques are less useful for more complex patterns, however, or in the presence of complicated encoding or encryption methods, in which case deep inspection of packets becomes much more difficult.

Some SaaS platforms feature DLP solutions that can be enabled to help your organization comply with business standards and industry regulations. Microsoft Office 365 and Google G Suite are two notable services that make DLP solutions available to be applied to media such as e-mails, word processing documents, presentation documents, spreadsheets, and compressed files. Many of these solutions require the configuration of rules that take into account data content, such as the exact type of data you're looking to monitor for, as well as the context, such as who is involved in the data exchange. With SaaS solutions, your organization may have to expose at least part of its data to the service provider, which may introduce unacceptable exposure in itself. Cloud service providers are in a unique position because they have to comply with privacy laws and data protection legislation that applies to data that is not their own. It's in their best interest to use DLP, in addition to many other technologies, to protect data in use, in transit, and at rest. It may be incumbent on you, as your organization's security lead, to read, understand, and communicate a cloud provider's terms of service and policies regarding data protection.

 EXAM TIP Data loss prevention is both a security management activity and a collection of technologies.

Data Inventories

A good first step is to find and characterize all the data in your organization before you even look at DLP solutions. If you've carefully considered your data types, their sensitivity and criticality, and the types of protection they require, you may already know what data is most important to your organization. Once you figure this out, you can start looking for that data across your servers, workstations, mobile devices, cloud computing platforms, and anywhere else it may live. Once you get a handle on your high-value data and where it resides, you can gradually expand the scope of your search to include less valuable, but still sensitive, data. As you keep expanding the scope of your search, you will reach a point of diminishing returns in which the data you are inventorying is not worth the time you spend looking for it.

Data Flows

Data that stays put is usually of little use to anyone. Most data will move according to specific business processes through specific network pathways. Understanding data flows at this intersection between business and IT is critical to implementing DLP. Many organizations put their DLP sensors at the perimeter of their networks, thinking that is where the leakages would occur. But if these sensors are placed in that location only, a large number of leaks may not be detected or stopped. Additionally, as we will discuss shortly when we cover network DLP, perimeter sensors can often be bypassed by sophisticated attackers.

Implementation, Testing, and Tuning

Assuming we've done our administrative homework and have a good understanding of our true DLP requirements, we can evaluate products. Once we select a DLP solution, the next interrelated tasks are integration, testing, and tuning. Obviously, we want to ensure that bringing the new toolset online won't disrupt any of our existing systems or processes, but testing needs to cover a lot more than that. The most critical elements when testing any DLP solution are to verify that it allows authorized data processing and to ensure that it prevents unauthorized data processing.

Finally, we must remember that everything changes. The solution that is exquisitely implemented, finely tuned, and effective immediately is probably going to be ineffective in the near future if we don't continuously maintain and improve it. Apart from the efficacy of the tool itself, our organizations change as people, products, and services come and go. The ensuing cultural and environmental changes will also change the effectiveness of our DLP solutions. And, obviously, if we fail to realize that users are installing rogue access points, using thumb drives without restriction, or clicking malicious links, then it is just a matter of time before our expensive DLP solution will be circumvented.

Network DLP

Network DLP (NDLP) applies data protection policies to data in motion. NDLP products are normally implemented as appliances that are deployed at the perimeter of an organization's networks. They can also be deployed at the boundaries of internal subnetworks and could be deployed as modules within a modular security appliance. Figure 1-14 shows how an NDLP solution might be deployed with a single appliance at the edge of the network and communicating with a DLP policy server.

Endpoint DLP

Endpoint DLP (EDLP) applies protection policies to data at rest and data in use. EDLP is implemented in software running on each protected endpoint. This software, usually called a DLP agent, communicates with the DLP policy server to update policies and report events. Figure 1-15 illustrates an EDLP implementation.

EDLP provides a degree of protection that is normally not possible with NDLP. The reason is that the data is observable at the point of creation. When a user enters personally identifiable information (PII) on the device during an interview with a client, for

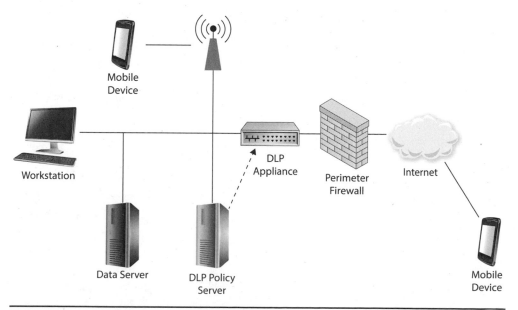

Figure 1-14   Network DLP

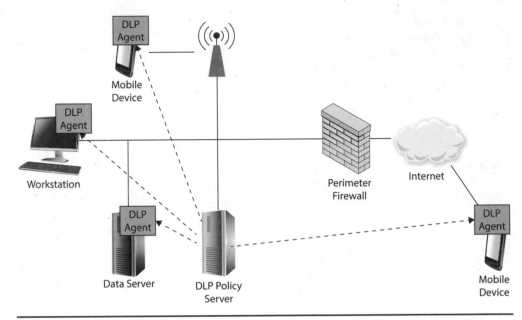

Figure 1-15 Endpoint DLP

example, the EDLP agent detects the new sensitive data and immediately applies the pertinent protection policies to it. Even if the data is encrypted on the device when it is at rest, it will have to be decrypted whenever it is in use, which allows for EDLP inspection and monitoring. Finally, if the user attempts to copy the data to a non-networked device such as a thumb drive, or if it is improperly deleted, EDLP will pick up on these possible policy violations. None of these examples would be possible using NDLP.

Hybrid DLP

Another approach to DLP is to deploy both NDLP and EDLP across the enterprise. Obviously, this approach is the costliest and most complex. For organizations that can afford it, however, it offers the best coverage. Figure 1-16 shows how a hybrid NDLP/EDLP deployment might look.

NOTE Most modern DLP solutions offer both network and endpoint DLP components, making them hybrid solutions.

Secure Sockets Layer and Transport Layer Security Inspection

Although the original Secure Sockets Layer (SSL) security protocol has been deprecated for several years now, security and IT personnel alike (as well as the formal exam objectives) still refer to the process of breaking certificate-based network encryption as *SSL inspection*. While there may be yet organizations and systems out there that still use SSL, it has

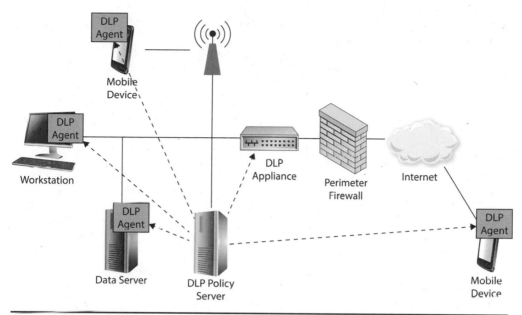

Figure 1-16   Hybrid DLP

been overwhelmingly replaced by the use of Transport Layer Security (TLS) due to glaring vulnerabilities that affected even the latest versions of the SSL protocol. For consistency purposes we will continue to refer to this process as the exam objectives do but understand that SSL is a thing of the past.

SSL/TLS inspection is the process of interrupting encrypted session between an end user and a secure web-based server for the purposes of breaking data encryption and inspecting the contents of the message traffic that is transmitted and received between the user and the web server. On the surface, this would seem to be a direct violation of privacy for the user, and that is a true statement. However, the primary reason organizations may engage in SSL/TLS inspection is to prevent sensitive data loss or exfiltration.

This is not an easy task, in that the organization must implement several complex technical measures to interrupt the session and become a proxy for the encrypted traffic by essentially forging a certificate on behalf of either the client or the server. There are several technical difficulties with SSL/TLS inspection, since many web servers will reject any attempts to masquerade as the end user or client. Additionally, SSL/TLS inspection introduces significant latency into the network, since it must decrypt all sessions and inspect the traffic, then re-encrypt the traffic and send it on to the destination. Combine those two issues with the fact that there must be a DLP solution set up that can inspect the decrypted traffic and alert if any prohibited data is being sent through the connection, which in turn must be managed by a human, and this can create a lot of work for cybersecurity analysts, as well as become taxing on the network. These technical difficulties alone mean that in practice, SSL/TLS inspection is not performed very often, except in very sensitive environments, and then only on very specific traffic meeting particular characteristics from sensitive or critical hosts.

Another consideration is that the organization attempting SSL/TLS inspection must be very clear on which encrypted communications sessions it will interrupt; privacy policies, as well as laws and regulations, may prevent an organization from intercepting certain protected communications sessions, such as those between a user and healthcare or financial provider, for instance.

 EXAM TIP   You may see references to SSL inspection on the exam, but in the practical world, SSL has been deprecated and is no longer considered secure. TLS is the preferred replacement for SSL applications.

Chapter Review

In this first chapter, we discussed several critical foundational concepts, such as network architecture, logging, identity access management, encryption, and protecting sensitive data.

Logging is a critical part of auditing and helps to ensure countability and nonrepudiation, since it records events that have taken place across the infrastructure and ties those events to a particular entity. It's important that we have an accurate time source so that audit logs can be correlated with each other and a timeframe where a series of events can be constructed. Log ingestion can be simplified by the use of advanced tools such as security event information management systems.

Operating systems directly control hardware and software applications and serve as an intermediary between the user, the hardware device, and applications that run on that device. The operating system consists of critical system files, as well as the libraries and utilities that perform critical functions and tasks on the system. Configuration information for Windows hosts is stored in the registry, while Linux hosts use plaintext files stored in the /etc directory. System hardening is the process of locking down a host with tight security configurations and patch management. The file structure on a system is dependent on the operating system that runs on the host and is responsible for file storage and access to media. System processes are activities that run in the background to support applications and the operating system. The hardware architecture that makes up a complete system consists of, at a minimum, CPU, RAM, and storage media, among other components.

Network architectures vary between on-premises devices and cloud-based models. Key concepts in constructing networks include segmentation of sensitive or critical hosts as well as zero trust, which essentially means that trust must be initially established by frequent reverification in the event a host becomes compromised. Many networks use software-defined networking versus hardware networking so they can be more effectively secured and reconfigured when necessary. A Secure Access Secure Edge system combines the concepts of software-defined wide area networking and zero trust to ensure that systems that are separated geographically are secured. Cloud service models include Software as a Service, Platform as a Service, and Infrastructure as a Service, along with many other type of services. Cloud deployment models include public, private, community, and hybrid, and they focus on the level of sharing that goes on within the cloud deployment model as well as who owns the infrastructure.

Concepts that can affect how you manage the infrastructure in its security processes include virtualization, containerization, and serverless architecture. These processes can help isolate and protect systems as well as applications and services running on the network.

We also discussed key points regarding identity and access management, including the case for multifactor authentication or any other passwordless authentication method. Single sign-on reduces the requirement for users to remember multiple usernames and passwords, since they will be able to use only one method of authentication to access multiple resources, assuming those resources trust the source of the authentication. Federated ID management means that a third-party brokers identification and authentication services between resources across multiple organizations.

The building blocks of encryption include both symmetric and asymmetric cryptography, which when combined enable the formal Public Key Infrastructure that assists in managing digital certificates and signatures.

Finally, we also discussed the protection of sensitive data, including personally identifiable information, personal health information, and cardholder data. We discussed each of these data types in detail, as well as the necessity for implementing a data loss prevention program and technologies in the organization.

Questions

1. During routine log reviews, you notice that certain events that should take place before others are out of sequence. Which of the following should you check to see if it is an issue?

   A. Network time synchronization

   B. Misconfiguration of auditing for certain security events

   C. Inadequate permissions for accessing log files

   D. Log ingestion issues with the security event information management (SIEM) system

2. Which architecture would you choose if you were particularly interested in adaptive control of how data moves around the network?

   A. Software-defined

   B. Physical

   C. Serverless

   D. Virtual private network

3. Best practices for managing privileged accounts include all of the following *except* which one?

   A. Maintain an accurate, up-to-date account inventory.

   B. Monitor and log all privileged actions.

   C. Ensure that you have only a single privileged account.

   D. Enforce multifactor authentication.

4. Which of the following statements most accurately describes the Windows registry?

   A. Open for any authenticated user or application to view and edit

   B. Stored in the /etc directory

   C. Proprietary hierarchical database containing all configuration items

   D. Plaintext file containing all configuration items

5. You are configuring authentication policies for hosts on the network. You have learned about zero trust and how it works. Which of the following should you include in your authentication policy to ensure that zero trust has been implemented on your network?

   A. Disallow authentication between all hosts, as they are not trusted by default.

   B. Eliminate the requirement for hosts authenticate to each other.

   C. Periodically perform reauthentication between hosts.

   D. Ensure that single sign-on is turned on for your network.

6. You wish to install an application on the network, but it would be the only application running on the server. You are looking for a more efficient way to run the application without the overhead of a full physical server. Which of the following would meet your needs?

   A. Infrastructure as a Service

   B. Platform as a Service

   C. Serverless architecture

   D. Containerization

7. To improve user authentication and secure access to several subscription services provided by a third-party infrastructure, which of the following technologies would be most helpful?

   A. Asymmetric cryptography

   B. Cloud access security broker

   C. Public key infrastructure

   D. Serverless architecture

8. Which of the following is not a normal part of system hardening?

   A. Increase the number of administrative user accounts on the host in case the default administrator account is inadvertently locked.

   B. Apply security policies.

   C. Change the default passwords for all system accounts.

   D. Apply the latest operating system and application patches.

Answers

1. **A.** The first item you should check is network time synchronization. If events are out of sequence, it could be that the time synchronization for the network or one of the hosts is off.

2. **A.** A software-defined network architecture provides the most adaptability when it comes to managing traffic flows. You could also accomplish this in some VPCs, but that would not be as flexible and was not an option.

3. **C.** Though you certainly want to minimize the number of privileged accounts, having only one means one of two things are certain to happen: either you'll have multiple people sharing the same account, or you'll be locked out of making any changes to your environment if the account holder is not willing or able to do the job.

4. **C.** The Windows registry is a proprietary hierarchical database that is only allowed to be read by specific privileged users and applications.

5. **C.** To implement zero trust on the network, all hosts, after their initial authentication, should be required to reauthenticate to each other on a periodic basis.

6. **D.** In this scenario, the only thing you need to run is an application in its own virtualized container. You don't need a full operating system, and the application will be run on the premises. It is not a serverless architecture since it is a full application instead of a simple service.

7. **B.** A cloud access security broker is likely the appropriate solution since it will control user authentication and secure access to subscription services offered through a third party. These services are likely cloud-based.

8. **A.** Increasing the number of privileged accounts on a host is not normally part of system hardening; this is actually the opposite and opens up the system to a wider attack surface.

Standardizing and Streamlining Security Operations

In this chapter you will learn about:
- Streamlining and standardizing security operations
- Integrating security technologies and tools
- The role of automation technologies in modern security operations
- Best practices for employing orchestration technologies
- Best practices for building automation workflows and playbooks

No one can whistle a symphony. It takes an orchestra to play it.

—H. E. Luccock

In this chapter we discuss how to make our security operations work as a well-tuned machine. This is accomplished by having standardized processes and procedures that are well documented, as well as having personnel who are well trained on those procedures. Processes and procedures should be efficient and manage resources such as money, equipment, and people resources well. In addition to being efficient, however, security operations should also be effective, meaning that they should not only do the job well but should also do the right job to the maximum extent possible. This is where streamlining operations comes into play; manual processes and procedures should be examined to see if they can be made more effective by better organizing, managing, and automating them. Finally, it's important to discuss aspects of integrating security technologies and tools that collect and analyze security data as well as perform critical tasks and connect disparate applications and systems. This chapter continues our discussion on security operations as well as addresses Objective 1.5, "Explain the importance of efficiency and process improvement in security operations."

Streamlining Security Operations

Security processes can be tedious and repetitive. Whether you're testing software functionality for vulnerabilities or responding to frequently occurring incidents, you'll find a certain level of automation to be helpful, particularly for activities that do not require a

45

great amount of analyst intervention. The goal is not to move the entire security process to full automation but rather to create the conditions that enable the analyst to focus brainpower on complex activities. Vulnerability management analysts can automate repeated security testing cases, for example, and instead focus their energies on exploring the in-depth weaknesses in critical services and validating complex logic flaws. Even the best analysts make mistakes, and although they work their best to secure systems, they do introduce limitations and occasional inconsistencies that may lead to catastrophic results. As systems get more and more complex, the number of steps required to perform a remediation may scale accordingly, meaning that the sheer number of actions needed to secure a system correctly grows, as do the demands on an analyst's attention.

To assist with this, we'll cover several automation concepts. Automation, in the context of security operations, refers to the application of technologies that leverage standards and protocols to perform specific, common security functions for a fixed period or indefinitely. One of the primary driving forces in high efficiency productions systems such as lean manufacturing and the famously effective Toyota Production System is the principle of *jidoka*. Loosely translated as "automation with a human touch," *jidoka* enables machines to identify flaws in their own operations or enables operators in a manufacturing environment to quickly flag suspicious mechanical behaviors. This principle has allowed for operators to be freed from continuously controlling machines, leaving the machines free to operate autonomously until they reach an error condition, at which point a human has the opportunity to exercise judgement to diagnose and remediate the issue. Most importantly, at least for efficiency, is that *jidoka* frees the human worker to concentrate on other tasks while the machines run. We can apply *jidoka* concepts to security to take advantage of standardization, consistent processes, and automation to reduce the cognitive burden on an analyst. Using specifications on how to interface with various systems across the network, along with using automated alerting and report delivery mechanisms, we can see massive increases in efficiency while experiencing fewer mistakes and employee turnover as a result of burnout. Additionally, the use of specifications and standards means that troubleshooting becomes more effective, more accurate, and less costly, while allowing for easy auditing of systems.

Automation and Orchestration

Automation proves itself as a crucial tool for security teams to address threats in a timely manner, while also providing some relief for analysts in avoiding repetitive tasks. However, to be truly effective, automation is often confined to systems using the same protocol. Although many analysts, including the authors, find success using scripting languages such as Python to interact with various system interfaces, there are challenges with managing these interactions at scale and across homogeneous environments. Keeping tabs with how actions are initiated and under what conditions, and what reporting should be provided, gets especially tricky as new systems and technologies are added to the picture. Orchestration is the step beyond automation that aims to provide an instrumentation and management layer for systems automation. Good security orchestration solutions not only connect various tools seamlessly, but they do so in a manner that enables the tools to talk to one another and provide feedback to the orchestration system without requiring major adjustments to the tools themselves. This is often achieved by making use of the tools' application programming interfaces (APIs).

 EXAM TIP Keep in mind the difference between automation and orchestration. Automation allows a sequence of tasks to be programmed into a tool, such as an API or a script, and orchestration is a level above automation that provides overall instrumentation, control, and management for automated processes.

Security Orchestration, Automation, and Response

As teams begin to integrate and automate their suites of security tools, they invariably come up against the limitations of specialized scripting and in-house expertise. Getting disparate security systems to work nicely together to respond to suspicious activity is not a trivial task, so a market for security orchestration, automation, and response (SOAR) tools has emerged to meet this need. Described by IT research firm Gartner as "technologies that enable organizations to collect security threats data and alerts from different sources, where incident analysis and triage can be performed leveraging a combination of human and machine power to help define, prioritize and drive standardized incident response activities according to a standard workflow," SOAR tools enable teams to automate frequent tasks within a particular technology as well as coordinate actions from different systems using repeatable workflows. Like security information and event management (SIEM) platforms, SOAR solutions often include comprehensive dashboard and reporting capabilities; in many cases, they work alongside SIEM solutions to help security teams maximize analyst productivity.

Acquired by Splunk in 2018 and renamed Splunk Phantom, the orchestration platform formerly known as Phantom Cyber is one of the most comprehensive SOAR platforms in the industry. Coupled with customizable dashboard functionality, the Phantom platform aims to address two of the major challenges facing security teams: back-end integration and front-end presentation. Offered in both commercial and community versions, Phantom provides out-of-the-box integration with hundreds of data sources, instances, and devices by way of apps. Figure 2-1 shows a snapshot of a few popular apps and the supported actions related to those technologies. It's also possible to create custom app integrations with third-party services and APIs.

As far as dashboard options are concerned, Phantom provides a multitude of metrics to help you gain a better understanding of both system and analyst performance, as shown in Figure 2-2. Analysts can get a sense of what kinds of events are in the pipeline, what playbooks are used most often, and the return on investment (ROI) associated with these events and actions. ROI, measured in both time and dollars saved, can be particularly powerful for a team in communicating the value of investment in orchestration platforms and training.

Orchestration Playbooks

Playbooks are workflows that help you visualize and execute processes across your security footprint in accordance with your orchestration rules. Also referred to as *runbooks,* these steps can be fully automated, or they can require human intervention at any point along

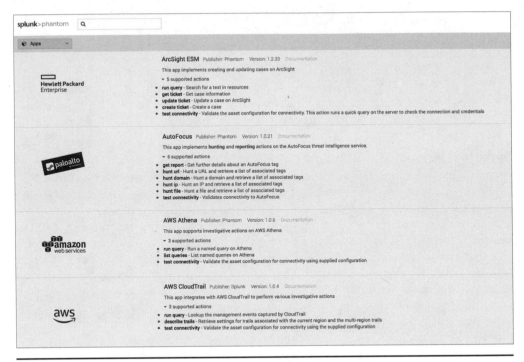

Figure 2-1 A portion of Splunk Phantom's supported apps

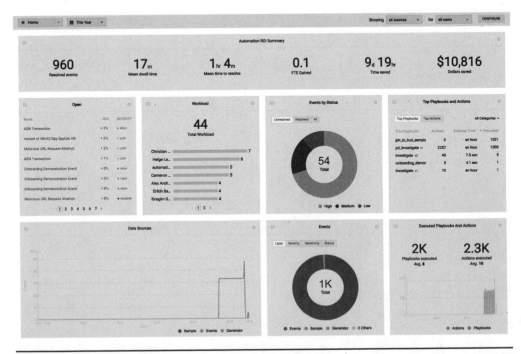

Figure 2-2 A portion of the Splunk Phantom dashboard

the process. Much like a recipe, a playbook prescribes the steps to be taken in a formulaic, often highly scalable, manner. In viewing their security process like an algorithm, security teams can eliminate much of the need for manual intervention, save for the most critical decision points. Playbooks are also discussed from an incident response and management perspective in Chapter 14.

To be complete, all playbooks must have a few key components. The first is the *initiating condition,* or the rules that must be triggered to begin the steps within the rest of the playbook. Often, this is the presence of artifacts that meet whatever your organization defines as a security incident. Sometimes, the condition may be preventative in nature and be initiated on some schedule. This initial condition may set off a series of actions across many security devices, each of which would normally take a bit of human interaction. This step alone significantly reduces the investment in analyst resources—an investment that may not always lead to anything actionable.

Next are the *process steps* that the playbook will invoke by interacting with the various technologies across the organization. In many cases, security orchestration solutions have software libraries that enable the platform to interact seamlessly with technology. For some of the more popular orchestration solutions, these libraries are written in coordination with the service provider to ensure maximum compatibility. For the analyst, this means minimal configuration on the front end, while in other cases, libraries may need to be initially set up manually within the orchestration software.

Finally, an *end state* must be defined for the playbook. Whether this comes in the form of an action to remediate or an e-mailed report, ensuring that a well-defined outcome is reached is important for the long-term viability of the playbook. It may well be the case that the outcome for one playbook is the initiating activity for another. This is the concept of *chaining,* in which multiple playbook actions originate from a single initiating condition. This final stage of a playbook's operation will often include some kind of reporting and auditing functionality. While these products may not be directly applicable to the remediation effort itself, they are incredibly valuable for improving overall orchestration performance as well as meeting any regulatory requirements your organization may have.

Orchestration is not only a tremendous time-saver, but it also facilitates a diversity of actions, such as technical and nontechnical, to be included in an overall security strategy. For example, a process such as an e-mail phishing investigation will benefit from a number of orchestration-enabled tasks. Enriching e-mail addresses and suspicious links by pulling data from threat intelligence data sets and then forwarding those domains to a deny-listing service, should they have a negative verdict, are tasks well suited for automation. Furthermore, trend reports can be generated over time and sent automatically to a training and communications team for use in improving user training. These kinds of tasks replace what may normally be a few hours of cutting, pasting, and formatting. When these tasks are chained within an orchestration tool, an initial signal about a suspicious e-mail can begin several processes without the need of any manual intervention from the security team, as shown in Figure 2-3.

Many modern SOAR platforms include the ability to design playbooks both textually and visually. Using the previous phishing workflow, you can see an example of the visual breakout of a playbook related to phishing in Figure 2-4. Named phishing_investigate_ and_respond, this playbook extracts various artifacts from suspected phishing messages

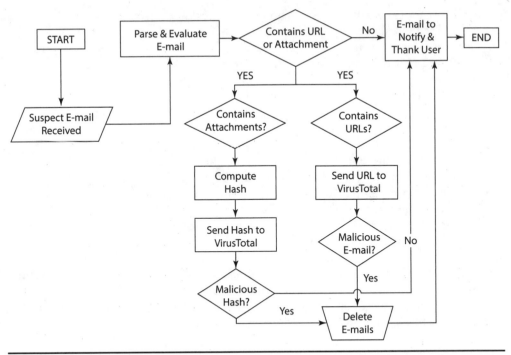

Figure 2-3 Example playbook for automated processing of suspected phishing e-mail

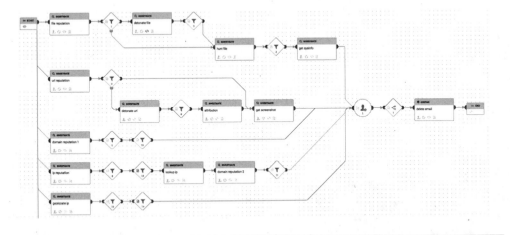

Figure 2-4 Splunk Phantom visual playbook editor

and uses them as input in querying enrichment sources, or data sources, that can give additional context to the artifacts. Any attachments, for example, are submitted to file reputation providers for a verdict, while URLs, domains, and IP addresses are passed to sources that can provide details on those aspects.

Figure 2-5 Splunk Phantom visual playbook editor showing a human prompt for action

Depending on how the playbooks are configured, they may call upon one or more apps to interact with data sources or devices. Playbook design becomes crucially important as event volume increases to ensure that the processes remain resilient while not overly consuming outside resources, such as API calls.

In some situations, your organization may require that a human take action because of the potential for adverse impact in the case of a false positive. Imagine for a moment that your organization has a highly synchronized identity management system, and a number of playbooks are related to account takeover actions. If one of these is written to perform a fully automated account reset, to include session logouts, password and token resets, and multifactor authentication (MFA) reset, it could cause catastrophic effects if initiated on a low-quality signal, such as the presence of suspicious language in an e-mail. A full account reset, therefore, is an action for which a fully automated action might not be the best; it makes sense to check and double-check that the action is warranted, however. Another action that may benefit from human interaction is blocking domains. Depending on your organization's network access policies, you may want to fully domain block or prompt an analyst for review. Domains, as you may know, often have associated reputations. This reputation can change over time, or it may be the case that a domain has earned a malicious reputation as a result of a temporary loss of control but has since recovered. Considering these possibilities, it may be prudent to require analyst input into the blocking process, as shown in Figure 2-5. Phantom's editor allows for prompts to team members for approval.

 EXAM TIP You do not have to be familiar with the playbook construction or format from any particular security tool; however, you should be familiar with the general concepts and characteristics of playbooks, such as initiating condition, process steps, and end state.

Process Standardization

Efficiency is said to be the measure of how well something is performed, such as a task, or even overall management of a process. We think of efficiency in terms of performing a task faster, with less time, money, labor, or materials, or with fewer required steps to complete it. Effectiveness, on the other hand, looks at a much higher view and is focused on the level of quality of the work produced by the task or process, and if it is the right activity in the first place.

Standardizing IT and security processes in the infrastructure is bound to produce both efficiency and, hopefully, effectiveness. It's not just a matter of performing a task well; it's a matter of making sure it's the right task in the first place and that it's producing quality results that make a difference. Standardization ensures that everyone is performing an activity the same way and that it is formally defined, repeatable, and documented. It reduces duplicative work and hopefully also reduces errors and eliminates the possibility of rework.

One of the ways that processes can be standardized is through automation. Automation helps us use our IT and security tools more efficiently and effectively by reducing human error and performing tasks faster and with less labor. This directly contributes to our security program being more effective at protecting people, systems, data, and other assets. It also reduces risk and uses resources more efficiently.

 NOTE The primary reason for standardizing processes in your security management program is to ensure that they are both efficient in terms of resource usage, such as time, money, and materials, and effective in terms of quality results.

Identification of Tasks Suitable for Automation

More modern technologies, as well as security and IT tools, generally offer easier ways to connect to each other and automate tasks between technologies than older ones. The interfacing capabilities of the technology or tool, in that case, may make a difference in how easy it is to automate tasks as well as exchange data between technologies and applications. Some tools and technologies offer interoperability and compatibility with other tools right out of the box; using standardized protocols, data exchange formats, and user interfaces can make automating tasks much easier. When applications don't necessarily make it easier to automate data exchange or task performance between them, this is when you may need to look at developing methods to do so. This involves creating links between technologies that may use APIs or scripting, for instance. We will discuss both of those methods later on in the chapter. An even bigger question may be how does an organization determine what should be automated if a tool or technology does not automatically provide the capability to automate a task or process? The organization has to decide what requirements it will use for determining if a task could or should be automated.

There are several criteria an organization may establish to determine if a task, process, or activity should be included in its automation efforts. These include, but are not limited to, the following:

- Simplicity of a task or activity
- Time, labor, or other resources spent performing an activity manually
- Activities performed in a repetitive manner
- Requirements for human decision-making
- Need to minimize human interaction with the process for efficiency or to reduce errors

- Integration of disparate technologies or security tools (for example, common protocols, programming languages, and data formats)
- Need for building data or control interfaces between technologies or applications (for example, creating scripts that transform data between applications or APIs used to invoke processes between applications)

EXAM TIP Identifying areas for automation helps to support the efficiency and effectiveness of security processes and management. Any task that is tedious, time-consuming, or repetitive is ripe for automation. Critical tasks that require human intervention and decision-making should be manually performed.

Minimizing Human Engagement

One of the primary reasons for automation and orchestration is to minimize the human factor in security operations. There are several good reasons for this. First of all, humans make mistakes. That's not to say that computers and devices don't as well; however, their mistakes are generally the result of poor programming on the part of human beings in the first place. When humans perform a task, it can be nonstandardized and unpredictable. They may not perform the same task consistently the same way over and over. Therefore, it's better to have a standardized way, using automation such as scripts, that can guarantee the tasks are performed the same way every single time.

Additionally, many security tasks, when performed by humans, do not get done as quickly or as efficiently as when automation is used. Automation can help bear the load by performing mundane, tedious, and time-consuming tasks far more quickly. This can free up human security analysts to focus on important tasks that require human intervention and critical decision-making.

EXAM TIP Remember that the primary reasons for minimizing human intervention in security processes are to reduce errors, perform tasks more efficiently, and better utilize people for other critical tasks that require human decision-making or human intervention.

Team Coordination to Manage and Facilitate Automation

In both small and large organizations, managing a technical workforce can be problematic, for different reasons. In a smaller organization, where there may not be many trained people available to perform tasks due to workloads, it can be difficult to assign tasks to the right person and avoid over-tasking them. In larger organizations, where the infrastructure can be far more complex, the same problem exists, but it's because there may only be one or two "experts" on a specific technology or process. In either case, the organization needs to be able to hire the right people who are adequately trained to perform all tasks, while at the same time efficiently and effectively scheduling their workload around the priorities of the organization.

This is yet another area where automation can be helpful, but it also stands to reason that there should be knowledgeable staff who can create and manage the automation methods implemented into the organizational infrastructure. Someone has to be able to write the scripts or manage the APIs that can help automate security tasks and activities. Once automation has become embedded in security and IT processes, managers have to make decisions about how to effectively employ and utilize knowledgeable personnel for other activities that require human intervention and decision-making. Obviously, no one wants it to happen, but frequently automation can eliminate the need for a person performing a particular task, so it's a good idea to manage the human resources such that people are not only trained on maintaining the overall automation process but are also trained on performing those technical tasks that don't require or are not suited for automation.

 CAUTION Process automation may eliminate the need for personnel to perform many repetitive tasks, but you will still need to keep qualified people on staff who can maintain and develop automation tools as well as understand how to perform the tasks in case those automated processes fail and require manual intervention.

Technology and Tool Integration

Both large and small businesses have a wide variety of technologies incorporated into their IT infrastructures. Each of these technologies likely has its own user interface and management utilities. However, as we have discussed, it's much more efficient to get all of these tools and utilities working under one large umbrella of management through orchestration. Integrating technologies together, which may use widely disparate interfaces, commands, utilities, data formats, and protocols, can be very difficult at best, and impossible at worst. There are many different techniques for integrating all of these disparate management tools and utilities, including using data exchange formats and protocols that are common to different applications. It's also possible to develop in-house APIs that can exchange data between applications and to develop customized interfaces. However, it's also worth discussing basic scripting using powerful scripting languages that can help query systems, extract data, convert that data into another usable format, and send that data to another application. Scripting can greatly assist in automating processes and tasks in bridging the gap between different management utilities. We'll discuss scripting next.

 EXAM TIP You should make every effort possible to leverage common protocols and data formats used by technologies and tools to assist in automation and orchestration efforts. When making the decision to purchase and implement new technologies, keep interoperability and integration with other security technologies in mind.

Scripting

Scripting has always been an effective way to delve into the inner workings of operating systems and applications. When working with operating systems, scripting normally takes place at the command line, and it involves using routine commands you may find built into the operating system or application. Commands can be run interactively, meaning that you can type in a command, execute it, and get results back. However, these commands can also be included in what is known as a *script,* which is typically a text file with the commands stored in the file sequentially, in a specific logical order. When the script is executed, the commands contained in the script are automatically executed one by one, in what is known as a *batch.* In fact, early scripting was called *batch programming,* and early Windows scripts were sometimes called *batch files* because they contained a batch of commands that would be executed as a group. You'll also hear the term *shell scripting,* which is more often associated with Linux and Unix variants, since scripting is performed from the command shell. Application scripting can also use basic text files, or it can be part of a management interface or utility designed to allow you to include a series of application-specific commands executed as a sequential batch of commands. A good example of application scripting is simple SQL programming, sometimes included in the interface of a relational database management system (RDBMS). The SQL statements are the commands that make up the script, and they perform a series of database functions when the script is executed.

Commands executed in a script can be very simple or complex; the results of one command can also be used as an input or parameter for the next command in the sequence. Scripts can be used for a wide variety of tasks. Scripts may be written to automatically carry out a series of commands that an administrator might find tedious to type in one by one. Scripts can be used to run backups on systems, create and provision user accounts, extract data from a system, and so on. The list of possibilities is endless. Scripting is very useful for automating tasks that may be tedious, repetitive, time-consuming, or otherwise be error-prone if performed manually. This makes it perfect for contributing to automation and orchestration processes.

While we have only discussed the general aspects of writing scripts here, note that scripting is also discussed in the context of determining malicious activity in Chapter 6.

 EXAM TIP   You will not be expected to write any scripts on the CySA+ exam; however, you should be able to determine what function a script is fulfilling. The particulars of scripting languages, such as those used in shell scripting, as well as Python and PowerShell, are discussed in Chapter 5.

Application Programming Interface

Application programming interfaces (APIs) have ushered in several major improvements in how applications communicate with each other. APIs are becoming the primary mechanism for both standard user interactions and systems administration for a number of reasons. First, APIs simplify how systems integrate with each other, because they provide a standard language with which to communicate while maintaining strong security and control over the system owner's data. APIs are also efficient, since providing API access often means that the content and the mechanism to distribute the content can be created once using accepted standards and formats and then published to those users with access. This means that the data is able to be accessed by a broader audience than just those with knowledge about the supporting technologies behind the data. Therefore, APIs are often used to distribute data effectively to a variety of consumers without the need to provide special instructions and without negatively impacting the requestor's workflow. Finally, APIs provide a way for machines to communicate at high volume in a scalable and repeatable fashion, which is ideal for automation.

As API usage has increased across the Web, two popular ways to exchange information emerged to dominate Internet-based machine-to-machine communications. The first is the Simple Object Access Protocol (SOAP). APIs designed with SOAP use Extensible Markup Language (XML) as the message format and transmit through HTTP or SMTP. The second is Representational State Transfer (REST). We'll take a deeper look into REST here because it is the style you'll most likely interface with on a regular basis and it offers flexibility and a greater variety of data formats.

 EXAM TIP You should understand the purpose and function of application programming interfaces; they are constructed to facilitate communications and data exchange between disparate applications. They will typically use programming languages, data formats, and protocols common to or supported by each application.

Representational State Transfer

Representational State Transfer (REST) is a term coined by computer scientist Dr. Roy Fielding, one of the principal authors of the HTTP specification. In his 2000 doctoral dissertation, Dr. Fielding described his designs of software architecture that provided interoperability between computers across networks. Web services that use the REST convention are referred to as *RESTful* APIs. Though many think of REST as a protocol, it is, in fact, an architectural style and therefore has no rigid rules. REST interactions are characterized by six principles, however:

- **Client/server** The REST architecture style follows a model in which a client queries a server for particular resources, communicated over HTTP.

- **Stateless** No client information is stored on the server, and each client must contain all of the information necessary for the server to interpret the request.

- **Cacheable** In some cases, it may not be necessary for the client to query the server for a request that has already occurred. If the server's response is marked as cacheable, a client may store it for reuse later on.

- **Uniform interface** Simplicity is a guiding principle for the architectural style and is realized with several constraints:

  - **Identification of resources** Requests identify resources (most often using URLs), which are separate from what is returned from the servers (represented as HTML, XML, or JSON).

  - **Manipulation of resources through representations** A client should have enough information to modify a representation of a resource.

  - **Self-descriptive messages** Responses should contain enough information about how to interpret them.

  - **Hypermedia as the engine of application state** There is no need for the REST client to have special knowledge about how to interact with the server, because hypermedia, most often HTTP, is the means of information exchange.

- **Layered system** A client will not be able to tell if it's connected directly to the end server, an intermediary along the way, a proxy, or load balancer. This means that security can be strongly applied based on system restrictions and that the server may respond in whatever manner it deems most efficient.

- **Code on demand (optional)** REST enables client functionality to be extended by enabling servers to respond to applets or scripts that can be executed on the client side.

RESTful APIs use a portion of the HTTP response message to provide feedback to a requestor about the results of the response. Status codes fall under one of the five categories, as listed in Table 2-1.

Category	Description
1xx: Informational	Communicates transfer protocol–level information
2xx: Success	Indicates that the client's request was accepted successfully
3xx: Redirection	Indicates that the client must take some additional action to complete its request
4xx: Client Error	Indicates that the client takes responsibility for the error status codes
5xx: Server Error	Indicates that the server takes responsibility for the error status codes

Table 2-1   HTTP Response Message Categories Used by RESTful APIs

Error Code	HTTP Code	Description
AlreadyExistsError	409	The resource already exists.
AuthenticationRequiredError	401	The operation requires an authenticated user. Verify that you have provided your API key.
BadRequestError	400	The API request is invalid or malformed. The message usually provides details about why the request is not valid.
ForbiddenError	403	You are not allowed to perform the requested operation.
InvalidArgumentError	400	Some of the provided arguments are incorrect.
NotFoundError	404	The requested resource was not found.
QuotaExceededError	429	You have exceeded one of your quotas (per minute, daily, or monthly). Daily quotas are reset every day at 00:00 UTC.
TooManyRequestsError	429	There are too many requests.
UserNotActiveError	401	The user account is not active. Make sure you've properly activated your account by following the link sent to your e-mail.
WrongCredentialsError	401	The provided API key is incorrect.
TransientError	503	This is a transient server error; a retry might work.

Table 2-2 VirusTotal Error Codes for RESTful APIs

Furthermore, you may be able to recover more detailed error messages depending on what API service is being used. VirusTotal, for example, provides a detailed breakout of error codes that can be used to troubleshoot problematic interactions, as summarized in Table 2-2.

 EXAM TIP   The CySA+ exam does not require you to have in-depth knowledge of HTTP response and error codes, but understanding how to use them in troubleshooting automation is important. Knowing where to adjust your code based on the HTTP responses is a critical skill for API automation.

Automating API Calls

Many tools can assist you with crafting an API call and then converting it to code for use in other systems or as a subordinate function in custom software and scripting. Postman, Insomnia, and Swagger Codegen are three popular API clients that can assist with generating API calls for automation. We'll use the VirusTotal API and Insomnia to show

```
* Preparing request to https://www.virustotal.com/api/v3/domains/google.com
* Using libcurl/7.69.1 OpenSSL/1.1.1g zlib/1.2.11 brotli/1.0.7 libidn2/2.1.1 libssh2/1.9.0 nghttp2/1.40.0
* Current time is 2020-06-09T00:23:48.991Z
* Disable timeout
* Enable automatic URL encoding
* Enable SSL validation
* Enable cookie sending with jar of 0 cookies
* 17 bytes stray data read before trying h2 connection
* Found bundle for host www.virustotal.com: 0x7fea1b5fa6b0 [can multiplex]
* Re-using existing connection! (#0) with host www.virustotal.com
* Connected to www.virustotal.com (74.125.34.46) port 443 (#0)
* Using Stream ID: 7 (easy handle 0x7fea2810ba00)

> GET /api/v3/domains/google.com HTTP/2
> Host: www.virustotal.com
> user-agent: insomnia/2020.2.1
> x-apikey: ████████████████████████████████████████████
> accept: */*

< HTTP/2 200
< cache-control: no-cache
< content-type: application/json; charset=utf-8
< x-cloud-trace-context: 73b8c77b7392d832b0a17829136c7098
< date: Tue, 09 Jun 2020 00:23:49 GMT
< server: Google Frontend
< content-length: 35387
```

Figure 2-6   Request sent to the VirusTotal domain enrichment API endpoint via API client

some of the most common capabilities of these API clients. According to the VirusTotal documentation, the API endpoint associated with domain enrichment requires a **GET** HTTP method. In many cases, you can copy the commands provided via the API documentation or use the code that follows in your API client. Here's an example:

```
curl --request GET \
  - url https://www.virustotal.com/api/v3/domains/{domain} \
  --header 'x-apikey: <your API key>'
```

This **curl** request automatically gets parsed by the client. After the appropriate credentials are added via an API key, OAuth credentials, login/password pair, bearer token, or other means, the request is ready to send. Figure 2-6 shows a complete request sent to the VirusTotal domain enrichment endpoint. You'll notice the HTTP 200 response, indicating that the exchange was successful.

The full contents of the HTTP response can be found under the Preview tab in this client, as shown in Figure 2-7. In this case, 92 verdicts are returned for the domain Google, with 83 being "harmless" and 9 being "undetected."

Once you're satisfied with the exchange between the client and server, you can export this request to many popular programming languages or scripting formats. Insomnia comes with the built-in ability to generate client code in several languages, some with

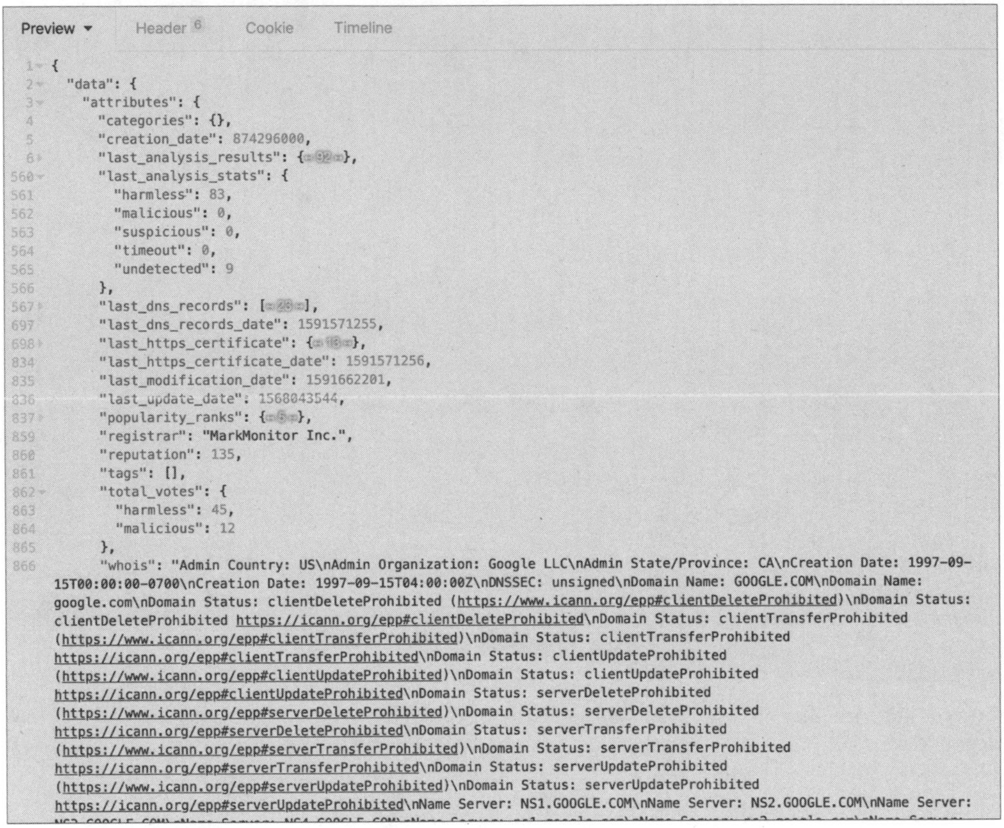

Preview ▾   Header 6   Cookie   Timeline

```
1  {
2    "data": {
3      "attributes": {
4        "categories": {},
5        "creation_date": 874296000,
6        "last_analysis_results": {...92...},
560      "last_analysis_stats": {
561        "harmless": 83,
562        "malicious": 0,
563        "suspicious": 0,
564        "timeout": 0,
565        "undetected": 9
566      },
567      "last_dns_records": [...28...],
697      "last_dns_records_date": 1591571255,
698      "last_https_certificate": {...18...},
834      "last_https_certificate_date": 1591571256,
835      "last_modification_date": 1591662201,
836      "last_update_date": 1568043544,
837      "popularity_ranks": {...8...},
859      "registrar": "MarkMonitor Inc.",
860      "reputation": 135,
861      "tags": [],
862      "total_votes": {
863        "harmless": 45,
864        "malicious": 12
865      },
866      "whois": "Admin Country: US\nAdmin Organization: Google LLC\nAdmin State/Province: CA\nCreation Date: 1997-09-15T00:00:00-0700\nCreation Date: 1997-09-15T04:00:00Z\nDNSSEC: unsigned\nDomain Name: GOOGLE.COM\nDomain Name: google.com\nDomain Status: clientDeleteProhibited (https://www.icann.org/epp#clientDeleteProhibited)\nDomain Status: clientDeleteProhibited https://icann.org/epp#clientDeleteProhibited\nDomain Status: clientTransferProhibited (https://www.icann.org/epp#clientTransferProhibited)\nDomain Status: clientTransferProhibited https://icann.org/epp#clientTransferProhibited\nDomain Status: clientUpdateProhibited (https://www.icann.org/epp#clientUpdateProhibited)\nDomain Status: clientUpdateProhibited https://icann.org/epp#clientUpdateProhibited\nDomain Status: serverDeleteProhibited (https://www.icann.org/epp#serverDeleteProhibited)\nDomain Status: serverDeleteProhibited https://icann.org/epp#serverDeleteProhibited\nDomain Status: serverTransferProhibited (https://www.icann.org/epp#serverTransferProhibited)\nDomain Status: serverTransferProhibited https://icann.org/epp#serverTransferProhibited\nDomain Status: serverUpdateProhibited (https://www.icann.org/epp#serverUpdateProhibited)\nDomain Status: serverUpdateProhibited https://icann.org/epp#serverUpdateProhibited\nName Server: NS1.GOOGLE.COM\nName Server: NS2.GOOGLE.COM\nName Server:
```

Figure 2-7   Preview of the API response in the Insomnia API client

multiple library options. Figure 2-8 shows the client code for both Python using the requests library and the PowerShell Invoke–WebRequest cmdlet (pronounced "command-let"). This can be used as-is or added to existing code to extend functionality.

Webhooks

One of the tricky issues with automation is sending data back and forth between applications because not all applications use compatible messaging or interfacing technologies. This is especially true with proprietary applications as well as some web-based applications. Enter the concept of *webhooks,* which are simple messages and data that are transferred back and forth between applications. These messages are usually automated on-demand as applications request or send data to and from each other. Webhooks can also be used to send instructions back and forth between applications so that, in a truly automated and properly orchestrated environment, the user only has to control various applications from a single interface.

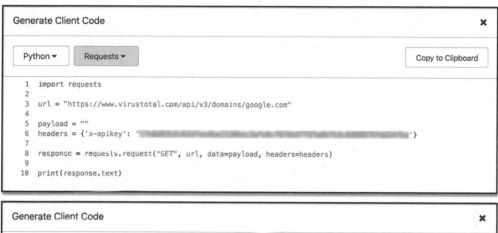

Figure 2-8 Two examples of API client code–generation features

Although webhooks are subset of APIs, they are much more simple and typically more automated than APIs. APIs generally use a manual trigger from a process or a user and can be more difficult to implement due to the complexity of the application code as well as the data and instructions transferred back and forth between applications. Webhooks normally take the form of a URL that a receiving application provides so that other applications can send data to and from it, typically in JSON or XML format.

EXAM TIP Although webhooks are a subset of APIs, understand that the main difference between the two is that APIs are most often triggered manually through some user interaction, and webhooks are almost always automatic. Webhooks are also much smaller pieces of code and are less complex than APIs. You will typically see a webhook in the form of a URL provided by the receiving application.

Plug-Ins

A *plug-in* is a piece of code developed to provide additional functionality or enhanced functionality to an application. Many applications come bundled with plug-ins, but third parties can also provide plug-ins that are compatible with an application.

A good example in the security tool realm is Nessus, the vulnerability scanner. Nessus comes out of the box with many different types of tests and can scan a wide variety of applications and operating systems. However, sometimes different functionality may be needed that can be developed as a plug-in using compatible languages. In Nessus, plug-ins are coded in the Nessus Attack Scripting Language (NASL), which is a very flexible language able to perform virtually any check imaginable. Figure 2-9 shows a portion of a NASL plug-in that tests FTP servers that allow anonymous connections. Security personnel skilled in application programming can also develop their own plug-ins for their tools.

 EXAM TIP Plug-ins are just smaller pieces of code written to be compatible with a larger application to provide additional functionality.

Figure 2-9
NASL script that tests for anonymous FTP logins

```
#
# The script code starts here :
#

include("ftp_func.inc");

port = get_kb_item("Services/ftp");
if(!port)port = 21;

if (get_kb_item('ftp/'+port+'/backdoor')) exit(0);

state = get_port_state(port);
if(!state)exit(0);
soc = open_sock_tcp(port);
if(soc)
{
 domain = get_kb_item("Settings/third_party_domain");
 r = ftp_log_in(socket:soc, user:"anonymous", pass:string("nessus@", domain));
 if(r)
 {
  port2 = ftp_get_pasv_port(socket:soc);
  if(port2)
  {
   soc2 = open_sock_tcp(port2, transport:get_port_transport(port));
   if (soc2)
   {
    send(socket:soc, data:'LIST /\r\n');
    listing = ftp_recv_listing(socket:soc2);
    close(soc2);
    }
  }
 }

 data = "
This FTP service allows anonymous logins. If you do not want to share data
with anyone you do not know, then you should deactivate the anonymous account,
since it may only cause troubles.
```

Orchestrating Threat Intelligence Data

In Chapter 8, we cover various types of threat data that can be used to support incident response, vulnerability management, risk management, reverse engineering, and detection efforts. The sheer number of observables, indicators, and context continuously pulled from internal and external sources often requires an abstraction layer to normalize and manage so much data. Since it's often not possible to affect the format in which threat feeds arrive, analysts spend a lot of time formatting and tuning feeds to make them most relevant to the operational environment. Understanding what an indicator may mean to your network, given the right context, cannot always be automated, but a good deal of the processing and normalization that occurs before analysis can be handled by automation. This includes pulling in threat feeds via APIs, extracting unstructured threat data from public sources, and then parsing that raw data to uncover information relevant to your network. Storing the data in a manner that can be easily referenced by security teams is not a trivial task, but with proper automation, a great deal of strain can be taken off the analysts.

Putting new threat intelligence into operation is often a manual and time-consuming process. These activities, which include searching for new indicators across various systems, are especially well-suited for automation. Once the threat data is analyzed, analysts can share threat intelligence products automatically to response teams and lead the enforcement of new rules across the entire network. Improvements such as changes to firewall rules can often be managed by the team's SIEM and SOAR platforms. Note that in-depth discussions on threat intelligence and threat feeds are provided in Chapters 7 and 8.

Data Enrichment

A major part of any security analyst's day is tracking down and investigating suspicious activity. Investigation into the source and meaning behind observables is a core skill of any detection analyst, incident responder, threat hunter, or threat intelligence analyst. *Enrichments* are the actions that lead to additional insights into data, and they involve a set of tasks that can be a draw on resources. Often repetitive, enrichment is a perfect candidate for automation. Any way we can make it easier for analysts to initiate an enrichment request means more time for them to focus on really challenging tasks. Depending on how automation is set up, enrichment may even occur as the initial data is delivered, meaning that the analyst sees the original data coupled with useful context to make a far more informed decision. This practice leads not only to far lower response times but also a reduced chance for human error because there are fewer areas for humans to interact directly in the process.

Single Pane of Glass

As security operations and the associated technologies used to manage security in the organization have matured, the need for centralized information, provided to the operator in the right place at the right time, has evolved into a concept called *single pane of glass* (SPOG). This concept essentially means that the various data feeds and sources of security information that flow into an organization should be parsed, correlated, and analyzed to a certain degree before the user even sees them. The security analyst must have all the information they need, typically in real time, at their fingertips, and this information must be presented to them in a fashion that not only makes sense but allows them to make good decisions quickly based on the information they are getting.

Moving away from the conceptual into the practical, the phrase *single pane of glass* has also come to spark visions of high-tech security operations centers where there are dozens of large screens all presenting applets and windows of information scrolling by in real time. That's not necessarily an incorrect vision; it's very useful to have all the information a security analyst needs in front of them arranged in a logical, useful manner so they can make real-time decisions based on real-time data. The single pane of glass concept is only made possible through some of the automation and orchestration concepts, as well as the maturity of security tools, we have discussed in this chapter.

Use of Automation Protocols and Standards

The use of automation to realize industry best practices and standards has been in practice for years in the commercial and government spaces. As an early developer of hardening standards, the Defense Information Systems Agency (DISA) has made significant investments in the promotion of these standards through products such as the Security Technical Implementation Guides (STIGs). STIGs, are meant to drive security strategies as well as prescribe technical measures for improving the security of networks and endpoints. Although STIGs describe how to minimize exposure and improve network resilience through proper configuration, patch management, and network design, they don't necessarily define methods to ensure that this can be done automatically and at scale. This is where automation standards come into play.

 EXAM TIP   For the exam, understand that the concept of SOAR is the overall integration and orchestration of disparate security tools and data under one central management interface. Automation protocols and standards, such as SCAP (discussed next), simply help facilitate an organization's implementation of SOAR.

Security Content Automation Protocol

How do you ensure that your security management process complies with all relevant regulatory and policy requirements *regardless of which security tools you use?* Each tool, after all, may use whatever standards (such as rules) and reporting formats its developers desire. This lack of standardization led the US National Institute of Standards and Technology (NIST) to team up with industry partners to develop the Security Content Automation Protocol (SCAP). SCAP uses specific standards for exchanging security data, such as the results of the assessment and reporting of vulnerabilities in the information systems of an organization, for instance. As of this writing, the current final version of SCAP is 1.3, with version 2.0 in draft form. SCAP incorporates about a dozen different components that standardize everything from the asset reporting format (ARF) to Common Vulnerabilities and Exposures (CVE), to the Common Vulnerability Scoring System (CVSS).

 EXAM TIP   You likely will not be asked any particulars about SCAP on the exam, but you are expected to know details about the Common Vulnerability Scoring System (CVSS), which is used by SCAP. We will go into detail on CVSS in Chapter 11.

At its core, SCAP leverages baselines developed by NIST and its partners that define minimum standards for security management. If, for instance, you want to ensure that your Windows 10 workstations are complying with the requirements of the Federal Information Security Management Act (FISMA), you would use the appropriate SCAP module that captures these requirements. You would then provide that module to a certified SCAP scanner (such as Nessus), and it would be able to report this compliance in a standard language. As you should be able to see, SCAP enables full automation of the vulnerability management process, particularly in regulatory environments.

The current technical specification of SCAP, version 1.3, is covered by NIST SP 800-126 Revision 3. SCAP 1.3 comprises 12 component specifications in five categories:

- **Languages**   The collection of standard vocabularies and conventions for expressing security policy, technical check techniques, and assessment results:
  - Extensible Configuration Checklist Description Format (XCCDF)
  - Open Vulnerability and Assessment Language (OVAL)
  - Open Checklist Interactive Language (OCIL)
- **Reporting formats**   The necessary constructs to express collected information in standardized formats:
  - Asset Reporting Format (ARF)
  - Asset Identification (AID)
- **Identification schemes**   The means to identify key concepts such as software products, vulnerabilities, and configuration items using standardized identifier formats as well as to associate individual identifiers with additional data pertaining to the subject of the identifier:
  - Common Platform Enumeration (CPE)
  - Software Identification (SWID) Tags
  - Common Configuration Enumeration (CCE)
  - Common Vulnerabilities and Exposures (CVE)

- **Measurement and scoring systems** Evaluation of specific characteristics of a security weakness and any scoring that reflects their relative severity:
  - Common Vulnerability Scoring System (CVSS)
  - Common Configuration Scoring System (CCSS)
- **Integrity** An SCAP integrity specification that helps to preserve the integrity of SCAP content and results:
  - Trust Model for Security Automation Data (TMSAD)

The standardized data exchange and reporting formats allow for easy communication between disparate security tools and technologies, enabling better automation and orchestration efforts.

 EXAM TIP For the exam, understand the scenarios in which SCAP would be helpful, such as when you're integrating tools that speak the same language for sharing data and when you need to export data from or import data to different tools that may support SCAP.

Chapter Review

In this chapter, we have discussed the benefits of developing security management processes that are both efficient and effective. We discussed the need for streamlining security operations, using the concepts of automation and orchestration. Automation is the process of offloading tedious, repetitive, or complex tasks onto systems using a variety of methods, including application programming interfaces, scripting, and built-in tools. Orchestration is the overall management and control of all these different automated processes. Security orchestration, automation, and response (SOAR) is a concept that describes unifying all these tools and technologies into single manageable interfaces.

Process standardization benefits the organization by ensuring that security processes are performed in a consistent, repeatable manner. Automation lends itself to process standardization by reducing human errors and minimizing human involvement.

Integrating various technologies and tools used for security management can be a daunting task. However, if these various technologies and tools use standardized interfaces, data exchange formats, and other common protocols, this can greatly facilitate automating and orchestrating security processes. Some tools that make technology integration possible include scripting and application programming interfaces. Scripting includes various command-line utilities and tools and is a quick way to automate tasks that use basic commands built into operating systems and applications. Scripting will also be covered more in detail in Chapter 5. Application programming interfaces come in many forms and use different methods. These include Representational State Transfer (REST) and webhooks. Plug-ins are written in code native to an application and allow analysts to gain additional functionality from the application.

Orchestrating threat intelligence data means automating the processes that use threat feeds and providing those feeds to SOAR and SIEM platforms. These platforms can also contribute to data enrichment, which typically means giving the threat intelligence organizationally focused context. This enriched threat intelligence is often provided to the end user, the analyst, through what is known as a "single pane of glass." This concept means that an analyst has all the information they need, typically in real time, available at their fingertips.

Questions

1. Which of the following is *not* an example of an identification scheme in SCAP 1.3?

   A. Common Platform Enumeration (CPE)

   B. Common Data Enumeration (CDE)

   C. Software Identification (SWID) Tags

   D. Common Vulnerabilities and Exposures (CVE)

2. What describes the first event of a playbook process that triggers the rest of the steps?

   A. Reporting

   B. Process steps

   C. End state

   D. Initiating condition

3. In the REST architecture style, which of the following is *not* one of the commonly returned data types in server responses?

   A. XML

   B. SCAP

   C. HTML

   D. JSON

4. Which HTTP status code indicates some kind of client error?

   A. 100

   B. 202

   C. 301

   D. 403

5. Which of the following primarily uses built-in operating system commands sequenced and executed as a batch?

   A. Scripts

   B. SCAP

   C. XML

   D. Playbooks

6. Which of the following hypothesis types is developed to address the inherently dynamic nature of a network and its changing qualities?

   A. The playbook may result in additional work for the analyst.

   B. The playbook may cause a significant impact to the end user in the case of a false positive.

   C. The playbook actions may change over time and require human tuning.

   D. Orchestration systems require that a human be present during the full duration of its operation.

7. Which of the following is provided for data exchange via a uniform resource locator (URL) by a receiving application?

   A. Playbook

   B. API

   C. Python script

   D. Webhook

8. Which of the following is the NIST framework that supports automated data exchange and reporting based on specific standards?

   A. STIG

   B. SCAP

   C. XCCDF

   D. BASS

9. Which of the following can be created from an application's native programming language to provide additional functionality in an application?

   A. Plug-in

   B. Script

   C. Playbook

   D. API

10. Which of the following is the process of providing additional organizationally focused context for threat intelligence data?

    A. Automation

    B. Orchestration

    C. Data enrichment

    D. Scripting

Answers

1. **B.** Common Data Enumeration (CDE) is not part of SCAP 1.3 identification schemes, which include Common Platform Enumeration (CPE), Software Identification (SWID) Tags, Common Configuration Enumeration (CCE), and Common Vulnerabilities and Exposures (CVE).

2. **D.** The initiating condition can be defined as the rules that must be completed to trigger the remaining steps in the playbook.

3. **B.** SCAP is not a data type. Although REST does not mandate a data type, the most commonly returned response data types are XML, HTML, and JSON.

4. **D.** HTTP status codes (RFC 7231) in the 400 range indicate a client error. In this case, 403 (Forbidden) indicates that the server understood the request but is refusing to fulfill it because of insufficient privileges.

5. **A.** Scripting uses commands that are built into either operating systems or applications. These commands are included in a file sequentially and executed together as a batch.

6. **B.** In some situations, such as a full account reset, your organization may require that a human take action because of the potential for adverse impacts in the case of a false positive.

7. **D.** Webhooks are simple messages and data that are transferred back and forth between applications. These messages are usually automated on-demand as applications request or send data to and from each other.

8. **B.** The Security Content Automation Protocol (SCAP) is an NIST framework that uses specific standards for the automated exchange of data and reporting between the tools and technologies in an organization.

9. **A.** A plug-in is a piece of code written in an application's native programming language to provide additional functionality for the application.

10. **C.** Data enrichment is the process of using automation and orchestration to glean additional context for threat intelligence data based on the needs of the organization.

Attack Methodology Frameworks

In this chapter you will learn:

- Attack frameworks and their use in leveraging threat intelligence
- The MITRE ATT&CK framework
- The Diamond Model of Intrusion Analysis
- The Cyber Kill Chain
- The Open Source Security Testing Methodology Manual
- The OWASP Web Security Testing Guide

The hacker didn't succeed through sophistication. Rather he poked at obvious places, trying to enter through unlock(ed) doors. Persistence, not wizardry, let him through.

—Clifford Stoll

Through modern television and films, we are often fooled into thinking that the hacker's actions are arbitrary or even instinctual in nature. A malicious attack on an infrastructure that may take an hour during a prime time television series may actually take weeks or even months in the real world. Hackers don't just arbitrarily execute actions against a network. Sophisticated attacks require patience, persistence, and planning. There is a method to their madness, and often this method comes from attack frameworks that have been carefully developed, tested, and documented.

In this chapter we will discuss various attack methods and frameworks, including the MITRE ATT&CK framework, the Diamond Model of Intrusion Analysis, and the Cyber Kill Chain. We will also look at two open source attack methodologies: the Open Source Security Testing Methodology Manual and the OWASP Web Security Testing Guide.

Note that while attack frameworks are specifically called out in Objective 3.1, we want to discuss them in this early chapter so that you will have the right context throughout the book. We will also discuss the relevance of attack frameworks to incident response in Part III of the book.

Attack Frameworks

An attack framework is a structured methodology used by security analysts to model and understand the tactics, techniques, and procedures (TTPs) used by cyberattackers. Such frameworks help security analysts identify, prioritize, and mitigate potential security threats to an organization's information systems.

Attack frameworks typically break down a cyberattack—from initial reconnaissance to final exfiltration of data—into a series of discrete steps or phases. They provide detailed descriptions of the tools and techniques attackers are likely to use at each stage of the attack, as well as guidance on how to detect and respond to those techniques.

Attack frameworks are an essential tool for understanding the nature and scope of cyber threats. By studying the TTPs used by attackers, security analysts can better anticipate and prepare for potential attacks and can develop more effective security controls and incident response plans. By using attack frameworks to identify vulnerabilities and potential attack vectors, security analysts can help to minimize the risk of successful cyberattacks and protect sensitive data and critical infrastructure.

MITRE ATT&CK

The MITRE ATT&CK framework is a comprehensive knowledge base of tactics and techniques used by cyberattackers. It provides a standardized language and methodology for describing and categorizing cyber threats, and it helps organizations better understand and defend against those threats. The framework is composed of multiple matrices, each of which focuses on a particular type of threat, such as the Enterprise matrix, which covers a wide range of tactics and techniques used in targeted attacks against enterprise-level networks. Within each matrix, the framework includes detailed information on the TTPs used by attackers, along with guidance on mitigations that organizations can implement to prevent or reduce the impact of an attack. The MITRE ATT&CK framework is widely used by security analysts and cybersecurity professionals to identify and mitigate cyber threats and has become an essential tool in the fight against cybercrime.

ATT&CK Components

The MITRE ATT&CK framework is composed of multiple components, including matrices, tactics, techniques, data sources, mitigations, groups, software, campaigns, and resources. These components work together to provide a structured methodology for modeling and understanding the TTPs used by cyberattackers. By utilizing these components, security analysts can better identify, prioritize, and mitigate potential security threats to an organization's information systems. In the following section, we will explore each of these components in more detail and examine how they contribute to the overall effectiveness of the MITRE ATT&CK framework:

- **Matrices** The MITRE ATT&CK framework is composed of multiple matrices, each of which focuses on a particular type of threat. The primary matrix is the Enterprise matrix, which covers a wide range of tactics and techniques used in targeted attacks against enterprise-level networks. Other matrices include Mobile, PRE-ATT&CK, ICS, and Cloud.

- **Tactics**   The high-level goals attackers are trying to achieve, such as gaining initial access, persistence, or exfiltrating data.

- **Techniques**   The specific methods and procedures attackers use to achieve their goals. Each technique is mapped to a specific tactic and may be used in multiple attack campaigns.

- **Data sources**   The types of information that can be used to detect or prevent attacks. Examples of data sources include logs, network traffic, and endpoint data.

- **Mitigations**   The defensive measures organizations can implement to prevent or reduce the impact of an attack. MITRE ATT&CK provides guidance on which mitigations are effective against specific techniques.

- **Groups**   The threat actors or attacker groups that use specific tactics and techniques. Each group is assigned a unique identifier and mapped to the techniques they have been observed using.

- **Software**   The malware or other tools used by attackers to execute specific techniques. Each software is assigned a unique identifier and is mapped to the techniques it has been observed using.

- **Campaigns**   The specific instances of attacks carried out by threat actors. Each campaign is assigned a unique identifier and mapped to the tactics and techniques used in that campaign.

- **Resources**   Any additional information and documentation that can be used to better understand and defend against specific threats. This can include research papers, blog posts, and other resources that provide insight into the tactics and techniques used by attackers.

EXAM TIP   While it's unlikely you will be tested on every component within the MITRE ATT&CK framework, it's important to have a solid understanding of the topics covered in the framework. Therefore, you should be familiar with the components and how they fit into the larger framework.

ATT&CK Usage Scenarios

The ATT&CK framework can be utilized by cybersecurity analysts in a variety of scenarios to better understand, prevent, and respond to cyber threats. Here are three scenarios that illustrate how the framework can be used:

- **Incident response**   When responding to a security incident, a cybersecurity analyst can use the MITRE ATT&CK framework to quickly identify the tactics and techniques used by the attacker. By mapping the observed behavior to the appropriate technique within the framework, the analyst can gain a better understanding of the attacker's goals and motivations. The analyst can then use the framework to identify other areas of the network that may have been compromised and to prioritize remediation efforts based on the severity of the attack.

- **Threat hunting**   In a proactive threat hunting scenario, a cybersecurity analyst can use the MITRE ATT&CK framework to identify potential threats before they have a chance to cause damage. By analyzing logs and other data sources for signs of suspicious activity, the analyst can map that activity to specific tactics and techniques within the framework. This can help the analyst identify potential weaknesses in the organization's security posture and prioritize remediation efforts accordingly.

- **Risk assessment**   The MITRE ATT&CK framework can also be used to conduct a comprehensive risk assessment of an organization's information systems. By mapping the organization's security controls to the tactics and techniques within the framework, cybersecurity analysts can identify potential gaps in their security posture and develop a prioritized plan to address those gaps. This approach can help organizations better understand their overall security risk and allocate resources more effectively to address the most critical issues.

Overall, ATT&CK is a versatile framework that can be used in a wide range of cybersecurity scenarios. By leveraging the framework to gain a deeper understanding of cyber threats and better defend against them, cybersecurity analysts can help protect their organization's sensitive data and critical infrastructure.

Enterprise ATT&CK

The Enterprise ATT&CK matrix is the primary matrix within the MITRE ATT&CK framework, and it covers a wide range of tactics and techniques used in targeted attacks against enterprise-level networks. This matrix is generally considered the most important for cybersecurity analysts because it provides a comprehensive view of the types of threats and attack vectors that are most likely to be encountered by organizations.

The Enterprise ATT&CK matrix is organized into 11 different tactics, each of which represents a high-level goal that an attacker may be trying to achieve. Here is a list of the tactics, along with a brief description of each:

1. *Initial access.* Tactics used by attackers to gain a foothold within a target network or system, such as phishing e-mails or exploiting vulnerabilities.

2. *Execution.* Techniques used by attackers to execute malicious code on a target system, such as through the use of a dropper or backdoor.

3. *Persistence.* Techniques used by attackers to maintain access to a compromised system over time, such as by installing a rootkit or creating a scheduled task.

4. *Privilege escalation.* Techniques used by attackers to gain higher levels of access or privileges within a compromised system, such as exploiting a vulnerability in a privilege escalation tool.

5. *Defense evasion.* Techniques used by attackers to evade detection or bypass security controls, such as through the use of encryption or obfuscation.

6. *Credential access.* Techniques used by attackers to steal or obtain credentials that can be used to access a target system, such as by harvesting credentials from memory or using brute-force attacks.

7. *Discovery.* Techniques used by attackers to gather information about a target system or network, such as through network scanning or Active Directory enumeration.

8. *Lateral movement.* Techniques used by attackers to move laterally within a compromised network, such as through the use of pass-the-hash or Remote Desktop Protocol.

9. *Collection.* Techniques used by attackers to collect data or information from a compromised system, such as through keylogging or screenshotting.

10. *Exfiltration.* Techniques used by attackers to move data or information out of a compromised network, such as through the use of command and control (C2) servers or external storage devices.

11. *Command and control.* Techniques used by attackers to communicate with compromised systems, such as through the use of a remote access Trojan or a web shell.

Overall, the Enterprise ATT&CK matrix provides a detailed view of the tactics and techniques used by attackers in targeted attacks against enterprise-level networks. By understanding these tactics and the techniques associated with them, cybersecurity analysts can better identify and mitigate potential threats to an organization's information systems.

EXAM TIP   It's important to have a good understanding of the tactics and techniques covered in the MITRE ATT&CK framework, as well as how they fit into the larger framework. While you may not be tested on every tactic specifically, having comprehensive knowledge of the framework can help you better understand and analyze cyber threats.

Working with ATT&CK

To facilitate working with the framework, MITRE has developed several tools that help analysts visualize, analyze, and incorporate the framework into their workflows. Here are some of the key tools:

- **ATT&CK Navigator**   The ATT&CK Navigator is a web-based tool that allows analysts to visualize and explore the MITRE ATT&CK framework. It provides an interactive interface that allows analysts to filter, sort, and search through the various components of the framework as well as to create customized views of the data based on their specific needs.

- **ATT&CK Workbench**   The ATT&CK Workbench is a desktop application that allows analysts to analyze and document specific instances of attacks using the MITRE ATT&CK framework. It provides a customizable workspace where analysts can create and modify tactics and techniques and link them to specific data sources and artifacts.

- **STIX/TAXII** STIX (Structured Threat Information eXpression) and TAXII (Trusted Automated eXchange of Indicator Information) are standards developed by MITRE that allow organizations to share and exchange threat intelligence in a standardized format. By using STIX/TAXII, organizations can share information about TTPs used by attackers, helping to improve overall situational awareness and enhance threat intelligence.

- **mitreattack-python library** The mitreattack-python library is a Python package that provides a programmatic interface to the MITRE ATT&CK framework. It allows analysts to search, filter, and analyze the framework using Python code, making it easier to incorporate the framework into automated workflows and other tools.

Overall, these tools help analysts work more efficiently with the MITRE ATT&CK framework, enabling them to better understand and defend against cyber threats. By providing standardized interfaces and workflows, these tools help to promote collaboration and information sharing within the cybersecurity community.

ATT&CK Summary

The ATT&CK framework is a comprehensive knowledge base of tactics and techniques used by cyberattackers, organized into multiple matrices that cover a range of different threat types. The framework includes components such as tactics, techniques, data sources, mitigations, groups, software, campaigns, and resources that work together to provide a structured methodology for modeling and understanding the tactics, techniques, and procedures used by attackers. The Enterprise ATT&CK matrix is the primary matrix within the framework and is particularly important for cybersecurity analysts, as it covers a wide range of tactics and techniques used in targeted attacks against enterprise-level networks. Security analysts can use the framework in various scenarios, such as incident response, threat hunting, and risk assessment, and tools such as the ATT&CK Navigator, ATT&CK Workbench, STIX/TAXII, and the mitreattack-python library can facilitate their work with the framework. Overall, the ATT&CK framework is a versatile tool that can help security analysts gain a deeper understanding of cyber threats and develop more effective strategies for defending against them.

The Diamond Model of Intrusion Analysis

While looking for an effective way to analyze and track the characteristics of cyber intrusions by advanced threat actors, security professionals Sergio Caltagirone, Andrew Pendergast, and Christopher Betz developed the Diamond Model of Intrusion Analysis, shown in Figure 3-1, which emphasizes the relationships and characteristics of four basic components: adversary, capability, victim, and infrastructure. The components are represented as vertices on a diamond, with connections between them. Using the connections between these entities, you can use the model to describe how an adversary uses a capability in an infrastructure against a victim. A key feature of the model is that enables defenders to pivot easily from one node to the next in describing a security event. As entities are populated in their respective vertices, an analyst will be able to read

Figure 3-1
The Diamond
Model

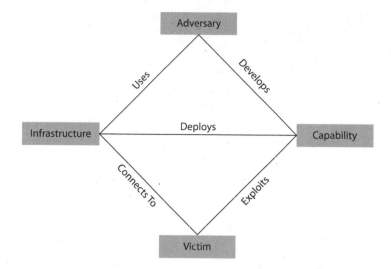

across the model to describe the specific activity (for example, FIN7 [the adversary] uses phish kits [the capability] and actor-registered domains [the infrastructure] to target bank executives [the victim]).

It's important to note that the model is not static but rather adjusts as the adversary changes TTPs, infrastructure, and targeting. Because of this, this model requires a great deal of attention to ensure that the details of each component are updated as new information is uncovered. If the model is used correctly, analysts can easily pivot across the edges that join vertices in order to learn more about the intrusion and explore new hypotheses.

As we use this model to capture and communicate details about malicious activity we may encounter, we should also consider the seven axioms that Caltagirone describes as capturing the nature of all threats. Table 3-1 lists the axioms and what they mean for defenders.

Axiom	What It Means for Defenders
For every intrusion event, there exists an adversary taking a step toward an intended goal by using a capability over infrastructure against a victim to produce a result.	Every security incident has the four components of adversary, infrastructure, capability, and victim. We use the Diamond Model to build strategies for detecting, tracking, and mitigating malicious activity.
There exists a set of adversaries (insiders, outsiders, individuals, groups, and organizations) that seek to compromise computer systems or networks to further their intent and satisfy their needs.	Threat actors are constantly trying to gain access to systems for specific reasons. If we can determine those reasons, we may be able to defend our systems more effectively.
Every system, and by extension every victim asset, has vulnerabilities and exposures.	Assume that no technology, and by extension no system, is safe from vulnerabilities and exploits.

Table 3-1   Diamond Model Axioms

Axiom	What It Means for Defenders
Every malicious activity contains two or more phases that must be successfully executed in succession to achieve the desired result.	Dependencies need to be fulfilled for an attack to be successful. The kill chain is one model that describes the phases of an attack.
Every intrusion event requires one or more external resources to be satisfied prior to success.	If we determine the adversary's external requirements, we may develop methods to deny the adversary access to them to frustrate their efforts.
A relationship always exists between the adversary and their victim(s), even if distant, fleeting, or indirect.	Because gaining access can be a difficult undertaking, adversaries will always have a reason to dedicated time and resources to a particular victim.
There exists a subset of the set of adversaries that have the motivation, resources, and capabilities to sustain malicious effects for a significant length of time against one or more victims while resisting mitigation efforts. Adversary-victim relationships in this subset are called *persistent adversary relationships*.	Depending on the nature of the operations, some adversaries need long-term access to their victims to be successful. Determining the nature of these operations will be helpful in developing techniques to deter or prevent persistence.

Table 3-1   Diamond Model Axioms *(continued)*

EXAM TIP   Remember the four components of the Diamond Attack Model: adversary, capability, victim, and infrastructure.

Kill Chain

The *kill chain* is a phase-based model that categorizes the activities an enemy may conduct in a kinetic military operation. One of the first and most commonly used kill chain models in the military is the 2008 F2T2EA, or Find, Fix, Track, Target, Engage, and Assess. Driven by the need to improve response times for air strikes, then–Air Force Chief of Staff General John Jumper pushed for the development of an agile and responsive framework to achieve his goals, and thus F2T2EA was born. Similar to the military kill chain concept, the Cyber Kill Chain defines the steps used by cyberattackers in conducting their malicious activities. The idea is that by providing a structure that breaks an attack into stages, defenders can pinpoint where along the lifecycle of an attack an activity is and deploy appropriate countermeasures. The kill chain is meant to represent the deterministic phases adversaries need to plan and execute in order to gain access to a system successfully.

The Lockheed Martin Cyber Kill Chain is perhaps the most well-known version of the kill chain, as applied to cybersecurity operations. It was introduced in a 2011 whitepaper authored by security team members Michael Cloppert, Eric Hutchins, and Rohan Amin. Using their experience from many years on intelligence and security teams, they describe a structure consisting of seven stages of an attack. Figure 3-2 shows the progression from stage to stage in the Cyber Kill Chain. Since the model is meant to approach

Figure 3-2
The Lockheed
Martin Cyber
Kill Chain

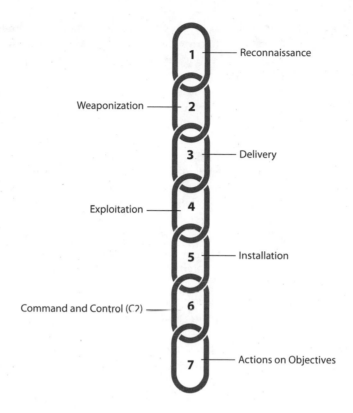

1 — Reconnaissance

Weaponization — 2

3 — Delivery

Exploitation — 4

5 — Installation

Command and Control (C2) — 6

7 — Actions on Objectives

attacks in a linear manner, if defenders can stop an attack early on at the exploitation stage, they can have confidence that the attacker is far less likely to have progressed to further stages. Defenders can therefore avoid conducting a full incident response plan. Furthermore, understanding the phase progression, typical behavior expected at each phase, and inherent dependencies in the overall process allows for defenders to take appropriate measures to disrupt the kill chain.

The kill chain begins with the *Reconnaissance* phase—the activities associated with getting as much information as possible about a target. Reconnaissance will often show the attacker focusing on gaining understanding about the topology of the network and key individuals with system or specific data access. As described in Chapter 1, reconnaissance actions (sometimes referred to as *recon*) can be passive or active in nature. Often an adversary will perform passive recon to acquire information about a target network or individual without direct interaction. For example, an actor may monitor for new domain registration information about a target company to get technical points of contact information. Active reconnaissance, on the other hand, involves more direct methods of interacting with the organization to get a lay of the land. An actor may scan and probe a network to determine technologies used, open ports, and other technical details about the organization's infrastructure. The downside (for the actor) is that this type of activity may trigger detection rules designed to alert defenders on probing behaviors.

It's important for the defender to understand what types of recon activities are likely to be leveraged against the organization and develop technical or policy countermeasures to mitigate those threats. Furthermore, detecting reconnaissance activity can be very useful in revealing the intent of an adversary.

With the knowledge of what kind of attack may be most appropriate to use against a company, an attacker would move to prepare attacks tailored to the target in the *Weaponization* phase. This may mean developing documents with naming schemes similar to those used by the company, which may be used in a social engineering effort at a later point. Alternatively, an attacker may work to create specific malware to affect a device identified during the recon. This phase is particularly challenging for defenders to develop mitigations for, because weaponization activity often occurs on the adversary side, away from defender-controlled network sensors. It's nonetheless an essential phase for defenders to understand because it occurs so early in the process. Using artifacts discovered during the Reconnaissance phase, defenders may be able to infer what kind of weaponization may be occurring and prepare defenses for those possibilities. Even after discovery, it may be useful for defenders to reverse the malware to determine how it was made. This can inform detection efforts moving forward.

The point at which the adversary goes fully offensive is often at the *Delivery* phase. This is the stage when the adversary transmits the attack. This can happen via a phishing e-mail or Short Message Service (SMS), by delivery of a tainted USB device, or by convincing a target to switch to an attacker-controlled infrastructure, in the case of a rogue access point or physical man-in-the-middle attack. For defenders, this can be a pivotal stage to defend. It's often measurable since the rules developed by defenders in the previous stages can be put into use. The number of blocked intrusion attempts, for example, can be a quick way to determine whether previous hypotheses are likely to be true. It's important to note that technical measures combined with good employee security awareness training continually proves to be the most effective way to stop attacks at this stage.

In the unfortunate event that the adversary achieves successful transmission to their victim, they must hope to somehow take advantage of a vulnerability on the network to proceed. The *Exploitation* phase includes the actual execution of the exploit against a flaw in the system. This is the point where the adversary triggers the exploit against a server vulnerability, or when the user clicks a malicious link or executes a tainted attachment, in the case of a user-initiated attack. At this point, an attack can take one of two courses of action. The attacker can install a *dropper* to enable them to execute commands, or they can install a *downloader* to enable additional software to be installed at a later point. The end goal here is often to get as much access as possible to begin establishing some permanence on the system. Hardening measures are extremely important at this stage. Knowing what assets are present on the network and patching any identified vulnerabilities improves resiliency against such attacks. This, combined with more advanced methods of determining previously unseen exploits, puts defenders in a better position to prevent escalation of the attack.

For the majority of attacks, the adversary aims to achieve *persistence,* or extended access to the target system for future activities. The attacker has taken a lot of steps to get to this point and would likely want to avoid going through them every time they want access to the target. *Installation* is the point where the threat actor attempts to emplace a backdoor or implant. This is frequently seen during insertion of a web shell on a compromised web server, or a remote access Trojan (RAT) on a compromised machine. Endpoint detection is frequently effective against activities in the stage; however, security analysts may sometimes need to use more advanced logging interpretation techniques to identify clever or obfuscated installation techniques.

In the *Command and Control* (C2) phase, the attacker creates a channel in order to facilitate continued access to internal systems remotely. C2 is often accomplished through periodic beaconing via a previously identified path outside of the network. Correspondingly, defenders can monitor for this kind of communication to detect potential C2 activity. Keep in mind that many legitimate software packages perform similar activity for licensing and update functionality. The most common malicious C2 channels are over the Web, Domain Name System (DNS), and e-mail, sometimes with falsified headers. For encrypted communications, beacons tend to use self-signed certificates or custom encryption to avoid traffic inspection. When the network is monitored correctly, it can reveal all kinds of beaconing activity to defenders hunting for this behavior. When looking for abnormal outbound activities such as this, we must think like our adversary, who will try to blend in with the scene and use techniques to cloak his beaconing. To complicate things more, beaconing can occur at any time or frequency—from a few times a minute to once or twice weekly.

The final stage of the kill chain is *Actions on Objectives,* or the whole reason the attacker wanted to be there in the first place. It could be to exfiltrate sensitive intellectual property, encrypt critical files for extortion, or even sabotage via data destruction or modification. Defenders can use several tools at this stage to prevent or at least detect these actions. Data loss prevention software, for example, can be useful in preventing data exfiltration. In any case, it's critical that defenders have a reliable backup solution that they can restore from in the worst-case scenario. Much like the Reconnaissance stage, detecting activity during this phase can give insight into attack motivations, albeit much later than is desirable.

While the Cyber Kill Chain enables organizations to build defense-in-depth strategies that target specific parts of the kill chain, it may fail to capture attacks that aren't as dependent on all of the phases to achieve end goals. One such example is the modern phishing attack, in which the attacker relies on the victim to execute an attached script. Additionally, the kill chain is very malware-focused and doesn't capture the full scope of other common threat vectors such as insider threats, social engineering, or any intrusion in which malware wasn't the primary vehicle for access.

Open Source Security Testing Methodology Manual

The Open Source Security Testing Methodology Manual, or OSSTMM, is a widely recognized methodology for security testing and analysis in the information technology and cybersecurity industries. It was developed by the Institute for Security and Open Methodologies (ISECOM) and is distributed as an open source project.

The OSSTMM is designed to provide a structured and systematic approach to security testing, with an emphasis on accuracy, completeness, and reliability. It defines a set of guidelines and procedures for security testing, including vulnerability assessment, penetration testing, and security auditing.

The methodology is organized into six main areas, which cover specific topics and provide detailed guidance for testing and analysis:

- **Information security management**   This area covers topics such as security policies, risk management, and incident response. It provides guidance on how to assess an organization's security posture and identify areas for improvement.

- **Human security testing**   This area focuses on the evaluation of people-related security issues such as social engineering, password policies, and user awareness. It provides guidance on how to assess an organization's vulnerability to these types of attacks.

- **Physical security testing**   This area involves the assessment of physical security measures such as access control, CCTV, and alarms. It provides guidance on how to test the effectiveness of these measures.

- **Telecommunications security testing**   This area focuses on evaluating the security of telecommunications systems such as VoIP, PSTN, and fax. It provides guidance on how to test the security of these systems and identify potential vulnerabilities.

- **Data network security testing**   This area involves testing the security of network infrastructure, protocols, and devices such as routers, switches, and firewalls. It provides guidance on how to identify and address vulnerabilities in these areas.

- **Wireless security testing**   This area focuses on evaluating the security of wireless networks, including Wi-Fi and Bluetooth. It provides guidance on how to test the security of these networks and identify potential vulnerabilities.

In practice, the OSSTMM is used in a variety of real-world applications. Here are some examples:

- **Penetration testing**   The OSSTMM is often used as a guide for performing penetration testing, which involves simulating an attack on a system or network to identify vulnerabilities and weaknesses. The methodology provides detailed guidelines for conducting comprehensive and accurate penetration testing that can help organizations identify and address security risks.

- **Security auditing**   The OSSTMM is also used for security auditing, which involves assessing the security posture of an organization's systems and infrastructure. The methodology provides a structured approach to auditing that can help organizations identify vulnerabilities and assess the effectiveness of their security controls.

- **Compliance and certification**   The OSSTMM is recognized by several international standards organizations as a reliable and effective methodology for security testing. As a result, many organizations use the OSSTMM to meet compliance requirements and achieve security certifications, such as ISO 27001.

- **Security training**   The OSSTMM can also be used as a training tool for security professionals. The methodology provides a structured approach to security testing that can help professionals develop and refine their skills and knowledge in the field.

Overall, the OSSTMM is a versatile and widely used methodology for security testing and analysis that provides a valuable resource for organizations and security professionals looking to improve their security posture and help mitigate security risks. More information can be found at https://www.isecom.org/research/osstmm.html.

OWASP Web Security Testing Guide

The OWASP Web Security Testing Guide is a comprehensive framework for testing the security of web applications. It is designed to provide a standardized and structured approach for identifying and addressing web application security vulnerabilities. The methodology is based on the OWASP Top 10, which is a list of the top 10 most critical web application security risks.

The OWASP Web Security Testing Guide covers all phases of testing, including initial planning, scoping, testing, and reporting. The methodology includes specific testing techniques and procedures for identifying and exploiting web application security vulnerabilities, such as SQL injection, cross-site scripting (XSS), and broken authentication and session management.

The methodology includes six phases:

1. *Planning and Preparation.* In this phase, the objectives of the test are defined and the scope of the test is determined. This phase involves reviewing the application architecture and identifying the testing tools and techniques that will be used.

2. *Information Gathering.* In this phase, information about the application is gathered, such as the application's functionality, input/output requirements, and potential attack vectors.

3. *Vulnerability Identification.* In this phase, potential security vulnerabilities are identified and verified. This phase includes testing for vulnerabilities such as SQL injection, XSS, and broken authentication and session management.

4. *Exploitation.* In this phase, vulnerabilities that have been identified are exploited to determine the potential impact of a successful attack. This phase includes testing for the ability to execute arbitrary code, escalate privileges, and exfiltrate data.

5. *Post-Exploitation.* In this phase, the tester assesses the level of access gained and the potential damage that could be caused if an attacker were to exploit the vulnerability.

6. *Reporting.* In this phase, the test results are documented and presented to the stakeholders. The report includes details of the vulnerabilities identified, the level of risk associated with each vulnerability, and recommendations for remediation.

EXAM TIP While the exam may not extensively cover the OWASP Web Security Testing Guide, it's important to have a good understanding of web application attacks and how to defend against them. Make sure you're familiar with the OWASP Top 10 and the different phases of testing for identifying and remediating vulnerabilities. This knowledge can help you better analyze and address web application security threats.

The OWASP Web Security Testing Guide can be leveraged in the real world by security practitioners and organizations to improve the security of web applications. By following the methodology, organizations can identify and address critical security risks, meet compliance requirements, and improve the overall security posture of their web applications.

More information can be found here: https://owasp.org/www-project-web-security-testing-guide/.

Chapter Review

The use of attack frameworks is an essential component of modern cybersecurity. The frameworks discussed in this chapter, including MITRE ATT&CK, the Diamond Model of Intrusion Analysis, Lockheed Martin Cyber Kill Chain, OSSTMM, and the OWASP Web Security Testing Guide, offer a structured and standardized approach to understanding and responding to cyber threats.

MITRE ATT&CK provides a comprehensive knowledge base of tactics, techniques, and procedures (TTPs) used by cyberattackers. It allows cybersecurity analysts to categorize threats and identify vulnerabilities, helping organizations to develop effective defense strategies.

The Diamond Model of Intrusion Analysis provides a structured approach to analyzing cyberattacks. Its four components—adversary, capability, infrastructure, and victim—provide a comprehensive view of an intrusion, allowing analysts to identify attackers' goals and motivations, their tactics and techniques, and the infrastructure they rely on.

The Lockheed Martin Cyber Kill Chain is another framework that describes the various stages of a cyberattack. By understanding each stage of the Cyber Kill Chain, cybersecurity analysts can develop strategies to stop attacks before they reach their final stages, preventing data exfiltration and other harmful outcomes.

The OSSTMM provides a standardized testing methodology for software security. It helps organizations to identify and address security vulnerabilities in their software, ensuring that critical assets are protected from cyber threats.

Finally, the OWASP Web Security Testing Guide offers a comprehensive approach to web application security testing. By using standardized security testing techniques, organizations can identify and address vulnerabilities before they can be exploited by attackers.

Overall, the attack frameworks discussed in this chapter provide a standardized language and methodology for understanding and responding to cyber threats. They help organizations to identify vulnerabilities, develop effective defense strategies, and prevent harmful outcomes. Cybersecurity analysts should make use of these frameworks to stay up to date with the latest threats and ensure that critical assets are protected from cyberattacks.

Questions

1. Which of the following tactics does MITRE ATT&CK *not* cover?

   A. Lateral movement

   B. Initial access

   C. Data exfiltration

   D. Encryption

2. The Diamond Model of Intrusion Analysis uses which of the following components to provide a comprehensive view of an intrusion?

   A. Attacker motivation, attack surface, infrastructure, and victimology

   B. Adversary, capability, infrastructure, and victim

   C. Reconnaissance, weaponization, delivery, exploitation, installation, command and control, and actions on objectives

   D. Initial access, execution, persistence, privilege escalation, defense evasion, credential access, discovery, lateral movement, collection, exfiltration, and command and control

3. Which of the following is *not* a stage in the Lockheed Martin Cyber Kill Chain?

   A. Command and Control

   B. Reconnaissance

   C. Exploitation

   D. Intrusion

4. Which area of the OSSTMM focuses on the assessment of physical security measures such as access control, CCTV, and alarms?

   A. Information security management

   B. Human security testing

   C. Physical security testing

   D. Telecommunications security testing

5. In which phase of the OWASP Web Security Testing Guide is cross-site scripting (XSS) commonly identified?

   A. Planning and Preparation

   B. Information Gathering

   C. Vulnerability Identification

   D. Exploitation

6. Which component of the MITRE ATT&CK framework provides step-by-step processes or sequences of tactics and techniques used by attackers?

   A. Matrices

   B. Tactics

   C. Techniques

   D. Procedures

7. Which of the following is *not* covered by the OWASP Web Security Testing Guide?

   A. Network intrusion detection

   B. Cross-site scripting (XSS)

   C. SQL injection

   D. Denial-of-service (DoS) attacks

8. What is the purpose of the Cyber Kill Chain model?

   A. To capture all possible attack vectors in a cyberattack

   B. To provide a linear structure that breaks an attack into stages

   C. To identify all possible vulnerabilities in a system

   D. To provide a framework for patching vulnerabilities in a system

Answers

1. **D.** MITRE ATT&CK does not cover encryption.

2. **B.** The Diamond Model uses adversary, capability, infrastructure, and victim.

3. **D.** Intrusion is not a stage in the Lockheed Martin Cyber Kill Chain.

4. **C.** This area of the methodology involves the assessment of physical security measures, including access control, CCTV, and alarms, to determine their effectiveness and identify any potential vulnerabilities.

5. **C.** Cross-site scripting (XSS) is a common web application vulnerability that can be identified during the vulnerability identification phase of the OWASP Web Security Testing Guide.

6. **D.** Procedures in the MITRE ATT&CK framework describe the step-by-step processes or sequences of tactics and techniques used by attackers to achieve their objectives. Procedures can be thought of as the "attack playbook" that a threat actor follows during an attack.

7. **A.** The OWASP Web Security Testing Guide includes specific testing techniques and procedures for identifying and exploiting web application security vulnerabilities, such as cross-site scripting (XSS), SQL injection, and denial-of-service (DoS) attacks, but does not cover network intrusion detection.

8. **B.** The Cyber Kill Chain model provides a linear structure that breaks an attack into stages and is specifically designed to capture the stages used by cyberattackers in conducting their malicious activities.

Analyzing Potentially Malicious Activity

In this chapter you will learn:

- How to diagnose incidents by examining network activity
- How to diagnose incidents by examining host activity
- How to diagnose incidents by examining application activity

Diagnosis is not the end, but the beginning of practice.

—Martin H. Fischer

The English word "diagnosis" comes from the Greek word *diagignōskein,* which literally means "to know thoroughly." Diagnosis, then, implies the ability to see through the myriad of irrelevant facts, homing in on the relevant ones, and arriving at the true root cause of a problem. Unlike portrayals in Hollywood, in the real world, security incidents don't involve malware in bold-red font, conveniently highlighted for our benefit. Instead, our adversaries go to great lengths to hide behind the massive amount of benign activity in our systems, oftentimes leading us down blind alleys to distract us from their real methods and intentions. The CySA+ exam, like the real world, will offer you plenty of misleading choices, so it's important that you stay focused on the important symptoms and ignore the rest. In this chapter we will discuss potentially malicious system activities and symptoms that may also become indicators of compromise (IoCs) once we establish their cause and intent. This includes examining activities related to network traffic, host-related processes and activities, applications, and other suspicious events that can occur on the infrastructure. In this chapter we will cover the requirements for Objective 1.2, "Given a scenario, analyze indicators of potentially malicious activity."

Network-Related Indicators

We'll begin our exploration of network-related indicators as you typically would when searching for potential adversaries—from the outside in. Network sensors often provide the first hints that something might be amiss in your infrastructure. Equipped with this information, you can investigate hosts and the processes running on them more thoroughly.

Throughout our discussion, we'll assume that your network is designed with an array of diverse sensors, and we'll use their outputs to describe potential attack indicators.

Keep in mind that network-related indicators often serve as the first line of defense against cyber threats. By closely monitoring and analyzing these indicators, you can identify and address potential vulnerabilities and ongoing attacks before they escalate and cause significant damage to your organization's IT infrastructure. Therefore, building a strong understanding of network-related indicators is essential for maintaining an effective and resilient network security posture.

Network-related potential indicators are crucial pieces of information that signal possible security incidents or breaches in a network. They play a vital role in an analyst's efforts to identify, investigate, and respond to potential cyber threats. By monitoring and analyzing network-related indicators, an analyst can discover threats before they escalate and cause significant damage to the organization's IT infrastructure.

Some common network-related potential indicators include the following:

- **Unexpected protocol usage** Attackers may use atypical or unauthorized protocols, such as transferring data over DNS, to avoid detection by traditional security measures.

- **Suspicious DNS requests** A high volume of DNS requests to a particular domain, especially if it's associated with known malicious activities, may indicate command-and-control (C2) server communication or malware infection.

- **Unusual network device behavior** Devices acting as network nodes, such as routers or switches, may exhibit abnormal behavior in the case of compromise, including configuration changes, altered routing tables, or unauthorized logins.

- **Geographically improbable access** Multiple logins or access attempts from disparate geographic locations within a short time frame may signal account compromise or the use of virtual private networks (VPNs) or proxies by attackers.

- **Unauthorized use of network services** Unauthorized access to or modification of network services, like file shares, databases, or e-mail servers, could indicate a breach or ongoing attack.

- **Malware-related activity** Network traffic patterns indicative of malware infections, such as connections to known malicious domains, C2 servers, or data exfiltration channels, warrant further investigation.

Later in this chapter, we'll explore more network-related indicators, such as bandwidth consumption, beaconing, irregular peer-to-peer communication, rogue devices on the network, scans/sweeps, unusual traffic spikes, and activity on unexpected ports.

Bandwidth Consumption

Monitoring and analyzing bandwidth consumption can provide valuable insights into the health and security of your network. Unusual changes in consumption patterns may indicate potential security incidents, such as data exfiltration, distributed denial-of-service (DDoS) attacks, or malware infections.

Src IP	Src Port	Dst IP	Dst Port	Protocol	Packets	Bytes/Pkt
10.0.0.3	54902	192.168.0.7	80	TCP	2491	740
10.0.0.6	55097	172.31.21.3	443	TCP	100227	1528
10.0.0.12	993	10.0.0.3	48450	TCP	2210	762
10.0.0.6	443	10.0.0.7	54122	TCP	2271	1040
10.0.0.6	443	10.0.0.3	53112	TCP	1022	810

Figure 4-1   NetFlow report demonstrating suspicious bandwidth usage

Bandwidth consumption refers to the amount of data transmitted or received over a network within a specific period. As a cybersecurity analyst, it's essential to establish a baseline for normal bandwidth usage within your organization. This baseline will help you identify anomalies that could signal potential threats. To establish a baseline, monitor bandwidth consumption during regular and peak business hours, as well as during periods of low activity. Analyzing flow logs can also provide valuable insights into network traffic patterns and help you understand your network's typical bandwidth consumption.

Flow logs are a valuable resource for monitoring bandwidth consumption. They are records of network traffic that provide details about the source and destination IP addresses, ports, packet sizes, and more. By analyzing flow logs, you can gain a comprehensive understanding of your network's traffic patterns and identify deviations from the baseline that may indicate potential security threats.

Figure 4-1 shows a suspicious pattern of NetFlow activity. Though one host (10.0.0.6) is clearly consuming more bandwidth than the others, this fact alone can have a multitude of benign explanations. It is apparent from the figure that the host is running a web server, which is serving other hosts in its own subnet. What makes it odd is that the traffic going to the one host in a different subnet is two orders of magnitude greater than anything else in the report. Furthermore, it's puzzling that a web server is connecting on a high port to a remote web server. When looking at bandwidth consumption as an indicator of compromise, you should look not only at the amount of traffic but also at the endpoints and directionality of the connection.

Beaconing

Beaconing is a communication pattern often associated with malware and command and control (C2) that uses periodic, often regular communication between a compromised device and a C2 server. Malware-infected devices may send beacons to their C2 server to signal their presence, receive commands, or exfiltrate data. Attackers use C2 servers to maintain control over compromised devices and orchestrate their activities, such as launching DDoS attacks, stealing sensitive information, and spreading further infections.

Beaconing can be challenging to detect, as attackers often use various techniques to obfuscate their communication and blend in with legitimate network traffic. However, identifying beaconing patterns can provide valuable insights into potential threats and help you respond to them proactively. When it comes to monitoring your network for beaconing behavior, staying vigilant and utilizing network analysis tools are key. Some strategies for detecting beaconing include analyzing jitter to uncover C2 communications with variable intervals.

NOTE   Focusing solely on specific intervals can lead to both false positives (FPs) and false negatives (FNs). To address this, cybersecurity analysts should employ a combination of detection methods and continually refine their approaches to stay ahead of evolving threats. Understanding the nuances of jitter and using various network analysis tools can improve your ability to identify and defend against C2 communications.

Irregular Peer-to-Peer Communication

Peer-to-peer (P2P) communication involves data transfer between devices in a network without relying on a centralized server. While P2P networks have legitimate uses, they can also be exploited by cybercriminals to conceal malicious activities, such as lateral movement within a network.

Irregular P2P communication occurs when devices on a network engage in unusual or unexpected data transfers. This could involve excessive data exchange between devices, the use of nonstandard ports, or communication patterns that suggest lateral movement. Cybercriminals can leverage irregular P2P communication to distribute malware, exfiltrate sensitive data, or establish covert communication channels.

Attackers may use a variety of tools and techniques to facilitate lateral movement within a network. Some common methods include the following:

- **PsExec**   A Microsoft tool that allows system administrators to execute processes on remote systems. Attackers often misuse PsExec to run commands or execute malware on remote machines.

- **SSH (Secure Shell)**   A cryptographic network protocol commonly used for secure remote access. Cybercriminals can exploit SSH to move laterally within a network, transferring files or executing commands on remote systems.

- **WMI (Windows Management Instrumentation)**   A powerful management framework in Windows that enables administrators to query and manipulate system settings. Attackers can misuse WMI to gather information, execute commands, or deploy malware on remote systems.

- **Pass-the-Hash (PtH)**   A technique used by attackers to authenticate to remote systems using password hash values rather than the original password. This method allows adversaries to move laterally within a network without needing to crack the actual password.

- **Remote Desktop Protocol (RDP)**   A proprietary protocol developed by Microsoft that enables users to connect to remote systems and control them. Attackers can exploit RDP for lateral movement by gaining unauthorized access to remote systems and executing commands or installing malware.

By gaining a thorough understanding of your network architecture, topology, and protocols, you can better identify irregular P2P communication within your network. Part of this process involves monitoring for the use of common lateral movement tools and techniques, such as PsExec, SSH, WMI, Remote Desktop Protocol (RDP), and Pass-the-Hash (PtH) attacks.

NOTE P2P traffic is common in enterprise networks, enabling direct communication between devices for tasks such as file sharing, service discovery, load balancing, and container orchestration. P2P communication can improve efficiency and reduce reliance on central servers, but it can also be used for malicious purposes and may use encryption and obfuscation techniques to evade detection. In addition to these use cases, P2P communication is also used in video conferencing platforms to improve call quality and reduce latency. Security analysts need to understand both the legitimate and potentially malicious uses of P2P traffic.

Rogue Devices on the Network

Rogue devices are unauthorized or unmanaged hardware connected to your network, potentially posing significant security risks. Identifying and mitigating the threat of rogue devices are essential for maintaining a secure and resilient network security posture.

Rogue devices can be anything from unauthorized laptops, smartphones, and tablets to unauthorized access points, routers, or Internet of Things (IoT) devices. These devices can introduce vulnerabilities to your network, serve as entry points for attackers, or be used for data exfiltration, eavesdropping, or other malicious activities. Bring-your-own-device (BYOD) policies, while convenient, can further increase the risk of rogue devices on your network if not properly managed and secured.

In order to detect and mitigate rogue devices, it's essential to implement network access control (NAC), software-defined networking (SDN), identity and access management (IAM), and endpoint detection and response (EDR) systems. Furthermore, the importance of maintaining a comprehensive IT service management (ITSM) system and configuration management database (CMDB) cannot be overstated, as these tools allow for effective tracking and management of authorized devices within your network.

Detecting, protecting, and mitigating rogue devices on a network requires a combination of tools and techniques. Here are some key use cases associated with various tools:

- **Endpoint detection and response (EDR)**   EDR solutions can help detect rogue devices on a network by continuously monitoring endpoints for suspicious activity. EDR tools can also provide endpoint visibility and allow for threat hunting, incident response, and remediation.

- **Network access control (NAC)**   NAC solutions can help prevent rogue devices from accessing a network by enforcing security policies and authentication protocols. NAC solutions can also provide network visibility and real-time threat detection as well as quarantine and remediation capabilities.

- **Identity and access management (IAM)**   IAM solutions can help prevent unauthorized access to network resources by enforcing access controls and authentication protocols. IAM tools can also provide identity verification and user behavior monitoring as well as audit trails and compliance reporting.

- **IT service management (ITSM)**   ITSM solutions can help track and manage network assets and incidents, including rogue devices. ITSM tools can provide inventory and asset management, incident management, and problem management as well as change and configuration management.

- **Configuration management database (CMDB)**   A CMDB can provide a central repository for managing network assets, including rogue devices. A CMDB can help track asset ownership, inventory, and dependencies as well as provide change management and audit trails.

Scans/Sweeps

Network scanning and sweeping are techniques used by attackers to discover available network resources, probe for vulnerabilities, and enumerate network devices. Detecting and managing these activities can help you maintain a secure and resilient network security posture.

Network scanning involves probing individual hosts or network devices to gather information about open ports, running services, and potential vulnerabilities, while network sweeping sends packets to a range of IP addresses to identify active hosts on a network. Both techniques are used by malicious actors and legitimate tools like vulnerability scanners and asset discovery tools.

Detecting scans or sweeps targeting externally facing assets can be noisy and may not always provide high-value data, but logging these activities can be useful during an investigation. In contrast, detecting port scanning behavior internally could be associated with malicious behavior, so it's crucial to differentiate between legitimate and malicious activities.

To detect and manage network scanning and sweeping, consider monitoring ARP queries; scanners tend to generate a large number of ARP queries when sweeping a network, as shown in Figure 4-2. Implementing network segmentation can also help by dividing your network into smaller, more manageable segments, limiting the scope of potential scanning and sweeping activities. This approach isolates critical assets and reduces the risk of compromise in the event of an attack.

Time	Source	Destination	Protocol	Length	Info	
1.88519600	Vmware_4a:58:30	Broadcast	ARP	42	who has 192.168.192.162?	Tell 192.168.192.6
1.88528900	Vmware_4a:58:30	Broadcast	ARP	42	who has 192.168.192.163?	Tell 192.168.192.6
1.88540000	Vmware_4a:58:30	Broadcast	ARP	42	who has 192.168.192.164?	Tell 192.168.192.6
1.88555900	Vmware_4a:58:30	Broadcast	ARP	42	who has 192.168.192.165?	Tell 192.168.192.6
1.88566200	Vmware_4a:58:30	Broadcast	ARP	42	who has 192.168.192.166?	Tell 192.168.192.6
1.88574400	Vmware_4a:58:30	Broadcast	ARP	42	who has 192.168.192.167?	Tell 192.168.192.6
1.88583400	Vmware_4a:58:30	Broadcast	ARP	42	who has 192.168.192.168?	Tell 192.168.192.6
1.88591000	Vmware_4a:58:30	Broadcast	ARP	42	who has 192.168.192.169?	Tell 192.168.192.6
1.88601800	Vmware_4a:58:30	Broadcast	ARP	42	who has 192.168.192.170?	Tell 192.168.192.6
1.88610000	Vmware_4a:58:30	Broadcast	ARP	42	who has 192.168.192.171?	Tell 192.168.192.6
1.88618800	Vmware_4a:58:30	Broadcast	ARP	42	who has 192.168.192.172?	Tell 192.168.192.6
1.88626800	Vmware_4a:58:30	Broadcast	ARP	42	who has 192.168.192.173?	Tell 192.168.192.6
1.88643300	Vmware_4a:58:30	Broadcast	ARP	42	who has 192.168.192.174?	Tell 192.168.192.6
1.88654100	Vmware_4a:58:30	Broadcast	ARP	42	who has 192.168.192.175?	Tell 192.168.192.6
1.88663100	Vmware_4a:58:30	Broadcast	ARP	42	who has 192.168.192.176?	Tell 192.168.192.6
1.88671500	Vmware_4a:58:30	Broadcast	ARP	42	who has 192.168.192.177?	Tell 192.168.192.6

Figure 4-2   ARP queries associated with a scan sweep

Unusual Traffic Spikes

Keeping an eye on network traffic patterns for sudden changes in volume or frequency can help you detect possible security incidents or breaches. By staying alert and employing the right strategies, you can spot unusual traffic spikes and act proactively to tackle potential threats.

Unusual traffic spikes represent sudden and unexpected surges in network traffic, which could point to various security concerns. These spikes might be connected to ongoing attacks, data exfiltration attempts, or even DDoS attacks. Recognizing the potential consequences of these traffic anomalies and responding accordingly is essential for maintaining a secure network environment.

For unusual traffic spikes, consider using anomaly detection techniques, such as algorithms and machine learning, to identify deviations from normal traffic patterns.

Activity on Unexpected Ports

Activity on unexpected ports refers to network traffic occurring on ports that deviate from their standard or designated use. Monitoring and analyzing port usage is crucial for detecting and addressing potential security incidents or breaches.

Network ports are the gateways through which data is transmitted between devices and systems. Typically, specific ports are designated for certain services and protocols, such as HTTP traffic on port 80 or HTTPS traffic on port 443. You can identify standard ports by referring to resources such as the /etc/services file on Unix-based systems, the IANA Service Name and Transport Protocol Port Number Registry, and online databases of well-known port numbers. However, attackers may use unexpected or nonstandard ports to evade detection or bypass security measures. They might also tunnel legitimate protocols through nonstandard ports to conceal their activities, such as tunneling SSH over HTTPS.

Network-Related Indicators Summary

In this section, we have explored a variety of network-related potential indicators that play a vital role in a daily effort to detect, investigate, and respond to cyber threats. We have discussed several, including bandwidth consumption, beaconing, irregular peer-to-peer communication, rogue devices on the network, network scanning and sweeping, unusual traffic spikes, and activity on unexpected ports.

Throughout these discussions, we have highlighted the importance of knowing your network, utilizing monitoring and detection tools, and staying vigilant to identify and react to potential threats. We also compiled a list of common detection strategies that can be applied across various network-related indicators:

- **Establish a baseline**   Understand normal network behavior, port usage patterns, and device connections to detect anomalies more readily.
- **Use network monitoring tools**   Leverage tools to continuously analyze network traffic, port usage patterns, and device connections, providing real-time data on potential threats.

- **Configure alerts and thresholds**   Set up alerts and thresholds within your network monitoring tools to notify you of unusual activity, allowing you to respond more quickly to potential threats.

- **Examine the nature of the traffic or activity**   Investigate the detected anomalies to determine if they are related to a legitimate event or a security incident, looking for connections to known malicious IP addresses, domains, and other indicators of compromise.

- **Review logs and packet captures**   Analyze logs and packet captures to gain further insight into the unusual activity, helping you determine whether it is malicious or benign.

- **Initiate incident response procedures**   If you determine that the activity is a security concern, begin your incident response procedures to contain and remediate the threat.

Host-Related Indicators

We'll continue our exploration of indicators by focusing on host-related indicators, which concentrate on individual systems within your network. These indicators are vital for detecting and responding to threats that directly impact your network's devices and the processes running on them. Host-related indicators serve as a critical line of defense against cyber threats, offering valuable insights into potential vulnerabilities and ongoing attacks. Host-related potential indicators of compromise are essential pieces of information that signal possible security incidents or breaches within individual systems. They play a crucial role in cybersecurity analysts' (CySA+) efforts to identify, investigate, and respond to potential cyber threats. Here are some common host-related indicators that we will not discuss in further detail but are still important to consider:

- **Unusual login patterns**   Multiple failed login attempts, logins at odd hours, or logins from unusual locations can indicate unauthorized access attempts or successful breaches.

- **Persistence mechanisms related to services**   The presence of malware or scripts designed to maintain persistence on the compromised host through the creation of new services.

- **Unusual user account activity**   The creation of new user accounts or modification of existing ones, especially those with elevated privileges, could signify unauthorized access.

- **Unusual system or application crashes**   Repeated crashes or errors may signal the presence of malware or an ongoing attack.

- **Anti-forensic activities**   The use of tools or techniques to erase logs, modify timestamps, or otherwise hinder digital forensic investigations.

Later in this section, we'll explore more host-related indicators in detail, such as capacity consumption, unauthorized software, malicious processes, memory contents, unauthorized changes, unauthorized privileges, data exfiltration, abnormal OS process behavior, file system changes or anomalies, registry changes or anomalies, and unauthorized scheduled tasks. We will discuss effective detection strategies for maintaining a strong security posture within your network.

Capacity Consumption

We have already seen how the various indicators of threat activity can consume network resources. In many cases, attacker behavior will also create spikes in capacity consumption on the host, whether it is memory, CPU cycles, disk space, or local bandwidth. Part of your job as an analyst is to think proactively about where and when these spikes would occur, based on your own risk assessment or threat model, and then provide the capability to monitor resources so that you can detect the spikes. Many tools can assist with establishing your network and system baselines over time. The CySA+ exam will not test you on the proactive aspect of this process, but you will be expected to know how to identify these anomalies in a scenario. You are likely to be presented with an image like Figure 4-3 and will be asked questions about the resources being consumed and what they may be indicative of. The figure, by the way, is of a Windows 10 system that is mostly idle and not compromised.

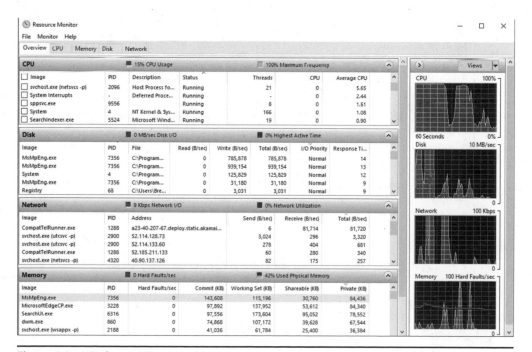

Figure 4-3 Windows 10 Resource Monitor

EXAM TIP You will likely encounter exam scenarios where the objective will be to identify hosts that are compromised. The indicators outlined in this chapter should be top of mind when you perform your analysis. Analysts should also attempt validate their findings with additional data sources such as associated log files whenever possible.

When faced with unexplained capacity consumption, you should refer to the steps we described for analyzing processes, memory, network connections, and file systems. The unusual utilization will be a signal, but your response depends on which specific resource is being used. The following are a few examples of warning signs related to abnormal consumption of various types of system resources.

Memory:

- **Persistent high memory consumption** If memory usage remains consistently high despite low system usage or no active user interaction, it could indicate a hidden process or malware consuming system resources.

- **Unusual memory allocation** Processes allocating an unusually large amount of memory or allocating memory in nonstandard regions could be indicative of malicious activities, such as a buffer overflow attack or memory-resident malware.

- **Unexpected memory access patterns** Processes attempting to read from or write to memory areas they should not access, or attempting to perform memory operations at a higher rate than expected, might be signs of malicious behavior.

- **Memory artifacts** The presence of suspicious strings, code, or data patterns within memory might point to malware or other threat activities. For instance, finding known signatures of malware or signs of data exfiltration within memory can help detect ongoing attacks.

- **Memory injection** The unauthorized injection of code or data into the memory space of another process is a common technique used by malware or attackers to evade detection and gain persistence. Monitoring for memory injection events can help identify malicious activities.

- **Unusual memory spikes** Sudden and unexplained spikes in memory usage, especially when they coincide with other suspicious events or network activities, might be indicative of an attack or malware infection.

Drive Capacity:

- **Sudden drop in available free space** A significant decrease in available disk space without any apparent reason, such as during a period of increased network activity or file transfers, could indicate data exfiltration, unauthorized file downloads, or the presence of malware.

- **Unexplained files or directories** The presence of new files or directories, particularly those with unusual names, extensions, or locations, can be a sign of unauthorized access, data exfiltration, or malware installation.

- **Unusual file growth**   Rapid or unexpected growth of files or directories, especially system files, logs, or databases, could indicate a potential security issue, such as a log flooding attack, data tampering, or unauthorized data storage.

- **Temp files accumulation**   A large number of temporary files, particularly those related to known malicious activities or created by suspicious processes, could signify an ongoing attack or malware infection.

- **Disk usage by unauthorized processes**   Unusual disk space consumption by unfamiliar or unauthorized processes can indicate the presence of malware or a compromised application.

- **Persistent low disk space**   Consistently low available disk space despite regular clean-up efforts or no apparent reason for the consumption can signal an underlying issue, such as malware or unauthorized activities.

Processor:

- **Prolonged periods of high processor usage**   Sustained high CPU usage despite no active user interaction or scheduled tasks could indicate the presence of malware, a compromised application, or a resource-intensive unauthorized process.

- **Unusually high processor consumption by unfamiliar tasks**   High CPU usage by unknown or suspicious processes can be a sign of malware infection, a cryptocurrency miner, or a compromised application.

- **Spikes in processor usage during idle periods**   Sudden increases in CPU usage when the system is expected to be idle or during low activity periods may signal unauthorized activity or malware execution.

- **Inconsistent processor usage patterns**   Processor usage that frequently fluctuates between extremely high and low levels, without apparent reason, can indicate the presence of a hidden malicious process or an ongoing attack.

- **High CPU usage by system processes**   Unusual CPU consumption by legitimate system processes could be a sign of process hollowing or other injection techniques employed by malware or attackers to evade detection.

Network:

- **Unusual network connections**   A high number of unexpected or unauthorized connections to external IP addresses or domains may indicate malware communication, data exfiltration, or C2 server interaction.

- **Uncharacteristic network traffic spikes**   Sudden increases in network traffic during idle periods or low activity times can be a sign of ongoing unauthorized activities, such as data exfiltration or malware communication.

- **Persistent high network throughput**   Prolonged periods of high network utilization, despite no active user interaction or scheduled tasks, could be indicative of a compromised system or ongoing unauthorized processes.

- **Network traffic to known malicious destinations**   Communication with known malicious IP addresses, domains, or URLs may signal an ongoing attack, malware infection, or C2 server interaction.

- **Unusual port usage**   Network traffic on unexpected or nonstandard ports can indicate attempts to evade detection, unauthorized services, or the tunneling of legitimate protocols through nonstandard ports to conceal activities.

- **Anomalous data transfer volumes**   Large volumes of data being transferred to or from a host, especially to external destinations, can be a sign of data exfiltration or unauthorized access to sensitive information.

 NOTE   Some malware, such as a rootkits, will alter its behavior or the system itself so as not to show signs of its existence in utilities such as Resource Monitor and Task Manager.

Unauthorized Software

The presence of unauthorized software on a system can serve as a strong indicator of compromise (IoC) or indicator of attack (IoA) in host-related security analysis. Unauthorized software can include a wide range of programs, such as unapproved applications, potentially unwanted programs (PUPs), or malicious software like viruses, Trojans, and ransomware. These programs can pose a significant risk to an organization's security, as they may lead to unauthorized access, data exfiltration, or other harmful activities.

To monitor and detect unauthorized software on your network, consider the following strategies:

- **Implement an application approved list**   By defining a list of approved applications and only allowing them to execute, you can reduce the risk of unauthorized software running on your systems.

- **Regular software inventory**   Conduct routine software inventories on all devices within your network to identify any unauthorized or unapproved programs.

- **Endpoint security solutions**   Employ endpoint security tools, such as antivirus software and endpoint detection and response (EDR) systems, to scan for and remove unauthorized software.

- **User education and awareness**   Train users about the risks associated with unauthorized software and the importance of adhering to your organization's software policies.

- **Monitor for unusual process behavior**   Keep an eye on processes running on your systems and investigate any that exhibit abnormal behavior or are associated with unrecognized applications.

- **Centralized software deployment and management**   Use centralized software deployment and management tools to control the installation and updating of applications, ensuring that only approved software is installed on your devices.

Malicious Processes

Someone once said, "Malware can hide, but it has to run." When you're responding to an incident, one of your very first tasks should be to examine the running processes. Malicious processes often attempt to disguise themselves to avoid detection, making it crucial to monitor system activities and identify any unusual or suspicious behavior.

Common techniques for disguising malicious processes include the following:

- **Using legitimate-sounding names**   Attackers may name their malicious processes to resemble legitimate system processes or applications, making it more challenging to spot them.

- **Masquerading as system processes**   Malicious processes may attempt to mimic system processes, either by modifying legitimate processes or by creating new ones with similar names or attributes.

- **Hiding process activity**   Some malware employs rootkit techniques to hide their processes from system utilities and monitoring tools, making them difficult to detect using standard methods.

To monitor and detect malicious processes on your network, consider the following strategies:

- **Use system utilities**   Leverage native system utilities like **ps**, **netstat**, **top**, and **lsof** on Unix-based systems or Task Manager and Resource Monitor on Windows systems to gain insights into running processes, open network connections, and resource usage. The output of the **top** utility is shown in Figure 4-4.

- **Monitor for unusual process behavior**   Keep an eye on processes running on your systems and investigate any that exhibit abnormal behavior, such as high CPU or memory usage, unexpected network connections, or unusual file system activities.

- **Implement endpoint security solutions**   Employ endpoint security tools, such as antivirus software and endpoint detection and response (EDR) systems, to scan for and remove malicious processes.

- **Analyze process dependencies**   Examine process parent-child relationships and investigate any unexpected or unusual dependencies that may indicate malicious activity.

- **Regularly update security software**   Keep your security software up to date with the latest signatures and behavioral analysis rules to better detect emerging threats and malicious processes.

EXAM TIP   For many of us, we first look at the processes running on a system before we decide whether to capture its volatile memory. For the exam, it is always preferable to capture memory first and then look at running processes.

```
● ● ●                🔲 brent — brent@budgie-dev: ~ — ssh budgie — 96×32
top - 13:57:45 up 1 min,  1 user,  load average: 1.21, 0.43, 0.16
Tasks: 213 total,   3 running, 118 sleeping,   0 stopped,   0 zombie
%Cpu(s): 71.7 us,  9.0 sy,  0.0 ni,  0.0 id, 19.3 wa,  0.0 hi,  0.0 si,  0.0 st
KiB Mem :  2017476 total,   177344 free,   296300 used,  1543832 buff/cache
KiB Swap:  2097148 total,  2097148 free,        0 used.  1546188 avail Mem

  PID USER      PR  NI    VIRT    RES    SHR S %CPU %MEM     TIME+ COMMAND
 2004 root      20   0  455936 127864  60280 S  7.3  6.3   0:00.46 unattended-upgr
12106 root      39  19   98884  22364  12376 R  2.0  1.1   0:00.06 apt-check
  619 message+  20   0   50708   5248   3980 S  0.3  0.3   0:00.09 dbus-daemon
 1730 root      20   0  454940 196912 129388 S  0.3  9.8   0:06.24 unattended-upgr
 7189 brent     20   0   47952   4100   3364 R  0.3  0.2   0:00.02 top
    1 root      20   0  159784   9068   6796 S  0.0  0.4   0:00.85 systemd
    2 root      20   0       0      0      0 S  0.0  0.0   0:00.00 kthreadd
    3 root      20   0       0      0      0 I  0.0  0.0   0:00.00 kworker/0:0
    4 root       0 -20       0      0      0 I  0.0  0.0   0:00.00 kworker/0:0H
    5 root      20   0       0      0      0 I  0.0  0.0   0:00.00 kworker/u256:0
    6 root       0 -20       0      0      0 I  0.0  0.0   0:00.00 mm_percpu_wq
    7 root      20   0       0      0      0 S  0.0  0.0   0:00.10 ksoftirqd/0
    8 root      20   0       0      0      0 R  0.0  0.0   0:00.09 rcu_sched
    9 root      20   0       0      0      0 I  0.0  0.0   0:00.00 rcu_bh
   10 root      rt   0       0      0      0 S  0.0  0.0   0:00.00 migration/0
   11 root      rt   0       0      0      0 S  0.0  0.0   0:00.00 watchdog/0
   12 root      20   0       0      0      0 S  0.0  0.0   0:00.00 cpuhp/0
   13 root      20   0       0      0      0 S  0.0  0.0   0:00.00 kdevtmpfs
   14 root       0 -20       0      0      0 I  0.0  0.0   0:00.00 netns
   15 root      20   0       0      0      0 S  0.0  0.0   0:00.00 rcu_tasks_kthre
   16 root      20   0       0      0      0 S  0.0  0.0   0:00.00 kauditd
   17 root      20   0       0      0      0 S  0.0  0.0   0:00.00 khungtaskd
   18 root      20   0       0      0      0 S  0.0  0.0   0:00.00 oom_reaper
   19 root       0 -20       0      0      0 I  0.0  0.0   0:00.00 writeback
   20 root      20   0       0      0      0 S  0.0  0.0   0:00.00 kcompactd0
```

Figure 4-4   Output from the top task manager utility in Ubuntu Linux

Memory Contents

Everything you can discern about a computer through the techniques discussed in the previous section can also be used on a copy of its volatile memory. Analyzing memory contents can reveal unauthorized or malicious processes, injected code, and other suspicious activities that could indicate a security incident or breach. By monitoring memory contents, you can uncover crucial information that may not be visible through other methods of investigation.

 NOTE   There are tools used by threat actors that reside only in memory and have no components stored on the file system. These sophisticated tools all but require incident responders to rely on memory forensics to understand them.

Some common memory-related indicators include the following:

- **Unusual process memory**   The presence of processes with unexpected memory consumption or memory regions with unusual permissions (for example, executable memory in a data region) can indicate malware or unauthorized activities.

PART I

- **Memory injection**   The presence of injected code or data in a legitimate process's memory space may signify an attacker's attempt to evade detection or maintain persistence. Memory injection can also be associated with advanced malware techniques, such as process hollowing or reflective DLL injection, where malicious code is loaded into the memory space of a legitimate process.

- **Hidden or unlinked processes**   Malware or attackers may attempt to hide their activities by unlinking processes from the process list, making them difficult to detect through standard process monitoring tools. These hidden processes can be engaged in a variety of malicious activities, such as keylogging, data exfiltration, and C2 communication.

- **Decoded strings or suspicious artifacts**   Memory analysis can reveal decoded strings or other artifacts that are obfuscated on disk but become visible in memory during execution. These artifacts can provide valuable information about the attacker's intent, such as C2 server addresses, encryption keys, or exfiltration methods.

Several common tools can help you analyze memory contents across different operating systems. For Linux, macOS, and Windows systems, Volatility and Rekall are powerful open source memory forensics frameworks. Linux systems can benefit from LiME (Linux Memory Extractor), a kernel module used for acquiring memory dumps. MacMemoryReader is a simple command-line tool for acquiring memory dumps from macOS systems. For Windows, WinDbg serves as a powerful debugger for kernel debugging and memory dump analysis, while FTK Imager is a popular digital forensics tool for acquiring memory dumps and analyzing various types of digital evidence.

 EXAM TIP   For the purposes of the exam, you do not need to understand how to perform memory forensics; however, you should understand why they are important as well as the forementioned indicators associated with memory dumps.

Unauthorized Changes

Unauthorized changes to system configurations, files, or settings can serve as potential sources of indicators. Detecting and investigating these changes can help identify ongoing attacks, breaches, or unauthorized access attempts.

Some common unauthorized changes that might indicate malicious activity include the following:

- **Changes to system or application configurations**   Modifications to critical configuration files or settings, which may impact the security of the system or enable further exploitation by attackers.

- **Unauthorized file modifications**   Alterations to files, including the creation, deletion, or modification of files, without proper authorization or knowledge could be indicative of an attack or compromise.

- **Overwriting or sideloading of DLLs**   Unauthorized replacement or manipulation of dynamic-link library (DLL) files can indicate attempts to inject malicious code or compromise system components.

- **Changes to security policies or permissions**   Unauthorized changes to access controls, user permissions, or security policies may allow attackers to gain elevated privileges or access restricted resources.

- **Modifications to scheduled tasks or services**   Unauthorized additions, deletions, or modifications to scheduled tasks or services could be a sign of an attacker attempting to maintain persistence on the compromised host.

To monitor and detect unauthorized changes, consider implementing the following strategies:

- **Regularly review logs**   Analyze system, application, and security logs for any unusual activity or changes made without proper authorization.

- **Use file integrity monitoring (FIM) tools**   Employ FIM tools to track changes to critical files and configurations, alerting analysts to unauthorized modifications in real time.

- **Implement change management processes**   Establish a robust change management process that requires approval and documentation for any changes to critical systems or configurations.

- **Perform routine system audits**   Regularly audit systems for unauthorized changes, comparing current configurations with known baselines to identify any discrepancies.

- **Enable Windows object access auditing**   Configure Windows object access auditing to track access and changes to critical system objects, including files, folders, and registry keys, thus providing valuable insights into unauthorized activity. Figure 4-5 shows the explanation associated with file system object access.

 NOTE   The word *artifact* is frequently used in forensics, and, though there is no standard definition for it in this context, it generally denotes a digital object of interest to a forensic investigation.

Unauthorized Privileges

When attackers successfully infiltrate a system, they often seek to escalate their privileges, granting themselves greater access to sensitive resources and enabling broader control over the compromised environment. In many cases, attackers may not directly target accounts with high levels of privilege but rather pivot to accounts with lower privileges that can provide a stepping stone for further exploitation. By compromising these less privileged accounts, attackers can gradually gain access to systems or accounts with higher privileges, ultimately achieving their desired level of control while potentially evading detection.

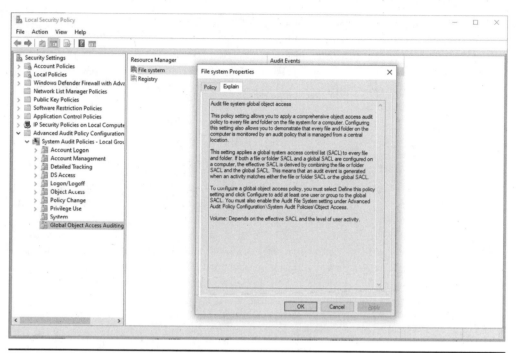

Figure 4-5   Windows 10 local security policy audit options for the file system

Examples of unauthorized privileges may include the following:

- **Privilege escalation**   Gaining higher-level access on a compromised system, such as escalating from a standard user account to an administrative account.
- **Unauthorized use of admin accounts**   Logging in to systems using compromised or stolen administrative credentials.
- **Creation of new accounts with elevated privileges**   Attackers may create new user accounts with high-level access rights to maintain persistence within the network.

To monitor and detect unauthorized privileges, consider implementing the following approaches:

- **Regularly review user accounts and permissions**   Periodically audit user accounts and their associated permissions to identify any unauthorized or unnecessary privileges.
- **Implement the principle of least privilege**   Limit user accounts and applications to the minimum level of access needed to perform their functions.
- **Monitor account activity**   Continuously track user account activity, focusing on privileged accounts and unusual patterns of behavior.

- **Use security tools and solutions**   Employ security tools such as security information and event management (SIEM) systems, intrusion detection systems (IDSs), or endpoint detection and response (EDR) solutions to monitor and alert on unusual activity related to privileges or account usage.

- **Enable logging and auditing**   Configure systems to log and audit events related to user account activity, especially for privileged accounts. Regularly review these logs to identify any unauthorized actions or changes in privileges.

Data Exfiltration

Data exfiltration refers to the unauthorized transfer of sensitive information from a compromised system to an external location, typically controlled by an attacker. This can include the theft of intellectual property, confidential documents, customer data, or financial information. Cybercriminals may use various techniques to exfiltrate data, such as encrypted communication channels, covert channels, or even social engineering tactics. Data exfiltration has become a prevalent threat in today's cybersecurity landscape, with data breaches and ransomware attacks becoming increasingly common.

The 2022 Verizon Data Breach Investigations Report (DBIR) analyzed 23,896 security incidents, of which 5,212 were confirmed data breaches. Ransomware-related breaches were up by 13 percent, highlighting the critical need for organizations to implement robust data protection strategies. Cybercriminals are continually refining their techniques to infiltrate organizations, steal sensitive data, and hold it for ransom or sell it on the dark web.

Some common indicators of data exfiltration include the following:

- **Unusual data transfer patterns**   Large or unexpected data transfers during off-hours or to unfamiliar destinations may indicate exfiltration attempts.

- **Connections to known malicious domains or IP addresses**   Communication with known malicious infrastructure can be a sign of data exfiltration in progress.

- **Compression or encryption of data**   Attackers usually compress or encrypt data before exfiltration to avoid detection and reduce the transfer size.

- **Unusual file access patterns**   Frequent or atypical access to sensitive files or directories may suggest an attacker is gathering data for exfiltration.

Data exfiltration monitoring and detection strategies can include the following:

- **Establish data loss prevention (DLP) policies**   Implement DLP tools to detect and prevent sensitive data from being transferred outside the organization.

- **Monitor network traffic**   Regularly analyze network traffic patterns for anomalies that may indicate data exfiltration attempts.

- **Implement intrusion detection and prevention systems (IDPSs)**   Use IDPS solutions to detect and block unauthorized data transfers.

- **Restrict outbound connections**   Limit outbound connections to trusted networks and enforce the use of secure communication protocols.
- **Train employees on social engineering tactics**   Educate employees about the risks associated with social engineering and how to identify and report potential attacks.

Data Exfiltration: A Real-World Case

One of the tactics used by the threat actor alternatively known as APT28 and Fancy Bear is as effective as it is low tech. This group is known to create a fake Outlook Web Access (OWA) page that looks identical to that of the target organization, has a message indicating the OWA session timed out, and prompts the users to reenter their credentials. The page is hosted on a domain that has a name very similar to the target's (for example, mail.state.qov instead of state.gov). The target is sent a spearphishing e-mail with a link to the decoy site that seems interesting and appropriate to the target. When the user clicks the link within OWA, it forwards the OWA tab to the fake timed-out page and opens the decoy site on a new tab. When the user closes or switches out of the decoy tab, they see the (fake) OWA prompt and then reenter their credentials. The fake page then forwards them to the (still valid) OWA session. At this point, the threat actor simply creates an IMAP account on some computer and uses the user's credentials to synchronize their folders and messages. This is data exfiltration made easy. Apart from the phony OWA domain name, everything else looks perfectly legitimate and is almost impossible to detect as an attack unless you are aware of this specific tactic.

Registry Change or Anomaly

The Windows Registry serves as a vital component of the operating system, storing configuration settings, information about installed software, and system preferences. Unauthorized changes or anomalies within the registry can be indicative of malicious activity, as attackers often manipulate registry entries to establish persistence, escalate privileges, or evade detection.

Detecting unauthorized registry changes or anomalies requires an understanding of the registry structure and the ability to recognize deviations from normal behavior. This can be challenging, as the registry is vast, complex, and unintuitive. However, by focusing on critical areas of the registry that are commonly targeted by attackers, you can significantly improve your ability to identify potential threats.

Some common indicators of compromise related to registry changes or anomalies include the following:

- **Unexpected registry key modifications**   The creation or modification of registry keys associated with malware or unauthorized software

- **Unusual startup entries**   The addition of new entries to the registry's startup locations, enabling malware to automatically execute upon system startup
- **Changes to security settings**   Unauthorized modifications to registry entries governing system security settings, which may weaken the system's defenses or grant attackers greater access
- **Hidden registry keys or values**   The use of obscure or unconventional naming conventions to conceal malicious registry entries from security tools and analysts

Here is an incomprehensive list of common Windows Registry locations that are often targeted by attackers:

- **Run and RunOnce keys**   These keys specify programs or scripts that should be executed automatically when a user logs in. They are common targets for malware to establish persistence.
  - HKEY_CURRENT_USER\Software\Microsoft\Windows\CurrentVersion\Run
  - HKEY_CURRENT_USER\Software\Microsoft\Windows\CurrentVersion\RunOnce
  - HKEY_LOCAL_MACHINE\Software\Microsoft\Windows\CurrentVersion\Run
  - HKEY_LOCAL_MACHINE\Software\Microsoft\Windows\CurrentVersion\RunOnce
- **Shell extensions and context menu entries**   These keys store information about shell extensions and context menu items, which can be abused by malware to integrate itself into the system.
  - HKEY_CLASSES_ROOT*\shellex\ContextMenuHandlers
  - HKEY_CLASSES_ROOT\Directory\shellex\ContextMenuHandlers
  - HKEY_CLASSES_ROOT\Directory\Background\shellex\ContextMenuHandlers
- **Browser helper objects (BHOs)**   These keys store information about BHOs, which are DLLs that extend the functionality of Internet Explorer. Malware can register itself as a BHO to intercept and manipulate web traffic.
  - HKEY_LOCAL_MACHINE\SOFTWARE\Microsoft\Windows\CurrentVersion\Explorer\Browser Helper Objects
- **Services**   These keys store information about system services, including their configuration and startup settings. Attackers may create or modify service entries to establish persistence or escalate privileges.
  - HKEY_LOCAL_MACHINE\SYSTEM\CurrentControlSet\Services

- **Security settings**   These keys store configuration information related to system security settings, such as User Account Control (UAC) and firewall policies. Attackers may attempt to modify these settings to weaken a system's defenses or gain additional access.
    - HKEY_LOCAL_MACHINE\SOFTWARE\Microsoft\Windows\CurrentVersion\Policies\System
    - HKEY_LOCAL_MACHINE\SYSTEM\CurrentControlSet\Control\SecurityProviders
    - HKEY_LOCAL_MACHINE\SOFTWARE\Policies\Microsoft\WindowsFirewall

Strategies for monitoring and detecting registry changes or anomalies may include the following:

- **Regularly audit critical registry locations**   Monitor key areas of the registry that are commonly targeted by attackers, such as startup locations and security settings.
- **Use security software with registry monitoring capabilities**   Employ security solutions that include real-time registry monitoring and alerting to notify you of suspicious changes.
- **Implement strict access controls**   Restrict write access to the registry to limit the potential for unauthorized modifications.
- **Perform regular system backups**   Maintain up-to-date backups of your system, including the registry, to facilitate recovery in the event of an incident.

Unauthorized Scheduled Task

Unauthorized scheduled tasks are a common technique used by attackers to maintain persistence, execute malware, and perform other malicious activities within a compromised system, regardless of the operating system in use. To help you monitor and detect unauthorized scheduled tasks on different platforms, we'll discuss how to review scheduled tasks on macOS, Linux, and Windows systems.

In Windows, scheduled tasks are managed through the Task Scheduler. You can access the Task Scheduler by searching for it in the Start menu or by using the **taskschd.msc** command in the Run dialog. Figure 4-6 shows the Windows 10 Task Scheduler.

You can also use the **schtasks** command in the Command Prompt or PowerShell to view and manage tasks:

```
schtasks
schtasks /query /taskname:taskname
```

On Linux systems, scheduled tasks are often managed using cron jobs, the **at** command, and **anacron**. You can review cron jobs by using the **crontab** command:

```
crontab -l
crontab -e
```

Figure 4-7 shows an overview and the basic syntax of cron table entries.

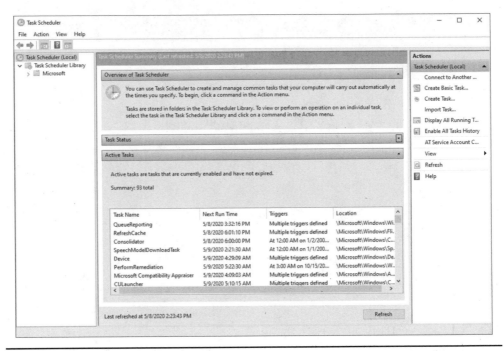

Figure 4-6   Windows 10 Task Scheduler

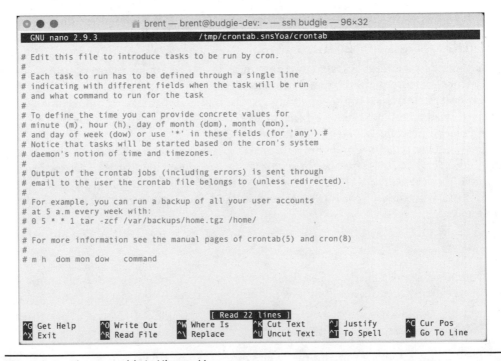

Figure 4-7   The cron table in Ubuntu Linux

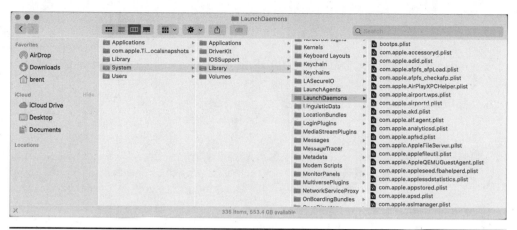

Figure 4-8   Contents of the System/Library/LaunchDaemons/ directory containing system daemons

To view tasks scheduled with the **at** command, you can use the following:

```
atq
```

Another scheduling tool used on Linux systems is **anacron**, which is particularly useful for running tasks on systems that may not always be powered on. The **anacron** configuration file can typically be found at **/etc/anacrontab**, where you can review the scheduled tasks.

On macOS, scheduled tasks are managed through various methods, such as LaunchAgents, LaunchDaemons, Login Items, and kernel extensions (kexts). The contents of the System/Library/LaunchDaemons/ directory are shown in Figure 4-8. To review tasks managed through LaunchAgents and LaunchDaemons, you can use the **launchctl** command, like so:

```
launchctl list
launchctl show /path/to/.plist
```

Additionally, you can check Login Items in System Preferences | Users & Groups | Login Items tab.

Application-Related Indicators

As we continue our examination of indicators, we'll now focus on application-related indicators. These indicators are vital for detecting and responding to threats that exploit widely used applications within your network. They serve as a critical line of defense against cyber threats, offering valuable insights into potential vulnerabilities and ongoing attacks.

Application-related indicators play a crucial role in the work of cybersecurity analysts, helping them identify, investigate, and respond to potential cyber threats targeting common software applications.

Here are some common application-related indicators we will not discuss in further detail but are still essential to consider:

- **Unauthorized application modifications**   Unexpected changes to application binaries or configuration files can signal tampering or malware infection.

- **Malicious plug-ins or extensions**   The presence of unauthorized or malicious plug-ins and extensions in web browsers or other applications can indicate an ongoing attack.

- **Privilege escalation**   Unauthorized elevation of application privileges can indicate attempts to gain control over a system or access sensitive resources. This will be partially addressed within the context of "Introduction of New Accounts" later in this section.

Later in this chapter, we'll explore more application-related indicators in detail, such as anomalous activity, introduction of new accounts, unexpected output, unexpected outbound communication, service interruption, and application logs. We will also discuss how to monitor, mitigate, and detect these indicators.

It's essential to be aware of the most commonly targeted or abused applications in relation to this topic. Some of the most frequently exploited applications include, but are not limited to:

- Microsoft Office suite
- Adobe Acrobat Reader
- Web browsers (for example, Google Chrome, Mozilla Firefox, and Microsoft Edge)
- E-mail clients (for example, Microsoft Outlook and Thunderbird)

By understanding the various application-related indicators and keeping a close eye on these commonly targeted applications, organizations can better detect and respond to potential cyber threats, thus enhancing their overall security posture.

Anomalous Activity

Identifying and addressing anomalous activity in applications is a critical aspect of safeguarding your organization from potential threats. Cybercriminals frequently target widely used applications such as Microsoft Office, Adobe Acrobat, PowerShell, and web browsers due to their extensive reach and access to sensitive information. Recognizing the expected behavior patterns of these applications and staying alert to any deviations can contribute to detecting suspicious activity and defending your organization against attacks.

Monitoring the relationships between processes, particularly grandparent, parent, and child relationships, can be a valuable method for detecting unusual activity. By establishing a baseline of normal process hierarchies, security analysts can more effectively identify deviations that may signal malicious behavior.

Here are a few examples of anomalous activity related to the top four most abused and targeted applications.

Microsoft Office:

- **Unusual macro activity**   Execution of macros with uncommon behavior, such as attempting to download external files or making unexpected network connections

- **Unexpected document access**   Access to sensitive or restricted documents by unauthorized users or from unusual locations

Adobe Acrobat:

- **Suspicious PDF attachments**   PDF files containing embedded scripts or unusual content that could be indicative of an exploit

- **Unexpected behavior**   Acrobat attempting to execute external programs or establish unusual network connections

PowerShell:

- **Suspicious scripts**   Execution of unknown or obfuscated scripts that could be indicative of malicious activity

- **Unusual command-line arguments**   PowerShell commands with unusual arguments or parameters that may indicate attempts to bypass security controls or execute malicious code

Web browsers:

- **Unusual browser extensions or plug-ins**   Installation of unauthorized extensions or plug-ins that could be malicious or compromise user privacy

- **Unexpected network connections**   Browser-initiated connections to unfamiliar or known malicious domains, which could indicate command and control (C2) communication or attempts to download additional malware

It's important to monitor these applications for anomalous activity and have a clear understanding of their expected behavior.

Introduction of New Accounts

The creation of new user accounts, particularly those with elevated privileges, can be a significant indicator of compromise in the context of application-related security. Attackers often attempt to introduce new local or domain admin accounts, or abuse service accounts, to maintain unauthorized access, escalate privileges, and execute malicious actions within an organization's network.

Service accounts are used to run applications, services, or processes and often have elevated privileges to access resources required for their operation. Since these accounts may not be as closely monitored as regular user accounts, attackers can exploit them to gain unauthorized access and perform malicious activities.

Monitoring for the introduction of new accounts, especially local and domain admin accounts, as well as service accounts, should be a priority for security analysts. The following strategies can help detect unauthorized account creation:

- **Regularly review user account lists**   Periodically check for new or modified user accounts, with a focus on those with elevated privileges. Pay close attention to any accounts that were created or changed outside of standard procedures.

- **Implement user account management policies**   Establish clear guidelines for user account creation, modification, and removal. This includes setting up processes for granting elevated privileges and monitoring account activity.

- **Enable logging and auditing**   Configure logging and auditing settings for user account management actions. Regularly review logs for suspicious activity, such as the creation of new local or domain admin accounts.

- **Implement least privilege principles**   Restrict the number of users with elevated privileges and ensure that users have the minimum level of access necessary to perform their job functions. This limits the potential impact of compromised accounts.

- **Monitor for suspicious activity**   Keep an eye on unusual login patterns, privilege escalation attempts, or other indicators of potential unauthorized access. Promptly investigate any suspicious behavior to determine if it's the result of a security incident.

Unexpected Output

Unexpected output from applications or systems can serve as an important indicator of potential security issues. This includes pop-up windows, system alerts on macOS, User Account Control (UAC) alerts on Windows, error messages, and unexpected changes in the behavior of applications.

Pop-up windows can be a sign of malicious activity, especially if they appear suddenly or request sensitive information, such as login credentials or financial data. Attackers may use these pop-ups to deceive users into disclosing sensitive information or inadvertently granting permissions to malicious software.

On macOS, system alerts prompt users for making system changes or running untrusted software. These alerts are similar to UAC alerts on Windows and can serve as a valuable warning sign of unauthorized activity. If a system alert appears unexpectedly, it could indicate that a malicious process is attempting to gain elevated privileges or execute untrusted software on your system.

UAC alerts on Windows are triggered when a program or process attempts to make changes to your system that require administrative permissions. If a UAC alert appears unexpectedly, as shown in Figure 4-9, it could indicate that a malicious process is attempting to gain elevated privileges on your system.

Figure 4-9
User Account
Control pop-up
for unsigned
software

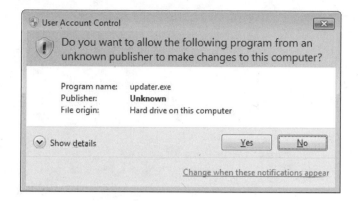

To monitor and detect unexpected output, consider implementing the following strategies:

- Educate users about the dangers of pop-ups and instruct them to report any suspicious or unexpected occurrences.

- Use an application approval list to prevent unauthorized or unknown applications from running on your systems.

- Implement endpoint detection and response (EDR) solutions to identify and remediate unexpected output or anomalies in real time.

- Regularly review system and application logs to identify unusual patterns or discrepancies in output.

Unexpected Outbound Communication

Unexpected outbound communication from applications or systems can indicate a security threat, such as data exfiltration, command and control (C2) communication, or malware infection. Detecting and analyzing unusual network traffic patterns can provide valuable insights into potential cyberattacks and help protect sensitive information from being compromised.

Here are some common tools and techniques used to initiate unexpected outbound communication:

- **BITS admin**   Used for managing file transfers between systems and can be used to download and execute malicious payloads

- **CertUtil**   Used for various certificate and cryptography-related functions and can be abused to download and execute malicious payloads

- **PowerShell**   A powerful scripting language that can be used to download and execute malicious payloads or execute malicious code already present on a system

- **mshta**   A Microsoft utility that can execute HTML applications and can be used to download and execute malicious payloads

Other examples of unexpected outbound communication include the following:

- **Unusual DNS requests**   DNS requests to known malicious domains or an unusually high volume of requests could indicate communication with C2 servers or attempts at data exfiltration.

- **Uncommon ports or protocols**   Communication using nonstandard ports or protocols may be an attempt to bypass security measures or obfuscate malicious traffic.

- **Data transfers to unfamiliar IP addresses**   Data transfers to unfamiliar or untrusted IP addresses could suggest data exfiltration or unauthorized remote access.

- **Encrypted traffic**   Although encryption is essential for protecting sensitive data, it can also be used by attackers to hide their activities. Monitor encrypted traffic for unusual patterns that may indicate malicious activity.

Monitor and detection techniques of unexpected outbound communication may include the following:

- **Network monitoring**   Utilize network monitoring tools to collect and analyze network traffic, identify anomalies, and detect unauthorized communication attempts.

- **Baseline network behavior**   Establish a baseline of normal network behavior, which will help in identifying deviations from the expected communication patterns.

- **Intrusion detection systems (IDSs) and intrusion prevention systems (IPSs)**   Deploy IDS and IPS solutions to detect and prevent unauthorized network traffic based on predefined rules or behavioral analysis.

- **Firewall configuration**   Regularly review and update firewall rules to ensure that only authorized applications and services can communicate with external networks.

- **Endpoint detection and response (EDR)**   Implement EDR solutions to monitor and detect unusual communication patterns on individual systems within your network.

- **Security information and event management (SIEM)**   Integrate SIEM systems to correlate network traffic data with other security events, providing a more comprehensive view of potential threats.

 EXAM TIP   The fact that an application suddenly starts making unusual outbound connections, absent any other evidence, is not necessarily malicious. During exam simulations, for example, look for indicators of new (authorized) installations or software updates to assess benign behavior.

Service Interruption

Service interruption occurs when a system or application becomes unresponsive or fails to function as intended, leading to potential service downtime or loss of functionality. This can be caused by a range of issues, including software bugs, hardware failure, and cyberattacks.

In some cases, attackers may force services to reload or restart as a tactic to gain control over a system or to bypass security controls. For example, an attacker may exploit a vulnerability to inject malicious code into a running service, causing it to crash or restart. By doing so, they may be able to gain elevated privileges, evade detection, or execute further malicious activity.

Here are a few examples to detect and respond to service interruptions:

- **Monitor system and application logs** By regularly reviewing system and application logs, you can quickly identify any unusual events or service interruptions that may indicate a security threat.

- **Use performance monitoring tools** Performance monitoring tools can help you identify service interruptions caused by hardware or software issues, such as memory leaks or CPU spikes.

- **Implement intrusion detection and prevention systems** IDS and IPS solutions can help detect and prevent unauthorized service interruptions by identifying and blocking traffic from known malicious sources or based on predefined rules.

- **Regularly update and patch systems and applications** Ensuring that systems and applications are updated with the latest security patches and software versions can help prevent service interruptions caused by known vulnerabilities.

- **Conduct regular vulnerability assessments and penetration testing** Regularly testing systems and applications for vulnerabilities can help identify potential attack vectors that could lead to service interruptions and allow you to address them proactively.

Memory Overflows

Memory overflows are a type of software vulnerability that can be exploited by attackers to execute arbitrary code, crash an application or system, or gain elevated privileges. A memory overflow occurs when a program writes more data to a memory buffer than it can hold, causing the extra data to overwrite adjacent memory locations. Attackers can take advantage of this vulnerability to inject malicious code into the affected system's memory, leading to a wide range of threats.

Memory overflow attacks can be challenging to detect and mitigate. Here are some common indicators of memory overflow attacks:

- **Application crashes or hangs** Unexplained crashes or hangs in an application could be a sign of a memory overflow attack.

- **Unusual system behavior** Unexpected system behavior or errors, such as the appearance of pop-up windows or missing functionality, can indicate a memory overflow attack.

- **Suspicious network activity**   Unusual network activity or communications from an affected system could indicate a memory overflow attack attempting to establish a connection with a C2 server.

- **Increased system resource consumption**   Elevated CPU usage or high memory consumption can be a sign of an attack in progress.

- **New or unusual processes**   The presence of new or unusual processes in the system task manager could indicate a memory overflow attack.

Mitigation techniques associated with memory overflow attacks include the following:

- **Use secure coding practices**   Develop applications using secure coding practices that can help prevent memory overflows.

- **Conduct regular security testing**   Utilize dynamic application security testing (DAST) and static application security testing (SAST) to identify and address memory overflow vulnerabilities during the development process.

- **Perform regular security updates**   Keep systems and applications up to date with the latest security patches to address known vulnerabilities.

- **Use runtime protection**   Deploy runtime application self-protection (RASP) technologies that can detect and block memory overflow attacks in real time.

- **Use sandboxes**   Deploy applications within a sandbox or virtual environment that can help isolate and contain the effects of a memory overflow attack.

- **Implement intrusion detection and prevention systems (IDPSs)**   Implement intrusion detection and prevention systems that can monitor network traffic and identify signs of a memory overflow attack.

- **Deploy endpoint detection and response (EDR) solutions**   Implement EDR solutions to monitor and detect memory overflow attacks on individual systems within your network.

If a memory overflow is suspected, it may be necessary to take a memory dump of the affected process or system. Memory dumps capture a snapshot of the system's memory at a given point in time and can be analyzed using specialized tools to identify potential threats or vulnerabilities.

Some tools that can be used to analyze memory dumps include Volatility, Rekall, and WinDbg. These tools can help identify potential malware or malicious activity as well as vulnerabilities that could be exploited in future attacks.

Application Logs

Application logs are used to identify potential security threats such as data exfiltration, malware infections, and unauthorized access. Analyzing application and OS logs can provide insights into user activity, system performance, and system events, allowing security teams to quickly detect and respond to potential security incidents.

Application and OS logs can be a valuable source of information when it comes to detecting and investigating security incidents. By reviewing logs, security teams can identify potential indicators and gain insights into the activities of attackers, including the following:

- **Unusual login attempts or failed authentication**   Monitoring login attempts and authentication failures can help identify potential brute-force attacks or other attempts at unauthorized access.

- **Abnormal user activity**   Unusual or suspicious user activity, such as accessing files or resources outside of normal patterns, could indicate a potential breach.

- **Unusual application crashes or errors**   Unexpected crashes or errors in applications could be a sign of a security threat.

- **Unexplained application errors or warnings**   Unexplained errors or warnings in application logs could indicate malicious activity.

- **High resource consumption**   Elevated resource consumption, such as high CPU or memory usage, could indicate an attack in progress.

- **Suspicious network activity**   Unusual network activity or communications from an application could indicate a security threat attempting to establish a connection with a C2 server.

- **Unusual system behavior**   Unexpected system behavior or errors related to application functionality, such as missing or modified features, can indicate a security threat.

- **Application error logs and dumps**   Analysis of application error logs and dumps can provide valuable insights into potential security threats, including vulnerabilities and malicious code.

- **Operating system errors related to memory, CPU, or disk space**   Errors related to system resources, such as memory, CPU, or disk space, could indicate an application-based security threat attempting to exploit system vulnerabilities.

Other Indicators

Social engineering attacks and obfuscated links can pose significant threats to an organization's security. Unlike the previous categories of host, network, and application-based indicators, these attacks don't necessarily rely on technical vulnerabilities. Instead, they target human factors such as trust, curiosity, and fear to deceive individuals and trick them into compromising sensitive information or granting unauthorized access. In this section, we will discuss some common signs of social engineering attacks and obfuscated links as well as some strategies to mitigate their impact.

Social Engineering

Social engineering attacks rely on manipulating human psychology to trick individuals into divulging sensitive information or performing actions that can compromise their security.

These attacks can be difficult to detect and prevent, as they often exploit human vulnerabilities rather than technical vulnerabilities.

Here are some common indicators of social engineering attacks:

- **Unusual or unexpected messages**   Messages from unknown or unexpected sources, or messages that contain unusual content or requests, could indicate a social engineering attack.
- **Urgency or pressure**   Messages that create a sense of urgency or pressure to act quickly or without question may indicate a social engineering attack.
- **Suspicious links or attachments**   Messages containing links or attachments from unknown or unexpected sources should be treated with caution, as they could contain malicious content.
- **Requests for personal information**   Messages requesting personal information, such as passwords or account information, should be treated with caution, as they could be part of a social engineering attack.

To mitigate the risks associated with social engineering attacks, organizations should consider the following strategies:

- **Employee training**   Provide regular employee training on social engineering attacks and how to detect and prevent them.
- **Policy enforcement**   Enforce strict policies for handling sensitive information and verify all requests for personal or sensitive information.
- **Security awareness**   Promote security awareness among employees and encourage them to report any suspicious activity or messages.

Obfuscated Links

Obfuscated links are links that have been modified or disguised to hide their true destination or purpose. These links can be used in phishing attacks or other types of cyberattacks to trick users into clicking them and inadvertently downloading malware or revealing sensitive information.

Here are some common indicators of obfuscated links:

- **Suspicious or unusual content**   Links containing unusual or suspicious content, such as random letters or symbols, may be obfuscated.
- **Unexpected or unusual sources**   Links from unexpected or unknown sources should be treated with caution, as they could be obfuscated.
- **Mismatched destinations**   Links that appear to go to one destination but lead to a different destination may be obfuscated.

To mitigate the risks associated with obfuscated links, organizations may consider implementing the following:

- **URL filtering**   Implement URL filtering to block access to known malicious or suspicious websites.

- **Employee training**   Provide regular employee training on how to identify and avoid obfuscated links.

- **Link verification**   Use link verification tools to check the destination of links before clicking them.

- **Antivirus software**   Deploy antivirus software that can detect and block malicious links and content.

Chapter Review

When it comes to detecting and responding to potential security threats, it's important to monitor a range of indicators across your network, hosts, and applications.

Network-based indicators can include unusual network traffic patterns, unexplained spikes in network activity, and attempts to communicate with known malicious domains or IP addresses. Monitoring network traffic, establishing baselines for normal network behavior, and deploying intrusion detection and prevention systems (IDPSs) can help detect and mitigate these types of threats.

Host-based indicators can include unexpected system reboots, changes to system settings or configurations, and suspicious process behavior. Monitoring system logs, implementing security measures such as endpoint detection and response (EDR) solutions and antimalware software, and regularly reviewing system configurations and settings can help detect and prevent these types of attacks.

Application-based indicators can include unusual application crashes or hangs, suspicious system resource consumption, and unexpected changes to application behavior. Monitoring application logs, implementing secure coding practices, deploying runtime protection technologies and web application firewalls (WAFs), and regularly reviewing and updating software can help detect and prevent these types of attacks.

Additionally, social engineering attacks and obfuscated links can be used to exploit human vulnerabilities and can be more challenging to detect. Social engineering attacks can include phishing e-mails, fake websites, and pretexting, while obfuscated links can disguise malicious URLs in legitimate-looking links. Educating employees on these types of attacks, implementing e-mail filtering solutions, and using website reputation services can help mitigate the risk of these types of threats.

To protect your organization from potential security threats, it's important to take a proactive, multilayered approach to security. This can include implementing secure coding practices, regularly updating software and systems, establishing baselines for normal behavior, and using a combination of network and host-based monitoring tools and techniques.

An important consideration in both the real world and the CySA+ exam is to look at the aggregated evidence before reaching any conclusions. As you go through this investigative process, keep in mind Occam's razor: the simplest explanation is usually the correct one.

Questions

1. Which of the following is an indicator of network-related threats?
   A. Data exfiltration
   B. Processor consumption
   C. Unauthorized software
   D. Drive capacity consumption

2. Which of the following is an indicator of host-related threats?
   A. Adding new accounts
   B. Activity on unexpected ports
   C. Unexpected outbound communication
   D. Obfuscated links

3. Which of the following is an indicator of application-related threats?
   A. Scans/sweeps
   B. Unauthorized privileges
   C. Unexpected output
   D. Social engineering

4. What is a common technique that attackers use to establish persistence in a network?
   A. Buffer overflows
   B. Adding new user accounts
   C. Phishing
   D. Beaconing

5. Which of the following is *not* an area to investigate when looking for indicators of threat activity?
   A. Network speed
   B. Memory usage
   C. CPU cycles
   D. Disk space

6. What is a useful method to curb the use of rogue devices on a network?
   A. SSID
   B. FLAC
   C. WPA
   D. NAC

Use the following scenario to answer Questions 7–10:

You receive a call from the head of the R&D division because one of her engineers recently discovered images and promotional information of a product that looks remarkably like one that your company has been working on for months. As she read more about the device, it became clear to the R&D head that this is, in fact, the same product that was supposed to have been kept under wraps in-house. She suspects that the product plans have been stolen. When inspecting the traffic from the R&D workstations, you notice a few patterns in the outbound traffic. The machines all regularly contact a domain registered to a design software company, exchanging a few bytes of information at a time. However, all of the R&D machines communicate regularly to a print server on the same LAN belonging to Logistics, sending several hundred megabytes in regular intervals.

7. What is the most likely explanation for the outbound communications from all the R&D workstations to the design company?

   A. Command and control instructions

   B. Exfiltration of large design files

   C. License verification

   D. Streaming video

8. What device does it make sense to check next to discover the source of the leak?

   A. The DNS server

   B. The printer server belonging to Logistics

   C. The mail server

   D. The local backup of the R&D systems

9. Why is this device an ideal choice as a source of the leak?

   A. This device may not arouse suspicion because of its normal purpose on the network.

   B. This device has regular communications outside of the corporate network.

   C. This device can emulate many systems easily.

   D. This device normally has massive storage resources.

10. What is the term for the periodic communications observed by the R&D workstations?

   A. Fingerprinting

   B. Chatter

   C. Footprinting

   D. Beaconing

Answers

1. **A.** Unusual data transfers to unfamiliar or untrusted IP addresses can suggest data exfiltration or unauthorized remote access.

2. **A.** Unauthorized account creation is a sign of a host-related threat and could be an indicator of malicious activity.

3. **C.** Unexpected application output or system behavior can indicate a potential application-related threat.

4. **B.** A clever method that attackers use for permanence is to add administrative accounts or groups and then work from those new accounts to conduct additional attacks.

5. **A.** Spikes in memory CPU cycles, disk space, or network usage (not necessarily network speed) may be indicative of threat activity. It's important that you understand what the normal levels of usage are so that you can more easily identify abnormal activity.

6. **D.** Network access control (NAC) is a method to ensure that each device is authenticated, scanned, and joined to the correct network. NAC solutions often give you fine-grained controls for policy enforcement.

7. **C.** Some types of software, particularly those for high-end design, will periodically check licensing using the network connection.

8. **B.** A common approach to removing data from the network without being detected is first to consolidate it in a staging location within the target network. As you note the size of the transfers to the print server, it makes sense for you to check to see if it is serving as a staging location and communicating out of the network.

9. **A.** This device is a good choice because an administrator would not normally think to check it. However, because a print server normally has no reason to reach outside of the network, it should alert you to investigate further.

10. **D.** Beaconing is a periodic outbound connection between a compromised computer and an external controller. This beaconing behavior can be detected by its two common characteristics: periodicity and destination. Beaconing is not always malicious, but it warrants further exploration.

Techniques for Malicious Activity Analysis

In this chapter you will learn:

- Various techniques for analyzing patterns of malicious activity
- How to use log analysis and correlation tools like SIEM and SOAR
- Tools used in endpoint detection and response (EDR) to monitor and detect malicious activity on individual systems
- Core concepts of file-based analysis
- Various behavior analysis techniques
- How to analyze e-mail headers and embedded links to investigate suspicious e-mail activity
- Various programming languages and their importance to security analysis and analytics

The computer is incredibly fast, accurate, and stupid. Man is incredibly slow, inaccurate, and brilliant. The marriage of the two is a force beyond calculation.

—Leo Cherne

In today's interconnected digital landscape, the frequency and sophistication of cyberattacks continue to rise. Detecting and responding to these threats requires comprehensive knowledge of security tools and techniques as well as the ability to analyze various types of data. In this chapter, we will explore some of the key tools and techniques used in the analysis of malicious activity, including packet capture, log analysis and correlation, endpoint security, DNS and IP reputation analysis, file analysis, and sandboxes. We'll also discuss common techniques such as pattern recognition and user behavior analysis as well as programming and scripting languages. By understanding these tools and techniques, you'll be better equipped to identify and respond to malicious activity in your environment. This chapter will help you better understand exam Objective 1.3, "Given a scenario, use appropriate tools or techniques to determine malicious activity."

Capturing Network Traffic

Packet capture is the process of intercepting and logging traffic that traverses a network. The captured data can then be analyzed for troubleshooting network issues, investigating security incidents, or gaining insights into network performance.

The captured network traffic data is typically stored in pcap (short for Packet Capture) files, which is a widely used industry standard for storing network traffic captures. Another file format that has been introduced recently is "pcapng," which is an improvement over the original pcap format and offers more advanced features such as support for capturing metadata and annotations.

Packet capturing can be performed using a variety of tools and techniques. Some of the most common packet capture tools include Wireshark, tcpdump, and TShark, which allow for real-time packet analysis and filtering. These tools can capture packets from a wide range of network interfaces, including Ethernet, Wi-Fi, and Bluetooth.

When you're capturing packets, it is important to note the difference between promiscuous and non-promiscuous mode. In non-promiscuous mode, the network card will only capture traffic specifically destined for that interface. However, in promiscuous mode, the network card captures all traffic on the network segment, regardless of destination. While promiscuous mode can provide more comprehensive packet capture, it can also increase the amount of data captured and may pose a security risk if not used carefully.

 EXAM TIP   In a switched network environment, traffic captures may be more difficult, since by their nature switches limit traffic that can be picked up to only that between the switch port and the host. To capture traffic in a switched environment, you must normally be plugged into a spanning port on the switch.

Packet capture is a valuable tool for network analysis and security monitoring. By capturing and analyzing network traffic, you can detect and investigate security incidents, troubleshoot network issues, and gain insights into network performance. However, packet capture can generate large amounts of data, so it's important to use filtering and compression techniques to manage the size of the capture files.

 NOTE   Performing full packet captures can have legal implications regarding privacy. Ensure that you consult your legal counsel before you start capturing.

Log Analysis and Correlation

In addition to packet capture and analysis, log analysis and correlation is a critical component of cybersecurity. Security information and event management (SIEM) and security orchestration, automation, and response (SOAR) are two powerful tools used for log analysis and correlation.

SIEM collects, aggregates, and analyzes log data from various sources in near real time to detect and respond to security events. It uses correlation rules to identify patterns and anomalies in log data and generate alerts when a security event is detected. SIEM also provides forensic capabilities, allowing analysts to investigate and remediate security incidents.

SOAR is a newer technology that builds on the capabilities of SIEM by adding automation and orchestration. It enables security teams to automate incident response workflows and orchestrate actions across multiple security tools and systems. SOAR can help reduce response times, increase efficiency, and improve overall security posture.

In the following sections, we will explore the key features and capabilities of SIEM and SOAR, and how they can be used to improve log analysis and correlation in a cybersecurity environment.

Security Information and Event Management

SIEM is a centralized approach to security management that involves collecting, analyzing, and correlating log data from various sources across an organization's network. By using a SIEM solution, security teams can gain a comprehensive view of their organization's security posture and identify potential threats.

One of the key functions of a SIEM is log collection and parsing. Logs can come from various sources, such as network devices, operating systems, databases, applications, and more. A SIEM solution typically includes pre-built parsers for common log types, which can help to normalize the data and make it easier to analyze.

In addition to log collection and parsing, SIEMs also include a correlation engine that analyzes the log data to identify potential security incidents. The correlation engine uses rules and algorithms to identify patterns and anomalies in the log data that could indicate a potential security threat. Once a threat is identified, the SIEM can trigger alerts to notify security teams or initiate automated response actions.

To help with log normalization and analysis, SIEM solutions often incorporate common information models (CIMs), which are standardized data models that define common log formats and fields, making it easier to parse and correlate log data across different systems and applications.

Several popular SIEM solutions are available on the market, including Splunk, QRadar, LogRhythm, and Graylog. Each of these solutions has its own strengths and weaknesses, and the choice of SIEM solution will depend on the specific needs and resources of the organization. Figure 5-1 demonstrates a Splunk dashboard.

Security Orchestration, Automation, and Response

We discussed the fundamental concepts of SOAR back in Chapter 2. SOAR allows us to integrate many disparate security tools and processes, both manual and automated, into a holistic set. A SOAR platform can be utilized to automate various security-related tasks, such as alert triaging, incident investigation, and response. One example of using a SOAR platform is to leverage it to process threat intelligence data from various sources, such as a cyber threat intelligence (CTI) feed. The platform can be programmed to automatically parse, extract, and prioritize threat intelligence and then use that data to create

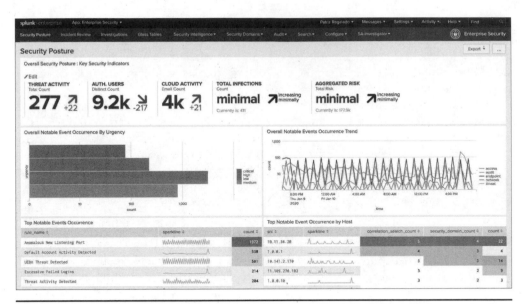

Figure 5-1 A dashboard created using the Splunk Enterprise Security SIEM to display security data

correlation rules and alerts. This can help to reduce the time it takes for security teams to detect and respond to potential threats.

Another scenario where a SOAR platform can be useful is in automating the incident response process. A SOAR platform can be configured to respond to specific types of incidents automatically. For example, when a new security alert is triggered, the SOAR platform can be programmed to perform initial analysis and enrichment and then initiate a predefined response playbook. This can help to reduce the time it takes to respond to an incident and improve the overall efficiency of the incident response process.

Popular SOAR platforms include Splunk Phantom, IBM Resilient, Swimlane, and Cortex XSOAR. These platforms provide a range of capabilities, such as automated response playbooks, incident response workflows, and threat intelligence management.

SOAR platforms can also be utilized to automate various routine security tasks, such as user provisioning, access control management, and audit log review. By automating these tasks, security teams can free up time to focus on more complex security challenges while also ensuring that routine tasks are performed consistently and without errors.

A common use case is in automating the investigation of phishing incidents. The platform can be programmed to analyze the e-mail headers, contents, and links and then to generate an incident report. Based on the report, the SOAR platform can automatically take actions such as blocking the malicious IP addresses, quarantining the affected user accounts, and initiating an investigation process.

Another usage example is in the automation of the vulnerability management process. SOAR can be programmed to identify and prioritize vulnerabilities based on the severity and criticality of the affected systems. The platform can also generate automated tickets for the IT team to patch the vulnerabilities or mitigate them using other means. This can help to reduce the risk of exploitation by threat actors and improve the overall security posture of the organization.

EXAM TIP You should not be asked specifics of how to perform SOAR tasks on the test. However, you should be familiar with common use cases and scenarios when leveraging a SOAR platform.

Endpoint

Endpoint security is a critical component of any organization's cybersecurity strategy. Endpoint security refers to the practice of protecting endpoints such as laptops, desktops, and mobile devices from cybersecurity threats. Endpoint security solutions are designed to detect and prevent various types of attacks, including malware, ransomware, and advanced persistent threats (APTs). EDR solutions are designed to provide real-time monitoring and response capabilities for endpoints, detect suspicious activity, and respond to potential threats in real time, reducing the time it takes to detect and respond to security incidents.

Endpoint Detection and Response

Endpoint detection and response (EDR) solutions take the monitoring and detection aspects of traditional antimalware technologies and add investigation, response, and mitigation functionalities. EDR is an evolution in security tools designed to protect the endpoints in a network. Given that these solutions operate at the edges of the network, with the requirement to work on a diverse set of systems and configurations, EDRs solutions are often built to be highly scalable, lightweight, and cross-platform. EDRs include an array of tools that provide the following capabilities:

- **Monitor** Log and aggregate endpoint activity to facilitate trend analysis.
- **Detect** Find threats with the continuous analysis of monitored data.
- **Respond** Address malicious activity on the network by stopping activity or removing the offending asset.

EDR solutions can monitor and record system events and user activity on endpoints, including file modifications, network connections, process executions, and more. By analyzing this data, EDR solutions can detect and respond to various types of endpoint threats, including malware infections, fileless attacks, and insider threats.

Some popular EDR solutions in the market today include CrowdStrike Falcon, Carbon Black, Symantec Endpoint Detection and Response, and Microsoft Defender for Endpoint. These solutions offer various features and capabilities, such as behavior analysis, threat hunting, and integration with other security tools.

 EXAM TIP Similarly to SOAR, you should not be asked specifics of how to perform EDR tasks on the test. However, you should be familiar with common use cases and scenarios when leveraging an EDR platform.

Reputation Analysis

Reputational analysis is a technique used to determine the reputation of an IP address or domain. It involves checking a database of known malicious IP addresses and domains to see if the given IP address or domain has been previously associated with malicious activity. Reputational analysis is a quick-and-easy way to identify potentially malicious IPs and domains, as the databases are constantly updated with the latest threat intelligence.

One advantage of reputational-based analysis is its speed and ease of use. It requires minimal technical expertise and can be performed quickly using free or commercial tools. Another advantage is that it can be used to quickly identify IPs and domains that are known to be associated with malicious activity, allowing security teams to take action to block or quarantine them.

However, a major disadvantage is the potential for false positives. Because the databases used for reputational analysis are constantly updated, an IP or domain that was previously associated with malicious activity may no longer be malicious but could still be flagged as such. Additionally, attackers can easily change IPs and domains, making reputational analysis less effective over the long term.

Reputational analysis is a key component of the Pyramid of Pain, a framework used to prioritize IoCs based on their value to attackers. IP addresses and domain names are relatively easy to change and are therefore low in the pyramid, meaning they are less valuable to attackers. However, it is equally easy for defenders to update watchlists and blocklists, making reputational analysis is a quick and effective method to detect and block know malicious IP addresses and domains.

File Analysis

File analysis is an essential practice that involves examining and scrutinizing different attributes of a file to gain insights into its behavior, purpose, and potential impact on a system. Several types of file analysis techniques and tools are available, each serving a specific purpose in understanding files and their potential risks.

Static Analysis

Static analysis focuses on examining the file without executing or running it. It involves reviewing the file's structure, metadata, and contents to identify potential indicators of malicious behavior.

Static analysis techniques include the following:

- **Signature analysis** This technique involves examining the file's signature, also known as the file header or magic number. The signature provides information about the file type and can help determine if it matches the expected format.

- **Metadata analysis** Metadata analysis involves extracting and analyzing information embedded within the file, such as author name, creation date, and revision history. This information can provide insights into the file's origin and help identify any suspicious or unauthorized modifications.

- **File structure analysis**   Analyzing the structure of a file involves examining its internal components, such as headers, sections, and data segments. This analysis can reveal any abnormalities or hidden elements that may indicate malicious behavior.
- **File entropy analysis**   File entropy measures the randomness or predictability of data within a file. High entropy values may suggest encrypted or compressed data, while low entropy values may indicate uniform or repetitive data, which can be indicative of malicious content.

Dynamic Analysis

Dynamic analysis involves executing or running the file in a controlled environment to observe its behavior and interactions with the system. It provides real-time insights into the file's actions, including any malicious or suspicious activities.

Dynamic analysis techniques include the following:

- **Sandboxing**   Sandboxing involves running the file in an isolated environment, known as a sandbox, where its activities can be monitored and analyzed without affecting the host system. Sandboxing provides a safe way to observe the file's behavior and identify any malicious actions.
- **Behavior analysis**   Behavior analysis focuses on monitoring the file's interactions with the system, such as file system modifications, network connections, and system calls. This analysis helps identify any unauthorized or suspicious activities performed by the file.

File Reputation Analysis

File reputation analysis involves assessing the reputation and trustworthiness of a file based on its prevalence and characteristics. It often involves utilizing reputation databases or services that maintain information about known-good and known-malicious files. One widely used tool for file reputation analysis is VirusTotal, which scans files against multiple antivirus engines and provides detailed reports on potential threats.

Code Analysis

Code analysis involves examining the underlying code or script within a file, such as analyzing scripts written in languages like JavaScript, PowerShell, and Python. This analysis helps identify any malicious or vulnerable code constructs that could be exploited.

Behavior Analysis

Behavior analysis plays a pivotal role in modern cybersecurity, enabling organizations to detect and respond to potential threats by analyzing the behavior of entities within their systems. By closely monitoring and analyzing the actions, interactions, and patterns exhibited by users, entities, processes, and devices, security analysts can gain valuable insights into potential security incidents, anomalous behavior, and emerging threats.

Behavior analysis encompasses various techniques and approaches that aim to identify and understand deviations from normal behavior. It focuses on detecting suspicious activities, unusual patterns, and indicators of compromise that may indicate malicious intent or compromised systems. By analyzing behavior across different dimensions, such as user behavior, entity behavior, and access patterns, security analysts can effectively identify and address security threats that may otherwise go undetected.

User Behavior Analysis

User behavior analysis (UBA) is a technique used in cybersecurity to detect and identify potential threats based on the behavior of users on a network or system. This technique involves creating a baseline of normal behavior for users and then analyzing deviations from that baseline to identify suspicious or malicious activity.

To create a baseline, analysts typically analyze log data to identify common patterns of behavior, such as the times of day when users typically log in, the applications they use, and the websites they visit. This baseline can then be used to identify anomalies or deviations from normal behavior that may indicate a security incident.

Trend analysis is another important aspect of user behavior analysis. By analyzing trends over time, analysts can identify patterns of behavior that may indicate a potential security incident. For example, an increase in failed login attempts or the volume of data being accessed by a user could be a sign of a compromised account or malicious activity.

It's also important to consider the context of the behavior being analyzed. For example, certain activities that might be considered abnormal for one user or department might be perfectly normal for another. In certain environments, such as cloud environments or those with identity and access management (IAM) systems, user behavior analysis can be particularly tricky. This is because users may assume different roles and access different resources based on their permissions, which can result in vastly different behaviors. In these cases, involving stakeholders from across the organization in the analysis process becomes even more critical to ensure that the baseline and analysis are relevant and accurate.

Entity Behavior Analysis

Entity behavior analysis (EBA) is a cybersecurity technique that extends the principles of user behavior analysis (UBA) to analyze the behavior of specific entities within a network or system. By focusing on entities like web servers or domain controllers, EBA can identify and detect potential security threats based on their behavior.

Let's consider a web server as an example. The baseline behavior for a web server may include patterns such as receiving HTTP requests, serving web pages, and logging access information. However, in the context of EBA, we can also look for anomalies that may indicate a compromise or suspicious activity.

For instance, if the web server suddenly starts making outbound connections to known-malicious IP addresses or communicating over nonstandard ports, it may suggest unauthorized communication with external entities. Additionally, a significant increase in outgoing traffic or unusual patterns of data transfer from the web server may indicate data exfiltration or the presence of a command and control (C2) channel.

Furthermore, unexpected changes in file integrity, such as the modification of critical system files or the presence of unknown or unauthorized files, could be a sign of a compromised system. Similarly, a sudden spike in failed login attempts or unauthorized access to sensitive directories might indicate an attempted breach or unauthorized activity.

NOTE In recent years, user behavior analytics (UBA) and entity behavior analytics (EBA) have increasingly been integrated into a unified solution known as user and entity behavior analytics (UEBA). UEBA combines the capabilities of UBA and EBA into a single product, offering a comprehensive approach to detecting and mitigating insider threats, anomalous behaviors, and other security risks.

EXAM TIP EBA and UEBA are not part of the CYSA+ exam objectives and are included here for the sake of completeness.

Abnormal Account Activity

Abnormal activity refers to actions taken by a user that are outside of their normal pattern of behavior. Some common examples of abnormal activity include multiple failed login attempts, unusual access to sensitive data or applications, changes to account settings or permissions, and the use of uncommon executables or API calls. These can all be signs of a compromised account or malicious activity.

One approach to detecting abnormal account activity is to use a scoring system, where points are assigned to various types of behavior based on their risk level. For example, a failed login attempt might be assigned a low score, while accessing sensitive data or executing uncommonly used executables or API calls might be assigned a high score. By monitoring these scores over time, analysts can identify when a user's score exceeds a certain threshold, indicating abnormal activity.

Another approach is to use machine learning algorithms to identify patterns of behavior that are indicative of abnormal activity, including unusual times of day and the use of uncommon executables or API calls. These algorithms can be trained on historical data to identify common patterns and then applied in real time to detect anomalies.

Commercial UBA solutions are increasingly popular among organizations looking to enhance their security posture by detecting and responding to potential insider threats. These solutions typically leverage advanced machine learning and artificial intelligence techniques to analyze large volumes of data from a variety of sources, including user behavior logs, network traffic, and endpoint activity. Some commercial UBA solutions can also integrate with other security tools, such as SIEMs and SOARs, to provide a more comprehensive threat detection and response workflow. However, it's important to note that commercial UBA solutions can be expensive and require significant resources to implement and maintain.

Impossible Travel

Impossible travel refers to instances where a user account is used to log in to a system or application from two different geographic locations within a short amount of time. This can be an indicator of compromised credentials, as it would be impossible for a user to travel between the two locations within the time frame observed.

To detect impossible travel, UBA tools can be configured to track logins from various locations and identify instances where a single user account logs in from two locations that are geographically distant from each other within a short period of time.

Impossible travel can be particularly challenging to detect in cloud environments, where users may be accessing systems and applications from multiple devices and locations. Additionally, it's important to consider other factors that could explain the behavior, such as the use of a virtual private network (VPN) and other remote access technologies.

E-mail Analysis

Depending on the size of your organization, you may see thousands or even millions of e-mails traverse your networks. Within that massive set of traffic are malicious messages that threat actors use to target employees of your organization. Hoping to gain access to internal systems or sensitive personal and financial information, these threat actors craft their messages to be as realistic as possible. Phishing remains a top attack vector for threat actors of all sophistication levels. Furthermore, many modern phishing e-mails are made using techniques that make the messages indistinguishable from legitimate e-mail. A scalable and automated e-mail analysis process, therefore, is required to provide the most protection against increasingly convincing phishing attempts.

Malicious Payload

Using a technique as old as e-mail itself, attackers can attach malicious files to e-mail, hoping they are downloaded and executed on a host machine. Modern e-mail systems automatically scan e-mail content and block a significant number of malicious messages, especially those that are obviously so. However, attackers will often conceal malware inside other types of commonly e-mailed files, such as word processing documents, compressed ZIP files, media files, and Adobe PDF documents. In some cases, these exploits take advantage of software vulnerabilities to enable the malicious content to surface on the host machine. Flaws in PDF readers, for example, have been exploited to enable the execution of malicious code without the user's knowledge.

Attackers may also use social engineering to trick users into enabling functionality that would be harmful to their systems. These attackers embed a malicious script or macro into a legitimate-looking document and try to trick the user into enabling functionality to get their malware in the door. In other cases, the document itself may contain URLs to malicious websites, which might bring up a fake prompt for password "verification." In the latter example, there would be no indication from the attachment that anything unusual was happening since there may not be malicious content in the document itself.

DomainKeys Identified Mail

The DomainKeys Identified Mail (DKIM) standard was introduced as a way for e-mail senders to provide a method for recipients to verify messages. It specifically offers three services: identity verification, identification of an identity as known or unknown, and determination of an identity as trusted or untrusted. DKIM uses a pair of keys, one private and one public, to verify messages. The organization's public key is published to DNS records, which will later be queried for and used by recipients. When sending a message using DKIM, the sender includes a special signature header in all outgoing messages. The DKIM header will include a hash of the e-mail header, a hash of some portion of the body, and information about the function used to compute the hash, as shown here:

```
DKIM-Signature: v=1; a=rsa-sha256; d=example.com; s=test;
c=relaxed/relaxed; q=dns/txt; t=1126524832; x=1149015927;
h=from:to:subject:date:keywords:keywords;
bh=kWwVkljr4/RXuFhWzCWO8PPyulPPHzyVhGYICEk1NWg=;
b=dzdVyOfAKCdLXdJOc9G2q8LoXSlEniSbav+yuU4zGeeruD001szZVoG4ZHRNiYzR
```

Upon receiving a message, the destination server will look up the previously published public key and use this key to verify the message. With this process, DKIM can effectively protect against spam and spoofing, and it can also alert recipients to the possibility of message tampering. Importantly, DKIM is not intended to give insight into the intent of the sender, protect against tampering after verification, or prescribe any actions for the recipient to take in the event in a verification failure.

Sender Policy Framework

The Simple Mail Transfer Protocol (SMTP) enables users to send e-mails to recipients and explicitly specify the source without any built-in checks. This means that anyone can send a message claiming to be from anyone. This default lack of verification has enabled spammers to send messages claiming to be from legitimate sources for decades. The Sender Policy Framework (SPF) enables domain owners to prevent such e-mail spoofing using their domains by leveraging DNS functionality. An SPF TXT record lists the authorized mail servers associated with a domain. Before a message is fully received by a recipient server, that server will verify the sender's SPF information in DNS records. Once this is verified, the entirety of the message can be downloaded. If a message is sent from a server that's not in that TXT record, the recipient's server can categorize that e-mail as suspicious and mark it for further analysis. SPF TXT information can be manually queried for, as shown in Figure 5-2, which shows the Google public DNS server, 8.8.8.8, reporting several TXT records for the domain comptia.org, including SPF information.

Domain-Based Message Authentication, Reporting, and Conformance

Domain-based Message Authentication, Reporting, and Conformance (DMARC) is an e-mail authentication protocol designed to give e-mail domain owners the ability to prevent spoofing and reduce the spam that appears to originate from their domain.

```
● ● ●                             🏠 brent — -zsh — 120×32
[brent@█████ ~ % nslookup -type=txt comptia.org 8.8.8.8
;; Truncated, retrying in TCP mode.
Server:        8.8.8.8
Address:       8.8.8.8#53

Non-authoritative answer:
comptia.org     text = "v=spf1 a ip4:198.134.5.0/24 ip4:68.70.162.0/24 include:spf.protection.outlook.com include:email.
freshservice.com include:mailer.comptia.org include:mozu.com include:mail.zendesk.com include:informz.net include:mail.c
ertmetrics.com  ?all"
comptia.org     text = "google-verification=651gV0C0AQQGiqt62732e01LB-DKAA12HCKJsQmGQjg"
comptia.org     text = "MS=ms77829986"
comptia.org     text = "atlassian-domain-verification=riU6JTmRJr0Kf8gK1HvFKiJPkzC31LjJpEjcvqO=aih2djsA0DNL+IbmLfwDraE5"
comptia.org     text = "JEcCx2j153dri/TC2MxLToeSprhLauj8f4QUoGGtMfpAoCW1fzs2Hbejgjptmm0nJdjK7qg4maDfncJZyAGpvw=="
comptia.org     text = "v=DMARC1; p=none; fo=1; rua=mailto:f22deb33@mstoolbox.dmarc-report.com; ruf=mailto:f22deb33@fore
nsics.dmarc-report.com;"

Authoritative answers can be found from:
```

Figure 5-2   TXT records from a DNS lookup of comptia.org highlighting an SPF entry

Like SPF, an entry is created in the domain owner's DNS record. DMARC can be used to tell receiving servers how to handle messages that appear to be spoofed using a legitimate domain. DMARC uses SPF and DKIM to verify that messages are authentic, so it's important that both SPF and DKIM are correctly configured for the DMARC policy to work properly. Once the DMARC DNS entry is published, any e-mail server receiving a message that appears to be from the domain can check against DNS records, authenticated via SPF or DKIM. The results are passed to the DMARC module along with message author's domain. Messages that fail SPF, DKIM, or domain tests may invoke the organization's DMARC policy. DMARC also makes it possible to record the results of these checks into a daily report, which can be sent to domain owners, usually on a daily basis. This allows for DMARC policies to be improved or other changes in infrastructure to be made. As with SPF, DMARC TXT information can be manually queried for using any number of DNS utilities. Figure 5-3 shows the DMARC entry from a DNS lookup.

 EXAM TIP   When deployed together, SPF, DKIM, and DMARC form a powerful defense against phishing attacks. SPF ensures that only authorized servers can send e-mails on behalf of a domain, DKIM adds a digital signature to verify e-mail integrity, and DMARC provides policies for handling failed authentication checks.

Header

An e-mail header is the portion of a message that contains details about the sender, the route taken, and the recipient. Analysts can use this information to detect spoofed or suspicious e-mails that have made it past filters. These headers are usually hidden from

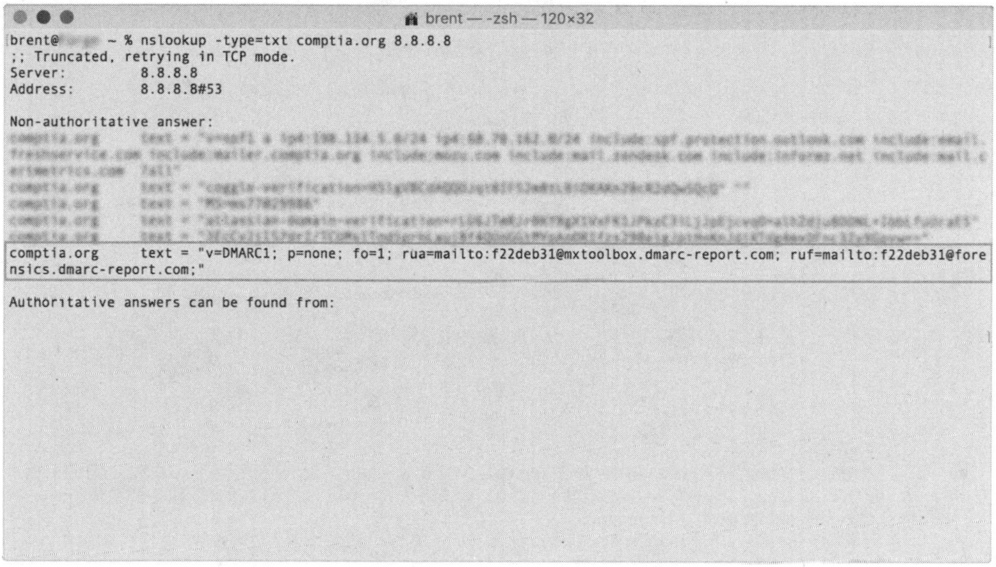

Figure 5-3 TXT records from a DNS lookup of comptia.org highlighting a DMARC entry

view, but mail clients or web services will allow the message header to be viewed with no more than a few clicks. Figure 5-4 is an excerpt of an e-mail header featuring several details about the message's journey from sender to recipient inbox. Note the SPF and DKIM verdicts are captured in the header information, along with various server addresses.

Phishing

Many attackers know that the best route into a network is through a careless or untrained employee. In a social engineering campaign, an attacker uses deception, often influenced by the profile they've built about the target, to manipulate the target into performing an act that may not be in their best interest. These attacks come in many forms—from advanced phishing e-mails that seem to originate from a legitimate source, to phone calls requesting personal information. Phishing attacks continue to be a challenge for network defenders because they are becoming increasingly convincing, fooling recipients into divulging sensitive information with regularity. Despite the most advanced technical countermeasures, the human element remains the most vulnerable part of the network. Handling phishing is no trivial task. Attacker techniques are evolving, and although several best practices have been established for basic protection, the very nature of e-mail is such that there aren't always visible indicators you can use to ensure that a message is genuine, especially at scale.

Forwarding

Some larger organizations have dedicated inboxes to review suspicious e-mails that have somehow passed through e-mail filters. Encouraging users who've received these kinds of messages to forward them to a special inbox may help analysts determine what changes

```
Delivered-To: *******@gmail.com
Received: by 10.80.176.68 with SMTP id i62csp9339161edd;
        Thu, 28 Dec 2017 13:53:30 -0800 (PST)
X-Received: by 10.200.50.206 with SMTP id a14mr43214491qtb.59.1514498010046;
        Thu, 28 Dec 2017 13:53:30 -0800 (PST)
ARC-Seal: i=1; a=rsa-sha256; t=1514498010; cv=none;
        d=google.com; s=arc-20160816;
        b=a70ETRryKuMDlF6QOgYwid5R45Raxn4p9VhYYyxt+uEaZxl8hSSWCQ0DamwY7KSuwW
              RBKXtQhx         XyYrolYz         me8jhgwb         R2HXDxSxT         FKEt3ajA
        arc=p           EJEC        r di      head       coun        .com
Retu   Path:
<32WdFWggTD5YDE-H4FBO022EKDJI.6EE6B4.2ECA4DD4J7C0IKJ0PK6C08B.2EC@scoutcamp.bounces.google.
com>
Received: from mail-sor-f69.google.com (mail-sor-f69.google.com. [209.85.220.69])
        by mx.google.com with SMTPS id l46sor25230779qtc.113.2017.12.28.13.53.29
        for <*******@gmail.com>
        (Google Transport Security);
        Thu, 28 Dec 2017 13:53:30 -0800 (PST)
Received-SPF: pass (google.com: domain of
32wdfwggtd5yde-h4fbo022ekdji.6ee6b4.2eca4dd4j7c0ikj0pk6c08b.2ec@scoutcamp.bounces.google.
com designates 209.85.220.69 as permitted sender) client-ip=209.85.220.69;
Authentication-Results: mx.google.com;
        dkim=pass header.i=@google.com header.s=20161025 header.b=RZ0mFn+4;
        spf=pass (google.com: domain of
32wdfwggtd5yde-h4fbo022ekdji.6ee6b4.2eca4dd4j7c0ikj0pk6c08b.2ec@scoutcamp.bounces.google.
com designates 209.85.220.69 as permitted sender)
smtp.mailfrom=32WdFWggTD5YDE-H4FBO022EKDJI.6EE6B4.2ECA4DD4J7C0IKJ0PK6C08B.2EC@scoutcamp.
bounces.google.com;
        dmarc=pass (p=REJECT sp=REJECT dis=NONE) header.from=accounts.google.com
DKIM-Signature: v=1; a=rsa-sha256; c=relaxed/relaxed;
        d=google.com; s=20161025;
        h=mime-version:date:reply-to:feedback-id:message-id:subject:from:to;
        bh=XYYcYIdqi70DvBTOHbIrzfOLsG8K+kZQDQ2ohki1Qao=;
        b=RZ0mFn+49r+Y/csjnRzyT6x405/wNDFbg8NIn+iMqdqhqXAta+yfv4ALV660R2r4bx
         7D909058kwsrIL2l3iwvjeargmPkLWMAaFIEkipinwm42NX7BPrSFUM5C4Vgl+quLDBA
         /AHMF/d5+N2oaR9OsCQYwpdaDwsXX8EX/4VUdofzfhwzdjpo4cDYHwMlHEXUHxMqYTo8
         oRUItOIdgiYpSsuNBUClK9TdsLIy6e1eLrazCrM0yuEJrFv3MWNJdbd08NUPQWT4C0yr
         nFGL6c19Cfaw+AnUuwVCN30zHHcGIevM1nwh+C8rLt8lnKsP+LUIaePRXGxHlJHz+BzG
         MbbA==
X-Google-DKIM-Signature: v=1; a=rsa-sha256; c=relaxed/relaxed;
        d=1e100.net; s=20161025;
        h        message        :mime-v        :date:r       o:feedb
A        KCQjU        uKfc0        e3lR1       3V91d        t4+ny        Hd80=
MIME-version: 1.0
X-Received: by 10.200.27.122 with SMTP id p55mr23522587qtk.53.1514498009758; Thu, 28 Dec
2017 13:53:29 -0800 (PST)
Date: Thu, 28 Dec 2017 21:53:27 +0000 (UTC)
Reply-To: Google <no-reply@accounts.google.com>
X-Google-Id: 196013
Feedback-ID: 91-anexp#rmd-standalone:account-notifier
X-Account-Notification-Type: 91-anexp#rmd-standalone
X-Notifications:
GAMMA:<c252089a83cb90e8.1514498009303.100215992.10009979.en.859a425a228ae17a@google.com>
Message-ID:
<c252089a83cb90e8.1514498009303.100215992.10009979.en.859a425a228ae17a@google.com>
Subject: Security alert
From: Google <no-reply@accounts.google.com>
To: *******@gmail.com
Content-Type: multipart/alternative; boundary="94eb2c0b29f6e27cf605616d8b72"
```

Figure 5-4   Sample e-mail header

need to be made to e-mail rules to prevent these e-mails from getting through in the future. It's also useful to analyze reports in aggregate to assist in identifying large-scale or targeted attacks. This technique is useful not only in helping security teams identify false negatives, or bad e-mails that have marked as good, but false positives as well. It can just be frustrating to have legitimate e-mails continuously sent to a junk folder.

 TIP Users provide the most useful information to a security team by forwarding an e-mail in its entirety, with headers and body intact, rather than just copying and pasting the text within the e-mail. It's also often possible for users to attach multiple e-mails in a forwarded message.

Digital Signatures and Encryption

A digital signature provides sender verification, message integrity, and nonrepudiation (that is, the assurance that a sender cannot deny having sent a message). This kind of signature requires the presence of public and private cryptographic keys. When crafting a message, the sender signs the message locally with their private key. Upon receipt, the recipient verifies it on their device by using the sender's public key. Digital messages are used today in much the same way that sealing wax was used centuries ago to seal documents. Wax sealant was used to verify that documents were unopened, and when stamped with a custom signet ring, the sealant could also be used to verify the sender's identity. Because these rings were difficult to replicate, recipients could have reasonable certainty that the message was legitimate if they recognized the seal.

Secure/Multipurpose Internet Mail Extensions (S/MIME) and Pretty Good Privacy (PGP) are the most common protocols used on the Internet for authentication and privacy when sending e-mails. PGP offers cryptographic privacy and authentication for many kinds of transmissions, but it is widely used for signing, encrypting, and decrypting electronic data to protect e-mail content. S/MIME is included in many browsers and e-mail clients and also supports encryption, key exchanges, and message signing. S/MIME and PGP can both provide authentication, message integrity, and nonrepudiation. In practice, S/MIME is often used in commercial settings, while PGP tends to be used by individuals.

 CAUTION It's critical for your end users to understand that a digital signature is not the same as the signature block routinely used in outgoing messages. Signature block content is simply additional text that is automatically or manually inserted with messages to enable users to share contact information. It offers no security advantage, whereas a digital signature provides verification of the sender's authenticity and message integrity.

Embedded Links

Some security devices perform real-time analysis of inbound messages for the presence of URLs and domains and then modify the messages so that links are either disabled or redirected to a valid domain. Some Software as a Service (SaaS) e-mail platforms, such as Microsoft Office 365 and Google Gmail, offer functionality to identify links behind standard and short URLs, scan linked images for malicious content, and intercept user clicks to untrusted domains.

Impersonation

It might be easy to think that almost every phishing e-mail contains malicious URLs, a malware attachment, or some other malicious technical content. This is not always the case, however, as we look at how effective impersonation attacks have been over the past few years. Impersonation attacks are highly targeted efforts designed to trick victims into performing actions such as wiring money to attacker accounts. Often these victims are directly connected to key decision-makers, such as members of a finance team and executive assistants. By pretending to be a CEO, for example, an attacker may use tailored language to convince their targets to perform the requested task without thinking twice. Detecting and blocking these types of attacks cannot be done with technical tools alone. Key staff must be aware of current attacker trends and take the required training to resist them.

 CAUTION   It is common for attackers to pretend to be an executive who is e-mailing from a personal e-mail address (for example, jane.doe@gmail.com). This is typically followed by some pretext of why they are using a personal e-mail address and not a corporate address, such as "I'm on my personal device," "I'm on vacation," or "I've been locked out." Although this author has seen executives exhibit this bad practice, you should definitely proceed with extreme caution, verify the claim, and get a second opinion before proceeding with anything being asked of you. Additionally, in many cases the executive's admin assistant should be able to reach the executive in question.

Programming Languages

Programming languages are a crucial aspect of cybersecurity. Many security tools, including SIEM, SOAR, and malware analysis platforms, require knowledge of programming languages to customize and automate their functionality. Additionally, many attacks involve exploiting vulnerabilities in software, making it essential for cybersecurity professionals to have knowledge of programming languages in order to understand, detect, and remediate detect these vulnerabilities and exploits.

As a CYSA+ professional, having a strong foundation in programming languages can improve your ability to analyze, detect, and respond to security threats. In the following sections, we discuss several programming languages commonly used in cybersecurity: XML, JSON, shell scripting, regular expressions, PowerShell, and Python.

Extensible Markup Language

XML, or Extensible Markup Language, is a markup language used to encode documents in a format that is both human- and machine-readable. XML is commonly used for data exchange and storage and has been widely used in web development for building websites and web applications, particularly SOAP (Simple Object Access Protocol) applications.

XML documents consist of elements, which are enclosed in opening and closing tags, and may contain attributes that provide additional information about each element. The structure of an XML document is defined by a schema, which specifies the types and structure of the elements that can be used in the document.

XML is often used for exchanging threat intelligence information between different security tools and platforms. In fact, the Structured Threat Information eXpression (STIX) language, which is commonly used for representing and sharing cyber threat intelligence, uses XML for its data format. Many security tools, such as SIEMs and threat intelligence platforms, also use XML to represent and exchange threat intelligence data, making it an important format for sharing and integrating threat intelligence across different systems.

JavaScript Object Notation

JSON, or JavaScript Object Notation, is a lightweight data interchange format that is easy for humans to read and write and for machines to parse and generate. It has become a popular alternative to XML due to its simplicity and flexibility. JSON documents consist of key-value pairs enclosed in curly braces, with values represented as strings, numbers, arrays, or objects. The structure of a JSON document is informally defined by a schema or data model, which specifies the types and structure of the elements that can be used in the document.

JSON is commonly used in web development for building web applications and services, particularly those that are REST based. It is also used in the exchange and storage of data between different systems and platforms, including in the field of cybersecurity. For instance, the latest version of STIX uses JSON for its data format. Many security tools and platforms, such as SIEMs and threat intelligence platforms, also use JSON for representing and exchanging threat intelligence data, making it an important format for sharing and integrating threat intelligence across different systems.

Shell Scripting

Shell scripting is the process of writing scripts using command-line shells, such as Bash, that can be executed in Unix and Unix-like operating systems. These scripts can automate repetitive tasks, such as system maintenance, file manipulation, and process control.

One of the key advantages of shell scripting is its versatility. Since shell scripts are written in a command-line interface, they can be easily integrated with other tools and technologies. This makes shell scripting a ubiquitous tool for security professionals who need to work with a variety of different systems and platforms. Also, shell scripting is a lightweight and efficient solution, making it a useful tool for performing tasks on remote or resource-constrained systems.

Some common use cases for shell scripting in cybersecurity include automating system hardening tasks, monitoring system logs for suspicious activity, and performing network analysis and monitoring tasks. Shell scripts can also be used to automate the deployment and management of security tools, such as intrusion detection systems and vulnerability scanners. Additionally, many endpoint detection systems log shell script contents, making it important for analysts to know how to read and interpret shell scripts.

Regular Expressions

Regular expressions, or regex, comprise a powerful tool widely used in cybersecurity for text processing, which allows you to search for and match patterns in text. In particular, it is used to search through log files, network traffic, and other data sources to extract relevant information and identify potential security incidents. Regex patterns can be used to match specific strings, characters, or sequences of characters. For example, a regex pattern could be used to match a specific IP address, a particular URL, or a password format. Regex can be combined with other tools, such as scripting languages like Python, to automate text processing and analysis.

However, it's important to note that regex can be challenging to use, particularly for those who are unfamiliar with the syntax and capabilities. Before attempting to use regex for security analysis, it's important to have a good understanding of regex basics, such as character classes, quantifiers, and anchors.

Furthermore, there are different standards for regular expressions, with the most common being POSIX (Portable Operating System Interface) and PCRE (Perl Compatible Regular Expressions). Some tools and platforms may use one standard over the other, so it's important to understand the differences between the two and how they may affect regular expression patterns. PCRE supports additional syntax and functionality that are not available in POSIX, making it a more powerful option for some use cases.

Some common regex tools used in cybersecurity include the command-line tool grep, which is used to search through files and directories for specific patterns, and the online regex tester regex101, which allows you to test and experiment with different regex patterns. It's worth mentioning that regular expressions are widely used in various tools and platforms, including Yara, Snort, Suricata, Burp Suite, and Splunk, as well as various antivirus and endpoint detection and response (EDR) solutions.

PowerShell

PowerShell is an object-oriented scripting language developed by Microsoft for automating and managing Windows environments. It provides a command-line shell and scripting environment that can be used to perform a variety of tasks, such as system administration, network configuration, and automation of routine tasks.

One of the advantages of PowerShell is its tight integration with the Windows operating system, which enables it to interact with various system components, including the registry, file system, and network. PowerShell scripts can also interact with COM objects, .NET classes, and other PowerShell scripts. Not only does this make PowerShell a powerful tool for administrators, it makes an equally powerful tool for attackers. In fact, PowerShell is widely used in various exploit and post-exploit frameworks like BloodHound, Mimikatz, Metasploit, PowerSploit, Posh, and Empire, among many others.

It is common for endpoint detection systems to log PowerShell commands and scripts, making it important for cybersecurity analysts to be able to read and interpret PowerShell scripts in order to detect malicious activity. Additionally, PowerShell has a number of built-in security features, such as execution policies and constrained language mode, which can be used to limit the scope of what PowerShell scripts can do and prevent malicious scripts from running.

NOTE PowerShell downgrade attacks are used by attackers to bypass security controls that restrict the use of PowerShell. These attacks take advantage of the fact that PowerShell before version 5.0 allows the execution of scripts and commands without digital signatures. Attackers can use this vulnerability to force a downgrade of PowerShell to an earlier version and then execute malicious code or commands that would otherwise be blocked by the more secure modern versions of PowerShell.

Python

Python is a versatile programming language that is widely used in cybersecurity for various tasks, such as scripting, automation, data analysis, and machine learning. Its readability, simplicity, and ease of use make it an attractive option for both beginners and experienced developers.

Python is commonly used in cybersecurity for several purposes, including vulnerability scanning, malware analysis, network scanning and reconnaissance, web application penetration testing, and data analysis. Its built-in libraries, such as Requests for HTTP requests and Beautiful Soup for web scraping, make it easy to automate tasks and gather information from various sources. Moreover, Python's vast collection of third-party libraries and modules, including those for cryptography, network analysis, and machine learning, allows cybersecurity professionals to build custom tools and applications that can be tailored to specific needs.

Python's popularity in data science and machine learning has made it an essential tool for security analysts, particularly in the field of security analytics. The SciPy library, which includes tools such as NumPy and Pandas, is widely used in security analytics for data manipulation and analysis. Pandas, in particular, is a popular library for working with data in a tabular format, such as log data. Machine learning can be used for tasks such as anomaly detection and classification of threats, and the scikit-learn library provides a range of tools for classification, regression, clustering, and more.

In recent years, Jupyter Notebooks have become increasingly popular in threat hunting and other cybersecurity applications. Jupyter Notebook is an open source web application that allows users to create and share documents that contain live code, equations, visualizations, and narrative text. Analysts can easily combine data, code, and visualization into a single interactive document, making it easier to explore and analyze data and communicate findings to others. In security analytics, Jupyter Notebooks are often used in combination with popular Python libraries such as Pandas, NumPy, and SciPy to perform data analysis, statistical modeling, and machine learning. This allows analysts to interactively explore data in real time, enabling them to quickly identify and respond to emerging threats. Jupyter Notebooks also allow for easy collaboration and sharing of analysis and findings with others in the organization, thus enhancing the efficiency and effectiveness of threat hunting and other security analytics tasks.

EXAM TIP While machine learning and data science tools and libraries are quite powerful, particularly within the context of threat hunting, they will not be covered in the exam and are only provided here as a reference to the reader.

Python's flexibility and ease of use make it a popular choice for integrating with vendor APIs, such as those provided by CrowdStrike, VirusTotal, and Splunk. These APIs enable analysts to automate various tasks, such as submitting files for analysis, retrieving threat intelligence data, and integrating security data across different tools and platforms. Python is also used in SOAR platforms to automate incident response workflows and connect different security tools.

Chapter Review

Acquiring data through continuous network monitoring is only the beginning. The real work is in analyzing that data and turning it into information. In this chapter, we covered a multitude of approaches and tools you can use to perform basic security operations and monitoring, along with some security analytics. There is no one-size-fits-all answer for any of this, so it is critical that, as cybersecurity analysts, we have enough familiarity with our options to choose the right one for a particular job. The topics brought up in this chapter are by no means exhaustive, but they should serve you well for the CySA+ exam and, perhaps more importantly, as a starting point for further lifelong exploration.

Questions

1. What is a potential use case for a SOAR platform?

   A. Automating incident response

   B. Manual alert triaging

   C. Manual user provisioning

   D. Manual audit log review

2. What is an EDR solution designed to do?

   A. Monitor and analyze server traffic

   B. Monitor and detect endpoint threats

   C. Monitor and detect network vulnerabilities

   D. Monitor and analyze firewall logs

3. What types of endpoint threats can EDR solutions detect and respond to?

   A. DDoS attacks

   B. SQL injection attacks

   C. Rogue access points

   D. Malware infections

4. Which of the following is a technique used to determine the reputation of an IP address or domain?

   A. Impossible travel

   B. Cyber threat intelligence feeds

   C. Reputation analysis

   D. Abnormal account activity

5. What is sandboxing?

   A. A technique used to monitor network traffic to understand how malware behaves

   B. A technique used to customize the analysis environment for malware analysis

   C. A technique used to detect IoCs in various sources, including e-mail attachments, network traffic, and disk images

   D. A technique used to isolate and analyze potentially malicious files or programs in a secure environment without risking the integrity of the host system

6. What is the purpose of DKIM?

   A. To prevent e-mail spoofing

   B. To provide encryption for e-mails

   C. To verify the authenticity of messages

   D. To prevent phishing attacks

7. What is the purpose of DMARC?

   A. To provide encryption for e-mails

   B. To prevent e-mail spoofing

   C. To prevent phishing attacks

   D. To verify the authenticity of messages

8. Which of the following is an example of abnormal account activity?

   A. Multiple failed login attempts

   B. Unusual access to sensitive data or applications

   C. Changes to account settings or permissions

   D. All of the above

9. Which of the following is a lightweight data interchange format that is commonly used in web development and has become a popular alternative to XML?

   A. JSON

   B. Bash

   C. PowerShell

   D. Python

10. Which programming language is commonly used for vulnerability scanning, malware analysis, network scanning and reconnaissance, web application penetration testing, and data analysis in cybersecurity?

   A. XML

   B. JSON

   C. Bash

   D. Python

Answers

1. **A.** Automating incident response. A SOAR platform can be configured to respond to specific types of incidents automatically, which can help to reduce the time it takes to respond to an incident and improve the overall efficiency of the incident response process.

2. **B.** An EDR is designed to monitor and detect endpoint threats.

3. **D.** An EDR solution can detect and respond to malware infections.

4. **C.** Reputation analysis is a technique used to check a database of known malicious IP addresses and domains to see if the given IP address or domain has been previously associated with malicious activity.

5. **D.** Sandboxing is a technique used to isolate and analyze potentially malicious files or programs in a secure environment without risking the integrity of the host system.

6. **C.** The purpose of DKIM is to verify the authenticity of messages.

7. **B.** The purpose of DMARC is to prevent e-mail spoofing.

8. **D.** Multiple failed login attempts, unusual access to sensitive data or applications, and changes to account settings or permissions are all signs of abnormal account activity.

9. **A.** JSON, or JavaScript Object Notation, is a lightweight data interchange format that has become a popular alternative to XML due to its simplicity and flexibility.

10. **D.** Python is commonly used for vulnerability scanning, malware analysis, network scanning and reconnaissance, web application penetration testing, and data analysis in cybersecurity.

Tools for Malicious Activity Analysis

In this chapter you will learn:

- How to use packet capture tools like Wireshark and tcpdump to capture and analyze network traffic
- How to use DNS and IP reputation services like WHOIS and AbuseIPDB to investigate suspicious network activity
- How to analyze files using tools like Strings and VirusTotal to identify potential malware
- About sandboxing tools like Joe Sandbox and Cuckoo Sandbox to safely analyze malware in an isolated environment

Give me a lever long enough and a fulcrum on which to place it,
and I shall move the world.

—Archimedes

In this chapter, we will explore a set of tools that are invaluable for analyzing and investigating malicious activities. These tools empower security professionals to delve deep into network traffic and file analysis, enabling them to uncover potential threats, vulnerabilities, and indicators of compromise.

Network Analysis Tools

In this section, we will cover tools that allow for the capture and analysis of network traffic, providing insights into the behavior and patterns of malicious activities. These tools enable the examination of packet-level details, protocol analysis, and the identification of suspicious network behavior.

BPF

In our discussion of network analysis tools, it's important to start with BPF (Berkeley Packet Filter). BPF is a critical low-level filtering technology that forms the backbone of various network analysis tools, including Wireshark, TShark, and tcpdump. By delving into BPF first, we can establish a solid understanding of its capabilities and inner workings.

This knowledge will serve as a foundation for our subsequent discussions on tcpdump and Wireshark.

BPF filters can be applied strategically to filter out packets that are not necessary for the analysis, which can improve performance and processing speed on downstream tools like Wireshark and tcpdump. By reducing the volume of traffic that is captured, filtered, and analyzed, BPF filters can also improve storage and memory usage, making it easier to manage large datasets.

For example, a network analyst may apply a BPF filter to capture only traffic to or from a specific IP address or port number. This can reduce the size of the capture file and make it easier to identify relevant packets during the analysis. Similarly, a security analyst may apply a BPF filter to capture only packets that match a specific pattern or contain certain keywords, reducing the volume of data that needs to be analyzed.

BPF operates by using a filter expression to match packets based on their content, protocol, or other characteristics. Filter expressions use Boolean logic, allowing for complex filtering conditions. For example, a filter expression can include multiple conditions combined with AND, OR, and NOT operators.

The following list enumerates the various types of filters and provides an example of each:

- **Direction filter** Capture outbound packets.
  Example: outbound

- **Host filters** Capture packets to or from specific hosts.
  Example: host 192.168.0.1 or host 192.168.0.2

- **Port filters** Capture packets associated with specific source or destination ports.
  Example: tcp port 80 or tcp port 443

- **Payload filters** Analyze packet payloads for specific patterns or content.
  Example: tcp[((tcp[12:1] & 0xf0) >> 2):4] = 0x47455420 (matches packets
  with "GET " in the TCP payload, indicating HTTP GET requests)

- **Time filters** Capture packets during specific time intervals.
  Example: after 2023-01-01 00:00:00 and before 2023-01-31 23:59:59
  (captures packets within the time period from January 1, 2023, to January 31, 2023)

Let's put that all together in a single expression:

```
outbound and (host 192.168.0.1 or host 192.168.0.2) and (tcp port 80 or
tcp port 443) and (tcp[((tcp[12:1] & 0xf0) >> 2):4] = 0x47455420) and
(after 2023-01-01 00:00:00 and before 2023-01-31 23:59:59)
```

In this example, we are capturing outbound packets to or from the hosts with IP address 192.168.0.1 or 192.168.0.2, on TCP port 80 or 443, with an HTTP GET request in the TCP payload within the time period from January 1, 2023, to January 31, 2023. This demonstrates how you can use BPF filters to precisely capture and analyze network traffic based on specific criteria, such as payload content and time intervals.

Wireshark, TShark, and tcpdump all utilize BPF filters to selectively capture and analyze network traffic. For example, a Wireshark user may apply a BPF filter to capture only HTTP traffic or filter out packets from a specific IP address. Similarly, tcpdump users can apply a BPF filter to capture only ICMP traffic or filter packets by protocol or destination.

In addition to the standard BPF implementation, a newer, more advanced version called eBPF (extended BPF) is emerging. eBPF allows for more flexible and powerful filtering capabilities, as well as the ability to execute custom code within the kernel. This can be particularly useful for advanced network analysis and security monitoring.

Wireshark and TShark

Wireshark and TShark are two of the most powerful and widely used packet capture tools available. Wireshark is a graphical user interface (GUI) tool that provides real-time network traffic monitoring, analysis, and packet capture. TShark is a command-line tool that is part of the Wireshark suite and provides similar packet capture and analysis capabilities in a lightweight, scriptable form.

Here are some of the key features of Wireshark and TShark:

- Packet capture and analysis for a wide range of network protocols
- Advanced filtering and search capabilities to isolate specific packets or types of traffic
- Customizable profiles and color-coding to highlight important information and make analysis more efficient
- Support for SSL/TLS decryption to view encrypted traffic
- Ability to isolate, filter, and follow protocol streams
- Export reassembled payloads
- Integration with other security tools and technologies, such as intrusion detection systems and network analyzers
- Scriptable automation and analysis through the use of custom Lua scripts and other programming languages

With TShark, you can capture and analyze network traffic from the command line, which makes it a great choice for scripting and automation. For example, TShark can be used to output packet and payload information into other formats, such as CSV and JSON, and can be configured to capture specific types of traffic using BPF filters. Additionally, TShark can be used to decrypt SSL/TLS traffic and save the payloads to a JSON file.

Here are a couple of examples of TShark usage. First, suppose you want to capture HTTPS traffic on your network and save the decrypted payloads to a JSON file. You can use TShark with the following command:

```
tshark -r capture.pcapng -o "ssl.desegment_ssl_records: TRUE" -o "ssl.keys_list:
TCP,443,http,keyfile.pem" -Y "http.request.method == POST" -T json > output.json
```

This command reads the capture file capture.pcapng, decrypts SSL traffic using the key-file keyfile.pem for TCP traffic on port 443, filters for POST requests, and outputs the payloads in JSON format to a file called output.json.

Now, let's suppose you suspect that someone is attempting to bypass network controls by sending SSL or SSH traffic over port 53. You can use TShark with the following command:

```
tshark -r capture.pcapng -Y "udp.port == 53 and (ssl || ssh)"
```

This command reads the capture file capture.pcapng and filters for UDP traffic on port 53 that contains SSL or SSH packets.

Overall, Wireshark and TShark are essential tools for any network administrator or security analyst who needs to capture, analyze, and troubleshoot network traffic. With their advanced features and flexibility, they provide a powerful and versatile set of capabilities for monitoring and securing networks. Figures 6-1 and 6-2 illustrate Wireshark packet captures.

 EXAM TIP You may encounter test scenarios where you will be asked to identify port scans, port sweeps, and brute-force attacks by reviewing the output of these tools.

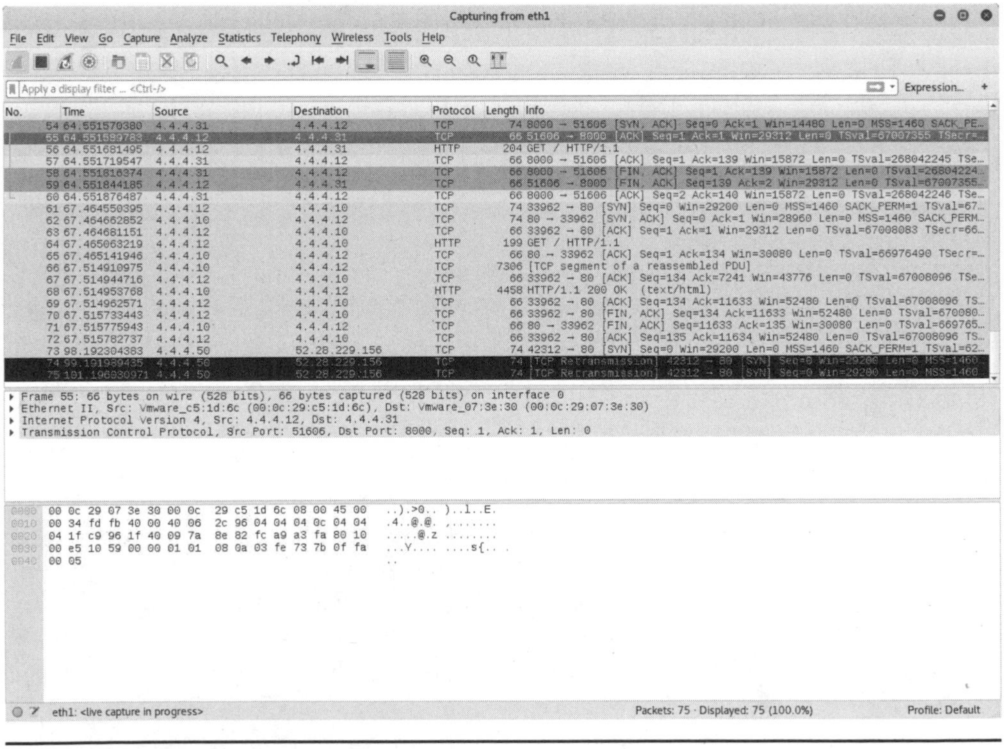

Figure 6-1 Typical Wireshark packet capture

```
Wireshark · Packet 64 · wireshark_eth1_20170420144701_EYJg2W                    ⊖ ⊡ ⊗
▶ Frame 64: 199 bytes on wire (1592 bits), 199 bytes captured (1592 bits) on interface 0
▶ Ethernet II, Src: Vmware_c5:1d:6c (00:0c:29:c5:1d:6c), Dst: Vmware_2b:16:2a (00:0c:29:2b:16:2a)
▶ Internet Protocol Version 4, Src: 4.4.4.12, Dst: 4.4.4.10
▼ Transmission Control Protocol, Src Port: 33962, Dst Port: 80, Seq: 1, Ack: 1, Len: 133
    Source Port: 33962
    Destination Port: 80
    [Stream index: 4]
    [TCP Segment Len: 133]
    Sequence number: 1      (relative sequence number)
    [Next sequence number: 134      (relative sequence number)]
    Acknowledgment number: 1      (relative ack number)
    Header Length: 32 bytes
  ▶ Flags: 0x018 (PSH, ACK)
    Window size value: 229
    [Calculated window size: 29312]
    [Window size scaling factor: 128]
    Checksum: 0x10c9 [unverified]
    [Checksum Status: Unverified]
    Urgent pointer: 0
  ▶ Options: (12 bytes), No-Operation (NOP), No-Operation (NOP), Timestamps
  ▶ [SEQ/ACK analysis]
▶ Hypertext Transfer Protocol

0000  00 0c 29 2b 16 2a 00 0c  29 c5 1d 6c 08 00 45 00   ..)+.*.. )..l..E.
0010  00 b9 b9 b0 40 00 40 06  70 71 04 04 04 0c 04 04   ....@.@. pq......
0020  04 0a 84 aa 00 50 a1 de  cf fc 35 d2 8a 72 80 18   .....P.. ..5..r..
0030  00 e5 10 c9 00 00 01 01  08 0a 93 fe 76 53 03 fd   ........ ....vS..
0040  fa ea 47 45 54 20 2f 20  48 54 54 50 2f 31 2e 31   ..GET / HTTP/1.1
0050  0d 0a 55 73 65 72 2d 41  67 65 6e 74 3a 20 57 67   ..User-A gent: Wg
0060  65 74 2f 31 2e 31 38 20  28 6c 69 6e 75 78 2d 67   et/1.18 (linux-g
0070  6e 75 29 0d 0a 41 63 63  65 70 74 3a 20 2a 2f 2a   nu)..Acc ept: */*
0080  0d 0a 41 63 63 65 70 74  2d 45 6e 63 6f 64 69 6e   ..Accept -Encodin
0090  67 3a 20 69 64 65 6e 74  69 74 79 0d 0a 48 6f 73   g: ident ity..Hos
00a0  74 3a 20 34 2e 34 2e 34  2e 31 30 0d 0a 43 6f 6e   t: 4.4.4 .10..Con
00b0  6e 65 63 74 69 6f 6e 3a  20 4b 65 65 70 2d 41 6c   nection:  Keep-Al
00c0  69 76 65 0d 0a 0d 0a                               ive....

No.: 64  Time: 67.465063219  Source: 4.4.4.12  Destination: 4.4.4.10  Protocol: HTTP  Length: 199  Info: GET / HTTP/1.1

Help                                                                              Close
```

Figure 6-2 Wireshark capture showing packet details

tcpdump

The command-line tool tcpdump allows you to capture and analyze network traffic in real time. Unlike Wireshark and TShark, tcpdump is lightweight and does not require a GUI, making it a great option for use on remote systems and in scripts. One of the main advantages of tcpdump over TShark is its speed: it can capture packets at a much faster rate and with less processing overhead.

tcpdump uses a syntax similar to BPF to filter and capture packets based on various criteria. For example, to capture only ICMP packets on a particular network interface, you could use the following command:

```
tcpdump -i eth0 icmp
```

In addition to filtering, tcpdump can also be used to rotate capture files based on size or time. This can be useful for long-term monitoring or capturing large amounts of data. For example, the following command will capture traffic and rotate the capture file every 10MB:

```
tcpdump -I eth0 -C 10 -w /var/log/capture/capture.pcap
```

WHOIS

WHOIS is a tool and protocol used to obtain information about domain name registration records, IP address assignments, and other information related to Internet resources.

It is a command-line utility that sends a query to a WHOIS server, which in turn responds with information about the queried domain name or IP address.

Some of the advantages of using WHOIS include the ability to obtain important information about a domain, such as the registrar, registration date, and contact information for the registrant. This information can be useful in identifying potential threat actors and for conducting investigations into malicious activity. However, there are also some disadvantages to using WHOIS, such as the potential for inaccurate or incomplete information, as well as the possibility of revealing sensitive information to attackers.

For security analysts, WHOIS can be a useful tool for gathering information about a domain or IP address, such as the registration date, the name of the registrar, and the name of the registrant. This information can be used to identify and track malicious activity as well as to determine if a domain or IP address is associated with a particular threat actor or campaign.

Some of the major regional WHOIS providers include the following:

- **InterNIC**   InterNIC is the primary registry for .com, .net, and .edu domain names in the United States.
- **LACNIC**   LACNIC is responsible for managing IP addresses in Latin America and the Caribbean.
- **RIPE NCC**   The Réseaux IP Européens Network Coordination Centre is responsible for managing IP addresses in Europe, the Middle East, and Central Asia.
- **APNIC**   The Asia-Pacific Network Information Centre is responsible for managing IP addresses in the Asia-Pacific region.
- **AFRINIC**   The African Network Information Centre is responsible for managing IP addresses in Africa.
- **IANA**   The Internet Assigned Numbers Authority is responsible for managing the global IP address space as well as domain names, protocol parameters, and other aspects of the Internet's infrastructure.

The WHOIS command-line utility can be used to query WHOIS servers and retrieve information about domain names and IP addresses. Here are two examples of how to use WHOIS on the command line.

- To retrieve information about a domain name (in this case, google.com), use the following command, which will send a WHOIS query to the server responsible for the .com top-level domain and retrieve information about the domain name google.com:

```
whois google.com
```

- To retrieve information about an IP address, us the following command, which in this case will send a WHOIS query to the server responsible for the IP address range containing 8.8.8.8 and retrieve information about the assigned network and organization:

```
whois 8.8.8.8
```

By using WHOIS to gather information about domains and IP addresses, security analysts can gain insights into potential threats and take proactive measures to protect their organizations.

 EXAM TIP Registrar specifics will not be part of the exam. The details here are provided for the sake of reference and completeness.

AbuseIPDB

AbuseIPDB is a website that allows users to report and track IP addresses and domains associated with malicious activity on the Internet. It maintains a community-driven database of reported artifacts, along with information on the types of abuse reported and the severity of the abuse. The website allows users to search the database for IP addresses and domains that have been reported as abusive as well as to view statistics on the most commonly reported IP addresses. The site also provides an API for programmatic access to its data, which will be discussed later.

Users can report abuse by providing the IP address or domain currently under review and selecting the appropriate category of abuse from a drop-down menu. At the time of this writing, AbuseIPDB has a total of 23 different categories, some of which are listed here:

- **DDoS attack** Distributed denial of service attack is a type of cyberattack that aims to make a website or online service unavailable by overwhelming it with traffic from multiple sources.
- **Hacking** Attempts to gain unauthorized access to a computer system or network.
- **Phishing** Attempts to trick individuals into providing sensitive information, such as login credentials or personal information, through fraudulent communication.
- **Spam** Unsolicited messages sent in large quantities, often for the purpose of promoting a product or service or spreading malware.
- **Web spam** Unsolicited messages sent through the Internet, often for the purpose of promoting a product or service or spreading malware.
- **SSH** Attempts to gain unauthorized access to a computer system using the SSH (Secure Shell) protocol.
- **IoT targeted** Attempts to compromise Internet of Things (IoT) devices, such as routers and cameras, for the purpose of using them in a botnet or for other malicious activities.

Users can also provide a comment about the reported IP address or domain and can choose the severity of the abuse; this will help other users to evaluate the risk and take appropriate actions.

It is worth reiterating that this website is a community-driven platform. Therefore, users should confirm any information obtained from it with other tools and techniques before taking any action.

AbuseIPDB APIs

AbuseIPDB provides APIs that allow users to access its data programmatically. These APIs can be used to automate the process of reporting and searching for IP addresses that have been reported as abusive as well as to retrieve statistics on the most commonly reported IP addresses.

Users can access the APIs by making HTTP requests to specific endpoints and can include various parameters in their requests to filter the data returned.

Here are some examples of the functionality provided by the APIs:

- **Report an IP address as abusive** This can be done by making a POST request to the /report endpoint, providing the IP address, the abuse category, and a comment.

- **Check an IP address's reputation** This can be done by making a GET request to the /check endpoint, providing the IP address and any additional parameters.

- **Retrieve information about an IP address** This can be done by making a GET request to the /info endpoint, providing the IP address.

- **Retrieve statistics on the most commonly reported IP addresses** This can be done by making a GET request to the /stats endpoint, providing any additional parameters.

Users can also retrieve data in bulk, such as all the reports made on a certain date or all the reports made on a certain category of abuse.

AbuseIPDB's API documentation provides more details on the endpoints, authentication, and parameters available for each request.

 EXAM TIP Although the AbuseIPDB APIs will not be covered directly on the exam, the details are provided here for the sake of reference and completeness.

File Analysis Tools

In this section, we will explore a range of utilities that facilitate the examination and understanding of potentially malicious files. These tools help extract valuable information from files, such as readable strings, and generate cryptographic hash values to verify file integrity. We will also discuss specialized platforms that provide comprehensive analysis, sandboxing, and threat intelligence capabilities to detect and understand the nature of malicious files.

Strings

Strings is a utility used in cybersecurity to analyze binary and executable files for human-readable text strings. This can include anything from plaintext passwords to debugging information. The strings utility is available on many operating systems, including Windows, Linux, and macOS.

When it comes to identifying indicators of compromise (IoCs) and tactics, techniques, and procedures (TTPs), the strings utility can be instrumental in uncovering specific details and artifacts. Analysts can search for various types of strings, including the following:

- **Registry keys**   Malicious software often creates registry entries for persistence or configuration purposes. Analysts can use strings to search for suspicious registry keys or values that may be indicative of malicious activity.

- **Filenames and paths**   Malware may use specific filenames, directories, or paths for installation or execution. By examining strings related to filenames, analysts can identify potential IoCs and gain insights into the malware's behavior.

- **Hostnames and IP addresses**   Strings can reveal hostnames and IP addresses that malware communicates with for command and control (C2) purposes. These indicators can help identify malicious servers or compromised systems involved in the attack.

- **URLs and web resources**   Malware and malicious activities often involve communication with remote servers or the retrieval of web-based resources. Analysts can use strings to search for URLs or specific web-related strings that may point to malicious infrastructure.

- **Encryption keys and algorithms**   Some malware employs encryption techniques to obfuscate communication or payload. The strings utility can uncover strings related to encryption keys or algorithms, providing insight into the encryption mechanisms employed by the malware.

- **Suspicious system commands**   Malware can leverage system commands or shellcode to execute malicious actions. Strings can help identify suspicious commands, shellcode snippets, or command-line arguments that indicate potential malicious activity.

Here are a few command-line examples of using strings:

- **strings malware.exe**   This command will output all of the strings contained in the malware.exe executable file.

- **strings -n 10 malware.exe**   This command will output all strings that are at least ten characters long.

- **strings -a malware.exe**   This command will output all printable ASCII strings in the malware.exe file.

The strings utility also has some common pitfalls and decoding issues. For example, strings may not be able to identify strings that are obfuscated or encoded using custom encoding schemes. Additionally, strings may output false positives or irrelevant data, which can make analysis more challenging. As such, it's important to use strings in conjunction with other analysis tools and techniques to get a full picture of a potential threat.

Hashing Utilities

When it comes to file integrity and verification, the generation of hash values plays a crucial role. Hash values serve as unique digital fingerprints for files, allowing you to verify their integrity and authenticity. By generating hash values for files and comparing them against known values, you can ensure that the files have not been tampered with or corrupted during transfer or storage.

Different platforms, such as Windows, Linux, and macOS, have built-in command-line utilities for generating hash values. We will explore these utilities in the following sections.

Windows Hashing

Windows has several built-in utilities for generating MD5, SHA-256, and SHA-512 signatures, including CertUtil, PowerShell, and File Explorer.

CertUtil   CertUtil is a command-line utility available in Windows that provides various cryptographic operations, including file hashing. It is a versatile tool commonly used for managing certificates, but it also offers functionality for generating hash values of files. With CertUtil, you can calculate hash values using different algorithms, such as MD5 and SHA-256.

For example, you can use the following command to generate an MD5 hash:

```
certutil -hashfile <filename> MD5
```

To generate an SHA-256 hash, use the following command:

```
certutil -hashfile <filename> SHA256
```

Get-FileHash   In Windows environments. the PowerShell cmdlet Get-FileHash can also be used to calculate the hash values of files.

For example, you can use the following command to generate an MD5 hash:

```
Get-FileHash -Algorithm MD5 -Path <filename> | Select-Object -ExpandProperty
Hash
```

To generate an SHA-256 hash, use the following command:

```
Get-FileHash -Algorithm SHA256 -Path <filename> | Select-Object -ExpandProperty
Hash
```

Linux Hashing

Linux provides several built-in command-line tools that can be used to generate MD5 and SHA-256 hash values for files. The two most commonly used are md5sum and sha256sum.

To generate an MD5 hash, use the following command:

```
md5sum <filename>
```

To generate an SHA-256 hash, use the following command:

```
sha256sum <filename>
```

macOS

In Mac environments, the md5 and shasum utilities can be used generate cryptographic hashes. The shasum command can compute hash values using different algorithms, including SHA-256, which is control by the **-a** command-line flag.

For example, to generate an MD5 hash, use the following command:

```
md5 <filename>
```

To generate an SHA-256 hash, use the following command:

```
shasum -a 256 <filename>
```

VirusTotal

VirusTotal is a free online service that allows users to scan files and URLs for potential malware. The service aggregates numerous antivirus engines and threat intelligence feeds to provide a comprehensive analysis of a given file or URL.

To use VirusTotal, users can simply upload a file or enter a hash value to scan. The service will then analyze the file or URL and provide a detailed report on its findings. The report includes information within the following sections: Detection, Details, Relations, Behavior, and Community.

The Detection section provides information on how many antivirus engines flagged the file or URL as malicious, as well as the names of those engines. The Details section includes more in-depth information on the file or URL, such as its size, type, and any embedded digital signatures. The Relations section shows any related files or URLs that are similar or related to the one being analyzed. The Behavior section provides a more dynamic analysis of the file or URL, showing any behaviors or activities it exhibits when executed. This can include things like network connections, system modifications, and processes started. Finally, the Community section allows users to leave comments and feedback on the file or URL, adding to the collective knowledge of the community.

File Uploads

When you're submitting a file to VirusTotal, it's important to consider the metadata that is shared with everyone. Uploading a file that has not been uploaded before can provide a significant amount of information to an attacker, including the organization or person who uploaded the file, the geographic location of the uploader, and the file's content and purpose. Therefore, it is preferred to use the file hash to check if a submission already exists in VirusTotal before uploading the file. This helps to avoid tipping off the attacker and compromising the integrity of the analysis process. By using the hash, analysts can check the reputation of the file and the detection rates of different antivirus engines without revealing any additional information to potential attackers. Figure 6-3 demonstrates a hash matching a malicious file on VirusTotal.

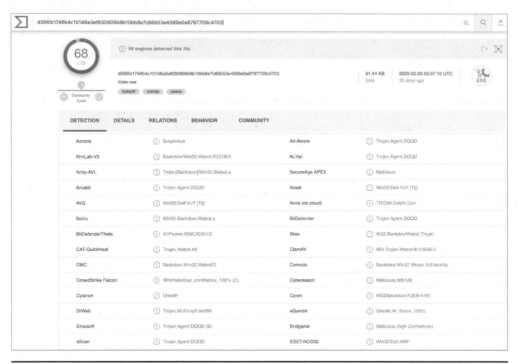

Figure 6-3 VirusTotal showing the given hash corresponds to a malicious file

VT API

The VirusTotal API provides powerful features for security analysts looking to automate their workflows. The API allows for the submission of files and hashes as well as provides access to the results of previous scans. Here are some of the most commonly used or useful endpoints for security analysts:

- **File scanning** The file scanning endpoint allows you to upload a file and receive the analysis results. You can also specify parameters such as notify_url to receive a webhook when the analysis is complete. This endpoint is useful for automating the scanning of files as part of a larger workflow.

- **File behavior** The file behavior endpoint provides information about the behavior of a file when it is executed. This can include network connections made by the file, registry changes, and other indicators of malicious behavior. This endpoint is useful for understanding the impact of a file on a system.

- **File relationships** The file relationships endpoint provides information about other files that are related to a particular file. This can include files that are similar to the original file, or files that have been identified as being part of the same malware family. This endpoint is useful for understanding the scope of a particular threat.

PART I

- **Hash scanning**   The hash scanning endpoint allows you to submit a hash and receive the analysis results. This is useful for determining the reputation of a file without actually uploading the file itself.

- **Hash relationships**   The hash relationships endpoint provides information about other hashes that are related to a particular hash. This can include hashes that are similar to the original hash as well as hashes that have been identified as being part of the same malware family.

Before moving on, it is worth noting that this chapter has only scratched the surface of VirusTotal's capabilities. The tool offers a range of additional features, such as the ability to scan IP addresses, domains, and URLs as well as a powerful hunting capability.

As a security analyst, it is highly likely that you will encounter VirusTotal on a regular basis, and we encourage you to get hands-on experience with the tool to explore its full potential.

 EXAM TIP   Although the VirusTotal API will not be covered directly on the exam, the details are provided here for the sake of reference and completeness.

Joe Sandbox

Joe Sandbox is a malware analysis tool that provides a secure environment for analyzing samples and generating detailed reports on their behavior and capabilities. Joe offers a wide range of capabilities that help improve malware detection, analysis, and response. By using Joe Sandbox, you can hunt for IoCs in various sources, customize your analysis environment, and leverage machine learning algorithms to enhance your malware detection capabilities. Additionally, its collaboration and integration capabilities allow you to work with others and automate threat detection and response workflows. Here are some of the most prominent capabilities of Joe Sandbox:

- **Malware analysis**   Joe Sandbox analyzes malware behavior and provides detailed reports on the malware's activities and capabilities.

- **Sandboxing**   Joe Sandbox provides a secure environment for running malware samples without risking damage to the host system.

- **Threat hunting**   Joe Sandbox can automatically hunt for IoCs in a wide range of sources, including e-mail attachments, network traffic, and disk images.

- **Customization**   Joe Sandbox allows users to customize the analysis environment, including the use of custom virtual machines and network configurations.

- **Collaboration**   Joe Sandbox allows users to share analysis results and collaborate on malware analysis with others.

- **Integration**   Joe Sandbox can be integrated with other security tools and platforms, such as security information and event management (SIEM) systems and security orchestration, automation, and response (SOAR) solutions, to automate threat detection and response workflows.

- **Machine learning** Joe Sandbox leverages machine learning algorithms to enhance its malware detection capabilities.

- **API** Joe Sandbox provides a powerful API that enables users to automate various tasks, such as malware submission and analysis retrieval.

Cuckoo Sandbox

Cuckoo is an open source malware analysis platform that allows security analysts to examine suspicious files and URLs in a secure and isolated environment. It has become a popular choice for malware analysis due to its extensible architecture and the wide range of features it provides. With Cuckoo, you can analyze various file formats, including PDFs, executables, and Office documents, and monitor network traffic to understand how the malware behaves.

Cuckoo provides a range of analysis options and customization features that allow security analysts to tailor their analyses to meet their specific needs. Additionally, it has powerful integration capabilities that enable it to work with other security tools and platforms to automate the analysis process and enhance threat detection and response workflows.

Here are some of the most prominent capabilities of Cuckoo:

- **Malware analysis** Cuckoo analyzes malware behavior and provides detailed reports on the malware's activities and capabilities.

- **Sandboxing** Cuckoo provides a secure environment for running malware samples without risking damage to the host system.

- **Threat hunting** Cuckoo can automatically hunt for IoCs in a wide range of sources, including e-mail attachments, network traffic, and disk images.

- **Customization** Cuckoo allows users to customize the analysis environment, including the use of custom virtual machines and network configurations.

- **Collaboration** Cuckoo allows users to share analysis results and collaborate on malware analysis with others.

- **Integration** Cuckoo can be integrated with other security tools and platforms, such as SIEMs and SOARs, to automate threat detection and response workflows.

- **Reporting** Cuckoo provides detailed and customizable reports on malware analysis results.

- **API** Cuckoo provides a powerful API that enables users to automate various tasks, such as malware submission and analysis retrieval.

 EXAM TIP The specific capabilities of Joe Sandbox and Cuckoo Sandbox will not be covered on the test. However, the reader should be familiar with the high-level capabilities provided by these tools.

Chapter Review

In this chapter, we explored various network and file analysis tools that are instrumental in identifying and investigating potential threats.

In the "Network Analysis Tools" section, we delved into the power of tools like BPF, tcpdump, Wireshark, TShark, WHOIS, and the AbuseIPDB platform. These tools enable security analysts to capture and analyze network traffic, allowing them to inspect packets, identify suspicious activities, and extract valuable information for further investigation. Whether it's filtering packets based on specific criteria, examining protocol details, or uncovering network-related IoCs, these tools offer in-depth visibility into network communications.

The "File Analysis Tools" section focused on the critical role of tools such as strings, hashing utilities, Joe Sandbox, Cuckoo Sandbox, and the VirusTotal platform. These tools empower analysts to perform static and dynamic analysis of files, uncover hidden information, and identify malicious attributes. From extracting human-readable strings to generating file hashes, conducting malware scans, and executing files in sandbox environments, these tools provide invaluable insights into the behavior and nature of potentially malicious files.

Throughout the chapter, we emphasized the importance of these tools in detecting, analyzing, and understanding malicious activities. By utilizing network analysis tools, analysts can uncover suspicious network behavior, identify IoCs, and gain visibility into the techniques employed by attackers. On the other hand, file analysis tools enable the extraction of valuable artifacts, identification of malicious files, and the assessment of their potential impact on systems and networks.

Questions

1. How does Wireshark support SSL/TLS decryption?

   A. Wireshark supports SSL/TLS decryption through the use of filters.

   B. Wireshark supports SSL/TLS decryption through the use of custom Lua scripts.

   C. Wireshark supports SSL/TLS decryption through the use of SSL/TLS keys.

   D. Wireshark does not support SSL/TLS decryption.

2. What is the purpose of the strings utility?

   A. To encrypt and decrypt sensitive data in malware samples

   B. To analyze human-readable text strings in binary and executable files

   C. To scan for malware infections on a network

   D. To monitor network traffic in real time

3. What are some of the hashing utilities available on Windows, Linux, and Mac?

   A. WHOIS and VirusTotal

   B. CertUtil, shasum, and md5sum

   C. Symantec Endpoint Detection and Response and Carbon Black

   D. awk, sed, and grep

4. What is the purpose of using a file hash to check if a submission already exists in VirusTotal before uploading the file?

   A. To avoid tipping off the attacker and compromising the integrity of the analysis process

   B. To identify whether or not a file is malicious

   C. To automate file scanning as part of a larger workflow

   D. To provide access to the results of previous scans

5. What is the advantage of using BPF filters in network analysis tools?

   A. Improved performance and processing speed

   B. Reduction in storage and memory usage

   C. Precise filtering based on specific criteria

   D. All of the above

6. What is one of the categories of abuse that can be reported on AbuseIPDB?

   A. Software vulnerabilities

   B. E-mail spam

   C. Website design flaws

   D. Network latency issues

Answers

1. **C.** Wireshark supports SSL/TLS decryption through the use of SSL/TLS keys.

2. **B.** The purpose of the strings utility is to analyze human-readable text strings in binary and executable files.

3. **B.** Some of the hashing utilities available on Windows, macOS, and Linux are CertUtil, shasum, and md5sum, respectively.

4. **A.** The purpose of using a file hash to check if a submission already exists in VirusTotal before uploading the file is to avoid tipping off the attacker and compromising the integrity of the analysis process.

5. **D.** Some advantages of using BPF filters in network analysis tools are improved performance and processing speed, reduction in storage and memory usage, and precise filtering based on specific criteria.

6. **D.** AbuseIPDB is an IP reputation service and is therefore focused on the reporting of potential malicious activities, not flaws or network-related issues.

Fundamentals of Threat Intelligence

In this chapter you will learn:

- The fundamentals of threat intelligence
- Characteristics of various threat actors
- Common intelligence sources and the intelligence cycle
- Information sharing best practices
- Effective use of indicators of compromise

Every battle is won before it is ever fought.

—Sun Tzu

Modern networks are incredibly complex entities whose successful and ongoing defense requires a deep understanding of what is present on the network, what weaknesses exist, and who might be targeting them. Getting insight into network activity allows for greater agility in order to outmaneuver increasingly sophisticated threat actors, but not every organization can afford to invest in the next-generation detection and prevention technology year after year. Furthermore, doing so is often not as effective as investing in quality analysts who can collect and quickly understand data about threats facing the organization.

Threat data, when given the appropriate context, results in the creation of *threat intelligence,* or the knowledge of malicious actors and their behaviors; this knowledge enables defenders to gain a better understanding of their operational environments. Several products can be used to provide decision-makers with a clear picture of what's actually happening on the network, which makes for more confident decision-making, improves operator response time, and, in the worst case, reduces recovery time for the organization in the event of an incident. Additionally, this knowledge has the effect of making it much more difficult for an adversary to gain a foothold in the network in the first place. Sergio Caltagirone, coauthor of "The Diamond Model of Intrusion Analysis" (2013), defines cyber threat intelligence as "actionable knowledge and insight on adversaries and their malicious activities enabling defenders and their organizations to reduce harm through better security decision-making." Without a doubt, a good threat intelligence program is a necessary component of any modern information security program. Formulating a

Discipline	Description
SIGINT	*Signals intelligence* is intelligence gathering done via intercepts of communications and electronic and/or instrumentation transmissions.
HUMINT	*Human intelligence* is derived from human sources through overt, covert, or clandestine methods.
OSINT	*Open source intelligence* is the collection and analysis of publicly available information appearing in print or electronic form.
MASINT	*Measurement and signature intelligence* is intelligence derived from data other than imagery and SIGINT.
GEOINT	*Geospatial intelligence* is the analysis of imagery and geospatial data concerning security-related activities on the earth.
All Source	This intelligence is derived from every available source on a subject or topic.

Table 7-1 A Sample of Intelligence Disciplines

brief definition of so broad a term as "intelligence" is a massive challenge, but fortunately we can borrow from decades of studies on the primitives of intelligence analysis for the purposes of defining threat intelligence.

 EXAM TIP   When applying context to a situation and where threat intelligence can provide immediate positive impact, consider how an enterprise may do vulnerability management for its production systems. For example, if patching critical systems, a security analyst could use valid threat intelligence to help assess risks, prioritize workloads, and guide the teams' prioritization of key systems that need to be remediated.

Foundations of Intelligence

Traditional intelligence involves the collecting and processing of information about foreign countries and their agents. Usually conducted on behalf of a government, intelligence activities are carried out using nonattributable methods in foreign areas to further foreign policy goals and support national security. Another key aspect is the protection of the intelligence actions, the people and organizations involved, and the resulting intelligence products, such as threat assessments and other reports, against unauthorized disclosure. Classically, intelligence is divided into the areas from which it is collected, as shown in Table 7-1. Functionally, a government may align one or several agencies with an intelligence discipline.

Threat Classification

Before we go too deeply into the technical details regarding threats you may encounter while preparing for or responding to an incident, you need to understand the term *incident,* which we use to describe any action that results in direct harm to your system or increases the likelihood of unauthorized exposure of your sensitive data. Your first step in knowing that something is harmful and out of place is to understand what "normal" looks like. In other words, establishing a baseline of your systems is the first step in preparing for an incident. If you don't know what normal is, it becomes incredibly difficult for you to see the warning signs of an attack. Without a baseline for comparison, you will likely know that you've been breached only when your systems go offline. Making a plan for incident response isn't just a good idea—it may be compulsory, depending on your operating environment and line of business. As your organization's security expert, you will be entrusted to implement technical measures and recommend policy that keeps personal data safe while keeping your organization out of court.

Known Threats vs. Unknown Threats

In attempting to find malicious activity, antivirus software and more sophisticated security devices work by using signature-based and anomaly-based methods of detection. Signature-based systems rely on prior knowledge of a threat, which means that these systems are only as good as the historical data companies have collected. Although these systems are useful for identifying threats that already exist, they don't help much with regard to threats that constantly change form or have not been previously observed; these will slip by, undetected.

The alternative is to use a solution that looks at what the executable is doing, rather than what it looks like. This kind of system relies on *heuristic analysis* to observe the commands the executable invokes, the files it writes, and any attempts to conceal itself. Often, these heuristic systems will sandbox a file in a virtual operating system and allow it to perform what it was designed to do in that separate environment.

As malware is evolving, security practices are shifting to reduce the number of assumptions made when developing security policy. A report that indicates that no threat is present just means that the scanning engine couldn't find a match, and a clean report isn't worth much if the methods of detection aren't able to detect the newest types of threats. In other words, the absence of evidence is not evidence of absence. Vulnerabilities and threats are being discovered at a rate that outpaces what traditional detection technologies can spot. Because threats still exist, even if we cannot detect them, we must either evolve our detection techniques or treat the entire network as an untrusted environment. There is nothing inherently wrong about the latter; it just requires a major shift in thinking about how we design our networks.

Zero-Day

The term *zero-day*, once used exclusively among security professionals, is quickly becoming part of the public dialect. It refers to either a vulnerability or exploit never before seen in public. A *zero-day vulnerability* is a flaw in a piece of software that the vendor is unaware of and therefore has not issued a patch or advisory for. The code written to take advantage of this flaw is called the *zero-day exploit*. When writing software, vendors often focus on providing usability and getting the most functional product out to market as quickly as possible. This often results in products that require numerous updates as more users interact with the software. Ideally, the number of vulnerabilities decreases as time progresses, as software adoption increases, and as patches are issued. However, this doesn't mean that you should let your guard down because of some sense of increased security.

Rather, you should be more vigilant; even if an environment has protective software in place, it's defenseless should a zero-day exploit be used against it.

The Emergence of the Exploit Marketplace

Zero-day exploits were once extremely rare, but the security community has observed a significant uptick in their usage and discovery. As security companies improve their software, malware writers have worked to evolve their products to evade these systems, creating a malware arms race of sorts. Modern zero-day vulnerabilities are viewed as extremely valuable to some malicious users and criminal groups, and as with anything else of perceived value, markets have formed. Black markets for zero-day exploits exist with ample participation from criminal groups. On the opposite end of the spectrum, vendors have used *bug bounty* programs to supplement internal vulnerability discovery, inviting researchers and hackers to actively probe their software for bugs in exchange for money and prizes. Even the US Pentagon, a traditionally bureaucratic and risk-averse organization, saw the value in crowd-sourcing security in this way. In March 2016, it launched the "Hack the Pentagon" challenge—a pilot program designed to identify security vulnerabilities on public-facing Department of Defense sites.

Preparing to face unknown and advanced threats like zero-day exploits requires a sound methodology that includes technical and operational best practices. The protection of critical business assets and sensitive data should never be trusted to a single solution. You should be wary of solutions that suggest they are one-stop shops for dealing with these threats, because you are essentially placing the entire organization's fate in a single point of failure. Although the word "response" is part of your incident response plan, your team should develop a methodology that includes proactive efforts as well. This approach should involve active efforts to discover new threats that have not yet impacted the organization. Sources for this information include research organizations and threat intelligence providers. The SANS Internet Storm Center and the CERT Coordination Center at Carnegie Mellon University are two great resources for discovering the latest software bugs. Armed with new knowledge about attacker trends and techniques, you may be able to detect malicious traffic before it has a chance to do any harm. Additionally, you will give your security team time to develop controls to mitigate security incidents in the case a countermeasure or patch is not available.

Threat Actors

Threat actors are not equal in terms of motivation and capability; neither are they all necessarily overtly malicious. You will learn that the term "threat actor" is wide-ranging and can be categorized by sophistication as well as intent. We'll describe threat actors using several groups, but it's important for you to understand that these classifications are not mutually exclusive. Threat actors and threat actor groups may span multiple classifications, usually depending on the targets and time frame of the activity we're considering.

Advanced Persistent Threats

In 2003, analysts discovered a series of coordinated attacks against the Department of Defense, Department of Energy, NASA, and the Department of Justice. Discovered to have been in progress for at least three years by that point, the actors appeared to be on a mission and took extraordinary steps to hide evidence of their existence. These events, known later as "Titan Rain," would be classified as the work of an advanced persistent threat (APT), which refers to any number of stealthy and continuous computer hacking efforts, often coordinated and executed by an organization or government with significant resources. The goal for an APT is to gain and maintain persistent access to target systems while remaining undetected. Attack vectors often include spam messages, infected media, social engineering, and supply-chain compromise. The support infrastructure behind their operations, their tactics, techniques, and procedures (TTPs) during operations, and the types of targets they choose are all part of what makes APTs stand out. It's useful to analyze each word in the APT acronym to identify the key discriminators between APT and other actors.

Advanced

The operators behind these campaigns are often well equipped and use techniques that indicate formal training and significant funding. Their attacks indicate a high degree of coordination between technical and nontechnical information sources. These threats are often backed with a full spectrum of intelligence support—from digital surveillance methods to traditional techniques focused on human targets.

Persistent

Because these campaigns are often coordinated by government and military organizations, it shouldn't be surprising that each operator is focused on a specific task rather than rooting around without direction. Operators will often ignore opportunistic targets and remain focused on their piece of the campaign. This behavior implies strict rules of engagement and an emphasis on consistency and persistence above all else.

Threat

APTs do not exist in a bubble. Their campaigns show capability and intent—aspects that highlight their use as the technical implementation of a political plan. Like a military operation, APT campaigns often serve as an extension of political will. Although their code might be executed by machines, the APT framework is designed and coordinated by humans with a specific goal in mind. Because of the complex nature of APTs, it may be difficult to handle them alone. The concept of automatic threat intelligence sharing is a recent development in the security community. Because speed is often the discriminator between a successful and an unsuccessful campaign, many vendors provide solutions that automatically share threat data and orchestrate technical countermeasures for them.

 NOTE Advanced persistent threats, regardless of affiliation, are characterized by resourcing, consistency, and a military-like efficiency during their actions to compromise systems, steal data, and cover their tracks.

Hacktivists

Hacktivists are threat actors that typically operate with less resourcing than their nation-state counterparts but nonetheless work to coordinate efforts to bring light to an issue or promote a cause. They often rely on readily available tools and mass participation to achieve their desired effects against a target. Though not always the case, their actions often have little lasting damage to their targets. Hacktivists are also known to use social media and defacement tactics to affect the reputation of their targets, hoping to erode public trust and confidence in their targets. Unlike other threat actors, hacktivists rarely seek to operate with stealth and look to bring attention to their cause along with notoriety for their own organization. As defenders, knowing that hacktivists frequently employ techniques to affect the availability of a system, we can use defensive techniques to mitigate denial-of-service (DoS) attacks. Furthermore, we can reduce the likelihood of successful social engineering efforts or unauthorized access to services and applications by enforcing multifactor authentication on system and social media accounts.

Organized Crime

Threat actors operating on behalf of organized crime groups are becoming an increasingly visible challenge for enterprise defenders to confront. Whether targeting theft of intellectual property or personal user data, these criminals' primary objective is to make money by selling stolen data. When compared to nation-state actors, organized crime may have a more moderate sophistication level, but as financial gain is often the goal, attacks will many times include the use of cryptojacking, ransomware, and bulk data exfiltration techniques. Despite having a well-understood operational model, organized crime threat actors still contribute to a significant percentage of security incidents. This is due in part to the comparatively low-risk, high-reward nature of their activities and the ease with which they can hide their activities online. Moreover, the rise in usage of digital currencies worldwide has allowed for these criminals to launder vast sums of money more easily.

Nation-States

Nation-state threat actors are frequently among the most sophisticated adversaries, with dedicated infrastructure, training resources, and operational support behind their activities. Their activities are characterized by extensive planning and coordination and often reflect the strong government or military influence behind them. Like many government-supported operations, nation-state threat actor activities are often conducted to achieve political, economic, or strategic military goals. Identifying and tracking these actors can be difficult, since many of the individuals involved use common techniques across teams, operate behind robust infrastructure, and use methods to actively obfuscate their behavior. Alternatively, they may use toolsets that are not often seen or impossible to detect at the time of the security event, such as a zero-day exploit.

There are a few interesting notes about nation-state operations that make them unique. The first is that, depending on the countries involved, businesses can quickly become a part of the activity in either a direct or supporting capacity. Second, more sophisticated threat actors may incorporate false flag techniques, performing activities that lead defenders to falsely attribute their activity to another. Given the high degree of coordination that some nation-state actor activities require, this is becoming a frequent challenge for defenders to address. Finally, there's an aspect of perspective worth noting here: one nation's intelligence apparatus is another nation's malicious actor.

Script Kiddies

The term "script kiddie" was coined to describe inexperienced or "wannabe" hackers who have very minimal skills. These novices essentially cut-and-paste exploit code or use pre-built GUI tools developed by more experienced hackers without understanding the intricacies of the tool or the attack itself. They will often use easy-to-run exploits that are also simple to defend against. Script kiddies may or may not develop into more knowledgeable, experienced hackers, depending on their motivation. Some of these novices may only be interested in seeing what fun they can have or trouble they can get into without really thinking about the consequences of their actions. Many will quickly become disinterested in hacking after a few unsuccessful attempts and move on to another pastime, but some will learn from their mistakes and eventually come to understand the finer details of exploitation, developing more sophisticated tools on their own.

Insider Threats

Insider threat actors work within an organization and represent a particularly high risk of causing catastrophic damage due to their privileged access to internal resources. Because access is often an early goal for insider threat actors, having access as result of a role or position in a company often means that traditional perimeter-focused security mechanisms are not effective in detecting and stopping their destructive activity. To address internal threats, it's critical that the security program is designed in a way that adheres to the principle of least privilege as it relates to access. Furthermore, network security devices should be configured to allow or deny access based on robust access control rules and not simply as a result of a device's location within the network. Insider threats are unique in that they may be influenced by a combination of factors—from personal to organizational and technical. Accordingly, the solution to address them cannot be one-dimensional and must include policies, procedures, and technologies to mitigate the overall threat. For example, mandating annual training on cybersecurity awareness along with implementing technical controls to prevent unauthorized file access have been shown to reduce the occurrence and impact of insider threat events.

Intentional

Intentional insider threat actors may be employees, contractors, or business partners with established access to internal service, or any of these who have severed ties with the organization but have not lost access. Intentional actors behave in a manner that may be damaging to the organization, through data theft, data deletion, or vandalism. In many cases, these malicious insiders look to acts against the organization with the goal of personal financial gain, revenge, or both. Malicious insiders looking to steal intellectual property in order to facilitate a secondary income source will typically remove data slowly to avoid detection. A disgruntled employee, on the other hand, may work deliberately to sabotage an organization's critical systems. As defenders, we should be aware of anomalous activity such as high-volume network activity or indiscriminate file access attempts, especially following an employee's resignation or firing.

Unintentional

It's easy to think of insider threats as actors with malicious intent, but other factors may lead to an increased insider threat risk. Lack of security education, negligence, and human error are among the top contributors to unintentional insider security events. Such actions, though unwitting, may cause as much harm as those done intentionally by other threat actors. Hanlon's razor famously expresses that one shouldn't attribute to malice that which can be adequately explained by ignorance (or stupidity, per the actual adage). Mistakes happen, and it may be counterproductive for a security team to treat every user who is responsible for a security incident as a willful malicious actor. Not only would this ensure that the user would have a difficult learning experience, but it may lull the security team into the perception that the root issue is sufficiently addressed. If, for example, there are ten occurrences of data spillage that all point to a similar type of user error, perhaps the problem is less about the user and more about the usability of the system.

Supply Chain Threats

A source of threats that has only really been considered and analyzed in the past decade is the supply chain for organizations. This includes sources from which an organization receives its hardware, software, and other supplies and can include primary, secondary, or tertiary providers who can threaten organizations from anywhere along the chain, even a few indirect links away from the organization. Supply chain threats not only can come from suppliers but can also be inadvertently passed along to an organization's customers, who receive *their* hardware, software, or supplies from the organization. If a piece of hardware is compromised—for example, with eavesdropping capabilities embedded into its computer chips—an organization may load the hardware with its own software and unknowingly pass that compromised system on to its customer.

Commodity Malware

Commodity malware includes any pervasive malicious software that's sold to threat actors. Often made available in underground communities, this type of malware enables criminals to focus less on improving their technical sophistication and more on optimizing their illegal operations. There's a well-known military axiom that states that great organizations do routine things routinely well. Correspondingly, commodity malware may not always be the most advanced or stealthy software, and good security teams will know how to handle this malware quickly and effectively.

Malware as a Service

Economic theory dictates that when there is a high demand for something, enterprising individuals will work toward creating the supply. This concept applies to malware in the rise of a phenomenon known as Malware as a Service (MaaS), which is malware designed, built, and sold to customers based on their individual specifications. Like any other piece of software, this malware software may offer customer support and release periodic updates, complete with bug fixes and improvements. Moreover, many of these tools are offered as a subscription service and based in the cloud, making it more attractive for potential "customers" to acquire, access, and suspend these services.

Tactics, Techniques, and Procedures

It would take far more than this book to discuss all the tactics, techniques, and procedures (TTPs) used to collect, analyze, and make use of threat intelligence; however, there are a few key concepts you should understand, particularly for the exam. You should be familiar with which characteristics define good threat intelligence as well as how trustworthy that intelligence can be.

Characteristics of Intelligence Source Data

Despite the many claims from vendors, there is no one solution for every organization when it comes to threat data and intelligence. Organizations must be able to map the threat intelligence products they acquire or produce to some distinct aspect of their threat profile. In short, analysts must prioritize data that is most relevant to their specific environment to ensure that they are not bogged down in unmanageable noise and that they can produce actionable, timely, and consistent results. Generic threat intelligence developed for environments that are too dissimilar from those in which the team is operating will not satisfy the organization's unique requirements. Furthermore, developing intelligence for environments that are not specific enough may result in a waste of resources. Security analysts working in a manufacturing environment, for example, must understand their environment and seek out and obtain threat intelligence products specific to manufacturing networks, in addition to general threat information. Intelligence must include context and provide recommendations if it is to have maximum value for decision-makers.

Good threat intelligence provides three critical elements to analysts so that they can appropriately provide answers to decision-makers. The intelligence must describe the threat using consistent and clear language, illustrate the impact to the business in terms that are relevant to the business, and provide a clear set of recommended actions. In addition to being complete, good threat intelligence often has three other characteristics: timeliness, relevancy, and accuracy. Teams that can effectively use quality threat intelligence are able to address known gaps in their security posture and apply this data and context to nearly every aspect of their security operations; this will improve detection, enhance response, and strengthen prevention. Furthermore, the rate of noise generation and intelligence failure is inversely proportional to the timeliness, relevancy, and accuracy of the threat intelligence information.

Timeliness

All intelligence, whether in a traditional military operation or as it applies to information security, has a temporal dimension. After all, intelligence considers environmental conditions as a part of context, so it makes sense that it is most useful given the time-related stipulations within the intelligence requirements. You may find that intelligence may be extremely useful at one time and completely useless at another. Accordingly, intelligence that is not delivered in a timely manner is not as useful to decision-makers.

Relevancy

As discussed earlier, internal network data invariably yields the most useful threat intelligence because it reflects the nuances of an organization. Additionally, relevancy varies based on the levels of operation, even within the same organization. It is therefore important to prepare threat intelligence products for the correct audience. Details about the exact nature of an adversary's technical capabilities, for example, may not be as useful for a strategic audience as they may be for a detection team analyst. This is an easy point to overlook, but intelligence requires human attention to consume and process, so irrelevant information is costly in terms of time and resources. Providing inconsequential intelligence is distracting, but it may be counterproductive as well.

Accuracy

Although it may seem self-evident in a field such as information security, accuracy is critical to enable a decision-maker to draw reliable conclusions and pursue a recommended course of action. The information must be factually correct. Acknowledging that it may be unrealistic to have an exact understanding of the operational environment at any given time, an analyst must at minimum convey facts as they exist.

 NOTE Bias is a reality of human nature and is a deeply complicated matter. As humans, we attempt to make the world simpler by introducing assumptions to allow for quick decisions, particularly in a dangerous or confusing situation. As security analysts, it's important for us to recognize that although it may be impossible to remove all of our biases, we must account for them in our analysis process. We can limit bias by surrounding ourselves with teammates who bring a diversity of thought and backgrounds during the analysis process as well as by using structured analytical techniques.

Confidence Levels

In a continuous effort to apply more rigorous standards to analytical assessment, intelligence providers often use three levels of analytic confidence made using *estimative language*. Estimative language aims to communicate intelligence assessments while acknowledging the existence of incomplete or fragmented information. The statements should not be seen as fact or proof but rather as judgments based on the analysis of collected information. As described next, *confidence levels* reflect the scope and quality of the information supporting these judgments:

- A *high* confidence level means that threat assessments are based on high-quality information, and/or the nature of the issue makes it possible to render a solid judgment. The judgement is not to be interpreted as fact and still has a possibility of being incorrect.

- A *moderate* confidence level means that the information is credibly sourced and plausible but is not of sufficient quality or lacks corroboration to warrant a higher level of confidence.

- A *low* confidence level means that the information acquired is questionable or implausible and may be too fragmented or poorly corroborated to make solid analytic inferences. Additionally, significant concerns about sources may exist.

Similar to, and somewhat related to confidence levels, *threat ratings* rank a threat's potential danger level. This is often measured on a scale of 0 to 5, with 5 representing the most critical type of threat. The confidence rating (level) is a ranking of how confident we are that a threat rating is accurate. This is often measured on a scale of 0 to 100, with 100 representing the highest level of confidence. Note that confidence levels only apply to our trust in the source of threat information, not the likelihood that a threat will materialize.

Our ability to classify threats into confidence levels is largely dependent on three things:

- Our ability to directly observe the threat
- The threat's feasibility
- Whether or not the threat can be corroborated with legitimate sources

A higher confidence rating in a threat grants us reasonable assurance that our cybersecurity response to the threat will not be in vain. Table 7-2 correlates threat types with confidence ratings.

Table 7-2
Threat Types and Their Confidence Ratings

Threat Type	Confidence Rating
Unknown	0
Discredited	1
Improbable	2–29
Doubtful	30–49
Possible	50–69
Probable	70–89
Confirmed	90–100

Collection Methods and Sources

Threat intelligence teams outside of the government do not often have the luxury of the on-call intelligence assets available to those within government. Energy companies and Internet service providers (ISPs) do not deploy HUMINT agents or have SIGINT operations, but they will focus on using whatever public, commercial, or in-house resources are available. Fortunately, there are a number of free and paid sources to help teams meet their intelligence requirements, including commercial threat intelligence providers, industry partners, and government organizations. And, of course, there's also broad monitoring of social media and news for relevant data.

Open Source

There are many ways to acquire free data associated with actor activity, be it malicious or benign. A common way to do this without interacting with threat actors is by gathering open source intelligence (OSINT), which is free information that's collected in legitimate ways from public sources such as news outlets, libraries, and search engines. Using OSINT, practitioners can begin to answer questions critical to the intelligence process. How can I create actionable threat intelligence from a variety of data sources? How can I share this threat information with the broader community, and what mechanism should I use? How can I use public information to limit the organization's exposure while enabling my understanding of what adversaries know about the organization?

There are several additional benefits to developing OSINT skills. Threat analysts often use OSINT sources to help them keep pace with security industry trends and discussions in near real time. This is a useful way for practitioners to understand what may be coming around the corner, even if the content comes in an irregular or inconsistent manner. Additionally, many security analysts rely on publicly available data sets to perform research on common threat indicators and mitigating controls. The information gleaned may also help in post-incident forensics efforts or in support of penetration testing activities.

From an adversary point of view, it is almost always preferable to get information about a target without directly touching it. Why? Because the less it is touched, the fewer fingerprints (or log entries) are left behind for the defenders and investigators to find. In an ideal case, adversaries gain all the information they need to compromise a target successfully without visiting it once by using OSINT techniques. *Passive reconnaissance,* for example, is the process by which an adversary acquires information about a target network without directly interacting with it. This technique can be focused on individuals as well as companies. Just like individuals, many companies maintain a public face that can give outsiders a glimpse into their internal operations. In the sections that follow, we describe some of the most useful sources of OSINT with which you should be familiar.

Google

Google's vision is to organize all the data in the world and make it accessible for everyone in a useful way. It should therefore not be surprising that Google can help an attacker gather a remarkable amount of information about any individual, organization, or network.

Operator	Restricts Search Results to	Example
site:	The specified domain or site	site:apache.org
inurl:	Having the specified text in the URL	inurl:/administrator/index.php
filetype:	The indicated type of file	filetype:xls
intitle:	Pages with the indicated text in their title	intitle:vitae
link:	Pages that contain a link to the indicated site or URL	link:www.google.com
cache:	Google's latest cached copies of the results	cache:www.eff.org

Table 7-3   Useful Google Search Operators

The use of this search engine for target reconnaissance purposes drew much attention in the early 2000s, when security researcher Johnny Long started collecting and sharing examples of search queries that revealed vulnerable systems. These queries made use of advanced operators that are meant to allow Google users to refine their searches. Though the list of operators is too long to include in this book, Table 7-3 lists some of the ones we've found most useful over the years. Note that many others are available from a variety of online sources, and that some of these operators can be combined in a search.

Suppose your organization has a number of web servers. A potentially dangerous misconfiguration would be to allow a server to display directory listings to clients. This means that instead of seeing a rendered web page, the visitor could see a list of all the files (HTML, PHP, CSS, and so on) in that directory within the server. Sometimes, for a variety of reasons, it is necessary to enable such listings. More often, however, they are the result of a misconfigured and potentially vulnerable web server. If you wanted to search an organization for such vulnerable server directories, you would type the following into your Google search box, substituting the actual domain or URL in the space delineated by angle brackets:

```
site:<targetdomain or URL> intitle:"index of" "parent directory"
```

This would return all the pages in your target domain that Google has indexed as having directory listings.

You might then be tempted to click one of the links returned by Google, but this would directly connect you to the target domain and leave evidence there of your activities. Instead, you can use a page cached by Google as part of its indexing process. To see this page instead of the actual target, look for the downward arrow immediately to the right of the page link. Clicking it will give you the option to select "Cached" rather than connecting to the target (see Figure 7-1).

Figure 7-1   Using Google cached pages

EXAM TIP You will not be required to know the specific symbols and words required for advanced Google searches, but it's useful as a security analyst to understand the various methods of refining search engine results, such as Boolean logic, word order, and search operators.

Internet Registries

Another useful source of information about networks is the multiple registries necessary to keep the Internet working. Routable Internet Protocol (IP) addresses as well as domain names need to be globally unique, which means that there must be some mechanism for ensuring that no two entities use the same IP address or domain. The way we, as a global community, manage this deconfliction is through the nonprofit corporations described next. They offer some useful details about the footprint of an organization in cyberspace.

Regional Internet Registries As Table 7-4 shows, five separate corporations control the assignment of IP addresses throughout the world. They are known as the *regional Internet registries* (RIRs), and each has an assigned geographical area of responsibility. Thus, entities wishing to acquire an IP address in Canada, the United States, or most of the Caribbean would deal (directly or through intermediaries) with the American Registry for Internet Numbers (ARIN). The activities of the five registries are coordinated through the Number Resource Organization (NRO), which also provides a detailed listing of each country's assigned RIR.

EXAM TIP You do not need to know the RIRs, but you do need to understand what information is available through these organizations together with the Internet Corporation for Assigned Names and Numbers (ICANN).

Domain Name System The Internet could not function the way it does today without the Domain Name System (DNS). Although DNS is a vital component of modern networks, many users are unaware of its existence and importance to the proper functionality of the Web. DNS is the mechanism responsible for associating domain names, such as www.google.com, with their server's IP address(es), and vice versa. Without DNS, you'd be required to memorize and input the full IP address for any website you wanted to visit instead of the easy-to-remember uniform resource locator (URL). Using tools such as nslookup, host, and dig in the command line, administrators troubleshoot

Table 7-4 The Regional Internet Registries	Registry	Geographic Region
	AFRINIC	Africa and portions of the Indian Ocean
	APNIC	Portions of Asia and portions of Oceania
	ARIN	Canada, many Caribbean and North Atlantic islands, and the United States
	LACNIC	Latin America and portions of the Caribbean
	RIPE NCC	Europe, the Middle East, and Central Asia

DNS and network problems. Using the same tools, an attacker can interrogate the DNS server to derive information about the network. In some cases, attackers can automate this process to reach across many DNS servers in a practice called *DNS harvesting*.

At times, it may be necessary to replicate a DNS server's contents across multiple DNS servers through an action called a *zone transfer*. With a zone transfer, it is possible to capture a full snapshot of what the DNS server's records hold about the domain; this includes name servers, mail exchange records, and hostnames. Zone transfers are a potential vulnerable point in a network because the default behavior is to accept any request for a full transfer from any host on the network. Because DNS is like a map of the entire network, it's critical to restrict leakage to prevent DNS poisoning or spoofing.

NOTE DNS zone transfers are initiated by clients—whether from a secondary DNS server or network host. Because DNS data can be used to map out an entire network, it's critical that only authorized hosts be allowed to request full transfers. This is accomplished by implementing access control lists (ACLs). Zone transfers to unrecognized devices should *never* be allowed.

Whenever a domain is registered, the registrant provides details about the organization for public display. This may include name, telephone, and e-mail contact information; domain name system details; and mailing address. This information can be queried using a tool called WHOIS (pronounced *who is*). Available in both command-line and web-based versions, WHOIS can be an effective tool for incident responders and network engineers, but it's also a useful information-gathering tool for spammers, identity thieves, and any other attacker seeking to get personal and technical information about a target. For example, Figure 7-2 shows a report returned from ICANN's WHOIS web-based service.

Showing results for: google.com
Original Query: google.com

Contact Information

Registrant Contact
Name: Dns Admin
Organization: Google Inc.
Mailing Address: Please contact contact-admin@google.com, 1600 Amphitheatre Parkway, Mountain View CA 94043 US
Phone: +1.6502530000
Ext:
Fax: +1.6506188571
Fax Ext:
Email:dns-admin@google.com

Admin Contact
Name: DNS Admin
Organization: Google Inc.
Mailing Address: 1600 Amphitheatre Parkway, Mountain View CA 94043 US
Phone: +1.6506234000
Ext:
Fax: +1.6506188571
Fax Ext:
Email:dns-admin@google.com

Tech Contact
Name: DNS Admin
Organization: Google Inc.
Mailing Address: 2400 E. Bayshore Pkwy, Mountain View CA 94043 US
Phone: +1.6503300100
Ext:
Fax: +1.6506181499
Fax Ext:
Email:dns-admin@google.com

Figure 7-2 A report returned from ICANN's WHOIS web-based service

You should be aware that some registrars (the service that you go through to register a website) provide *private* registration services, in which case the registrar's information is returned during a query instead of the registrant's. Although this may seem useful to limit an organization's exposure, the tradeoff is that in the case of an emergency, it may be difficult to reach that organization.

Job Sites

Sites offering employment services are a boon for information gatherers. Think about it: the user voluntarily submits all kinds of personal data, a complete professional history, and even some individual preferences. In addition to providing personally identifiable characteristics, these sites often include indications of a member's role in a larger network. Because so many of these accounts are often identified by e-mail address, that address can often be the common link in the course of investigating a suspicious entity.

In understanding what your public exposure is, you must realize that it's trivial for attackers to automate the collection of artifacts about a target. They may perform activities to broadly collect e-mail addresses, for example, in a practice called *e-mail harvesting*. An attacker can use this to their benefit by taking advantage of business contacts to craft a more convincing phishing e-mail.

Beyond the social engineering implications for the users of these sites, companies themselves can be targets. If a company indicates that it's in the market for an administrator of a particular brand of firewall, then it's likely that the company is using that brand of firewall. This can be a powerful piece of information because it provides clues about the makeup of the company's network and potential weak points.

Social Media

Social media sites can be rich sources of threat data. Twitter and Reddit, for example, are two platforms that often provide useful artifacts during high-impact events. Company or even personal blogging sites can also be a source of useful information during these events. In addition, community and user forums covering a wide variety of topics can be used to glean insight on threat events. As a vehicle to quickly spread news of major emergencies, these platforms can be leveraged as a source for indicators about cyberattacks. They can also be highly targeted sources for personal information. As with employment sites, defenders can learn quite a bit about an attacker's social network and tendencies, should the attacker have a public persona. Conversely, an attacker can gain awareness about an individual or company using publicly available information. The online clues captured from personal pages enable an attacker to conduct *social media profiling,* which uses a target's preferences and patterns to determine their likely actions. Profiling is a critical tool for online advertisers hoping to capitalize on highly targeted ads. This information is also useful for an attacker in identifying which users in an organization may be more likely to fall victim to a *social engineering* attack, in which the perpetrator tricks the victim into revealing sensitive information or otherwise compromising the security of a system.

Many attackers know that the best route into a network is through a careless or untrained employee. In a social engineering campaign, an attacker uses deception, often influenced by the profile they've built about the target, to manipulate the target into performing an act that might not be in their best interest. These attacks come in many forms—from advanced phishing e-mails that seem to originate from a legitimate source, to phone calls requesting additional personal information. Phishing attacks continue to be a challenge for network defenders because they are becoming increasingly convincing, fooling recipients into divulging sensitive information with regularity. Despite the most advanced technical countermeasures, the human element remains the most vulnerable part of the network.

OSINT in the Real World

One of the authors of this book was asked to teach a class in an allied country to members of its nascent cyberspace workforce. The goal of the one-week course was to expose students to some open domain offensive techniques that they would have to master as a prerequisite to building their own capabilities. The first block of instructions was on reconnaissance, and the teachers of the class were given authorization to be fairly aggressive, as long as we didn't actually compromise any systems. In preparation for the class, the author performed a fairly superficial OSINT-gathering exercise and found a remarkable amount of actionable information.

Starting from the regional Internet registry, we were able to identify an individual named Daniel who appeared to be a system administrator for the target organization. We then looked him up on LinkedIn and confirmed his affiliation, but we were also able to learn all his experience, skills, and accomplishments. We then looked up the organization in a handful of prominent job sites and were able to confirm (and even refine) the tools the organization was using to manage its networks. We noted that one of the tools was notorious for having vulnerabilities. Finally, we looked up Daniel on Facebook and found a recent public post from his mother wishing him a happy birthday. At this point, we could have sent him an e-mail with a PDF resume attachment or an e-mail with a very convincing message from his "mother" with references to his three siblings and a link to a video of the birthday party. Either way, the probability of Daniel opening a malware-laden attachment or clicking a link would have been fairly high—and all it took was about 15 minutes on the Web.

Government Bulletins

Threat intelligence can come from federal, state, and local governments. This may include law enforcement sources, the Department of Defense, the Department of Homeland Security, or other agencies. These organizations often have superior threat collection and analysis resources and may dispense threat intelligence freely across different industries. Typically, broad threat intelligence applying to a wide audience that does not specify the source of the intelligence may be dispersed to everyone; however, understand that sometimes intelligence that comes from government agencies can also be more refined and targeted toward specific industries or organizations. Additionally, intelligence that comes from government bulletins is more likely less specific when it is dispersed through an open source feed; that same intelligence may be more detailed and contain additional sensitive information when it is sent to organizations such as other government agencies, law enforcement, and so on.

 NOTE Threat intelligence that comes from government sources could be either open source or closed source, depending on the level of sensitivity of the threat intelligence and the intended audience.

Response Team Intelligence

Very often, response teams such as computer emergency response teams (CERTs) and cybersecurity incident response teams (CSIRTs) may publish threat intelligence as open source based on current threats they have encountered or investigations they are conducting. These teams could be private, belonging to a commercial organization, or even government teams. Open source versions of threat intelligence may be in the form of threat bulletins that go out to a wide community; however, like government intelligence feeds, depending on the specific audience and the sensitivity of the threat data, these teams may also release threat intelligence through closed source or proprietary feeds as well.

Deep/Dark Web

The so-called *deep* or *dark web* is used by both law enforcement agencies and hackers alike. This is the part of the Internet that most casual users don't see, but it can be accessed by technically savvy criminals, terrorists, and other unscrupulous people. On the dark web, many malicious and illegal activities are conducted, such as theft, drug trade, human trafficking, and so on. For our purposes in cybersecurity, there are many things that go on in the dark web that directly affect our profession. Pirated software can be purchased, and dangerous software such as exploit code and malware is plentiful. Naturally, however, the dark web is also a good source of threat intelligence for those who are technically adept and able to access it. Not only do hackers and other malicious entities access this type of threat intelligence, but governments, law enforcement agencies, and professional security consultants do as well.

Closed Source

One of the key tenets of intelligence analysis is never relying on a single source of data when attempting to confirm a hypothesis. Ideally, analysts should look at multiple artifacts from multiple sources that support a hypothesis. Similarly, open source data is best used with corroborating data acquired from closed sources. Closed source data is any data collected covertly or as a result of privileged access. Common types of closed source data include internal network artifacts, dark web communications, details from intelligence-sharing communities, and private banking and medical records. Since closed source data tends to be higher quality, an analyst can confidently assess and verify findings using any number of intelligence analysis methods and tools. An added benefit of using multiple sources is that the practice reduces the effect of confirmation bias, or the tendency for an analyst to interpret information in a way that supports a prior strongly held belief.

Internal Network

Your organization's network will inherently have the most relevant threat data available of all the sources we'll discuss. Despite internal threat data being completely germane to every security function, many organizations eschew this data in favor of external data feeds. As an analyst, you must remember that by leveraging threat data from your own network, you can identify potential malicious activity with far greater speed and confidence than generic threat data. The most common sources for raw threat-related data include events, DNS, virtual private networks (VPNs), firewalls, and authentication system logs. By establishing a baseline of normal activity, analysts can use historical knowledge of past incident responses to improve awareness of emerging threats or ongoing malicious activity.

Classified Data

When handling closed source data, you must consider several important factors. In some cases, the mere disclosure of the data may jeopardize access to the source information, or worse, the individuals involved in the collection and analysis process. Since closed source data is sometimes not meant to be openly available to the public, there may be some legal stipulations regarding its handling. *Classified data,* or data whose unauthorized disclosure may cause harm to national security interests, is protected by several statutes that restrict its handling and sharing to trusted individuals. Those individuals undergo formal security screening to achieve clearance, or the minimum eligibility required for them to handle or access classified data. Accordingly, leaks of classified data may result in steep administrative or criminal penalties. It will be your responsibility, should you encounter classified data, to handle it appropriately and to safeguard it against unauthorized disclosure.

Traffic Light Protocol

The Traffic Light Protocol (TLP) was created by the UK government's National Infrastructure Security Coordination Centre (NISCC) to enable greater threat information sharing between organizations. It includes a set of color-coded designations that are used to guide responsible sharing of sensitive information to the appropriate audience while also protecting the information's sources. As shown in Table 7-5, the four color designations are meant to be easily understood among participants since their usage closely mirrors the colors of traffic lights around the world. Despite its usage as a data-sharing guideline, TLP is not a classification or control scheme, nor is it designed to be used as a mechanism to enforce intellectual property terms or how the data is to be used by the recipient.

Threat Intelligence Subscriptions

Commercial threat feeds that an organization subscribes to and pays for are considered closed source. This is because the feeds are not available for just anyone. The advantage of these threat feed subscriptions is that they are curated, are sometimes more detailed and of higher quality than open source threat intelligence, and are customized for the organization's business needs. For example, many commercial threat intelligence subscriptions are specially created for certain industries, such as banking and finance or healthcare.

Color	When Should It be Used?	How May It be Shared?
TLP:RED Not for disclosure; restricted to participants only	Use TLP:RED when information cannot be effectively acted upon by additional parties and could lead to impacts on a party's privacy, reputation, or operations if misused.	Recipients may not share TLP:RED information with any parties outside of the specific exchange, meeting, or conversation in which it was originally disclosed. In the context of a meeting, for example, TLP:RED information is limited to those present at the meeting. In most circumstances, TLP:RED information should be exchanged verbally or in person.
TLP:AMBER Limited disclosure; restricted to participants' organizations	Use TLP:AMBER when information requires support to be effectively acted upon, yet carries risks to privacy, reputation, or operations if shared outside of the organizations involved.	Recipients may share TLP:AMBER information only with members of their own organization as well as with clients or customers who need to know the information to protect themselves or prevent further harm. Sources are at liberty to specify additional intended limits of the sharing; these must be adhered to.
TLP:GREEN Limited disclosure; restricted to the community	Use TLP:GREEN when information is useful for the awareness of all participating organizations as well as with peers within the broader community or sector.	Recipients may share TLP:GREEN information with peers and partner organizations within their sector or community, but not via publicly accessible channels. Information in this category can be circulated widely within a particular community. TLP:GREEN information may not be released outside of the community.
TLP:WHITE Unlimited disclosure	Use TLP:WHITE when information carries minimal or no foreseeable risk of misuse, in accordance with applicable rules and procedures for public release.	Subject to standard copyright rules, TLP:WHITE information may be distributed without restriction.

Table 7-5 Traffic Light Protocol Designations (source: US Department of Homeland Security CISA website, https://www.us-cert.gov/tlp)

This means they more accurately address the threats those organizations face. Obviously, the disadvantage is their cost, which can be a low monthly fee or can get quite expensive. Many of these threat intelligence subscriptions are part of a larger package, however. For instance, purchasing and installing a next-generation firewall that has built-in intrusion detection capabilities also means you may get a threat intelligence feed subscription with that purchase. However, these types of subscriptions are typically more generic and more applicable to the type of equipment purchased.

PART I

 EXAM TIP A security analyst's main role in preventing attacks is in assessing threat intelligence. This is made difficult because there can be multiple feeds to review and assess. To make this process quicker, analysts may reduce complexity, speed up time, and increase probability by assessing a client's attack surface and then look up attacks that have taken place that may match that same industry peer company.

Threat Intelligence Sharing

As we just discussed, threat intelligence can come from a wide variety of sources. This implies that threat intelligence is shared among different organizations, whether it is between the government and commercial organizations, between private companies and communities, and so on. To effectively share threat intelligence, there must be some sort of formalized information exchange structure in place. Different organizations must be authorized to receive specific types of threat intelligence from various sources, and threat intelligence that is shared must be in a commonly understood format. Threat intelligence can certainly be shared using manual methods, but as with all other data types, automated tools can be used to share threat intelligence between organizations. Those organizations sharing this type of information must have the means to ingest and, in turn, push out threat intelligence data. In this part of the discussion on threat intelligence, we will talk about the different communities that share threat intelligence data.

Information Sharing and Analysis Communities

Information sharing communities were created to make threat data and best practices more accessible by lowering the barrier to entry and standardizing how threat information is shared and stored between organizations. While information sharing occurs frequently between industry peers, it's usually in an informal and ad hoc fashion. One of the most effective formal methods of information sharing comes through information sharing and analysis centers (ISACs). ISACs, as highlighted in Table 7-6, are industry-specific bodies that facilitate sharing of threat information and best practices relevant to the specific and common infrastructure of the industry.

 EXAM TIP There are a few questions relating to knowing about ISAC and its versions. Make sure you remember these versions and what specific resource information they provide. For example, if a security analyst is creating a threat-hunting and intelligence team in their enterprise, ISAC would more likely be used. If there is a medical- or dental-related focus, H-ISAC would more likely be used. Make sure you remember the different versions and what makes them different.

Another mechanism to achieve similar goals has been made possible via a 2015 executive order by then US president Barack Obama in the creation of information sharing and analysis organizations (ISAOs). These public information sharing organizations are similar to ISACs but without the alignment to a specific industry. ISAOs, by definition, are

ISAC	Description
Automotive (Auto-ISAC)	Founded in 2015, Auto-ISAC is the primary mechanism for global car manufacturers to share information about threats, vulnerabilities, and best practices related to connected vehicles.
Aviation (A-ISAC)	Open to trusted global private aviation companies, A-ISAC works with public aviation entities to ensure resilience of the shared global air transportation network.
Communications (NCC)	Also known as the National Coordinating Center for Communications, NCC facilitates the sharing of threat and vulnerability information among communications carriers, ISPs, satellite providers, broadcasters, vendors, and other stakeholders.
Electricity (E-ISAC)	Working with the US Department of Energy and the Electricity Subsector Coordinating Council (ESCC), the E-ISAC establishes awareness of incidents and threats relevant to the electricity sector.
Elections Infrastructure (EI-ISAC)	Established in 2018, EI-ISAC enables election bodies, from local municipalities to the federal government, to ensure the security and integrity of elections. The EI-ISAC is spearheaded by the nonprofit Center for Internet Security (CIS) and routinely collaborates with the Department of Homeland Security's Cybersecurity and Infrastructure Security Agency and the Election Infrastructure Subsector Government Coordinating Council (GCC).
Financial Services (FS-ISAC)	As one of the oldest ISACs, the FS-ISAC has existed in support of the resilience and continuity of the global financial services infrastructure with information sharing, education, and collaboration initiatives between private firms and government agencies.
Health (H-ISAC)	With membership comprising patient care providers, health IT companies, pharmaceutical companies, medical device manufacturers, and labs, H-ISAC exists to maintain the continuity of the health sector against cyber and physical threats.
Information Technology (IT-ISAC)	Operating since 2001, IT-ISAC has provided a forum for members of the IT sector to continuously share high-volume indicators related to their sector.
MultiState (MS-ISAC)	The MS-ISAC provides resources for information sharing for the nation's state, local, tribal, and territorial governments focused on response to and recovery from security events.

Table 7-6   A List and Description of Several ISACs

designed to be voluntary, transparent, inclusive, and flexible. Additionally, they are strongly encouraged to provide actionable products. Threat intelligence sharing is also discussed in Chapter 8 in the context of applying threat intelligence to organizational security.

Managing Indicators of Compromise

In discussing threat data, the term *indicator* will come up often to describe some observable characteristic, effect, or artifact encountered on the network. Note that an indicator is not just data on its own. Indicators must include some context describing an aspect of an event, indicating *something* related to the intrusion of concern. Think about a time when someone asked for your help in answering a question related to something you knew a lot about. If the question begins with "What can you tell me about...," you're almost certainly going to ask follow-up questions to try to get as much information and context as possible before you provide an answer. Analyzing threat data is similar, in that context matters: a domain name is not an indicator on its own, but a domain name with the added context that is it used for phishing *is* an indicator. Indicators can take the form of log entries, behavioral patterns, file artifacts, and so on.

Note that indicators can come in the form of indicators of activity (IoAs) or indicators of compromise (IoCs). IoAs are bits of information that indicates that a security attack or attempted attack may be in progress. They are typically derived from observed patterns of activity, such as unusual network traffic, user behavior, or system activity, whereas IoCs include malicious IP addresses, domain names, and file hashes associated with known malware or threat actors.

 CAUTION Note that a single indicator alone does not mean a threat or a compromise has materialized. By itself, an indicator is simply something that shows than an event has take place, such as a failure or other issue. Indicators of compromise must be examined contextually, alongside correlating information such as unusual network traffic patterns, suspicious user behavior, or unexpected system activity, in order to determine whether a compromise has occurred.

Indicator Lifecycle

In working as an analyst toward completing the picture of what's happened during an incident, you will want to turn a newly discovered indicator into something actionable for remediation or detection at a later point. Your first step is to vet the indicator (the process of deciding whether the indicator is valid), researching the originating signal, and determining its usefulness in actually detecting the malicious activity you expect to find in your environment. Characteristics you may want to consider during vetting include the reliability of the indicator source and additional details about the artifact that you're able to uncover with follow-up research.

Indicators often have value beyond just your organization, even when they are derived from internal network data. Many financial service organizations use the same supporting technologies, have similar internal operations processes, and face the same kind of threat actors on a regular basis. It follows, therefore, that these organizations would be keenly interested in how others in the same space are detecting and responding to malicious activity. Sharing threat data is a key component of success of any security operations effort. Threat intelligence shared among partners, peers, and other trusted groups often helps focus detection efforts and prioritize the use of limited resources. As we mentioned earlier, automated threat intelligence sharing relies on standardized formats and structures, some of which we will discuss in the upcoming sections.

Structured Threat Information Expression

The *Structured Threat Information Expression,* or STIX, is a collaborative effort managed by the OASIS Cyber Threat Intelligence Technical Committee (CTITC) to communicate cyber threat intelligence (CTI) using a standardized lexicon. To represent threat information, the STIX 2.1 framework uses a structure consisting of 18 key STIX Domain Objects (SDOs) and two STIX Relationship Objects (SROs). In describing an event, an analyst may show the relationship between one SDO and another using an SRO. The goal is to allow for flexible, extensible exchanges while providing both human- and machine-readable data. STIX information can be represented visually for analysts or stored as JSON (JavaScript Object Notation) for use in automation.

Attack Pattern

Attack patterns are a class of TTPs that describes attacker tendencies in how they employ capabilities against their victims. This SDO is helpful in generally categorizing types of attacks, such as spear phishing. Additionally, these objects may be used to add insight into exactly how the attacks are executed. Using the spear phishing example, an attacker would identify a high-value target, craft a relevant phishing message, attach a malicious document, and send the message with the hope that the target downloads and opens the attachment. Each of these individual actions viewed together make up an attack pattern.

Campaign

A *campaign* is a collection of malicious actor behaviors against a common target over a finite time frame. Campaign SDOs are often identified through various attributions methods to tie them to specific threat actors, but more important than the *who* behind the campaign is the identification of the unique use of tools, infrastructure, techniques, and targeting used by the actor. Tying this in with our phishing example, a campaign could be used to describe a threat actor group's attack that used a specially tailored phish kit to target specific executives of a multinational energy company over the course of eight weeks in the past winter.

Course of Action

A *course of action* is a preventative or response action taken to address an attack. This SDO describes any technical changes, such as a modification of a firewall rule, or policy changes, such as mandatory annual security training. To address the effectiveness of spear phishing, a security team may choose a course of action that includes enhanced phishing detection, automated attachment scanning, and link sanitization.

Grouping

A *grouping* indicates that the relevant STIX objects have a commonly shared context. It is used to indicate that other objects have some common characteristics between them. Note that this is a new SDO in the STIX 2.1 specification that was released in 2021.

Identity

An *identity* is an SDO that represents individuals, organizations, or groups. It can be specific and named, such as John Doe or Acme Corporation, or broader to refer to an entire sector, for example. In the act of collecting identifying information about the individuals and organizations involved in an incident, you may derive previously unseen patterns. The individuals that were the target of the specially crafted phishing message would be represented as identity objects using this framework.

Indicator

Similar to the previously defined indicator, the indicator SDO describes an observable characteristic that can be used to detect suspicious activity on a network or an endpoint. Again, this specific observable or pattern of observables must be accompanied with contextual data for it to be truly useful in communicating interesting aspects of a security event. Indicators found in spear phishing messages often include links with phishing domains, generic form language, or the use of ASCII homographs.

Infrastructure

This SDO, also new to STIX 2.1, describes any infrastructure pieces, such as systems or software, that are included in the attack itself or that are targeted by the attack. This could include both virtual or physical infrastructure. This is a collection of related data objects in context to the attack.

Intrusion Set

An *intrusion set* is a compilation of behaviors, TTPs, or other properties shared by a single entity. As with campaigns, the focus of an intrusion set is on identifying common resources and behaviors rather than just trying to figure out who's behind the activity. Intrusion set SDOs differ from campaigns in that they aren't necessarily restricted to just one time frame. An intrusion set may include multiple campaigns, creating an entire attack history over a long period of time. If a company has identified that it was the target of multiple phishing campaigns over the past few years from the same threat actor, that activity may be considered an intrusion set.

Location

Location is also an SDO new to STIX 2.1. It represents a physical geographic location, such as a region, country, or even latitude and longitude. The location SDO can be used to indicate either the origin of an attack or the target of the attack. It is most often associated to the identity or intrusion set SDOs.

Malware

Malware is any malicious code or malicious software used to affect the integrity or availability of a system or the data contained therein. Malware may also be used against a system to compromise its confidentiality, enabling access to information not otherwise available to unauthorized parties. In the context of this framework, malware is considered a TTP, most often introduced into a system in a manner that avoids detection by the user. As a STIX object, the malware SDO identifies samples and families using plain language to describe the software's capabilities and how it may affect an infected system. Examples of how these objects may be linked include connections to other malware objects to demonstrate similarities in their operations as well as connections to identities to communicate the targets involved in an incident. The specific malicious code delivered in a phishing attempt can be described using the malware object.

Malware Analysis

Malware analysis is an SDO that represents the results of a malware analysis and metadata related to that analysis. This is a new SDO, published under the STIX 2.1 specification.

Note

Introduced in STIX 2.1, a *note* is an SDO that relays informative data and provides additional context outside of that assigned to another SDO value. Notes can be added to other SDOs to provide additional information. Notes can be added by anyone, not just the original object creator.

Observed Data

The *observed data* SDO is used to describe any observable collected from a system or network device. This object may be used to communicate a single observation of an entity or the aggregate of observations. Importantly, observed data is not intelligence, or even information, but rather is raw data, such as the number of times a connection is made or the summation of occurrences over a specified time frame. The observed data object could be used in a phishing event to highlight the number of requests made to a particular phishing domain over the course of an hour.

Opinion

An *opinion,* as you would expect, is an SDO that provides an accuracy assessment of the information in a STIX object created by someone else. It uses a fixed numeric system to express subjective assessments on the agreement or disagreement with another entity's SDO. The opinion SDO was introduced in 2021 under STIX 2.1.

Report

Reports are finished intelligence products that cover some specific detail of a security event. Reports can give relevant details about threat actors believed to be connected to an incident, the malware they may have used, and the methodologies used during a campaign. For example, a narrative that describes the details of the phish kits used in targeting energy company executives may be included in a report SDO. The report could include references to any of the other objects previously described.

Threat Actor

The *threat actor* SDO defines individuals or groups believed to be behind malicious activity. They conduct the activities described in campaign and intrusion set objects using the TTPs described in malware and attack pattern objects against the targets identified using identity objects. Their level of technical sophistication, personally identifiable information (PII), and assertions about motives can all be used in this object. If a determination can be made about the goals of the actors behind our fictional series of phishing messages, it could be included in the threat actor object along with any information about the individuals or groups involved.

Tool

The *tool* SDO describes software used by a threat actor in conducting a campaign. Unlike software described using the malware object, tools are legitimate utilities such as PowerShell and the terminal emulator. Tool objects may be connected to other objects describing TTPs to provide insight into levels of sophistication and tendencies. Understanding how and when actors use these tools can provide defenders with the knowledge necessary for developing countermeasures. Since the software described in tool objects is also used by power users, system administrators, and sometimes regular users, the challenge moves from simply detecting the presence of the software to detecting unusual usage and determining malicious intent. A caveat in using the tool object, in addition to avoiding using it to describe malware, is that this object is not meant to provide details about any software used by defenders in detecting or responding to a security event.

Vulnerability

A *vulnerability* SDO is used to communicate any mistake in software that may be exploited by an actor to gain unauthorized access to a system, software, or data. Whereas malware objects provide key characteristics about malicious software and when they are used in the course of an attack, vulnerability objects describe the exact flaw being leveraged by the malicious software. The two may be connected to show how a particular malware object targets a specific vulnerability object.

Relationship

The *relationship* SRO can be thought of as the connective tissue between SDOs, linking them together and showing how they work with one another. In the previous description of vulnerability, we highlighted that there may be a connection made to a malware object to show how the malicious software may take advantage of a particular flaw. Using the relationship SRO relationship type *target*, we can show how a source and target are related using this framework. Table 7-7 highlights some common associations between a source SDO and target SDO using a relationship SRO.

Table 7-7
A Sample of Commonly Used Relationships

Source SDO	Relationship SRO	Target SDO
campaign	attributed to	threat actor
malware	targets	identity
attack pattern	uses	malware
course of action	mitigates	vulnerability
indicator	indicates	tool

Sighting

A *sighting* SRO provides information about the occurrence of an SDO such as indicator or malware. It's effectively used to convey useful information about trends and can be instrumental in developing intelligence about how an attacker's behavior may evolve or respond to mitigating controls. The sighting SRO differs primarily from the relationship SRO in that it can provide additional properties about when an object was first or last seen, how many times it was seen, and where it was observed. The sighting SRO is similar to the observed data SDO in that they both can be used to provide details about observations on the network. However, you may recall that an observed data SDO is not intelligence and provides only the raw data associated with the observation. While you would use the observed data SDO to communicate that you observed the presence of a particular piece of malware on a system, you'd use the sighting SRO to describe that a threat actor is likely to be behind the use of this malware given additional context.

Trusted Automated Exchange of Indicator Information

Trusted Automated Exchange of Intelligence Information (TAXII) defines how threat data may be shared among participating partners. It specifies the structure for how this information and accompanying messages are exchanged. Developed in conjunction with STIX, TAXII is designed to support STIX data exchange by providing the technical specifications for the exchange API.

TAXII 1.0 was designed to integrate with existing sharing agreements, including access control limitations, using three primary models: hub and spoke, source/subscriber, and peer-to-peer, as shown in Figure 7-3.

The most current version of TAXII, 2.1, defines two primary services—namely, collections and channels—to facilitate exchange models. Collections are an interface to a logical store of threat data objects hosted by a TAXII server. Channels, maintained by the TAXII server, provide the pathway for TAXII clients to subscribe to the published data. Figure 7-4 illustrates the relationship between the server and clients for the collection and channel services.

OpenIOC

OpenIOC is a framework designed by Mandiant, an American cybersecurity firm. The goal of the framework is to organize information about an attacker's TTPs and other indicators of compromise in a machine-readable format for easy sharing and automated follow-up. The OpenIOC structure is straightforward, consisting three of main components: IOC metadata, references, and the definition. The metadata component provides useful indexing and reference information about the IOC, including author name, the IOC name, and a description of the IOC. The reference component is primarily meant to enable analysts to describe how the IOC fits in operationally with their specific environments. As a result, some of the information may not be appropriate to share because it may refer to internal systems or sensitive ongoing cases. Analysts should be particularly careful to verify that reference information is suitable for sharing before sharing it externally. Finally, the definition component provides the indicator content most useful for

Figure 7-3
Primary models
for TAXII

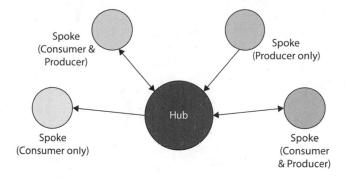

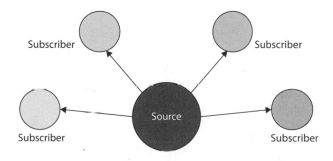

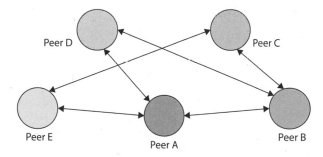

investigators and analysts. The definition often contains Boolean logic to communicate the conditions under which the IOC is valid. For example, the requirement for an MD5 hash *and* a file size attribute above a certain threshold would have to be fulfilled for the indicator to match.

MISP and Open CTI

MISP and OpenCTI are two open source platforms used for sharing and analyzing cyber threat intelligence. MISP allows organizations to collect, share, and collaborate on threat intelligence data, while OpenCTI provides advanced capabilities for correlation,

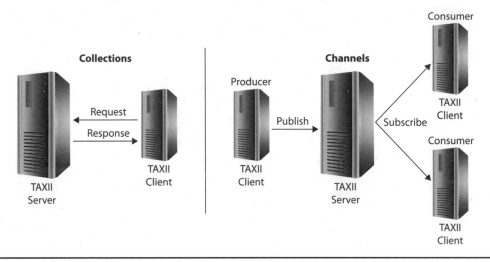

Figure 7-4   Collections and channel service architecture for TAXII 2.1

contextualization, and visualization of CTI data. These platforms enable organizations to improve their CTI capabilities by facilitating more efficient sharing, collaboration, and analysis of CTI data, which can help organizations stay ahead of emerging threats and respond more effectively to potential security incidents.

Intelligence Cycle

The *intelligence cycle* is a core process used by most government and business intelligence and security teams to process raw signals into finished intelligence for use in decision-making. Depending on the environment, the process is a five- or six-step method of adding clarity to a dynamic and ambiguous environment. Figure 7-5 shows the five-step cycle. Among the many benefits of its application are the increased situational awareness about the environment and the delineation of easily understood work efforts. Importantly, the intelligence cycle is also continuous and does not require perfect knowledge about one phase to begin the next. In fact, the cycle is best used when output from one phase is used to feed the next while also refining the previous. For example, you may discover a new bit of information at a later stage that can be used to improve the inputs into the overall cycle.

Requirements

The requirements phase involves the identification, prioritization, and refinement of uncertainties about the operational environment that the security team must resolve to accomplish its mission. It includes key tasks related to the planning and direction of the overall intelligence effort. In simple terms, requirements are steps that are *needed*. The results of this phase are not always derived from authority but are determined by aspects of the customer's operations as well as the capabilities of the intelligence team. As gaps in

Figure 7-5
The five-step
intelligence cycle

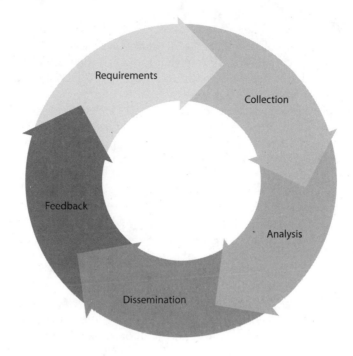

understanding are identified and prioritized, analysts will move on to figuring out ways to close these gaps, and a plan is set forth as to how they will get the data they need. This in turn will drive the collection phase.

Collection

At this phase, the plan that was previously defined is executed, and data is collected to fill the intelligence gap. Unlike a collection effort at a traditional intelligence setting, this effort at a business will likely not involve the dispatching of HUMINT or SIGINT assets but will instead mean the instrumentation of technical collection methods, such as setting up a network tap or enabling enhanced logging on certain devices. The sources of the raw data arrive from outside of the network, from news reports, social media, and public documents, or from closed and proprietary sources.

Indicators are often collected incidentally through routine data gathering activities such as log collection and analysis, host examination, malware detection, and so on. In a mature organization, security information and event management (SIEM) systems are often programmed to automatically collect and display indicators that meet specific patterns or behaviors. Even manual analysis can discover indicators of compromise during routine security activities.

Outside of routine security activities, indicators of compromise are often discovered when an analyst is looking for something specific—usually caused by a system or application failure or another unusual event that takes place on the host. Once an analyst discovers unusual or abnormal behavior on the infrastructure, indicators are collected, categorized, and analyzed for patterns that may indicate malicious activities.

Analysis

Analysis is the act of making sense of what you observe. With the use of automation, highly trained analysts will try to give meaning to the normalized, decrypted, or otherwise processed information by adding context about the operational environment. They then prioritize it against known requirements, improve those requirements, and potentially identify new collection sources. The product of this phase is finished, actionable intelligence that is useful to the customer. Analysis can be a difficult process, but there are many structured analytical techniques analysts may use to mitigate the effects of biases, to challenge judgments, and to manage uncertainty.

Once a set of suspicious indicators is collected, each indicator is examined individually and in context with other indicators and events to determine if malicious activities are happening on the network or host. Log files are reviewed, both system and user behaviors are examined, and an analyst may look for resulting events, such as the introduction of malware, file exfiltration, system degradation, and so on. Sometimes it can be difficult to distinguish between an indicator of compromise and the compromise itself; often, indicators may look themselves like the end result of compromise but are in fact symptoms of a larger incident.

The analyst has to determine whether an indicator is in fact part of a pattern that shows malicious behaviors or simply shows that there is an infrastructure problem, such as failing hardware, an unstable application, or a misconfigured operating system. Often indicators also show simple user noncompliance or negligence. In any event, the analyst will have to determine the seriousness of the event as well as what the indicators really show. The analyst may compare the set of indicators they have with indicators that show a known attack is taking place, or that, at a minimum, activities on the infrastructure may lead to negative consequences if allowed to continue.

Dissemination

Distributing the requested intelligence to the customer occurs at the dissemination phase. Intelligence is communicated in whichever manner was previously identified in the requirements phase and must provide a clear way forward for the customer. The customer, who may be the security team itself, can then use these analytical products and recommendations to improve defense, gain a greater understanding of an adversary's social or computer network for counterintelligence, or even move toward legal action. This also highlights an important concept in intelligence: the product provided must be useful. The words "actionable intelligence" are often misused because intelligence is always meant to be actionable.

Feedback

Once intelligence is disseminated, more questions may be raised, which leads to additional planning and direction of future collection efforts. At each phase of the cycle, analysts are evaluating the quality of their input and outputs, but explicitly requesting feedback from consumers is extremely important to enable the security team to improve its activities and better align products to meet consumers' evolving intelligence needs.

This phase also enables analysts to review their own analytical performance and to think about how to improve their methods for soliciting information, interacting with internal and external partners, and communicating their findings to the decision-makers.

 EXAM TIP The exam may ask questions about where in the intelligence cycle a security analyst may be when engaged in incident response. It would be helpful to remember that if an analyst is helping support an incident, they may be doing analysis work and collection planning. The intelligence cycle is also crucial when an analyst is required to follow steps such as data collection, evaluation, processing, and more.

Application of the Intelligence Cycle

A set of indicators that match known attack patterns isn't just taken at face value; these indicators are analyzed and confirmed through both manual and automated means by experienced analysts to determine if an attack is, in fact, taking place. If this is the case, the incident response cycle begins, and the attack or other negative event is dealt with. If indicators show that the issue comes from non-malicious sources, such as a hardware or application failure, those events are also dealt with likewise. A mature organization will record and catalog indicators and events to help analyze future events and negative trends. The organization may develop new processes or procedures that are put into place when the same indicators show up in the future.

Chapter Review

The usefulness of threat intelligence to your business depends on how well integrated business requirements are with intelligence requirements and the security operations effort. It's vital that you understand the basic concepts of threat intelligence. In this chapter, we discussed the foundations of threat intelligence. We discussed various threat actors, including advanced persistent threats, hacktivists, organized crime, nation-states, script kiddies, and insider threats. We also discussed threats that come from supply chains. We explained characteristics of intelligence source data that make it valuable, such as its timeliness, relevancy, and accuracy. Confidence levels are assigned to threat intelligence to express their relative reliability. There are various sources of threat intelligence information, such as those that come from both open and closed sources. These include the Internet, social media, government bulletins, incident response teams, and of course the dark web. Closed sources include internal networks, classified data sources, and threat intelligence subscriptions. Threat intelligence is shared by government agencies, proprietary sources, and between like organizations. We also discussed threat indicators and their lifecycles, as well as some of the common threat indicator data exchange formats. Finally, we talked about the intelligence cycle itself, which includes the requirements, collection, analysis, dissemination, and feedback phases.

Questions

1. Which of the following is *not* considered a form of passive or open source intelligence reconnaissance?

   A. Google hacking

   B. nmap

   C. ARIN queries

   D. nslookup

2. Which of the following is the term for the collection and analysis of publicly available information appearing in print or electronic form?

   A. Signals intelligence

   B. Covert intelligence

   C. Open source intelligence

   D. Human intelligence

3. Information that may not be shared with parties outside of the specific exchange, meeting, or conversation in which it was originally disclosed is designated by which of the following?

   A. TLP:RED

   B. TLP:AMBER

   C. TLP:GREEN

   D. TLP:WHITE

4. Which of the following sources will most often produce intelligence that is most relevant to an organization?

   A. Open source intelligence

   B. Deep and dark web forums and communications platforms

   C. The organization's network

   D. Closed source vendor data

5. Which of the following is *not* a characteristic of high-quality threat intelligence source data?

   A. Timeliness

   B. Transparency

   C. Relevancy

   D. Accuracy

6. In the STIX 2.0 framework, which object may be used to represent individuals, organizations, or groups?

    A. Campaign

    B. Persona

    C. Intrusion set

    D. Identity

7. In which phase of the five-step intelligence cycle would an analyst communicate their findings to the customer?

    A. Communication

    B. Dissemination

    C. Collection

    D. Feedback

8. Threat actors whose activities lead to increased risk as a result of their privileged access or employment are best described by what term?

    A. Unwilling participant

    B. Nation-state actor

    C. Hacktivist

    D. Insider threat

Answers

1. **B.** Nmap is a scanning tool that requires direct interaction with the system under test. All the other responses allow a degree of anonymity by interrogating intermediary information sources.

2. **C.** Open source intelligence, or OSINT, is free information that's collected in legitimate ways from public sources such as news outlets, libraries, and search engines. It should be used alongside intelligence gathered from closed sources to answer key intelligence questions.

3. **A.** TLP:RED information is limited to those present at a particular engagement, meeting, or joint effort. In most circumstances, TLP:RED should be exchanged verbally or in person. The use of TLP:RED outside of approved parties could lead to impacts on a party's privacy, reputation, or operations if misused.

4. **C.** An organization's network will inherently have the most relevant threat data available of all the sources listed.

5. **B.** Transparency is not a characteristic of high-quality threat intelligence source data. In addition to being complete, good threat intelligence often has the characteristics of timeliness, relevancy, and accuracy.

6. D. An identity is a STIX domain object that represents individuals, organizations, or groups. The object may be specific and may include the names of the person or organization referenced, or it may be used to identify an entire industry sector, such as transportation.

7. B. Distributing the requested intelligence to the customer occurs at the dissemination phase. The product may be used to gain a greater understanding of an adversary's motivation, to strengthen internal defenses, or to support legal action.

8. D. Insider threat actors are those who work within an organization and represent a particularly high risk of causing catastrophic damage due to their privileged access to internal resources.

Applying Threat Intelligence in Support of Organizational Security

In this chapter you will learn:

- The types of threat intelligence
- The various attack frameworks and their use in leveraging threat intelligence
- The threat modeling methodologies
- How threat intelligence is best used in other security functions
- The tactics of threat hunting

> *By "intelligence" we mean every sort of information about the enemy and his country—the basis, in short, of our own plans and operations.*
>
> —Carl von Clausewitz

Depending on the year and locale, fire departments may experience around a 10 percent false alarm rate resulting from accidental alarm tripping, hardware malfunction, and nuisance behavior. Given the massive amount of resources required for a response and the scarce and specialized nature of the responders, this presents a significant issue for departments to manage. After all, they cannot respond to a perceived emergency with anything less than their full attention. As with fire departments, false alarms are more than just an annoyance for security operations teams. As the volume of data that traverses the network increases, so do the alerts and logs that have to be triaged, interpreted, and actioned—and the chance for any of those alerts being a false alarm also rises. Unfortunately, the growth of specialized security teams that work endlessly to protect an enterprise from threats isn't growing at the same pace.

Although organizations invest in new types of threat detection technologies, they may only add to the already overwhelming amount of noise that exists, resulting in *alert fatigue*. Not only are analysts simply unable to assess, prioritize, and act upon every alert that comes in, but they may often ignore some of them because of the high rate of false positives. Much like the townspeople who responded to the boy crying "wolf!" only to learn that there was no wolf, security responders may learn to ignore alarm bells over time if no malicious activity exists.

One effective way to mitigate the dangers of overwhelming alerts and the often-associated alert fatigue is to integrate a threat intelligence program into all aspects of security operations. As covered in Chapter 7, threat intelligence is about adding context to internal signals to make risk-based decisions. Whether these choices occur at the tactical level in the security operations center or at the strategic level in the boardroom, good threat intelligence makes for a far better-informed security professional. In this chapter, we'll explore threat intelligence and the practices for integrating it into your security program to improve operations at every level.

Levels of Intelligence

In his doctrine on characterizing the adversary, famed Prussian general Carl von Clausewitz states that the adversary is a thinking, animate entity that reacts to the decisions of his enemy. The essence of developing a strong operational plan is to discover the enemy's strategy, develop your own plan to confront the enemy, and execute it with precision. The delineation of *levels of war* has become a keystone in the military decision-making process for armies throughout the world. The key concepts of providing intelligence at these levels can also be applied to cybersecurity.

At the highest level, organizations think about their conduct in a *strategic* manner, the results of which should impair adversaries' abilities to carry out what they're trying to do. Strategic effects should aim to disrupt the enemies' ability to operate by neutralizing their centers of gravity or key resource providers. Strategic threat intelligence therefore should support decisions at this level by delivering products that are anticipatory in nature. These products will provide a comprehensive view of the environment, identify the key actors, and offer a glimpse into the future based on recommended courses of action or inaction. This type of intelligence is often designed to inform the decisions of senior leaders in an organization and is accordingly not overtly technical. It's aimed at addressing the concerns of that particular audience, covering topics such as regulatory and financial impacts to the organization.

The application of a company's cybersecurity strategy occurs at the *operational* level, and planning will address concepts such as what the organization is trying to defend, from whom, for what duration, and with what capabilities. Before defining exactly how all this is to happen, defenders must determine what major efforts need to be in place to accomplish strategic goals, what resources might be needed, and what defines the nature of the problem. Without this direction, organizations will fail to adequately confront the challenges posed by the adversary, possibly squandering resources and frustrating security analysts. Operational threat intelligence products will provide insight into conditions particular to the environment that the organization is looking to defend. Products of this type will inform decision-makers about how best to allocate resources to defend against specific threats.

Finally, at the lowest level of war are the engagements between attacker and defender. Decisions at the *tactical* level are focused on how, exactly, a defender will engage with the adversary, including any technical countermeasures. The results of these activities may sometimes ripple out broadly to affect operational and strategic decision-making.

For example, a decision to block a service on a network may be required in response to a particularly damaging ongoing attack. If that decision then affects legitimate operations, or how the organization shares data with a strategic partner, it clearly extends beyond the immediate engagement at hand, and its second- and third-order effects will need to be considered moving forward. Tactical threat intelligence focuses on attacker tactics, techniques, and procedures (TTPs) and relates to the specific activity observed. These products are highly actionable, and the results of the follow-up decisions they inform will be used by operational staff to ensure that technical controls and processes are in place to protect the organization moving forward.

Threat Research

Thanks to the increasing acceptance of intelligence concepts across security teams and the use of attack frameworks, threat research is gaining the analytic rigor and completeness required to be a repeatable and scalable practice. Though threat research can be used to enrich alerts raised with existing detection technologies, it can also be used to uncover novel attacker TTPs within an environment not already discovered by detection rules. As an analyst coming across an artifact, you should work to answer a few initial questions about it: Is this benign? Has anyone seen this before and, if so, what do they have to say about it? Why is this present in my system? There are many different approaches we can use to get answers to these questions, but often we must conduct some sort of initial enrichment to determine the next steps. Conducting threat research is a critical part of the threat intelligence process, and we'll step through a few effective methods to getting answers to those questions.

Reputational

Security team members need valid malware signatures and reputation data about IPs and domains to help filter the vast amount of data that flows through the network. They use this information to enable firewalls, gateways, and other security devices to make decisions that prevent attacks while maintaining access for legitimate traffic. There are many free and commercial services that assign reputation scores to URLs, domains, and IP addresses across the Internet. Scores that correlate to the highest risk are associated with malware, spyware, spam, phishing, command and control (C2), and data exfiltration servers. Reputation scores can also be assigned to computers and websites that have already been identified as compromised. Google's Safe Browsing is a useful service that enables users to check the status of a website manually. The service also allows for automatic URL deny-listing for users of the Chrome, Safari, and Firefox web browsers, helping them identify whether they are attempting to access web resources that contain malware or phishing content.

Cisco's threat intelligence team, Talos, provides excellent reputational lookup features in a single dashboard in its Reputation Center service. Figure 8-1 is a snapshot of the report page generated for a suspicious IP address. Included in the report are details about location, blocklist status, and IP address owner information. For the Reputation Details section,

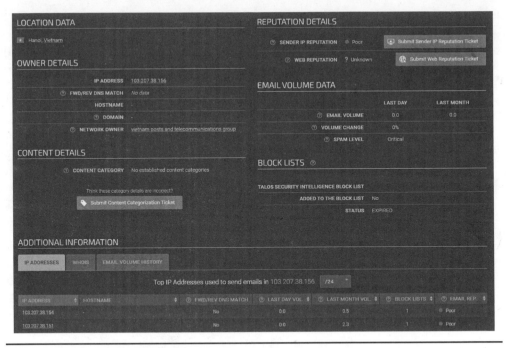

Figure 8-1 Talos Reputation Center report

Talos breaks the reputational assessments out by e-mail, malware, and spam, with historical information to give a sense of trends associated with the IP address. Finally, at the bottom of the report is a section for additional information. In this case, the IP address carried "critical" and "very high" spam levels from the previous day and month, respectively. The Additional Information section in this case provides daily e-mail volume information to give some historical context to the rating.

For high-volume reputational information, VirusTotal, a security-focused subsidiary of Google, is one of the most reliable services. VirusTotal aggregates the results of submitted URLs and samples from more than 70 antivirus scanners and URL/domain block-listing services to return a verdict about the likelihood of content being malicious. In addition to the web-based submission method shown in Figure 8-2, users may submit samples programmatically using any number of scripting options via VirusTotal's application programming interface (API).

Behavioral

Sometimes we are unable or unwilling to invest the effort into reverse engineering a binary executable, but we still want to find out what it does. This is where an isolation environment, or *sandbox*, comes in handy. Unlike endpoint protection sandboxes, this tool is usually instrumented to assist the security analyst in understanding what a running executable is doing as samples of malware are executed to determine their behaviors.

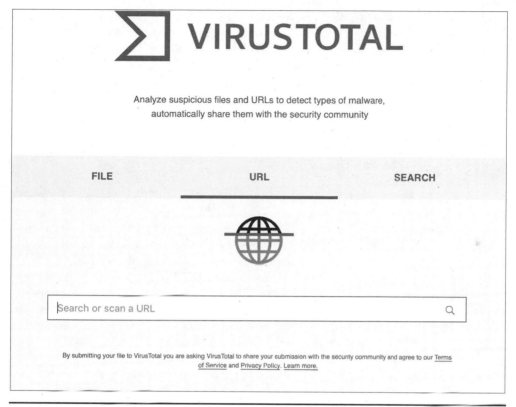

Figure 8-2 VirusTotal homepage

Cuckoo Sandbox is a popular open source isolation environment for malware analysis. It uses either VirtualBox or VMware Workstation to create a virtual computer on which to run the suspicious binary safely. Unlike other environments, Cuckoo is just as capable in Windows, Linux, macOS, or Android virtual devices. Another tool with which you may want to experiment is REMnux, which is a Linux distribution loaded with malware reverse engineering tools.

Using these tools, we may get insight into how a particular piece of software behaves when executed in the target environment. Be aware that malware writers are increasingly leveraging techniques to detect sandboxes and control various malware activities in the presence of a virtualized environment.

Indicator of Compromise

An indicator of compromise (IoC) is an artifact that indicates the possibility of an attack or compromise. IoCs need two primary components: data and context. Of the countless commercial feeds available to security teams, the most appropriate one to use depends on the industry and specific organizational requirements. As for free sources of IoC, we'll highlight a few high-quality sources. In addition to the ISACs covered in

Chapter 7 (https://www.it-isac.org/), the Computer Incident Response Center Luxembourg (CIRCL) operates several open source malware information sharing platforms, or MISPs, to facilitate automated sharing of IoCs across private and public sectors. Domestically, the FBI's InfraGard Portal provides historical and ongoing threat data relevant to 16 sectors of critical infrastructure.

 EXAM TIP Make sure as a security analyst you are aware of how to develop a threat hunting and intelligence capability and which resources would be required to do so. Make sure you know the difference between IoC feeds, CVSS (discussed next), and ISAC.

Security architect David Bianco developed a great model to categorize IoCs. His model, the Pyramid of Pain, shown in Figure 8-3, is used to show how much cost we can impose on the adversary when security teams address indicators at different levels. Hashes are easy to alert upon with high confidence; however, they are also easy to change and can therefore cause a trivial amount of pain for the adversary if detected and actioned. Changing IP addresses is more difficult than changing hashes, but most adversaries have disposable infrastructure and can also change the IP addresses of their hop points and command and control (C2) nodes once they are compromised. The bottom half of the pyramid contains the indicators that are most likely uncovered using highly automated solutions, while the top half includes more behavioral-based indicators.

As security professionals, we want to operate right at the top whenever possible, where the TTPs, if identified, require that attackers change nearly every aspect of how they operate. As you can probably guess, it is more difficult to alert on network and host artifacts and TTPs as well, but if we can address these high-confidence indicators, it will have a lasting impact on the security of our networks.

Figure 8-3
Bianco's Pyramid
of Pain

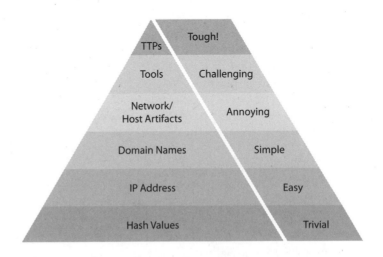

Common Vulnerability Scoring System

A well-known standard for quantifying severity is the Common Vulnerability Scoring System (CVSS). As a framework designed to standardize the severity ratings for vulnerabilities, this system ensures accurate quantitative measurement so that users can better understand the impact of these weaknesses. With the CVSS scoring standard, members of industries, academia, and governments can communicate clearly across their communities.

EXAM TIP The Common Vulnerability Scoring System is the de facto standard for assessing the severity of vulnerabilities. Therefore, you should be familiar with CVSS and its metric groups: base, temporal, and environmental. These groups represent various aspects of a vulnerability. Base metrics are those characteristics that do not change over time, temporal metrics describes those that do, and environmental metrics represents those that are unique to a user's environment.

Threat Modeling Methodologies

Threat modeling promotes better security practices by taking a procedural approach to thinking like the adversary. At their core, threat modeling techniques are used to create an abstraction of the system, develop profiles of potential attackers, and bring awareness to potential weaknesses that may be exploited. Exactly how the threat modeling activity is conducted depends on the goals of the model. Some threat models may be used to gain a general understanding about all aspects of security, while others may be focused on related aspects such as user privacy.

To gain the greatest benefit from threat modeling, it should be performed early and continuously as an input directly into the software development lifecycle (SDLC). Not only might this prevent a catastrophic security issue in the future, but it may lead to architectural decisions that help reduce vulnerabilities without sacrificing performance. For some systems, such as industrial control systems and cyber-physical systems, threat modeling may be particularly effective, because the cost of failure is not just monetary. By promoting development with security considerations, rather than security as an afterthought, defenders should have an easier time with incident response because of their increased awareness of the software architecture. Threat modeling examines several facets of a threat actor and threat event, including adversary capability, attack surface, attack vector, the likelihood that a threat will be successful in exploiting a weakness, and the impact if it does. These facets are described in the following sections, in addition to the popular threat modeling methodologies STRIDE and PASTA.

Adversary Capability

Understanding what a potential attacker is capable of can be a daunting task, but it is often a key competency of any good threat intelligence team. The first step in understanding adversary capability is to document the types of threat actors that would likely be threats, what their intent might be, and what capabilities they might bring to bear in the event of a security incident. As previously described, we can develop an understanding of adversary TTPs with the help of various attack frameworks and resources such as MITRE ATT&CK. Remember that the MITRE ATT&CK framework was discussed in Chapter 3.

Total Attack Surface

The attack surface is the logical and physical space that can be targeted by an attacker. Logical areas include infrastructure and services, while physical areas include server rooms and workstations. Mapping out what parts of a system need to be reviewed and tested for security vulnerabilities is a key part of understanding the total attack surface. As each component is addressed, defenders need to keep track of how the overall attack might change as compensating controls are put into place. Analysis of the attack surface is usually conducted by penetration testers, software developers, and system architects, but as a security analyst, you will have significant influence in the architecture decisions as the local expert on security operations in the organization.

Attack Vector

With a potential adversary in mind and critical assets identified, the natural next step is to determine the most likely path for the adversary to get their hands on the goods. This can be done using visual tools, as part of a red-teaming exercise, or even as a tabletop exercise. The goals of mapping out attack vectors consist of identifying realistic or likely paths to critical assets and identifying which security controls are in place to mitigate specific TTPs. If no mitigation exists, security teams can put compensating controls in place while they work out a long-term remediation plan.

Likelihood

The possibility of a threat actor successfully exploiting a vulnerability that results in a security incident is referred to as *likelihood*. The Nation Institute of Standards and Technology, or NIST, provides a formal definition of likelihood as it relates to security operations as "a weighted factor based on a subjective analysis of the probability that a given threat is capable of exploiting a given vulnerability or a set of vulnerabilities."

Impact

Impact is simply the potential damage to an organization in the case of a security incident. Impact types can include but aren't limited to physical, logical, monetary, and reputational. Impact is used across the security field to communicate risk to an organization. We'll cover various aspects of impact later in the book when discussing risk analysis.

Threat	Property Affected	Definition	Example
Spoofing	Authentication	Impersonating someone or something else	A outside sender pretending to be HR in an e-mail
Tampering	Integrity	Modifying data on disk, in memory, or elsewhere	A program modifying the contents of a critical system file
Repudiation	Nonrepudiation	Claiming to have not performed an action or have knowledge of who performed it	A user claiming that they did not receive a request
Information disclosure	Confidentiality	Exposing information to parties not authorized to see it	An analyst accidentally revealing the inner details of the network to outside parties
Denial of service	Availability	Denying or degrading service to legitimate users by exhausting resources needed for a service	Users flooding a website with thousands of requests a second, causing it to crash
Elevation of privilege	Authorization	Gaining capabilities without the proper authorization to do so	A user bypassing local restrictions to gain administrative access to a workstation

Table 8-1 STRIDE Threat Categories

STRIDE

STRIDE is a threat modeling framework that evaluates a system's design using flow diagrams, system entities, and events related to a system. The framework name is a mnemonic, referring to the security threats in the six categories shown in Table 8-1. Invented in 1999 and developed over the last 20 years by Microsoft, STRIDE is among the most used threat modeling methods, suitable for application to logical and physical systems alike. Microsoft has also developed a freely available threat modeling tool based on STRIDE that anyone can use.

PASTA

PASTA, or the Process for Attack Simulation and Threat Analysis, is a risk-centric threat modeling framework originally developed in 2012. Focused on communicating risk to strategic-level decision-makers, the framework is designed to bring technical requirements in line with business objectives. Using the seven stages shown in Table 8-2, PASTA encourages analysts to solicit input from operations, governance, architecture, and development.

Stage	Key Tasks
Define Objectives	Identify business objectives. Identify security and compliance requirements. Perform business impact analysis.
Define Technical Scope	Record infrastructure, application, and software dependencies. Record scope of the technical environment.
Application Decomposition	Identify use cases. Identify actors, assets, services, roles, and data sources. Create data flow diagrams.
Threat Analysis	Analyze attack scenarios. Perform threat intelligence correlation and analytics.
Vulnerability and Weaknesses Analysis	Catalog vulnerability reports and issues. Map existing vulnerabilities. Perform design flaw analysis.
Attack Modeling	Analyze complete attack surface.
Risk and Impact Analysis	Qualify and quantify business impact. Catalog mitigating strategies and techniques. Identify residual risk.

Table 8-2   PASTA Stages

Threat Intelligence Sharing with Supported Functions

The end goal of using threat intelligence is to protect assets and reduce the possibility of threats infiltrating your infrastructure. As such, threat intelligence can be used to support critical security functions in your organization, such as incident detection and response, managing vulnerabilities, and overall risk management. Proactive use of threat intelligence can also be used in security engineering to design secure systems from the beginning. Integrating threat intelligence concepts enables responders to act more quickly in the face of uncertainty and frees them up to deal with new and unexpected threats when they arise.

Incident Response

Incident responders have some of the most sought-after skills required by any organization because of their ability to rapidly and accurately address potentially wide-ranging issues on a consistent basis. Although many incident responders thrive in stressful environments, the job can be challenging for even the most seasoned security professionals. Looking at the upward trend of security event volume and complexity, there will likely be a constant demand for responders well into the future. Incident response is not usually an entry-level security function because it requires such a diverse skill set—from malware analysis to forensics to network traffic analysis. Furthermore, at the core of a responder's modus operandi is speed—speed to confirm a potential incident, speed to remediate, and speed to address the root cause. When we take a look at what's required across the skill spectrum from an incident responder, and combine that with the need for speed, it becomes clear why reducing response time and moving toward proactive measures are so important.

As security teams attempt to move away from a reactive nature, they must do whatever they can to prepare themselves for the possibility of a security event. Many teams are using playbooks, or predefined sets of automated actions, more and more in their response efforts. Although it may take some time to understand the company's IT environment, the entities involved, and the external and internal threats posed against the company, preparation pays off in several ways. Threat intelligence information is a critical part of the preparation phase because it enables teams to more accurately develop strong, consistent processes to cope with issues should they arise. These not only dramatically reduce the time needed to respond, but as repeatable and scalable processes, they reduce the likelihood of analyst error. Incident response activities are covered in detail in Part III.

Vulnerability Management

Vulnerability management teams are all about making risk-based decisions. Thinking back to one of the axioms of the Diamond Model of Intrusion Analysis, we're reminded that "every system, and by extension every victim asset, has vulnerabilities and exposures." Vulnerabilities seem to be a fact of life, but that doesn't mean that a team can forsake its responsibility to identify vulnerable assets and deploy patches.

Throughout the book so far, we've referred to useful sources for threat data, many of them providing vulnerability information. Another database, NIST's National Vulnerability Database (NVD), makes it easy for organizations to determine whether they are likely to be affected by disclosed vulnerabilities. But the NVD and other databases miss a key feature that threat intelligence adds. Threat intelligence takes vulnerability management concepts a step further and provides awareness about vulnerabilities in an operational context—that is, answering the question, "Are these vulnerabilities actively being exploited?" Table 8-3 provides a short list of some of the authors' favorite types of free sources for intelligence related to vulnerabilities.

Type	Description
Information security sites	Vendor blogs and official vendor disclosure notices are a great source for up-to-date disclosure information.
Social media	"Security Twitter," the community of researcher and security-adjacent personas, is one of the best sources for vulnerability information and observations of exploitation in the wild.
Code repositories	GitHub is a popular platform for sharing proof-of-concept exploit code.
Paste sites	Pastebin, Ghostbin, and other free and anonymous services often host lists of exploitable vulnerabilities.

Table 8-3 Sources of Intelligence Related to Vulnerabilities

Threat intelligence communicates exploitation relevant to the organization instead of general exploitability. This is important, because thinking back to the scale of vulnerabilities across the enterprise, a vulnerability management team's core function is really prioritization. By identifying what *is* being exploited versus what *can be* exploited, these teams can make better decisions about where to place resources. Note that vulnerability management is covered in depth in Part II.

 NOTE Many times, vulnerabilities with high scores may not be the ones actually being exploited in the wild. There are a number of reasons for this— from technical complexity preventing the creation of a practical exploit to the fact that threat actors are going to use whatever works as long as they can, regardless of CVSS score.

Risk Management

As with vulnerability management teams, risk management teams speak the language of risk in terms of impact and probability. If we understand risk to mean the impact to an asset by a threat actor exploiting a vulnerability, we see that the presence of a threat actor is necessary in communicating risk accurately. Drilling down further, three components need to be present for a threat to be accurately described: capability, intent, and opportunity. Providing answers to these three components as they appear at present is exactly what threat intelligence is designed to do. Furthermore, good threat intelligence will also be able to predict what the threat will likely be in the future, or if there are likely to be more. Figure 8-4 highlights the various components necessary to describe a threat and how it all fits in with defining risk.

Predicting the future is what all risk team members want to do, and though that's not really possible, threat intelligence does provide answers to questions that risk managers and security leaders ask. Primary among these are identifying what type of attacks are becoming more or less prevalent and what assets attackers are likely to target in the future. In terms of quantifying the cost to an organization, risk teams may also want to know which of these attacks are likely to be most costly to the business. The logistics sector, for example, has a completely different cost of downtime than does the automotive industry.

Security Engineering

Security engineers of all flavors, whether on a product security or corporate security team, regularly benefit from threat intelligence data. Threat intelligence gathered from security research or criminal communities can offer insight into the effectiveness of security measures across a company. While the motivations of these two communities are very different, they both can provide a unique outlook on your organization's security posture. This feedback can then be analyzed and operationalized by your organization's security engineers.

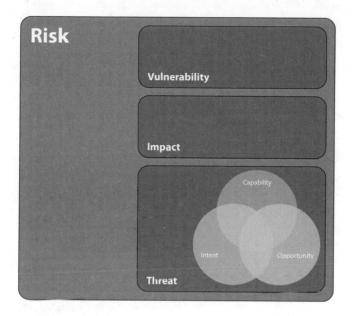

Figure 8-4
Relationship of
vulnerability,
impact, threat,
and risk

Detection and Monitoring

As discussed throughout Chapter 7, threat intelligence as applied to security operations is all about enriching internal alerts with the external information and context necessary to make decisions. For analysts working in a security operations center (SOC) to interpret incoming detection alerts, context is critical in enabling them to triage quickly and move on to scoping potential incidents. Because a huge part of a detection analyst's time is spent interpreting the output of dashboards, identifying relevant inputs early on reduces the cognitive load for the analyst down the line.

Let's explore a typical workflow for a detection analyst, where threat intelligence can significantly speed up the decision-making cycle. When an analyst receives an alert, they are getting only a headline of the activity and a few artifacts to support the alert condition. Attempting to triage this initial alert without access to enough context will not give the analyst a sense of what the true story is. Even if a repository exists and is made available to the analyst with all information, it would be impractical to perform the manual steps necessary to assimilate and correlate with other data related to the alert. Automated threat intelligence tailored to the needs of the detection team improves the analyst workflow by providing timely details. A great example is enrichment around suspicious domains. A detection team can easily leverage automation techniques to query threat intelligence data to extract reputation information, passive DNS details, and malware associations linked to that domain. Joining this information with what's already in the alert content provides so much more awareness for the analyst to make a call.

Threat Hunting

Every year, the SANS Institute conducts its Threat Hunting Survey to identify trends related to threat hunting programs from a variety of organizations. In noteworthy take-aways from the responses in the 2022 survey, SANS discovered that most organizations assess their own threat hunting capabilities as still maturing (62 percent). A surprising 68 percent of the respondents said that their organizations did not have the skilled personnel needed for threat hunting. This may have been the reason that 25 percent of the organizations responding to the survey said that they outsource their threat hunting capabilities. However, despite the obvious deficiencies in organizational threat hunting capabilities, 68 percent of the survey respondents said that their security posture experienced a 25–75 percent increase in effectiveness due to threat hunting efforts, and almost half indicated that they have experienced an improvement in the accuracy of threat detections with fewer false positives. (Fuchs and Lemon, "SANS 2022 Threat Hunting Survey: Hunting for a Standard Methodology for Threat Hunting Teams," July 2022.)

The majority of security concepts we cover in this book are reactive. Whether they involve tuning endpoint detection tools to identify potential incidents or blocking traffic based on how it is attempting to traverse the network, these techniques rely on your being able to observe behavior and make a call on whether it is good or bad—as it is happening or shortly thereafter. Threat hunting, on the other hand, is a proactive and iterative approach to defense, rooted in a mindset that the attacker is already in your system. Whether that's true or not, this approach means making fewer potentially damaging assumptions about your organization's security posture. Furthermore, just because a breach isn't visible doesn't mean it hasn't already occurred—it just means that your traditional methods of detection have failed. Often categorized as a type of active defense, threat hunting requires analysts to see beyond alerts and dig deep to find malicious actors in the network that may have slipped past defenses. Primarily driven by a human, threat hunting can benefit tremendously from technologies such as machine learning (ML) and user and entity behavior analytics (UEBA). The practice can never be fully automated, however, because hunting often requires analysts to step into the minds of attackers and see things from their point of view. This kind of assumed perspective helps us as defenders in determining the most likely techniques used by an attacker, and, combined with intelligence about motivations, can help clarify what exactly we need to look for in our network to uncover them. The best threat hunting efforts combine the data and capabilities of advanced security operations with the strong, individual analytical skills of those on the hunting team.

Though different from other key defense processes such as vulnerability management, incident response, digital forensics, and detection, threat hunting requires familiarity with these processes and the skills associated with them. As a result, many good threat hunting teams tend to be quite diverse, composed of members with rich experience in all of these domains. Hunting also requires that analysts have enhanced awareness about their network, including an accurate catalog of sensitive assets as well as an understanding of normal traffic patterns. Like threat intelligence analysts, so much of what differentiates threat hunters is their ability to add context to raw data to tell a story. Unlike threat intelligence analysts, however, threat hunters look for what already might be present and unseen instead of what might occur in the future. Ideally, this practice helps us find adversaries hiding in the network well before attackers have the chance to fully step through a kill chain and fulfill their goals.

For success in threat hunting, the analyst must develop the means to identify and distinguish the patterns of the target, track that target activity throughout the environment, and eventually take a successful shot at the threat. Any successful hunting campaign, therefore, requires identification of the target and comprehensive preparation on the part of the analyst. Before embarking on a threat hunting effort, you'll also need to have a comprehensive plan in place. Because so many time- and resource-consuming activities are associated with threat hunting, knowing what you're going to do and preparing for overall success are key to maximizing the chances of a fruitful effort. Like traditional hunters, analysts will put tremendous effort into preparing their tools, clarifying plans for how they will test their assumptions, and thinking about what to do after the hunt is complete.

At the very least, you should address the following questions before moving forward:

- What is the purpose of the hunt?
- Where will it be conducted?
- What resources do I need to conduct the hunt?
- Who are the key stakeholders?
- What is the desired outcome of the hunt?

You can visualize the entire threat hunting process in several ways, but for the sake of this exam, we'll use a four-stage cycle that's quite similar to the *intelligence cycle* described in Chapter 1. Many organizations already conduct hunting for threats in a manner similar to what we describe, whether they realize it or not. Ensuring that the process is repeatable and scalable is easier with a framework such as the one shown in Figure 8-5.

Figure 8-5
A four-phase threat hunting process

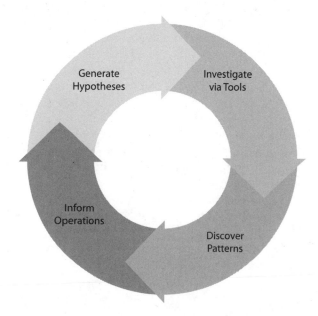

Assume Breach

For decades, security professionals operated with a primary focus on perimeter defense and incident response. Most believed that, with the right investment in outward-facing detection and prevention technologies, attackers would be thwarted most of the time. And in those rare occasions that something got through, incident responders would be able to home in on and evict attackers quickly from the network. This mindset, as the community has come to learn, is flawed in many ways. Attackers, it turns out, can be patient, clever, and, in some cases, very well resourced. In many cases, attackers had more knowledge of technical details and flaws in a target network than the owners did. Years of increasingly successful and stealthy breaches proved to defenders that not only were attackers capable of launching a successful attack, but the defenders themselves weren't nearly as situationally aware as they had once believed.

Enter the concept of *assumption of breach,* which is a simple acceptance of the possibly that an attacker is already in the network and working toward an end goal. This comes with an inherent acknowledgement that, as we've covered throughout the book so far, no system is entirely free of vulnerabilities. Accordingly, security professionals cannot accurately claim that there haven't been intruders in their networks in a given time frame.

Establishing a Hypothesis

With threat hunting goals identified, your first step in the hunting effort is to develop a hypothesis (or hypotheses) for the hunt. Each hypothesis will be a simple statement with your ideas about the threats in the environment and how you foresee identifying and removing them. Hypotheses can be seen as educated guesses that need two key components to be valid: The first is some observable aspect that goes beyond an analyst's hunch. There must be some phenomena occurring (or not occurring) on the network that can be captured in a consistent way. This ensures that the event can be analyzed and compared in a consistent way. This leads to the second component of every good hypothesis—it must be testable. Good hunters will know what technologies to leverage to get the signal they need to begin the analysis and testing of hypotheses. The initial signal for a hypothesis is often derived from one or more of the sources listed in Table 8-4.

Along with the two previously discussed components, keep in mind that, at some point, you may have to communicate your process, findings, or results to stakeholders. Your hypotheses, therefore, should be clear and concise. Attempting to move forward with an improperly formed hypothesis not only adds unnecessary confusion, but it may also result in dubious results. As with poor requirements in the intelligence cycle, poorly defined hypotheses can lead to a substantial waste of resources and time.

Type	Description	Example
Analytics-driven	Hypothesis informed by leveraging advanced technologies such as ML and UEBA	Your UEBA systems are showing significant spikes in outbound traffic from several workstations associated with members of your company's research and development arm, all of whom are currently out of the office at a technical conference. You suggest that all recent e-mails be checked for phishing messages and their endpoints scanned for unusual processes.
Situation-driven	Hypotheses developed with understanding of the organization's environment, network topology, and key assets as well as how they change over time	Your organization is in the final steps of acquiring a small startup with an inexperienced security team. This startup has been the victim of several attackers' campaigns over the last few years. Attackers will likely leverage their existing access to the startup's network and the new connections to your organization to facilitate attacks against your company. You suggest that enhanced monitoring be configured at those connection points.
Intelligence-driven	Hypotheses derived through the use of IOCs, adversary TTPs, and reports from vendors or internal threat intelligence teams	An external vendor recently sent a report describing the TTPs of a new organized crime outfit operating out of Eastern Europe. This group uses *bulletproof hosting* servers in the same region to send tailored phishing messages. You suggest that messages originating from that region undergo additional scrutiny or filtering based on the IOCs contained in the report.
Experience-driven	Hypotheses informed by lessons learned from previous hunts and knowledge gained from experiences in security operations	Having previously worked at a major ISP, you have firsthand experience with how the Border Gateway Protocol (BGP) is meant to operate. You have also observed suspicious behaviors purportedly conducted by a well-resourced, nation-level threat actor. You suggest that your current team develop and maintain an intelligence sharing agreement with your old team and with other ISP security teams to gain insight into recent BGP abuses.

Table 8-4   Types of Threat Hunting Hypotheses Sources

Profiling Threat Actors and Activities

In Chapter 3, we covered the MITRE ATT&CK framework, an important tool resource for understanding adversary tactics and techniques in the context of developing threat intelligence. As profiling attackers and their associated activities is a critical step in threat hunting, ATT&CK is incredibly useful. As a reminder, MITRE ATT&CK is meant to serve as a globally accessible knowledge base of adversary tactics and techniques based on real-world observations. It's the "real-world" feedback about the framework that adds so much relevancy to threat hunting efforts. Another major benefit of the ATT&CK framework is that it enables threat hunters to discover potential activity based on the stage of the attack lifecycle. Tactics and techniques are grouped within a matrix that can be used for confirming hunting hypotheses. The ATT&CK matrix includes the following categories:

- **Reconnaissance** The active or passive techniques used to gather information on the target
- **Resource development** The techniques used by the adversary to create, purchase, steal, or otherwise acquire resources supporting the attack
- **Initial access** The techniques used by the adversary to obtain a foothold within a network
- **Execution** The techniques that enable adversaries to run their code on a target system
- **Persistence** The techniques that enable an adversary to maintain long-term access to a target system
- **Privilege escalation** The techniques used by an adversary to gain higher level privilege, such as administrator or root
- **Defense evasion** The techniques used by attackers to circumvent security mechanisms or obfuscate their behavior to avoid detection
- **Credential access** The techniques developed to capture legitimate user credentials
- **Discovery** The techniques used by adversaries to obtain information about systems and networks, often to assist in targeting and exploit development
- **Lateral movement** The techniques that enable an attacker to move from one system to another within a network
- **Collection** The techniques used by an adversary to aggregate information about target systems
- **Command and control** The techniques leveraged by an attacker to enable communication between victim machines and those under their control
- **Exfiltration** The techniques used to get data out of a compromised network and into an environment controlled by the attacker
- **Impact** The techniques used by an attacker to impact legitimate users' access to a system

Threat hunting isn't spared from one of the biggest problems in defending modern systems: the volume and complexity of attacks. MITRE ATT&CK and other frameworks help hunters figure out what to focus on by providing a foundation that brings some order to the chaos. It provides a common language when describing attacker behavior that can be applied to long-term detection and remediation efforts, but it also means that new members are able to wrap their head about these activities and the impact they have more quickly.

 EXAM TIP The CySA+ exam does not focus exclusively on MITRE ATT&CK in the context of threat hunting, but this framework is used broadly across the domains covered in the test. ATT&CK provides an excellent model for thinking about all adversary behavior, and it will be useful for you to be able to describe adversary behavior and how you, as an analyst, might develop your hunting plan using its language.

Threat Hunting Tactics

Threat hunting, like nearly every other aspect of defense, benefits from automation and specialized tooling. Threat hunters can use a huge range of software tools to sift through the vast amount of data to help them make sense of what they are seeing and improve the hunting process. Getting started on threat hunting efforts does not often require additional investment in technology, because threat hunters often rely on existing security tools to achieve their key tasks. Firewalls, endpoint protection software, and intrusion detection systems (IDSs), for example, can be used to help reveal indicators of compromise. Additionally, hunters can use security information and event management (SIEM) solutions to aggregate vast amounts of log and traffic data to enable statistical analyses and visualization tools to present trends and highlight anomalies in useful ways. A security team doesn't have to spend significant amounts of money to get a threat hunting effort started. In fact, one of the simplest threat hunting tools is the spreadsheet, which can often be an effective tool for storing and retrieving observed data. Taking cues from the popularity and usefulness of tabular formats, the MITRE ATT&CK Navigator tool (https://mitre-attack.github.io/attack-navigator) presents its rich content in a manner similar to spreadsheet software to help defenders develop and execute their plans.

High-Impact TTPs

A common method of conducting a hunt is to go through every phase of an attack model and determine the areas or phases the team is most concerned with. The exact techniques your team will use to hunt malicious activity will depend largely on what you're trying to defend against. Each phase will involve several associated TTPs that an adversary may normally use. To hunt the adversary—and defend yourself—you must understand your enemy's tendencies. You can use the previously discussed techniques to uncover some common (but high-impact) TTPs as you begin your hunting efforts. We'll take some time to explore TTPs aligned with the ATT&CK categories; although this is by no means an exhaustive list, it will provide an excellent starting point for the hunt.

Initial Access and Discovery

The TTPs associated with initial access and discovery have a lot to do with how the adversary is targeting your systems and how they decide to go one way instead of another. Accordingly, behaviors associated with enumeration are the focus here. The attacker works to determine details about a local host, the larger networks, and their configuration. As a hunter, you're looking for artifacts that indicate that an attacker is trying to get the network layout, lists of users and groups, and lists of privileges allotted to particular users. Querying to look for the use of tools such as nmap and the Windows net.exe utility is a good start.

Persistence

Uncovering TTPs related to persistence is all about how attackers maintain access even after the host is rebooted. Quite often, attackers will use built-in functionality, such as Windows scheduled tasks execution and registry or macOS login items, to ensure that their malicious programs or scripts can maintain a long-term presence on the system. Tasks can also be scheduled remotely, provided that an attacker has the correct credentials via remote procedure calls. As another example of using built-in resources, adversaries will sometimes run malicious code by using a legitimate process to load and execute the code. In this case, an attacker would leverage the trusted relationship between the system and the process to hide the malicious activity. This method, often a dynamic-link library (DLL) injection in the Windows environment, can lead to attacks taking hold of a process's memory and permissions. The most common way malware persists on macOS is via a LaunchAgent, a component of the OS management service. Each macOS user can have LaunchAgents with configuration files stored in their own Library folder. These files specify the code that should be run every time that user logs in, or they may contain their own commands to execute directly.

Lateral Movement and Privilege Escalation

With some degree of confidence that they have established a foothold in a network, attackers will move to explore the network via lateral movement—attempting to access services beyond the level of the accounts they're currently in control of via some kind of privilege escalation. A common TTP associated with attackers looking to target credentials is a Pass-the-Hash (PtH) attack. This method involves capturing password hash values that can be used to authenticate against other systems at a later point. Importantly, PtH techniques do not require the actual password or even an attempt to crack the credentials. Another particularly effective means to traverse quickly across systems is a built-in functionality that's heavily used across many industries: Remote Desktop Protocol (RDP). As with the scheduled tasks and login items persistence techniques, attackers will use tools that they know are unlikely to be blocked because of their popularity. If RDP is enabled on a system and an attacker is in possession of those account credentials, they can access and exploit the target system in a manner that becomes very difficult to detect in most environments.

Command and Control

During the course of an attack, attackers may at some point need to have their malware reach out to get new instructions from them. In many cases, attackers will seek to hide in plain sight by blending in their command and control (C2) with routine network traffic and piping their instructions using standard ports and protocols that are unlikely to be blocked. Hoping that their communications are lost or ignored in the sheer volume of traffic, attackers rely on some assumptions made by the security team about where legitimate traffic resides. This reliance does have the possibility of backfiring, however, as may be the case if a detection team invests resources into deep inspection of traffic across heavily used ports and protocols. If this is known to be the case, an attack can bypass heavily monitored ports by sending data through uncommon ports to enable attackers to operate stealthily as they work toward their end goals.

Exfiltration

Many of the stealthier data exfiltration techniques rely on concepts similar to those used for sending and receiving C2 information. Domain Name System (DNS) tunneling, for example, is a method of sending data via encoded DNS queries. Because DNS is a critical and foundational protocol of the Internet, it's often untouched by network defenders. As long as the malicious encoding is consistent and the traffic conforms to DNS standards, it can be hard to detect. Hunters will need to keep an eye out for abnormal DNS queries or unusually high query volumes.

Although detecting abnormal domains may be straightforward for a human, it's not as simple for machines to read a string of characters and understand its significance linguistically or culturally. This is where we can leverage mathematical principles to assist us with identifying suspicious DNS queries. In the context of information, *entropy* is the measure of randomness in data. *High entropy domains* are those that have comparatively large amounts of randomness, and in terms of readability, these domains are likely to appear as gibberish to a human. As we cover later in the book, malware may use *domain generation algorithms* (DGAs) for its C2 exchanges to try to avoid detection. Because it is very difficult to block domains one at a time, this technique can be an effective way to facilitate that communication. The entropy associated with the generated domains is usually higher than that of standard domains. You can perform your own analysis by first collecting legitimate DNS logs and determining the frequencies for characters that appear in those domains' names to establish a threshold. Using entropy alongside other hunting techniques increases your confidence in the harm of a particular signal. For example, if you have uncovered an unsigned application on a host acting strangely, you can then look for network connections that appear to have a relatively high degree of entropy to reduce the likelihood of a false positive or false negative.

Content Delivery Networks

Although computer-generated domain names are often used by many malware strains to define their C2 channels, DGAs have legitimate uses in content delivery networks (CDNs). These cloud-based services have become extremely popular in recent years. Many websites use CDNs to deliver dynamic content such as video and images to customers across the globe. The challenge is that many CDN domains are generated using DGAs, though they usually include some clue as to who the CDN provider is. Keeping track of each CDN's unique characteristics and naming schemes will improve your hunt queries.

Searching

Armed with collection and aggregation capabilities, and a hypothesis that you hope to prove, you can begin the hunt by simply searching for data that answers your questions. Querying, as we've discussed throughout the book, is a core functionality of any security data aggregator that can yield quick results, assuming that the questions are well defined and that queries are well written. Searching rapidly scopes down the working data set and prevents analyst overload. Always keep in mind that searching too broadly for general entities may produce far too many results to be useful to an analyst, or it may present the analyst with extra work. On the other hand, searching too specifically can result in the network producing too few results in the hunt.

Clustering and Grouping

Two types of techniques are particularly useful for threat hunting: clustering and grouping. Borrowing from statistical analysis, both these techniques are effective when you're looking for shared features in very large data sets. *Clustering analysis* is a technique often used in statistics to identify groups of data points based on certain criteria, such as occurrence. Good clustering methods will result in groups that have high interclass similarity, meaning that they are indeed quite similar to one another based on the predefined criteria, as well as low interclass similarity, meaning that they can be sufficiently differentiated from other clusters.

Like clustering, *grouping* is a means to categorize similar data points by taking a set of unique features and determining the artifacts that fit the criteria. Grouping requires that these defining features be described in advance, whereas clustering does not require this to be the case. Often, one of the features used in a clustering criterion is time, as would be the case in looking for a particular type of command executed in a certain timeframe.

Stacking

Stacking, or stack counting, is a basic technique for identifying outliers in data. It involves counting the number of occurrences of a particular value, sorting them, and investigating the extreme outliers. Stacking is less useful with very large data sets because the outliers in these collections can themselves be quite large. Stacking is most effective with data sets that produce a finite number of results, when the criteria are carefully designed, and with the use of automation or statistics technology. This is a case where spreadsheet software can be very helpful in your hunting.

Delivering Results

Threat hunting is not a purely academic endeavor; there is the potential for immediate and massive operational impact as a result of your team's hunting efforts. In most cases, an analyst is conducting a hunt in a business environment, which is subject to the external influences of the organization, environmental restrictions, and business needs. Because of this, analysts must work to exhaust every possible avenue toward achieving well-defined criteria for success or completion of the hunt. Time is money, and hunting can be a costly undertaking. As important as knowing why you're starting the hunt in the first place is knowing when to stop. The criteria for ending the hunt should therefore be included when the scope of this hunt is defined.

Although hunts do not necessarily fall under the traditional incident response process, they will require similar levels of investment in personnel and technology. Unlike the incident response process, though, it's important that you accept that hunts may not yield results, and it may be difficult to determine when to stop. After all, it's expected that at any point during the hunt, an analyst may uncover a lead that will require more investigation. It's often impossible to tell at the onset what the exact time required for a particular hunt may be. Part science and part art, the process benefits from the freedom of an analyst to explore all possibilities and think "outside the box," but the process must also be sound and responsible. Good hunters will often know when they've hit the point of diminishing returns and need to refocus. If your security organization is just beginning its journey of building a threat hunting team, it may be worthwhile to prescribe periodic reviews to make sure your hunts are producing results.

Documenting the Process

Earlier in this chapter, we described the importance of developing your hypothesis when starting out on a hunt. Hypotheses are best guesses, and sometimes even the most educated guesses are incorrect. Threat hunters routinely get to a point at which they've exhausted all possibilities and resources and will just have to move on. Hunts are often short, lasting only a few days or weeks, and highly scoped, so the act of accepting a fruitless outcome will be necessary for a good threat hunting team to be prepared to tackle the next challenge. Even if a hunt results in no necessary action, it can nevertheless be very beneficial. Regardless of the outcome, documentation of the hypothesis, why it was or was not correct, any inhibitors to the process, and what you can do better next time will be useful for future efforts. Documentation is a crucial part of the hunt process, and if you forget to document every step you've taken, every lead you've tracked down, and everything you've learned, you'll simply have to reinvent the wheel the next time.

Integrating Vulnerability Management with Threat Hunting

We've learned from covering threat intelligence concepts in Chapter 7 that it's virtually impossible to defend something if you're not aware of its existence on your network. An area of improvement for any organization is its asset management. Network diagrams and asset catalogs are constantly in a state of evolution, and the natural lag between updates to that information and when the security team recognizes these changes creates a period of increased vulnerability. Threat hunting turns out to be an extremely effective way to gather knowledge about your network environment and its users.

Thinking as an attacker, you may often find it faster and more reliable to take advantage of known exploits, should a vulnerability present itself, rather than risk detection or failure with a new technique. This is in part why vulnerability scanners are such a useful part of the attacker's arsenal. Figure 8-6 shows the output from Nessus, a popular vulnerability scanner, listing the found vulnerabilities by hosts. Nessus, like many other vulnerability scanners, provides the final list of vulnerabilities, along with their type, count, and other details about exploitability in the scan results that can assist defenders in hardening their hosts (see Figure 8-7). Attackers can use the information from the various scan results to determine the priority of targets as they work toward their goals.

Figure 8-6 Nessus scan results organized by host

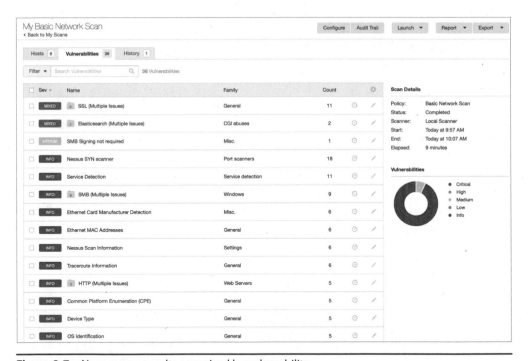

Figure 8-7 Nessus scan results organized by vulnerability

Attack Vectors

In studying how attackers make their way onto networks, hunters find the same handful of attack vectors time and time again. At a macro level, attackers gain access to systems using one or a combination of the following: malware, vulnerability exploitation, social engineering, or insiders. Beginning with malware, attackers have found lots of success with code designed to evade detection by antivirus software and security appliances. As these malware programs can often be aware of their surroundings, modern strains can even choose to become active only when they detect the correct environmental conditions, all while appearing benign in virtualized environments. Furthermore, much of the malware in use today is *polymorphic,* taking on a different look as it moves to and from infected systems. This common quality is rendering many legacy detection techniques ineffective.

Vulnerability exploitation, whether by way of a zero-day exploit or using well-known techniques, continues to prove useful for attackers. Zero-days, especially, give attackers a massive advantage in terms of time. Knowing that activity associated with a zero-day is far less likely to be detected using traditional methods, an attacker can often dwell in a system for months while defenders are none the wiser. Exploits of all kinds are particularly lucrative for attackers because they don't often require victim interaction. An attacker can scan a network, discover vulnerable conditions, launch the attack, and take advantage of the access. Another frequently observed technique is brute-force attacks for credentials.

For as long as attackers have been attempting to access networks, social engineering has been an integral part of their plan. By tricking their victims into divulging sensitive information or making decisions that weaken a part of the system, intruders use various methods such as pretexting, or communicating a false motive, to mislead and confuse. This is often very effective when used to deliver malware, because the privileged position gained as a result of a successful social engineering effort means fewer security hurdles to overcome for delivery of the malicious code.

If attackers cannot get an unwitting actor to help them gain access, they will sometimes resort to enticing willing insiders to do their bidding. Motivated by any number of factors, insider actors continue to pose a massive threat that attackers are all too eager to take advantage of. What's worse is that it's incredibly difficult to detect insider vectors because they "belong" on the network. Threat hunters will find that identifying insider behaviors related to attacker activities is among the most challenging categories of hunts.

Integrated Intelligence

Threat intelligence teams have a special relationship with threat hunters. Both are laser-focused on TTPs and want to know how attackers have behaved in the past and how they are likely to act in a given situation. Threat intelligence feeds inform threat hunters of the latest attacker TTPs, connected infrastructure, victimology, and attacker tendencies. Hunters, in pursuing these leads, can provide feedback to the intelligence team as to the effectiveness, accuracy, and relevance of the provided data. Additionally, they may also be able to feed back into the intelligence process so that the threat intelligence team can update their own products to reflect reality. In closing out a hunt, the team will want to communicate relevant malicious activity and new intelligence back to the operations and threat intelligence teams. In a sense, threat hunters are extensions of threat intelligence efforts, scouting for new information while verifying assumptions and assessments from the intelligence team.

Improving Detection Capabilities

A hunt, whether successful or not, will yield products that are directly relevant to detection efforts. At the very least, hunters will have a better understanding of TTPs and how they may be used against the environment. In the best scenario, the team can use examples of how TTPs were leveraged successfully to inform modifications to infrastructure, improvements to detection logic, and changes in policy. Technical modifications can result from discoveries about the network, servers, and endpoints during a hunt. One common change is the addition of security devices and sensors to areas in which the team lacks visibility. Additionally, a team may discover that a sensor is in place but is not correctly configured to catch the malicious behavior. Improvements to misconfigured sensors, network blind spots, and data collection not only help the hunting team should they have to embark on a similar venture in the future but also prepare the detection team to catch potentially malicious events and actors more effectively.

Following are a few benefits that a threat hunting team's output will provide to a detection team:

- Updated firewall and intrusion detection/prevention system (IDS/IPS) rules
- Updated alert logic for SIEM platforms
- Updated alert logic for endpoint detection and response (EDR) platforms
- Improvements to sensor placement across the network
- Improvements to asset visibility

Although not strictly within the purview of the detection team, the following benefits across the security team will affect the detection team's efficiency and reduce excess noise on the network:

- Changes in your organization's development process
- Changes to security training across the organization
- Changes to quality assurance and quality control processes

 TIP The threat hunting process often yields a plethora of new ideas for techniques to try and places to look. Be sure to record these ideas, as they will be great starting points for the next hunt.

Focus Areas

When performing threat hunting, you should always examine certain key areas of the infrastructure, both when looking for specific threats and when looking for anything in general that might indicate malicious activity. This of course includes unusual behavior patterns or unusual singular events. Some areas in the infrastructure warrant specialized or additional attention, such as device configuration, sensitive network segments, critical business processes, active defense controls, and security devices used to distract hackers. These areas are discussed next.

Configurations/Misconfigurations

Configuration of all network infrastructure devices, such as switches, routers, Voice over IP (VoIP), and security devices such as intrusion detection systems and firewalls, should all be under a standard configuration baseline. Different classes of hosts should also be under their own configuration baselines, based on intended function, criticality, and information sensitivity. For instance, user workstations may be under one baseline, while servers may be under a different one. In any case, baselining device configuration on your network and standardizing operating systems, applications, and access controls are two ways to detect when those devices are out of configuration.

In terms of threat hunting, you should review configuration files on a frequent basis. Most modern network devices and hosts have the ability, through agents installed on the host, to send information to a SIEM or other centralized monitoring facility to routinely report their health and configuration status. This would also include when configurations change, either as part of a routine or planned change or when the change occurs outside the normal procedures. A change in configuration, particularly one that has not been put through standard configuration and change management controls, may be indicative of malicious activity. Although most configuration changes can be monitored through automated means, manual configuration reviews also sometimes identify misconfigurations in devices that might not otherwise get noticed. These misconfigurations could lead to functionality and performance issues at best, but could also be indicative of malicious activity at worst. For example, a network device that has an unsecure port left open—either because it was not properly configured or because a malicious entity has opened the port—is worth examining. Here are a few configuration items you should pay particular attention to:

- Active Directory security policies
- User and group privilege assignments
- Rule sets configured on network security devices and host-based security services
- Open ports, protocols, and running services
- Application configuration settings
- Operating system configurations

Isolated Networks

Networks are often physically or logically isolated from other hosts and networks because of the sensitivity or criticality of the information that processes over them. These hosts can become higher value targets for malicious entities. Isolated network segments that are logically separated include those whose data may be encrypted to and from specific hosts on the network as well as those that are separated through the VLAN configuration, for example. You should pay more attention to these devices and networks since they are likely isolated for a reason. For isolated systems, you should focus on logical and physical system entry points, such as through firewalls, over specific ports, as well as traffic from and to specific hosts. Segments that are physically isolated may be less of a worry, unless these networks are ever connected, even infrequently, to the primary infrastructure or if an attacker physically gains access to these networks. In addition to rarely used network connections, you should also focus on physical access through uncontrolled removeable media, such as portable drives or USB sticks. There can be a tendency to lessen security controls on a physically isolated host since the belief is that it is harder to attack, but even isolated networks should be protected with essential security controls such as firewalls, restrictive access, controls, strong authentication, and encryption.

Business-Critical Assets and Processes

Beyond looking at the technical areas of the infrastructure, such as hosts and configuration items, you should also examine critical business processes and the systems that support those processes throughout the organization. A business process such as payroll, for example, or the process that initiates wire transfers from banks to other financial institutions, should be examined to determine if it has been compromised by an external entity. Business processes that handle critical or sensitive information are particularly vulnerable to these types of attacks. You should look at all administrative, technical, and even physical or operational controls that protect these processes. Any weaknesses in any of these types of controls make these business processes more vulnerable. You should look for abnormal transactions, unauthorized access, and unusual patterns of activity or behavior.

Active Defense

Employing active defenses is one way to reduce the viability of a threat exercising a vulnerability on the infrastructure. However, even your defenses can become targets of threats. You should review configuration and audit trails of security devices when engaging in active threat hunting. Attackers will almost always seek to disable or circumvent a security device or other security control before and during an attack. Intrusion detection systems, firewalls, SIEM systems, and other security-oriented systems are particularly vulnerable. These systems should require more stringent access control, and they should be more difficult to access remotely—only by only a limited number of personnel who have been carefully vetted and approved.

Honeypots and Honeynets

A *honeypot* is a device that is used to draw an attacker away from more sensitive portions of the infrastructure, since it seemingly is more interesting to the attacker or appears to be less protected. The reason for implementing a honeypot is that it gives the cybersecurity analyst an opportunity to observe attempts or an actual attack in progress. This allows the analyst time to scrutinize the attacker's methodology as well as to prevent them from accessing other parts of the infrastructure. A *honeynet* is a group of these devices that may reside on different segments within the infrastructure. Most honeynets are connected to perimeter networks, although there may be some merit to installing them at different points within the internal infrastructure. In any case, you should make use of this particular strategy in your threat hunting efforts to detect potentially malicious attacks and threats that may come into your infrastructure and are attracted to the honeypot first.

Chapter Review

Threat intelligence enables organizations to anticipate, respond to, and remediate threats. In some cases, organizations can use threat intelligence to speed up their decision-making cycle, causing increased cost to attackers conducting malicious activity, with continual improvements in their security posture and response efforts. Useful threat intelligence can be generated only after establishing a clear understanding of the organization's goals, the role of the security operations team within the organization, and the role of threat intelligence in supporting the security teams. Although the threat intelligence team may often reside within or adjacent to a security operations center, it serves customers throughout the organization. Risk managers, vulnerability managers, incident responders, financial analysts, and C-suite members can all benefit from threat intelligence products. Key to providing the best products possible is to have a baseline understanding of adversaries who may target the organization, what their capabilities are, and what motivates them. Understanding these aspects focuses the threat intelligence effort and ensures not only that the value delivered by the security team is in line with organizational goals but that it is also relevant and actionable.

Threat hunting is an analyst-centric process that enables organizations to look for malicious activity that may have slipped past detection and prevention mechanisms. It is a proactive process that relies on a skilled analyst to focus on attacker behavior and the evidence that they leave behind when they're moving about the network. Threat hunting is driven by a modern philosophy being adopted by more and more information security processionals: assume compromise and act accordingly. Accepting the very real possibility that no network is completely impenetrable and that attackers may have made it past defenses is a prudent mindset that demonstrates a mature and realistic view of security.

Conducting a hunt requires the smart application of tools and techniques to extract and make sense of highly detailed information across the environment. Part science and part art, the process is repeatable and scalable, while allowing for hunter intuition to guide the pursuit of signs of intrusion, no matter how insignificant they may seem. Bringing your analytical capacity and your understanding of the details will be more impactful than any single piece of technology. With the assistance of tools, you can bring threat hunting techniques to bear to find evil and discover attacks earlier in the attack cycle.

Questions

1. Which is *not* an example of a built-in resource in the Windows environment that attackers often leverage for persistence?

    A. LaunchAgent

    B. Windows registry modification

    C. DLL injection

    D. Scheduled task

2. Developed by Microsoft, which threat modeling technique is suitable for application to logical and physical systems alike?

   A. PASTA

   B. STRIDE

   C. The Diamond Model

   D. MITRE ATT&CK

3. What term is used for a key assumption that differentiates the threat hunter mindset from traditional security processes?

   A. Walled garden

   B. Defense in depth

   C. Least privilege

   D. Assume breach

4. Defining what a threat actor might be able to achieve in the event of an attack is also known as determining the actor's _____.

   A. means

   B. skillset

   C. intent

   D. capability

5. Details about domains that may include scoring information, blocklist status, and association with malware are also known as what kind of data?

   A. Behavioral

   B. Threat

   C. Reputational

   D. Malware

6. Accurately describing a threat includes all but which of the following components?

   A. Intent

   B. Capability

   C. Opportunity

   D. Operations

7. What is the primary difference between threat intelligence and threat hunting as they relate to security operations?

   A. Threat intelligence aims to add context to observed activity on the network, whereas threat hunting does not.

   B. Threat hunting requires an understanding of adversary TTPs, whereas threat intelligence does not.

    C. Threat intelligence requires skills and experience in all facets of security operations, whereas threat hunting is focused on forensics.

    D. Threat hunting focuses on what may have already occurred, whereas threat intelligence can be used to estimate an adversary's future behaviors.

8. Consisting of the two components of data and context, what term describes an artifact that indicates the possibility of an attack?

    A. Indicator of compromise

    B. Security indicators and event monitor

    C. Security information and event management

    D. Simulations, indications, and environmental monitors

9. Which of the following is an open framework for communicating the characteristics and severity of software vulnerabilities?

    A. STRIDE

    B. NVD

    C. CVSS

    D. CVE

Answers

1. A. LaunchAgent creation is the most commonly used method in the macOS environment, but it does not exist in Windows. In a Windows environment, registry modification, dynamic-link library (DLL) injection, and scheduled task execution are all methods that attackers use to maintain persistence.

2. B. STRIDE is a threat modeling framework that evaluates a system's design using flow diagrams, system entities, and events related to the system.

3. D. Assume breach is a strategy based on the assumption that an attacker is already in your network, or that your defenses may be insufficient to detect all attacker behavior. The "assume breach" mindset promotes ongoing testing and refinement of detection and response techniques.

4. D. Defining a threat actor's capability (that is, the ability to use skills and tools to perform an attack) helps indicate what the actor might be able to achieve in the event of an attack.

5. C. Reputational services often assign scores to URLs, domains, and IP addresses across the Internet that are generated based on the entity's links with malware, spyware, spam, phishing, C2, and data exfiltration servers.

6. D. Operations is not one of the three components that need to be present for a threat to be accurately described. The components are capability, intent, and opportunity.

7. **B.** Threat hunting requires an understanding of adversary TTPs, whereas threat intelligence does not.

8. **A.** An indicator of compromise (IoC) is an artifact consisting of context applied to observable data that indicates the possibility of an attack.

9. **C.** The Common Vulnerability Scoring System (CVSS) is the de facto standard for assessing the severity of vulnerabilities.

PART II

Vulnerability Management

Vulnerability Scanning Methods and Concepts

In this chapter you will learn:

- The importance of asset identification and discovery
- The industry frameworks that address vulnerability management
- The types of nontraditional IT that make up critical infrastructure
- The various considerations in vulnerability identification and scanning

Of old, the expert in battle would first make himself invincible and then wait for his enemy to expose his vulnerability.

—Sun Tzu

Managing vulnerabilities in the organization is a critical part of security program management. Without consistent proactive vulnerability management, there would be no point in maintaining the other security controls in the organization since these weaknesses will eventually be exploited by a variety of internal and external threats. One of the first and most important pieces of vulnerability management is identifying vulnerabilities in various assets in the organization. Vulnerabilities can be identified through formal or informal assessments, but likely you are going to use some sort of vulnerability scanning tools for the technical vulnerabilities. That's the focus of this chapter—discovering and identifying technical vulnerabilities. We will discuss mapping out the assets on the infrastructure and point out some nontraditional types of infrastructure that you should pay particular attention to because of the risk; these include operational technology (OT), industrial control systems (ICSs), and supervisory control and data acquisition (SCADA) systems. We will also discuss the characteristics of vulnerability scanning, including the different types of scans and the considerations you must weigh when implementing each of them. We'll also explain security frameworks that require (and can assist you in) vulnerability management. This chapter addresses the requirements of Objective 2.1, "Given a scenario, implement vulnerability scanning methods and concepts."

Asset Discovery

You cannot protect what you don't know you have. Though inventorying assets is not what most of us would consider glamorous work, it is nevertheless a critical aspect of managing vulnerabilities in your information systems. In fact, this aspect of security is so important that it is prominently featured at the top of the Center for Internet Security's list of critical security controls. Critical control number 1 applies to the inventory of authorized and unauthorized devices, and control number 2 deals with inventorying the software running on those devices.

Keep in mind that an asset is anything of value to an organization, regardless of whether that value is expressed in quantifiable terms, such as dollars, or qualitative terms, such as low- or high-value assets. Apart from hardware and software, assets include people, partners, equipment, facilities, reputation, and information. For the purposes of the CySA+ exam, we focus on hardware, software, and information. Determining the value of an asset can be difficult and is oftentimes subjective, but first you must discover what assets you have. For assets connected to the infrastructure, you can manually go through your facilities and count them (and sometimes you may have to do exactly that), but most of the time it's a much more efficient use of your time and resources to make the network do the work for you by scanning it for your connected devices.

Asset Mapping Scans and Fingerprinting

One of the most efficient ways to discover and identify assets is through scanning them on the network. If a device is connected, and the right tool is used, a mapping scan will find all of your hosts. The scanning tool, such as nmap (discussed in more detail later on in the chapter), sends traffic throughout the network, querying any devices. The devices respond in different ways, depending on the type of traffic that is sent. In some instances, Internet Control Message Protocol (ICMP) packets may be sent, causing the hosts to respond to "ping" packets. Other traffic, such as Address Resolution Protocol (ARP) requests, may be sent, eliciting a different response from hosts. In all cases, multiple types of traffic are usually transmitted over the network simultaneously, targeting specific ports on network hosts to see if they are running the services associated with those ports.

Not every host will respond to every type of network traffic sent to it; security configurations on the host may prevent them from responding to ICMP requests, for example. However, since a variety of different scanning techniques can be used, it is likely that at least one type of traffic sent will elicit a response from every active host on the network. Depending on how the various packets are crafted by the scanning tool, not only will the hosts respond but they will also give up information unique to the individual TCP/IP stack implementation running on it. This serves to "fingerprint" the device, returning information from the scan on which operating system and version it is running, which services are running, open and closed ports, IP address, MAC address, and so on. To account for hosts that may be turned off or temporarily disconnected from the network, discovery scans should be run on a frequent basis. Discovery scans can also be a good way of detecting rogue or unauthorized devices connected to the network.

 EXAM TIP Identifying assets is one of the most critical processes in most security programs, such as asset management, vulnerability identification, and risk management. You will likely see this emphasized on the exam, depending on the context of the question.

Industry Frameworks

Vulnerability management should not only be considered a critical part of your overall organizational security management program but is also often required by governance, such as laws, regulations, industry and professional standards, and internal organizational security policy. To assist you in meeting governance requirements with regard to vulnerability management, several industry and professional frameworks, control sets, and so on are available to provide more detailed guidance in this area. Note that none of the frameworks we mention here are mandatory unless a law or regulation specifically requires them or your organization has decided to formally adopt them as a matter of policy. We will address the regulatory environment as a special consideration for vulnerability scanning later in the chapter.

In this section, we discuss some of the most important frameworks with which you should be familiar in the context of vulnerability management. The following four standards are specifically called out in the CySA+ exam objectives but cover only a few of the examples of frameworks available to you.

Payment Card Industry Data Security Standard

The Payment Card Industry Data Security Standard (PCI DSS) applies to any organization involved in processing credit card payments using cards branded by the five major issuers: Visa, MasterCard, American Express, Discover, and JCB. Each of these organizations had its own vendor security requirements, so in 2006 they joined efforts and standardized these requirements across the industry. The PCI DSS requirements are periodically updated, and the standard is in version 4.0, as of March 2022, and has been renamed the "Payment Card Industry Data Security Standard: Requirements and Testing Procedures."

Requirement 11 of the PCI DSS deals with the obligation to "test security of systems and networks regularly." The requirements under this heading include 11.3.1 and 11.3.2, which address internal and external vulnerability scanning, respectively. Specifically, these two requirements state that the organization must perform two types of vulnerability scans every quarter: internal and external. Internal scans may be performed by qualified staff members of the organization, whereas external scans must be performed by approved scanning vendors (ASVs). It is important to know that the organization must be able to show that the personnel involved in the scanning have the required expertise to do so. Requirement 11 also states that both internal and external vulnerability scans must be performed whenever significant changes are made to the systems or processes.

Finally, PCI DSS requires that any "critical" vulnerabilities uncovered by either type of scan be resolved. After resolution, another scan is required to demonstrate that the risks have been properly mitigated.

 EXAM TIP You do not have to be familiar with each requirement for PCI DSS, but you should remember that Requirement 11 covers vulnerability scanning and management.

Center for Internet Security Controls

The Center for Internet Security (CIS) is a nonprofit organization that, among other things, maintains a list of 18 critical security controls designed to mitigate the threat of the majority of common cyberattacks. The 18 CIS controls, currently in version 8, are shown in Table 9-1.

Despite the use of the word "controls," you should really think of these 18 as major control areas or groupings. Under each of these 18 control areas are supporting subordinate controls, called *safeguards,* that are more granular and provide details on individual activities relevant to that group. For example, if we look into Control 7 of the CIS (Continuous Vulnerability Management), we can see the following seven safeguards (excerpted from CIS Critical Security Controls, Version 8, http://www.cisecurity.org/controls/, May 2021):

- **7.1 Establish and Maintain a Vulnerability Management Process**   Establish and maintain a documented vulnerability management process for enterprise assets. Review and update documentation annually or when significant enterprise changes occur that could impact this safeguard.

- **7.2 Establish and Maintain a Remediation Process**   Establish and maintain a risk-based remediation strategy documented in a remediation process, with monthly, or more frequent, reviews.

Table 9-1
The 18 CIS controls

Control	Number of Safeguards
1. Inventory and Control of Enterprise Assets	5
2. Inventory and Control of Software Assets	7
3. Data Protection	14
4. Secure Configuration of Enterprise Assets and Software	12
5. Account Management	6
6. Access Control Management	8
7. Continuous Vulnerability Management	7
8. Audit Log Management	12
9. Email and Web Browser Protections	7
10. Malware Defenses	7
11. Data Recovery	5
12. Network Infrastructure Management	8
13. Network Monitoring and Defense	11
14. Security Awareness and Skills Training	9
15. Service Provider Management	7
16. Application Software Security	14
17. Incident Response and Management	9
18. Penetration Testing	5

- **7.3 Perform Automated Operating System Patch Management**   Perform operating system updates on enterprise assets through automated patch management on a monthly, or more frequent, basis.

- **7.4 Perform Automated Application Patch Management**   Perform application updates on enterprise assets through automated patch management on a monthly, or more frequent, basis.

- **7.5 Perform Automated Vulnerability Scans of Internal Enterprise Assets**   Perform automated vulnerability scans of internal enterprise assets on a quarterly, or more frequent, basis. Conduct both authenticated and unauthenticated scans, using a SCAP-compliant vulnerability scanning tool.

- **7.6 Perform Automated Vulnerability Scans of Externally-Exposed Enterprise Assets**   Perform automated vulnerability scans of externally exposed enterprise assets using a SCAP-compliant vulnerability scanning tool. Perform scans on a monthly, or more frequent, basis.

- **7.7 Remediate Detected Vulnerabilities**   Remediate detected vulnerabilities in software through processes and tooling on a monthly, or more frequent, basis, based on the remediation process.

The CIS recognizes that not every organization will have the resources (or face the risks) necessary to implement all safeguards listed under each control. For this reason, safeguards are applicable and assigned to three Implementation Groups (IGs), which describe organizations based on size and resources. While every organization should strive for full implementation, this approach provides a way to address the most urgent requirements first and then grow over time.

- **IG1**   This group consists of small- to medium-sized organizations that have limited IT and cybersecurity personnel trained on staff. Controls assigned to this group are the minimum essential controls needed to protect these organizations.

- **IG2**   These organizations are larger and have more dedicated IT and cybersecurity personnel on staff, qualified to manage the organization's infrastructure. The additional safeguards assigned to this group enhance operational security.

- **IG3**   This group consists of large enterprise-level organizations that have a mature cybersecurity program with qualified IT and cybersecurity staff focused not only on day-to-day operations but also the more strategic aspects of cyber risk management. Safeguards assigned to this group are the more advanced, strategic controls needed to protect organizations at a higher level of maturity.

As an example, note that of the seven safeguards under Continuous Vulnerability Management, four apply to IG1 organizations, and all seven apply to IG2 and IG3 organizations.

EXAM TIP   You do not have to memorize the requirements of the CIS controls for the exam, but you should keep in mind the general requirements of Control 7, Continuous Vulnerability Management. You should also be familiar with how the CIS controls work within the implementation groups.

Open Web Application Security Project

The Open Web Application Security Project (OWASP) is an organization that deals specifically with web security issues. Along with a long list of tools, articles, and resources that developers can access to create secure software, OWASP also sponsors individual member meetings (chapters) throughout the world. The group provides development guidelines, testing procedures, and code review steps, but it is probably best known for its list of top ten web application security risks (known as the OWASP Top Ten). The top ten security risks identified by this group have evolved over time, and, as of the updated list in 2021 (and the writing of the third edition of this book in 2023), they are as follows:

1. A01:2021—Broken Access Control
2. A02:2021—Cryptographic Failures
3. A03:2021—Injection
4. A04:2021—Insecure Design
5. A05:2021—Security Misconfiguration
6. A06:2021—Vulnerable and Outdated Components
7. A07:2021—Identification and Authentication Failures
8. A08:2021—Software and Data Integrity Failures
9. A09:2021—Security Logging and Monitoring Failures
10. A10:2021—Server-Side Request Forgery (SSRF)

This list represents the most common vulnerabilities that reside in web-based software and are exploited most often. You can find out more information pertaining to these vulnerabilities at https://owasp.org/www-project-top-ten/.

 EXAM TIP You do not have to memorize the top ten vulnerabilities in OWASP, but you should be familiar with them enough to be able to identify them on the exam.

ISO/IEC 27000 Series

The International Organization for Standardization (ISO) and the International Electrotechnical Commission (IEC) 27000 series serves as industry best practices for the management of security controls in a holistic manner within organizations around the world. The list of standards that make up this series grows each year. Each standard has a specific focus (such as metrics, governance, auditing, and so on).

ISO 27001:2022

One of these ISO/IEC standards that is particularly relevant to our discussion is 27001. ISO/IEC 27001 applies to any organization, regardless of size, that wants to formalize its security activities through the creation of an information security management system (ISMS). This system documents the following, at a minimum:

- Who are the stakeholders and what are their expectations?
- What are the information security objectives?
- What are the risks to information systems?
- Which controls will be used to handle those risks?
- How are these controls to be implemented?
- How will the controls' effectiveness be continuously monitored?
- What is the process to continuously improve the ISMS?

ISO/IEC 27001 has 114 controls organized into 14 domains. While standards such as ISO 27001, PCI-DSS, NIST, and the CIS controls are compatible with each other, some of these standards focus only on controls, but the ISO/IEC standard deals with the overarching security program management as well. The 14 domains in ISO/IEC 27001 are listed here:

- Information security policies
- Organization of information security
- Human resource security
- Asset management
- Access control
- Cryptography
- Physical and environmental security
- Operations security
- Communications security
- System acquisition, development, and maintenance
- Supplier relationships
- Information security incident management
- Information security aspects of business continuity management
- Compliance

ISO 27001 and its related publications in the 27000 series call out vulnerability management controls, requirements, and best practices.

EXAM TIP You do not have to memorize the details of ISO/IEC 27001, CIS, or PCI DSS, but you need to know that there are regulatory environments that require vulnerability management, and you should be somewhat familiar with each of these frameworks. You may be required to differentiate one security framework from another based on the scenario given in the exam question.

Critical Infrastructure

Critical infrastructure is the broad name given to the set of technologies used throughout an entire country that run its core services, such as power, heating, water treatment, refineries, transportation systems, medical systems, and so on. While most of this structure is composed of traditional information technologies, such as WAN and LAN networks, servers, workstations, network devices, and other traditional hosts, some of these technologies are considered "nontraditional." Nontraditional technologies are those that historically were electromechanical in nature and did not include IT components in them. They were also not traditionally connected to a network of any type. However, in modern times, these technologies used to connect to electrical components and machinery that run critical services now not only have computerized components in them but have also been merged with traditional IT such that they now have CPUs, memory, hard drives, operating systems, and are even connected to each other via IP-based networks or the larger Internet. These systems are now popularly referred to as *cyber-physical* systems. These nontraditional technologies, which we will discuss in the following sections, include operational technology, industrial control systems, and supervisory control and data acquisition systems. Each has unique considerations when it comes to protecting assets, as well as inherent vulnerabilities.

Industrial Control Systems and Operational Technology

Industrial control systems (ICSs) are cyber-physical systems that enable specialized software to control their physical behaviors. For example, ICSs are used in automated automobile assembly lines, building elevators, and even HVAC (heating, ventilation, and air conditioning) systems. A typical ICS architecture is shown in Figure 9-1. At the bottom layer (level 0) are the actual physical devices, such as sensors and actuators, that control physical processes. These are connected to remote terminal units (RTUs) or programmable logic controllers (PLCs), which translate physical effects to binary data, and vice versa. These RTUs and PLCs at level 1 are, in turn, connected to database servers and human–machine interaction (HMI) controllers and terminals at level 2.

Vulnerabilities in Interconnected Networks

In what has become the most popular example of the vulnerabilities involved with connecting traditional IP-based networks and nontraditional control systems, we often point to the now-infamous Target breach. In late 2013, the consumer retail giant Target educated the entire world on a major vulnerability of interconnected networks. One of the largest data breaches in history resulting from nontraditional systems was accomplished not by attacking the retailer's data systems directly, but by using an HVAC vendor's network as an entry point. The vendor had access to the networks at Target stores to monitor and manage their HVAC systems, but the vulnerability introduced by the interconnection was not fully considered by Target's security personnel. In a world that has grown completely interconnected and interdependent, being completely aware of not only your own infrastructure, but also of other systems that may connect to your network, is essential.

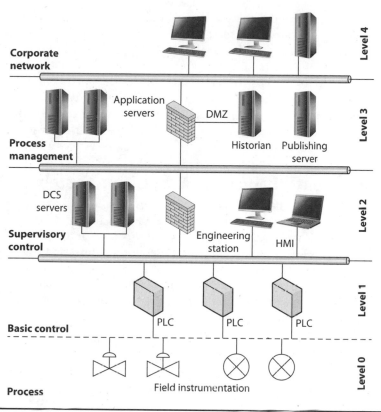

Figure 9-1 Simple industrial control system

Operational Technology

The three lower levels of the architecture we described earlier are known as the *operational technology* (OT) network. The OT network was traditionally isolated from the IT network that inhabits levels 3 and 4 of the architecture. For a variety of functional and business reasons, this gap between OT (levels 0 through 2) and IT (levels 3 and 4) is now frequently bridged, providing access to physical processes from anywhere on the Internet.

Much of the software that runs an ICS is burned into the firmware of devices such as programmable logic controllers (PLCs). In 2010, the Stuxnet worm targeted PLCs running uranium enrichment centrifuges. This is a source of vulnerabilities because updating the ICS software cannot normally be done automatically or even centrally. The patching and updating process, which is pretty infrequent to begin with, typically requires that the device be brought offline and manually updated by a qualified technician. Between the cost and effort involved and the effects of interrupting business processes, it should come as no surprise to learn that many ICS components are never updated or patched. To make matters worse, vendors are notorious for not providing patches at all, even when vulnerabilities are discovered and made public. Adding to the problem is the fact some vendors that built and supplied some of the older cyber-physical technologies are not even in business anymore.

Another common vulnerability with ICSs is the lack of authentication methods in older devices. Strong authentication methods were not considered for these technologies when they were first developed, and many legacy devices have weak authentication, such as simple passwords, or even no authentication at all. Sometimes the manufacturer of the ICS device would set a trivial password in the firmware, documenting it so all users (and perhaps abusers) knew what it was, and sometimes making it difficult, if not impossible, to change. In many documented cases, these passwords are stored in plaintext. Manufacturers are getting better at dealing with these issues, but many devices still have unchangeable simple passwords controlling critical physical systems around the world.

Supervisory Control and Data Acquisition Systems

A supervisory control and data acquisition (SCADA) system is a specific type of ICS characterized by its ability to monitor and control devices throughout large geographic regions. Whereas an ICS typically controls physical processes and devices locally in one building or a small campus, a SCADA system is used for pipelines and transmission lines covering hundreds or thousands of miles. SCADA is most commonly associated with energy (for example, petroleum or power) and utility (for example, water or sewer) applications. The general architecture of a SCADA system is depicted in Figure 9-2.

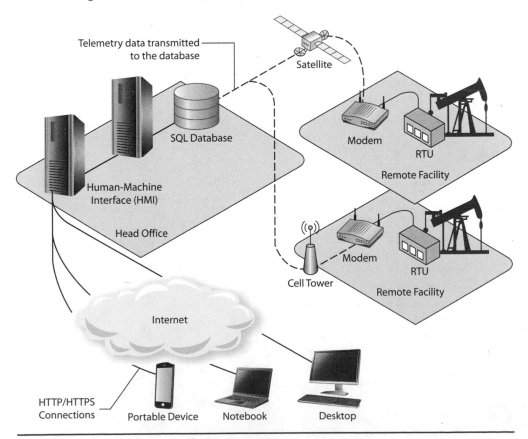

Figure 9-2 Typical architecture of a SCADA system

SCADA systems introduce two more types of common vulnerabilities in addition to those normally found in ICS. The first of these is induced by the long-distance communications links. For many years, most organizations using SCADA systems relied on the relative obscurity of the communications protocols and radio frequencies involved to provide a degree of, or at least the illusion of, security. In one of the first cases of attacks against SCADA systems, an Australian man apparently seeking revenge in 2001 connected a rogue radio transceiver to a remote terminal unit (RTU) and intentionally caused millions of gallons of sewage to spill into local parks and rivers. Though these wireless systems have mostly been modernized and hardened, they still present potential vulnerabilities.

The second weakness, particular to a SCADA system, is its reliance on isolated and unattended facilities. These remote stations provide attackers with an opportunity to gain physical access to system components. Though many of these stations are now protected by cameras and alarm systems, their remoteness makes responding significantly slower compared to that of most other information systems.

 EXAM TIP Although the exact protocols used may vary from standard networked devices, the concepts of network scanning, identification of vulnerable targets, and exploit delivery associated with ICS, OT, and SCADA infrastructures remain the same. For the CySA+ exam, you should focus on broad mitigation strategies for these types of activities.

Vulnerability Identification and Scanning

Vulnerability scanning, the practice of automating security checks against your systems, is a key part of securing a network. These checks help focus your efforts on protecting the network by pointing out the weak parts of the system. In many cases, scanning tools even suggest options for remediation.

Although we promote the regular use of vulnerability scanners, you should consider some important limitations of this practice before you use them. Many vulnerability scanners do a tremendous job of identifying weaknesses, but they are often single-purpose tools. Specifically, they often lack the functionality of capitalizing on a weakness and elevating to the exploit stage automatically. As a defender, you must understand that an actual attacker will combine the results from their own vulnerability scan, along with other intelligence about the network, to formulate a smart plan on how to get into the network. What's more, scanning tools will usually not be able to perform any type of advanced correlation on their own, and you'll likely require additional tools and processes to determine the overall risk of operating the network. This is due not only to the large variety of network configurations but also to other nontechnical factors such as business requirements, operational requirements, and organizational policy.

Consider a simple example—a discovery of several low-risk vulnerabilities across the network. Although the vulnerability scanner may classify each of these occurrences as "low risk," without the context of the security posture in other areas of the network, it's impossible for you to truly understand the cumulative effect of these low-risk vulnerabilities.

It may even turn out that the cumulative effect is beyond what the additive effect may be. In other words, the combined effect of several relatively low-severity vulnerabilities is amplified by the fact that they may be exploited together. A weak password used by an administrator and one used by a normal user are both problematic, but the potential effect of a compromise of an administrator's account can have far greater impact on the organization. No single tool is going to be able to provide such a depth of insight automatically, so it's important for you to understand the limitations of your tools and their capabilities.

Typically, organizations will have an issue-specific policy covering vulnerability management, but it is important to note that this policy is nested within the broader corporate security policy and may also be associated with system-specific policies. The point is that it is not enough to understand the vulnerability management policy (or develop one if it doesn't exist) in a vacuum. You must understand the organizational security context within which this process takes place. Over the next several sections, we will discuss some important factors regarding how you should frame your vulnerability management policy and procedures. These include considering risk, scope, regulatory requirements, technical constraints, workflow, and tools, among other considerations.

Passive vs. Active Scanning

Scanning is a method used to get more details about the target network or device by poking around and taking note of the target's responses. Attackers have scanned targets attempting to find openings since the early days of the Internet, starting with a technique called *war dialing.* By using a device to dial sequentially and automatically through a list of phone numbers and listen to the response, an attacker could determine whether it was a human or a machine on the other side. Back when many computers were connected to the Web via unprotected modems, war dialing was the easiest and most effective method for gaining access to these systems. In modern networks, *host scanning* remains an effective way to inventory and discover details of a system by sending a message to a host, and based on the response, either classifying that system or taking further exploratory measures. Scanners generally come in three flavors: network mappers, host (or port) scanners, and web app vulnerability scanners.

Passive scanning refers to the technique of scanning a host without triggering any intrusion detection alerts. This can be employed simply by listening to traffic coming from the host to gain information about its internal configuration, such as ports, protocols, and services in use, or by sending it innocuous traffic. *Active* scanning refers to intentionally sending specifically crafted traffic to a host to elicit a particular response. Active scanning is more likely to be detected by both network and host-based intrusion detection systems.

Mapping/Enumeration

Earlier in the chapter we discussed discovering assets such as hosts and other devices using a scanning tool such as nmap. This same technique can also be used to discover how the network is designed and architected. The goal of *network mapping* is to understand the topology of the network, including perimeter networks, demilitarized zones, and key network devices. The process used during network mapping is referred to as *topology discovery*.

The first step in creating a network map is to find out what devices exist by performing a "sweep." As with the example of war dialing, network sweeping is accomplished by sending a message to each device and recording the response. These messages are in the form of network traffic with particular characteristics, such as using specific combinations of protocols and ports. A popular tool for this is Network Mapper, more commonly referred to as nmap. In executing a network sweep, nmap's default behavior is to send an ICMP echo request, a TCP SYN to port 443, a TCP ACK to port 80, and an ICMP timestamp request. A successful response to any of these four methods is evidence that the address is in use. Some hosts may even require other specific types of network traffic in order to get a response. Nmap also has a traceroute feature that enables it to map out networks of various complexities using the clever manipulation of the time-to-live values of packets. After mapping a network, an adversary may have an inventory of the network but may want to fill in the details.

Port Scanning

Port scanners are programs designed to probe a host or server to determine what ports are open. They are an important tool for administrators. This method of enumerating the various services a host offers is one means of *service discovery*. It enables an attacker to add details to the broad strokes by getting insight into what services are running on a target. Because network-connected devices often run services on well-known ports such as 80 and 25, port scanning is a reliable source of information on these devices. Depending on the response time, the response type, and other criteria, the scanning software can identify which services are running—and some scanning tools, such as nmap, can even provide *OS fingerprinting* to identify the device's operating system. However, identifying the OS isn't perfect because the values that the software relies on for detection can change depending on the network configuration and other settings. With the information provided by the scanner, the attacker is in a better position to choose what kind of attack may be most effective. Note that nmap, like most general-purpose scanning tools, can be used to map devices and scan ports simultaneously.

 NOTE   OS fingerprinting is not an exact science. You should not conclude that a host is running a given OS simply because the scanner identified it as such.

Scanning Parameters and Criteria

With all these very particular vulnerabilities floating around, how often should you be checking for them? As you may have guessed, there is no one-size-fits-all answer to that question. The important issue to keep in mind is that the *process* is what matters. If you haphazardly do vulnerability scans at random intervals, you will have a much harder time answering the question of whether or not your vulnerability management is effective. If, on the other hand, you do the math up front and determine the frequencies and scopes of the various scans, given your list of assumptions and requirements, you will have much more control over your security posture.

Just as you must weigh a host of considerations when determining how often to conduct vulnerability scans, you also need to think about different but related issues when configuring your tools to perform these scans. Today's tools typically have more power and options than most of us will sometimes need. Our information systems may also impose limitations or requirements on which of these features can or should be brought to bear. When configuring scanning tools, you have a host of different considerations, but here we focus on the main ones you will be expected to know for the CySA+ exam. The list is not exhaustive, however, and you should probably grow it with issues that are specific to your organization or sector.

Schedule

One of the first criteria for a scan is its schedule. Simply running scans at any time of the day or night is not always the best policy because vulnerability scanning can interfere in the operations of critical devices or operations. Most of your scans also will not simply be run on an ad hoc basis, although those do occur. Routine scans will typically be scheduled and automated, to take into account both high and low network traffic usage times. This is because some devices, such as user workstations or portable devices, may be turned off or disconnected during non-business hours. Other devices, such as servers that process high loads, may not handle scans very well during high peak usage times, so you will likely have scans scheduled throughout the business day, during nights, or even on weekends, depending on the particular assets you are scanning and their availability. Additionally, scanning the entire network at once is usually not a good idea because of the massive volume of network traffic you could generate, which would impact the usability of the network for your users. Normally scans are scheduled based on asset criticality or usage.

There also may be considerations in scheduling during certain critical processing times, such end-of-month reports, or specific blackout dates when critical types of operations are performed, such as tax time or closeout of fiscal year. During these unique processing times, vulnerability scanning may have to be delayed to ensure that nothing goes wrong with critical business functions. You should also keep in mind downtime considerations for critical assets when developing your vulnerability scanning schedules.

Of course, you will have the occasional ad hoc scan, where you need to scan a particular device or even a subnet, to perform troubleshooting or to investigate a network security issue, for instance. These are typically manual scans that may occur anytime, but they usually focus on a very small subset of your network assets.

Scope

Whether you are running a scheduled or an ad hoc scan, you have to define its scope carefully and configure your tools appropriately. Though it would be simpler to scan everything at once at set intervals, the reality is that this is oftentimes not possible simply because of the load this places on critical nodes, if not the entire system. What may work better is to have a series of scans, each with a different scope and parameters.

Whether you are doing a global or targeted scan, your tools must know which nodes to test and which ones to leave alone. The set of devices that will be assessed constitutes the scope of the vulnerability scan. Deliberately scoping these events is important for a variety of reasons, but one of the most important ones is the need for credentials, which we discuss later in the chapter.

Framework Requirements

If you thought the approach to determining the frequency of scans based on risk appetite was not very definitive, the opposite is true of framework and regulatory requirements. Assuming you've identified all the applicable frameworks, policies, and regulations applicable to vulnerability management, the frequencies of the various scans may already be given to you. For instance, requirements 11.3.1 and 11.3.2 of the PCI DSS mandate vulnerability scans at least quarterly as well as after any significant change in the network. The Health Insurance Portability and Accountability Act (HIPAA), on the other hand, requires periodic vulnerability assessments but imposes no specific scanning frequency requirements. Still, to avoid potential problems, most experts agree that HIPAA-covered organizations should run vulnerability scans at least quarterly at minimum.

Vulnerability Feeds

Unless you work in a governmental intelligence organization, the odds are that your knowledge of vulnerabilities mostly comes from commercial or community feeds. These services have update cycles that range from hours to weeks and, though they eventually tend to converge on the vast majority of known vulnerabilities, one feed may publish a threat significantly before another. If you run hourly scans, you would obviously benefit from the faster services and may be able to justify the higher cost. If, on the other hand, your scans are weekly, monthly, or even quarterly, the difference may not be as significant. As a rule of thumb, you want a vulnerability feed that is about as frequent as your own scanning cycle.

If your vulnerability feed is not one with a fast update cycle, or if you want to ensure you are absolutely abreast of the latest discovered vulnerabilities, you can (and perhaps should) subscribe to alerts in addition to those of your provider. The National Vulnerability Database (NVD), maintained by the National Institute of Standards and Technologies (NIST), provides two such feeds. One will alert you to any new vulnerability reported, and the other provides only those that have been analyzed. The advantage of the first feed is that you are on the bleeding edge of notifications. The advantage of the second is that it provides you with specific products that are affected as well as additional analysis. A number of other professional and vendor organizations provide similar feeds that you should probably explore as well.

Assuming you have subscribed to one or more feeds (in addition to your scanning product's feed), you will likely learn of vulnerabilities in between scheduled scans. When this happens, you will have to consider whether to run an out-of-cycle (usually an ad hoc) scan that looks for that particular vulnerability or to wait until the next scheduled event to run the test. If the flaw is critical enough to warrant immediate action, you may have to perform an update from your scanner's service provider or, failing that, write your own plug-in to test the vulnerability. Obviously, this would require significant resources, so you should have a process by which to make decisions like these as part of your vulnerability management program.

Technical Constraints

Vulnerability assessments require resources such as personnel, time, bandwidth, hardware, and software, many of which are likely limited in your organization. Of these, the top technical constraints on your ability to perform these tests are qualified personnel and technical capacity. Here, the term *capacity* is used to denote computational resources expressed in cycles of CPU time, bytes of primary and secondary memory, and bits per second (bps) of network connectivity. Because any scanning tool you choose to use will require a minimum amount of such capacity, you may be constrained in both the frequency and scope of your vulnerability scans. For instance, a network with many devices but low bandwidth will make scans run slower and eat up valuable bandwidth for your users.

If you have no idea how much capacity your favorite scans require, quantifying it should be one of your first next steps. It is possible that in well-resourced organizations such requirements are negligible compared to the available capacity. In such an environment, it is possible to increase the frequency of scans to daily or even hourly for high-risk assets. It is more likely, however, that your scanning takes a noticeable toll on assets that are also required for your principal mission. In such cases, you want to balance the mission and security requirements carefully so that one doesn't unduly detract from the other.

Workflow

Another consideration when determining how often you conduct vulnerability scanning is established workflows of security and network operations within your organization. As mentioned earlier, qualified personnel constitute a limited resource. Whenever you run a vulnerability scan, someone will have to review and perhaps analyze the results to determine what actions, if any, are required. This process is best incorporated into the workflows of your security and/or network operations centers personnel.

A recurring theme in this chapter has been the need to standardize and enforce repeatable vulnerability management processes. Apart from well-written policies, the next best way to ensure this happens is by writing these processes into the daily workflows of security and IT personnel. If you work in a security operation center (SOC) and know that every Tuesday morning your duties include reviewing the vulnerability scans from the night before and creating tickets for any required remediation, then you're much more likely to do this routinely. The organization, in turn, benefits from consistent vulnerability scans with well-documented outcomes, which, in turn, become enablers of effective risk management across the entire system.

Tool Updates and Plug-Ins

Vulnerability scanning tools work by testing systems against lists of known vulnerabilities. These flaws are frequently being discovered by vendors and security researchers. Modern scanning tools can easily be configured to perform periodic updates to download the latest vulnerability lists on a weekly, daily, or even hourly basis. It stands to reason that if you don't keep your vulnerabilities lists up to date, whatever tool you use will eventually fail to detect vulnerabilities that are known by others, especially your adversaries. This is why it is critical to keep an eye on current vulnerabilities lists.

Figure 9-3
NASL script
that tests for
anonymous
FTP logins

```
#
# The script code starts here :
#

include("ftp_func.inc");

port = get_kb_item("Services/ftp");
if(!port)port = 21;

if (get_kb_item('ftp/'+port+'/backdoor')) exit(0);

state = get_port_state(port);
if(!state)exit(0);
soc = open_sock_tcp(port);
if(soc)
{
 domain = get_kb_item("Settings/third_party_domain");
 r = ftp_log_in(socket:soc, user:"anonymous", pass:string("nessus@", domain));
 if(r)
 {
  port2 = ftp_get_pasv_port(socket:soc);
  if(port2)
  {
   soc2 = open_sock_tcp(port2, transport:get_port_transport(port));
   if (soc2)
   {
    send(socket:soc, data:'LIST /\r\n');
    listing = ftp_recv_listing(socket:soc2);
    close(soc2);
    }
  }
 }

 data = "
This FTP service allows anonymous logins. If you do not want to share data
with anyone you do not know, then you should deactivate the anonymous account,
since it may only cause troubles.
```

A vulnerability scanner plug-in is a simple program that looks for the presence of one specific flaw. Most vulnerability scanners have the ability to accept programmed scripts to check for very specific vulnerability characteristics. In Nessus, for example, plug-ins are coded in the Nessus Attack Scripting Language (NASL), which is a very flexible language able to perform virtually any check imaginable. Figure 9-3 shows a portion of a NASL plug-in that tests for FTP servers that allow anonymous connections.

SCAP

How do you ensure that your vulnerability management process complies with all relevant regulatory and policy requirements *regardless of which scanning tools you use*? Each tool, after all, may use whatever standards (such as rules) and reporting formats its developers desire. Some of these rules and formats could be proprietary in nature. This lack of standardization led NIST to team up with industry partners to develop the Security Content Automation Protocol (SCAP). SCAP uses specific standards for the assessment and reporting of vulnerabilities in the information systems of an organization. Currently in version 1.3, SCAP incorporates about a dozen different components that standardize everything from an asset reporting format (ARF) to Common Vulnerabilities and Exposures (CVE) and the Common Vulnerability Scoring System (CVSS).

At its core, SCAP leverages baselines developed by NIST and its partners that define minimum standards for vulnerability management. If, for instance, you want to ensure that your Windows 10 workstations are complying with the requirements of the Federal Information Security Management Act (FISMA), you would use the appropriate SCAP module that captures these requirements. You would then provide that module to a certified SCAP scanner (such as Nessus), and it would be able to report this compliance in a standard language. As you should be able to see, SCAP enables full automation of the vulnerability management process, particularly in regulatory environments.

EXAM TIP You should be familiar with the different parameters and criteria used to configure scans, such as the schedule (time and frequency of scans), the scope (specific hosts or network segments), any control or framework requirements, updating vulnerability feeds before scanning, technical constraints, the scan workflow, and so on.

Types of Vulnerability Scans

Along with understanding the general characteristics of scanning tools, it's important that you understand the types of vulnerability scans available in most scanning tools. Frequently this is a function of the tool itself, but more often than not it's a function of your vulnerability scanning policy and the results you want to get out of the scan. You should make several different decisions before you run vulnerability scans, such as whether to use credentials, whether to have scans run from endpoint agents, and whether to scan from an internal scanner or an external one. The next few sections will discuss these choices you should make based on your vulnerability management goals and the results you wish to obtain from the vulnerability scans themselves.

Noncredentialed and Credentialed Scans

A noncredentialed vulnerability scan evaluates the system from the perspective of an outsider, such as an attacker just beginning to interact with a target. This is a sort of an "unknown environment" test in which the scanning tool doesn't get any special information on or access to the target. The information the scanner gets back from the host is more generic, and it can only get back information that does not require any special privileged access to the host. The advantage of this approach is that it tends to be quicker while still being fairly realistic. It may also be a bit more secure because there is no need for additional credentials on all tested devices. The disadvantage, of course, is that you will most likely not get full coverage of the target.

NOTE Noncredentialed scans look at systems from the perspective of the attacker but are not as thorough as credentialed scans because there is a great deal of information that can only be obtained from a system using the appropriate credentials.

To fully discover everything that is vulnerable in a host, you will typically need to provide the scanning tool with credentials so it can log in remotely and examine the inside as well as the outside. Credentialed scans will always be more thorough than noncredentialed ones, simply because of the additional information a login provides the tool. However, the tradeoff is that credentialed scans can take longer per host due to the increased amount of information the scanner is receiving. Whether this additional thoroughness is important to you is for you and your team to decide. An added benefit of credentialed scans is that they tend to reduce the amount of network traffic required to complete the assessment, particularly if used with agent-based scanning (discussed next).

NOTE Although most credentialed scans require some level of privileges to access certain aspects of the system (the Windows registry, for instance), it is very rare to need full domain admin credentials to perform a vulnerability scan. If you are performing credentialed scans, you should avoid using accounts with excessive privileges unless you are certain you cannot otherwise meet your requirements.

Apart from the considerations in a credentialed scan already discussed, the scanning tool must have the correct permissions on whichever hosts it is running, as well as the necessary access across the network infrastructure. It is generally best to have a dedicated account for the scanning tool or, alternatively, to execute it within the context of the user responsible for running the scan. In either case, minimally privileged accounts should be used to minimize risks (that is, do not run the scanner as root, unless you have no other choice).

EXAM TIP Remember that the difference between noncredentialed and credentialed scans is the amount of data you will get back on vulnerabilities from the host. Noncredentialed scans are generally easier and quicker to perform, but they do not produce a lot of data. Credentialed scans generate the most amount of data but can be slower.

Agent-Based vs. Agentless Scanning

Vulnerability scanners tend to use one of two methods for scanning hosts: those that require a running process (agent) on every scanned device, and those that do not. The difference is illustrated in Figure 9-4. A server-based (or agentless) scan consolidates all data and processes on one or a small number of scanning hosts, which depend on a fair amount of network bandwidth to run their scans. It has fewer components, which could

Figure 9-4
Server-based
and agent-based
vulnerability
scanner
architectures

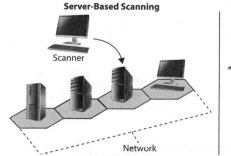

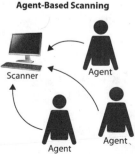

make maintenance tasks easier and help with reliability. Additionally, it can detect and scan devices that are connected to the network but do not have agents running on them (for example, new or rogue hosts).

Agent-based scans use preconfigured agents that run on each protected host and report their results back to the central scanner. Because only the results are transmitted, the bandwidth required by this architectural approach is considerably less than a server-based solution. Also, because the agents run continuously on each host, mobile devices can still be scanned even when they are not connected to the corporate network. Note that most modern scanners can use both of these methods as needed for different types of hosts.

 NOTE   While both agent-based and agentless scans are suitable for determining patch levels and missing updates, agent-based (or serverless) vulnerability scans are typically better for scanning mobile devices.

Internal vs. External Scanning

Many modern vulnerability scanning services allow for scanning of IP addresses on your network from an outside location or from within the corporate network. Internal scanners usually use appliances located within the network to perform the scanning activity, taking advantage of their privileged position to gain visibility of the devices across the network. With an external scan, it's possible to get a sense of what vulnerabilities exist from an outsider's point of view. In some cases, a larger organization may use external scanners combined with special access control rules to allow for elevated visibility into internal assets. In this way, they act as internal scanners, but there is no need to carve out internal resources.

Web App Vulnerability Scanning

A *web app vulnerability scanner* is an automated tool that specifically scans web applications to determine security vulnerabilities. Included in popular utilities are common tests such as those for SQL injection, command injection, cross-site scripting, and improper server configuration. As usage of these applications has increased over the years, so has the frequency of attacks by their exploitation. These scanners are extremely useful because they automatically check against many types of vulnerabilities across many systems on a network. The scans are often based on a preexisting database of known exploits, so it's important to consider this when using these types of scanners. Although vulnerability scanners in the strictest definition don't offer anything beyond identification of existing vulnerabilities, some scanners offer additional correlation features or can extend their functionality using plug-ins and APIs.

Special Considerations for Vulnerability Scans

We have discussed some specific aspects of vulnerability scans, such as scope, schedule, technical constraints, scanning tools, and so on. We've also talked about the different types of vulnerability scans, such as noncredentialed and credentialed scans, agent-based versus agentless scanning, and others. However, some special considerations apply to the entire infrastructure that should be carefully planned when you're implementing a vulnerability scanning and management strategy. We'll discuss several of these considerations in this section.

Asset Criticality

Earlier we discussed the necessity to inventory all the devices connected to your network to assist in both hardware and software accountability and vulnerability scanning. However, we also need to add asset criticality to our scanning considerations. A *critical asset* is anything that is absolutely essential to performing the primary functions of your organization. If you work at an online retailer, for example, critical assets would include your web platforms, data servers, and financial systems, among other things. They probably wouldn't include the workstations used by your web developers or your printers. Critical assets clearly require a higher degree of attention when it comes to managing vulnerabilities. This attention can be expressed in a number of different ways, but you should focus on at least two: the thoroughness of each vulnerability scan and the frequency of each scan.

A *noncritical asset,* though valuable, is not required for the accomplishment of your main mission as an organization. You still need to include these assets in your vulnerability management plan, but given the limited resources with which we all have to deal, you would give them a lower priority than critical assets.

Note that asset owners are those persons in the organization officially designated as the responsible and accountable entities that manage the assets. An asset owner could be appointed because of their position or role in the organization (for example, the vice president of finance could be appointed as the de facto owner of all accounting systems and data) or due to regulatory requirements. The asset owner has overall responsibility for protecting assets under their control and often makes recommendations for security controls to protect their assets. The asset owner is often the authority for determining the criticality or sensitivity of an asset.

 EXAM TIP In the context of vulnerability management, the CySA+ exam will require that you decide how you would deal with critical and noncritical assets.

Operations

While scanning for vulnerabilities is important, as with most security processes, it should not overly interfere in the normal business functions of the organization. Balancing security, functionality, resources, and operational considerations can be difficult; however, you must remember that the reason the business is in operation is not necessarily to keep its security processes going. In fact, the opposite is usually true: security processes, including vulnerability scanning, are there to support the functions of the business, so vulnerability scanning must often take a backseat or a lower priority during critical business operations, particularly around important processing times.

Ongoing Scanning and Continuous Monitoring

Where feasible, you should arrange for automated vulnerability scanning to occur on a periodic, regularly scheduled basis. Also, you should stagger scans such that you are scanning everything, but not all at the same time. You should devise a scanning frequency based on asset criticality and information sensitivity but ensure that you are scanning as often as practical. Depending on the types of networks you operate and your security policies, you may opt to perform scans more often, always using the most updated version of the scanning tool. You should pay extra attention to critical vulnerabilities and aim to remediate them within 48 hours. Recognizing that maintaining software, libraries, and reports can be tedious for administrators, some companies have begun to offer web-based scanning solutions. Qualys and Tenable, for example, both provide cloud-enabled web application security scanners that can be run from any number of cloud service providers. Promising increased scalability and speed across networks of various sizes, these companies provide several related services based on subscription tiers.

Performance

One of the concerns nontechnical people, such as managers, often have is that vulnerability scanning will interfere with the performance of devices connected to the infrastructure, such as workstations, servers, and so on. Many times, security personnel have been blamed for network slowdowns during a vulnerability scan, when the issue may have nothing to do with scanning. However, there may be some instances when vulnerability scans do create an excessive amount of network traffic, causing latency and giving the appearance of bogging down the network. This is something the network technicians and security personnel should be aware of and monitor during vulnerability scans, to ensure that the scans are not interfering too much with network or host responsiveness.

If you detect that vulnerability scans are causing excessive traffic that's interfering with business functions, you can approach the situation a few different ways. For instance, you could reschedule the scans for that particular network segment to a time when business functions are slower, or you could isolate that segment temporarily and scan it apart from the rest of the network. If the scans are interfering with the performance of a particular network device or a critical server, you should investigate the reason why the performance is being impacted; in some cases, the type of scan must be reconfigured.

Sensitivity Levels

Organizations typically assign different classifications or sensitivity levels to their data. We should keep in mind these data sensitivity levels as we configure our scanning tools to do their jobs while appropriately protecting our assets. When it comes to the information in our systems, we must take great care to ensure that the required protections remain in place at all times. For instance, if we are scanning an organization covered by HIPAA, we should ensure that nothing we do as part of our assessment in any way compromises protected health information (PHI). It's possible, although unlikely, that vulnerability assessment results could include sensitive data when scanning for a security flaw. Obviously, this is not desirable.

Besides protecting information, we also need to protect the systems on which it resides. Earlier we discussed critical and noncritical assets in the context of focusing attention on the critical ones. Now we'll qualify that idea by saying that we should scan these assets in a way that ensures they remain available to the business or other processes that made them critical in the first place. If an organization processes thousands of dollars each second and our scanning slows that down by an order of magnitude, even for a few minutes, the effect could be a significant loss of revenue that might be difficult to explain to the board. Understanding the nature and sensitivity of these assets can help us identify tool configurations that minimize the risks to them, such as scheduling the scan during a specific window of time in which no trading occurs.

Network and Security Device Considerations

Network access is also an important consideration, not so much because of the tool as because of the infrastructure, since network security configurations in the infrastructure may block the scans across the network. Because vulnerability scans are carefully planned beforehand, it should be possible to examine the network and determine what access control lists (ACLs), if any, need to be modified to allow the scanner to work. Similarly, network intrusion detection systems (IDSs) and intrusion prevention systems (IPSs) may be triggered due to the scanning activity unless they have been configured to recognize it as legitimate. This may also be true for host-based security systems (HBSSs), which might attempt to mitigate the effects of the scan.

Remember that the purpose of a security device is to block or redirect unwanted network traffic, while the purpose of a vulnerability scanner is to detect weaknesses in a system, sometimes using aggressive techniques that resemble attacks. See the conflict here? Firewalls and IDS/IPS devices can pose a serious problem for network vulnerability assessment efforts if they are not correctly configured to allow incoming traffic from the scanning device. It's generally good practice for the vulnerability management team to publish its schedule of scans to key asset owners and the infrastructure team, along with source device information, so that network security devices will be configured to allow traffic to and from the scan devices.

Network segmentation is also often a consideration during scanning since you want to use logical and physical segmentation to your advantage. As we mentioned before, scanning an entire network all at once is normally not a good idea because of the massive amounts of traffic it can create. This will definitely introduce latency into the network, which may become so bogged down that it is unusable for the duration of the scan. This is where segmentation can assist you. Scanning logical network segments, such as VLANs or physical segments, can help you focus on the assets you are concerned with at the moment. It can also help you segment critical devices and scan those at different schedules or times, and it can help you manage them based on the class of device, such as servers, workstations, network devices, and so on. Regardless of how you use segmentation to assist in your scanning, it's a good idea to consider it when planning your scanning strategy.

Regulatory Requirements

Earlier in the chapter we discussed how different frameworks, such as PCI DSS, can require a scanning frequency or type. Let's go a bit more in depth and discuss the regulatory environment in general where it concerns vulnerability management. A *regulatory environment* is an environment in which an organization exists or operates that is controlled to a significant degree by laws, rules, or regulations implemented by government (federal, state, or local), industry groups, or other organizations. In a nutshell, when you have to play by someone else's rules or else risk serious consequences, you're dealing with a regulatory environment. Regulatory environments commonly have enforcement groups and procedures in place to deal with noncompliance.

You, as a cybersecurity analyst, may have to take action in a number of ways to ensure compliance with one or more regulatory requirements. This can also include your vulnerability scanning strategy and processes. When developing your scanning strategy, you must ensure that your scanning operations have been approved by all of the data owners in the infrastructure, particularly if there are different owners who control specific types of sensitive data. For example, scanning assets that have protected health information or payment cardholder data may have different scanning requirements that you must meet for regulatory purposes. You must also ensure that the personnel performing vulnerability scans are allowed to access assets that may contain sensitive data. If those assets are on protected networks that not everyone has access to, you must ensure you have permission from the data owner to scan them.

Additionally, since many regulatory environments have particular vulnerability reporting procedures, you need to determine whether you should report vulnerabilities to the regulatory agency based on specific reporting requirements or based on specific criticality or sensitivity findings.

Security Baseline Scanning

Most routine vulnerability scanning will tell you if your systems are configured within your standardized security baselines. For example, if you have automated configuration and patching mechanisms in place that should patch vulnerabilities on a regularly scheduled basis, a scan will indicate whether this is actually being performed. The scan will tell you if devices are not operating within their standardized baselines so that you can correct any issues keeping those devices from remaining within the baseline. The results of baseline scans should tell you when brand-new vulnerabilities are discovered as well as whether they have been discovered consistently across the network. However, if you encounter vulnerabilities that only exist on one or two hosts and no others, that could tell you that those particular hosts are not being scanned or patched properly and are in fact out of configuration baseline control.

 EXAM TIP You will see questions on the exam that require you to make decisions about scanning while keeping some of these special considerations in mind, especially where it concerns normal business operations being affected, network performance, and regulatory requirements.

Risks Associated with Scanning Activities

Most IT processes and security processes introduce some level of risk into the organization. Vulnerability scanning is no different and introduces risks that security analysts must consider. Many of these risks can be mitigated by proper planning and a sound vulnerability scanning strategy. Risks introduced by vulnerability scanning include network latency due to high bandwidth usage, the possibility of interrupting business operations by using up bandwidth (sometimes making the network performance crawl to a halt), and scans temporarily disabling critical devices, causing slowdowns or reboots. Additionally, there is a risk of not properly configuring vulnerability scans to capture all the relevant vulnerability information necessary to make risk-based decisions on vulnerability mitigation.

As mentioned, almost all of these risks can be mitigated by proper planning. Scheduling scans for certain critical devices so that they take place during off-business hours is one way to keep from interrupting business processes. Configuring scans to target only specific segments at a time can help reduce network bandwidth usage while the scans are running. Properly configuring credentialed scans can ensure that you gather all the necessary vulnerability information from each host so that you can make good mitigation decisions.

NOTE Every security decision—including how, when, and where to conduct vulnerability assessments—must consider the risk implications of activities on the core business of the organization.

Generating Vulnerability Management Reports

Report generation is an important part of the incident response process and is particularly critical for vulnerability management. All vulnerability scanners perform reporting functions of some kind, but they don't all come with customization options. Nessus, like other vulnerability scanners, provides its reports in common formats such as PDF, HTML, and CSV. Additionally, you can also use Nessus's own formats.

As an administrator, it's important that you consider what kinds of reporting your utility is capable of and how you may automate the reporting process. Getting the pertinent information to the right people in a timely fashion is the key to capitalizing successfully on vulnerability scans.

Since vulnerabilities are considered sensitive information, it is important that the right permissions must be set for reports. It is ironic that some organizations deploy vulnerability scanners but fail to secure the reporting interfaces properly. This allows users who should be unauthorized to access the reports at will. Although this may seem like a small risk, consider the consequences of adversaries being able to read your vulnerability reports. This ability would save them significant effort because it would enable them to focus on the targets you have already listed as vulnerable. As an added bonus, they would know exactly how to attack the hosts. There are also other considerations that should contribute to your vulnerability scan reporting processes, some of which are discussed in the next few sections.

Types of Data Included in Reports

As you configure your scanning tool, you must consider the information that should or must be included in the report, particularly when dealing with regulatory compliance scans. This information will drive the data that your scan must collect, which in turn affects the tool configuration. Keep in mind that each report (and there may be several as outputs of one scan) is intended for a specific audience. This affects both the information in the report as well as the manner in which it is presented.

Automated vs. Manual Report Distribution

Creating reporting templates enables you to rapidly prepare customized reports based on vulnerability scan results, which can then be forwarded to the necessary points of contact. For example, you can have all the web server vulnerabilities automatically collected and sent to the web server administrator. Similarly, you can have occurrences of data storage violations sent to your spillage team for faster action. Unless there is only one administrator, it may make sense to automate the report delivery process to prevent the primary administrator from having to manage every report manually. The service administrators can be more efficient because they are getting the reports that are most relevant to their role.

 CAUTION Vulnerability data is very sensitive and should only be reviewed by authorized technical and management personnel. Ensure that your vulnerability scan reports are only accessed by people who have a valid need for that information.

Software Vulnerability Assessment Tools and Techniques

Scanning for software vulnerabilities deserves some additional discussion because there are some considerations that apply to applications, in addition to the previously discussed issues, as well as concerns with network vulnerability scanning. As software becomes larger and more complex, the potential for vulnerabilities increases. Software vulnerabilities are part of the overall attack surface, and attackers waste no time discovering what flaws exist—in many cases using the same techniques we'll describe shortly. Software vulnerability detection methods usually fall into the categories of static analysis, dynamic analysis, reverse engineering, and fuzzing. These methods can be done separately or, ideally, together and as a part of a comprehensive software assessment process.

Static Analysis

Static code analysis is a technique meant to help identify software defects or security policy violations. It is carried out by examining the code without executing the program (hence the term *static*). The term *static analysis* is generally reserved for automated tools that assist analysts and developers, whereas manual inspection by humans is generally referred to as *code review*. Because it is an automated process, static analysis enables developers and security staff to scan their source code quickly for programming flaws and vulnerabilities.

Figure 9-5 shows an example of a tool called Lapse+, which was developed by OWASP to find vulnerabilities in Java applications. This tool is highlighting an instance where user input is directly used, without sufficient validation, to build a SQL query against

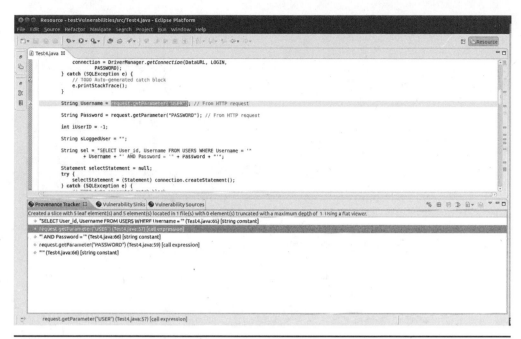

Figure 9-5   Code analysis of a vulnerable web application (source: www.owasp.org)

a database. In this particular case, the query is verifying the username and password. This insecure code block would allow a threat actor to conduct a SQL injection attack against the system. The actor could likely gain access by providing the string `'foo' OR 1==1 --` if the database is on a MySQL server.

Automated static analysis like that performed by Lapse+ provides a scalable method of security code review and ensures that secure coding policies are being followed. There are numerous manifestations of static analysis tools, ranging from tools that simply consider the behavior of single statements to tools that analyze the entire source code at once. However, you should keep in mind that static code analysis cannot usually reveal logic errors or vulnerabilities (that is, behaviors that are evident only at runtime) and therefore should be used in conjunction with manual code review to ensure a more thorough evaluation.

Dynamic Analysis

Dynamic analysis doesn't really care about what the binary *is* but rather what the binary *does*. This method often requires a sandbox in which to execute the software. The sandbox creates an environment that looks like a real operating system to the software and provides such things as access to a file system, network interface, memory, and anything else the software might need. Each request is carefully documented to establish a timeline of behavior that enables us to understand what it does. The main advantage of dynamic analysis is that it tends to be significantly faster and requires less expertise than alternatives. It can be particularly helpful for code that has been heavily obfuscated or is difficult to interpret. The biggest disadvantage is that dynamic analysis doesn't reveal all that the software does but rather all that it did during its execution in the sandbox. Note that this method is also used to examine suspected malware in a protected environment.

 EXAM TIP Keep in mind the difference between static and dynamic analysis for the exam; static analysis only involves automated and manual reviews of the code itself, without executing it. Dynamic analysis requires code execution and is more concerned with the behavior of the code while it is running.

Reverse Engineering

Reverse engineering is the detailed examination of a product to learn what it does and how it works. In this approach to understanding what software is doing, a highly skilled analyst will either disassemble or decompile the binary code to translate its 1's and 0's into assembly language or whichever higher level language the code was created in. This enables a reverse engineer to see all possible functions of the software, not just those exhibited during a limited run in a sandbox. It is then possible, for example, to understand what kind of input is expected, discover dependencies, and highlight inefficient or dangerous techniques. It can be argued that static analysis is a subset, or supporting function, of an overall reverse engineering effort.

Engineering and Reversing Software

Computers can understand only sequences of 1's and 0's (sometimes represented in hexadecimal form for our convenience), which is why we call this representation of software *machine language*. It would be tedious and error-prone to write complex programs in machine language, which is why we invented *assembly language* many decades ago. In this language, the programmer uses operators (such as push and add) and operands (such as memory addresses, CPU registers, and constants) to implement an algorithm. The software that translates assembly language to machine language is called an *assembler*. Though assembly language was a significant improvement, we soon realized that it was still rather ineffective, which is why we invented higher-level programming languages such as C/C++. This higher-level source code is translated into assembly language by a compiler before being assembled into binary format, as shown here.

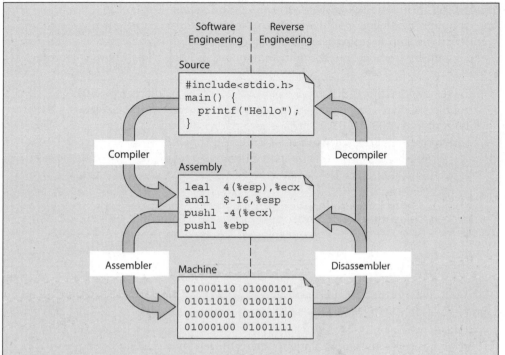

When reverse engineering binary code, we can translate it into assembly language using a tool called a *disassembler*. This is the most common way of reversing a binary. In some cases, we can also go straight from machine language to a representation of source code using a *decompiler*. The problem with using decompilers is that there are infinitely many ways to write source code that will result in a given binary. The decompiler makes educated guesses as to what the original source code looked like, but it's unable to replicate it exactly.

Fuzzing

Fuzzing is a technique used to discover flaws and vulnerabilities in software by sending large amounts of malformed, unexpected, or random data to the target program in order to trigger failures. Attackers could manipulate these errors and flaws to inject their own code into the system and compromise its security and stability. Fuzzing tools are commonly successful at identifying buffer overflows, denial-of-service (DoS) vulnerabilities, injection weaknesses, validation flaws, and other activities that can cause software to freeze, crash, or throw unexpected errors. Figure 9-6 shows a popular fuzzer called American Fuzzy Lop (AFL) crashing a targeted application.

Fuzzers don't always generate random inputs from scratch. Purely random generation is known to be an inefficient way to fuzz systems. Instead, they often start with an input that is pretty close to normal and then make lots of small changes to see which ones seem

```
                        american fuzzy lop 1.86b (test)
┌─ process timing ──────────────────────────┐┌─ overall results ─────┐
│        run time : 0 days, 0 hrs, 0 min, 2 sec ││   cycles done : 0     │
│   last new path : none seen yet           ││   total paths : 1     │
│ last uniq crash : 0 days, 0 hrs, 0 min, 2 sec ││  uniq crashes : 1     │
│  last uniq hang : none seen yet           ││    uniq hangs : 0     │
├─ cycle progress ──────────────┬─ map coverage ────────────────────┤
│ now processing : 0 (0.00%)    │    map density : 2 (0.00%)        │
│ paths timed out : 0 (0.00%)   │ count coverage : 1.00 bits/tuple  │
├─ stage progress ──────────────┼─ findings in depth ───────────────┤
│ now trying : havoc            │ favored paths : 1 (100.00%)       │
│ stage execs : 1464/5000 (29.28%) │  new edges on : 1 (100.00%)   │
│ total execs : 1697            │ total crashes : 39 (1 unique)     │
│ exec speed : 626.5/sec        │   total hangs : 0 (0 unique)      │
├─ fuzzing strategy yields ─────┴─ path geometry ───────────────────┤
│   bit flips : 0/16, 1/15, 0/13 │      levels : 1                  │
│  byte flips : 0/2, 0/1, 0/0   │      pending : 1                  │
│ arithmetics : 0/112, 0/25, 0/0 │    pend fav : 1                  │
│  known ints : 0/10, 0/28, 0/0 │   own finds : 0                  │
│  dictionary : 0/0, 0/0, 0/0   │    imported : n/a                │
│       havoc : 0/0, 0/0        │    variable : 0                  │
│        trim : n/a, 0.00%      └──────────────────────────────────┘
└───────────────────────────────┘        [cpu: 92%]
```

Figure 9-6   A fuzzer testing an application

more effective at exposing flaws. Eventually, an input will cause an interesting condition in the target, at which point the security team will need a tool that can determine where the flaw is and how it could be exploited (if at all). This observation and analysis tool is often bundled with the fuzzer because one is pretty useless without the other.

 NOTE   Both reverse engineering and fuzzing are highly specialized techniques and typically require advanced skill sets and software tools.

untidy   *Untidy* is a popular Extensible Markup Language (XML) fuzzer. Used to test web application clients and servers, untidy takes valid XML and modifies it before inputting it into the application. The untidy fuzzer is now part of the Peach Fuzzer project.

Peach Fuzzer   The Peach Fuzzer is a powerful fuzzing suite that's capable of testing a wide range of targets. Peach uses XML-based modules, called *pits,* to provide all the information needed to run the fuzz. These modules are configurable based on the testing needs. Before conducting a fuzz test, the user must specify the type of test, the target, and any monitoring settings desired.

Microsoft SDL Fuzzers   As part of its security development lifecycle (SDL) toolset, Microsoft released two types of standalone fuzzers designed to be used in the verification phase of the SDL: the MiniFuzz File Fuzzer and the Regex Fuzzer. However, Microsoft has dropped support and no longer provides these applications for download.

Chapter Review

This chapter focused on the concepts associated with managing vulnerability scanning. We discussed the importance of asset discovery, using mapping scans and fingerprinting, to determine which assets you have on the network that should be scanned. We also covered industry frameworks that have scanning requirements and controls built into them. These include the Payment Card Industry Data Security Standard, the CIS controls, OWASP, and ISO/IEC 27000 series.

We also touched on the different types of critical infrastructure, primarily nontraditional devices, that require special considerations when managing vulnerabilities. These include industrial control systems, operational technology, and SCADA systems. These nontraditional systems often have older, proprietary security mechanisms and protocols or even little to no security controls implemented in them, and they can be difficult to update.

We also discussed basic concepts of vulnerability identification and scanning. We talked about some of the risks associated with scanning activities, such as network latency and interfering with critical operations. We discussed the basics of passive and active scanning as well as how mapping/enumeration and port scanning work. We also talked about the various scanning parameters and criteria used to configure scans, including scheduling, asset scope, vulnerability feeds, technical constraints, scanning workflow, and tool updates and plug-ins. We also discussed standardization of reporting and data formats contained in SCAP. We covered the basic types of vulnerability scans as well, including the difference between noncredentialed and credentialed scans, agent-based versus agentless scanning, and internal versus external scanning, with discussions on when and how to use each of these types of scans. We also briefly described web application vulnerability scanning.

Often, vulnerability scans must be carefully planned, taking into account considerations such as scanning critical assets, not interfering with business operations, and performing continuous scanning and monitoring. We also talked about the impact scanning may have on infrastructure performance. System criticality and sensitivity levels often have an impact on how scans are planned and managed on the network. We also considered the need to reconfigure the network and security devices to allow scans to take place without being unnecessarily interrupted by security devices. Other special considerations for vulnerability scan management include following any regulatory requirements imposed on the organization as well as ensuring that security baselines are being followed by all scanned devices. We also discussed vulnerability scan reporting, including the types of data you should use in reports and how scan reports must be controlled and issued using automated or manual means so that only the right people have permissions to access that information.

Finally, we discussed considerations involved with software vulnerability assessment tools and methods. We discussed the differences between static and dynamic analysis as well as the need for reverse engineering. Fuzzing is also a specialized technique used to send unformatted data to an application to discover security or performance issues in the software.

Questions

1. What popular framework aims to standardize automated vulnerability assessment, management, and compliance formats and languages among disparate security tools?

   A. PCI DSS

   B. SCAP

   C. CVE

   D. OWASP

2. Which of the following control frameworks requires vulnerability scanning for both internal and external networks on a quarterly basis?

   A. HIPAA

   B. International Organization for Standardization (ISO)

   C. PCI DSS

   D. CIS

3. Which of the following accurately describes the characteristics of credentialed and noncredentialed scans?

   A. Credentialed scans do not require administrative privileges and are faster.

   B. Noncredentialed scans are slower and require full administrative privileges on a host.

   C. Credentialed scans are faster and obtain much more vulnerability data than noncredentialed scans.

   D. Noncredentialed scans are faster but do not obtain as much vulnerability data as credentialed scans.

4. Which of the following is a risk that must be considered when planning vulnerability scans?

   A. Degrading network performance

   B. Data loss or corruption

   C. Unauthorized disclosure of sensitive information types, such as financial or health information

   D. Unintended changes to data permissions and other protections

5. Which of the following types of scans may be more effective in discovering specific vulnerabilities such as SQL injection and cross-site scripting?

   A. Agent-based scanning

   B. External scanning

   C. Web application scanning

   D. Noncredentialed scans

6. Which of the following is a reason that patching and updating occur so infrequently with ICS and SCADA devices?

   A. These devices control critical and costly systems that require constant uptime.

   B. These devices are not connected to networks, so they do not need to be updated.

   C. These devices do not use common operating systems, so they cannot be updated.

   D. These devices control systems such as HVAC that do not need security updates.

7. All of the following are important considerations when deciding the frequency of vulnerability scans *except* which one?

   A. Costs associated with scanning

   B. Asset criticality and vulnerability severity

   C. Regulatory compliance

   D. Scanning impact on business processes

Use the following scenario to answer Questions 8–10:

You are developing a vulnerability scanning strategy for your organization. You have a very large infrastructure, consisting of several classes of devices, including critical workstations, servers, network devices, mobile devices, web servers, and so on. Although employees work around the clock in shifts, there are some predictable time periods where network activity is lower than other times. You have several critical devices containing sensitive information that are segmented into protected subnets. You monitor several vulnerability feeds and ensure that your scanning tools are updated on a daily basis. Bandwidth usage and the desire to reduce impact to critical business operations must be considered in your scanning strategy.

8. What kind of vulnerability scanning method do you recommend be used in this environment?

   A. External

   B. Agentless

   C. Agent-based

   D. Noncredentialed

9. Which of the following scanning schedules would be most effective for this network?

   A. Constant scans of all network segments at once

   B. Separately scheduled scans for critical devices that run during off-peak hours

   C. Less-frequent scans for critical devices

   D. Hourly scheduled scans for all noncritical devices during peak hours

10. Which of the following types of scan parameters should you use to gain the most information possible from all hosts, using the minimum level of bandwidth necessary and creating the least impact to business operations?

   A. Agent-based credentialed scans scheduled during low network usage times

   B. Agentless noncredentialed scans configured to run during peak business times

   C. External agent-based credentialed scans configured to run during peak business times

   D. Internal agentless credentialed scans configured to run during low network usage times

Answers

1. **B.** The Security Content Automation Protocol (SCAP) is a method of standardizing vulnerability data and reporting formats across different scanning tools.

2. **C.** Requirement 11 of the PCI DSS requires both internal and external network vulnerability scans on a quarterly basis for those systems that process cardholder data.

3. **D.** Noncredentialed scans are faster but do not obtain as much vulnerability data as credentialed scans.

4. **A.** Risks that are incurred by vulnerability scanning include degrading network performance if the scans are not properly planned and executed.

5. **C.** Web application scanning is effective at discovering specific vulnerabilities associated with web applications, such as SQL injection and cross-site scripting.

6. **A.** The cost involved and potential negative effects due to interrupting business and industrial processes often dissuade device managers from updating and patching these systems.

7. **A.** Cost should not be a factor in determining the frequency of vulnerability scans; relevant factors include asset criticality, vulnerability severity, regulatory requirements, and impact to business operations.

8. **C.** You should use agent-based scanning whenever possible. Since the network is large, this will cut down on scanning times and use less bandwidth.

9. **B.** In order to minimize impact to business operations, you should schedule scans of critical devices separately, during nonpeak hours.

10. **A.** To minimize the use of bandwidth, scans should be agent-based so that they will send only minimal information across the network. To receive the most information possible concerning vulnerabilities on all hosts, scans should also be configured to use appropriate credentials. Although employees work in shifts, scans should be scheduled to run during the lowest periods of network usage, versus peak activity times. Scans should also be configured for the internal network instead of the external network since most critical hosts are on the inside.

CHAPTER 10

Vulnerability Assessment Tools

In this chapter you will learn:
- When and how you can use different vulnerability assessment tools
- How to choose among similar tools and technologies
- How to review and interpret results of vulnerability scan reports
- How to use vulnerability assessment tools for specialized environments

We shape our tools and thereafter our tools shape us.

—Father John Culkin

The purpose of this chapter is to introduce you to (or perhaps reacquaint you with) the vulnerability assessment tools with which you will need to be familiar for the CySA+ exam. We are not trying to provide a full review of each tool or even cover all the features. Instead, we give you enough information to help you understand the purpose of each tool and when you may want to use one over another. If you read about a tool for the first time in this chapter, you may want to spend more time familiarizing yourself with it before you take the exam. Given the diversity and scale of the modern network, making sense of the output of a vulnerability scan may be a daunting task. Fortunately, many tools deliver their comprehensive reports with visual tools and technical details behind the vulnerabilities they uncover. Understanding why vulnerabilities exist and how they can be exploited will assist you in analyzing the final scan report.

Some of the tools within a single category do pretty much the same thing, albeit in different ways. For each tool category, we provide an overview before comparing notable products in that class. We then provide an illustrative scenario that offers a more detailed description of each tool and how it fits in that scenario. Note that this chapter addresses Objective 2.2, "Given a scenario, analyze output from vulnerability assessment tools."

 EXAM TIP You do not need to know about these tools in detail for the exam, but you do need to know when and how you would use the different classes of tools in different scenarios.

Network Scanning and Mapping

Network scanning and mapping involve identifying the various devices, systems, applications, and segments that exist within a network. This is typically accomplished by sending specific network traffic to hosts and analyzing the responses received back from them. This network traffic contains specially crafted messages that allow the scanning software to identify the operating system, open ports, and other important characteristics of each device on the network.

The process of network scanning and mapping is important for several reasons. First, it can help organizations identify vulnerabilities in their network infrastructure and take steps to address them before they can be exploited by malicious actors. Additionally, it can help administrators identify unauthorized devices or software running on their network, which can be a sign of a security breach.

There are several types of network scanning and mapping techniques, including ping sweeps, port scans, and vulnerability scans. Ping sweeps involve sending ICMP echo requests to a range of IP addresses to determine which hosts are active on the network. Port scans involve sending packets to various ports on a target device to determine which ports are open and what services are running on them. Vulnerability scans go beyond simple port scanning and attempt to identify specific vulnerabilities in the target device or application. We will discuss vulnerability scanning later in this chapter.

Passive vs. Active Enumeration Techniques

Passive enumeration techniques are used to gain information about the target without interfacing with or interrogating the target directly. In fact, access to the target isn't necessarily required since alternative sources for target information are queried. Common examples include using a WHOIS query, nslookup, and specialized tools like dnsrecon. A useful application of these tools for the purpose of vulnerability assessment could be to assist in discovery of what an asset looks like to outsiders. Figure 10-1 shows a dnsrecon lookup against google.com and provides a good deal of insight into the records associated with the company.

Active enumeration techniques involve interfacing directly with the target system. Port scanning is one of the most widely used active scanning techniques and employs any number of tools and techniques directly against a target to discover open ports and available services.

nslookup

The name server lookup utility, better known as nslookup, can be thought of as the user interface for Domain Name System (DNS). It enables you to resolve the IP address corresponding to a fully qualified domain name (FQDN) of a host. Depending on the situation, it is also possible to do the inverse (that is, resolve the IP address of an FQDN). This tool allows you to specify a DNS server to be used, or you can use the system default. Finally, it is possible to fully interrogate the target server and obtain other record data, such as Mail Exchange (MX) for e-mail or Canonical Name (CNAME).

```
                                    kali@kali: ~/Desktop                        _ □ ×

  File  Actions  Edit  View  Help

  root@kali:/home/kali/Desktop# dnsrecon -d google.com
  [*] Performing General Enumeration of Domain: google.com
  [-] DNSSEC is not configured for google.com
  [*]     SOA ns1.google.com 216.239.32.10
  [*]     NS ns1.google.com 216.239.32.10
  [*]     NS ns1.google.com 2001:4860:4802:32::a
  [*]     NS ns2.google.com 216.239.34.10
  [*]     NS ns2.google.com 2001:4860:4802:34::a
  [*]     NS ns3.google.com 216.239.36.10
  [*]     NS ns3.google.com 2001:4860:4802:36::a
  [*]     NS ns4.google.com 216.239.38.10
  [*]     NS ns4.google.com 2001:4860:4802:38::a
  [*]     MX alt4.aspmx.l.google.com 173.194.175.26
  [*]     MX aspmx.l.google.com 64.233.179.26
  [*]     MX alt1.aspmx.l.google.com 172.253.112.27
  [*]     MX alt2.aspmx.l.google.com 173.194.77.26
  [*]     MX alt3.aspmx.l.google.com 64.233.177.27
  [*]     MX alt4.aspmx.l.google.com 2607:f8b0:400d:c0b::1a
  [*]     MX aspmx.l.google.com 2607:f8b0:4003:c12::1b
  [*]     MX alt1.aspmx.l.google.com 2607:f8b0:4023::1b
  [*]     MX alt2.aspmx.l.google.com 2607:f8b0:4023:401::1a
  [*]     MX alt3.aspmx.l.google.com 2607:f8b0:4002:c08::1a
  [*]     A google.com 216.58.217.14
  [*]     AAAA google.com 2001:4860:4802:38::75
  [*]     TXT google.com docusign=05958488-4752-4ef2-95eb-aa7ba8a3bd0e
  [*]     TXT google.com docusign=1b0a6754-49b1-4db5-8540-d2c12664b289
  [*]     TXT google.com facebook-domain-verification=22rm551cu4k0ab0bxsw536tlds4h95
  [*]     TXT google.com globalsign-smime-dv=CDYX+XFHUw2wml6/Gb8+59BsH31KzUr6c1l2BPvqKX8=
  [*]     TXT google.com v=spf1 include:_spf.google.com ~all
  [*] Enumerating SRV Records
  [*]     SRV _ldap._tcp.google.com ldap.google.com 216.239.32.58 389 0
  [*]     SRV _ldap._tcp.google.com ldap.google.com 2001:4860:4802:32::3a 389 0
  [*]     SRV _carddavs._tcp.google.com google.com 216.58.217.14 443 0
  [*]     SRV _carddavs._tcp.google.com google.com 2001:4860:4802:38::75 443 0
  [*]     SRV _caldav._tcp.google.com calendar.google.com 216.58.217.14 80 0
  [*]     SRV _caldav._tcp.google.com calendar.google.com 2607:f8b0:4000:804::200e 80 0
  [*]     SRV _caldavs._tcp.google.com calendar.google.com 216.58.217.14 443 0
  [*]     SRV _caldavs._tcp.google.com calendar.google.com 2607:f8b0:4000:804::200e 443 0
  [*]     SRV _xmpp-server._tcp.google.com alt4.xmpp-server.l.google.com 173.194.68.125 5269 0
  [*]     SRV _xmpp-server._tcp.google.com xmpp-server.l.google.com 64.233.179.125 5269 0
```

Figure 10-1 Output from dnsrecon performed against google.com

responder

In the Windows environment, the Link-Local Multicast Name Resolution (LLMNR) protocol or NetBIOS Name Service (NBT-NS) can be used to query local computers on a local area network (LAN) if a host is unable to resolve a hostname using DNS. If either of these two fallback protocols does not work, any host can respond with an answer that may be viewed as authoritative by the requesting machine. In this situation, responder is a powerful tool that can be used to gain remote access by poisoning name services to gather hashes and credentials from systems within a LAN. Figure 10-2 shows a snapshot of the responder reference page from the command-line-based tool.

Angry IP Scanner

Angry IP Scanner was first released in 1998. This scanner is designed to be fast, light-weight, and simple to use. Angry IP Scanner is cross-platform (available for Windows, macOS, and Linux) and can be run via a graphical interface or as a command-line tool.

Some of the features of Angry IP Scanner include the following:

- **Multithreaded scanning** The scanner uses multithreaded scanning technology that enables users to scan multiple IP addresses and ports simultaneously. This feature increases the speed of scanning, making it one of the fastest network scanners available.

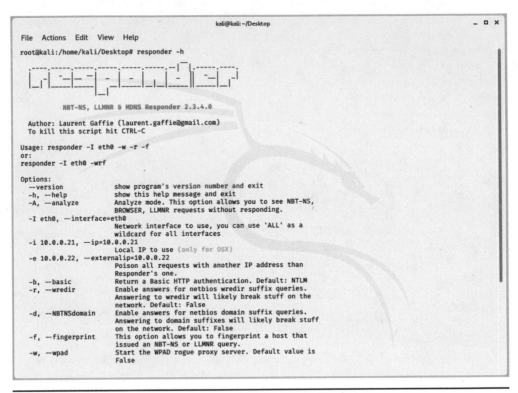

Figure 10-2   responder usage and options screen

- **Customizable scanning**   Users can choose which ports to scan, which IP addresses to include or exclude, and the number of threads to use for scanning.
- **Exportable results**   After scanning, the tool generates detailed reports of the results, which can be exported in various formats, including CSV, TXT, XML, and HTML.
- **User-friendly interface**   The scanner has a simple and user-friendly interface that users can easily navigate. The interface provides a summary of the scanning results, including the IP addresses and ports that were scanned and their status.

Maltego

Maltego is a powerful and versatile tool used for information gathering, network scanning and mapping, and data visualization. It is widely used by security professionals and investigators to obtain a comprehensive understanding of their target's digital footprint. Maltego provides a wide range of capabilities, including data transformation and integration, facilitating the correlation of diverse data sources, and transforming the data into a structured and visual form.

One of Maltego's primary strengths is its ability to enrich and contextualize data, thus providing in-depth insights into the target's network. This is achieved by performing data mining and data aggregation activities that help in identifying patterns and uncovering connections that may not be visible at first glance. Maltego can integrate with multiple data sources, such as WHOIS databases, social media networks, and publicly available data sets, to extract valuable information for analysis.

Maltego's network mapping and scanning capabilities are another strength of the tool. It can be used to perform a comprehensive scan of a network, identifying hosts, devices, and applications that are active and accessible. Maltego can also map network topologies and identify relationships between network nodes. This information can be crucial in identifying vulnerabilities and potential attack vectors that can be exploited.

Here is a list highlighting several of Maltego's most interesting features:

- **Pivoting**   Maltego allows you to pivot from one piece of data to another, enabling you to expand your investigation and uncover new relationships and connections.

- **Graph relationships**   Maltego presents data in a graphical format that allows you to easily visualize and analyze complex relationships and connections between different entities.

- **Transforms**   Maltego comes with a large library of built-in transforms that enable you to gather information from a wide range of sources and integrate it into your investigation. You can also create your own transforms using Maltego's developer tools.

- **Integration with other tools**   Maltego integrates with a wide range of other tools and services, allowing you to gather information from multiple sources and automate your investigation.

- **Data enrichment**   Maltego can enrich your scan data by adding context and additional information to each entity, such as location data, domain names, and social media profiles.

- **Collaboration**   Maltego enables you to collaborate with others on your investigation by sharing graphs and workspaces as well as by using built-in messaging and commenting features.

- **Customization**   Maltego is highly customizable, allowing you to tailor the tool to your specific needs and workflows. You can customize the interface, create your own transforms, and build integrations with other tools and services.

Web Application Scanners

Web application vulnerability scanners are automated tools that scan web applications, normally from the outside, and from the perspective of a malicious user. Like other vulnerability scanners, they will scan only for vulnerabilities and malware for which plug-ins have been developed. Here are some of the most common types of vulnerabilities that scanners look for:

- **Vulnerability scanning**   Involves scanning the web application to detect common vulnerabilities such as SQL injection, cross-site scripting (XSS), and directory traversal

- **Fuzz testing**   Involves sending random data or inputs to the web application to see if it can handle unexpected inputs and to identify any vulnerabilities
- **Authentication testing**   Used to determine if the web application can be accessed without proper authentication or if there are any authentication-related vulnerabilities
- **Session management testing**   Involves testing the web application's ability to manage user sessions and to identify any session-related vulnerabilities
- **Input validation testing**   Used to identify vulnerabilities that may arise from improper input validation or filtering

Many commercial and open source web application vulnerability scanners are available. In this section, we will discuss some of the most popular ones, including Burp Suite, Zed Attack Proxy (ZAP), Arachni, and Nikto. These scanners enable you to develop customized tests for your specific environment. Therefore, if you have some unique policies or security requirements that must be satisfied, it is worthwhile to learn how to write plug-ins or tests for your preferred scanner.

Burp Suite

Burp Suite is a web application security testing tool developed by PortSwigger. It is a widely used tool designed to help cybersecurity professionals automate many aspects of web application security testing. Some of the key capabilities of Burp Suite include the following:

- **Automated scanning**   Burp Suite can automatically scan web applications for vulnerabilities, including SQL injection, XSS, and more. The Burp Suite scanner can also be customized to perform scans with specific configurations.
- **Vulnerability reporting and analysis**   Burp Suite provides a comprehensive set of tools for analyzing the results of security tests. This includes identifying vulnerabilities and generating detailed reports with recommendations for remediation.
- **Collaboration**   Burp Suite allows multiple users to work together on the same project. This makes it easy to collaborate with team members on vulnerability testing and remediation.
- **Extensibility**   Burp Suite is highly extensible and has a large and active community of users who have developed plug-ins and add-ons to enhance its capabilities. This makes it possible to customize the tool to meet specific needs and requirements.
- **Intercepting proxy**   Burp Suite's Intercept feature allows you to capture and modify requests and responses between your browser and the web application. This makes it possible to modify parameters, headers, cookies, and more, and to see how the web application reacts.

In proxy mode, Burp will enable the user to manually inspect every request passing through from the user to the server. Options to forward or drop the request are shown in Figure 10-3.

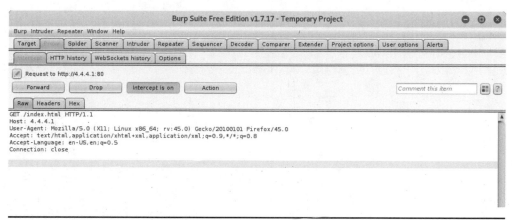

Figure 10-3 Burp Suite intercept screen and options in proxy mode

OWASP Zed Attack Proxy

The OWASP Zed Attack Proxy (ZAP) is one of the Open Web Application Security Project (OWASP) Foundation's flagship projects, popular because of its powerful features. ZAP uses its position between the user's browser and the web application to intercept and inspect user requests, modify the contents if required, and then forward them to a web server. This is exactly the same process that occurs during a man-in-the-middle attack. ZAP is designed to be used by security practitioners at all levels.

Here are some of the key features of ZAP:

- **Intercepting proxy** ZAP acts as an intercepting proxy, allowing you to capture and manipulate HTTP and HTTPS traffic between your web application and the client.

- **Active scanner** ZAP's active scanner automatically crawls your web application and attempts to identify vulnerabilities by sending malicious payloads and analyzing the response.

- **Passive scanner** ZAP's passive scanner continually monitors the traffic between the client and server for potential vulnerabilities and provides alerts when suspicious behavior is detected.

- **Fuzzer** ZAP includes a powerful fuzzer that can test for a wide range of vulnerabilities, including injection flaws, directory traversal, and file inclusion vulnerabilities.

- **AJAX spider** ZAP's AJAX spider is designed to handle the complexities of modern web applications and can crawl and test applications built using AJAX technologies.

- **Scripting** ZAP supports scripting in several languages, including Python, to automate and extend its functionality.

- **API** ZAP provides a rich API that can be used to integrate with other tools and automate testing workflows.

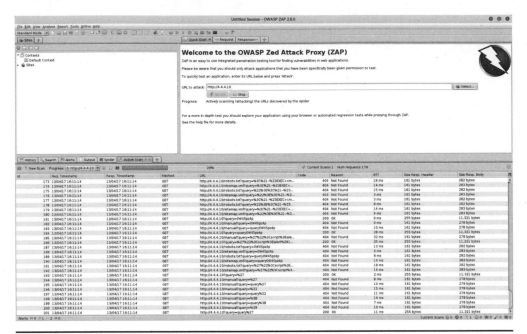

Figure 10-4 ZAP screen showing progress in an active scanning attack

Figure 10-4 shows the results of an attack conducted with nothing more than a target specified. In this example, ZAP rapidly fabricates a list of GET requests using known directories and files to test the site. These locations should not be publicly viewable, so the results here will inform an administrator of misconfigurations in the server and unexpected data exposure.

Arachni

Arachni is a Ruby-based, modular web app scanner with a special focus on speed. Unlike many other scanners, Arachni performs many of its scans in parallel, enabling the app to scale to large test jobs without sacrificing performance. The tool's developer, Tasos Laskos, designed Arachni to train itself throughout its audits using several techniques. Among them is the tool's ability to incorporate the feedback it gets from initial responses during the test to inform which new techniques should be used moving forward. In presenting the final results, Arachni is also able to reduce the occurrence of false positives through a process the author refers to as *meta-analysis,* which considers several factors from the tests responses. Arachni can perform audits for vulnerabilities, including SQL injection, cross-site request forgery (CSRF), code injection, LDAP injection, path traversal, file inclusion, and XSS.

Despite being fairly performant, Arachni has few requirements to operate. It needs only a target URL to get started and can be initiated via a web interface or command line.

Here are some of the key features of Arachni:

- **Comprehensive scanning**   Arachni can identify a wide range of vulnerabilities, including SQL injection, cross-site scripting (XSS), remote file inclusion (RFI), local file inclusion (LFI), and more.

- **Modular architecture**   Arachni uses a modular approach, allowing users to extend its functionality with custom plug-ins, also called "checks." This feature allows users to implement their own security checks and adapt the tool to their specific needs.

- **High performance**   The scanner is designed to be efficient and capable of handling large web applications. It can perform concurrent scans, reducing the time taken to analyze a web application.

- **RESTful API**   Arachni provides a RESTful API, which allows integration with other tools and services. This makes it easier to automate and incorporate the scanner into existing workflows and development pipelines.

- **Reporting**   Arachni generates detailed and customizable reports, including information on identified vulnerabilities, affected resources, and remediation suggestions. The scanner supports various reporting formats, such as HTML, JSON, XML, and more.

- **Browser-based crawling**   Arachni uses a real browser environment to crawl web applications, enabling it to detect vulnerabilities that may be missed by traditional spidering techniques. This approach increases the accuracy and effectiveness of the scan.

Nikto

Nikto is a web server vulnerability scanner whose main strength is finding vulnerabilities such as SQL and command-injection susceptibilities, XSS, and improper server configuration. Although Nikto lacks a graphical interface as a command-line-executed utility, it's able to perform thousands of tests very quickly and provides details on the nature of the weaknesses it finds. To conduct a scan against a web server, you specify the IP with the **–host** option enabled. By default, the results of the scan will be output to the same window. Although not practical for detailed analysis, Nikto is useful for quickly confirming the status of a host. By using other options on the command line, you can export the results to an output file for follow-up evaluation. Note that the output includes the type of vulnerability, a short description, and any reference information about the vulnerability.

 NOTE   We focus on specific vulnerability scanners in this chapter, but the workflow of vulnerability scanning execution, report generation, and report distribution is similar with nearly all other types of vulnerability scanners on the market.

Although its utility is limited to web servers, Nikto's strength is its speed in assessing software vulnerabilities and configuration issues. As a command-line utility, it's not as

```
root@kali:~# nikto -host 4.4.4.28 -port 3780
- Nikto v2.1.6
---------------------------------------------------------------------
+ Target IP:          4.4.4.28
+ Target Hostname:    4.4.4.28
+ Target Port:        3780
---------------------------------------------------------------------
+ SSL Info:           Subject:  /CN=CompanyX/O=bl
                      Ciphers:  ECDHE-RSA-AES256-GCM-SHA384
                      Issuer:   /CN=CompanyX/O=bl
+ Start Time:         2017-04-10 12:14:28 (GMT-7)
---------------------------------------------------------------------
+ Server: Product Information
+ The site uses SSL and the Strict-Transport-Security HTTP header is not defined.
+ Root page / redirects to: https://4.4.4.28:3780/login.jsp
+ No CGI Directories found (use '-C all' to force check all possible dirs)
+ Hostname '4.4.4.28' does not match certificate's names: CompanyX
+ Allowed HTTP Methods: GET, HEAD, POST, PUT, DELETE, OPTIONS
+ OSVDB-397: HTTP method ('Allow' Header): 'PUT' method could allow clients to save files
on the web server.
+ OSVDB-5646: HTTP method ('Allow' Header): 'DELETE' may allow clients to remove files on
the web server.
+ OSVDB-67: /_vti_bin/shtml.dll/_vti_rpc: The anonymous FrontPage user is revealed through
a crafted POST.
+ /login.html: Admin login page/section found.
+ 7499 requests: 0 error(s) and 7 item(s) reported on remote host
+ End Time:           2017-04-10 12:20:26 (GMT-7) (358 seconds)
---------------------------------------------------------------------
+ 1 host(s) tested
```

Figure 10-5   Nikto command-line output for a test against a web server located at IP 4.4.4.28

user friendly as some other tools. Nikto requires at least a target host to be specified, with any additional options, such as nonstandard ports, added in the command line. Figure 10-5 shows the command issued to perform a scan against a web team's new site, which operates on port 3780.

Nikto enables reports to be saved in a variety of ways, including HTML. An example of Nikto HTML test files is shown in Figure 10-6. This report includes a summary of the command issued, information about the servers tested, and hyperlinks to the relevant resources and their vulnerability data. Although this is good for technical teams to act on, it may not be as useful for nontechnical decision-makers.

Key features of Nikto include the following:

- **Plug-in architecture**   Nikto uses a plug-in architecture that allows users to extend its functionality and customize the scan to their specific needs.

- **SSL/TLS support**   Nikto supports scanning of SSL/TLS-encrypted web applications, allowing it to detect vulnerabilities related to encryption and secure communication.

- **Comprehensive coverage**   Nikto scans for a wide range of vulnerabilities, including outdated software versions, configuration issues, and common vulnerabilities such as XSS and SQL injection.

- **Multiple output formats**   Nikto supports multiple output formats, including HTML, XML, CSV, and Nessus' NBE file formats, allowing users to generate customized reports that meet their specific needs.

PART II

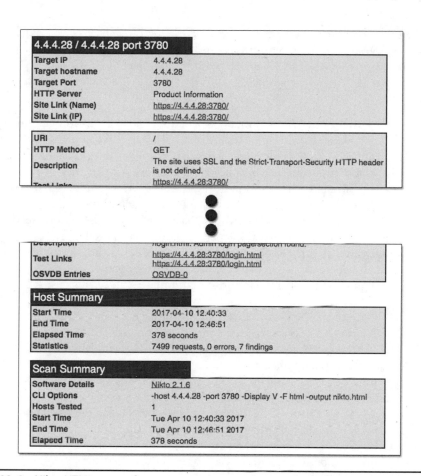

4.4.4.28 / 4.4.4.28 port 3780

Target IP	4.4.4.28
Target hostname	4.4.4.28
Target Port	3780
HTTP Server	Product Information
Site Link (Name)	https://4.4.4.28:3780/
Site Link (IP)	https://4.4.4.28:3780/

URI	/
HTTP Method	GET
Description	The site uses SSL and the Strict-Transport-Security HTTP header is not defined.
Test Links	https://4.4.4.28:3780/

Description	login.html: Admin login page/section found.
Test Links	https://4.4.4.28:3780/login.html https://4.4.4.28:3780/login.html
OSVDB Entries	OSVDB-0

Host Summary

Start Time	2017-04-10 12:40:33
End Time	2017-04-10 12:46:51
Elapsed Time	378 seconds
Statistics	7499 requests, 0 errors, 7 findings

Scan Summary

Software Details	Nikto 2.1.6
CLI Options	-host 4.4.4.28 -port 3780 -Display V -F html -output nikto.html
Hosts Tested	1
Start Time	Tue Apr 10 12:40:33 2017
End Time	Tue Apr 10 12:46:51 2017
Elapsed Time	378 seconds

Figure 10-6   Nikto HTML output from a test against a web server located at IP 4.4.4.28

- **Web server fingerprinting**   Nikto includes a built-in web server fingerprinting tool that can detect the type and version of the web server being used, as well as any known vulnerabilities associated with it.

Infrastructure Vulnerability Scanners

Modern scanners cannot find weaknesses they're not aware of or do not understand. The most popular vulnerability scanners have amassed enormous libraries of vulnerabilities that cover the vast majority of flaws most likely to be exploited. We'll discuss a few popular vulnerability scanners in the next few pages. Many of these tools enable analysts to get a picture of the network from the perspective of an outsider as well as from a legitimate user. In the latter case, the scanner will most often perform an *authenticated scan* in one of two primary ways. The first method is to install local agents on the endpoints to synchronize with the vulnerability scan server and provide analysis on the endpoint during the course of the scan. The second method is to provide administrative credentials directly to the scanner, which it will invoke as necessary during the scan. It's good practice to use both authenticated and unauthenticated scans during an assessment, because the use of one type may uncover vulnerabilities that would not be found by the other.

Nessus

Nessus, a popular and powerful scanner, began its life as an open source and free utility in the late 1990s and has since become a top choice for conducting vulnerability scans. With more than 80,000 plug-ins, Tenable's Nessus enables users to schedule and conduct scans across multiple networks based on custom policies. Nessus includes basic port-scanning functionality. Its real power, however, lies in its multitude of features for vulnerability identification, misconfiguration detection, default password exposure, and compliance determination. The standard installation includes the Nessus server, which will coordinate the vulnerability scan, generate reports, and facilitate the vulnerability management feature. It can reside on the same machine as the Nessus web client or can be located elsewhere on the network. The client is designed to be run from the web interface, which enables the administrator to manipulate scan settings using any browser that supports HTML5.

Figure 10-7 shows the Nessus architecture being used against several targets on the network. Located on the Nessus server are the various plug-ins used in conducting assessments against the targets. With registration, Tenable provides updates of plug-ins and the server software often, usually once a day.

Assuming the server is running on the same local machine as the client, as is often the case, you can access the Nessus web interface by pointing your browser to http://localhost:8834, as shown in Figure 10-8. When you start Nessus for the first time, there is a bit of a delay for initial configuration, registration, and updating. Be patient, and you'll soon be ready to conduct your first scan.

Once the initial setup is complete, you can specify the details for any type of scan from the same interface. By default, the most popular scans are already enabled, but it's good practice to walk through all the settings to learn what exactly will be happening on your network. Figure 10-9 shows the general Settings page, which provides space for a name and description of the scan. Scans created here can be used for immediate or scheduled action. Targets can be specified in one of several ways, including via a single IPv4 address, a single IPv6 address, a range of IPv4 or IPv6 addresses, or a hostname. In addition, the

Figure 10-7
Nessus
client/server
architecture
shown against
several network
targets

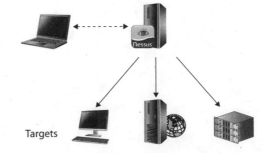

Targets

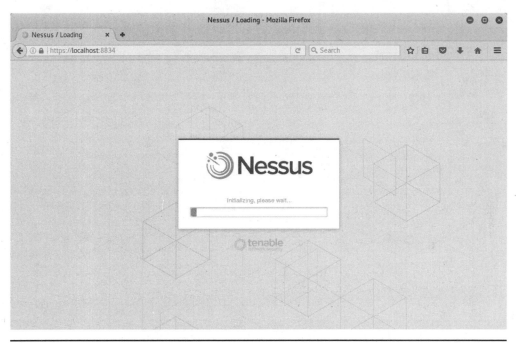

Figure 10-8   View of Nessus loading from a standard web browser

server will also correctly interpret classless inter-domain routing (CIDR) or netmask notation to specify IPv4 subnets. Nessus also provides a space to upload groups of specific target machines in ASCII text format, making it easy to reuse pre-populated lists. In this Settings page, you can also set schedules for scans, adjust notification preferences, and define certain technical limits for the scan. Nessus classifies some plug-ins as dangerous, meaning that their use may cause damage to some systems in certain conditions. When you're preparing to execute a scan, it may be useful to use the Nessus "safe checks" option to avoid launching potentially destructive attacks. We'll step through setting up a basic Nessus scan over the next few pages.

Nessus allows for great flexibility and depth in the scanning process. You can configure Nessus to pass along any credentials that may be useful. In the Credentials page, shown in Figure 10-10, there is space to configure credentials for Windows hosts. Nessus supports passing authentication for a wide range of cloud services, databases, hosts, network devices, and hypervisors.

In the Compliance page, shown in Figure 10-11, you can configure compliance checks for the scan. Included in the default installation are many preconfigured checks developed in-house or based on industry best practices and benchmarks. As an admin, you can also develop and upload your own custom configuration, called an *audit file,* for use in the compliance check. The audit file gives instructions used to assess the configuration of endpoints and network device systems against a compliance policy or to check for the presence of sensitive data.

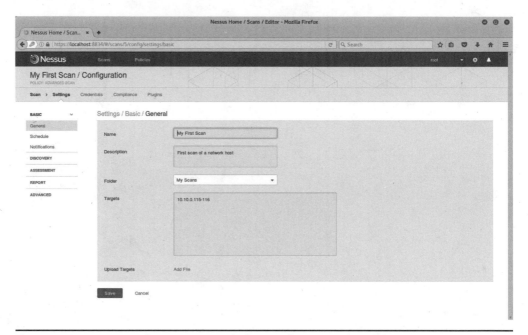

Figure 10-9 Nessus configuration screen before conducting a vulnerability scan

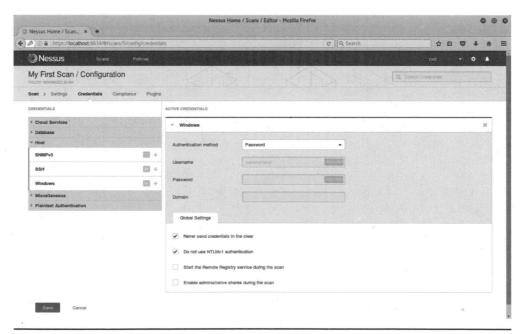

Figure 10-10 Nessus Credentials page

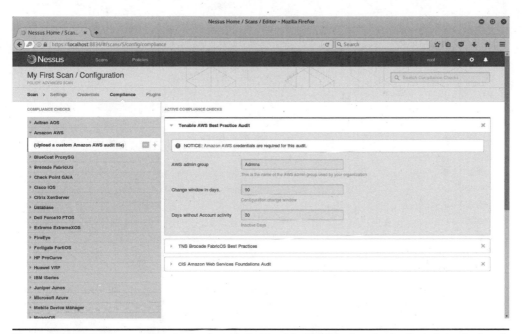

Figure 10-11 Nessus compliance checks with the Tenable AWS Best Practice Audit options displayed

When using compliance checks, you should be aware of some of the tradeoffs. Enabling these checks may slow down the scan because many more aspects of the target system will be checked, and potentially at a deeper level. In some cases, active scanning may reduce functionality of both the client and target machines. Furthermore, these compliance checks may be interpreted as intrusive by the target, which may trigger alerts on intermediate security devices and endpoint software.

On the next page, Plugins, you can see the status of all the plug-ins available for scanning. Nessus maintains a library of these small programs that checks for known flaws. Plug-ins are written in the Nessus Attack Scripting Language (NASL) and contain information about the vulnerability, its remediation steps, and the mechanism that the plug-in uses to determine the existence of the vulnerability. Usually released within 24 hours of a public disclosure, plug-ins are constantly updated as part of the Nessus subscription. As shown in Figure 10-12, you can activate (or deactivate) any plug-ins required for the scan, or you can just get details into what exactly is performed by the plug-in during the assessment.

With all the necessary settings saved, you can begin scanning targets for vulnerabilities. When Nessus discovers a vulnerability, it assigns a severity level to it in the scan results, as shown in Figure 10-13.

Technical details for each vulnerability, the method used in identifying it, and any database references are displayed here. Nessus is particularly strong at assessing compliance using its library of compliance checks. These compliance checks, or any other type of scan, can be scheduled to occur as desired, fulfilling your CISO's desire to conduct

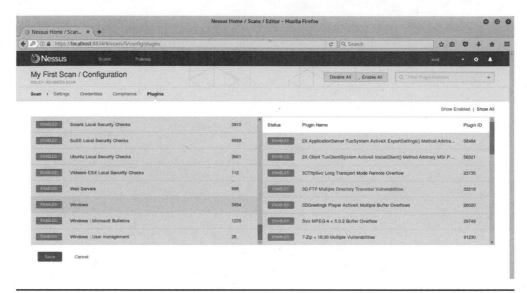

Figure 10-12 Nessus plug-in selection interface

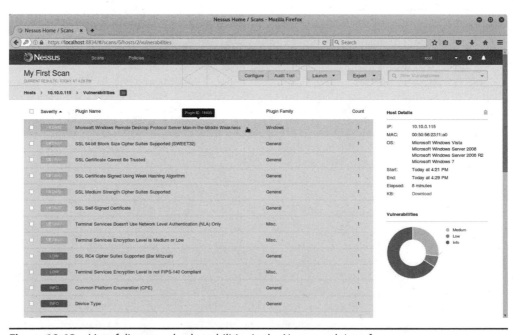

Figure 10-13 List of discovered vulnerabilities in the Nessus web interface

periodic scans automatically. As for reports, Nessus offers several export options, as shown in Figure 10-14.

Nessus can generate reports that list only vulnerabilities with an associated exploit, alongside suggested remediation steps. For an audience such as company leaders,

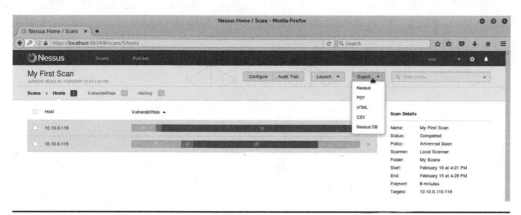

Figure 10-14   Nessus export options for report generation after a vulnerability scan

explaining in plain language the concrete steps that may be taken to improve organizational security is key. Nessus provides these suggestions for individual hosts as well as for the network at large.

The following are some of the key features of Nessus:

- **Advanced vulnerability scanning**   Nessus is known for its advanced vulnerability scanning capabilities, which include detecting known and potentially unknown vulnerabilities across a range of devices and platforms.

- **Plug-in architecture**   Nessus uses a plug-in architecture that allows for customization and extensibility. Users can write their own plug-ins or leverage third-party plug-ins to extend the functionality of the scanner.

- **Policy creation and enforcement**   Nessus allows for the creation and enforcement of customized security policies, which can be applied to specific devices or groups of devices. Policies can include requirements for patching, configuration settings, and other security controls. Nessus can also perform compliance checks against various security frameworks and policies, such as PCI DSS and CIS.

- **Continuous monitoring**   Nessus can be used for the continuous monitoring of devices and systems, providing ongoing visibility into vulnerabilities and security posture. It can also generate alerts and notifications when new vulnerabilities are detected.

- **Agent-based scanning**   Nessus offers the option for agent-based scanning, which allows for more granular scanning of devices and systems. Agents can be deployed to endpoints and used for scanning when devices are offline or disconnected from the network.

- **Asset discovery**   Nessus can be used for asset discovery, allowing for the identification and tracking of devices and systems on the network.

- **Cloud support**   Nessus supports scanning of cloud-based environments, including AWS and Azure.

- **Reporting and analytics**   Nessus provides detailed reporting and analytics capabilities, including customizable dashboards, executive reports, and compliance reports. Reports can be generated in typical formats, such as PDF, HTML, and CSV.

OpenVAS

The Open Vulnerability Assessment System, or OpenVAS, is a free framework that consists of several analysis tools for both vulnerability identification and management. OpenVAS is a fork of the original Nessus project that began shortly after Tenable closed development of the Nessus framework. OpenVAS is similar to Nessus in that it supports browser-based access to its OpenVAS Manager, which uses the OpenVAS Scanner to conduct assessments based on a collection of more than 47,000 network vulnerability tests (NVTs). Results of these NVTs are then sent back to the Manager for storage.

You can access OpenVAS's interface by using a standard browser to access http://localhost:9392. Figure 10-15 shows the welcome screen from which an admin can access all settings for both the OpenVAS Manager and OpenVAS Scanner. There is also an empty field on the right side of the screen that can be used to launch quick scans.

OpenVAS also provides details on active NVTs used in the scan, as shown in Figure 10-16. You can see the status of each of the tests and, as with Nessus, get details on the test itself. In addition to the summary of the NVT, a vulnerability score is given, plus a level of confidence assigned to the detection method.

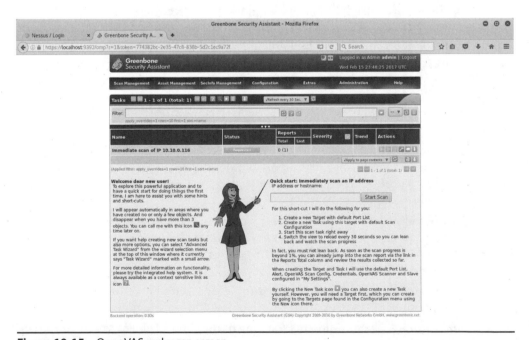

Figure 10-15   OpenVAS welcome screen

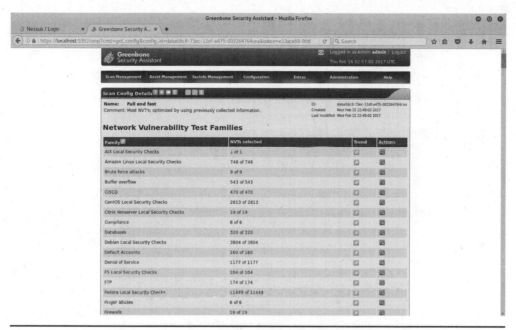

Figure 10-16   OpenVAS network vulnerability test families

Some of the key OpenVAS features are listed here:

- **Open source**   OpenVAS is a fully open source vulnerability scanner, making it accessible to a wide range of users and organizations.

- **Command-line and web-based interfaces**   OpenVAS provides both a command-line interface and a web-based graphical user interface (GUI), allowing users to choose the interface that best suits their needs and experience.

- **Support for multiple platforms**   OpenVAS is compatible with various operating systems, including Linux, Mac, and Windows.

- **Comprehensive reporting**   OpenVAS generates detailed reports that include a summary of identified vulnerabilities, affected hosts and systems, and recommendations for remediation. The scanner supports typical reporting formats, such as HTML, PDF, and XML.

Qualys

QualysGuard is a product of the California-based security company Qualys, an early player in the vulnerability management market. The company currently provides several cloud-based vulnerability assessment and management products through a Software as a Service (SaaS) model. For internal scans, a local virtual machine conducts the assessment and reports to the Qualys server. Figure 10-17 shows a QualysGuard dashboard with various options under the vulnerability management module.

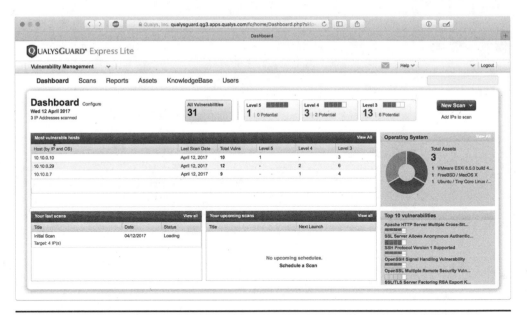

Figure 10-17 The QualysGuard dashboard for managing its cloud-based vulnerability assessment and management tasks

All network discovery, mapping, asset prioritization, scheduling, vulnerability assessment reporting, and remediation tracking tasks can be accessed via the web-based UI. The platform can generate detailed reports using several templates. Included in the default installation is a template called "Executive Report," which provides just the type of data needed by a CISO. A portion of the results of this report is shown in Figure 10-18.

Some key features of QualysGuard include the following:

- **Cloud based** QualysGuard is a cloud-based solution, which means that there is no need to install any software or hardware on-premises.

- **Asset management** QualysGuard provides an inventory of an organization's assets, including physical, virtual, and cloud-based assets. It also provides detailed information about each asset, such as operating system, installed applications, and network topology.

- **Vulnerability assessment** QualysGuard can perform both authenticated and unauthenticated scans of an organization's assets to identify vulnerabilities.

- **Compliance management** QualysGuard includes pre-built templates for various compliance regulations, such as PCI DSS, HIPAA, and ISO 27001. It can also generate reports as evidence of compliance with these regulations.

- **Threat protection** QualysGuard integrates with threat intelligence feeds to provide real-time protection against known threats.

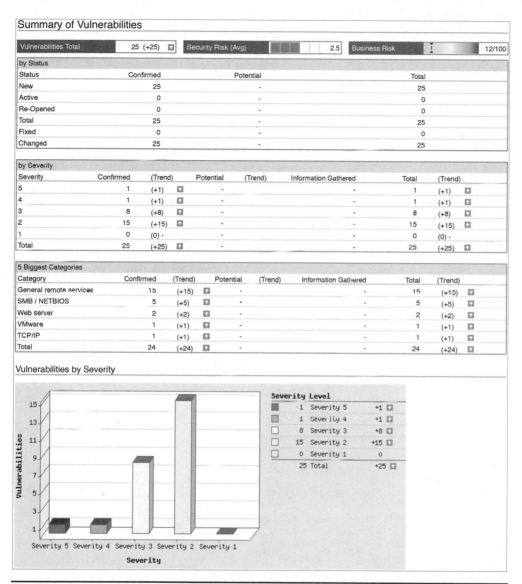

Figure 10-18   A portion of the QualysGuard report generated from the "Executive Report" template

- **Patch management**   QualysGuard provides a patch management module that allows users to identify missing patches and deploy them automatically.

- **Reporting**   QualysGuard offers a wide range of customizable reporting options, including dashboards, executive reports, and detailed technical reports.

- **API integration**   QualysGuard provides an API that allows users to integrate the tool with other systems and applications.

Multipurpose Tools

Network enumeration is the interrogation of a set of hosts to look for specific information. A horizontal network scan, for instance, sends messages to a set of host addresses asking the question, "Are you there?" Its goal is to determine which addresses correspond to active (responding) systems. A vertical scan, on the other hand, sends messages to a set of protocol/port combinations (for example, UDP 53 or TCP 25) asking the same question, with the goal of determining which ports are listening for client connection attempts. It is possible to combine both horizontal and vertical scans, as shown in Figure 10-19. The point of a network scan of any flavor is to find out who is listening (and responding) on a network. This is useful in finding systems that are not behaving as they ought to.

Consider the case in which a software development team sets up a test web server to ensure that the web app on which the team members are working is functioning properly.

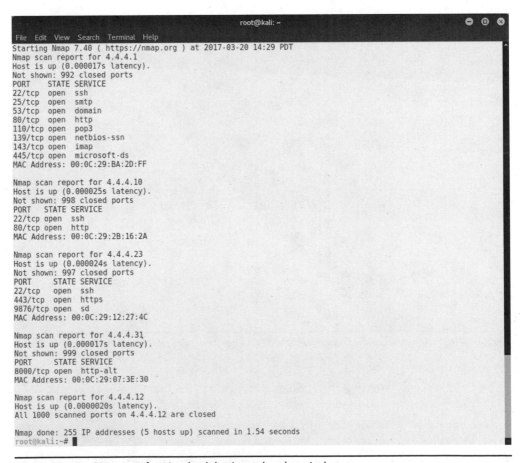

Figure 10-19 Nmap performing both horizontal and vertical scans

There is no malice, but not knowing that this server is running (and how) could seriously compromise the integrity of the defenses. On the other hand, we can sometimes find evidence that a host has been compromised and is now running a malicious service. Though these situations should be rare in a well-managed network, scanning is one of the quintessential skills of any security professional because it is one of very few ways to know and map what is really on our networks.

nmap

Nmap, one of the most popular tools used for the enumeration of a targeted host, is synonymous with network scanning. The name is shorthand for "network mapper," which is an apt description of what it does. Nmap works by sending specially crafted messages to the target hosts and then examining the responses. This can tell not only which hosts are active on the network and which of their ports are listening, but it can also help us determine the operating system, hostname, and even patch level of some systems. Though nmap is a command-line interface (CLI) tool, a number of front ends provide a GUI, including Zenmap (Windows), NmapFE (Linux), and Xnmap (macOS).

Nmap scan results are not as rich in diverse content as those of other data sources, but they offer surgical precision for the information they do yield. Moreover, successive runs of nmap with identical parameters, together with a bit of scripting, enable the user to quickly identify changes to the configuration of a target. Attackers may be interested in new services because they are likelier to have exploitable configuration errors. Defenders, on the other hand, may be interested in new services because they could indicate a compromised host. Nmap is even used by some organizations to inventory assets on a network by periodically doing full scans and comparing hosts and services to an existing baseline.

 NOTE One of the most important defensive measures you can take is to maintain an accurate inventory of all the hardware and software on your network. Nmap can help with this, but various open source and commercial solutions are also available for IT asset management.

Nmap is a comprehensive scanner. The following list enumerates just some of its features:

- **Host discovery**   Nmap uses a range of techniques to discover hosts on a network, including ping sweeps, ARP scans, and DNS resolution.
- **Port scanning**   Nmap can scan for open ports on a target system, allowing users to identify services that may be vulnerable to attack.
- **Service detection**   Nmap can identify the type of services running on a target system as well as the version and other details about those services.
- **Operating system detection**   Nmap can also identify the operating system running on a target system, using a range of techniques such as TCP/IP fingerprinting and DHCP requests.

- **NSE scripts**   The Nmap Scripting Engine, NSE, allows users to write scripts that can automate a wide range of tasks, such as vulnerability scanning, brute-force attacks, and banner grabbing. NSE scripts are written in the Lua programming language.

- **Scriptable interaction**   Nmap can be scripted to interact with other tools and systems, allowing for more sophisticated and automated attacks. For example, nmap can be used to launch attacks against web applications using the OWASP ZAP proxy or to automate the exploitation of vulnerabilities using Metasploit.

- **Stealth scanning**   Nmap offers a range of options for performing stealthy scans, such as TCP SYN scanning and idle scanning, which can be useful for avoiding detection.

- **Customizable output**   Nmap can generate output in a range of formats, including XML, grepable text, and HTML.

hping

Designed to provide advanced features beyond those offered from the built-in ping utility, hping is a useful enumeration tool that enables users to craft custom packets to assist with the discovery of network flaws, or it can be used by attackers to facilitate targeted exploit delivery. In addition to providing the packet analysis functionality of TCP, UDP, and ICMP traffic, hping includes a traceroute mode and supports IP fragmentation. Figure 10-20 shows the output of a basic hping command targeting the loopback address.

Here's a list of some of hping's features:

- **Packet crafting**   Hping allows users to craft custom packets and manipulate packet fields, such as source and destination IP addresses, TCP flags, and more. This can be useful for testing firewall rules and filtering as well as for creating specialized network traffic for testing and reconnaissance.

- **Traceroute**   Hping can perform traceroute functionality, allowing users to trace the path of packets through a network and identify potential network issues or misconfigurations.

- **Port scanning**   Hping includes several port scanning modes, including TCP connect, SYN stealth, FIN stealth, and UDP. It also allows users to define custom scan types and options.

- **OS fingerprinting**   Hping includes an OS fingerprinting feature, which can be used to identify the operating system of a target host based on its responses to specific packets.

- **Network mapping**   Hping can be used for network mapping and discovery, allowing users to identify hosts, services, and potential vulnerabilities within a network.

- **Scripting**   Hping includes a scripting language utilizing Tcl that allows users to automate tasks and perform more advanced packet manipulation and network analysis.

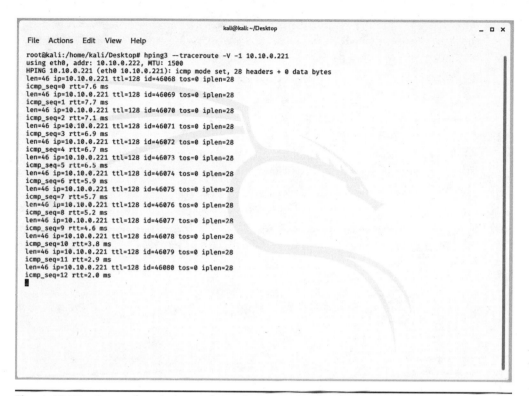

```
                                    kali@kali:~/Desktop                              _ □ ✕
 File   Actions   Edit   View   Help

root@kali:/home/kali/Desktop# hping3 —traceroute -V -1 10.10.0.221
using eth0, addr: 10.10.0.222, MTU: 1500
HPING 10.10.0.221 (eth0 10.10.0.221): icmp mode set, 28 headers + 0 data bytes
len=46 ip=10.10.0.221 ttl=128 id=46068 tos=0 iplen=28
icmp_seq=0 rtt=7.6 ms
len=46 ip=10.10.0.221 ttl=128 id=46069 tos=0 iplen=28
icmp_seq=1 rtt=7.7 ms
len=46 ip=10.10.0.221 ttl=128 id=46070 tos=0 iplen=28
icmp_seq=2 rtt=7.1 ms
len=46 ip=10.10.0.221 ttl=128 id=46071 tos=0 iplen=28
icmp_seq=3 rtt=6.9 ms
len=46 ip=10.10.0.221 ttl=128 id=46072 tos=0 iplen=28
icmp_seq=4 rtt=6.7 ms
len=46 ip=10.10.0.221 ttl=128 id=46073 tos=0 iplen=28
icmp_seq=5 rtt=6.5 ms
len=46 ip=10.10.0.221 ttl=128 id=46074 tos=0 iplen=28
icmp_seq=6 rtt=5.9 ms
len=46 ip=10.10.0.221 ttl=128 id=46075 tos=0 iplen=28
icmp_seq=7 rtt=5.7 ms
len=46 ip=10.10.0.221 ttl=128 id=46076 tos=0 iplen=28
icmp_seq=8 rtt=5.2 ms
len=46 ip=10.10.0.221 ttl=128 id=46077 tos=0 iplen=28
icmp_seq=9 rtt=4.6 ms
len=46 ip=10.10.0.221 ttl=128 id=46078 tos=0 iplen=28
icmp_seq=10 rtt=3.8 ms
len=46 ip=10.10.0.221 ttl=128 id=46079 tos=0 iplen=28
icmp_seq=11 rtt=2.9 ms
len=46 ip=10.10.0.221 ttl=128 id=46080 tos=0 iplen=28
icmp_seq=12 rtt=2.0 ms
```

Figure 10-20   Output from hping performed against a host on the LAN

Metasploit Framework

Metasploit is an open source framework that is widely used in penetration testing and security research. It provides a set of tools and utilities that can be used to identify vulnerabilities, exploit them, and gain access to systems. The framework is designed to be modular and flexible, allowing users to customize and extend it to suit their needs.

One of the key features of Metasploit is its ability to automate the process of identifying vulnerabilities and exploiting them. This is done through the use of "exploits," which are pieces of software that can be used to take advantage of a specific vulnerability. Metasploit includes a large database of exploits that can be searched and filtered to find the ones relevant to a particular target.

The Metasploit Framework (MSF) consists of several components, including the following:

- **msfconsole**   The primary interface for interacting with the framework, msfconsole provides a command-line environment for executing exploits and payloads as well as managing sessions.

- **msfvenom**   A tool for generating payloads and encoding them to avoid detection.

- **Meterpreter**   A post-exploitation tool that provides a remote shell on the target system and allows the attacker to perform various tasks, such as escalating privileges and pivoting to other systems on the network.
- **Exploit modules**   Pre-built code that can exploit specific vulnerabilities in target systems.
- **Payload modules**   Code that can be delivered to a target system after an exploit has been successful, allowing for further exploitation and control.
- **Auxiliary modules**   Modules that do not exploit vulnerabilities but perform other useful tasks such as information gathering, brute forcing, and scanning.
- **NOPS**   No-operation payloads that are used to create padding in exploit code and avoid detection by intrusion detection systems (IDSs) and antivirus software.
- **Post-exploitation modules**   Modules that provide additional capabilities once a system has been compromised, such as keylogging, port forwarding, and pivoting to other systems.

As mentioned previously, msfconsole is the primary interface for interacting with the Metasploit Framework. Here is an example of how to use msfconsole to exploit a known vulnerability in a web application:

1. Launch msfconsole by opening a terminal and typing

   ```
   msfconsole
   ```

2. Set the target host by typing

   ```
   set RHOST <target_ip_address>
   ```

3. Select an exploit. For example, if the target web application is vulnerable to SQL injection, we would type

   ```
   use exploit/multi/http/sqli
   ```

4. Set any required options for the selected exploit. For example, we may need to set the URL of the vulnerable page by typing

   ```
   set URI <vulnerable_url>
   ```

5. We may also need to set the payload we want to use. For example, to use the Meterpreter payload, we would type

   ```
   set payload windows/meterpreter/reverse_tcp
   ```

6. Finally, to run the attack, type

   ```
   exploit
   ```

If the exploit is successful, we will have a remote shell on the target machine. We can then use Metasploit's built-in tools to gather information, escalate privileges, and perform other actions on the compromised machine.

 EXAM TIP   You will not need to know how to perform an attack with Metasploit for the exam. However, you should be aware of its utility and general use.

Recon-ng

Recon-ng is an open source framework used for reconnaissance and intelligence gathering. Similar to the Metasploit framework, it is designed to automate and streamline the process of gathering information about targets, which is a critical step in the process of penetration testing and vulnerability assessment. However, whereas Metasploit is primarily focused on exploiting vulnerabilities, Recon-ng is geared toward the discovery and mapping of potential targets and their associated infrastructure.

Recon-ng includes a modular architecture that allows users to extend its functionality with custom modules. It includes a variety of modules for performing reconnaissance on a wide range of targets and platforms, including social media, DNS, web applications, and more.

Like Metasploit, Recon-ng provides a command-line interface (CLI) and is operated through a series of commands and options. Once a target has been identified, users can choose from a variety of modules to extract additional information about the target. These modules range from simple port scanning and banner grabbing to more complex enumeration and fingerprinting. Additionally, users can create custom modules tailored to their specific needs, allowing them to expand the functionality of the framework to suit their requirements.

The Recon-ng CLI provides a number of built-in commands for performing reconnaissance tasks. To launch Recon-ng, type the following command into the terminal:

```
recon-ng
```

First, we can list the available modules by typing

```
show modules
```

To use a module, type use and the module name. For example, to use the recon/domains-hosts/brute_hosts module, type

```
use recon/domains-hosts/brute_hosts
```

Next, we can set the required options. For example, to set the SOURCE option to a file containing a list of target IP addresses, type

```
set SOURCE /path/to/targets.txt
```

Once the required options have been set, we can run the module by typing

```
run
```

Recon-ng will now begin brute forcing the target hosts and display the results in real time. Once the module has finished executing, we can view the results by typing

```
show hosts
```

This will display a list of all hosts that were discovered during the scan. We can then use the **use** command to select another module and continue our reconnaissance.

EXAM TIP You will not need to know how to perform reconnaissance with Recon-ng for the exam. However, you should be aware of its utility and general use.

Wireless Assessment Tools

It is difficult to run any kind of corporate network without considering the implications of wireless networks. Even if you don't allow wireless devices at all (not even mobile phones) in your building, how would you know that the policy is being followed by all employees, all the time? Admittedly, most organizations will not (and often cannot) implement such draconian measures, which makes wireless local area network (WLAN) auditing and analysis particularly important.

To conduct a WLAN analysis, you must first capture data. Normally, when a WLAN interface card connects to a wireless access point (WAP), the client device will be in managed mode and the WAP will be in infrastructure mode. Infrastructure mode (also known as *master* mode) means that the interface will be responsible for managing all aspects of the WLAN configuration, such as channel and service set ID (SSID). The client in managed mode is being managed by the access point and thus will change channels or other settings when told to do so. Wireless interfaces can also communicate directly in *mesh* mode, enabling the interface to establish direct connections with other interfaces without the need for access point-based hierarchies (also known as ad hoc mode). In each of these three modes, the interface will be limited to one connection to one network. To monitor multiple networks simultaneously, we need a fourth mode of operation. In *monitor* mode, the wireless interface will be able to see all available WLANs and their characteristics without connecting to any of them. This is the mode we need in order to perform a WLAN audit. Fortunately, WLAN analyzers, such as Kismet, take care of these details and enable us simply to run the application and see what is out there.

The most important step as a security analysis of your WLANs is to know your devices. Chief among these, of course, are the WAPs, but you must also keep track of wireless clients. How would you know that something odd is going on? Quite simply, by keeping track of what "normal" looks like. When analyzing the structure of WLANs, you must start from a known-good list of access points and client devices. Because, presumably, your organization installed (or had someone install) all the WAPs, you should have a record of their settings (for example, protocol, channel, and location) as well as their MAC and IP addresses. As you conduct your periodic audits, you will be able to tell if a new WAP shows up in your scan, potentially indicating a rogue access point.

Looking for rogue or unauthorized clients is a bit tricky because it is not difficult to change the MAC address on many networked devices. Indeed, all major operating systems have built-in tools that enable you to do just that. Because the main indicator of an end device's identity is so susceptible to forgery, you may not be able to detect unauthorized nodes unless you implement some form of authentication, such as implementing WPA Enterprise and IEEE 802.1x. Absent authentication, you will have a very difficult time identifying all but the most naïve intruders connected to your WLAN.

Aircrack-ng

Aircrack-ng is the most popular open source wireless network security tool. Despite the name, the tool is actually a full-featured suite of wireless tools. It's used primarily for its ability to audit the security of WLANs through attacks on WPA keys, replay attacks, de-authentication, and the creation of fake access points, as shown in Figure 10-21. In support of all of this functionality, Aircrack-ng also allows for indiscriminate wireless monitoring, packet captures, and, if equipped with the correct hardware, wireless injection.

Reaver

It's well known that many wireless security protocols have significant flaws associated with them, which may allow for an attacker to gain foothold into a network that's within reach of a wireless signal. Reaver takes advantage of a vulnerability that exists in access points that use the Wi-Fi Protected Setup (WPS) feature. The WPS protocol emerged in the 2000s as a way for users to get set up on a network without having to remember complicated passwords or configuration settings. Unfortunately, a major flaw

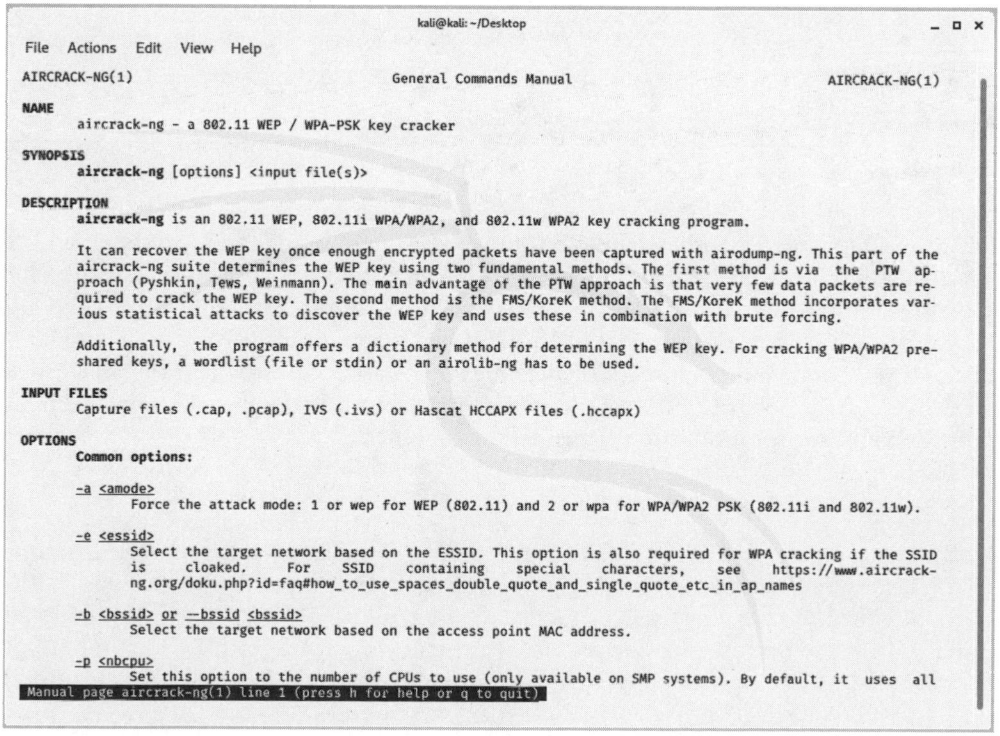

Figure 10-21   Aircrack-ng description and option screen

```
                                        kali@kali: ~/Desktop                              _ □ ×

  File  Actions  Edit  View  Help

  Copyright (c) 2011, Tactical Network Solutions, Craig Heffner <cheffner@tacnetsol.com>

  Required Arguments:
        -i, --interface=<wlan>        Name of the monitor-mode interface to use
        -b, --bssid=<mac>             BSSID of the target AP

  Optional Arguments:
        -m, --mac=<mac>               MAC of the host system
        -e, --essid=<ssid>            ESSID of the target AP
        -c, --channel=<channel>       Set the 802.11 channel for the interface (implies -f)
        -s, --session=<file>          Restore a previous session file
        -C, --exec=<command>          Execute the supplied command upon successful pin recovery
        -f, --fixed                   Disable channel hopping
        -5, --5ghz                    Use 5GHz 802.11 channels
        -v, --verbose                 Display non-critical warnings (-vv or -vvv for more)
        -q, --quiet                   Only display critical messages
        -h, --help                    Show help

  Advanced Options:
        -p, --pin=<wps pin>           Use the specified pin (may be arbitrary string or 4/8 digit WPS pin)
        -d, --delay=<seconds>         Set the delay between pin attempts [1]
        -l, --lock-delay=<seconds>    Set the time to wait if the AP locks WPS pin attempts [60]
        -g, --max-attempts=<num>      Quit after num pin attempts
        -x, --fail-wait=<seconds>     Set the time to sleep after 10 unexpected failures [0]
        -r, --recurring-delay=<x:y>   Sleep for y seconds every x pin attempts
        -t, --timeout=<seconds>       Set the receive timeout period [10]
        -T, --m57-timeout=<seconds>   Set the M5/M7 timeout period [0.40]
        -A, --no-associate            Do not associate with the AP (association must be done by another application)
        -N, --no-nacks                Do not send NACK messages when out of order packets are received
        -S, --dh-small                Use small DH keys to improve crack speed
        -L, --ignore-locks            Ignore locked state reported by the target AP
        -E, --eap-terminate           Terminate each WPS session with an EAP FAIL packet
        -J, --timeout-is-nack         Treat timeout as NACK (DIR-300/320)
        -F, --ignore-fcs              Ignore frame checksum errors
        -w, --win7                    Mimic a Windows 7 registrar [False]
        -K, --pixie-dust              Run pixiedust attack
        -Z                            Run pixiedust attack

  Example:
        reaver -i wlan0mon -b 00:90:4C:C1:AC:21 -vv
```

Figure 10-22   Reaver standard and advanced options screen

lies in the how WPS handles validation of the personal identification number (PIN). After splitting up the PIN into two halves, WPS validates each portion separately. This method significantly reduces the sample space, which Reaver leverages to guess the full password. As you can see from Figure 10-22, usage is straightforward. The analyst simply calls the command from the CLI, specifies the interface over which the attack will be delivered, and identifies the target access point. From a vulnerability management point of view, the solution is to disable WPS altogether.

Hashcat

Hashcat is a popular password cracking tool that has gained a reputation for being one of the fastest and most powerful tools in its category. Developed by Jens Steube, hashcat is designed to take advantage of modern hardware, particularly graphics processing units (GPUs), to perform high-speed password cracking operations. This is important because GPUs are designed to perform many calculations in parallel, making them ideal for password cracking tasks, where typically billions of calculations are required to guess a password. With the help of GPUs, hashcat can perform password cracking operations orders of magnitude faster than traditional CPU-based methods, making it an essential tool for security professionals.

Hashcat supports several operating modes:

- **Straight**   This is the simplest mode, where hashcat tries to crack one hash from the provided list of hashes.
- **Combination**   In this mode, hashcat combines two wordlists to create password candidates and then tries to crack hashes with them.
- **Brute-force**   This mode tries all possible combinations of characters until it finds the correct password.
- **Hybrid**   This mode combines a wordlist with rules to create password candidates and then tries to crack hashes with them.
- **Mask**   This mode lets the user define a custom character set and password length to generate password candidates.

Additionally, at the time of this writing, hashcat supports over 350 hash types and hashing algorithms. Here are several of the most prominent:

- **MD5**   A hashing algorithm that produces a 128-bit hash value.
- **SHA1**   A hashing algorithm that produces a 160-bit hash value.
- **SHA2**   A family of hashing algorithms that includes SHA-224, SHA-256, SHA-384, and SHA-512. These algorithms produce hash values of varying bit lengths.
- **SHA3**   The latest hashing algorithm in the SHA family, which produces hash values of 224, 256, 384, or 512 bits.
- **PBKDF2**   A key derivation function that uses a hash function (such as SHA1 or SHA2) to derive a key from a password.
- **bcrypt**   A password hashing algorithm that uses a modified form of the Blowfish cipher.
- **scrypt**   A password-based key derivation function that is designed to be "memory-hard," making it more difficult to perform brute-force attacks.
- **NTLM**   A proprietary hashing algorithm used by Microsoft for password storage.
- **WPA/WPA2**   Hashing algorithms used for Wi-Fi network authentication.
- **MySQL**   Hashing algorithms used for MySQL database authentication.

Figure 10-23 shows the output after initiating a dictionary brute-force attack on a list of hashes. Upon starting, hashcat identifies suitable processor candidates to perform the

```
● ● ●                        📁 Desktop — -bash — 128×56
hashcat (v5.1.0) starting...

OpenCL Platform #1: Apple
==========================
* Device #1: Intel(R) Xeon(R) CPU E5-1680 v2 @ 3.00GHz, skipped.
* Device #2: AMD Radeon HD - FirePro D700 Compute Engine, 1536/6144 MB allocatable, 32MCU
* Device #3: AMD Radeon HD - FirePro D700 Compute Engine, 1536/6144 MB allocatable, 32MCU

Hashes: 5 digests; 5 unique digests, 1 unique salts
Bitmaps: 16 bits, 65536 entries, 0x0000ffff mask, 262144 bytes, 5/13 rotates
Rules: 1

Applicable optimizers:
* Optimized-Kernel
* Zero-Byte
* Precompute-Init
* Precompute-Merkle-Demgard
* Meet-In-The-Middle
* Early-Skip
* Not-Salted
* Not-Iterated
* Single-Salt
* Raw-Hash

Minimum password length supported by kernel: 0
Maximum password length supported by kernel: 31

Watchdog: Hardware monitoring interface not found on your system.
Watchdog: Temperature abort trigger disabled.

Dictionary cache hit:
* Filename..: rockyou.txt
* Passwords.: 14344384
* Bytes.....: 139921497
* Keyspace..: 14344384


Session..........: hashcat
Status...........: Cracked
Hash.Type........: MD5
Hash.Target......: test.txt
Time.Started.....: Tue Feb 18 20:31:39 2020 (1 sec)
Time.Estimated...: Tue Feb 18 20:31:40 2020 (0 secs)
Guess.Base.......: File (rockyou.txt)
Guess.Queue......: 1/1 (100.00%)
Speed.#2.........:    44116.2 kH/s (1.62ms) @ Accel:256 Loops:1 Thr:256 Vec:1
Speed.#3.........:        0 H/s (0.00ms) @ Accel:256 Loops:1 Thr:256 Vec:1
Speed.#*.........:    44116.2 kH/s
Recovered........: 5/5 (100.00%) Digests, 1/1 (100.00%) Salts
Progress.........: 4195254/14344384 (29.25%)
Rejected.........: 950/4195254 (0.02%)
Restore.Point....: 0/14344384 (0.00%)
Restore.Sub.#2...: Salt:0 Amplifier:0-1 Iteration:0-1
Restore.Sub.#3...: Salt:0 Amplifier:0-1 Iteration:0-1
Candidates.#2....: 123456 -> rogabac
Candidates.#3....: SALCIDO -> roeiend
```

Figure 10-23   Hashcat in operation against a list of MD5 hashes using two GPUs

password cracking. It then lists the unique digests, or hashes, on which the utility will operate. For the duration of the cracking operation, hashcat will output useful statistics about its performance. This includes the estimated time of completion, cracking speed, and successfully recovered passwords.

In this example, we've specified that the successfully cracked passwords be outputted to a text file, shown in Figure 10-24. Note that the hash and its plaintext equivalent are placed side by side.

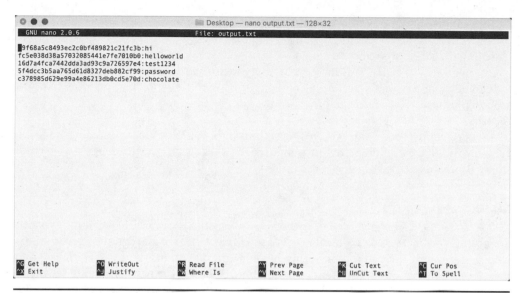

Figure 10-24 Contents of the hashcat output file

Debuggers

Debuggers are essential tools in the field of cybersecurity and software development. They provide a way to analyze and understand the internal workings of a program, helping in tasks such as identifying bugs, analyzing crashes, and investigating security vulnerabilities. Debuggers allow developers and security analysts to step through code, inspect variables, and track the flow of execution, providing valuable insights into the behavior of a program. Although debuggers are most widely used in the context of development and reverse engineering, we will explore their use in vulnerability assessment.

Debugger Scenario

Suppose you have a web server application that unexpectedly crashed and generated a core dump file. As a security analyst, your task is to investigate the cause of the crash and determine if it was triggered by a vulnerability.

Using a debugger, you can load the core dump file and examine the program's state at the time of the crash. One common vulnerability you might encounter is a stack-based buffer overflow, which occurs when a program writes more data into a buffer than it can hold, leading to memory corruption.

By analyzing the core dump, you notice that the crash occurred while processing an incoming HTTP request. Leveraging a debugger, you can inspect the values of relevant variables and registers to identify any anomalies. In this case, you discover that the length of the user-supplied request exceeds the buffer size allocated to store it.

By examining the memory layout and the stack, you find that the excessive input overflows into adjacent memory regions, potentially leading to the execution of arbitrary code or a denial-of-service condition.

Through this analysis, you have successfully identified a stack-based buffer overflow vulnerability in the web server application. Armed with this information, you can now work with the development team to patch the vulnerability and enhance the application's security.

By performing core dump analysis, even junior to midlevel security analysts can gain valuable insights into potential vulnerabilities without needing an in-depth understanding of programming languages or assembly.

GDB

GDB, the GNU Debugger, is an open-source debugger that can be leveraged for dynamic analysis, allowing users to set breakpoints and closely examine a program's execution. By stepping through the code, monitoring memory modifications, and inspecting register values, analysts can uncover potential vulnerabilities within the software. GDB's capability to inspect program memory during execution is useful in detecting memory corruption issues and other security risks.

GDB plays a crucial role in analyzing core dump files generated during program crashes or errors. Loading a core dump into GDB enables analysts to investigate the program's state at the time of the crash, aiding in the identification of potential vulnerabilities and security implications. By examining the memory, stack trace, and variable values from the core dump, analysts can gain insights into the cause of the crash and identify areas of the program that may be susceptible to exploitation.

Here's a list of prominent features in GDB that are relevant to vulnerability analysis:

- **Breakpoints and watchpoints** Set breakpoints at specific memory addresses or functions, enabling you to pause program execution and examine the state of the system at that point.
- **Memory examination** Inspect the contents of memory, allowing you to examine the values of variables, data structures, and buffers.
- **Disassembly and instruction stepping** Disassemble machine code instructions, allowing you to analyze the low-level execution flow.
- **Core dump analysis** Load and analyze core dump files, which capture the state of a program at the time of a crash or abnormal termination, discovering security vulnerabilities.
- **Stack tracing and backtraces** Generate stack traces and backtraces, providing information about the call hierarchy and function stack frames.
- **Dynamic code analysis** GDB allows you to dynamically modify program execution, change variable values, and observe the effects in real time.
- **Multi-architecture support** GDB supports a wide range of processor architectures and executable formats, making it a versatile tool for analyzing binaries and debugging software on various platforms.

Immunity Debugger

Immunity, a powerful debugger specifically designed for the security industry, offers a range of features that make it highly valuable for security analysts. Similar to GDB, Immunity excels in performing dynamic analysis of applications. Security analysts can leverage Immunity to set breakpoints, step through code, and monitor the execution flow of a program. Again, by closely examining the behavior of the application at runtime, analysts can identify potential vulnerabilities and gain insights into how they can be exploited. Immunity provides capabilities to track and manipulate registers, memory, and stack frames, allowing analysts to delve deep into the inner workings of an application and uncover critical security information.

In addition to dynamic analysis, Immunity offers advanced searching and scripting capabilities. Analysts can search for specific patterns or strings within an application's memory, registers, or stack. This feature is particularly useful for identifying sensitive information, such as passwords or encryption keys, that may be stored in memory. Immunity's scripting support allows analysts to automate repetitive tasks, customize the debugging environment, and develop complex analysis routines.

The following are some of Immunity's most relevant features:

- **Breakpoints and watchpoints**   Set breakpoints and watchpoints to pause program execution and monitor changes in variables or memory addresses of interest.

- **Memory examination**   Analyze the contents of memory to gain insights into variables, data structures, and buffers.

- **Disassembly and instruction stepping**   Disassemble machine code instructions and step through them to understand the low-level execution flow.

- **Core dump analysis**   Load and analyze core dump files, which capture the state of a program during a crash or termination.

- **Stack tracing and backtraces**   Generate stack traces and backtraces to understand the call hierarchy and function stack frames.

- **Dynamic code analysis**   Modify program execution dynamically, change variable values, and observe real-time effects.

- **Python integration**   Immunity Debugger offers integration with the Python programming language, allowing security analysts to leverage the extensive capabilities of Python for automation, customization, and analysis.

- **Python graphing**   Immunity Debugger provides built-in Python graphing capabilities, allowing security analysts to visualize complex data and relationships.

EXAM TIP   You should not be asked specifics of how to operate a debugger on the CySA+ test. However, you should be familiar with common usage in relation to vulnerability assessment.

Cloud Infrastructure Assessment Tools

Although the elastic nature of cloud computing and storage makes for rapid scalability and efficiency, its dynamic nature also means you need to think about tracking and prioritizing vulnerabilities in a different way. Thankfully, with the rise of cloud services, several fantastic tools are now available to assess cloud host vulnerabilities caused by misconfigurations, access flaws, and custom deployments. Many of these tools automate monitoring against industry standards, compliance checklists, regulatory mandates, and best practices to prevent common issues such as data spillage and instance takeover.

Scout Suite

Scout Suite is an open source auditing tool developed by NCC Group, a security consulting company that specializes in verification, auditing, and managed services. With support for Amazon Web Services (AWS), Microsoft Azure, and Google Cloud Platform, the tool enables security teams to determine the security posture of their cloud assets. It works by managing the interactions with cloud assets via the platform API and gathering information to make determinations of potentially vulnerable configurations. The results can be easily prepared for manual inspection or follow-up orchestration because of its structured format.

Here are some of the most prominent features of Scout Suite:

- **Multicloud support**   Scout Suite supports multiple cloud providers, including AWS, Azure, and GCP, allowing users to monitor their security posture across different cloud environments.

- **Automated scanning**   Scout Suite automatically scans cloud accounts for potential misconfigurations, security risks, and compliance violations, reducing the manual effort required to manage cloud security.

- **Customizable scans**   Users can customize the scan to focus on specific areas of their cloud environment or exclude certain resources, tailoring the scan to their unique requirements.

- **Detailed reporting**   Scout Suite generates detailed and customizable reports, providing users with a clear overview of their cloud security posture, including identified vulnerabilities, affected resources, and remediation suggestions.

- **Integration with third-party tools**   Scout Suite integrates with other security tools and services, such as SIEM and ticketing systems.

- **Compliance checks**   Scout Suite includes compliance checks for various standards and regulations, such as CIS AWS Foundations Benchmark, HIPAA, and GDPR, helping users meet their compliance obligations.

The tool requires a bit of preparation in the way of terms of service agreements and environmental setup, but usage is straightforward once configuration is in place. While Scout Suite ships with a default set of rules, the framework enables an analyst to provide custom rules to change the breadth of coverage during a scan. As shown in Figure 10-25, the rules are captured in a JSON file, which can be adjusted to the needs of the vulnerability team and specified during the utility's execution.

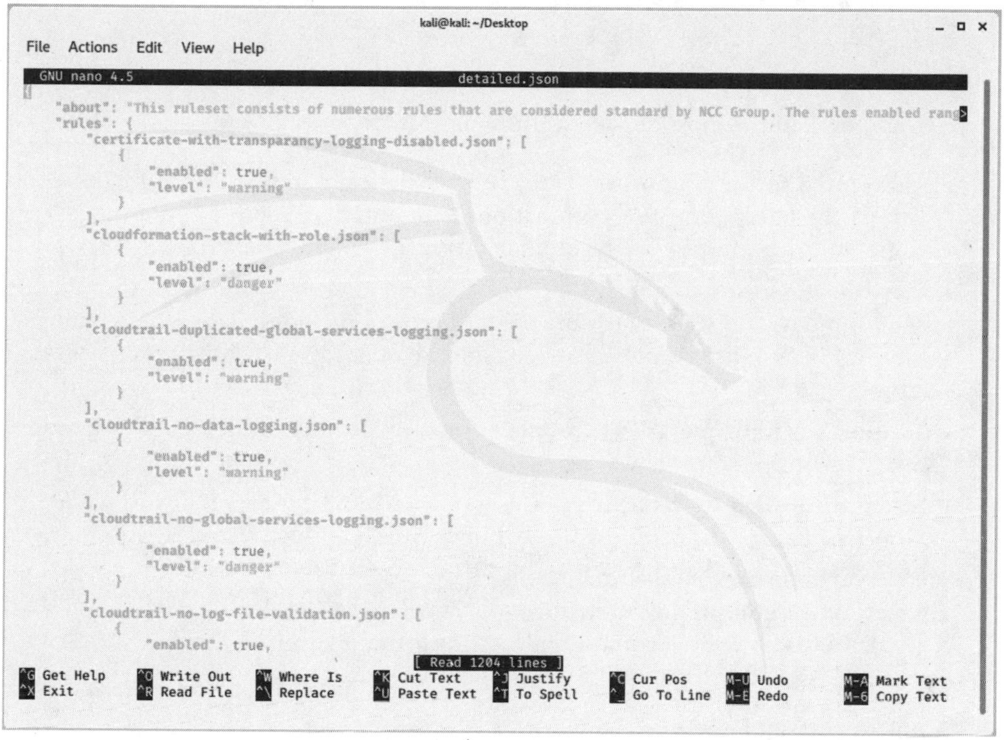

Figure 10-25 JSON file containing Scout Suite ruleset

Prowler

Similar to Scout Suite, Prowler is a framework designed as a scalable and repeatable method of acquiring measurable data related to the security readiness of your organization's cloud infrastructure. Prowler assesses cloud assets based in part on the Center for Internet Security (CIS) best practices for configuring security options for various AWS resources. Like Scout Suite, Prowler offers a fair amount of configuration to allow the tool programmatic access via the Amazon API. Additionally, the AWS CLI will have to be installed on the machine or instance running the tool. Prowler allows for the definition of custom checks, but by default it ships with the following best practice test configurations, or "groups":

- Identity and Access Management
- Logging
- Monitoring
- Networking
- CIS Level 1
- CIS Level 2
- Forensics

- GDPR
- HIPAA

Here are some of the most notable features of Prowler:

- **Automated security auditing**   Prowler automatically audits AWS configurations against the latest CIS AWS Foundations benchmark to identify potential vulnerabilities and provide recommendations for remediation.
- **Flexible and customizable**   Prowler can be customized to suit specific AWS environments and security requirements. The tool provides the option to run specific checks, include or exclude certain AWS services or regions, and generate custom reports.
- **Support for multiple AWS accounts**   Prowler can audit multiple AWS accounts simultaneously.
- **Integration with AWS Security Hub**   Prowler can be integrated with AWS Security Hub to automatically ingest Prowler findings into Security Hub for further analysis and correlation with other AWS security findings.
- **Continuous compliance monitoring**   Prowler can be scheduled to run on a regular basis, providing continuous monitoring and ensuring that any new AWS resource is evaluated against the latest CIS benchmark.

Pacu

Rhino Security Labs, a boutique security services firm made famous by its cutting-edge cloud penetration testing services, released the AWS exploitation framework Pacu in 2018. Pacu is open source and has a modular architecture based on common syntax and data structure to allow for simple expansion of its features. A key difference between Pacu and other cloud-focused assessment tools is that it's meant to be used in penetration tests and not just compliance checks. Accordingly, the framework makes it easy to document and export results in a manner familiar to those who frequently perform security engagements. Pacu is available via Rhino Lab's GitHub page, along with all the documentation and initial configurations needed to get started testing instances and services.

Here's a list of some of the most prominent features of Pacu:

- **Automated enumeration**   Pacu can automatically enumerate all the AWS resources and services that are accessible to a user, including S3 buckets, EC2 instances, RDS databases, and IAM roles.
- **Comprehensive AWS attacks**   Pacu provides a large number of preconfigured attacks that target various AWS services, including privilege escalation, data exfiltration, and lateral movement.
- **Cloud security posture assessment**   Pacu can also be used for security posture assessment of AWS environments, which involves identifying and addressing vulnerabilities and misconfigurations in the cloud infrastructure.

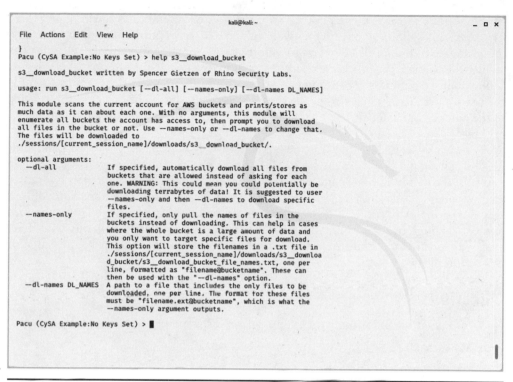

```
                                    kali@kali: ~                              _ □ ✕

 File  Actions  Edit  View  Help

 }
 Pacu (CySA Example:No Keys Set) > help s3__download_bucket

 s3__download_bucket written by Spencer Gietzen of Rhino Security Labs.

 usage: run s3__download_bucket [--dl-all] [--names-only] [--dl-names DL_NAMES]

 This module scans the current account for AWS buckets and prints/stores as
 much data as it can about each one. With no arguments, this module will
 enumerate all buckets the account has access to, then prompt you to download
 all files in the bucket or not. Use --names-only or --dl-names to change that.
 The files will be downloaded to
 ./sessions/[current_session_name]/downloads/s3__download_bucket/.

 optional arguments:
   --dl-all            If specified, automatically download all files from
                       buckets that are allowed instead of asking for each
                       one. WARNING: This could mean you could potentially be
                       downloading terrabytes of data! It is suggested to user
                       --names-only and then --dl-names to download specific
                       files.
   --names-only        If specified, only pull the names of files in the
                       buckets instead of downloading. This can help in cases
                       where the whole bucket is a large amount of data and
                       you only want to target specific files for download.
                       This option will store the filenames in a .txt file in
                       ./sessions/[current_session_name]/downloads/s3__downloa
                       d_bucket/s3__download_bucket_file_names.txt, one per
                       line, formatted as "filename@bucketname". These can
                       then be used with the "--dl-names" option.
   --dl-names DL_NAMES A path to a file that includes the only files to be
                       downloaded, one per line. The format for these files
                       must be "filename.ext@bucketname", which is what the
                       --names-only argument outputs.

 Pacu (CySA Example:No Keys Set) > █
```

Figure 10-26 Pacu's Help screen detailing the usage of a plug-in module

- **Extensive reporting** Pacu generates comprehensive reports that document the results of the attack, including the vulnerabilities discovered, the attack vectors used, and recommendations for mitigating the risks.

- **Integrated exploitation** Pacu integrates with other exploitation frameworks, such as Metasploit and Empire, to extend its attack capabilities.

Pacu ships with more than 30 modules that enable a range of attacks, including user privilege escalation, enumeration, and attacking vulnerable Lambda functions. Each of the modules has comprehensive details about its usage, as shown in Figure 10-26.

Chapter Review

Vulnerability scanning is a key responsibility of any security team. Taking the steps to understand and track the vulnerabilities your network faces is important in determining the best mitigation strategies. Keeping key stakeholders involved in the effort will also enable you to make decisions that are in the best interests of the organization. When you increase the visibility of the vulnerability status of your network, you ensure that your security team can focus its efforts in the right place and that leadership can devote the right resources to keeping the network safe. We covered several tools, including Nessus, OpenVAS, and Nikto, all of which provide vulnerability scan information using continuously updated libraries of vulnerability information. Some of these tools also offer the ability to automate the process and output in formats for ingestion in other IT systems. Vulnerability scanning is a continuous process, requiring your security team to monitor the network regularly to determine changes in detected vulnerabilities, gauge the efficacy of the patches and compensating controls, and adjust its efforts accordingly to stay ahead of threats.

As a CySA+, you should at least be familiar with every tool we described here, and, ideally, you should be proficient with each. Our goal in this chapter was not to provide you with the depth of knowledge we believe you should possess on these tools but rather to give you a high-level survey of the essential tools of the trade. We hope you will use this as a springboard for your own self-study into any products with which you are not familiar. Though the exam will require that you have only a general familiarity with these tools, your real-world performance will likely be enhanced by a deeper knowledge of these tools of the trade.

Questions

1. Which of the following is an example of an infrastructure vulnerability scanner?

    A. Bro

    B. Aircrack-ng

    C. OpenVAS

    D. Burp Suite

2. To what class of tools does Reaver belong?

    A. Wireless assessment tools

    B. Interception proxies

    C. Enumeration tools

    D. Exploitation frameworks

3. What are some of the unique features of Maltego?

    A. Graphical representation of relationships between entities

    B. Extensive library of transforms for data manipulation

    C. Pivoting to discover additional targets

    D. All of the above

4. Which of the following is not a component of Metasploit?

    A. msfconsole

    B. msfvenom

    C. msfscan

    D. Meterpreter

5. What is the purpose of the Recon-ng framework?

    A. To launch exploits on vulnerable systems

    B. To gather information on targets

    C. To perform brute-force attacks

    D. To perform brute-force attacks

Use the following scenario to answer Questions 6–8:

Your company's internal development team just created a new web application for deployment onto the public-facing web server. You are trying to ensure that it conforms to best security practices and does not introduce any vulnerabilities into your systems.

6. Which would be the best tool to use if you want to ensure that the web application is not transmitting passwords in cleartext?

    A. Nikto

    B. Hashcat

    C. Burp Suite

    D. Aircrack-ng

7. If you wanted to scan the web server for known vulnerabilities, what open source tool is most specifically aligned with that task?

    A. Nikto

    B. hping

    C. nmap

    D. Nessus

8. Your developer team is preparing to roll out a beta version of the software tomorrow and wants to quickly test for vulnerabilities, including SQL injection, path traversal, and cross-site scripting. Which of the following tools do you recommend to the team?

    A. nmap

    B. Arachni

    C. Hashcat

    D. nslookup

9. Which utility provides advanced features beyond those offered by the built-in network tools?

    A. OpenVAS

    B. Zed Attack Proxy

    C. hping

    D. nslookup

10. You have a list of password hashes, and you want to quickly assess and recover a password from each one. Which is the most appropriate tool to use for this operation?

    A. Hashcat

    B. ifconfig

    C. nslookup

    D. MD5

11. Of the cloud infrastructure assessment tools covered in this chapter, which is designed as both a compliance assessment tool and penetration testing framework?

    A. Pacu

    B. Scout Suite

    C. Reaver

    D. Prowler

Answers

1. **C.** OpenVAS (in addition to Qualys, Nessus, and Nikto) is an infrastructure vulnerability scanner with which you should be familiar.

2. **A.** Reaver is a wireless assessment tool that takes advantage of a vulnerability that exists in access points that use the Wi-Fi Protected Setup (WPS) feature.

3. **D.** A few of the unique features of Maltego are graphical representation of relationships between entities, an extensive library of transforms for data manipulation, and the ability to pivot to discover additional targets

4. **C.** Msfscan is not a component of the Metasploit framework.

5. **B.** The purpose of the Recon-ng framework is to gather information on targets.

6. **C.** Burp Suite is an integrated web application testing platform often used to map and analyze a web application's vulnerabilities. It is able to intercept web traffic and enables analysts to examine each request and response.

7. **A.** Nikto is an open source vulnerability scanner that is specifically tailored to web servers. Nessus may seem like a good option, but it is no longer open source.

8. **B.** Arachni has the ability to incorporate the feedback it gets from initial responses during the test to inform what new techniques should be used moving forward. In presenting the final results, Arachni is also able to reduce the occurrence of false positives through a process its author refers to as *meta-analysis,* which considers several factors from the tests responses.

9. **C.** Hping is a free packet generator and network analyzer that supports TCP, UDP, and ICMP, and it includes a traceroute functionality.

10. **A.** Hashcat can be used to recover passwords from a list of hashes.

11. **A.** Cloud infrastructure assessment tools assess cloud host vulnerabilities caused by misconfigurations, access flaws, and custom deployments, many times checking against industry standards and compliance checklists. Pacu performs these assessments and also enables penetration testers to exploit any configuration flaws discovered.

CHAPTER 11

Analyzing and Prioritizing Vulnerabilities

In this chapter you will learn:

- How the Common Vulnerability Scoring System works
- How to validate vulnerabilities and separate actual vulnerabilities from false positives
- How the different contexts of vulnerabilities can affect their severity

To kill an error is as good a service as, and sometimes even better than, the establishing of a new truth or fact.

—Charles Darwin

Simply collecting vulnerability data is of no use unless you actually do something with the data. This certainly means collecting it by scheduling and performing vulnerability scans and assessments, but it also requires you to analyze the vulnerability data that comes from your assessments. Vulnerability analysis means that you must examine the vulnerabilities that exist on the system, determine their impact to the system and organization, and then categorize and prioritize them for remediation. You also make risk-based decisions on which vulnerabilities can realistically be addressed and which ones can't. Not every vulnerability will always be mitigated immediately. This may be due to several factors, including available resources, but it also comes down to how you categorize and prioritize the vulnerabilities for remediation. As we will see in this chapter, this depends largely on the severity of the vulnerability and the criticality of the asset.

In this chapter, we will examine how vulnerabilities are categorized and prioritized for remediation, along with discussing those instances where they can't be immediately addressed and what the long-term consequences of that are. This chapter covers the CySA+ exam objective 2.3, "Given a scenario, analyze data to prioritize vulnerabilities."

Common Vulnerability Scoring System

A well-known standard for quantifying vulnerability severity is the Common Vulnerability Scoring System (CVSS). As a framework designed to standardize the severity ratings for vulnerabilities, this system ensures accurate qualitative measurement so that users can better understand the impact of these weaknesses. With the CVSS scoring standard, members of industries, academia, and governments can communicate vulnerability severity metrics clearly across their communities. Note that CVSS only provides a qualitative measurement for vulnerability severity and should not be used as a measurement for overall risk.

CVSS uses three metric groups: *base, temporal,* and *environmental.* The base group is the foundational group of metrics. It describes the basic characteristics of a vulnerability that do not depend on changes over time or the environment in which the vulnerability resides. The temporal and environmental groups are used to further define and modify the base score of a vulnerability, based on changing contexts. We will discuss all three metrics groups in the upcoming sections.

The CVSS is managed by FIRST.org, a professional organization focused on assisting computer security incident response teams (https://www.first.org/cvss/).

Base Metric Group

The base metric group of the CVSS is the group that generates the overall numerical score indicating the severity of a particular vulnerability. This group describes characteristics of a vulnerability that do not change over time and are consistent across user environments. It consists of three sets of metrics: exploitability metrics, scope, and impact metrics. Exploitability metrics describe the details of how exploitable a particular vulnerability may be. It includes Attack Vector, Attack Complexity, Privileges Required, and User Interaction. Impact metrics describe how the standard three goals of security—confidentiality, integrity, and availability—are affected. The Scope metric describes how one vulnerability can affect another. These metrics are all described next.

Attack Vector

The Attack Vector (AV) metric describes how exploitation of a given vulnerability could happen. There are five potential values for the AV metric, based on whether the attack vector occurs remotely, locally, or physically. Note that the more remote the attack vector is, the higher score the AV metric receives. The possible values for the AV metric are as follows:

- **Network (N)**   The vulnerability is connected in some way to the network stack and can be exploited remotely.
- **Adjacent (A)**   The vulnerability is connected to the network stack but is limited to the protocol used or to a logically adjacent network.
- **Local (L)**   The vulnerability is not connected to the network stack, and the attack vector is executed via permission or privileges assigned to the resource, such as the ability to read, write, or execute locally, or via a remote connection.
- **Physical (P)**   For the vulnerability to be exploited, the attacker must physically interact with the vulnerable component.

Attack Complexity

The Attack Complexity (AC) metric characterizes any factors that are not within the attacker's control and must be favorable for the exploit to be successful. Some of these factors are also their own metrics, such as whether user interaction is required or the level of privileges that must be used to exploit the vulnerability. Other factors could include the ability to evade detection controls, the ease of traversing the network, and so on. There are only two values for the AC metric. A value of Low (L) means that there are generally no external unfavorable conditions that exist that might prevent the attacker from being successful; in other words, the attack does not rely on a complex set of circumstances for execution. The other value is High (H), which means that a successful attack depends on factors that the attacker cannot control or affect but may have to navigate in order to be successful.

Privileges Required

Privileges Required (PR) is the metric that indicates the level of privileges an attacker will require before they are successful in exploiting a vulnerability. Metric values here are None (N), which indicates that the attacker requires no special privileges; Low (L), indicating that the attacker requires only basic user or resource owner privileges; and High (H), which indicates that the attacker requires significant privileges, such as administrative rights, to execute the attack. As a general rule, the less privileges that are required for the attacker to execute a given vulnerability, the higher the potential base score.

User Interaction

The User Interaction (UI) metric describes the requirement for a user to interact with the exploit, either intentionally or inadvertently, to cause a successful exploitation of the vulnerability. This indicates whether user interaction may be required (such as a user clicking a link or executing a malicious program locally on the system). The possible metric values are None (N) and Required (R), indicating, respectively, that the vulnerability could be exploited without any user action or that user interaction is required for the successful exploitation of the vulnerability. Note that if no user interaction is required, this results in a much higher base score.

Scope

The scope metric indicates whether a vulnerability in one area may affect a vulnerable component in another area. This means that the vulnerability of a component in a specific security domain, or *security scope* (as described by CVSS documentation), could possibly impact components or resources in another security domain or scope. This metric tells you whether or not a vulnerability is isolated to only its own security context. For example, security controls in a particular host, operating system, or application should be able to limit the effects of the exploitation of that vulnerability to only that system or application's context. If a vulnerability in a particular application could affect other components or resources of another application or system, then its scope increases. The two possible values for the scope metric are Unchanged (U) and Changed (C). A value of Changed, indicating that the vulnerability can affect components outside of its own security scope, causes the base score to be higher.

Impact

CVSS measures impact in the base metric group with regard to confidentiality, integrity, and availability, but not necessarily the same way. Confidentiality and integrity values measure impacts that affect the data itself. The availability values refer to the actual operation of a system or service, not the availability of the data itself.

The confidentiality metric, measuring the impact on information access or disclosure by unauthorized entities, can have a value of High (H), Low (L), or None (N), indicating a total loss of confidentiality, some loss of confidentiality, or no loss of confidentiality within the system or environment, respectively.

The integrity metric measures any change of data integrity within the system. As with confidentiality, the metric values are High (H), Low (L), and None (N), indicating a total loss of integrity, a possible loss of integrity, or no loss of integrity within the impact environment.

Unlike confidentiality and integrity metrics, which apply to the data itself, the availability metric applies to the loss of availability of the service or system affected by the vulnerability. Consistent with confidentiality and integrity, however, the metric values are High (H), Low (L), and None (N), indicating, as you would expect, a total loss of availability, a reduction in performance or interruption to availability, or no impact to availability for the service or system, respectively.

Temporal Metric Group

The temporal metric group describes vulnerability characteristics that may change over time. This group consists of three metrics: Exploit Code Maturity (E), Remediation Level (RL), and Report Confidence (RC).

Exploit Code Maturity

The Exploit Code Maturity (E) metric describes the likelihood of the vulnerability being attacked and successfully exploited, in relation to the availability of exploitable code. There are five possible values for this metric:

- **High (H)** Functional exploit code exists, is reliable, and is widely available; there is no exploit required, and the code works in every environment.

- **Functional (F)** There is functional exploit code available, and the code commonly works in systems where the vulnerability exists.

- **Proof-of-Concept (P)** Proof-of-concept exploit code is available but may or may not work in all situations and may require substantial modification, depending on the system and its environment.

- **Unproven (U)** The exploit is only theoretical, or there is no known exploit code available.

- **Not Defined (X)** This value indicates there is insufficient information to select one of the other values.

Remediation Level

Remediation Level (RL) refers to the availability of a workaround, temporary fix, or official vendor solution, such as a patch, to remediate a vulnerability. Generally, the more permanent and official the remediation available, the lower the temporal score, which contributes to a lower overall vulnerability score in the base group. The five possible values for RL are as follows:

- **Unavailable (U)**   There is no known remediation solution available, or it cannot be applied.
- **Workaround (W)**   There is a temporary fix available, but it's not officially supported by the vendor and may come from non-vendor sources.
- **Temporary Fix (T)**   A temporary fix, officially released by the vendor, is available. This may take the form of a temporary hotfix, tool, or other workaround.
- **Official Fix (O)**   An officially released vendor solution is available, typically in the form of an official patch or upgrade.
- **Not Defined (X)**   There is insufficient information available to select one of the other values.

Report Confidence

The Report Confidence (RC) metric indicates the degree of confidence that the vulnerability actually exists and the veracity of its technical details. This metric describes the uncertainty inherent to new vulnerabilities, where the security community or the vendor does not have much information to go on. Neither the overall impact of the vulnerability nor how the vulnerability is exploited may not be completely understood. The four possible metric values for RC include the following:

- **Confirmed (C)**   Detailed information on the vulnerability exists that indicates the vulnerability, and its exploitation can be reproduced; vulnerability research can be independently verified or the vendor has verified the vulnerability.
- **Reasonable (R)**   Significant details regarding the vulnerability have been researched and published, but the root cause is not completely known, or researchers do not have full access to the source code to confirm all the details that may lead to exploitation of the vulnerability; reasonable confidence exists that the exploit is reproducible and verifiable.
- **Unknown (U)**   There are anecdotal indications that the vulnerability is present and can be exploited, but those assertions are unverifiable and uncertain; there is little confidence in the validity of any research related to the vulnerability.
- **Not Defined (X)**   There is insufficient information to select one of the other possible values for this metric.

Any of these metrics in the temporal group can change over time, resulting in an increased or even decreased base score. For example, the exploit code used to take advantage of the vulnerability may change over time as the code evolves or is updated to counteract security measures put in place to prevent exploitation. The same can be said of the remediation level since the ability to prevent or mitigate the exploit will also change over time.

Environmental Metric Group

The environmental metric group allows the end user to modify the CVSS base score as it applies to their unique environment. The key to this modification is how the organization values confidentiality, integrity, and availability, which are indicated in the score as CR, IR, and AR, respectively. The values assigned to each of the three elements in this metric group are High (H), Medium (M), Low (L), and Not Defined (X). These values are assigned based on the effect that a loss of confidentiality, integrity, or availability would have on the organization. For example, a value of High would be assigned if the loss of confidentiality, integrity, or availability would be likely to have a catastrophic impact on the organization. A value of Medium would be assigned if a loss of any of those three elements were to cause a serious impact to the organization, and, of course, a value of Low would be assigned if a loss of any of the three would only cause a limited impact to the organization. Note that both temporal group and environmental group metrics are optional in CVSS scoring.

Overall CVSS scores are derived by expressing what is called a *vector*, which essentially describes all of these factors in the shorthand notation detailed previously. For example, a vulnerability with base metric values of "Attack Vector: Local, Attack Complexity: High, Privileges Required: High, User Interaction: None, Scope: Changed, Confidentiality: Moderate, Integrity: Low, Availability: None" and no expressed temporal or environmental group metrics would be expressed as the following vector:

CVSS:3.1/AV:L/AC:H/PR:H/UI:N/S:C/C:M/I:L/A:N

The process required for developing the final numerical CVSS score is beyond the scope of this text, but you can easily find and read about it at the FIRST.org CVSS information site (https://www.first.org/cvss/).

 EXAM TIP The Common Vulnerability Scoring System is the de facto standard for assessing the severity of vulnerabilities. Therefore, you should be familiar with CVSS and its metric groups: base, temporal, and environmental. These groups represent the various aspects of a vulnerability. Base metrics are those characteristics that do not change over time, temporal describes those that do, and environmental represents those that are unique to a user's environment. For the exam, you should be able to read a CVSS vector and identify the individual metrics and their possible values.

Validating Vulnerabilities

No vulnerability scanning software is perfect; scanners do not always pick up every single vulnerability, nor do they always accurately detect vulnerabilities. This may be due to several factors. First, if the vulnerability scanning software does not have the current updates and signatures, it may miss the most current vulnerabilities that exist out in the wild. Second, systems are not always configured in such a way that the vulnerability scanning software can accurately analyze its settings or patch levels. In Chapter 9 we discussed the necessity for credentialed scans as a way to gain more accurate information about a system. If the correct level of credentials is not used, or they are not accurate for all systems, vulnerability information may not be accurately collected or reported.

It is up to the analyst to review and make sense of vulnerability data and findings before passing that information on to others in the organization. The two most important outcomes of the review process are to determine the validity of reported vulnerabilities and to determine exceptions to policies that may affect how vulnerabilities are mitigated. The aim is to have the most accurate information about your network because it means more confidence in the decisions made by your technical staff and company leadership. With vulnerabilities accurately identified and the most appropriate courses of action developed and refined through open lines of communication, you can prioritize responses that have minimal impact throughout the company.

True Positives

A true positive is a piece of data that can be verified and validated as correct. An example would be when a vulnerability scan indicates the vulnerability exists, and it can be verified using other methods. This is as opposed to a false positive, which, as described below, means that there is in fact no vulnerability when a scanning tool says that there is. Distinguishing true positives from false positives, as well as their opposites, true and false negatives, can be a tricky part of vulnerability remediation and prioritization. In the next few sections we will discuss these types of positive and negative findings in greater detail.

Once you receive data from vulnerability scan reports, you may find that verifying the results is a fairly straightforward process. Figure 11-1 shows the output for an uncovered vulnerability on a Windows host located at 10.10.0.115 that's related to the Remote Desktop functionality.

The protocol was found to have a weakness in its implementation of the cryptographic exchange during identity verification. As a solution, Nessus suggests that we either force the use of SSL for the service or enable Network Level Authentication. When we check the System properties of the same Windows host identified in Figure 11-2, we can see that the option for the use of Network Level Authentication is available for us to select.

Here we see that the vulnerability scanner successfully identified the less-secure state of the Windows host. Fortunately for us, we don't have to manually verify and adjust for every occurrence; this can all be automated by enforcing a new group policy or by using any number of automated remediation solutions.

NOTE The goal of major databases such as the National Vulnerability Database (NVD) is to publish common vulnerabilities and exposures (CVEs) for public awareness. These databases are incredibly useful but do not always have complete information because many vulnerabilities are still being researched. Therefore, you should use supplemental sources in your research, such as Bugtraq, OWASP, and CERT.

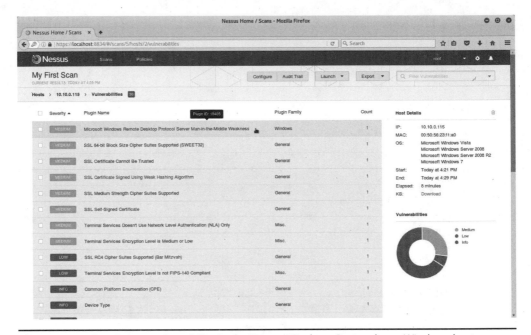

Figure 11-1   Details on a vulnerability in the Remote Desktop Protocol on a Windows host

Figure 11-2
The Remote
Desktop options
in the System
Properties
dialog for a
Windows 10 host

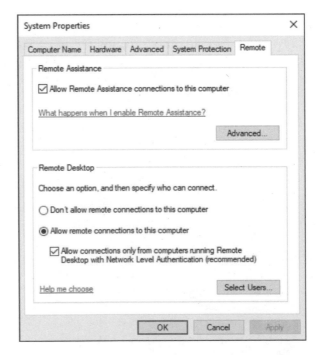

False Positives

A false positive (sometimes called a Type I error) is data that shows that a particular vulnerability exists, but in fact, it does not. Usually these issues arise from a misconfigured system, application, or even the vulnerability scanning tool. An example of this would be if the vulnerability tool shows a misconfiguration in the Apache web server on a system, when in reality Apache is not installed on that system. This may have happened because the HTTPD service is running, for instance, but there is no actual web server installed on the system.

False positives with vulnerability scanners are particularly frustrating because the effort required to remediate a suspected issue can be resource intensive. A false positive rate of 2 percent may not be a problem for smaller organizations, but the same rate on a large network with thousands of endpoints will cause significant problems for the security staff. Although it's important that you quickly produce a solution to an uncovered vulnerability, you should take a moment to consider the reasons why a scanner might cry wolf. Sometimes the logic that a check, network vulnerability test (NVT), or plug-in uses is flawed, resulting in a report of a vulnerability that does not exist.

Understand that the check for a particular vulnerability is written with certain assumptions about a system because it is impossible to write logic in such a way that it applies perfectly to every system. There is no way for the authors of a vulnerability test to know the details of your network, so they must create rules that are sometimes less granular, which may lead to false positives. In this case, it may be useful for you to customize your own test after a false positive has been discovered. Another reason for a false positive could be that you've already determined the appropriate compensating control for an issue but have not correctly disposed of the alert.

Note that in addition to the results from vulnerability scans, false positives are often presented through security protection mechanisms, such as alerts from intrusion detection systems that may have older signatures, security information and event management (SIEM) data, and various tools and components included in a security orchestration, automation, and response (SOAR) implementation.

NOTE Although vulnerability scanners have improved over the years, operating system (OS) and software detection in vulnerability scanners isn't perfect. This makes detection in environments with custom operating systems and devices particularly challenging. Many devices use lightweight versions of Linux and Apache web server that are burned directly onto the device's read-only memory. You should expect to get a higher number of alerts in these cases because the vulnerability scanner may not be able to tell exactly what kind of system it is. However, you should also take care not to dismiss alerts immediately on these systems either. Sometimes a well-known vulnerability may exist in unexpected places because of how the vulnerable software packages were ported over to the new system.

True Negatives

A true negative is an odd instance to understand. This is when the vulnerability scanner does not detect an issue, and it's because the issue truly doesn't exist. So why would this be of concern? Based on research and other indicators from the system, you may suspect that a vulnerability is there, so you test for it. When the vulnerability scanner detects no actual vulnerability, it may cause you to wonder if the tool is reporting accurately. You may be experiencing issues from the system, such as too much bandwidth consumption or high processor utilization. While troubleshooting these issues, it's not uncommon to scan using a vulnerability tool. The true negative rules out the possibility that any vulnerabilities you suspect exist are actually on the system. This is when you should start looking at other causes—possibly hardware or software failures. It's *very* important, however, that you understand that proving a true negative is almost impossible. Without getting into a deep discussion about the intricacies of informal logic, we can look to the old aphorism for assistance: "Absence of evidence is not evidence of absence."

False Negatives

A false negative, also referred to as a Type II error, is a result that indicates that no vulnerability is present when, in fact, a vulnerability does actually exist. Reasons behind this outcome include a lack of technical capability to detect the vulnerability. It could well be that a vulnerability is too new and that detection rules for the scanner do not yet exist. Or perhaps an incorrect type of vulnerability scan was initiated by the analyst. As troublesome as false positives are in terms of the effort expended to prove they are false, a false negative is far worse, because in this case a vulnerability actually exists but is undetected, so it will not be remediated and will be possibly exploitable. If other indicators lead you to believe that there is an actual vulnerability present but the scanning tool does not detect it, you may have to do further research and look at other indicators that could confirm the existence of the vulnerability, such as critical file changes, processor utilization, bandwidth utilization, changes to privileges, and so on. The worst false negative is the one that you never even know exists.

 EXAM TIP When validating vulnerabilities, keep in mind that true positives are actual vulnerabilities and should be included in your remediation strategy. False positives may use up a lot of your time and energy simply to prove that they aren't real vulnerabilities. True negatives occur because there actually isn't a vulnerability, but you may be led to believe that there is one due to performance issues related to hardware or software. False negatives are the worst of all vulnerabilities because there may in fact be a vulnerability that exists in the system that cannot be detected through normal vulnerability scanning. You'll likely see many scenarios on the exam that focus on false positives, so understanding how to interpret data to determine if a false positive exists is important.

Examining True Positives

Once you have validated that vulnerabilities are, in fact, true positives, there are some additional steps you should take. Sometimes this involves additional research you should perform to verify more details of the vulnerabilities and how they are affecting your system. You should also compare the vulnerabilities to your regulations and policies to see how they actually affect compliance. These additional steps, and the others discussed next, will also help you make better informed decisions regarding vulnerability mitigation and prioritization.

Compare to Best Practices or Compliance

Several benchmarks for industry, academia, and government are available for you to use to improve your network's security. One of the most widely used examples of this is the Center for Internet Security (CIS) benchmarks. As another example, on military networks, the most widely used set of standards is developed by the Defense Information Systems Agency (DISA). Its Security Technical Implementation Guides (STIGs), combined with the National Security Agency (NSA) guides, are the configuration standards used on US Department of Defense (DoD) information systems. Both of these benchmarks are best practice security configuration guides that you can use to compare the current state of your systems and applications to the desired state of best practices.

In addition to these guides, however, you must also compare the state of your systems with regulatory governance or other policies mandated by your organization. When your system configurations conflict with what governance requires, based on the results of your vulnerability data, you must take action to remediate those issues or obtain documented exceptions to policy. These exceptions to policy are risk-based decisions that are made if a vulnerability cannot be immediately remediated for some reason. Frequently, the reason is diminished functionality or the inability to take a critical system offline. Some vulnerability mitigations may in fact cause the intended functionality of the system to be reduced, so a decision must be made as to whether the vulnerability is so severe that it must be mitigated versus the requirement to maintain the functionality needed to support a critical business process. Often, other mitigations may have to be put in place if the primary mitigation, such as patching, can't be implemented. This is a good example of compensating controls, which we have discussed elsewhere in the book. In any event, the decision for this exception to policy should be made by well-informed managers and documented, along with a long-term solution to the problem.

Reconcile Results

If there's one thing that's certain in incident response and forensic analysis, it's that taking thorough notes will make your job much easier in the end. These notes include the steps you take to configure a device, validate its configuration, verify its operation, and, of course, test for vulnerabilities. Taking notes on how you uncovered and dealt with a vulnerability will aid in continuity, and it might be required based on the industry in which you operate. Both Nessus and OpenVAS provide ways to track how the corrective actions perform on systems they have scanned, including available patches and configuration changes needed. Should your network activity be examined by an investigation, it's also good to know you've taken thorough notes about every action you performed to make the network safer.

Review Related Logs and/or Other Data Sources

When reviewing the vulnerability report, you should also review event logs and network data. You can compare running services, listening ports, and open connections against a list of authorized services to identify any abnormal behavior. Correlating the vulnerability scan output with historical network and service data serves several functions. First, it verifies that your logging mechanism is capturing the activities related to the vulnerability scans, because these scans will often trigger logging. Second, you should be able to see changes in the network based on the patches or changes you've made because of compensating controls. Finally, the logs may give insight into whether any of the uncovered vulnerabilities have been acted upon already. SIEM tools can assist tremendously with validation because they will likely be able to visualize all the scanning activity. And because you are likely already ingesting other log data, these tools provide a useful place to begin correlation.

Determine Trends

Using either the built-in trending functionality or other software, you can track how vulnerabilities in the network have changed over time. Trending improves context and enables your security response team to tailor its threat mitigation strategies to its efforts more efficiently. Additionally, you can also determine whether any of your solutions are taking hold and are effective. Linking the vulnerability scanners with existing SIEM platforms isn't the only option; you can also track progress on fixing problems using existing trouble ticket software. This helps with the internal tracking of the issues and allows for visibility from leadership, in case outside assistance is required to enforce a policy change.

 EXAM TIP Gaining as much information as possible about true-positive vulnerabilities will assist you in making better remediation strategy decisions for them. Of particular importance is determining how a vulnerability affects your compliance with governance since regulations or policy may require that you mitigate a vulnerability faster, regardless of severity, system criticality, or other factors.

Context Awareness

In addition to gathering all the possible information about a vulnerability, such as its severity and the CVSS scoring information regarding the attack vector, exploit code, and so on, the decision to prioritize vulnerabilities for remediation also depends on several other factors. The key word here is "depends" because, all else being equal, context is important. This simply means that you must make decisions on vulnerability remediation and prioritization based on the situation. In some situations, for instance, a vulnerability may reside on a highly protected system that is isolated away from other networks and the general user population. While the vulnerability, considered alone, may have a high severity, the actual risk associated with exploiting that particular vulnerability may be very low, as mitigating factors may make it next to impossible for an attacker to even connect to the system that has the vulnerability. Context awareness is another way of saying that you should weigh the likelihood of the vulnerability actually being exploited, given the situation, versus its impact if it is exploited. Infrastructure architecture and design weighs heavily on the situation in this case. Whether the system that may contain the vulnerability is an internal system, an external system, or even physically or logically isolated, the risk should be weighed in prioritizing vulnerability remediation.

Internal

Typically, internal systems contain the most sensitive information and are the most critical to business operations. It only makes sense, then, that they would also be the most well protected. This means that, if we go back to basic risk concepts, the impact to the system if it were compromised by exploiting a vulnerability residing on that system would likely be very high. But the likelihood of an attacker being able to exploit the system may be very low due to mitigations such as strong authentication and encryption controls, restrictive permissions, multiple layers of defense, and so on. These factors should be considered in the situation when deciding how quickly a vulnerability must be remediated. Critical systems, in particular, must have high availability, and the time it takes to bring the system down, remediate the vulnerability, and bring it back up to operational status may have unacceptable impacts on business processes.

External

External systems likely contain less sensitive information and may be less critical business operations. This may not be the case, however, for publicly available web servers where customers input transactions such as ordering goods and services, for instance. Therefore, these external systems should also be highly protected, given the sensitivity of the information that is processed on them, as well as the criticality to key business processes. These systems may require much faster vulnerability remediation as well since they are more exposed to attacks than internal systems and may be reasonably expected to be compromised a bit faster. Again, it really depends on two primary factors: information sensitivity and criticality to business processes.

Isolated

Isolated systems are those that are logically and physically segmented or otherwise separated from other networks and hosts. They may be completely physically separated, with no external connections, or architected such that they only have minimum unidirectional connections to the internal network and are separated by internal firewalls or other security devices, VLANs, or other logical means. These segments are typically harder for an attacker to reach, except for a malicious insider, and may not fall victim to the typical network-based attacks. Due to their isolation, the risk is much lower, because the likelihood of a vulnerability being exploited on one of these hosts is much lower. Vulnerabilities on these hosts may be prioritized at a lower remediation priority than others since they are not easily exploitable, but they should still be mitigated as soon as practical.

 EXAM TIP   The architecture of your infrastructure should be a factor in making remediation decisions and prioritizing vulnerabilities for mitigation. Internet-facing hosts with sensitive information will likely be your highest priority, while isolated systems that are better protected may be able to wait a bit longer for remediation.

Exploitability and Weaponization

Another consideration in determining how quickly you need to remediate a vulnerability is how easily the vulnerability is exploitable and weaponized. This relates somewhat to attack complexity, so the CVSS Attack Complexity metric and other research you perform about the vulnerability will help inform this decision. Generally, the more complex the attack required for exploitation is, the less likely it is to succeed, and the less likely the vulnerability is to be exploited.

Asset Value

Asset value is a very important consideration in the decision-making process for vulnerability remediation and prioritization. Obviously, the higher value the asset, the more you will focus on remediating vulnerabilities that are found in the system and its software. Asset value, remember, is related to two important factors: sensitivity and criticality. Sensitivity refers to the confidentiality of the information or system, in that the more sensitive the information, the more you will want to protect it from unauthorized access. Criticality is different from sensitivity. Criticality means that the asset is very important to your business processes. Most of the time, assets will be both sensitive and critical, but this is not always the case. For example, personal information that resides on the system may be collected incidentally to the business but is not very critical to its processes. However, that information still has to be stringently protected. Conversely, critical systems may not contain sensitive information. They may just be critical for performing business processes, such as inventory, ordering supplies and equipment, and so on.

In any case, asset value is likely one of the most important factors in determining how quickly you should remediate vulnerabilities and the process for doing so. In addition to sensitivity and criticality, availability is a concern in that critical assets must be available almost constantly. If there are redundancies in assets, such as a server cluster or multiple copies of a database that are online, this isn't so much of an issue. But if you must take down a critical server for several hours to install patches or make configuration changes to remediate a vulnerability, then you must balance the need to keep the server up and running with the need to take it down to mitigate its vulnerabilities. Often this is more of a management decision than a technical one.

EXAM TIP   Asset sensitivity and criticality, along with vulnerability severity, are likely the most important factors in making vulnerability remediation decisions. These are risk-based decisions that must account for the possibility of unauthorized access to sensitive information and the unavailability of systems needed for critical business processes. Either of these factors could drastically increase the priority of remediating vulnerabilities, but it has to be balanced with the need for users to access systems while they are down for remediation.

PART II

Zero-Day

The term *zero-day*, once used exclusively among security professionals, is quickly becoming part of the public dialect. It refers to either a vulnerability or exploit never before seen in public. A *zero-day vulnerability* is a flaw in a piece of software that the vendor is unaware of and has not issued a patch or advisory for. The code written to take advantage of this flaw is called the *zero-day exploit*. When writing software, vendors often focus on providing usability and getting the most functional product out to market as quickly as possible. This often results in products that require numerous updates, as more users interact with the software. Ideally, the number of vulnerabilities decreases as time progresses, as software adoption increases, and as patches are issued. However, this doesn't mean that you should let your guard down because of some sense of increased security. Rather, you should be more vigilant; even if an environment has protective software in place, it's defenseless should a zero-day exploit be used against it.

The Emergence of the Exploit Marketplace

Zero-day exploits were once extremely rare, but the security community has observed a significant uptick in their usage and discovery. As security companies improve their software, malware writers have worked to evolve their products to evade these systems, creating a malware arms race of sorts. Modern zero-day vulnerabilities are viewed as extremely valuable to some malicious users and criminal groups, and as with anything else of perceived value, markets have formed. Black markets for zero-day exploits exist with ample participation from criminal groups. On the opposite end of the spectrum, vendors have used *bug bounty* programs to supplement internal vulnerability discovery, inviting researchers and hackers to actively probe their software for bugs in exchange for money and prizes. Even the US Pentagon, a traditionally bureaucratic and risk-averse organization, saw the value in crowdsourcing security in this way. In March 2016, it launched the "Hack the Pentagon" challenge, a pilot program designed to identify security vulnerabilities on public-facing Department of Defense sites.

Preparing for Zero-Days

Preparing to face unknown and advanced threats like zero-day exploits requires a sound methodology that includes technical and operational best practices. The protection of critical business assets and sensitive data should never be trusted to a single solution. You should be wary of solutions that suggest they are one-stop shops for dealing with these threats because you are essentially placing the entire organization's fate in a single point of failure. Although the word "response" is part of your incident response plan, your team should develop a methodology that includes proactive efforts as well. This approach should involve active efforts to discover new threats that have not yet impacted the organization. Sources for this information include research organizations and threat intelligence providers. The SANS Internet Storm Center and the CERT Coordination Center at Carnegie Mellon University are two great resources for discovering the latest software bugs. Armed with new knowledge about attacker trends and techniques, you may be able to detect malicious traffic before it has a chance to do any harm. Additionally, you will give your security team time to develop controls to mitigate security incidents, should a countermeasure or patch not be available.

 EXAM TIP Zero-day vulnerabilities must be carefully and constantly monitored because often they are of sufficient severity to warrant immediate remediation, especially when discovered on sensitive or critical systems.

Chapter Review

In this chapter, we discussed the need for vulnerability analysis. Primarily we focused on the need to categorize and prioritize vulnerabilities for remediation, given factors such as severity, criticality of assets, and so on. Each of these factors has several considerations.

The Common Vulnerability Scoring System is a standardized, formal way of categorizing vulnerabilities to determine their severity. It uses factors such as attack vectors, attack complexity, the privileges required to exploit the vulnerability, user interaction, and scope. We also must consider the impact to the system and information it processes in terms of confidentiality, integrity, and availability.

It's also important to validate whether vulnerabilities are real. By "real," we mean are they actual vulnerabilities or simply ghosts? We categorize them in terms of true or false positives or negatives. A true positive is a vulnerability that actually exists that you should address. A false positive is data that presents as a vulnerability, even though it doesn't really exist. This could be a limitation of the system, the vulnerability, scanning software, or the updates to any of those. A true negative is one where the scanning software doesn't show vulnerability, and it's because there really isn't one. This may show up as hardware or software performance issues. A false negative, on the other hand, may be the most dangerous type of vulnerability that should be validated. This is when the scanning software does not show that there's a vulnerability but one truly exists. This can only be discovered by using multiple types of scanning software and making sure your signatures are updated. You may, however, have other indications that a vulnerability is present on the system, even if you can't detect it through vulnerability scanning.

Another consideration for prioritizing vulnerabilities is context awareness. This basically means that you should look at the factors that exploiting the vulnerability, or its overall severity, may depend on. For instance. where the vulnerability comes from, and which assets it affects, such as internal assets, external assets, or isolated assets, makes a difference in how important it is to remediate the vulnerability. Asset criticality and location within the infrastructure, such as on critical or isolated network segments, may help drive how this contributes to decision-making.

You should also look at other factors for determining severity and prioritization of vulnerabilities. Can the vulnerability be easily exploited or weaponized? Is it a vulnerability that already has a patch or other remediation produced by the vendor, or is it one that could be considered a zero-day, or a vulnerability for which there is no known mitigation?

Finally, you should look at asset value and criticality when you determine the process for remediating vulnerabilities. The asset may be unavailable for a period of time while vulnerabilities are mitigated, either through patching, configuration management, or even software or hardware upgrades. If the asset or business processes it supports must be kept available constantly, you should consider the impact to the business on taking the asset offline while its vulnerabilities are mitigated. If there are redundancies built in the infrastructure that can keep the asset up and functioning while other identical assets are mitigated, then you can likely afford to take the system offline for a while. These are all considerations you must consider when analyzing data to determine how to prioritize vulnerabilities for mitigation.

Questions

1. Which of the following CVSS metric groups are dependent on the system on which the vulnerability is present?

   A. Base group

   B. Temporal group

   C. Environmental group

   D. Attack Vector group

2. Which of the following CVSS base group metrics addresses factors that are not within the attacker's control?

   A. Attack Complexity (AC)

   B. Attack Vector (AV)

   C. Scope (S)

   D. Impact (I)

3. Which CVSS metric refers to the availability of a workaround, temporary fix, or official vendor solution, such as a patch, to remediate a vulnerability?

   A. Scope (S)

   B. Remediation Level (RL)

   C. Impact (I)

   D. Attack Complexity (AC)

4. Which of the following CVSS metric values is designated with a value of "X"?

   A. Unproven

   B. Unavailable

   C. Unknown

   D. Not defined

5. You are reviewing vulnerability scan data and discover an application vulnerability for a Windows system. Upon reviewing the baseline information for the system, you learn that the application is in fact not actually running on the system. Which of the following types of findings would this be considered?

   A. False positive

   B. False negative

   C. True positive

   D. True negative

6. During routine monitoring, you discover that a critical system is experiencing some unusual issues with memory utilization, unexpected reboots, and other negative behaviors. You research these behaviors as symptoms of a vulnerability and discover that a zero-day vulnerability with the same symptoms has been discovered. You update your vulnerability scanner and scan all systems for the zero-day. The scanner results indicate that your systems are not vulnerable to this issue, but other research indicates that they are. What type of finding is this?

   A. True negative

   B. False positive

   C. False negative

   D. True positive

7. Which of the following is a consideration when determining vulnerability remediation prioritization with regard to situation and context?

   A. CVSS score

   B. Vulnerability severity

   C. Asset criticality

   D. Vulnerability exploitability

8. Which of the following should be considered as part of context awareness in terms of physical and logical architecture of systems?

   A. CVSS score

   B. True positives and false negatives

   C. Exploitability of the vulnerability

   D. Level of protection and asset criticality

Answers

1. **C.** The environmental group contains metrics that can affect the base group scores and are dependent on the user's system and the environment it operates within.

2. **A.** The Attack Complexity (AC) metric characterizes any factors that are not within the attacker's control that must be favorable for the exploit to be successful.

3. **B.** Remediation Level (RL) refers to the availability of a workaround, temporary fix, or official vendor solution, such as a patch, to remediate a vulnerability.

4. **D.** The Not Defined metric value, which appears as a value in several of the CVSS metrics, is designated in shorthand by a value of "X."

5. **A.** Since the vulnerability has been detected but does not in fact exist, this would be considered a false positive.

6. **C.** This is a false negative since the scanner shows the system is not vulnerable but you can prove that it is in fact vulnerable.

7. **C.** Asset criticality must be considered when determining the priorities for vulnerability remediation since this varies based on situational or contextual factors.

8. **D.** In terms of context or situational awareness, the physical and logical location of the asset, as well as its level of protection, must be considered.

Mitigating Vulnerabilities

In this chapter you will learn:

- How common attacks may threaten your organization
- Best practices for securing environments from commonly used attacks
- Common classes of vulnerabilities
- Mitigating controls for common vulnerabilities

The attacker only needs to be right once, but defenders must be right all the time.

—Unknown

The threat of a cyberattack is a fact of life in our connected world. As new vulnerabilities are discovered, attackers will often look to take advantage of them using custom and/or commodity attack tools. Given the scale of these threats, operating in a strictly response capacity, or not at all, is not a prudent option. Protecting your organization's operations and brand by establishing strong security habits combined with forward-looking practices will yield the best results. It's useful for you to understand both the mechanics of common attacks as well as the trends associated with their usage in preparing your proactive and reactive defense plans. Additionally, having a full understanding of how common vulnerabilities may be exploited will prepare you for defending against future attacks not yet observed in the wild. This chapter will help you prepare for Objective 2.4, "Given a scenario, recommend controls to mitigate attacks and software vulnerabilities."

Attack Types

There are seemingly countless ways for a bad actor to gain access to privileged systems, and often a single flaw can be exploited to cause a nightmare. Many times, the exploited vulnerabilities are already well known. Hackers know that despite hardware and software vendors' various disclosure mechanisms and security best practices, the targets may still be completely unaware of their malicious activities. In this section, we'll cover common classes of attacks and how they are used to create the conditions that enable attackers to get in easily.

Injection Attacks

In injection attacks, attackers execute malicious operations by submitting untrusted input into an interpreter that is then evaluated. Security flaws may enable system calls into the operating system, where they invoke scripts and outside functionality or requests to back-end databases via database languages. Any time a web application uses an interpreter to assess untrusted data, it is potentially vulnerable to injection attacks. Injection attacks can take many forms, depending on what the attacker is trying to do and what target system is available. Injection vulnerabilities, though sometimes obscure, can be very easy to discover and exploit. The results of a successful injection attack range from a nuisance denial of service to, under certain circumstances, complete system compromise.

Remote Code Execution

Remote code execution (RCE) describes an attacker's ability to execute malicious code on a target platform, often following an injection attack. RCE is widely considered one of the most dangerous types of computer vulnerabilities, because it may allow for arbitrary command execution and does not require physical connectivity.

Here's an example: An attacker may achieve RCE using a PHP built-in function called **system()**. If the attacker, through some reconnaissance, can determine that a web server is vulnerable to an injection attack, they might be able to invoke a shell on the server by wrapping the shell command in what is otherwise a legitimate PHP command:

```
http://victimwebsite.com/?code=system('whoami');
```

RCE attacks can be incredibly costly. One recent example was in the Log4j library for Java, which is widely used in enterprise software applications. It was discovered that a critical vulnerability, known as CVE-2021-44228, existed in the library that could allow RCE attacks. Additionally, the RCE condition was trivial for attackers to execute. The vulnerability has a severity score of 10 out of 10, indicating the high risk it poses. It is estimated that hundreds of thousands of applications and services were affected by this vulnerability. The potential cost of the vulnerability has been estimated to be in the billions of dollars, with the average cost for incident response amounting to roughly $90,000, according to security vendor Arctic Wolf. More details can be found at https://arcticwolf.com/resources/blog/log4j-retrospective/.

Here are some common tools and techniques for directly mitigating RCE:

- **Input validation and sanitization**   This involves verifying that user input is safe before processing it, by checking it against a set of allowed values or patterns, which can help prevent attackers from injecting malicious code into an application.

- **Application firewalls**   These are designed to monitor and filter incoming and outgoing traffic to an application, blocking any traffic that appears suspicious or malicious.

- **Runtime application self-protection (RASP)**   RASP solutions monitor the runtime behavior of an application and can help detect and prevent RCE attacks in real time by monitoring the application for suspicious behavior and blocking any attempts to execute malicious code.

- **Containerization and virtualization**   Containerization and virtualization provide a layer of isolation between an application and the host operating system, preventing an attacker from accessing or executing code on the host system. This approach can help limit the impact of an RCE vulnerability.

Extensible Markup Language Attack

Extensible Markup Language (XML) injection is a class of attack that relies on manipulation or compromise of an application by abusing the logic of an XML parser to cause some unwanted action. XML injections that target vulnerable parsers generally take two forms: XML bombs and XML External Entity (XXE) attacks.

An XML bomb is an attack designed to cause the XML parser or the application it supports to crash by overloading it with data. A common XML bomb attack, the Billion Laughs attack, uses nested entities, each referring to another entity that itself may contain several others. When triggered, the parser will attempt to evaluate the input, expand the entities, and eventually run out of resources. The resulting crash can cause denial of service and application downtime. Figure 12-1 shows an example of code behind a Billion Laughs attack.

XXE can be used to initiate denial of service, conduct port scanning, and perform server-side request forgery (SSRF) attacks. The attack works though abuse of the XML parser to execute functions on behalf of the attacker, using a reference to an external entity. One feature of the XML standard is that it can be used to reference outside resources. By providing an input referencing an external entity, an attacker may be able to get a vulnerable XML parser to read and process normally protected data. In doing so, the parser could inadvertently leak sensitive information.

Here are some common tools and techniques for XXE mitigation:

- **Input validation** Validate input to ensure that it does not contain malicious XML code. This can be done by filtering out specific XML elements or by using a schema to validate the XML structure.

- **Disabling external entities and DTDs** This prevents an attacker from referencing external entities and Document Type Definitions (DTDs) within the XML document, thus eliminating the ability to read local files and execute arbitrary code. Disabling Document Type Definitions also makes the parser secure against denial of services (DoS) attacks such as Billion Laughs.

- **Using a secure XML parser** Some XML parsers have built-in protections against XXE attacks. For example, the SAX and StAX parsers in Java have security features that can help prevent XXE attacks.

```
1    <?xml version="1.0"?>
2    <!DOCTYPE lolz [
3     <!ENTITY lol "lol">
4     <!ELEMENT lolz (#PCDATA)>
5     <!ENTITY lol1 "&lol;&lol;&lol;&lol;&lol;&lol;&lol;&lol;&lol;&lol;">
6     <!ENTITY lol2 "&lol1;&lol1;&lol1;&lol1;&lol1;&lol1;&lol1;&lol1;&lol1;&lol1;">
7     <!ENTITY lol3 "&lol2;&lol2;&lol2;&lol2;&lol2;&lol2;&lol2;&lol2;&lol2;&lol2;">
8     <!ENTITY lol4 "&lol3;&lol3;&lol3;&lol3;&lol3;&lol3;&lol3;&lol3;&lol3;&lol3;">
9     <!ENTITY lol5 "&lol4;&lol4;&lol4;&lol4;&lol4;&lol4;&lol4;&lol4;&lol4;&lol4;">
10    <!ENTITY lol6 "&lol5;&lol5;&lol5;&lol5;&lol5;&lol5;&lol5;&lol5;&lol5;&lol5;">
11    <!ENTITY lol7 "&lol6;&lol6;&lol6;&lol6;&lol6;&lol6;&lol6;&lol6;&lol6;&lol6;">
12    <!ENTITY lol8 "&lol7;&lol7;&lol7;&lol7;&lol7;&lol7;&lol7;&lol7;&lol7;&lol7;">
13    <!ENTITY lol9 "&lol8;&lol8;&lol8;&lol8;&lol8;&lol8;&lol8;&lol8;&lol8;&lol8;">
14    ]>
15    <lolz>&lol9;</lolz>
```

Figure 12-1 Sample XML code designed to trigger a Billion Laughs attack

- **Containerization and virtualization**   Running applications in containers or virtual machines can help prevent XXE attacks by isolating the application from the host system.

- **Using a web application firewall**   A web application firewall (WAF) can help protect against XXE attacks by filtering out malicious input.

- **Using a dedicated XML parser**   Some programming languages provide dedicated XML parsers that have built-in protections against XXE attacks. For example, the ElementTree library in Python has a DTD parser that can prevent XXE attacks.

- **Regularly updating software**   Keeping software up to date can help prevent XXE attacks by ensuring that known vulnerabilities are patched.

Structured Query Language Injection

SQL injection (SQLi) is a popular form of injection in which an attacker injects arbitrary SQL commands to extract data, read files, or even escalate to an RCE. To exploit this vulnerability, the attacker must find a legitimate input parameter that the web app passes through to the SQL database. The attacker then embeds malicious SQL commands into the parameter and hopes that those SQL commands passed on for execution in the back end. These attacks are not particularly sophisticated, but the consequences of their successful usage are particularly damaging, because an attacker can obtain, corrupt, or destroy database contents.

Attackers can use several different types of SQL injection attacks to compromise a web application. Here are some of the most common types of SQL injection attacks:

- **Union-based SQL injection**   Uses the UNION SQL operator to combine the results of two SELECT statements

- **Error-based SQL injection**   Exploits SQL errors to extract information from the database

- **Blind SQL injection**   Exploits SQL vulnerabilities without displaying any error messages or other indications of success or failure

- **Time-based SQL injection**   Exploits SQL vulnerabilities by introducing time delays to the application's response to determine the presence or absence of a vulnerability

- **Out-of-band SQL injection**   Exploits SQL vulnerabilities by triggering outbound communication from the server to an external system under the attacker's control

- **Second-order SQL injection**   Involves injecting malicious SQL code into the application, which is then stored in the database and executed at a later time

- **Inference-based SQL injection**   Attempts to infer information about the database by exploiting vulnerabilities in the application's response to input

PART II

EXAM TIP   You will not need to be an expert in the various forms of SQLi attacks. However, as an analyst, it is important to be familiar with the concepts in order to identify these types of attacks when encountered. For example, if you are examining logs, you should be able to recognize why a query such as **SELECT * FROM table WHERE id=1-SLEEP(15)** looks suspicious.

The following are some common tools and techniques for SQLi mitigation:

- **Input validation**   Validate all user input to ensure that it does not contain malicious SQL code by filtering out specific SQL commands or by using prepared statements and parameterized queries.

- **Sanitization of user inputs**   Sanitize all user inputs to remove any special characters, escape quotes, and other characters that could be used in SQL injection attacks.

- **Parameterized queries**   Use parameterized queries instead of plain SQL statements. Parameterized queries are pre-compiled statements that can prevent SQL injection by separating the SQL code from the user input data.

- **Least privilege access**   Ensure that database users only have the minimum level of access necessary to perform their tasks. This can help limit the damage that can be caused by SQLi attacks.

- **Database firewalls (DBFWs) and proxies**   Use a database firewall or proxy to monitor and filter incoming database traffic, blocking any SQL injection attacks.

- **Regularly updating software**   Keeping software up to date can help prevent SQL injection attacks by ensuring that known vulnerabilities are patched.

- **Database encryption**   Encrypt sensitive data in the database to protect it in the case of a breach.

- **Database activity monitoring**   Use database activity monitoring tools to detect and alert on any suspicious database activity. This can help with SQLi attacks as well as other types of attacks.

- **Using stored procedures**   Use stored procedures to access the database instead of allowing direct access to the database. Stored procedures can help prevent SQL injection attacks by limiting the ability of an attacker to execute arbitrary SQL code.

NOTE   While some may think that NoSQL databases are inherently safe from injection attacks due to their schema-less nature, this is a common misconception. NoSQL Injection attacks are still possible; in fact, they can be even more devastating than SQL injection attacks due to the distributed and decentralized nature of NoSQL databases. In a NoSQL injection attack, an attacker can modify the input in a way that the application does not expect, leading to unauthorized access to the database, data leaks, and even complete server compromise. Therefore, it is imperative to ensure proper input validation and sanitization measures are in place to protect NoSQL databases as well.

Cross-Site Scripting

Cross-site scripting (XSS) is a type of injection attack that leverages a user's browser to execute malicious code that can access sensitive information such as passwords and session information. Because the malicious code resides on the site that the user accesses, it's often difficult for the user's browser to know that the code should not be trusted. XSS thus takes advantage of this inherent trust between browser and site to run the malicious code at the security level of the website.

XSS comes in two forms: persistent and nonpersistent. With persistent attacks, malicious code is stored on a site, usually via message board or comment postings. When other users attempt to use the site, they unwittingly execute the code hidden in the previously posted content. Nonpersistent attacks, also referred to as *reflected* XSS, take advantage of a flaw in the server software. If an attacker notices an XSS vulnerability on a site, they can craft a special link that, when passed to and clicked on by other users, would cause the browser to visit the site and reflect the attack back onto the victim. This could cause an inadvertent leak of session details or user information to whatever server the attacker specifies. These links are often passed along through e-mail and text messages and appear to be innocuous and legitimate.

Another type of attack, called a DOM-based XSS attack, occurs when an attacker injects a malicious script into the client-side HTML being parsed by a browser. The DOM, or Document Object Model, is the standard by which a client—or more specifically, the browser—interacts with HTML. If website code either does not properly validate input or does not encode data correctly, it creates the opportunity for an attacker to modify code en route to initiate an XSS attack. Importantly, no server resources are affected using the method. The page, its HTML contents, and the associated HTTP response do not change, but the modifications that result from the malicious script cause the client to execute abnormally. Detecting DOM-based attacks using server-side tools is impossible because the traffic will look identical to legitimate traffic. Defense against DOM-based XSS involves sanitizing client-side code through inspection of DOM objects and using intrusion prevention systems that are able to inspect inbound traffic to determine if unusual parameters are being passed.

The following are several tools and techniques for XSS prevention and mitigation:

- **Input validation** Validate all user input to ensure that it does not contain script or other malicious code.
- **Output encoding** Encode all output to prevent script injection.
- **Contextual output encoding** Encode output based on the context in which it will be displayed. For example, encoding in JavaScript may differ from encoding in HTML.
- **Content Security Policy (CSP)** CSP is a browser security feature that allows web developers to specify which resources a browser should trust. It can help mitigate XSS attacks by blocking inline scripts and restricting which scripts can be executed.
- **HTTPOnly cookies** HTTPOnly cookies are not accessible to client-side scripts, which helps prevent session hijacking attacks.

- **X-XSS-Protection header**   The X-XSS-Protection header is an HTTP header that can be set by the server to instruct the browser to enable its built-in XSS filter.

- **Web application firewall**   A WAF can help protect against XSS attacks by filtering out malicious input.

- **Security testing**   Regularly testing web applications for vulnerabilities, including XSS, can help identify and mitigate potential attacks.

- **Regularly updating software**   Keeping software up to date can help prevent XSS attacks by ensuring that known vulnerabilities are patched.

Cross-Site Request Forgery

Cross-site request forgery (CSRF) is an attack that exploits the trust a website has in a user's browser. The attack works by tricking a user into performing an action on a website without their knowledge or consent. This is achieved by a malicious actor crafting a request that is sent to the target website and is designed to mimic a legitimate request. When the victim interacts with the website, the browser will send the crafted request, causing the website to perform an unintended action. The victim will be unaware of the attack, as the attacker is able to piggyback on the victim's previously authenticated session. CSRF attacks can lead to a wide range of consequences, including unauthorized transactions, disclosure of sensitive information, and changes to account settings. Common techniques for exploiting CSRF vulnerabilities include the use of hidden form fields, image tags, and script tags, as well as embedding malicious JavaScript in a web page.

In 2018, Facebook suffered a massive CSRF attack affecting nearly 50 million users. The vulnerability exploited Facebook's "View As" feature and allowed an attacker to create an access token for a victim's account and gain control of it. The attacker could access personal information, post on the victim's timeline, and carry out further attacks. The attack was due to a flaw in Facebook's implementation of CSRF protection, allowing the attacker to bypass the protection by manipulating the OAuth flow of the "View As" feature. This underscores the significance of proper implementation of CSRF mitigations.

Here are some tools and techniques for preventing and mitigating CSRF attacks:

- **HTTP Referer**   The HTTP Referer header can be used to check whether a request is coming from an expected source, which can help by ensuring that requests are coming from an expected source.

- **SameSite attribute**   Setting the SameSite attribute in cookies to "Strict" or "Lax" can help prevent CSRF attacks by preventing the cookie from being sent with a cross-site request.

- **CAPTCHAs**   CAPTCHAs can be used to verify that the request is being made by a human and not a script or bot.

- **CSRF tokens**   Include a unique token with each user request to ensure that it originated from a legitimate source. This token can be checked by the server to verify the legitimacy of the request.

- **CSRF protection frameworks**   Some web development frameworks include built-in protection against CSRF attacks.

- **Double-submit cookies**   Double-submit cookies involve setting a cookie that contains a random value, and then embedding that value in a hidden form field. When the form is submitted, the value of the cookie and the hidden form field are compared. If they match, the request is considered legitimate.

- **User re-authentication**   Require the user to re-authenticate for sensitive operations or after a period of inactivity to prevent unauthorized requests.

- **Multifactor authentication**   Requiring additional factors such as a one-time code sent to the user's phone or e-mail can help prevent CSRF attacks.

- **Web application firewall**   A WAF can help protect against CSRF attacks by filtering out malicious requests.

- **Regularly updating software**   Keeping software up to date can help prevent CSRF attacks by ensuring that known vulnerabilities are patched.

Directory Traversal

A directory traversal attack enables an attacker to view, modify, or execute files in a system that they wouldn't normally be able to access. For web applications, these files normally reside outside of the web root directory and should not be viewable. However, if the server has poorly configured permissions, a user may be able to view other assets on the server. If an attacker determines a web application is vulnerable to directory traversal attack, they may use one or more explicit Unix-compliant directory traversal character sequences (**../**) or an encoded variation of it to bypass security filters and access files outside of the web root directory. Figure 12-2 shows the execution of a simple directory traversal attack against a vulnerable server. In this example, an attacker uses the wget utility to crawl up and down the file system to recover the unprotected /etc/passwd file.

Here are some common tools and techniques for preventing and mitigating directory traversal attacks:

- **Input validation**   Validate user input and ensure it does not contain directory traversal sequences.

- **Principle of least privilege**   Set up proper file and directory permissions to prevent unauthorized access. Restrict access to sensitive files and directories to authorized users only.

- **Filename sanitization**   Sanitize filenames to remove any directory traversal sequences or other potentially malicious characters.

- **Secure coding practices**   Develop applications using secure coding practices to prevent directory traversal attacks and other types of security vulnerabilities.

- **Web application firewall**   A WAF can help protect against directory traversal attacks by filtering out malicious input.

- **Regularly updating software**   Keeping software up to date can help prevent directory traversal attacks by ensuring that known vulnerabilities are patched.

- **File-handling libraries**   Use a dedicated file-handling library that has built-in protections against directory traversal attacks.

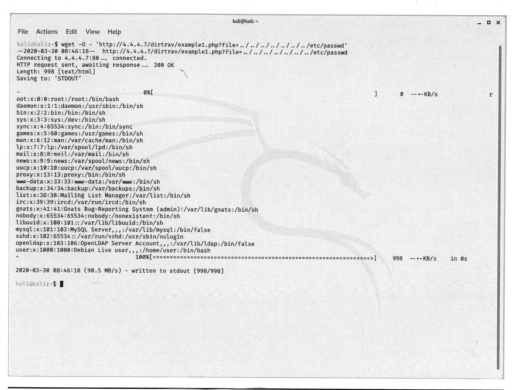

Figure 12-2   Output from a successful directory traversal

- **Reverse proxy**   A reverse proxy can be used to protect web applications from directory traversal attacks by intercepting requests and filtering out malicious input.

- **Process isolation**   Running applications in chroot jails or containers can help prevent directory traversal attacks by isolating the application from the host system.

Server-Side Request Forgery

SSRF, or server-side request forgery, refers to a vulnerability that arises when a web application allows a user to specify a URL to fetch a remote resource, without properly validating the URL. This can allow an attacker to send a crafted request to an unexpected destination, potentially bypassing firewalls, virtual private networks (VPNs), and other network access controls. SSRF attacks have become more prevalent as web applications provide more features for fetching URLs and can be especially severe in the context of cloud services and complex architectures.

A well-known SSRF exploit is the Capital One data breach in 2019. In this attack, the hacker exploited an SSRF vulnerability in Capital One's server to steal the personal information of over 100 million customers. The attacker was able to send requests to the metadata service of the AWS cloud infrastructure used by Capital One, which contained sensitive information such as access keys and credentials. The attacker was then able to use this information to gain access to Capital One's stored data in S3. The vulnerability was caused by a misconfigured web application firewall that allowed the attacker to send requests to the metadata service. This attack underscores the severity of the consequences associated with these vulnerabilities—a single SSRF vulnerability can lead to a large-scale data breach with significant financial and reputational costs.

Common tools and techniques for prevention and mitigation of SSRF are as follows:

- **Input validation**   Validate user input and ensure that it does not contain URLs with unexpected destinations or any other malicious input.

- **Principle of least privilege**   Set up proper network and application permissions to prevent unauthorized access. Restrict access to sensitive resources to authorized users only.

- **URL validation and sanitization**   Sanitize URLs to remove any potentially malicious characters and validate that they only reference expected hosts or IP addresses.

- **Secure coding practices**   Develop applications using secure coding practices to prevent SSRF attacks and other types of security vulnerabilities.

- **Web application firewall**   A WAF can help protect against SSRF attacks by filtering out malicious input.

- **Regularly updating software**   Keeping software up to date can help prevent SSRF attacks by ensuring that known vulnerabilities are patched.

- **Dedicated libraries and frameworks**   Use a dedicated HTTP client library or framework that has built-in protections against SSRF attacks.

- **Reverse proxy**   A reverse proxy can be used to protect web applications from SSRF attacks by intercepting requests and filtering out malicious input.

- **Process isolation**   Running applications in containers or virtual machines can help prevent SSRF attacks by isolating the application from the host system.

Buffer Overflow Vulnerabilities

Attackers often will write malware that takes advantage of some quality or operation of main memory. Memory is an extremely complex environment, and malicious activities are prone to disrupt the delicate arrangement of elements in that space. The temporary space that a program has allocated to perform operating system or application functions is referred to as the *buffer*. Buffers usually reside in main memory, but they may also exist in hard drive and cache space. You may be familiar with the type of buffer used by video-streaming services. Streaming services often uses buffers to ensure smooth video playback and to mitigate the effects of an unexpected drop in connectivity. As the video is playing, upcoming portions are saved to memory in a sliding window. If the connection is dropped, the video can be played directly from the buffer until the connection resumes; the more buffer space the system has, the longer it is able to maintain the temporary streaming. Buffers in software enable operating systems to access data efficiently since RAM is among the fastest types of storage.

When the volume of data exceeds the capacity of the buffer, the result is *buffer overflow*. If this occurs, a system may attempt to write data past the limits of the buffer and into other memory spaces. Attackers will sometimes find ways to craft input into a program in a way that will cause the program to attempt to write too much data to a buffer. If the boundaries of data are well understood, an attacker may be able to overwrite legitimate executable data and replace it with malicious code.

Buffer overflows affect nearly every type of software and can result in unexpected results if not managed correctly. Even though these types of attack are well understood, they are still fairly common. If an attacker is off by even a byte when writing to memory, this could cause memory errors that terminate processes and display some sort of message indicating this condition to the user. This type of symptom is particularly likely if the exploit is based on buffer overflow vulnerabilities. Fortunately, these messages sometimes indicate that the attack failed. Your best bet is to play it safe and take a memory dump so you can analyze the root cause of the problem.

To understand how specific types of buffer attacks work, it's useful to understand the different types of memory allocation techniques. Generally, system memory is divided into two parts: the stack and the heap. The *stack* is a type of data structure that operates on the principle of last-in, first out (that is, the data that was last added to the stack is the first removed during a read operation). The stack is a structured, sequential memory space that is statically allocated for specific operations. The *heap,* in contrast, is an unstructured body of memory that the computer may use to satisfy memory requests. Heap memory allocation is done on a dynamic basis as space becomes available to use. A useful resource is security legend Elias Levy's 1996 article, "Smashing the Stack for Fun and Profit," a seminal piece for understanding and exploiting various buffer overflow vulnerabilities.

Here is a list of prevention and mitigation techniques for buffer overflow vulnerabilities:

- **Input validation**   Validate user input to ensure that it conforms to expected formats and length limits. Check boundaries to ensure that inputs fall within the expected range of values.

- **Principle of least privilege**   Reduce the attack surface by restricting access to sensitive resources and functions to only authorized users or processes.

- **Secure coding practices**   Use secure coding practices such as bounds checking to prevent buffer overflows. Rust and Ada programming languages have built-in safety mechanisms to prevent buffer overflows.

- **Runtime application self-protection**   A RASP solution can monitor and protect against buffer overflows by detecting and preventing the execution of malicious code.

- **Stack canaries**   Use stack canaries to detect buffer overflows that overwrite return addresses on the stack. This can help prevent stack-based buffer overflows.

- **Address space layout randomization (ASLR)**   Use ASLR to randomize the location of key memory segments, making it harder for an attacker to exploit a buffer overflow.

- **Data execution prevention (DEP)**   Use DEP to mark memory pages as nonexecutable, preventing an attacker from executing code on the stack or heap.

- **Code signing**   Use code signing to ensure that only trusted code is executed. This can help prevent integer overflows and other types of code injection attacks.

- **Heap randomization**   Heap randomization strategically shuffles objects in the heap, making it more difficult for attackers to predict the location of objects in memory.

Stack-Based Attacks

Stack-based buffer overflows work by overwriting key areas of the stack with too much data to enable custom code, located elsewhere in memory, to be executed in place of legitimate code. Stack-based overflows are the most common and well known of all buffer overflow attacks, and the terms are often used interchangeably. Stack-based attacks have a special place in security history. The first widely distributed Internet worm was made possible through a successful stack-based buffer attack. The Morris Worm, written by graduate student Robert Tappan Morris from Cornell University in the late 1980s, took advantage of a buffer overflow vulnerability in a widely used version of fingerd, a daemon for a simple network protocol used to exchange user information. In short, the worm's main purpose was to enumerate Internet-connected computers by connecting to a machine, replicating itself, and sending that copy on to neighboring computers. Morris's activity also resulted in the first conviction under the 1986 Computer Fraud and Abuse Act.

Heap-Based Attacks

Attacks targeting the memory heap are usually more difficult for attackers to implement because the heap is dynamically allocated. In many cases, heap attacks involve exhausting the memory space allocated for a program. To make things more complicated for attackers, the success of a heap-based overflow does not always mean a successful exploit because data in the heap must be corrupted rather than just overwritten.

Integer Attacks

An integer overflow takes advantage of the fixed architecture-defined memory regions associated with integer variables. In the C programming language, the integer memory regions are capable of holding values of up to 4 bytes, or 32 bits. This means the integer value range is −2,147,483,648 to 2,147,483,647. If a value is submitted that is larger in size than the 4-byte limit, the integer buffer may be exceeded. The challenge with an integer overflow lies in its difficulty of detection because there may not be an inherent way for a process to determine whether a result it calculated is correct. Most integer overflows are not exploitable because memory is not being overwritten, but they can lead to other types of overflow conditions. Real-life examples of exploits are rare but not unheard of.

In 2001, the CERT Coordination Center released Vulnerability Note VU#945216, which described a flaw in the SSH1 protocol that could allow for remote code execution. Curiously, the fault existed in a function designed to detect cyclic redundancy check (CRC) attacks. The function made use of a hash table to store connection information used in determining abuse patterns. With a specially crafted packet of a length greater than the function's integer buffer, an attacker could create a null-sized table, or one with no value, that allowed the attacker to modify arbitrary addresses within the daemon. Even worse, this attack could be executed before any authentication occurred, meaning the system might essentially have no defenses against it.

Broken Access Control

Broken access control is a term used to describe the failure of access controls to prevent unauthorized access to sensitive data or functionality. This vulnerability can occur when an application fails to properly enforce access controls, such as authentication or authorization. According to OWASP's Top 10 report of web application security risks for 2021, broken access control is the most common web application security risk, with 43 percent of organizations being affected by this type of vulnerability.

The impact of broken access control can be severe, allowing attackers to access sensitive information, modify data, or execute unauthorized actions on behalf of legitimate users. Common examples of broken access control vulnerabilities include vertical privilege escalation, horizontal privilege escalation, insecure direct object references, and lack of user session management.

Broken Object Level Authorization

When exposing services via APIs, some servers fail to authorize on an object basis, potentially creating the opportunity for attackers to access resources without the proper authorization to do so. In some cases, an attacker can simply change a URI to reflect a target resource and gain access. Broken object level authorization (BOLA) checks should always be implemented and access granted based on the specific role of the user. Additionally, universally unique identifiers (UUIDs) should be implemented in a random manner to avoid the chance that an attacker can successfully enumerate them.

Here is a list of common tools and techniques for mitigating and preventing broken object level authorization:

- **Role-based access control (RBAC)** Use RBAC to restrict access to resources based on a user's role in the organization.

- **Attribute-based access control (ABAC)** Use ABAC to restrict access to resources based on specific attributes or characteristics of the user, such as job title or location.

- **Least privilege** Limit access to only the resources and data necessary for a user to perform their job.

- **Access control testing** Test access control measures regularly to ensure they are effective and not easily bypassed.

- **Proper error handling** Implement proper error handling to prevent attackers from obtaining information about the system or gaining unauthorized access.

- **Session management** Implement proper session management to ensure that sessions cannot be hijacked or taken over by unauthorized users.

- **Regular software updates** Keep software up to date to ensure that known vulnerabilities are patched.
- **Web application firewall** Implement a WAF to filter out malicious traffic and protect against attacks that exploit access control vulnerabilities.
- **Business object level authorization** Also referred to as BOLA, business object level authorization restricts access to specific business objects or resources rather than just pages or features.
- **Business flow level authorization** Also referred to as BFLA, business flow level authorization ensures that users can only perform actions that are appropriate for their role and the current stage of the business process.

Broken User Authentication

Authentication mechanisms exist to give legitimate users access to resources, provided they are able to present the correct credentials. When these mechanisms fail to validate credentials correctly, allow credentials that are too weak, accept credentials in an insecure manner, or allow brute forcing of credentials, they create conditions that an attacker can take advantage of.

Broken user authentication is a critical security risk that consistently ranks as one of the top 10 vulnerabilities according to OWASP. This vulnerability arises when user authentication mechanisms are improperly implemented or fail to provide adequate protection against authentication-related attacks. Attackers exploit these vulnerabilities to gain unauthorized access to sensitive data or functionality, compromising user accounts and other critical assets. One of the most common examples of broken user authentication is when weak passwords are used, making it easier for attackers to guess or brute force their way into user accounts. A recent study by Verizon found that compromised credentials were involved in over 80 percent of data breaches in 2022, highlighting the critical importance of secure authentication mechanisms.

Broken Function Level Authorization

Broken function level authorization (BFLA) is a critical security risk that occurs when an application fails to properly restrict access to certain functionality based on the user's role or privileges. This can lead to unauthorized access to sensitive data or functionality, including the ability to modify or delete data, execute commands, or perform other malicious actions. According to OWASP, this vulnerability is consistently ranked as one of the top 10 security risks in web applications. In addition, the vulnerability can also be exploited in the form of insecure direct object reference (IDOR) attacks, where an attacker can directly access and manipulate resources that they are not authorized to access.

The vulnerability arises when an application relies solely on client-side checks to enforce access control policies or when access control policies are not properly designed or implemented. This can allow an attacker to modify requests or perform actions that they should not be authorized to do. Attackers can exploit this vulnerability through a variety of means, including direct manipulation of URLs or parameters, forging HTTP requests, and by exploiting known vulnerabilities in the application.

Cryptographic Failures

Cryptographic failures are vulnerabilities or weaknesses in a system's cryptographic algorithms, protocols, or key management. Attackers can exploit these weaknesses to bypass or break cryptographic protections, such as encryption or digital signatures, and gain unauthorized access to sensitive information or systems. Cryptographic failures are consistently ranked as a top security risk by OWASP and can lead to significant data breaches and other security incidents.

One of the main causes of cryptographic failures is the improper implementation or use of cryptographic techniques. For example, weak or outdated encryption algorithms, poor key management practices, and using the same key for multiple purposes can all create vulnerabilities in a system's cryptographic protections.

One of the most high-profile incidents involving cryptographic failures was the Heartbleed bug, which was discovered in 2014. Heartbleed was a vulnerability in the widely used OpenSSL cryptography library that allowed an attacker to read sensitive information from the memory of a vulnerable server. This information could include private keys, passwords, and other sensitive data. The vulnerability was caused by a flaw in the implementation of the Transport Layer Security (TLS) heartbeat extension, which is used to keep a TLS connection alive. The vulnerability affected an estimated 17 percent of all web servers, and it was estimated that over 500,000 websites were potentially vulnerable to attack at the time.

Here is a list of common mitigations and prevention techniques for cryptographic failures:

- **Algorithm selection** Always use strong and up-to-date encryption algorithms, such as AES and RSA, to protect sensitive data.

- **Key management** Proper key management is essential for ensuring the security of cryptographic systems; keys should be securely stored and managed throughout their entire lifecycle.

- **Password storage** Passwords should be securely hashed and salted to prevent attackers from easily cracking them. Passwords should also be periodically updated.

- **Secure random number generators** Secure random number generators should be used to ensure that keys and other cryptographic elements are truly random and cannot be easily guessed or predicted.

- **Certificate pinning** Certificate pinning can help prevent man-in-the-middle attacks by verifying that a server's certificate matches a known and trusted certificate.

- **Digital signatures** Digital signatures can help verify the authenticity and integrity of data, messages, and other important information.

- **Application firewalls** An application firewall can help filter out malicious traffic and protect against attacks that exploit cryptographic vulnerabilities.

- **Regularly updating software and firmware** Keeping software and firmware up to date can help prevent cryptographic failures by ensuring that known vulnerabilities are patched.

Data Poisoning

Data poisoning is an attack that involves the manipulation of training data used to create machine learning (ML) or artificial intelligence (AI) models. The goal of the attacker is to introduce biased or malicious data into the training set, which can then result in incorrect or harmful decisions by the model. As ML and AI continue to become more prevalent in cybersecurity, data poisoning attacks are becoming an increasingly concerning threat.

Attackers can conduct data poisoning attacks through a variety of methods, including injecting biased or malicious data directly into the training set, manipulating data sources or sensors to produce biased data, and manipulating human input used to label or classify data. The impact of a successful data poisoning attack can be severe, ranging from incorrect or inaccurate decisions by the model to potentially dangerous actions taken based on the model's output.

The following are some tools and techniques that can be used in the prevention and mitigation of data poisoning attacks:

- **Data quality controls**   Implement data quality controls to detect anomalies and inconsistencies in input data, which can be indicative of data poisoning attacks.

- **Data monitoring**   Regularly monitor input data and log any suspicious activity or unexpected patterns. This can help detect data poisoning attacks early.

- **Outlier detection**   Implement outlier detection techniques to identify and remove data points that fall outside of normal parameters. This can help prevent data poisoning attacks that involve injecting anomalous data.

- **Model validation and testing**   Validate and test models to ensure that they are resilient to data poisoning attacks. This can include using adversarial testing to identify weaknesses in the model's ability to identify and handle malicious inputs.

- **Data preprocessing**   Implement data preprocessing techniques such as normalization and scaling to reduce the impact of potentially malicious data inputs on the model's output.

- **Access controls**   Implement proper access controls to restrict access to data and models to authorized users only. This can help prevent data poisoning attacks that involve unauthorized access to the system.

- **Regular software updates**   Keep software up to date to ensure that known vulnerabilities are patched and models are updated with the latest security features.

- **Input validation**   Validate input data to ensure that it conforms to expected formats and length limits. Check boundaries to ensure that inputs fall within the expected range of values.

- **Principle of least privilege**   Reduce the attack surface by restricting access to sensitive resources and functions to only authorized users or processes.

Privilege Escalation

Privilege escalation is simply any action that enables a user to perform tasks they are not normally allowed to do. This often involves exploiting a bug, implementation flaw, or misconfiguration. Escalation can happen in a *vertical* manner, meaning that a user gains the privileges of a higher privilege user. Alternatively, *horizontal* privilege escalation can be performed to get the access of others in the same privilege level. Attackers will use these privileges to modify files, download sensitive information, or install malicious code.

Here is a list of common mitigations and protections against privilege escalation:

- **Least privilege**   Limit user access to only the resources and data necessary to perform their job functions. This can prevent attackers from gaining access to sensitive data or functions in the event of a breach.

- **Role-based access control (RBAC)**   Implement RBAC to restrict access to resources based on a user's role in the organization. This can help ensure that users only have access to the resources necessary for their job functions.

- **Attribute-based access control (ABAC)**   Implement ABAC to restrict access to resources based on specific attributes or characteristics of the user, such as job title or location. This can provide an additional layer of access control beyond RBAC.

- **Segmentation and isolation**   Segment and isolate critical systems and data to prevent unauthorized access or lateral movement by attackers. This can involve network segmentation or the use of virtualization or containerization technologies.

- **Logging and monitoring**   Implement logging and monitoring to detect and respond to suspicious activity or attempts to escalate privileges. This can include monitoring of user activity, system logs, and network traffic.

- **Regular software updates**   Keep software up to date to ensure that known vulnerabilities are patched. This can help prevent attackers from exploiting vulnerabilities to escalate privileges.

- **Penetration testing**   Regularly conduct penetration testing to identify vulnerabilities and potential privilege escalation issues. This can help identify areas where access controls may be weak or where additional protections may be needed.

- **Application firewalls**   Implement application layer firewalls to filter out malicious traffic and protect against attacks that exploit privilege escalation vulnerabilities. This can include the use of signatures or heuristics to detect and block known attack patterns.

> ### Jailbreaking and Rooting
>
> Jailbreaking, the act of bypassing Apple iOS restrictions, uses privilege escalation to enable users to perform functions that they normally could not. Jailbreaking enables Apple mobile device users to install custom software or modified operating systems. Similarly, "rooting" an Android device gives a user privileged access to the device's subsystem. Developing these kinds of exploits is a big deal because mobile device manufacturers expend enormous resources to standardize their devices. While gaining freedom to install additional apps and modify a mobile device seems like a good idea, it makes the device less secure because it's likely that the protections that could prevent malicious activity were removed to achieve the jailbreak or root in the first place.

Identification and Authentication Attacks

In securing authentication systems, the main challenge lies in identifying and communicating just the right amount of information to the authentication system to make an accurate decision. These are machines, after all, and they will never truly know who we are or what our intentions may be. They can form a decision based only on the information we give them and the clues about our behavior as we provide that data. If an attacker is clever enough to fabricate a user's information sufficiently, they are effectively the same person in the eyes of the authentication system.

Some prevention techniques for identification and authentication attacks are as follows:

- **Strong password policy**   Implement a strong password policy that requires complex and unique passwords and enforces regular password changes.
- **Multifactor authentication (MFA)**   Implement MFA to add an additional layer of security to the authentication process, making it harder for attackers to gain unauthorized access.
- **CAPTCHA**   Implement CAPTCHA to prevent automated attacks such as credential stuffing and password spraying.
- **Rate limiting**   Implement rate limiting to prevent brute-force attacks by limiting the number of login attempts or requests per user, device, or IP.
- **Session management**   Implement proper session management to prevent session hijacking and ensure that sessions are properly invalidated after logout or after a period of inactivity.
- **Encryption**   Use encryption to protect sensitive user data such as passwords and authentication tokens from being intercepted by attackers using man-in-the-middle (MITM) attacks.
- **Access control**   Implement access control to restrict access to sensitive resources and functionality to only authorized users or roles.

- **User education** Educate users on safe authentication practices, including the importance of creating strong passwords, using multifactor authentication, recognizing phishing attempts, and other social engineering attacks that attempt to steal login credentials.

Password Spraying

Password spraying is a type of brute-force technique in which an attacker tries a single password against a system and then iterates though multiple systems on a network using the same password. In doing so, an attacker may avoid account lockouts from a single system. Detecting spraying attempts is much easier if there is a unified interface, such as that provided by a security information and event management (SIEM) solution, on which an analyst can visualize events from a range of security information sources.

Common techniques to detect password spraying include the following:

- High number of authentication attempts within a defined period of time across multiple systems
- High number of bad usernames, or usernames that don't match company standard
- High number of account lockouts over a defined period of time
- Multiple successful logins from a single IP in a short time frame
- Multiple failed logins from a single IP in a short time frame

Credential Stuffing

Credential stuffing is a type of brute-force attack in which credentials obtained from a data breach of one service are used to authenticate to another system in an attempt to gain access. Given the scale and rate of data breaches, credential stuffing continues to be a major problem for the security and safety of organizations and data. Recent data breaches have each exposed hundreds of thousands to millions of credentials. When aggregated as "collections," these numbers can easily top billions. If even a small fraction of a credentials list can be used to gain access to accounts, it's worth it from the attacker's vantage point, especially with the use of automation. For organizations, mandating MFA is effective in slowing the effectiveness of attacks, especially those that are automated.

Impersonation

Sometimes attackers will impersonate a service to harvest credentials or intercept communications. Fooling a client can be done one of several ways. First, if the server key is stolen, the attacker appears to be the server without the client possibly knowing about it. Additionally, if an attacker can somehow gain trust as the certificate authority (CA) from the client, or if the client does not check to see if the attacker is actually a trusted CA, then the impersonation will be successful.

Man-in-the-Middle

Essentially, man-in-the-middle, or monkey-in the-middle (MITM), attacks are impersonation attacks that face both ways: the attacker impersonates both the client to the real server and the server to the real client. Acting as a proxy or relay, the attacker will use

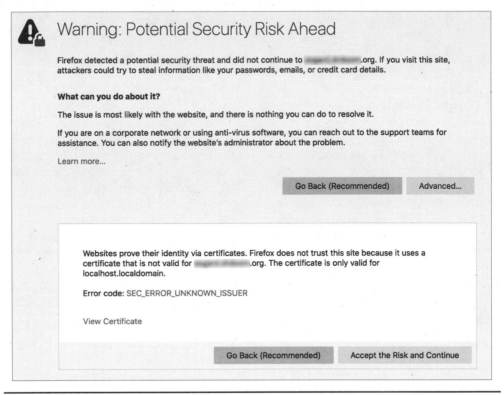

Figure 12-3   Firefox warning displaying information regarding a website's certificate validity

their position in the middle of the conversation between parties to collect credentials, capture traffic, or introduce false communications. Even with an encrypted connection, it's possible to conduct an MITM attack that works similarly to an unencrypted attack. In the case of HTTPS, the client browser establishes a Secure Sockets Layer (SSL) connection with the attacker, and the attacker establishes a second SSL connection with the web server. The client may or may not see a warning about the validity of the client, as shown in Figure 12-3.

If a warning appears, it's very likely that the victim may ignore or click though the warning. The tendency for users to ignore warnings highlights the importance of user training. The Firefox browser attempts to give as much information to the user about what's happening as plainly as possible. Firefox offers detailed information about the certificate for more technical users to use in troubleshooting any potential issues. Note that the certificate details shown in Figure 12-4 are valid only for certain domains, which prompted the initial warning from the browser. It's possible for the warning not to appear at all, which would indicate that the attacker has managed to get a certificate signed by a trusted CA.

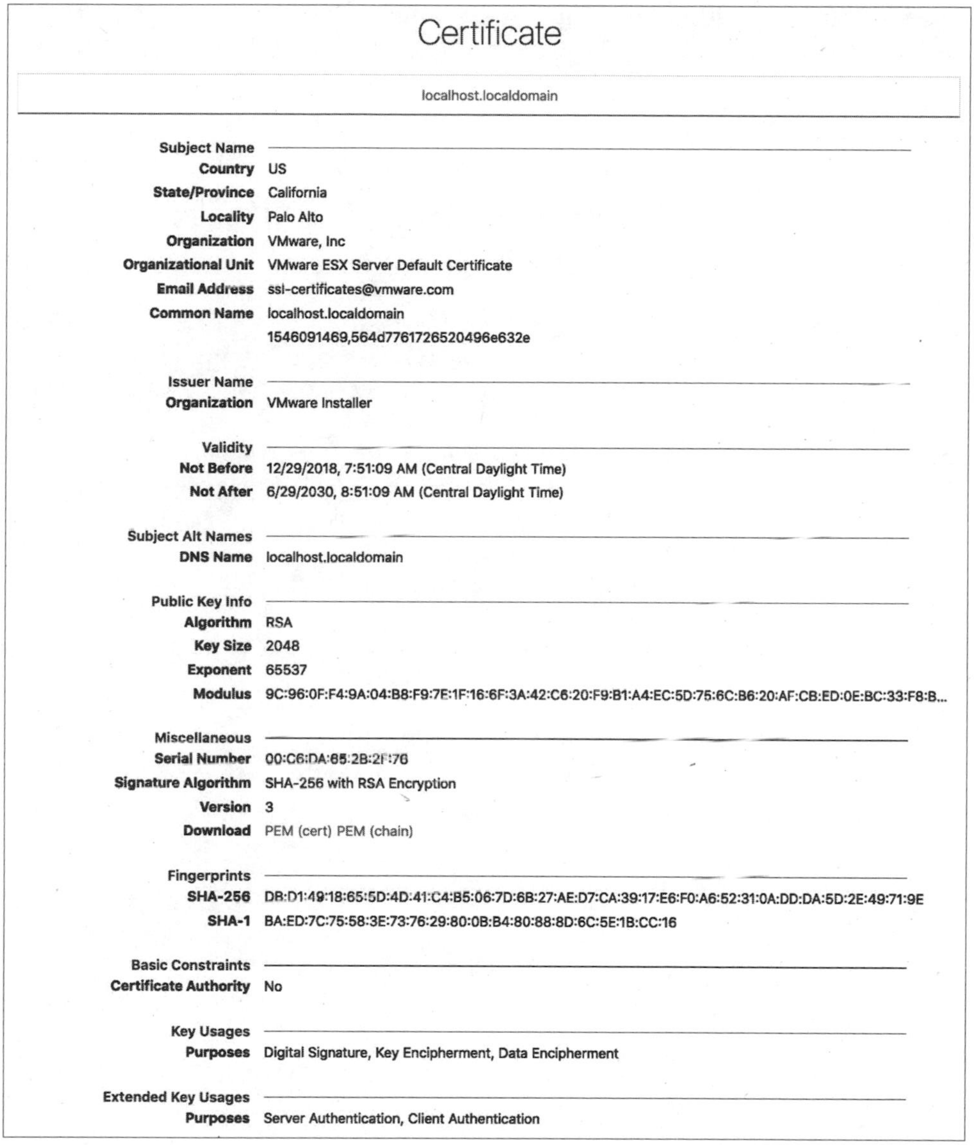

Certificate

localhost.localdomain

Subject Name	
Country	US
State/Province	California
Locality	Palo Alto
Organization	VMware, Inc
Organizational Unit	VMware ESX Server Default Certificate
Email Address	ssl-certificates@vmware.com
Common Name	localhost.localdomain
	1546091469,564d7761726520496e632e
Issuer Name	
Organization	VMware Installer
Validity	
Not Before	12/29/2018, 7:51:09 AM (Central Daylight Time)
Not After	6/29/2030, 8:51:09 AM (Central Daylight Time)
Subject Alt Names	
DNS Name	localhost.localdomain
Public Key Info	
Algorithm	RSA
Key Size	2048
Exponent	65537
Modulus	9C:96:0F:F4:9A:04:B8:F9:7E:1F:16:6F:3A:42:C6:20:F9:B1:A4:EC:5D:75:6C:B6:20:AF:CB:ED:0E:BC:33:F8:B...
Miscellaneous	
Serial Number	00:C6:DA:65:2B:2F:76
Signature Algorithm	SHA-256 with RSA Encryption
Version	3
Download	PEM (cert) PEM (chain)
Fingerprints	
SHA-256	DB:D1:49:18:65:5D:4D:41:C4:B5:06:7D:6B:27:AE:D7:CA:39:17:E6:F0:A6:52:31:0A:DD:DA:5D:2E:49:71:9E
SHA-1	BA:ED:7C:75:58:3E:73:76:29:80:0B:B4:80:88:8D:6C:5E:1B:CC:16
Basic Constraints	
Certificate Authority	No
Key Usages	
Purposes	Digital Signature, Key Encipherment, Data Encipherment
Extended Key Usages	
Purposes	Server Authentication, Client Authentication

Figure 12-4 Firefox certificate details screen

Session Hijacking

Session hijacking is a class of attacks by which an attacker takes advantage of valid session information, often by stealing and replaying it. HTTP traffic is stateless and often uses multiple TCP connections, so it uses sessions to keep track of client authentication.

Session information is just a string of characters that appears in a cookie file, the URL itself, or other parts of the HTTP traffic. An attacker can get existing session information through traffic capture, an MITM attack, or by predicting the session token information. By capturing and repeating session information, an attacker may be able to take over, or hijack, the existing web session to impersonate a victim.

Local File Inclusion/Remote File Inclusion Attacks

Local file inclusion (LFI) and remote file inclusion (RFI) attacks are a common vulnerability found in web applications. LFI occurs when an attacker is able to include a file located on the server in a web page, allowing them to view sensitive information or execute arbitrary code. RFI is similar to LFI, but instead of including a file on the server, an attacker is able to include a file located on a remote server, giving them even more control over the targeted system.

LFI attacks occur when an attacker can manipulate user input to include files that reside on the server. RFI attacks, on the other hand, occur when an attacker can manipulate user input to include remote files from a malicious source. Both can happen when the application doesn't properly validate user input or restrict access to sensitive files or remote resources. Attackers can leverage these vulnerabilities to access sensitive files or execute malicious code on the server.

Some common mitigations and prevention techniques for LFI/RFI attacks are as follows:

- **Input validation** Validate user input to ensure that it does not contain directory traversal sequences or other malicious characters.

- **Access controls** Implement proper access controls to restrict access to sensitive files and directories to authorized users only.

- **Filename sanitization** Sanitize filenames to remove any directory traversal sequences or other potentially malicious characters.

- **Secure coding practices** Develop applications using secure coding practices to prevent directory traversal attacks and other types of security vulnerabilities. Avoid using user input to construct file paths or include remote files.

- **Web application firewall** A WAF can help protect against LFI/RFI attacks by filtering out malicious input.

- **Regularly updating software** Keeping software up to date can help prevent LFI/RFI attacks by ensuring that known vulnerabilities are patched.

- **File-handling libraries** Use a dedicated file-handling library that has built-in protections against LFI/RFI attacks.

Rootkits

Rootkits are among the most challenging types of malware because they are specially designed to maintain persistence and root-level access on a system without being detected.

As with other types of malware, rootkits can be introduced by an attacker leveraging vulnerabilities to achieve privilege escalation and clandestine installation. Alternatively, they may be presented to a system as an update to BIOS or firmware. Rootkits are difficult to detect because they sometimes reside in the lower levels of an operating system, such as in device drivers and in the kernel, or even in the computer hardware itself, so the system cannot necessarily be trusted to report any modifications it has undergone.

A few protection and mitigation techniques for rootkits are as follows:

- **Regular system updates**   Keep your operating system and software up to date with the latest security patches and updates to prevent vulnerabilities that can be exploited by rootkits.

- **Endpoint protection**   Install and regularly update endpoint protection software to detect and remove rootkits from your system.

- **Secure boot process**   Use the secure boot process to prevent rootkits from being loaded during bootup.

- **Kernel patch protection**   Use kernel patch protection to prevent rootkits from modifying the kernel code.

Insecure Design Vulnerabilities

Attackers often use software vulnerabilities to get around an organization's security policies intended to protect its data. Sometimes the flaws exist in how the rules are written, how the mechanism is implemented, or what functions are called in the operation of the software. All computer systems have vulnerabilities, but depending on the number and type of compensating controls in place, they may or may not result in damage if exploited. As we describe these errors, it's important for you to remember that all of the vulnerabilities have some relevance to the secure operation of your company's software and network. They aren't just mistakes that inhibit usability or the look of the software but rather enable attackers to do something they wouldn't otherwise be able to do. They will sometimes result in unexpected and often undesirable behavior, but in many cases, they can be addressed using secure coding practices and thoughtful review processes before code ever goes to production.

Here are some common prevention and mitigation techniques for insecure design:

- **Secure development lifecycle (SDLC)**   Incorporate security into the software development process from the beginning, including threat modeling, secure coding practices, and security testing.

- **Component analysis**   Perform software composition analysis (SCA) to identify and manage vulnerabilities in third-party components and libraries.

- **Static application security testing (SAST)**   Use SAST tools to identify security vulnerabilities in the source code, including issues such as insecure use of functions and potential race conditions.

- **Dynamic application security testing (DAST)**   Use DAST tools to identify vulnerabilities in the running application, including issues such as insecure object references and sensitive data exposures.

- **Runtime application self-protection (RASP)**   Implement a RASP solution to detect and prevent attacks in real time, including issues such as insecure object references and race conditions.

- **Access controls**   Implement proper access controls to prevent unauthorized access to sensitive data and functionality.

- **Error handling**   Implement proper error handling to prevent information leakage that could be used by attackers.

- **Configuration management**   Implement secure configuration management practices to prevent misconfigurations that could lead to security vulnerabilities.

- **Regular software updates**   Keep software up to date to ensure that known vulnerabilities are patched.

- **Logging and monitoring**   Implement proper logging and monitoring to detect and respond to security events, and regularly monitor and remediate insecure logging and monitoring practices.

- **Application firewalls**   Implement application layer firewalls to filter out malicious traffic and protect against known attacks.

Improper Error Handling

Error handling is an important and normal function in software development. Although developers work to identify problems quickly, consistently, and early, errors related to memory, network, systems, and databases routinely pop up in a production environment. Improper error handling can be a security concern when too much information is disclosed about an exception to outside users. When internal error messages such as stack traces, database dumps, and error codes are displayed to the user, they may reveal details about internal network configuration or other implementation details that should never be revealed. For attackers, this kind of information can provide the situational awareness they need to craft very specific exploits.

Sometimes error messages don't reveal a lot of detail, but they can still provide clues to help attackers. Notices about file unavailability, timeout conditions, and access denial could reveal the presence or non-presence of a resource or indications about a file system's directory structure. As part of a secure coding practice, policies on error handling should be documented, including what kind of information will be visible to users and how this information is logged. Messages should be simple, conveying only what's needed in a consistent way to avoid disclosing too much about the platform.

Dereferencing

A dereferencing vulnerability, or null point dereference, is a common flaw that occurs when software attempts to access a value stored in memory that does not exist. A null pointer is a practice in programming used to direct a program to a location in memory that does not contain a valid object. This vulnerability has legitimate uses when used as a special marker, but security issues arise when it is dereferenced or accessed. Often, dereferencing results in an immediate crash and subsequent instability of an application. Attackers will try to trigger a null pointer dereference in the hopes that the resulting errors enable them to bypass security measures or learn more about how the program works by reading the exception information.

Insecure Object Reference

Insecure object reference vulnerabilities occur when the object identifiers in requests are used in a way that reveals a format or pattern in underlying or back-end technologies, such as files, directories, database records, and URLs. If database records are stored in a sequential manner and referenced directly by a function, for example, an attacker may be able to use this predictable pattern to identify resources to target directly, thereby saving them time and effort.

Rather than referencing sources directly, developers can avoid exposing resources by using an indirect reference map. With this method, a random value is used in place of a direct internal reference, preventing inadvertent disclosure of internal asset locations. Enforcing access controls at the object level also addresses the primary issue with this vulnerability: insufficient or missing access check. While client-side validations for access may be useful, server-side validations will be more effective at verifying that the current user owns or is allowed to access the requested data.

Race Condition

A race condition vulnerability is a defect in code that creates an unstable quality in the operation of a program arising from timing variances produced by programming logic. These deviations from timing could mean that a program that relies on sequential execution of a series of actions may experience two actions attempting to complete at the same time, or actions that attempt to complete out of order. A subclass of race condition vulnerabilities, time-of-check to time-of-use (TOCTOU), is often leveraged by attackers to cause issues with data integrity. TOCTOU is used by software to check the state of a resource before its use. If the state of the resource is changed between the checking and usage window, it may result in unexpected behavior from the software.

All kinds of software are vulnerable to race condition attacks. One way that an attacker may target this vulnerability is to bypass any restrictions imposed by an access control list (ACL). CVE-2016-7098 refers to such a possibility in its description of a flaw in wget, a popular command-line tool that allows file retrieval from servers. This vulnerability affects the way that wget applies its ACLs during the download process. In this case, if a download is initiated with recursive options, the utility will wait until the completion of the download to apply the rules. An attacker may take advantage of this by inserting malicious code or altering a file mid-download before the application has a chance to finish the transfer. Because the file gets deleted only after the connection closes, the attacker could keep the connection open and make use of the malicious file before its deletion.

Sensitive Data Exposure

Sensitive data exposure vulnerabilities occur when an application or system does not adequately protect data from access to unauthorized parties. Data can include authentication information, such as logins, passwords, and tokens, as well as personally identifiable information (PII), protected health information (PHI), or financial information. Recent advances in legislation and privacy laws, such as the European Union's General Data Protection Regulation (GDPR), attempt to enhance protections around this kind of sensitive data. To help identify vulnerabilities in the space, you may find it useful to go through a few questions related to the data your organization handles:

- Is any data transmitted in cleartext across your networks?
- Are any old, weak, or custom cryptographic algorithms and libraries used in your organization's code?
- Are default cryptographic keys in use?
- Are cryptographic keys rotated on a regular basis?
- Is encryption enforced across services?
- Do clients properly verify server certificates?

At the minimum, all organizations can follow a set of practices to ensure baseline protections against exploits of data exposure vulnerabilities. The process begins with identifying which data is sensitive according to privacy laws, regulatory requirements, or your organization's own definitions. As the data is introduced into various systems and applications for processing and transmission, there needs to be a way to identify these various levels of sensitivity by some technical means. From this point, it's straightforward for the data to be processed, stored, and transmitted in accordance with these standards. Furthermore, auditing can be made easier if the technical foundation is in place.

In terms of data storage, it's important to collect and store only the minimum amount of data needed to fulfill a business requirement. It's important that sensitive information be stored only as long as necessary and not beyond its usefulness. Stored data should be encrypted using strong standard algorithms and protocols. Private keys should be stored in a way that protects their disclosure and integrity. Strong encryption is also critical for all data in transit. When possible, your organization should promote usage of standards such as Transport Layer Security (TLS) with perfect forward secrecy (PFS) ciphers and HTTP Strict Transport Security (HSTS).

Insecure Components

Though modern software development practices make use of open source and external components to speed up the software development process, overreliance on these components, especially when they're not fully examined from a security aspect, can lead to dangerous exposure of your organization's data. Developers need to know what these components are doing, how they're interacting with internal assets and data, and what compensating controls can be put into place to address security issues related to their use. Some vulnerabilities related to insecure components may lead to minor impacts in performance, but others can lead to major security events. What's more, promises about the security of an external component may even lead to a false sense of security, making the impact potentially worse because there was some expectation of protection.

Insufficient Logging and Monitoring

Earlier in the chapter, we touched on the concept of errors as a way for developers to get feedback about their software and find ways to improve performance and stability. Like errors, logging gives critical feedback about the state of a system, enabling analysts to trace events back to their beginning as they work to determine root cause. The main vulnerability with logging is the nonexistence of logging mechanisms at key points within the network that would give insight into malicious and abusive behaviors. Nearly all network devices, operating systems, and other types of hosts provide one or more options for logging, often at various levels of detail (or verbosity). However, developers might disable or misconfigure logging during development and never turn it back on. Good logging practice is also much more than just having the feature enabled—it's about setting the conditions under which logs can be ingested, understood, and operationalized easily. This may include developing intermediate steps such as setting up specialized servers and normalizing the data. Security without logging is so much harder because, as with asset visibility, you cannot defend what you cannot see.

As best practice, the Open Web Application Security Project (OWASP) recommends that logging be configured for the following activities:

- Input validation failures, such as invalid parameter names and values, and protocol violations
- Output validation failures such as invalid data encoding
- Authentication successes and failures
- Access control failures
- Session management failures
- Application and component syntax and runtime errors
- Connectivity problems
- Malware detection
- Configuration modifications
- Application and related system startups and shutdowns
- Logging functionality and state changes
- Actions by administrative accounts

It's also important to define what to exclude for logging. Data that is not legally sanctioned, or that may have serious privacy implications for users, should not be part of the logging effort. This usually includes some types of privileged communications, data collected without consent, payment card holder data, encryption keys, sensitive PII, access tokens, passwords, and intellectual property data. Keep in mind that local laws may explicitly forbid the collection of certain classes of data.

Security Misconfiguration

A *vulnerability window* is the time between the disclosure of a flaw from a vendor and the moment an organization is able to patch the flaw. Attackers will often attempt to exploit unpatched flaws during this time, or they may perform actions to cause a system to revert to a weakened state. Though Microsoft aimed to stop the cat-and-mouse game between attackers and defenders by modifying its predictable "Patch Tuesday" release model, attackers nevertheless pay close attention to disclosure announcements on a continual basis to maximize the vulnerability window.

Often attackers will attempt to take advantage of default accounts and settings in the hopes that administrators have not changed them. Security misconfigurations like this can exist at any level—from a factory password left on a wireless access point to static credentials left on enterprise devices. In some cases, despite a security team's best effort, these credentials may not be able to be changed. An example of this last condition is described in an advisory issued by Cisco in 2019 and covered in CVE-2019-1723. There was a flaw in a previous version of the Cisco Common Service Platform Collector (CSPC), a tool used for gathering information from Cisco devices on a network, that allowed anyone to access and control the tool using a static default password.

Downgrade Attack
Some kind of attacks, such as a downgrade attack, attempt to take advantage of the backward-compatibility features offered by certain services by causing them to operate in a mode that offers lower levels of security. One common example of a downgrade attack occurs when an attacker redirects a visitor from an HTTPS version of a website to an HTTP version. When this occurs, a user loses all of the benefit of strong encryption between the client and server. Downgrade attacks are often used to enable MITM attacks, in which the switch to a lower version of crypto enables an attacker to eavesdrop on communications. One such vulnerability existed in a previous version of the popular OpenSSL service that could allow for an attacker to negotiate a lower version of TLS between the client and server.

Use of Insecure Functions

Even with a major focus on secure coding practices across the development industry, the use of insecure and dangerous functions is still a common occurrence. This vulnerability occurs when a function is invoked by a program that introduces a weakness into a system based on its implementation or inherent qualities. These functions may be used to perform the job they were designed for, but at greater risk to the organization employing them. Sometimes, the function can never be guaranteed to be used safely. This is the case with **gets()**, an inherently unsafe C function that operates by blindly copying all input from STDIN to the buffer without checking size. This is problematic because it may enable the user, intentionally or unwittingly, to provide input that is larger than the buffer size, resulting in an overflow condition.

strcpy

The **strcpy()** function simply copies memory contents into the buffer, ignoring the size of the area allocated to the buffer. This attribute can easily be misused in a manner that could enable an attacker to cause a buffer overflow. A short example of how this may occur is shown here:

```
char str1[10];
char str2[]="AStringThatIsClearlyTooMuchForTheBuffer";
strcpy(str1,str2);
```

Although there are some alternatives to some of these functions advertised as safe, those functions may themselves be vulnerable to other types of attacks. The **strncpy()** function, for example, is said to be a safer version of **strcpy()** because it enables a maximum size to be specified. However, the **strncpy()** function doesn't null-terminate the destination if the buffer is completely filled, which may lead to stability problems in code. As a security analyst, it's important that you not take alternative recommendations for granted. Doing so can give you a false sense of security and may introduce additional vulnerabilities.

End-of-Life or Outdated Components

End-of-life or outdated components are a significant security risk to applications. When software components are no longer supported by the vendor or have not been updated with security patches, they can leave web applications vulnerable to known exploits and attacks. In many cases, attackers will target known vulnerabilities in outdated components in order to gain access to sensitive data or execute malicious code on the server.

One of the key steps to mitigating the risk of end-of-life or outdated components is to maintain an accurate and up-to-date software bill of materials (SBOM). An SBOM is a detailed inventory of all the software components and libraries used in a web application, including their version numbers and dependencies. By maintaining an accurate SBOM, developers can quickly identify which components are outdated or have reached their end of life and then prioritize updates accordingly.

Software composition analysis (SCA) tools can also help identify outdated or vulnerable components. SCA tools automate the process of identifying and tracking software components and their dependencies, providing developers with real-time information about potential vulnerabilities or issues.

In addition to maintaining an accurate SBOM and using SCA tools, developers should also stay up to date on the latest security vulnerabilities and patches for the components they use. They should regularly monitor vendor websites and security advisories for updates and prioritize updates for critical components.

Chapter Review

The chapter has provided an overview of some of the most common and critical security risks facing applications today, as well as some of the most common mitigation and prevention techniques. It is important to note that this is not an exhaustive list because new vulnerabilities and attack techniques are constantly being discovered. As such, developers and security practitioners should stay up to date on the latest security best practices and trends and continue to incorporate new techniques and technologies into their processes.

To that end, a wealth of resources is available to developers looking to improve the security of their applications. In addition to the OWASP Top 10 and other OWASP resources, organizations such as the National Institute of Standards and Technology (NIST) and the SANS Institute offer guidance and best practices for securing applications. In addition, numerous commercial tools and services are available for security testing, including static application security testing (SAST), dynamic application security testing (DAST), software composition analysis (SCA), and runtime application self-protection (RASP). By leveraging these resources and staying current on emerging threats and best practices, we can help ensure that our applications remain secure and resilient in the face of evolving threats.

Questions

1. What kind of attack takes advantage of compatibility functionality provided by a program or protocol to force a user into operating in a less secure mode?

   A. Downgrade attack

   B. Side-channel attack

   C. Passthrough attack

   D. Hijacking

2. Attacks that rely on an interpreter to evaluate untrusted input and execute tasks on an attacker's behalf are known by what name?

   A. Injection attacks

   B. Authentication attacks

   C. Exhaustion attacks

   D. Overflow attacks

3. What is the primary difference between a memory heap and memory stack?

   A. The stack allows for memory reservations beyond the limits of the buffer, while the heap does not.

   B. The stack is a structured, statically allocated memory space, while the heap space is not reserved in advance.

   C. The heap allows for memory reservations beyond the limits of the buffer, while the stack does not.

   D. The heap is a structured, statically allocated memory space, while the stack space is not reserved in advance.

4. Software that checks the status of a resource before using it, but allows a change between initial check and final usage, suffers from what kind of vulnerability?

   A. Buffer overflow

   B. Race condition

   C. Injection

   D. Derefencing

Use the following scenario to answer Questions 5–8:

Your security team is made aware of a massive data breach of a popular social media platform. According to analysts of the breach, the records include details such as credit card information, e-mail addresses, language preference, and passwords. Although there is no connection between the social media platform and your organization, you are concerned about the security implications to your company given the popularity of the platform.

5. You are aware that password reuse is a common occurrence and urge the team to issue a mandatory password reset for all users in hopes of preventing which kind of attack?

   A. Session hijacking

   B. Downgrade attack

   C. Password spraying

   D. Credential stuffing

6. Your security dashboard sends an alert indicating that in the last hour, the same user had several unsuccessful login attempts across eight internal systems. What type of attack has most likely occurred?

   A. Session hijacking

   B. Man-in-the-middle attack

   C. Password spraying

   D. Firehose attack

7. Security analysts investigating the breach have now indicated that attackers were able to target their attack to a specific system based on information recovered from an exception that was raised during their reconnaissance. Based on this information, what type of vulnerability did the attacks likely take advantage of?

   A. Improper error handling

   B. Insecure object reference

   C. Use of insecure functions

   D. Use of default configurations

8. The information recovered from the previously identified reconnaissance effort indicated the use of a public-facing security device known to have a static password in previous versions of its firmware. Analysts discovered that the firmware was never upgraded, and static credentials were used to get into the device. What flaw is likely to have been exploited?

A. Improper error handling

B. Insecure object reference

C. Use of insecure functions

D. Use of default configurations

Answers

1. **A.** Downgrade attacks are characterized by techniques that cause services to operate in a mode that offers lower levels of security, such as HTTP instead of HTTPS.

2. **A.** In injection attacks, attackers execute undesirable operations by submitting untrusted input into an interpreter that is then evaluated.

3. **B.** The stack is a type of reserved, sequential memory space that operates on the principle of last in, first out, while the heap is an unstructured body of memory that the computer may use as needed.

4. **B.** A race condition vulnerability is a flaw in the operation of a program that may allow two actions to attempt completion at the same time or for the actions to be performed out of order, resulting in integrity or stability issues.

5. **D.** Credential stuffing is a type of brute-force attack where credentials obtained from a data breach of one service are used to authenticate to another system.

6. **C.** Password spraying is a type of brute-force technique in which an attacker tries a single password against a system and then iterates though multiple systems on a network using the same password.

7. **A.** Improper error handling is a vulnerability that allows for too much information to be disclosed about an exception to outside users.

8. **D.** Default configurations exist at many levels, from standard factory passwords to static credentials on enterprise devices. Attackers will take advantage of these settings to get around other security mechanisms.

Vulnerability Handling and Response

In this chapter you will learn:
- The types and functions of security controls
- Patching and configuration management
- Risk management essentials
- Policies and governance
- Managing the attack surface
- Secure coding best practices and the secure development lifecycle

Security is always going to be a cat and mouse game because there'll be people out there that are hunting for the zero day award, you have people that don't have configuration management, don't have vulnerability management, don't have patch management.

—Kevin Mitnick

Vulnerability management is about much more than simply scanning systems since that is the method people think of most in terms of collecting information on vulnerabilities. However, not all vulnerabilities are system-related or even technical. Vulnerabilities can also be tied to the organizational level, including overall security program management, as well as the business process level. Additionally, it's not simply a matter of collecting vulnerability data, as you do during scanning, but also what you do with that data. The vulnerability management program should answer questions such as how you prioritize vulnerabilities for remediation and what do you do when you can't immediately address a vulnerability.

In this chapter we will discuss several topics critical to vulnerability management beyond scanning. Although some of these topics may seem unrelated, you'll find that when you are deep into managing system and organizational vulnerabilities, as well as overall risk, all these different topics will come together and are a part of vulnerability management. First, we're going to talk about governance, including policies that drive how we manage vulnerabilities. Then we will discuss security controls, including their type and function. We're also going to talk about patching, configuration management, system maintenance, and exceptions to policy, since these are some of the major ways we manage vulnerabilities, both on a strategic and day-to-day basis. Since vulnerability management is a subset of overall risk management, we will discuss foundational concepts of risk management, including the four methods organizations traditionally use to deal with risk. As a significant portion of vulnerabilities come from faulty software applications, we will also discuss secure coding best practices and methodologies, including the need for a secure software development lifecycle.

Finally, we will end the chapter with a discussion on the vulnerability management reporting and communication processes. We'll discuss the different considerations in communicating with various stakeholders and exactly what should be communicated to whom about the overall vulnerability management processes in the organization.

Note that this chapter addresses two separate exam objectives related to vulnerability management: Objective 2.5, "Explain concepts related to vulnerability response, handling, and management," and Objective 4.1, "Explain the importance of vulnerability management reporting and communication."

Vulnerability Management Governance and Policy

We have discussed governance throughout this book and will continue to do so. However, in the context of this chapter, we should discuss governance in terms of how it directs vulnerability management. Both external governance, in terms of laws and regulations, and internal governance, in the form of organizational policies and requirements, direct that vulnerabilities must be managed properly.

External governance and standards often require that a vulnerability management program be put into place. For instance, requirements 11.3.1 and 11.3.2 of the PCI DSS require quarterly vulnerability scans, and the HIPAA Security Rule (45 CFR §164.308(a) (1)(ii)(A) states that organizations must "conduct an accurate and thorough assessment of the potential risks and vulnerabilities to the confidentiality, integrity, and availability of electronic protected health information held by the covered entity." The Security rule also further states that organizations must "implement security measures sufficient to reduce risks and vulnerabilities to a reasonable and appropriate level" (Risk Management, 45CFR §163.308(a)(1)(ii)(B)).

Vulnerabilities must be discovered; they must be prioritized, and mitigated, according to an established, documented strategy and process. This is why it's critical to have a formalized, vulnerability management strategy, policy, and plan that dictate the requirement to manage vulnerabilities, the time frames in which they will be managed and prioritized, related roles and responsibilities, and the process itself.

 NOTE An effective vulnerability management process starts with appropriate strategy, policy, and procedures that are the foundation of the process.

Control Types and Functions

Security controls are the building blocks of protecting information and systems. Controls are essentially detailed security measures, implemented to address information protection requirements, mitigate vulnerabilities, reduce the likelihood of threats exploiting vulnerabilities, and reduce the impact to a system if a negative event does occur.

General examples of security controls include firewall configuration rules, the use of encryption algorithms, strong identification and authentication methods, policy elements, security fences around a facility, and so on. Anything that can be used to protect an asset could be considered a security control. Security controls can be extremely detailed or they can be overarching and general.

During this first part of the chapter we're going to discuss security controls in depth. We're going to talk about the different types of controls—in other words, how they are categorized—and then discuss their functions. It's important to note that there is no standardized definition for the types and functions of security controls within the security community. Depending on which book you read, which expert you listen to, and certainly which certification exam you are studying for, they may be categorized and referred to differently. Here in this book, to meet the current objectives of the CySA+ exam, we will refer to them as the exam does; however, we will also describe them, when appropriate, in general terms that you should be aware of since you will likely encounter these terms throughout your security career. First, we will discuss the three general types of controls—managerial, operational, and technical—as they are referred to by the CompTIA CySA+ exam objectives.

Managerial

Managerial controls, also referred to elsewhere as *administrative* controls, are the controls that are developed and implemented as part of the overall security management process. Many people refer to these as the "paper" or "soft" controls. They include policy and procedures, documentation, security training, personnel controls, and so on. For the most part, these controls do not directly interact with technical aspects of systems or facilities. However, for every managerial or administrative control, there is typically a corresponding technical, operational, and/or physical control. These controls typically dictate requirements about what should happen in terms of implementing a security control or how a system or information should be protected. Prime examples of managerial controls include the following:

- Account management policies
- Media and equipment use policies
- Acceptable use policies
- Incident response plans and procedures
- Security awareness and training
- Business continuity and disaster recovery plans

 NOTE Control types usually have corresponding controls between them. For instance, a policy that dictates that a sensitive system must be protected is a managerial control and will often have related or supporting technical and operational controls. The policy dictates the requirements, and the technical or operational control is implemented to carry out the policy through technical or physical means.

Technical

Technical controls (also frequently called *logical* controls) are the easiest type of controls for most cybersecurity professionals to understand. These are easily identifiable as controls that relate to the configuration and implementation of security devices and methods. As examples, firewalls, screening routers, web application firewalls, proxies, and so on are technical controls. So are encryption algorithms, strong identification and authentication methods, and authorization processes, including the assignment of rights, permissions, and privileges to individuals. Technical controls must be planned, implemented, configured, and monitored to ensure that they are constantly functioning properly. This is where configuration management, vulnerability scanning, patching, and so on come into play.

Operational

Traditionally, physical and operational controls were considered related but separate. Operational controls were typically thought to be more related to the integration of business processes and security functions and were considered as their own categorization or type, or even sometimes a subset of physical and environmental controls. However, there has been a movement in recent years, reflected by the updated CompTIA CySA+ exam objectives, to consider these types of controls as one. Physical controls encompass the elements of protecting facilities, equipment, people, and so on. Obvious examples of physical controls would be gates, fences, entry control points, guards, video surveillance, physical intrusion detection and alarm systems, temperature and humidity controls, and so on.

Operational controls can also encompass physical controls. In fact, operational controls can also encompass the other control types, such as managerial and technical. These relate to the actual processes in place to ensure that business and security functions are carried out. Operational controls can also be more overarching. For instance, an operational control may include elements of ensuring a critical business process is functioning while at the same time ensuring that it is secure. The operational control could be a process or set of procedures, for instance, that dictate how sensitive data is transferred from one business process application to another or to an outside entity such as a business partner. Faulty operational controls could result in unintended access to data or systems by unauthorized individuals.

 EXAM TIP   For the CySA+ exam, you should consider operational controls as a separate type, distinguished from managerial and technical controls. For the exam, operational controls also include physical and environmental controls. However, in the real world, these distinctions between physical and operational controls are often blurred, and you will almost always see the terms administrative, technical, and physical controls.

Control Functions

Under these broad categories of control types, we also have control *functions*. Control functions describe what a control actually does in terms of protecting information and systems. Some controls are proactive, meaning that they are put in place and work before an incident happens, in order to prevent or deter a negative event or malicious behavior. Other controls are reactive in nature, meaning that although we can plan for them and put them in place, they typically take effect only after an incident has taken place. Note that several of the control functions we will discuss tend to overlap. A security control could be considered both deterrent and detective, as is the case for video surveillance, for instance. We'll describe the proactive controls first: preventative and deterrent. It's important that you understand the difference between these two control functions as well.

Preventative

A preventative control does exactly what it sounds like it should: it prevents incidents, malicious behavior, and other negative things from happening to information systems, data, facilities, and so on. An acceptable use policy could be put into place warning users of what behavior is acceptable on the infrastructure and what is not. This is a preventative control because it seeks to ensure that users don't perform prohibited or malicious acts. Note that a preventative control does not have to be known to a user for it to be effective. For example, a firewall rule put into place to prevent users from communicating with a malicious IP address does not have to be known by that user in order for it to be effective. The firewall rule will still function whether the user knows about it or not. Contrast this to deterrent controls, which we will discuss next.

Deterrent

A deterrent control is also considered a preventive control, in that it seeks to prevent an incident from happening, typically by warning a user that the act is not allowed. When a deterrent control warns a user that an act is not allowed, it relies on the user making the determination that the negative consequences of performing an action outweigh the benefits of performing it. The key difference between a preventative control and a deterrent control is that for a deterrent control to be effective, the user or other entity must be *aware* of the control. If they're not aware of a deterrent control, it is ineffective in deterring them from performing a malicious act.

A policy is typically a deterrent control, since the policy should be known by all users and should specifically state what is allowed or not allowed in terms of actions. If the policy, a managerial control, states what the consequences will be from performing those prohibited actions, this should make the user think twice about those behaviors, since it will result in negative consequences. An example of a technical deterrent control would be a warning banner that is displayed to the user when they attempt to log in to a system, which also warns of prohibited actions and consequences. Yet another example would be the physical video surveillance cameras mentioned previously. Cameras that are visible and placed in the hall outside of a restricted processing area should deter individuals from the malicious act of attempting to break into the secure area, since they know they are being watched and recorded. They may, however, choose to ignore those facts and attempt malicious behavior anyway. In other words, deterrent controls are only effective if the person determines that the negative consequences outweigh the rewards of committing a malicious or prohibited act. Note that as mentioned earlier, in this case, video surveillance also serves as a detective control since it can also detect and record actions. We'll discuss detective controls next.

EXAM TIP Deterrent controls are not mentioned in the current CompTIA exam objectives; however, you should still understand the difference between them and preventative controls. Preventive controls work regardless of whether an individual is aware of them. Deterrent controls are simply preventive controls that must be known to an individual for them to be effective.

Detective

Detective controls also perform the functions you would think simply because of their function name. They are reactive controls, in that detective controls won't detect an action or event until it has already happened. However, they must be proactively put in place and configured properly to detect an event when it does occur. The most common example of detective controls is audit logs. If event logging is configured properly, then any action the user takes on a system or within a facility would be detected and logged. Auditing comes into play when the logged event is of sufficient importance to automatically notify someone or when someone is reviewing the logs specifically to look for unusual or malicious activities. Another example of a detective control is the aforementioned surveillance cameras. The surveillance cameras, regardless of whether they are visible and deterrent to the malicious actor, are detective in nature since they can detect an incident and record it for later review. This is an example of how controls can overlap different functions and fulfill more than one function at a time. Other examples of detective controls include motion sensors, network intrusion prevention/detection systems, and physical intrusion detection systems and alarms.

Responsive

Immediately following detective controls in logical order are responsive controls. Responsive controls can span all three of the major control types: managerial, technical, and operational. Responsive controls relate to what the organization will do upon detecting an incident or after a negative event happens, such as a natural disaster. Incident response processes and procedures are responsive controls. Restoring systems from backups, reconstituting systems, personnel evacuations, and business continuity operations are all considered responsive controls and could be very detailed down to the technical level, such as rebuilding a critical server, or include an overarching program or process, such as disaster recovery. Responsive controls can also include compensating and corrective controls, discussed next.

EXAM TIP Some texts and security professionals may refer to responsive controls as recovery controls, but for the purposes of the CySA+ exam objectives, you should remember them as responsive controls.

Compensating Control

Two key control functions that we should discuss in detail are compensating and corrective controls, since these terms are often confused and interchanged for each other. On the surface, they both seem to accomplish the same result.

A compensating control is put into place when the primary or more desirable control is not feasible or available. For instance, if it is infeasible to place video surveillance cameras completely around the perimeter of an organization, due to the environment, terrain, or regulatory restrictions, a compensating control might be to schedule regular guard patrols around a particular vulnerable or sensitive area of the perimeter. There would not necessarily be full 24-hour surveillance, but at least a guard patrol could monitor the area once per hour. That would be a compensating control that may have to be in place for a longer period of time, until video surveillance cameras can be placed in the area.

Another example might be where there are legacy systems on the network, such as Windows 7 hosts, that are no longer supported. The desired solution, of course, would be to pull those machines off the network and replace them with a much more current version of the operating system. However, there may be considerations such as interoperability and compatibility with legacy applications that may prevent this. Therefore, compensating controls may have to be implemented so that those systems are better protected, such as segmenting them on their own protected VLAN, encrypting all traffic between the legacy systems and other hosts, and allowing only specific users, hosts, or applications to communicate with those machines. That would be a longer-term compensating control until those machines can be removed from the infrastructure. Contrast this with corrective controls, which we will describe next.

Corrective

A corrective control is a temporary control that is quickly put in place to take care of an immediate security problem or issue. It is not designed to be implemented over the long term. You might implement a corrective control immediately after an incident to either stop the incident from occurring or prevent the loss of data or systems. Immediately after the incident is over, you should implement a longer-term solution for the corrective control, making it either a primary control or compensating control. For example, if your facility is struck by a natural disaster, such as a tornado, and a piece of secure perimeter fencing is torn away, it might take a week for the fencing company to come out and fix the hole in the fence. Rather than leave the hole open for anyone to walk through, you might have to implement a corrective control, such as stationing a guard there temporarily until the fence can be repaired. Stationing a guard by the hole in the fence is not a long-term solution, since it would be expensive and reduces the guard's availability for other critical areas, but it's something that is a quick fix to take care of an immediate security problem.

 EXAM TIP You should remember the difference between compensating and corrective controls. Compensating controls are longer term and typically put into place strategically when a primary or more desired control is not available. A corrective control is temporary in nature and usually only used to immediately correct a security issue.

Patching and Configuration Management

Two of the key ways we deal with vulnerabilities are to apply vendor-produced or vendor-approved patches or updates and to make changes to the functional or security configuration of a system. Patches normally are produced and released on a routine basis by the vendor of an operating system, application, or even a device. Although these patches are normally released on a routine basis, vulnerabilities that are discovered to be serious and could cause severe damage to a system or information may warrant a patch to be released outside of the normal release cycle and may require serious attention from cybersecurity analysts and managers. Configuration changes can be as simple as updating files, or they can require more significant changes, such as to the Windows registry, operating system, application configuration files, and so on. In any event, these two key processes are the major ones we use to manage vulnerabilities; therefore, they must be planned and managed carefully.

Testing

Testing is a critical part of patch and configuration management. Any changes implemented on a system, whether they are the result of routine or critical patches or configuration changes, should be tested prior to implementing them on production systems. This is because, even with the best of security intentions, patches and configuration changes could have detrimental effects on the functionality of a host and its applications. It's best to test changes in an environment that closely replicates the production environment. This way, you can see how the patches and configuration changes will interact with not only the host operating system and applications but also the overall functionality of the device involved. Many security changes have had to be reversed upon discovery that they reduced or completely eliminated functionality to the point where the business could not carry out critical activities. When patches and configuration changes have been adequately tested, and any issues resolved, then they can be safely implemented on the production system. Procedures will be in place to help mitigate any unforeseen issues.

Implementation

After testing, cybersecurity and IT personnel should implement patches and configuration changes according to their priority, as well as according to the criticality of the assets. This could be on a routine schedule or during emergency maintenance windows that are pre-programmed into the schedule for specific times. For instance, patches could be implemented at 2 A.M. on a Saturday morning, when normal business hours are slow and users do not depend on those resources. Additionally, prior to any patches or configuration changes being implemented on the system, a backup should be performed so that, in the event that something goes wrong, the system can be quickly restored to its unaltered state. This should also be part of the patch and configuration management plans.

Rollback

Assuming you have properly tested patches and configuration changes in a test environment, unforeseen issues should not occur when implementing the change in production. However, not everything can be predicted, and even if changes that have been installed on test systems show that there are no significant issues, there are always unpredictable events, even if they are minor, that could occur. It may sometimes be necessary to reverse or roll back changes that have been made to a system. This is the reason why we mentioned the need to back up a system in the previous section before implementing patches and configuration changes. Backups could range from a full system backup—which is likely the most desirable but may take the longest to restore—to small, targeted backups.

For instance, in Windows, you could perform a system state backup that saves only critical files changed before the installation of a patch or configuration change. You could also back up select parts of the operating system, such as the registry. User files could be backed up if necessary and restored. In today's environments that use cloud and virtualization technology, snapshots of entire systems can be both taken and restored quickly. Given the widespread use of these technologies, there's really no good reason not to back up systems to some degree to ensure recoverability in the event something goes wrong after a patch or configuration change.

If a rollback becomes necessary, this may involve uninstalling the patch or changing the configuration back to its previous state. This is why documentation during a change is very important, so that everyone will understand exactly what was changed, down to the individual registry key and value, process, or file version. This will make rolling back a change and restoring the system to a previous unaltered state much easier.

Validation

Assuming that a patch or configuration change works properly, and no security or functional issues arise, there should be no need for a rollback. Once it has been established that the system is functioning properly, you should validate the security patch update or configuration change. Validation means checking to see if the issue that needed a patch or change in the first place has been resolved or mitigated. You can do this a couple of different ways. First, you could scan the system again, using a vulnerability scanner to show that the vulnerability has been remediated and no longer shows up in the scan results. You could also review logs on the system to ensure that the system has booted properly and is accessing the network as it should. You could also put a sniffer on the network to capture traffic coming from the host to make sure that it looks normal and is within network traffic baselines. In any case, validating a patch or configuration change is important to ensuring that the vulnerability has been remediated and the issue is no longer a problem.

Maintenance Windows

A maintenance window is a scheduled time the system is taken offline or out of use so that patches or configuration changes can be made. Unless there is a serious emergency or critical patch that must be applied immediately, which may be the case during an actual attack, most patches, even for zero-day exploits, should wait until a scheduled maintenance window. This is a time when the system is not in heavy use, can be taken offline and worked on, and then restored to operation according to standardized procedures. There may be standard maintenance windows that are pre-programmed into the schedule, such as, again, 2 A.M. on a Saturday night, when there is no significant processing load and users do not require the use of the resource. This may be sufficient for routine patches and configuration changes as well as hardware or software upgrades.

However, there may also be critical or emergency maintenance windows built in to the schedule, even if they are not routinely used. For example, if a zero-day exploit comes out on a Wednesday, you may not wish to wait until the Saturday 2 A.M. routine maintenance window to fix the problem. It may be better to try for an emergency maintenance window that occurs at 11:00 P.M. the same night. For these emergency maintenance windows, you may need to let users know that you are taking the resource offline, how long the maintenance will take, and if there will be any issues with resource access. Note that sometimes informing users is not enough; sometimes critical processing must make use of the resource and will have to be delayed or rescheduled. If this is not possible, you may have to figure out a way to make the changes on one resource while users are able to use an alternate resource, such as what may occur in a load-balancing or clustered environment. In any case, maintenance windows are critical in the vulnerability management process since this is when patches and configuration changes are normally applied.

Exceptions

Security policies, procedures, and processes are not absolute. If they were, there would be no need to even manage vulnerabilities. However, since they are not absolute, you must consider the exceptions that happen. One critical part of the vulnerability management process is how exceptions are managed. Exceptions occur when a vulnerability cannot be mitigated, normally for reasons relating to resources (insufficient money, time, equipment, and such), system criticality, information sensitivity, and so on. Possibly there is not enough money to buy a required security device, or people do not have the expertise to implement the mitigation. Perhaps a needed patch will take down functionality to an unacceptable level, such that the business cannot maintain its critical processes. For whatever reason, exceptions do exist, and they must be considered.

Security policies and procedures should have exception management built in to them. This means that they should define the parameters of what is considered an exception by the organization and what the process will be to deal with it. For instance, the organization may not allow any exceptions for zero-day exploits or critical patches but may allow exceptions for routine patches that don't significantly affect system risk.

Once a range of exceptions is identified, it's important to know how to deal with them. For instance, if a patch cannot be installed on the system because it will break functionality within an application that is critical to business processes, you must consider if other mitigations can be implemented to reduce the risk due to the vulnerability that cannot be patched. This may mean implementing other security controls, such as the compensating controls we discussed previously. Compensating controls in this example could be encrypting specific traffic to or from the host, allowing only specific hosts to communicate with the vulnerable system, upgrading the operating system if possible, or even upgrading the application to a higher version. These last two may be drastic steps and require planning and resource allocation but may be necessary in the long term.

That leads us to discuss how long exceptions should be maintained. All exceptions should be documented, and even known exceptions that have been accepted by management should not last forever. There should be an active plan on how to deal with the exception and eventually bring the vulnerable system or application back to a secure baseline state. An exception may be allowed for one week, six months, or even a year, depending on how serious the exception raises risk to the system and the environment as well as how difficult it will be to implement the mitigation that will correct the issue. In any event, exceptions should be carefully considered, and there should be a standard process for identifying them, approving them, and eventually mitigating them.

Prioritization and Escalation

Both prioritization and escalation were discussed in Chapter 9, although in a different context. We discussed both of these concepts in the context of scheduling and prioritizing scanning activities, but as you will see, mitigation activities after scanning are equally as important. We won't belabor the point here, but, as we said then, you must prioritize vulnerabilities for remediation since you likely cannot remediate all vulnerabilities at once and apply the same level of resources (labor hours, time, money, etc.) to each. Prioritization means that you should consider managing vulnerabilities based on two criteria.

The first is the severity of the vulnerability. The most severe vulnerabilities (the ones that will cause catastrophic issues) and zero-day exploits (the ones for which there is no known patch or remediation) must be dealt with at the highest priority. This means they must be scheduled as quickly as possible, and resources must be devoted to them, such as labor hours, expenditures for software and equipment, and so on. Criticality is the other issue, and this relates directly to the criticality of the systems that are vulnerable. Some of these systems may be required to function on a 24/7 basis, and it would be very difficult to take them down for any length of time to remediate.

There must be a balance between these two factors of criticality and severity, however. Even for critical assets, you must be able to have the downtime to remediate severe or zero-day vulnerabilities. If vulnerabilities are considered non-severe or routine, this may not be such a concern. The maintenance windows we described earlier in the chapter are the perfect time to remediate vulnerabilities and must be built in to your vulnerability management plan.

Escalation is another issue we briefly mentioned in Chapter 9. Escalation means that sometimes a vulnerability is very severe or affects a critical asset, but the IT team can't necessarily make the decision on how, if, or when to remediate the vulnerability based on those two factors. Sometimes more resources are required, which likely requires management approval. Sometimes critical systems must be taken down, and users will be denied their functionality, which also must be a management decision. Escalating these issues to management doesn't necessarily relieve the IT personnel of their responsibilities in managing and fixing the issues, but it does expand out the level of decision-making to people who are both responsible and accountable for the decision.

Risk Management Principles

We could write entire books of information about risk management, and indeed there are many books devoted to the subject. However, for the purposes of the exam and your career as a cybersecurity analyst, you should at least be familiar with risk management foundations, which we will discuss here. This material will not make you an expert on risk management, but it will give you the foundational information you need to be able to understand risk and how to respond to it at a high level. First, we will discuss the elements of risk and then about gathering information and examining it during risk assessment and analysis. Then we will talk about the four traditional ways that organizations deal with risk.

Elements of Risk

No matter which risk theory or methodology for managing risk you subscribe to, there are some foundational concepts that are common to all risk management methodologies. One of these foundational concepts is the elements that make up risk, which we'll briefly describe here.

Threats

We discussed threats in depth in Chapters 7 and 8, but we will briefly mention them here as well, in the context that threats are one of the key factors that contribute to risk. Threats are negative events that exploit weaknesses in assets to create an impact to those assets. While vulnerabilities can be mitigated, and to some degree eliminated from a system, threats are usually outside the control of the organization and cannot be eliminated or reduced. The only thing you can do with a threat is defend against it. If the vulnerability the threat would exploit has been reduced or eliminated, the threat is unlikely to manifest itself. That is, of course, a simplistic view, since there are usually multiple threats that can exploit multiple vulnerabilities, lending to the complexity of the relationships between threat and vulnerabilities. Note that the threat actor or the source that initiates a threat is normally not considered an element of risk, and it also cannot be controlled by the organization.

Vulnerabilities

Since we are discussing vulnerability management in this chapter, we won't go too much in depth on what a vulnerability is. But for the sake of completeness, a vulnerability is a weakness inherent to an asset. Vulnerabilities can be found in systems, business processes, or even in the organization itself. In addition to being an inherent weakness, a vulnerability could also be considered the lack of security protections for an asset. An example of a weakness inherent in assets would be if a system has a weak encryption algorithm that has been known to be compromised or faulty code in an application that offers a backdoor into the system. An example of the lack of security protections that cause a weakness would be the lack of a strong identification and authentication mechanism, or the lack of a policy or procedure that dictates how security should be implemented. In either case, the vulnerability creates a situation such that a threat could take advantage of that weakness and cause harm to the asset or the organization.

Likelihood

While threats and vulnerabilities are contributing factors to risk, risk is really a measurable product of two other factors: likelihood and impact. Likelihood is the probability, from a range of zero to extremely high, that a given vulnerability will be exploited by a given threat, and that the exploitation will cause measurable damage to the system or organization. Likelihood, as one of the two major components of risk, goes hand-in-hand with impact, which we will discuss next, as well as the relationship between the two.

Impact

Impact is the level of damage caused to an asset, such as a system or even the organization, if a threat exploits a vulnerability. If such an occurrence happens, then the likelihood automatically goes to 100 percent, since it is now past tense and the event has indeed occurred. However, even if such an event happens, how bad will the impact be? Sometimes threats exploit vulnerabilities that have very little impact on the system because there may be security controls in place that serve to lessen the impact. Likewise, there may be an extremely small likelihood of a specific threat exercising a given vulnerability, but if that were to happen, there would be a significant impact. This means that the overall view of risk considers both likelihood and impact. There is a proportional relationship that risk has to both likelihood and impact factors, both separately and together, as detailed next:

- The higher the likelihood of a negative event occurring, the higher the risk will be.
- The higher the impact to an asset if a negative event occurs, the higher the risk will be.
- Raising *both* the likelihood of an event and the impact, should that event occur, significantly raises risk.
- Lowering *either* the likelihood or the impact also lowers the risk.
- Lowering *both* the likelihood of an event and the impact, should that event occur, significantly lowers the risk.

Risk can be measured and expressed in various ways, but usually it boils down to two different methods: quantitative and qualitative. Quantitative usually means that risk is expressed in hard numbers that can be calculated through data. For example, the impact to an organization may be expressed in terms of revenue lost or the cost to replace an asset that has been damaged or destroyed during a negative event. Both of these impacts can be expressed in the numerical form of dollars. Expressing risk in terms of qualitative values is more subjective and may be subject to interpretation. Although not any less accurate than expressing risk through quantitative or numerical terms, qualitative risk is often expressed by such values as "very low," "low," "moderate," "high," and "very high" to describe levels of likelihood, impact, and overall risk. Table 13-1 shows the relationship between likelihood and impact to qualitatively measure risk.

As an example, a very low likelihood of an event occurring, coupled with a very high impact if the event did occur, would only yield a low risk. A moderate likelihood of an event occurring, on the other hand, coupled with a very high impact, would yield a high risk. Note that the highest risk possible using this method is if a highly likely event occurred that had a severe impact on the asset, resulting in a very high risk.

Likelihood	Impact				
	Very Low	**Low**	**Moderate**	**High**	**Very High**
Very High	Very Low	Low	Moderate	High	Very High
High	Very Low	Low	Moderate	High	Very High
Moderate	Very Low	Low	Moderate	Moderate	High
Low	Very Low	Low	Low	Low	Moderate
Very Low	Very Low	Very Low	Very Low	Low	Low

Table 13-1   Qualitative Relationship Between Likelihood and Impact to Measure Risk

EXAM TIP   On the exam, you may be presented with scenarios and questions that ask how you would prioritize a risk for remediation. In addition to looking at the severity of the risk, you should consider factors such as compensating controls, cost to remediate a risk, and so on.

Risk Assessment and Analysis

To determine risk, you must gather a lot of information. Risk assessment and analysis are separate but related processes and can be very complex and tedious in terms of gathering information and determining risk. Risk can be analyzed at the smallest level possible, such as at the level of a particular vulnerability affecting an operating system, or it can be examined at the overall system level, business process level, or even at the entire organizational level. Additionally, to complicate matters, risk can be aggregated. A very high level risk for a system, coupled with a moderate risk for a business process, may result in high level risk for the organization, depending on how the organization assesses and analyzes risk.

Risk assessment is the collection of data leading to the determination of risk. This determination is the analysis portion. Risk assessments collect data on all the possible threats as well as all the vulnerabilities in the system and the organization, combined with collecting data on the likelihood of each of these events happening and how they affect each of the vulnerabilities in context. This analysis also requires data about the asset itself, to see what the impact to the asset and the organization would be. Again, if this is expressed quantitatively, it could be in terms of money, labor hours lost, people needed, and so on.

There is no perfect way to analyze risk: quantitative risk analysis can also have subjective elements to it, and qualitative risk analysis sometimes has objective elements involved in that type of effort. Some elements are better expressed qualitatively, such as customer confidence, company reputation, and so on, and some are best expressed using numerical values (in other words, quantitatively). Typically, the organization will determine a hybrid of these methods that works best for its own purposes.

Risk Appetite and Tolerance

Once an organization has conducted a risk assessment and analysis, it must determine how to deal with risk. Some risks may be more than the organization is willing to take. This brings us to a discussion about two terms that measure just that. These are *risk appetite* and *risk tolerance*. Risk appetite is the overall attitude from management that describes how much risk the organization is willing to take. In some organizations, taking risks is part of their business. Think of investment companies, for example, since there is some risk in every investment the company may make. However, the *amount* of risk they are willing to take, past a certain point, is called its *risk appetite*. In general, companies can be risk averse, or they may be willing to take risks if the rewards are high enough. This is normally not measured in terms of dollars but in a general attitude or culture from management.

Another term you will hear is *risk tolerance*. This is not the same thing as risk appetite, but it is related. Whereas risk appetite is the overall level of risk an organization is willing to take in general, risk tolerance is normally seen at a smaller level. For a particular business venture or investment, for instance, there could be a monetary value assigned to the risk tolerance levels that the organization is willing to take for that particular venture. For example, the organization may have a limit of $5 million in risk for investment. Past that amount, it is not willing to accept the risk. That is its risk tolerance level for that particular venture. This may be aligned with, or even a deviation from, its normal risk appetite, depending on whether or not the organization feels this particular venture is worth it.

 EXAM TIP   Remember that risk appetite is more general and reflects the attitude of management toward risk. Risk tolerance is specific to a particular business venture or effort and may have a monetary limit attached to it. Risk tolerance may or may not be aligned with the organization's risk appetite, especially if the organization feels the rewards are worth a high risk effort.

Risk Response

Risk response is how an organization deals with, or responds to, risk. The risk response an organization takes toward a particular risk, or even risk in general, is typically aligned with factors such as the cost to reduce the risk as well as its levels of risk appetite and risk tolerance, among other factors. Risk responses must bring the organization below the thresholds of its risk appetite and tolerance levels; otherwise, they will not be effective or desirable. There are generally four traditional ways that an organization can deal with risk. Keep in mind that the response for one risk may be different from the response for another risk, and it is likely that an organization will use any one or even all four at different times.

Risk Mitigation

Risk mitigation, sometimes referred to as risk reduction, is generally the first method that an organization will use to manage risk. This involves trying to reduce the risk using security controls. Security controls should either reduce the likelihood of an event occurring or reduce the impact if the event does occur. Reducing either or both of these will, of course, reduce risk. Examples of risk mitigations include the ones typically seen in vulnerability management, such as patching, configuration management, routine maintenance, software and hardware upgrades, and so on.

Risk Transference

Sometimes the cost to mitigate or reduce risk is far more than the organization can afford. After it has mitigated or reduced as much risk as it can, it may choose to transfer or share risk. The typical example of risk transference is the use of insurance. For example, if an organization cannot reduce the risk of a natural disaster destroying its data center, it may try to mitigate the risks by ensuring that the facility is well constructed and that there is redundant power, proper safety equipment, and protocols in place, and so on. But this doesn't fully reduce the risk enough, so it may insure its facility against monetary losses (impact) and transfer some of that risk to the insurance company. That way, if the disaster does strike, the organization has done its due diligence and can still recoup some of its money to rebuild.

Another example is the use of outsourcing services to a third-party provider. For example, an organization may outsource its security services to a vendor. The vendor would be responsible for perimeter security and maintaining devices such as firewalls, proxy servers, and so on. The vendor may also provide security operations center (SOC) services, where it monitors logs and alerts personnel in the event of an attack. While this is certainly sharing the risk with a third party, keep in mind that ultimately even when risk is shared, responsibility and accountability remain with the organization, particularly when sensitive data is involved. While contractual obligations might require the outsourced security service provider to fulfill due diligence and care requirements in protecting data, if the data is ultimately lost due to a breach, the company that owns the data is still responsible and accountable.

 EXAM TIP Using methods to transfer some of its risk, such as purchasing insurance or outsourcing services to a third party, does not relieve an organization of its responsibilities and accountability in the event of an incident.

Risk Avoidance

The term *risk avoidance* is sometimes a misnomer. Many people incorrectly believe that this means that the organization will simply ignore the risk. It definitely does not mean that. It means that a company may decide that the risk of performing an activity or engaging in a particular business venture is too risky and simply avoid the activities that lead to risk. Think of a company that may, after research, determine that a product it wants to develop and sell is too risky; it may be cost prohibitive or violate environmental regulations, for example. It may simply decide to not develop and sell that product.

Risk Acceptance

The term *risk acceptance* can also be a misnomer. It's not a matter of simply accepting the risk and, again, ignoring it; it's a matter of implementing all the previously discussed responses until the risk levels are below the risk appetite and tolerance levels. The organization may not be able to reduce or mitigate the risk any further, there may be no more risk to transfer, and it may have no choice but to pursue the business venture that incurs the risk. At this point, it must accept the risk. It's important to note that the risk that the organization should accept is called *residual risk*, and it is the risk left over after all other risk responses have been implemented. It's also important to know that risk should only be accepted after it falls below the risk appetite and tolerance levels.

 EXAM TIP Understand the different risk responses required for the exam: risk mitigation seeks to reduce risk, risk transference attempts to reduce an element of risk, such as impact (which in turn reduces risk), risk avoidance means that an organization will avoid activities that incur excessive risk, and, finally, risk acceptance means that after all other responses have been tried or implemented, the organization must accept whatever risk is left that falls below its risk appetite and tolerance levels (residual risk).

Attack Surface Management

An *attack surface* is the sum of all possible attack vectors into a system, a process, or an organization. A system can have attack surfaces in the form of the operating system, applications, and even the hardware. Attack surfaces can also be inherent to the business processes of an organization, as well as its people, its facilities, and so on. Since the attack surfaces is the sum of all possible attack vectors an adversary could attempt, it must be minimized as much as possible. An attack surface is exposed to malicious entities through a variety of means, including both physically and logically.

Attack surface management is more than simply minimizing and reducing the attack surface exposure. It also includes continuously monitoring and checking the attack surface, testing it to determine what vulnerabilities exist there, and attempting to eliminate the possible attack vectors a threat could use to target those vulnerabilities. That's what we're going to discuss in the next few sections.

Edge and Passive Discovery

Edge discovery takes the point of view of testing outside of your infrastructure, just as an attacker might do during the early stages of discovering how your infrastructure is designed from a security perspective, including its specific flaws. This means that you should perform external testing as well as conduct open source reconnaissance on your network, and even the entire organization. Because this is one of the first steps an attacker will take, typically these discovery actions will not be active. In other words, they will not actively touch your systems; instead, they will simply gather as much information passively as they can without triggering any types of alerts or alarms.

Edge and passive discovery can yield a great deal of information for an attacker, including possible attack vectors from the outside of the infrastructure to the inside, and give the attacker information on the types of operating systems, applications, patch levels, security configurations, and such that they desperately need in order to wage an attack on your organization. Gathering information about the organization itself, such as its personnel, organizational structure, and so on, can also give an attacker valuable information on security processes and how security is managed within the organization.

Security Controls Testing

While we do not go into the different types of assessments and tests in this section, there are particular types of testing that serve specific purposes. As part of the overarching subject of assessing risk, there are many different types of tests, including security controls testing, vulnerability testing, penetration testing, and more.

Security controls testing is a routine type of test that should be accomplished on a regularly recurring basis. During this type of test, the actual security controls implemented and put in place to protect assets are assessed. They may be tested for different aspects of security. The first might be for compliance, since many compliance vehicles, such as external laws and regulations or internal policies, may require that a specific security control be implemented to protect sensitive or critical data.

The other aspect of security controls testing involves effectiveness. It's simply not enough to implement a required security control for the sake of compliance with governance. The control must also be effective in protecting the system from assessed threats. Implementing a control for the sake of compliance may or not be sufficient to protect an asset, since effectiveness focuses more on the depth of implementation and the details of how the control is actually implemented.

Testing security controls for both compliance and effectiveness is necessary to determine the level of protection that sensitive assets get. Note that sometimes there is no defined boundary between what constitutes a security controls test, a vulnerability assessment, and a penetration test. Frequently all three of these types of tests can overlap, and security controls can be tested during a vulnerability assessment or penetration test.

Penetration Testing and Adversary Emulation

As you've already learned, vulnerability testing is the process of scanning or assessing what weaknesses may lie in the system or the environment, including the organization, as well as discovering which security controls may be missing or ineffective in protecting assets. A vulnerability assessment, however, only generates information used to remediate vulnerabilities. It does not necessarily give you an accurate, in-depth review of which of those vulnerabilities could actually be exploited. In other words, it provides theoretical information on exploitation but not practical information.

Penetration testing goes one step further than vulnerability testing. Whereas vulnerability testing seeks to only discover vulnerabilities that may or may not be exploitable by a threat actor initiating a threat against the organization, penetration testing actually attempts to exploit those discovered vulnerabilities. This is the difference between what is theoretical and what is actual. A theoretical vulnerability from an assessment may never be exploited but should be treated as if it would. The problem with this is, you will never know exactly how many resources you need to put toward remediating a vulnerability because you don't know exactly how likely it may be to be exploited. You may be seeing vulnerabilities listed in a scanner that are considered severe, but in practicality, they would be very difficult to exploit (reducing likelihood), actually lowering that risk significantly. Penetration testing and adversary emulation can give you a much better idea of the actual exploitability of a vulnerability in the practical world. Following a penetration test, you should know exactly which vulnerabilities you should focus on in terms of committing resources and prioritization.

Penetration testing seeks not only to exercise vulnerabilities to determine which ones can be practically exploited but also tends to emulate an adversary's actions. The best penetration tests are the ones that are threat faithful; in other words, they use the identical tools, techniques, and tactics that a true malicious entity would use. There are different methodologies for conducting a penetration test. These include the classic blind and double-blind test methods. A blind test is where the attacker has no inside information on the network and can only get information through open sources, passive reconnaissance, and data collection. In a double-blind test, the defender has knowledge of the test, so the test also exercises the ability of the defenders to detect and respond to simulated attacks.

Bug Bounty

A bug bounty is an effective way of rapidly discovering vulnerabilities, using a sort of crowdsourcing method. Bug bounties are often established and publicized by vendors as a means of allowing the security community at large to actively look for, discover, and report security flaws in operating systems and applications. While many of these bug bounties offer prizes and cash rewards, most of the people who participate in them are simply doing it for the betterment of the system security and the profession, as well as to prove their credentials in security analysis. Many severe and zero-day vulnerabilities have been discovered through bug bounty programs. The key thing to note about bug bounties is that in order for them to be effective, the analysts that hunt for these flaws must be ethical in their discovery, confidentiality, and reporting. Very often security flaws are discovered by malicious actors who do not report these flaws to the vendor but instead publish them as zero-day vulnerabilities to the hacker communities.

Attack Surface Reduction

All of the tools and techniques we have discussed in this section are focused toward one goal: reducing the attack surface of a system or even the organization. This is where controls testing, vulnerability assessments, and penetration testing come into play. The purposes of these activities are to discover if security controls have been implemented properly and are functioning effectively, to discover vulnerabilities or flaws in systems, and to see if those security flaws are exploitable, respectively. Attack surface reduction also heavily depends on how well you know your own infrastructure, such that you are aware of where the weaknesses in your systems may be. If you are aware of all vulnerabilities within the attack surface, you can take steps to reduce the likelihood of the vulnerability being exploited, eliminate the vulnerability altogether, and/or reduce the impact to the asset if the vulnerability were to be exploited. Being intimately familiar with your systems and the environment in which they operate will significantly reduce their attack surfaces. Again, this is a constant, consistent effort since vulnerabilities may appear in the wild every day.

Secure Coding Best Practices

A good many vulnerabilities we see are those found in the operating system or the applications installed on the system. As we have seen, correcting these vulnerabilities typically involves updating them with patches or configuration changes. This is definitely a reactive method of dealing with vulnerabilities. Possibly a more proactive method, however, is to build systems and software without those vulnerabilities in the first place. Enter secure software development methodologies and coding practices.

As a bit of historical context, perhaps the most important concept behind software development is that of *quality,* can be defined as fitness for purpose—in other words, how good something is at whatever it is meant to do. A quality car will be good for transportation. We don't have to worry about it breaking down or failing to protect its occupants in a crash or being easy for a thief to steal. When we need to go somewhere, we simply get in the car and count on it safely taking us to wherever we need to go. Similarly, we don't have to worry about quality software crashing, corrupting our data under unforeseen circumstances, or being easy for someone to subvert. Sadly, many developers still think of functionality first (or only) when thinking about quality. When we look at things holistically, we should see that both functionality and security are important concepts in developing quality software.

This, of course, is not a new problem. Secure software development has been a challenge for a few decades. Unsurprisingly, there is an established body of best practices to minimize the flaws and vulnerabilities in our code. You should be familiar with what some of the best-known advocates for secure coding recommend.

Input Validation

If there is one universal rule to developing secure software, it is this: don't *ever* trust any input entered by a user. This is not just an issue of protecting our systems against malicious attackers; it is equally applicable to innocent user errors. The best approach to validating inputs is to perform context-sensitive allow-listing. In other words, consider what is supposed to be happening within the software system at the specific points in which the input is elicited from the user and then allow only the values that are appropriate. For example, if you are getting a credit card number from a user, you would allow only 16 consecutive numeric characters to be entered. Anything else would be disallowed.

Perhaps one of the most well-known examples of adversarial exploitation of improper user input validation is Structured Query Language (SQL) injection, or *SQLi.* SQL is a language originally developed by IBM to query information in a database management system (DBMS). Because user credentials for web applications are commonly stored in a DBMS, many web apps will use SQL to authenticate their users. A typical *insecure* SQL query to accomplish this in PHP is shown here:

```
$result = mysql_query("SELECT * FROM userdb WHERE username='$form_username'
         AND password='$form_password'");
$num_rows = mysql_num_rows($result);
if($num_rows > 0){
    $authenticated = True;
else
    $authenticated = False;
```

Absent any validation of the user inputs, the user could provide the username **attacker'** **or 1=1 --** and **pwned** (or anything or nothing) for the password, which would result in the following query string:

```
"SELECT * FROM userdb WHERE username='attacker' or 1=1 --'
        AND password='pwned'"
```

If the DBMS for this web app is MySQL, that system will interpret anything after two dashes as a comment, which will be ignored. This means that the value in the password field is irrelevant because it will never be evaluated by the database. The username can be anything (or empty), but because the logical condition 1=1 is always true, the query will return all the registered users. Because the number of users is greater than zero, the attacker will be authenticated.

Clearly, we need to validate inputs such as these, but should we do it on the client side or the server side? Client-side validation is often implemented through JavaScript and embedded within the code for the page containing the form. The advantage of this approach is that errors are caught at the point of entry, and the form is not submitted to the server until all values are validated. The disadvantage is that client-side validation is easily negated using commonly available and easy-to-use tools. The preferred approach is to do client-side validation to enhance the user experience of benign users but double-check everything on the server side to ensure protection against malicious actors.

Output Encoding

Sometimes user inputs are displayed directly on a web page. If you've ever posted anything on social media or left a product review at a vendor's site, then you've provided input (your post or review) that a web application incorporated into an HTML document (the updated page). But what happens if your input includes HTML tags? This could be useful if you wanted to use boldface by stating you are <b>very</b> happy about your purchase. (The <b> tag in HTML denotes boldface.) It could just as easily be problematic if you included a <script> tag with some malicious JavaScript. The web browser will happily interpret benign and malicious HTML just the same.

Output encoding is a technique that converts user inputs into safe representations that a web browser cannot interpret as HTML. So, going back to our previous example, when you enter <b>very</b> in a purchase review, the HTML tags are "escaped" or rendered in a way that prevents the browser from interpreting them as valid HTML. This is the most important control to prevent cross-site scripting (XSS) attacks.

Session Management

As you may know, HTTP is a *stateless* protocol. This means that every web server is a bit of an amnesiac; it doesn't remember you from one request to another. A common way around this is to use cookies to sort of "remind" the server of who you are so that, even if you haven't authenticated, you can go from page to page on an online retail store and have the web application remember what you may have added to your shopping cart. Every time you request a resource (such as a web page or an image), your browser sends along a cookie so the web application can tell you apart from thousands of other visitors.

The cookie is simply a text file that usually contains some sort of unique identifier for you. This identifier is typically known as the *session ID*.

An HTTP session is a sequence of requests and responses associated with the same user, whereas session management is the process of securely handling these sessions. The word "securely" is critical because, absent security, sessions can easily be hijacked. Let's go back to the previous example of writing a session ID on a cookie to track a given user. That cookie is sent along with every request, so anyone who can sniff it off the network can impersonate the legitimate session user. All they would have to do is wait for you to send a request, intercept it, get the session ID from the cookie, and then send their own request to the server, pretending to be you.

Secure session management revolves around two basic principles: use HTTPS whenever a session is active and ensure that session IDs are not easy to guess. HTTPS is essential whenever any sensitive information is exchanged, and this is particularly true of a session ID. Even if attackers can't break your secure connection to steal your ID, they could still try to guess it. Suppose a web application assigns session IDs sequentially. You send a request and see that your session ID is 1000. You clear your cache and cookies and interact with the application again, noticing that your new session ID is 1002. It would be reasonable to assume that there is another active session with an ID of 1001, so you rewrite your cookie to have that value and send another request to the web application. Voilà! You just took over someone else's session. Secure session management involves using IDs that are hard to guess (such as pseudo-random), long enough to prevent brute-force attacks, and generic so that they are not based on any identifiable information.

Authentication

Most software systems, particularly distributed ones, require user authentication. Sadly, this is an area that is often given insufficient attention during the development process. Many programmers seem to think that authentication is pretty easy, and a surprising number of them prefer to implement their own. The problem with weak authentication mechanisms in distributed software systems is that they can turn the platform into an easy foothold into the trusted network for the attacker. Additionally, because many people reuse passwords in multiple systems, obtaining credentials on one (poorly built or protected) system often leads to unauthorized access to others. If at all possible, we should avoid building our own authentication and rely instead on one of the approaches to single sign-on (SSO) we've discussed before.

Regardless of whether you use your own or use someone else's authentication sources, here are some of the best practices for authentication in software systems:

- Use multifactor authentication (MFA) whenever possible.
- Enforce strong passwords with minimum lengths (to thwart brute-force attacks) as well as maximum lengths (to protect against long password DoS attacks).
- Never store or transmit passwords in plaintext anywhere (and use the appropriate cryptographic techniques to protect them).

- Implement failed-login account lockouts if at all possible (but beware of this making you vulnerable to account DoS attacks).

- Log all authentication attempts and ensure that the logs are periodically reviewed (or, better yet, generate appropriate alerts).

 NOTE We discussed authentication in general and SSO in particular in Chapter 1.

Data Protection

Passwords are not the only data we need to protect in our software systems. Depending on their functions, these applications can contain personal data, financial information, or trade secrets. Generally speaking, data exists in one of three states: at rest, in motion, or in use. These states and their interrelations are shown in Figure 13-1.

Data at Rest

Information in a software system spends most of its time waiting to be used. The term *data at rest* refers to data that resides in external or auxiliary storage devices, such as hard disk drives (HDDs), solid-state drives (SSDs), optical discs (CDs/DVDs), and even magnetic tape. A challenge with protecting data in this state is that it is vulnerable not only to threat actors attempting to reach it over our systems and networks but also to anyone who can gain physical access to the device. The best approach to protecting data at rest is to encrypt it. Every major operating system provides encryption means for individual files or entire volumes in a way that is almost completely transparent to the user. Similarly, every major database management system enables you to encrypt data deemed sensitive, such as passwords and credit card numbers.

Data in Motion

Data in motion is data that is moving between computing nodes over a data network such as the Internet. This is perhaps the riskiest time for our data—when it leaves the confines of our protected enclaves and ventures into other networks that we do not control, such as the Internet. The single best protection for our data while it is in motion (whether within or without our protected networks) is strong encryption such as that offered by Transport Layer Security (TLS) or IPSec, both of which support multiple cipher suites

Figure 13-1
The states of data

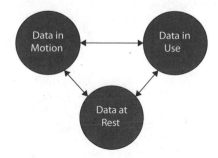

PART II

(though some of these are not as strong as others). By and large, TLS relies on digital certificates (we talked about those in Chapter 1 as well) to certify the identity of one or both endpoints. Another approach to protecting our data in motion is to use trusted channels between critical nodes. Virtual private networks (VPNs) are frequently used to provide secure connections between remote users and corporate resources. VPNs are also used to securely connect campuses or other nodes that are physically distant from each other. The trusted channels we thus create enable secure communications over shared or untrusted network infrastructure.

Data in Use

Data in use refers to data residing in primary storage devices, such as volatile memory (such as RAM), memory caches, or CPU registers. Typically, data remains in primary storage for relatively short periods of time while a process is using it. Note, however, that anything stored in volatile memory could persist there for extended periods (until power is shut down) in some cases. The point is that data in use is being touched by the CPU and will eventually go back to being data at rest or end up being deleted. Many people think this state is safe, but the Meltdown, Spectre, and BranchScope attacks that came to light in 2018 show how a clever attacker can exploit hardware features in most modern CPUs. Meltdown, which affects Intel and ARM microprocessors, works by exploiting the manner in which memory mapping occurs. Since cache memory is a lot faster than main memory, most modern CPUs include ways to keep frequently used data in the faster cache. Spectre and BranchScope, on the other hand, take advantage of a feature called speculative execution, which is meant to improve the performance of a process by guessing what future instructions will be, based on data available in the present. All three of these attacks go after data in use.

So, how do we protect our data in use? For now, it boils down to ensuring that our software is tested against these types of attacks. Obviously, this is a tricky proposition since it is very difficult to identify and test for every possible software flaw. In the near future, whole-memory encryption will mitigate the risks described in this section, particularly when coupled with the storage of keys in CPU registers instead of in RAM. Until these changes are widely available, however, we must remain vigilant to the threats against our data while it is in use.

Parameterized Queries

A common threat against web applications is the SQL injection (SQLi) class of attacks. We already covered them earlier here and in Chapter 12, but by way of review, SQLi enables an attacker to insert arbitrary code into a SQL query. This typically starts by inserting an escape character (such as a closing quote around a literal value), terminating the query that the application developer intended to execute based on the user input, and then inserting a new and malicious SQL command. The key to SQLi working is the insertion of user inputs directly into a SQL query. Think of it as cutting and pasting the input into the actual query that gets executed by the database.

A *parameterized query* (also known as a prepared statement) is a programming technique that treats user inputs as parameters to a function instead of substrings in a literal query. This means that the programmer can specify what values are expected (for example, a number, a date, and a username) and validate that they conform to whatever limits are reasonable (such as a value range and a maximum length for a username) before integrating them into a query that will be executed. Properly implemented, parameterized queries are the best defense against SQLi attacks. They also highlight the importance of validating user inputs and program parameters.

Secure Software Development Lifecycle

Although vulnerability management is by necessity a reactive process, there is a way to make it proactive in nature—that is to say, to eliminate vulnerabilities before they even make it into software through secure development processes. These processes are designed to build security into software in the first place. There are many approaches to building software, but they all follow some sort of predictable pattern called a *software development lifecycle* (SDLC). This lifecycle starts with identifying an unmet need and ends with retiring the software, usually so that a new system can take its place. Whether you use formal or agile methodologies, you still have to identify and track the user or organizational needs; design, build, and test a solution; put that solution into a production environment; keep it running until it is no longer needed; and, finally, dispose of it without breaking anything else. In the sections that follow, we present the generic categories of effort within this lifecycle, though your organization may call these by other names. Along the way, we'll highlight how this all fits into the CySA+ exam.

 EXAM TIP You do not need to memorize the phases of the SDLC, but you do need to know how a cybersecurity analyst would contribute to the development effort at different points in it.

Requirements

All software development should start with the identification of the requirements that the finished product must satisfy. Even if those requirements are not explicitly listed in a formal document, they will exist somewhere before the first line of code is written. Generally speaking, there are two types of requirements: functional requirements that describe *what* the software must do, and nonfunctional requirements (sometimes called performance requirements) that describe *how* the software must do these things or what the software must be like. Left to their own devices, many software developers will focus their attention on the functionality and only begrudgingly (if at all) pay attention to the rest.

Functional Requirements

A *functional requirement* defines a function of a system in terms of inputs, processing, and outputs. For example, a software system may receive telemetry data from a temperature sensor, compare it to other data from that sensor, and display a graph showing how the values have changed for the day. This requirement is not encumbered with any specific constraints or limitations, which is the role of nonfunctional requirements.

Nonfunctional Requirements

A *nonfunctional requirement* defines a characteristic, constraint, or limitation of the system. Nonfunctional requirements are the main input to architectural designs for software systems. An example of a nonfunctional requirement, following the previous temperature scenario, would be that the system must be sensitive to temperature differences of one-tenth of a degree Fahrenheit and greater. Nonfunctional requirements are also sometimes called *quality requirements.*

Security Requirements

The class of requirements in which we are most interested deals with security. A *security requirement* defines the behaviors and characteristics a system must possess to achieve and maintain an acceptable level of security by itself and in its interactions with other systems. Accordingly, this class includes both functional and nonfunctional aspects of the finished product.

Development

Once all the requirements have been identified, the development team starts developing or building the software system. The first step in this phase is to design an architecture that will address the nonfunctional requirements. Recall that nonfunctional requirements describe the characteristics of the system. On this architecture, the detailed code modules that address the features or functionality of the system are designed so that they satisfy the functional requirements. After the architecture and features are designed, software engineers start writing, integrating, and testing the code.

Testing is a critical part of developing secure code. Four types of software testing are usually involved: The first is *unit testing,* which ensures that specific blocks (or units) of code behave as expected. This is frequently automated and involves a range of inputs that are reasonable, absurd, and at the boundary between these two extremes. The next level of testing is *integration testing,* which involves ensuring that the outputs that one unit provides to another as inputs don't reveal any flaws. After integration testing, a product is usually ready for *system testing,* which is sort of like integration testing but for the entire system. Assuming everything is okay so far, we know that the product is built right (system verification). The final question to answer is whether we built the right product (system validation), and this is something only the intended user can determine. To take care of this final check, products go through formal *acceptance testing,* at which point the customer certifies that the software meets the needs for which it was developed. At the end of the development phase, the system has passed all unit, integration, and system tests and is ready to be rolled out onto a production network.

From a security perspective, we should test software to ensure that security mechanisms are both functional and effective. Each of the software tests we described can have security testing aspects as well. For instance, unit testing can also include code reviews to see if security functions are coded correctly. Integration and system testing can determine if data is transferred securely between components and interfaces, as well as if the components and systems are communicating securely.

Implementation

The implementation phase is when the system or application is introduced into the production network, available for users. This phase is often the point at which frictions between the development and operations teams can start to become real problems, unless these two groups have been integrated beforehand. The challenges in this transitory phase include ensuring that the software will run properly on the target hardware systems, that it will integrate properly with other systems (for example, Active Directory), that it won't adversely affect the performance of any other system on the network, and that it doesn't compromise the security of the overall information system. If the organization used DevOps or DevSecOps (which we'll describe shortly), most of the thorny issues will have been identified and addressed by this stage, which means implementation simply becomes an issue of provisioning and final checks.

From the security perspective, unfortunately this is also where vulnerabilities often appear for the first time. If the organization does not have a secure software development lifecycle and related processes, vulnerabilities may not be discovered until the system or application is already in use and cannot be easily reengineered to include security controls. It's at this point where security becomes "bolted on" instead of "baked in" to the system or application.

Operation and Maintenance

By most estimates, operation and maintenance (O&M) of software systems represents around 75 percent of the total cost of ownership (TCO). Somewhere between 20 and 35 percent of O&M costs are related to correcting vulnerabilities and other flaws that were not discovered during development. If you multiply these two figures together, you can see that typically organizations spend between 15 and 26 percent of the TCO for a software system fixing defects. This is the main driver for spending extra time in the design, secure development, and testing of the system before it goes into O&M. By this phase, the IT operations team has ownership of the software and is trying to keep it running in support of the business, while the software developers have usually moved on to the next project and see requests for fixes as distractions from their main efforts. This should highlight, once again, the need for secure software development before it ever touches a production network.

DevOps and DevSecOps

Historically, the software development and quality assurance teams would work together, but in isolation from the IT operations teams who would ultimately have to deal with the end product. Many problems have stemmed from poor collaboration between these two during the development process. It is not rare to have the IT team berating the developers because a feature push causes the former group to have to stay late, work on a weekend, or simply drop everything they were doing in order to "fix" something that the developers "broke." This friction makes a lot of sense when you consider that each team is incentivized by different outcomes. Developers want to push out finished code, usually under strict schedules. The members of the IT staff, on the other hand, want to keep the

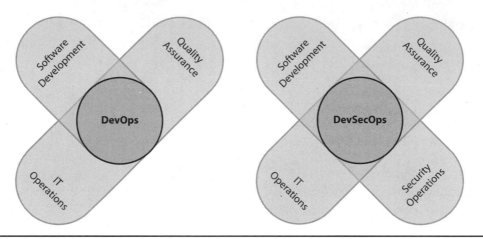

Figure 13-2   The functions involved in DevOps and in DevSecOps

IT infrastructure operating effectively. A good way to solve this friction is to have both developers and operations staff (hence the term DevOps) work together throughout the software development process. *DevOps* is the practice of incorporating development, IT, and quality assurance (QA) staff into software development projects to align their incentives and enable frequent, efficient, and reliable releases of software products. Recently, the cybersecurity team is also being included in this multifunctional team, leading to the increasing use of the term *DevSecOps,* as shown in Figure 13-2.

Vulnerability Management Reporting and Communication

While the other three domains of the CySA+ exam have their own distinct parts and chapters in this book, it makes sense that Objective 4.1, "Explain the importance of vulnerability management reporting and communication," should be included as part of our discussion on vulnerability management, so we included it here in Part III of the book. Many of the concepts and definitions discussed earlier about vulnerability management are also mentioned here at the risk of repeating them. The difference here, however, is that we want to discuss these pieces of vulnerability management in the context of reporting the ongoing process and status of vulnerability management to all the relevant stakeholders.

In this section, we will go over the finer points of reporting the progress of our vulnerability management program. We will discuss the mechanics of the report itself and how it may be focused on particular levels of stakeholders (for example, executives, managers, and technical personnel), as well as the critical highlights of the information that should be included in the reports, such as actual vulnerabilities, affected hosts, risk scoring, vulnerability mitigation, repeated instances of specific vulnerabilities, and prioritizing vulnerability remediation.

In addition to vulnerability reports, there may be specific instances where compliance reporting is required, so governance may require that vulnerabilities be communicated in the context of legal requirements, using specific requirements or formats. We will discuss this piece of vulnerability management reporting as well.

At the heart of vulnerability management is how the organization takes action to manage its vulnerabilities, minimize the risk from them, and remediate them. During this part of the chapter we will also discuss how those action plans are reported to management. Along with this, any inhibitors or barriers to managing vulnerabilities must also be brought to the attention of management. Finally, we will discuss the necessity for reporting how metrics such as key performance and risk indicators are faring in our vulnerability management processes.

Stakeholder Identification and Communication

Stakeholders are those entities, including people and other organizations, who have varying degrees of vested interest in aspects of your organization. The obvious general stakeholders include owners, members of management, other employees, customers, suppliers, partners, and regulatory organizations. Specific stakeholders, however, could be narrowed down to those who have an interest in a particular aspect of the organization. Stakeholders who have an interest in vulnerability management in your organization, for example, will definitely consist of members of management but also could include relevant department heads and asset owners as well as other technical personnel in the organization. All these stakeholders have an interest in how vulnerabilities are assessed, managed, remediated, and reported.

Note that the audience intended to receive the vulnerability report or communication will influence what level of technical detail you include in the report. If the report is a summary or more general in nature, it's likely not going to be very technical. These are the type of reports that go to managerial stakeholders. In this type of report, you typically communicate summaries, historical analysis, or general trends, and you request additional resources to assist in vulnerability management. For other technical personnel, however, particularly those who will be responsible for managing or remediating vulnerabilities, you will likely go into more technical detail. These stakeholders require the information needed to actually mitigate vulnerabilities, including some of the information we will explain later regarding vulnerability specifics, affected hosts, prioritization, and so on.

Vulnerability Reports

In general, vulnerability reports can take many forms, depending on how management chooses to communicate vulnerabilities within and outside of the organization. Vulnerability reports can be generated by the cybersecurity personnel in the trenches on either a regularly scheduled basis (for example, weekly or monthly) or an ad hoc basis, and they communicate specific vulnerabilities in assets and the remediation status of each. Vulnerability reports can also be generated on a longer-term basis, such as quarterly or annually, to show historic information or assist with trend analysis. Vulnerability reports can be targeted to specific groups; for instance, a vulnerability report that contains a great deal of technical information should be targeted toward those personnel who understand and can take action on the technical information provided. However, a report that is created specifically so management can determine the effectiveness of the cybersecurity program should likely be less targeted toward technical information and more toward the overall health of the cybersecurity program, possibly even with the focus on business efforts and how cybersecurity management is affecting those efforts. Vulnerability reports can also be focused on specific systems and, in turn, communicated to those system or data owners.

Another important consideration is what information a vulnerability report should contain. This, again, is dependent on the audience that will receive it as well as the purpose of the report. Depending on the level of technical detail required, the report could contain information on specific vulnerabilities and which hosts they affect, the severity of the risk involved with the vulnerabilities, the mitigation strategy (for example, patching or configuration changes), and how vulnerabilities should be prioritized for remediation. We will discuss each of these items, which may or may not be included in a vulnerability report, next.

NOTE Vulnerability reports are usually generated using an automated process from the tools that perform vulnerability scanning or using manual processes that may include information beyond simple scans. In either case, the information included in a vulnerability report should be configurable based on the needs of the organization.

Vulnerability reports, particularly those generated by an automated tool, may conform to standardized data formatting methods, such as the Security Content Automation Protocol (SCAP) mentioned in Chapter 9. These standardized data formats allow vulnerability data to be exchanged electronically with different systems and provide for consistent data elements.

Vulnerabilities

The vulnerabilities included in a report may depend on several factors. First, vulnerabilities are often included based on severity or system criticality. This means that the vulnerabilities that are more serious are usually given higher emphasis in the report, but vulnerabilities that are very minor might not be included at all. This is configurable in most automated vulnerability management systems and can be changed for manual systems and processes as well. The organization will usually decide what level of system criticality or severity of vulnerability should be reported, depending on the audience and the needs of the organization.

NOTE Although most vulnerabilities included in a vulnerability report are technical in nature, usually as the result of automated vulnerability scans, other weaknesses such as physical, environmental, and administrative vulnerabilities should also be included, particularly when a vulnerability report is addressed to higher levels of management or as part of a larger risk assessment. Vulnerability reporting is often the impetus to gain more management support (such as additional resources) for remediation efforts.

Affected Hosts

The hosts affected by various vulnerabilities are typically included in the more technically oriented reports to assist cybersecurity personnel in targeting specific endpoints for remediation and in identifying characteristics of hosts that are more likely to incur those weaknesses. For example, a vulnerability that affects only specific hosts running a particular version of Windows 10 would help the team further identify and remediate all hosts that could be affected by that vulnerability, even if it has not been discovered on them.

For non-technical reports, such as the ones that may go to management, summaries of affected hosts, typically by numbers of hosts affected, operating system, segment, criticality, and so forth, are often provided. Management doesn't necessarily need to know which particular host names and IP addresses are affected by a vulnerability; they are likely more interested in percentages of the infrastructure affected by vulnerabilities—particularly severe ones.

Risk Score

Automated tools that generate lists of findings, such as Nessus, Qualys, and OpenVAS, will often provide risk scores for vulnerabilities. At a basic level, the risk score normally consists of at least the severity level for the vulnerability. Most modern vulnerability scanners, however, provide additional information such as Common Vulnerabilities and Exposures (CVE) scoring. This information is useful in determining not only the seriousness of a vulnerability but how easily exploitable it could be.

 NOTE Common Vulnerabilities and Exposures (CVE) were mentioned in Chapter 9.

In addition to the predetermined vulnerability or risk scores provided by automated tools, the organization could also implement its own risk scoring methodology based on its infrastructure, risk appetite and tolerance levels, and mitigations already in place. For instance, the vulnerability tool output may indicate that a vulnerability is a severity level of "high," but the tool won't necessarily take into account mitigations that are in place that significantly reduce the risk of the vulnerability being exploited. This is where human beings must enter the picture and perform realistic risk assessment. With that in mind, tool findings and risk scores should not always be explicitly trusted and should be examined in context with the overall environment. Figure 13-3 illustrates risk scoring provided by the Nessus vulnerability scanner.

Mitigation

In addition to providing information on specific vulnerabilities, vulnerability reports should also provide detailed information on how to remediate a particular vulnerability. This may be something as simple as installing an updated version of software, applying a patch, or changing a configuration item on a host. Typically the more technically oriented vulnerability reports will contain detailed mitigation information for each discovered vulnerability, but a more generalized report intended for management may simply state that the mitigation is to assign more resources, such as personnel or equipment, to a vulnerability.

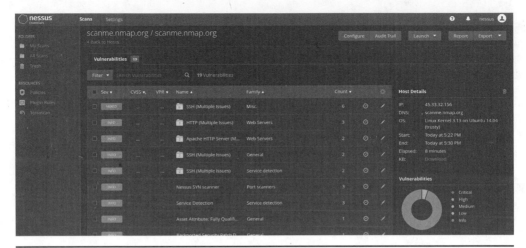

Figure 13-3   Nessus scoring output

Recurrence

If a vulnerability has been seen on multiple hosts, this can help technical personnel track down those hosts with the characteristics that allow the vulnerability to be present, such as operating system or application version, patch level, and so on. Most automated reports will list all such vulnerabilities, even if they are repeated across multiple hosts. Cybersecurity analysts also usually have the option in the vulnerability management tool to group vulnerabilities together for convenience in the report. Another issue with recurrence is if the vulnerability has been seen before and continually shows up in reports. If this is a known vulnerability and there has been no previous resolution in place to mitigate it, the organization has to make a decision on whether to allow it to continue to be an issue. If the risk has been accepted for the vulnerability, then the organization should expect that the same vulnerability will continually show up in the reports. If this is not the case, the organization should carefully review its vulnerability management strategy since its remediation efforts may not be effective.

Prioritization

Vulnerability management reports should include prioritization for remediation. This is typically based on the severity of the vulnerability and is often produced as part of an automated process from the vulnerability management or scanning tool. However, the organization certainly has the ability to prioritize vulnerabilities based on its own needs and infrastructure. Vulnerabilities should be prioritized for remediation based on several factors.

First, vulnerability severity is likely the most important factor. A zero-day vulnerability, for example, should be prioritized above all else and should be remediated as quickly as possible. Slightly less severe vulnerabilities, such as those in the critical and high categories, should also be considered for immediate remediation. Vulnerabilities that are in the medium, low, and routine categories of the vulnerability scoring system may be deferred until the next scheduled patching process, for example, or when resources (such as people) are available to implement those remediations.

Second, vulnerabilities may have to be prioritized based on system criticality. Even a vulnerability rated with a high severity may not be one that can be immediately remediated if the host requires constant availability. This could be because of the critical nature of the data it processes, but it could also be based on the critical processes that use the host. For example, remediating even a high vulnerability doing a critical processing time of the year for a business could have serious consequences. This should be considered in prioritizing vulnerabilities for mitigation, and it should normally be included in the report.

Finally, another factor that may go into reporting prioritization decisions for remediating vulnerabilities is available resources. If personnel are not available, or if the organization must purchase additional equipment to remediate a vulnerability and can't commit those resources, then that vulnerability might not be remediated for quite some time. In that event, the organization must look at compensating controls that can at least reduce the risk until such time as it is able to fully mitigate the weakness. Vulnerability remediation prioritization should be specifically spelled out in the organization's vulnerability management strategy and plan, and its status should be reported as needed.

CAUTION   Vulnerability prioritization is as much a risk-based decision as it is anything else. Although primarily based on vulnerability severity, the other factors such as system criticality and available resources contribute to the ability of an organization to immediately remediate vulnerabilities and should be considered accordingly.

Compliance Reports

Vulnerability reporting is often a standalone process; however, the requirement to report vulnerabilities and the progress of their mitigations is often a part of compliance requirements as well, so compliance must also be considered. A vulnerability report may be submitted to the right stakeholders (technical personnel, executives, system owners, and so on) as part of routine security processes, but it also may be submitted as part of a broader compliance report.

Vulnerability reports submitted as part of compliance reports usually follow some specific reporting and formatting requirements based on the governance vehicle. For example, a compliance report submitted to the Department of Health and Human Services from a healthcare provider that contains vulnerabilities will often require those vulnerabilities to be reported in a specific format and may levy additional requirements on the provider regarding the particulars of the vulnerabilities, such as how they directly impact the ability of the provider to deliver healthcare services to a patient. Other compliance requirements may also impose their own specific caveats on vulnerability reporting.

In any event, based on the requirements spelled out in the governance, the items we discussed earlier regarding vulnerabilities, mitigations, prioritization, and so on are also common to compliance reporting.

Action Plans

The action plan is a critical part of an organization's vulnerability management process. Regardless of the form it takes, the plan is focused on how the organization manages its vulnerabilities on an ongoing basis. This includes key concerns such as how often vulnerabilities are assessed, who gets the results of vulnerability scanning, which tools should be used, what manual processes are involved, how vulnerabilities are categorized in terms of severity, and how they are prioritized for mitigation. Mitigations tied to specific vulnerabilities may also be generally included in routine vulnerability reports and action plans. While there may be a specific action plan generated for a particular vulnerability assessment, action plans on a more general basis are prescribed in policy and usually include requirements for configuration management, patching, compensating controls, awareness and training (whenever human failure is determined to be the cause of the weakness), and any changes to business or security processes that may be needed to address the vulnerabilities. We will discuss each of these in the following sections.

Patching

A large percentage of discovered vulnerabilities require updates or patches to operating systems and applications. Patches are typically released by the associated vendor on a scheduled basis and are assigned a criticality or urgency level based on the severity of the vulnerability they address. With this in mind, patch management is an important process that must be carefully considered, given vulnerability severity, asset criticality, and the need to maintain functionality of hosts while at the same time ensuring the vulnerability is mitigated. Although we have discussed patching earlier in the chapter, the focus for Objective 4.1 is to ensure that patches are carefully considered and communicated to stakeholders as part of vulnerability management reporting. Patches that have the potential to impact the availability of an asset, or that must be at least managed through the configuration management process, should be part of routine vulnerability reporting and communications.

Compensating Controls

Remember from our discussion on control types and functions earlier in the chapter that a compensating control is used when a more desirable or primary control is not available for implementation. This could be due to a lack of resources, such as money, personnel, and so on, but it could also be due to the circumstances surrounding the system or the environment in which it or the organization operates. A compensating control, unlike a corrective control, is a longer-term control that may not be ideal but at least reduces risk to a minimum acceptable level. Compensating controls are typically implemented under the provision that a more desirable or primary control will be implemented when the organization can do so.

Compensating controls should be included in risk documentation and reported when required for vulnerability management. This is to inform managers and other stakeholders when a less than ideal mitigation has been implemented but to still assure stakeholders that risk is being addressed and mitigated to the extent that it can be.

Configuration Management

Configuration management ensures that configuration items across the infrastructure are carefully controlled in how they are planned, tested, and implemented. Configuration management ensures that when vulnerabilities in a system are remediated, the remediation process also goes through configuration control. For instance, when you are applying patches to a system, you should ideally put them through a process of documenting the patches and the reasons for them and then testing the patches before implementing them in the system, particularly if they have the potential to impact the infrastructure in a negative way. We all know from experience that this doesn't always happen; patches may be applied through automated means without ever being examined or tested by an administrator. However, configuration management also involves the ability to back up systems and restore them to a stable state that existed prior to the patch being applied, if necessary. Configuration management tends to be emphasized to a lesser degree when a patch is time sensitive or critical. Organizations frequently are more concerned about getting a patch on the system quickly to remediate a serious issue; however, this is exactly the time when configuration management is important, since installing the patch quickly, without careful evaluation, may do more damage than the issue it is supposed to fix. The same goes for configuration changes, which should also be vetted and documented in the configuration management process.

In terms of reporting, changes to systems that are implemented to mitigate vulnerabilities, such as patches and configuration changes, should be reported through the formal configuration management process as well as through the vulnerability management reporting process, since these are mitigations that should be documented.

Awareness, Education, and Training

Often, vulnerabilities are not technical in nature. Sometimes they relate to physical or environmental weaknesses, and other vulnerabilities are due to human weaknesses. For vulnerabilities involving personnel, typically the best course of action is initial or remedial training. We discussed awareness, education, and training programs elsewhere, so we won't go into great depth here. However, you should understand that for most vulnerabilities introduced by human beings, initially establishing a baseline of awareness, education, or training, as well as reinforcing that baseline periodically, is the best way to reduce, mitigate, or even eliminate those vulnerabilities. For example, social engineering is a threat that exploits human vulnerabilities, and those vulnerabilities can be mitigated through effective training programs. These programs should be done initially when an employee is hired into the organization, and then periodically to reinforce the training and ensure the employee remembers their responsibilities and how to prevent social engineering attacks. However, if an employee does fall victim to social engineering, remedial training can be used to mitigate the vulnerability, even after the damage has been done. For the purposes of vulnerability management and reporting, incidents that can be attributed to personnel due to faulty training should be reported, as well as any other weaknesses in personnel security programs.

Changing Business Requirements

Vulnerabilities aren't just inherent to an operating system, application, system, or the environment. Weaknesses can also be introduced when the organization changes its structure or its mission. Introducing new business requirements or opportunities often also introduces vulnerabilities into the organization, and these vulnerabilities flow down into the systems that must support those new business requirements. For example, partnering with a company for a new business venture may require that new security mechanisms be installed if the partner must have some level of access to an organization's internal network. Mitigating vulnerabilities involved with allowing access to sensitive information within an organization by outsiders can include establishing a separate VPN connection, creating a business partner extranet, enhancing security controls that protect sensitive information, and so on. This is also yet another example of potentially non-technical vulnerabilities that should be included in routine vulnerability management reporting.

Inhibitors to Remediation

Even a solid plan for remediation that has stakeholder buy-in sometimes faces obstacles. Many of the challenges arise from processes that have major dependencies on the IT systems or from a stale policy that fails to address the changing technological landscape adequately. In this section, we cover some common obstacles to remediation and how we can avoid them.

Memorandum of Understanding

The *memorandum of understanding* (MOU) outlines the duties and expectations of all concerned parties. As with a penetration test, a vulnerability scan should have a clearly defined scope, along with formal rules of engagement that dictate, above all else, what can be done during the assessment and in the event of a vulnerability discovery. For example, conducting a scan on production systems during times of high usage would not be suitable. There might also be a situation that, without a formal MOU in place, would leave too much ambiguity. It wouldn't be hard to imagine that the discovery of a vulnerability on your network may have implications on an adjacent network not controlled by you. Also, a misconfiguration of an adjacent network may have a direct impact on your organization's services. In either case, an MOU that covers such conditions will clarify how to proceed in a way that's satisfactory for everyone involved.

Service Level Agreement

Many IT service providers perform their services based on an existing service level agreement (SLA) between them and the service recipient. An SLA is a contract that can exist within a company (say, between a business unit and the IT staff) or between the organization and an outside provider. SLAs exist to outline the roles and responsibilities for the service providers, including the limits of the services they can perform. Unless remediation is explicitly part of an SLA, providers cannot be compelled to perform those steps.

Organizational Governance

Corporate governance is the system of processes and rules an organization uses to direct and control its operations. Corporate governance aims to strike a sensible balance among the competing priorities of company stakeholders. In some cases, governance may interrupt the application of remedial steps, because those actions may negatively affect other business areas. This highlights the importance of communicating your actions with corporate leadership so that they can factor in the effects of remedial action with other issues to make a decision. Strong communication enables timely decision-making in the best interest of the company.

Business Process Interruption

There's never a good time to apply a patch or take other remedial actions. Highly efficient business and industrial processes such as just-in-time manufacturing have enabled businesses to reduce process time and increase overall efficiency. Underpinning these systems are production IT systems that themselves are optimized to the business. A major drawback, however, is that some systems may be more susceptible to disruption because of their optimized states. This fear of unpredictably or instability in the overall process is often enough for company leadership to delay major changes to production systems, or to avoid them altogether. Although earlier in the chapter we mentioned that maintenance schedules appropriate for implementing vulnerability mitigation processes, such as patches, should be included in the overall plan, any potential business process interruptions due to those maintenance schedules should be reported.

Degrading Functionality

Although there's no equivalent to the Hippocratic Oath in network administration, we must always try to "do no harm" to our production systems. Sometimes the recommended treatment, such as quarantining key systems after critical vulnerabilities are discovered, may be deemed unacceptable by leadership. How much risk you and your leadership are willing to underwrite is a decision for your organization, but you should aim to have the most accurate information possible about the state of every vulnerability. If you discover that an important remedial action breaks critical applications in a test environment, the alternative isn't to avoid patching. Rather, you must report this instance to management and devise other mitigating controls to address the vulnerabilities until a suitable patch can be developed.

Legacy and Proprietary Systems

Legacy and proprietary systems are a unique challenge to manage. Often, the equipment is older than many of the analysts on staff or may have been built in such a complicated manner that businesses choose to keep them on board instead of replacing them completely. The equipment still works, but an upgrade is out of the question because of complex upgrade procedures, unique connectivity requirements, or the immense cost of making any kind of change. What's more, some specialized systems have their own proprietary communication protocols, and keeping tabs on these is a challenge in itself.

Such systems often leave vulnerabilities unpatched or lack modern security features such as Transport Layer Security (TLS). Though it's easy to think "if it ain't broke, don't fix it," simply repeating this does nothing to reduce risk. Addressing the challenges of having these systems on the network takes a focused and comprehensive approach that includes constant network monitoring, compensating controls, and multiple layered security mechanisms. As part of routine vulnerability management reporting, you should include these high-risk systems on which you may not be able to mitigate some severe vulnerabilities.

Metrics and Key Performance Indicators

When you are communicating about vulnerabilities and how well they are managed in the organization, offering nebulous or unclear information isn't helpful for remediating them or managing them through the lifecycle. That's why more often than not, management cares about metrics and how they are affecting different risk and performance indicators in the organization. For instance, management likely wants to know how many vulnerabilities were discovered, how many were remediated, how they are categorized by severity and system criticality, and so on. You will need to communicate this information to them in your vulnerability reporting. Examples of metrics you should keep track of with regard to vulnerabilities include the following:

- The number of new vulnerabilities identified on a weekly, monthly, or quarterly basis
- The number of vulnerabilities that fall into the different categories of severity, such as critical, high, medium, low, and informational
- The number of vulnerabilities that can be immediately remediated through simple patching or configuration management
- The number of vulnerabilities that must be deferred for mitigation until a decision on additional resources or system availability is made
- The number and type of critical systems affected by vulnerabilities

These are just examples of some of the metrics that should be collected and reported; however, your organization will typically identify specific metrics, how often they should be reported, and to whom.

Key performance indicators (KPIs) often aggregate metrics in the form of sums or averages over a period of time. These metrics show how cybersecurity controls are performing in terms of reducing or mitigating vulnerabilities from a longer-term or strategic standpoint. Indicators are often grouped into categories such as performance, risk, and control indicators, depending on the context management wishes to focus on.

Trends

Reporting vulnerability trends involves using information that comes from both within and outside the organization. Trends involving the number of discovered vulnerabilities on specific systems or applications, for instance, may help management identify problem areas within the organization. Trends involving information that comes from outside the organization, such as the number of vulnerabilities increasing for a particular market segment, may help identify areas in which your organization may want to be proactive and focus its vulnerability detection efforts. If everyone in the industry is using a specific software application package that is suffering from an increasing number of vulnerabilities, your organization could identify the software version number and implementation details (such as underlying platform or OS) and take steps to remediate those vulnerabilities before they affect your systems. Communicating trends is a proactive, versus reactive, form of vulnerability reporting. Note that trends can also show information over a period of time, such as a historical analysis, or information that can help an organization predict what will happen in the future in terms of vulnerabilities.

Top 10

Top 10 lists, discussed in Chapter 9, often help provide a context for management to understand the criticality or severity of vulnerabilities that are discovered in your organization's infrastructure. A vulnerability scanning tool output, for instance, may show that a discovered vulnerability has a severity rating of critical, but until management sees that a trusted list of vulnerabilities (such as the OWASP Top 10 or the CVE database) verifies that it's truly an issue, there may not be as much of an effort to take the vulnerability seriously. Additionally, those lists also provide context to help both technical personnel and management understand the specific details of identified vulnerabilities.

Critical Vulnerabilities and Zero-Days

Metrics that reflect critical vulnerabilities both introduced into and mitigated by the organization should also be communicated, often with some level of urgency. These may include the number vulnerabilities that are new, including zero-day vulnerabilities that are suddenly discovered, as well as any critical vulnerabilities that may not be immediately mitigated, for whatever reason. These critical vulnerabilities should definitely remain at the forefront of vulnerability reporting, especially since the organization may need to make fast decisions on allocating additional resources, balancing vulnerability remediation with availability, and so on. Metrics involved with reporting critical vulnerabilities and zero-days typically include how many new vulnerabilities in these categories have been identified, which systems they affect, how these vulnerabilities may affect system availability for the user population, how many have been remediated, and how many must be deferred until management decisions must be made on factors that may inhibit remediation, such as resource allocation or system availability.

Service Level Objectives

Not to be confused with the entire service level agreement (SLA), a *service level objective* (SLO) is clause in that agreement stating a particular requirement and how the requirement is satisfied by all parties. The SLA is typically between a customer and a third-party provider, so the agreement would specify requirements the third party has to meet as an obligation to the customer contracting its services. In terms of vulnerability management, requirements for how often vulnerabilities are assessed, how quickly they will be mitigated, and how they will be reported may be stipulated in the SLA.

The effectiveness of the third-party provider must be communicated to all stakeholders, particularly those in management who oversee these type of agreements and make security decisions in the organization.

Chapter Review

In this chapter, we have discussed a wide range of topics that directly relate to vulnerability management. Governance, in the form of external laws and regulations as well as internal policies and procedures, drives how an organization manages overall risk and vulnerabilities. These policies will determine how vulnerabilities are prioritized for remediation, as well as when issues must be escalated to higher management so that vulnerability management can be better resourced.

It's critical to understand how security controls are categorized, in terms of type and function, since vulnerabilities typically affect one or more of these controls. Security controls can be categorized into one of three types: managerial, operational, or technical controls. Controls can also be categorized in terms of what function they perform, such as preventive, detective, responsive, compensating, or corrective.

Vulnerabilities are managed on both a strategic and day-to-day basis for processes that include patching systems, configuration management, and system maintenance. Patches and configuration changes must be tested prior to implementation and then validated to ensure that they are effective and do not introduce new vulnerabilities that may bring harm to the system. There must be a rollback strategy for patches and configuration changes so that the system can be restored to its original secure and functioning condition. Exceptions to policies and other governance can be made if a vulnerability cannot be immediately addressed or mitigated. Vulnerabilities should also be considered in terms of priorities for remediation.

Vulnerabilities are a component of risk, along with threats, impact, and likelihood. Risk management principles are applied at the organizational level, the business process level, and, of course, the system or infrastructure level. Risk appetite and tolerance define how much risk an organization is willing to take overall and how much risk the organization can tolerate for a specific business venture or activity, respectively. There are three general ways that organizations deal with risk: they can transfer or share risk with another entity, they can avoid risk by ceasing an activity that would otherwise incur too much risk, and they can mitigate risk to reduce it to an acceptable level. At some point, however, the organization must accept whatever residual risk remains, since risk cannot be completely eliminated.

Attack surface management is a technique used to reduce vulnerabilities inherent to a system. This involves ensuring that every aspect of a system is tested and configured as securely as possible. Several techniques are used to discover and reduce the attack surface. Since a large number of vulnerabilities exist in software that has not been securely developed, we also discussed secure coding best practices and methodologies, including key best practices such as input validation, output encoding, session management, strong authentication, and more. We also discussed the necessity for a secure software development lifecycle. Vulnerability management reporting and communications are critical because stakeholders throughout the organization must be identified and communicated with regarding overall vulnerability measure processes as well as details for specific system vulnerabilities. We discussed the nature of vulnerability reports and the information that should be included in them, as well as specific types of reports, including compliance with governance. We also talked about the necessity for action plans in remediating vulnerabilities as well as items that could be inhibitors to remediation. Finally, we discussed the need for measuring how well we are managing vulnerabilities in our infrastructure.

Questions

1. Which of the following is *not* a category for security controls?

   A. Managerial

   B. Operational

   C. Virtual

   D. Logical

2. Which of the following is an example of a responsive control?

   A. Restoring a system from backup

   B. Reviewing logs to determine who completed an action

   C. Implementing a firewall rule to block certain network traffic

   D. Using a system warning banner to list prohibited actions upon login

3. Which of the following may be necessary if an untested patch has a severe performance impact on a system after its implementation?

   A. Testing

   B. Rollback

   C. Validation

   D. Maintenance

4. Which of the following factors make up risk?

   A. Threats and impact

   B. Threats and vulnerabilities

   C. Likelihood and impact

   D. Vulnerabilities and likelihood

5. Which of the following two factors directly influence how vulnerabilities are prioritized for remediation?

   A. Cost to remediate and system criticality

   B. Vulnerability severity and system criticality

   C. Vulnerability severity and likelihood of exploitation

   D. Likelihood and impact

6. Which of the following are inhibitors to vulnerability remediation that must be reported to the proper stakeholders?

   A. Patch management processes

   B. Configuration changes

   C. Routine maintenance windows

   D. Business process interruption

7. Which of the following types of tests is focused on actually exploiting weaknesses in systems?

   A. Penetration test

   B. Vulnerability assessment

   C. Security controls testing

   D. Risk assessment

8. Which of the following is a good example of a corrective control?

   A. Restricting access to a legacy system that cannot be immediately replaced

   B. Encrypting data between two hosts whose operating systems cannot be upgraded due to application incompatibility issues

   C. Installing video surveillance cameras for an area that does not have guard patrols

   D. Temporarily placing a critical system on a segregated network to stop an attack on it

Answers

1. **C.** Virtual is not one of the categories of access controls, which are the mechanisms put in place to protect the confidentiality, integrity, and availability of systems. Access controls are categorized as managerial, operational, and technical (aka logical).

2. **A.** Restoring a system from a backup is an example of a responsive control, since it is reacting to an incident and recovering the system.

3. **B.** If a system has issues after a patch is installed, regardless of whether it has been tested, the patch should be rolled back, restoring the system to an unaltered, functional state.

4. **C.** The two primary factors that directly compose risk are the likelihood of a negative event occurring and the resulting impact to an asset if it does occur.

5. **B.** The two factors that influence the prioritization of vulnerability remediation are the severity of the vulnerability itself and the criticality of the systems it affects.

6. **D.** Any interruptions to business processes within the organization caused by vulnerability remediation must be reported to the proper stakeholders, including management, system and data owners, and others, as appropriate.

7. **A.** Penetration testing focuses on the practicality of actually exploiting discovered vulnerabilities in the system.

8. **D.** Taking a system offline and placing it on a segregated network segment to stop an active attack is an example of a corrective control, since it is temporary and corrects an immediate security issue.

PART III

Incident Response

Incident Response Procedures

In this chapter you will learn:

- The major steps of the incident response cycle
- How to prepare for security incidents
- The importance of establishing communications processes
- Incident detection and analysis techniques
- How to contain, or reduce the spread, of an incident
- How to eradicate and recover from an incident

I am prepared for the worst, but hope for the best.

—Benjamin Disraeli

Although we commonly use the terms interchangeably, there are subtle differences between an *event*, which is any occurrence that can be observed, verified, and documented, and an *incident*, which is one or more related negative events that compromise an organization's security posture. *Incident response* is the process of negating the effects of an incident on an information system.

In Chapter 8, we covered the benefits of using the intelligence cycle in enabling us to understand and scale key intelligence tasks by breaking them down into distinct phases. As with generating and sharing intelligence, incident response benefits from using a framework to help us more easily understand an adversary's activities and respond to them using repeatable, scalable methods. The incident response cycle comprises the major steps required to prepare for an intrusion, identify the activities associated with it, develop and deploy the analytical techniques to understand it, and execute the plans to return the system to an operational state. In this chapter we'll cover these phases, which are shown in Figure 14-1, and we'll discuss techniques associated with each step and how these defensive efforts can make our responses more effective. Note that "Post-Incident Activities," the fifth phase of the cycle, is discussed in Chapter 15.

Figure 14-1
The incident
response cycle

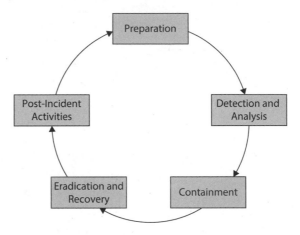

There are many incident response models, but all share some basic characteristics. They all require us to take some preparatory actions before anything bad happens, to identify and analyze an event to determine the appropriate counteractions, to correct the problem(s), and finally to keep the incident from happening again. Clearly, efforts to prevent future occurrences tie back to our preparatory actions, to create a cycle. This chapter, along with Chapters 15 and 16, addresses Objective 3.2, "Given a scenario, perform incident response activities," and Objective 3.3, "Explain the preparation and post-incident activity phases of the incident management life cycle."

 EXAM TIP You will be expected to understand the general phases of the incident response cycle, but you won't be tested on any particular incident response model.

Preparation

As highlighted several times throughout the book, preparing for security incidents requires a sound methodology that aims to reduce the amount of uncertainty as much as possible. By prescribing technical and operational best practices, we may effectively protect critical business from compromise and sensitive data from exposure by identifying key assets and response priorities. Though we do as much as we can to be proactive in stopping threats, we must face the reality that at some point, something will get through, so we must be prepared to recognize and remediate as quickly and completely as possible. In thinking about how a security team might approach preparing for the unknown, we need to keep a few things in mind. Because preparation will likely affect a wide range of teams outside of the security team itself, it's important that we get buy-in from all levels of the organization as soon as possible.

Preparation will involve many technical and nontechnical steps. For the purpose of the CySA+ exam, we'll cover several elements of preparation, including training, testing, and documentation. Although many of the technical steps associated with each element will not involve everyone in the organization, it will require the cooperation of teams directly impacted by changes to the network and its operations. For example, installing new security devices, deploying detection signatures, and ensuring that patches are applied may not need direct involvement from end users, but the organization's network architecture, systems administrators, and IT support teams must be aware so that they can make the appropriate modifications on their end to enforce and validate these changes. For all users in the organization, the processes and documentation techniques used must be as user-friendly as possible, particularly for a nontechnical audience.

The Incident Response Plan

The incident response plan (IRP) is the core document used to manage the entire incident response process. A policy dictates requirements for the plan and assigns roles and responsibilities. However, a policy is usually a short document that does not go into great detail but rather establishes the internal governance necessary to create the incident response capability. The incident response plan, on the other hand, is a much more comprehensive document that includes processes and procedures to carry out all incident response activities. This includes core incident response areas such as how the organization triages and declares an incident, escalation procedures, the communications process, as well as containment, eradication, and remediation processes. The incident response plan may also dictate how the plan is exercised and how the incident response team is staffed and trained.

 EXAM TIP You may find questions on the exam that require you to understand the purpose and content of the incident response plan, so you should know that the incident response plan is the overarching document that contains all the procedures and processes used during an actual response.

Establishing a Communication Process

One of the most important processes developed during in the incident response plan is the communications process. This process is vital to planning and executing effective incident response. A variety of team members and stakeholders are involved in incident response, each with different capabilities and priorities. Maintaining effective communications with them all can help you make the experience of responding to an incident far more manageable. Ineffective communication processes with internal and/or external stakeholders can endanger your entire organization, even if you have a textbook-perfect response to an incident.

We cannot be exhaustive in our treatment of how best to communicate during incident responses in this chapter, but we hope to convey the importance of interpersonal and interorganizational communications in these few pages. Even the best-handled technical incident response can be overshadowed very quickly by an organization's inability to communicate effectively—internally and/or externally. Note that this discussion on communications also covers a portion of Objective 4.2, "Explain the importance of incident response reporting and communication."

EXAM TIP When an incident does occur, an organization's goal when following the best practices outlined by its IRP should cover how the organization will handle both public and private communications, disclosures, and information flow during the incident. The plan should also outline how the organization will handle legal and other regulatory communication requirements.

Internal Communications

One of the key parts of any incident response plan is the process by which trusted internal parties are kept abreast of and consulted about an incident and how it will be dealt with. It is not uncommon, at least for the more significant incidents, to designate a command center where key decision-makers and stakeholders can meet for periodic updates and feedback regarding the incident response (IR). In between these meetings, the room can serve as a clearinghouse for information about the response activities, where at least one knowledgeable member of the incident response team (IRT) will be stationed for the duration of the response activity. The command center can be a physical space, but a virtual one may work as well, depending on your organization.

In addition to hosting regular meetings (formal or otherwise) in the command center, it may be necessary to establish a secure communications channel with which to keep key personnel up to date on the progress of the response. This could involve group texts, e-mails, and even a chat room—but it must include all the key personnel who may have a role or stake in the issue. When it comes to internal communications with stakeholders after an incident, there is no such thing as too much information. One important aspect of communications to consider is that the incident may require alternate or out-of-band communications, such as personal e-mail or smartphones, if the primary infrastructure has been destroyed or degraded to the point where internal communications using the existing infrastructure is impacted.

External Communications

Communications outside of the organization, on the other hand, must be carefully controlled. Sensible reports have a way of getting turned into misleading and potentially damaging sound bites. For this reason, a trained professional should be assigned the role of handling external communications. Some of these communications, after all, may be restricted by regulatory or statutory requirements.

The first and most important sector for external communications comprises government entities, which could include the US Securities Exchange Commission (SEC), the Federal Bureau of Investigation (FBI), regulatory agencies, and other government entity or law enforcement agency. If your organization is required to communicate with these entities in the course of an incident response, your legal team must assist in crafting any and all messages. If you manage to ignore these communication requirements, your organization will pay a price. This is not to say that government stakeholders are adversarial but that when the process is regulated by laws or regulations, the stakes are much higher.

Next on the list of importance are the customers. Though your organization may be affected by regulatory requirements with regard to compromised customer data, your focus here is on keeping the public informed so that it perceives transparency and trustworthiness from the organization. This is particularly important when the situation is interesting enough to make headlines or "go viral" on social media. Just as lawyers are critical to government communications, the organization's media relations (or equivalent) team will carry the day when it comes to communicating with the masses. The goal here is to assuage fears and concerns as well as to control the narrative to keep it factually correct. To this end, press releases and social media posts should be templated, even before an event occurs, to make it easier to push out information quickly.

Another group you may have to communicate with deliberately and effectively includes the key partners, such as business collaborators, select shareholders, and investors. The goal of this communications thrust is to convey the impact of the incident on the business's bottom line. If the event could drive down the price of the company's stock, the conversation has to include ways in which the company will mitigate such losses. If the event could spread to the systems of partner organizations, the focus should be on how to mitigate that risk. In any event, the business leaders should carry on these conversations, albeit with substantial support from the senior response team leaders.

 EXAM TIP The incident response plan should provide detailed provisions for both internal and external communications, both up and down the chain of command and laterally across the organization.

Training

While laying the groundwork for an effective response, you'll need to ensure that the first few steps performed by everyone involved are the right ones. After all, the more quickly and accurately a team can identify an issue, the better off you all will be as you work through the entire IR process. Seeing and interpreting the right indicators and signs becomes easier as you and your team gain experience, but providing good training on the fundamentals can save the organization time and money in the long run. This should include technical training for the IR team, college courses, or various professional education classes. Colleges and universities now offer many cybersecurity-related courses through distance learning, which makes it easier for students to access training opportunities.

In many cases, the nontechnical staff make up a majority of the organization, and invariably these users will be the ones who are most exposed to the signs of a potential security incident. Devising a defense against continuous and persistent threats such as phishing is imperative. The key to a collective defense is training users in how to identify such threats and how to handle situations in which they may have been tricked into providing sensitive information. To be clear, training nontechnical staff members who are targets of these types of malicious activities should include training in how to communicate what they observe. This will significantly raise the organization's level of preparation.

Testing

In IR, as with so many tasks in life, practice makes perfect, and getting to a state of proficiency takes time and discipline. Practice sessions are useful in gauging the team's ability to respond appropriately, identifying areas for improvement, and increasing team members' confidence in themselves and in the IR process. Without practice that simulates live conditions, incident responders may not be able to articulate their observations in a realistic manner. Through realistic testing, your team members can validate assumptions and dispel unhelpful preconceptions about the incidents they may face. Keep in mind that incident response testing closely relates to both business continuity planning and disaster recovery planning. Although they are all three closely related functions, and have many common processes and procedures in place, these are distinctly separate functions with different goals.

For the purposes of the exam, you should be aware of the four major types of exercises used to test the incident response capability in the organization. The four listed next can also be used to evaluate your organization's IR plan, procedures, and capabilities. The goals of IR exercises are to test strategies, vet procedures, and train personnel on IR tasks they must perform.

- **Documentation reviews**   Team members review incident response plans and procedures for familiarization with IR processes.

- **Tabletop exercises**   Tabletop exercise are live sessions in which members of the security team come together to discuss their roles and responses to hypothetical situations. The goal is to highlight how various teams execute their parts of the plan, what improvements may be needed, and what it's like to operate in uncertainty through discussion. A tabletop exercise is executed as a paperwork exercise, without actually leaving a conference room or involving systems, information, or other equipment.

- **Walkthrough**   Walkthroughs offer a basic kind of testing for team members that can be performed in a classroom setting, with little or no additional resources required. Walkthroughs are designed to familiarize participants with response steps, crisis communications plans, and their roles and responsibilities as defined in the plans. A walkthrough actually takes participants through the steps of an IR exercise, without using actual equipment, systems, or data. What separates tabletop exercises from walkthroughs is that participants are often guided through a scenario, complete with changes in the environment and simulated actor behaviors.

- **Full-scale exercises**   A full-scale exercise is an experience modeled as closely as possible to a real event. Often performed in real time, full-scale exercises test everything from the participants' detailed understanding of the organization's IR process to specific individual and team tasks. This type of exercise is useful in measuring performance compared to program objectives. Understand that full-scale incident response exercises are often difficult to perform unless the organization is very mature and uses resources such as purple teams and cyber ranges for these exercises.

NOTE Other types of tests, such as parallel and full interruption tests, are normally seen during disaster recovery exercises rather than incident response exercises, although it is possible that an incident response team can make use of these types of tests when responding to a disaster.

Keep in mind when formulating the testing plan that the tests and the testing process should be easy to understand for everyone involved. Understanding that plans are designed with little space for improvisation, you should design the exercises so that all participants can clearly understand the roles they play and the tasks they are expected to perform. It's also desirable for key leaders to be involved in testing by providing initial requirements and vision, participating in a tabletop event, observing a full-scale exercise, or simply providing feedback at the conclusion of the assessments. Although the results from training aren't always immediately apparent, judging the effectiveness of a response strategy by using a well-designed testing plan can tell you if your team is on the right path, and it provides clear steps forward if adjustments are necessary.

EXAM TIP You should know the difference between the different types of exercises that can be used to test the incident response capability. Due to the level of resources required, the most often seen incident response exercises are documentation reviews, tabletops, and walkthroughs.

Playbooks

We discussed playbooks extensively in Chapter 2; our discussion here will specifically focus on their use during incident planning and response. While procedures to complete individual tasks are useful, it may be more useful to develop what is known as a *playbook*. Remember that a playbook can be characterized by entire sets of interrelated procedures to complete a single task or, more often, a group of tasks. Note that playbooks are not always simply checklists or procedures; they also take the form of automated scripts that can perform one or many tasks needed through automation. The organization can develop standardized checklists, procedures, and processes, but a playbook puts them all together into a holistic set of tactics that can be run as a single task or a group of tasks. Playbooks are an important part of the incident response plan and its related processes and procedures. For example, a playbook may consist of several tasks, such as checking all the running processes on a set of servers, turning off certain services, combing through log files looking for particular events, and so on, during an incident. These playbooks free analysts to focus on other critical tasks, while those that can be automated are executed much more quickly and efficiently. Playbooks can also be integrated into and leverage existing tools such as security information and event management (SIEM) systems.

Documentation

All good processes need to be recorded so that they can be referenced, shared, and sometimes improved upon. Documentation is arguably the most important nontechnical tool at your team's disposal. Even for the most seasoned team, it pays to have well-documented steps ready. Documentation extends beyond just recording the steps of your organization's IR process; any information about systems that may be useful to responders throughout the process, such as network configurations, system settings, and system points of contact, should also be included.

Detection and Analysis

Detecting and analyzing events is the first step in putting practice into play. Often referred to as *identification,* this step in the process may use a number of automated detection techniques to increase team efficiency. An automated detection and analysis process is much more scalable and reliable than manual processes because it can be used consistently to highlight behavior patterns of interest that a human analyst may miss.

Incident Scope and Impact

It's important to have a clear reference point to know the true level of scope and impact during a suspected incident—simply noting that the network seems slow will not be enough to make a good determination regarding what to do next. As a responder, you must lay out a clear set of criteria to determine how to classify a security event. This classification process is usually based on criteria such as *scope* and *impact,* which is the formal determination of whether an event is enough of a deviation from normal operations to be called an incident, and the degree to which services have been affected. Keep in mind that some actions performed in the course of systems administrator duties may trigger security devices and appear to be an attack. Documenting these types of legitimate anomalies will reduce the number of false positives and enable you to have more confidence in your alerting system. In the case of a legitimate attack, you must collect as much data as possible from sources throughout your network, such as log files from network devices. Gathering as much information as possible in this step will help you decide on the next steps for your incident responders.

Once an event is confirmed to be legitimate, you should quickly communicate with your team to identify who needs to be contacted outside of your security group and key leadership. Whom you contact may be dictated by your local policy—and in some cases, laws or regulations. Opening communication channels early will also ensure that you get the appropriate support for any major changes to the organization's resources.

Indicators of Compromise

We've previously discussed indicators of compromise (IOCs) and indicators of activity (IOAs) throughout Part I. Indicators are often the first clue that alerts you to a potential issue. One of the key reasons to pay attention to IOCs and IOAs is to detect negative events before they become incidents. During the triage portion of your incident, when you're determining exactly what has happened, you'll likely see some indicators you must analyze to figure out whether they are telling you there has been a malicious event or there is simply a functional or performance problem with your infrastructure. Analyzing these indicators singularly may tell you there is something you should be concerned about, but analyzing them as a group will tell you if there is a pattern of behavior indicating something more serious than a malfunctioning piece of equipment.

Downtime

Networks exist to provide resources to those who need them when they need them. Without a network and services that are available when they need to be, nothing can be accomplished. Every metric in determining network performance, such as stability, throughput, scalability, and storage, requires the network to be up. The decision on whether to take a network completely offline to handle a breach is not a small one by any measure. Understanding that a complete shutdown of the network may not be possible, you should isolate infected systems to prevent additional damage. The priority here is to prevent additional losses and minimize impacts on the organization. This is not dissimilar to triage in a hospital emergency room: your team must work quickly to perform triage on your network to determine the extent of the damage and prevent additional harm, all while keeping the organization running.

The key is to determine which of the organization's critical systems are needed for survival and then estimate the outage time that can be tolerated by the organization as a result of an incident. The outage time that can be endured by an organization is referred to as the *maximum tolerable downtime* (MTD), which is illustrated in Figure 14-2.

Following are some sample MTD estimates for several systems arranged by criticality. These estimates will vary from organization to organization and from business unit to business unit:

- **Nonessential**   30 days
- **Normal**   7 days
- **Important**   72 hours
- **Urgent**   24 hours
- **Critical**   Minutes to hours

Each business function and asset should be placed in one of these categories, depending on how long the organization can survive without it. These estimates will help you

Figure 14-2
Maximum tolerable downtime

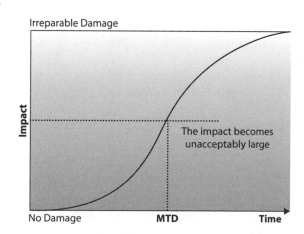

determine how to prioritize response team efforts to restore these assets. The shorter the MTD, the higher the priority of the function in question. For example, systems classified as Urgent should be addressed before those classified as Normal.

Recovery Time

Time is money, and the faster you can restore your network to a safe operating condition, the better it is for the organization's bottom line. Although there may be serious financial implications for every second a network asset is offline, you should not sacrifice speed for completeness. You should keep lines of communication open with organization management to determine acceptable limits to downtime. Having a sense of what the key performance indicators (KPIs) are for detection and remediation will help clear up confusion, manage expectations, and potentially enable you to demonstrate your team's preparedness should you exceed these limits. Setting recovery time limits may also be useful in the long run for the reputation of the team and may be useful in securing additional budgets for training and tools.

The recovery time objective (RTO) is oftentimes used, particularly in the context of disaster recovery, to denote the earliest time within which a business process must be restored after an incident to avoid unacceptable consequences associated with a break in business processes. The RTO value is smaller than the MTD value, because the MTD value represents the time after which an inability to recover significant operations will mean severe and perhaps irreparable damage to the organization's reputation or bottom line. The RTO assumes that there is a period of acceptable downtime. This means that an organization can be out of production for a certain period of time (RTO) and can still get back on its feet. But if it cannot get production up and running within the MTD window, the organization may be sinking too fast to recover properly.

Data Integrity

Taking down a network isn't always the goal of a network intrusion. For malicious actors, tampering with data may be enough to disrupt operations, and it may provide them with the outcome they were looking for. Financial transaction records, personal data, and professional correspondence are types of data that are especially susceptible to data tampering. There are cases when attacks on data are obvious, such as those involving ransomware. In these situations, malware will encrypt data files on a system so the users cannot access them without submitting payment for the decryption keys. However, it may not always be apparent that an attack on data integrity has taken place. It may be that you are able to discover the unauthorized insertion, modification, or deletion of data only after a detailed inspection. This illustrates why it's critical to back up data and system configurations as well as keep them sufficiently segregated from the network so that they are not themselves affected by the attack. An easily deployable backup solution will allow for very rapid restoration of services. The authors will caution, however, that much like Schrödinger's cat, the condition of any backup is unknown until a restore is attempted. In other words, having a backup alone isn't enough; it must be verified over time to ensure that it's free from corruption and malware.

Ransomware

Organized crime groups frequently set up malicious sites that serve malware convincingly disguised as games or other files. The malware contained in these files is often installed silently without user knowledge and encrypts a portion of the host's system, requiring payment for the decryption keys. For these groups, this is a source of significant and reliable income, because so many users and organizations have poor backup habits. Ironically, these groups rarely renege on an exchange, because it would be very damaging to their business model. After all, if you knew that you'd never see your data again, what would be the point of submitting payment? An industry that has sprung up with the proliferation of ransomware is *cyber insurance,* which an organization purchases to help offset the financial impact of a breach or a ransomware attack.

Economic Impacts

It's difficult to predict the second- and third-order effects of network intrusions. Even if some costs are straightforward to calculate, the complete economic impact of a network breach is difficult to quantify. A fine levied against an organization that had not adequately secured its workers' personal information is an immediate and obvious cost, but how does one accurately calculate the future losses due to identity theft, or the damage to the reputation of the organization resulting from the lack of confidence? It's critical to include questions like these in your discussion with stakeholders when determining courses of action for dealing with an incident.

Another consideration in calculating the economic scope of an incident is the value of the assets involved. The value placed on information is relative to the parties involved, what work was required to develop it, how much it costs to maintain, what damage would result if it were lost or destroyed, what enemies would pay for it, and what liability penalties could be endured. If an organization does not know the value of the information and the other assets it is trying to protect, it does not know how much money and time it should spend on protecting or restoring them. If the calculated value of a company's trade secret is x, then the total cost of protecting or restoring it should be some value less than x.

The previous examples refer to assessing the value of information and protecting it, but this logic also applies to an organization's facilities, systems, and resources. The value of facilities must be assessed, along with all printers, workstations, servers, peripheral devices, supplies, and employees. You do not know how much is in danger of being lost if you don't know what you have and what it is worth in the first place.

System Process Criticality

As part of your preparation, you must determine what processes are considered essential for the business's operation. These processes are associated with tasks that must be accomplished with a certain level of consistency for the business to remain competitive.

Each business's list of critical processes will be different, but it's important to identify those early so that they can be the first to be brought back up during a recovery. The critical processes list isn't restricted to technical assets only; it should include the essential staff required to get these critical systems back online and keep them operational. It's important to educate members across the organization as to what these core processes are, how their work directly supports the goals of the processes, and how they benefit from successful operations. This is effective in getting the appropriate level of buy-in required for successfully responding to incidents and recovering from any resulting damage.

 EXAM TIP   Criticality and probability are the primary components of risk analysis. Whereas *probability* describes the chance of a future event occurring, *criticality* is the impact of that future event. Criticality is often expressed by degree, such as high, moderate, or low. Low criticality indicates little impact to business operations, moderate indicates impaired or degraded performance, and high indicates a significant impairment of business functions. For the CySA+ exam, it's important to be able to describe incident response priorities based on factors such as criticality.

Data Correlation and Analysis

Security information and event management (SIEM) systems do a fantastic job of collecting and presenting massive amounts of data from disparate sources in a single view. They assist the analyst in determining whether an event is indeed malicious and what behaviors may be connected with the event. With a smart policy for how logs are captured and sent to a SIEM system, you can spend more time investigating what actually happened versus trying to figure out if the data you needed was even recorded. SIEM systems are critical when it comes to categorizing attacks. Because a primary goal of IR is to enable the organization to figure out what happened and get back to normal operations, it helps to be able to say with a fair degree of certainty that something you observe on the network is tied to some stage of an attack. If you're able to determine with confidence that an attack is early in its attack cycle, you can prioritize actions to remove it from the network. Compare this with finding evidence of exfiltration after the fact, and you can see why time is so critical in tying into and referencing across massive data sets.

Incident Declaration and Escalation

Based largely on the scope and impact of the incident, and considering the factors we discussed previously (IOCs, downtime, economic impact, criticality, and so on), a senior person in the organization (normally the IR team lead or on-site commander) makes the decision to declare the event as an incident and begin the response process. The criteria and procedures for declaring an incident should be detailed in the IR plan. This may involve alerting management, assembling the team, initiating the correct IR procedures, and so on.

Escalation is also based on the scope and impact factors discussed earlier. Decisions to escalate the incident, either to a higher level within the organization or outside the organization, are always made by the IR team lead at minimum, and sometimes even by higher-level management if it involves outside organizations, such as law enforcement or an outside contractor.

Reverse Engineering

Reverse engineering (RE) is the detailed examination of a product to learn what it does and how it works. In the context of IR, RE relates almost exclusively to malware. The idea is to analyze the binary code to find, for example, the IP addresses or host/domain names it uses for command and control (C2) nodes, the techniques it employs to achieve permanence in an infected host, or the unique characteristics that could be used as a signature for the malware.

Generally speaking, there are two approaches to reverse engineering malware. The first doesn't really care about what the binary *is* but rather with what the binary *does*. This approach, focused on behavioral analysis, is sometimes called *dynamic code analysis* and requires a sandbox in which to execute the malware. This sandbox creates a virtual environment that looks like a real operating system to the malware and provides such things as access to a file system, network interface, memory, and anything else the malware asks for. Each request is carefully documented to establish a timeline of behavior that enables you to understand what it does. The main advantage of dynamic malware analysis is that it tends to be significantly faster and requires less expertise than the alternative (described next). It can be particularly helpful for code that has been heavily obfuscated by its authors. The biggest disadvantage is that it doesn't reveal all that the malware does but rather all that it did during its execution in the sandbox. Some malware will actually check to see if it is being run in a sandbox before doing anything interesting. Additionally, some malware doesn't immediately do anything nefarious, waiting instead for a certain condition to be met (for example, a logic bomb that activates only at a particular date and time).

The alternative to dynamic code analysis is, unsurprisingly, *static code analysis*. In this approach to malware RE, a highly skilled analyst will either disassemble or decompile the binary code to translate its 1's and 0's into either assembly language or whichever higher-level language it was created in. This enables a reverse engineer to see all possible functions of the malware, not just the ones it exhibited during a limited run in a sandbox. It is then possible, for example, to see all the domains the malware would reach out to, given the right conditions, as well as the various ways in which it would permanently insert itself into its host. This last insight enables the IR team to look for evidence that any of the other persistence mechanisms exist in other hosts that were not considered infected up to that point.

Note that depending on how your incident response plan is constructed, as well as the availability of knowledgeable personnel who can perform reverse engineering, this activity may in fact wait until after the incident has been contained and eradicated. It is often actually performed during the forensics analysis portion of response, after the fact, in order to determine the root cause. Any reverse engineering that occurs during the actual incident is typically with the intent to halt the incident by understanding the nature of the malware involved.

Incident Response Tools

During Part I, and elsewhere in the book, we discussed specific tools used to determine malicious activities. These are the tools you will primarily use during incident response.

Additionally, you will make use of the same tools you use during the normal course of security operations in your infrastructure. These include logging, intrusion detection and prevention systems (IDPSs), and security information and event systems, among others. These will also typically include automated scripts that may perform specific tasks. We discussed these automated scripts in the context of incident response earlier when we talked about playbooks.

One specific IR-focused tool used during incidents that you might not otherwise use is an incident response management system. This type of system is where you go to centrally record and document specific details about the incident. This can often take the place of every team member having their own separate paper notebook in which they take their notes regarding the events. A centralized incident response management system enables all team members to input their notes, so they can be analyzed and correlated, and thus provide instant documentation for management on the status of the incident response. In any event, it is to your advantage to make use of these tools so you will have a more efficient and effective response.

Containment

Once you know that a threat agent has compromised the security of your information system, your first order of business is to keep things from getting worse. Containment comprises a set of actions that attempts to deny the threat agent the ability or means to cause further damage. The goal is to prevent or reduce the spread of this incident while you strive to eradicate it. This is akin to confining highly contagious patients in an isolation room of a hospital until they can be cured to keep others from becoming infected. A proper containment process buys the IR team time for a proper investigation and determination of the incident's root cause. The containment should be based on the category of the attack (that is, whether it was internal or external), the assets affected by the incident, and the criticality of those assets. Containment approaches can be proactive or reactive. Which is the best approach depends on the environment and the category of the attack. In some cases, the best action may be to disconnect the affected system from the network. However, this reactive approach could cause a denial of service or limit functionality of critical systems.

 NOTE Remember that preserving evidence is an important part of containment. You never know when a seemingly routine response will end up in court and require well-documented evidence that has been properly acquired.

Segmentation

A well-designed security architecture will segment your information systems by some set of criteria, such as function (for example, finance or HR) or sensitivity (for example, unclassified or secret). *Segmentation* divides a network into subnetworks (or segments) so that hosts in different segments are not able to communicate directly with each other.

This can be done by either physically wiring separate networks or by logically assigning devices to separate virtual local area networks (VLANs). In either case, traffic between network segments must go through some sort of gateway device, which is oftentimes a router with the appropriate access control lists (ACLs). For example, the accounting division may have its own VLAN that prevents users in the research and development (R&D) division from directly accessing the financial data servers. If certain R&D users had a legitimate need for such access, they would have to be added to the gateway device's ACL, which could place restrictions based on source/destination addresses, time of day, or even specific applications and data to be accessed. Note that VLANs can be implemented on physical layer 3 switches as well as use software-defined networking (SDN). Segmenting using VLANs isn't only limited to local subnets; compromised hosts located at another logical and physical site connected across wide area network (WAN) links can also be segmented away from other networks using Virtual eXtensible LANs (VXLANs) in larger, geographically dispersed organizations and those that use cloud-based infrastructures.

The advantages of network segmentation during IR should be pretty obvious: compromises can be constrained to the network segment in which they started. To be clear, it is still possible to go from one segment to another, as was the case with the R&D users example. Some VLANs may also have vulnerabilities that could enable an attacker to jump from one to another without going through the gateway. Still, segmentation provides an important layer of defense that can help contain an incident. Without it, the resulting "flat" network will make it more difficult to contain an incident.

Isolation

Although it is certainly helpful to segment the network as part of its architectural design, we already saw that this can still allow an attacker to move easily between hosts on the same subnet. As part of your preparations for IR, it is helpful to establish an isolation VLAN, much like hospitals prepare isolation rooms before any contagious patients actually need them. The IR team would then have the ability to move any compromised or suspicious hosts quickly to this VLAN until they can be further analyzed. The isolation VLAN would have no connectivity to the rest of the network, which would prevent the spread of any malware. This isolation would also prevent compromised hosts from communicating with external hosts such as C2 nodes. About the only downside to using isolation VLANs is that some advanced malware can detect this situation and then take steps to eradicate itself from the infected hosts. Although this may sound wonderful from an IR perspective, it does hinder your ability to understand what happened and how the compromise was executed so that you can keep it from happening in the future.

While a host is in isolation, the response team is safely able to observe its behaviors to gain information about the nature of the incident. By monitoring its network traffic, you can discover external hosts (for example, C2 nodes and tool repositories) that may be part of the compromise. This enables you to contact other organizations and get their help in shutting down whatever infrastructure the attackers are using. You can also monitor the compromised host's running processes and file system to see where the malware resides and what it is trying to do on the live system. All this helps you better understand the incident and come up with the best way to eradicate it. It also enables you to create indicators of compromise that you can then share with others, such as the computer emergency response team (CERT) or an information sharing and analysis center (ISAC).

Removal

At some point in the response process, you may have to remove compromised hosts from the network altogether. This can happen after isolation or immediately upon noticing the compromise, depending on the situation. Isolation is ideal if you have the means to study behaviors and gain actionable intelligence, or if you're overwhelmed by a large number of potentially compromised hosts that need to be triaged. Still, one way or another, some of the compromised hosts will come off the network permanently.

When you remove a host from the network, you need to decide whether you will keep it powered on, shut it down and preserve it, or simply rebuild it. Ideally, the criteria for making this decision are already spelled out in the IR plan. Here are some of the factors to consider in this situation:

- **Threat intelligence value**   A compromised computer can be a treasure trove of information about the tactics, techniques, procedures (TTPs) and the tools used by an adversary—particularly a sophisticated or unique one. If you have a threat intelligence capability in your organization and can gain new or valuable information from a compromised host, you may want to keep it running until its analysis has been completed.

- **Crime scene evidence**   Almost every intentional compromise of a computer system is a criminal act in many countries, including the United States. Even if you don't plan to pursue a criminal or civil case against the perpetrators, it is possible that future IR activities will change your mind and would benefit from the evidentiary value of a removed host. If you have the resources, it may be worth the effort to make forensic images of the primary storage (for example, RAM) before you shut it down and of secondary storage (for example, the file system) before or after you power it off.

- **Ability to restore**   It is not a happy moment for anybody in our line of work when we discover that, though we did everything by the book, we removed and disposed of a compromised computer that contained critical business information that was not replicated or backed up anywhere else. If we took and retained a forensic image of the drive, we could mitigate this risk, but otherwise, someone is going to have a bad day. This is yet another reason why you should, to the extent that your resources allow, keep as much of a removed host as possible.

The removal process should be well documented in the IR plan so that the right issues are considered by the right people at the right time. We address chain of custody and related issues in Chapter 16, but for now, suffice it to say that what you do with a removed computer can come back to haunt you if you don't do it properly.

Eradication and Recovery

Once the incident is contained, you turn your attention to the eradication and recovery process, in which you eliminate the compromise by removing malware, patching, and mitigating vulnerabilities and then return all systems to a known-good state. It is important that you gather evidence before you recover systems, because in many cases you won't know that you need legally admissible evidence until days, weeks, or even months after an incident. It pays, then, to treat each incident as if it will eventually end up in a court of justice.

Once all relevant evidence is captured, you can fix everything that was broken. The aim is to restore full, trustworthy functionality to the organization. For hosts that were compromised, the best practice is simply to reinstall the system from a gold master image and then restore data from the most recent backup that occurred prior to the attack.

Recovery in an IR is focused on ensuring that you have identified the corresponding attack vectors and implemented effective countermeasures against them. This stage presumes that you have analyzed the incident and verified the manner in which it was conducted. This analysis can be a separate postmortem activity or can take place in parallel with the response.

Remediation

Remediation involves correcting or mitigating any issues that may have led to the incident in the first place, whenever possible. It may not always mean that every single issue will be corrected, but it should mean that the most severe concerns that initiated or are continuing the incident are addressed. Remediation can come in many forms; which method of remediation used will depend on the circumstances involved with the incident, its severity, and the assets that must be recovered. Remediation can involve several aspects of correcting or updating a variety of administrative, technical, and physical controls. Examples of methods used to remedy an incident include containing and eradicating malware, repairing compromised physical controls, rerouting network traffic, changing firewall and IDS rules, and even logically or physically relocating assets.

Compensating Controls

It's important here to revisit a basic tenet of security controls. Ordinarily, we would have the most effective security controls we can have in place. Sometimes that's not always possible though, due to resources such as money and personnel availability. The principles of risk mitigation allow us to put other controls in place that may or may not be as effective but still reduce the risk significantly. Sometimes we must put multiple controls in place to have the same level of effect as a desired or primary control. Compensating controls are those that you put into place when a preferred control is not available for some reason. During an incident, it is possible that you may not have the primary control available and must put compensating controls in place. For example, if an attack has completely compromised one your security devices, you may not be able to put that device back online for quite some time, and it may even have to be replaced. However, you could install other devices in its place (as a compensating control) or reroute traffic until the device can come back online.

Note that compensating controls are typically temporary in nature, but longer term. As such, they are often confused with corrective controls. A corrective control is usually a quick fix to immediately solve a security issue and is temporary and short term in nature. For example, suppose that a larger piece of your perimeter fence is destroyed during a heavy storm. It will take a week or two to get the fence repaired, so in the meantime a corrective control would be to post guards outside the compromised fence section so that unauthorized personnel may not enter the facility grounds. The additional guards are a corrective control, temporary in nature, and short term. The ideal control would be to fully repair the fence as soon as possible. Contrast that, in the same situation, to a compensating control. In the event you can't immediately get the fence repaired, keeping guards there posted for weeks or even months on end would not be cost-effective. Therefore, a longer-term control may have to be implemented, such as constructing a temporary barrier around the destroyed fence section, increasing the frequency of guard patrols, placing video surveillance cameras around the compromised fence, and so on, until the fence can be fully repaired.

Vulnerability Mitigation

Recovering from an incident means not only getting things back to where they were but also not allowing your environment to be disrupted in the same way again. Mitigation involves eradicating the cause of any event or incident once it has been accurately identified. By definition, every incident occurs because a threat actor exploits a vulnerability and compromises the security of an information system. It stands to reason, then, that after recovering from an incident, you would want to scan your systems for other instances of that same (or a related) vulnerability.

Although it is true that you will never be able to protect against every vulnerability, it is also true that you have a responsibility to mitigate those that have been successfully exploited, whether or not you thought they posed a high risk before the incident. The reason is that you now know that the probability of a threat actor exploiting it is 100 percent, because it already happened. And if it happened once, it is likely to happen again absent a change in your controls. The inescapable conclusion is that, after an incident, you need to implement a control that will prevent a recurrence of the exploitation. You also need to develop a plug-in for your favorite scanner that will test all systems for any residual vulnerabilities.

For the best results, this process will require coordination with your vulnerability management process, since vulnerability mitigation activities will likely change your environment. Your team will need a method to determine, first, if the vulnerability was sufficiently addressed and, second, if any of these changes introduce new conditions that may make the system more vulnerable to attack. Your vulnerability management team will often be a great ally in advising IR efforts related to vulnerability mitigation because they will likely have the most experience and resources related to identifying, prioritizing, and remediating software flaws.

Sanitization

According to NIST Special Publication 800-88 Revision 1, "Guidelines for Media Sanitization," *sanitization* refers to the process by which access to data on a given medium is made infeasible for a given level of effort. These levels of effort, in the context of IR, can be cursory and sophisticated. What we call cursory sanitization can be accomplished by simply reformatting a drive. This may be sufficient against run-of-the-mill attackers who look for large groups of easy victims and don't put too much effort into digging their hooks deeply into any one victim. On the other hand, there are sophisticated attackers who may have deliberately targeted your organization and will go to great lengths to persist in your systems or, if repelled, compromise them again. This class of threat actor requires more advanced approaches to sanitization.

The challenge, of course, is that you don't always know which kind of attacker is responsible for the incident. For this reason, simply reformatting a drive is a risky approach. Instead, we recommend one of the following techniques, listed in increasing level of effectiveness at ensuring the adversary is definitely denied access to data on the medium:

- **Overwriting**   Overwriting data entails replacing the 1's and 0's that represent it on storage media with random or fixed patterns of 1's and 0's to render the original data unrecoverable. This should be done at least once (for example, overwriting the medium with 1's, 0's, or a pattern of these), but it may have to be done more than that to ensure that all data is destroyed.

- **Encryption**   Many mobile devices take this quick and secure approach to render data unusable. The data stored on the medium is encrypted using a strong key. To render the data unrecoverable, the system securely deletes the encryption key, which is many times faster than deleting the encrypted data. Recovering the data in this scenario is typically computationally infeasible.

- **Degaussing**   This is the process of removing or reducing the magnetic field patterns on conventional disk drives or tapes. In essence, a powerful magnetic force is applied to the media, which results in the wiping of the data and sometimes the destruction of the motors that drive the platters. Note that degaussing typically renders the drive unusable.

- **Physical destruction**   Perhaps the best way to combat data remanence is simply to destroy the physical media. The two most commonly used approaches to destroying media are to shred them or expose them to caustic or corrosive chemicals. Another approach is incineration.

Reconstruction

Once a compromised host's media is sanitized, your next step is to rebuild the host to its pristine state. The best approach to doing this is to ensure you have created known-good, hardened images of the various standard configurations for hosts on your network.

These images are sometimes called *gold masters* and facilitate the process of rebuilding a compromised host. This reconstruction is significantly more difficult if you manually reinstall the operating system, configure it so it is hardened, and then install the various applications and/or services that were in the original host. We don't know anybody who, having gone through this dreadful process once, doesn't invest the time to build and maintain gold images thereafter.

Another aspect of reconstruction is the restoration of data to the host. Again, there is one best practice here, which is to ensure you have up-to-date backups of the system data files. This is also key for quickly and inexpensively dealing with ransomware incidents. Sadly, in too many organizations, backups are the responsibility of individual users. If your organization does not enforce centrally managed backups of all systems, your only other hope is to ensure that data is maintained in a managed data store such as a file server.

Reimaging

Reimaging is a mitigation that must sometimes be considered if a system cannot be successfully recovered to a trusted state. If the infrastructure has been exposed to malware or is suspected of being compromised by an attacker, obviously the best course of action is to try to eliminate the malware completely and ensure that all systems are configured to their standard secure baselines. However, this is not always possible if the attack is widespread or complex. Sometimes the only course of action is to start from scratch and reimage a device with a trusted image. Ideally, if sensitive and critical data have been backed up on a regular basis, this should not be much of a problem. However, the danger of restoring a system from scratch is that valuable data will be lost and cannot be recovered from a backup. Another issue is that during the reimaging process, critical assets can be offline and unusable. While reimaging a device should be something that is carefully considered, the organization should have plans in place that permit regular critical data backups, and there should be solid, standardized procedures for reimaging devices when needed.

 NOTE An attacked or infected system should never be trusted because you do not necessarily know all the changes that have taken place and the true extent of the damage. Some malicious code could still be hiding somewhere. Systems should be rebuilt to ensure they are trustworthy again.

Virtualization Solutions

Because of the rapid adoption of virtualization technologies, those are also available for an organization to use to reconstitute its networks and hosts. Hosts don't have to simply be reimaged any longer, although that's still a viable option. Virtualized hosts can be reconstituted using snapshots of virtual hosts in near real time. Depending upon how often the snapshots are taken, the organization could conceivably restore virtualized hosts to a state very shortly before the incident took place, closing the gap on data loss if the snapshots are recent.

Other virtualization options for restoring hosts and entire networks include those where the hosts are cloud-based and can be restored easily—again, almost in real time—to a known trusted state using technologies such as Infrastructure as Code (IaC).

Secure Disposal

When you're disposing of media or devices as a result of an IR, any of the four techniques covered earlier (overwriting, encryption, degaussing, or physical destruction) may work, depending on the device. Overwriting is usually feasible only with regard to hard disk drives and may not be available on some solid-state drives. Encryption-based purging can be found in multiple workstation, server, and mobile operating systems, but not in all. Degaussing works on magnetic media only, but some of the most advanced magnetic drives use stronger fields to store data and may render older degaussers inadequate. Note that we have not mentioned network devices such as switches and routers, which typically don't offer any of these alternatives. In the end, the only way to dispose of these devices securely is by physically destroying them using an accredited process or service provider. This physical destruction involves the shredding, pulverizing, disintegration, or incineration of the device. Although this may seem extreme, it is sometimes the only secure alternative left.

Patching

Many of the most damaging incidents are the result of an unpatched software flaw. This vulnerability can exist for a variety of reasons, including failure to update a known vulnerability or the existence of a heretofore unknown vulnerability, also known as a *zero-day*. As part of the IR, the team must determine which cause is the case. The first would indicate an internal failure to keep patches updated, whereas the second would all but require notification to the vendor of the product that was exploited so a patch can be developed.

Many organizations rely on endpoint protection that is not centrally managed, particularly in a "bring-your-own-device" (BYOD) environment. As a result, if a user or device fails to download and install an available patch, it causes a vulnerability, which can become an incident. If this is the case in your organization and you are unable to change the policy to require centralized patching, you should also assume that some number of endpoints will fail to be patched, so you should develop compensatory controls elsewhere in your security architecture. For example, by implementing network access control (NAC), you can test any device attempting to connect to the network for patching, updates, antimalware, and any other policies you want to enforce. If the endpoint fails any of the checks, it is placed in a quarantine network that may allow Internet access (particularly for downloading patches) but keeps the device from joining the organizational network and potentially spreading malware.

If, on the other hand, your organization uses centralized patches and updates, the vulnerability was known, and still it was successfully exploited, this points to a failure within whatever system or processes you are using for patching. Part of the response would be to identify the failure, correct it, and then validate that the fix is effective at preventing a repeated incident in the future.

Restoration of Permissions

For many organizations, recovery is an effort to restore business operations quickly and efficiently, and it also addresses the issues that contributed to that incident. Although recovery operations will ideally leave you in a better place than before the incident, just getting access back at the same level is a win for many security teams. This often means that a reliable backup solution is in place and that backups have been tested and verified as part of the overall IR process. The rebuilding phase is not the time to discover that a backup you relied on was never verified.

Validation of Permissions

There are two principal reasons for validating permissions before you wrap up your IR activities. The first is that inappropriately elevated permissions may have been a cause of the incident in the first place. It is not uncommon for organizations to allow excessive privileges for their users. One of the most common reasons we've heard is that if the users don't have administrative privileges on their devices, they won't be able to install whatever applications they'd like to try out in the name of improving their efficiency. Of course, we know better, but this may be an organizational culture issue that is beyond your power to change. Still, documenting the incidents (and their severity) that are the direct result of excessive privileges may, over time, move the needle in the direction of common sense.

Not all permissions issues can be blamed on end users. Time and again, we've seen system or domain admins who do all their work (including surfing the Web) using their admin account. Furthermore, most of us have heard of (or had to deal with) the discovery that a system admin who left the organization months or even years ago still has a valid account. The aftermath of an IR provides a great opportunity to double-check on issues like these.

Finally, it is very common for interactive attackers to create or hijack administrative accounts so that they can do their nefarious deeds undetected. Although it may be odd to see an anonymous user in Russia accessing sensitive resources on your network, you probably wouldn't get too suspicious if you saw one of your fellow admin staff members moving those files around. If there is any evidence that the incident leveraged an administrative account, it would be a good idea to delete that account and, if necessary, issue a new one to the victimized administrator. While you're at it, you may want to validate that all other accounts are needed and protected.

Restoration of Services and Verification of Logging

The security team will be directly involved in two key aspects of restoring services. The first is developing and executing the testing processes for network service validation to certify that all systems are operational and provide the requisite level of service. The second, and less obvious aspect, is to ensure that, along with certifying that any vulnerable services are taken offline, the team has the necessary visibility and logging to detect any future issues.

Chapter Review

In this chapter we began our discussion of incident response. We discussed the phases of incident response, including preparation, detection and analysis, containment, eradication and recovery, and post-incident activities. Post-incident activities will be covered more in depth in Chapter 15.

The incident response plan is a critical piece of the response capability. It discusses processes, procedures, and how to actually implement the response. In the plan, you should establish a communication process that covers both internal and external organizations. The plan should also discuss training both incident response team members and general members of the organization on their incident responsibilities. The plan should also discuss testing incident capabilities using exercises such as documentation reviews, tabletop exercises, walkthroughs, and full exercises. The incident response plan also includes playbooks, which are step-by-step groups of tasks that must be performed during the incident. Playbooks also use automated scripts that can perform tasks as a group.

In the detection and analysis phase, the response team considers factors such as indicators of compromise, downtime, required recovery time, and maintaining data integrity to determine scope and impact. Scope and impact are also affected by different factors, including system criticality and economic impact to the organization. We also discussed the value of reverse engineering malware to discover how it is constructed and what its effects on the infrastructure may be. Incident response tools include many of the tools you use in the normal course of security operations to detect malicious activities, in addition to a good incident management system.

During the containment phase, the goal is to halt the incident and limit its damage. We discussed the value of segmenting affected hosts, isolating them, and, if needed, removing them from the network. This will help contain the spread of malware and may help prevent damage to critical hosts or information.

Finally, we discussed eradication and recovery activities. These consists of the activities needed to remediate hosts using a variety of methods, including implementing compensating controls when needed, mitigating any vulnerabilities that may have caused the incident, sanitizing media, and rebuilding hosts completely from scratch, through reimaging with trusted media. We also discussed securely disposing of assets so that their data cannot be recovered. Patching systems is likely a necessary task to eliminate vulnerabilities that may have contributed to the incident. When you're recovering systems, another goal is to validate and restore the necessary permissions for users and ensure that there are no unauthorized accounts or permissions on resources. Finally, we talked about restoring network services.

Questions

1. The process of dissecting a sample of malicious software to determine its purpose is referred to as what?

   A. Segmentation

   B. Frequency analysis

   C. Traffic analysis

   D. Reverse engineering

2. During the IR process, when is a good time to perform a vulnerability scan to determine the effectiveness of corrective actions?

   A. Change control process

   B. Reverse engineering

   C. Removal

   D. Eradication and recovery

3. What is the key goal of the containment stage of an IR process?

   A. To limit further damage from occurring

   B. To get services back up and running

   C. To communicate goals and objectives of the IR plan

   D. To prevent data follow-on actions by the adversary exfiltration

Use the following scenario to answer Questions 4–8:

You receive an alert about a compromised device on your network. Users are reporting that they are receiving strange messages in their inboxes and having problems sending e-mails. Your technical team reports unusual network traffic from the mail server. The team has analyzed the associated logs and confirmed that a mail server has been infected with malware.

4. You immediately remove the server from the network and route all traffic to a backup server. What stage are you currently operating in?

   A. Preparation

   B. Containment

   C. Eradication

   D. Validation

5. Now that the device is no longer on the production network, you want to restore services. Before you rebuild the original server to a known-good condition, you want to preserve the current condition of the server for later inspection. What is the first step you want to take?

   A. Format the hard drive.

   B. Reinstall the latest operating systems and patches.

   C. Make a forensic image of all connected media.

   D. Update the antivirus definitions on the server and save all configurations.

6. Your team has identified the strain of malware that took advantage of a bug in your mail server version to gain elevated privileges. Because you cannot be sure what else was affected on that server, what is your best course of action?

   A. Immediately update the mail server software.

   B. Reimage the server's hard drive.

    C. Write additional firewall rules to allow only e-mail-related traffic to reach the server.

    D. Submit a request for next-generation antivirus for the mail server.

7. Your team believes it has eradicated the malware from the primary server. You attempt to bring the affected systems back into the production environment in a responsible manner. Which of the following tasks will *not* be a part of this phase?

    A. Applying the latest patches to server software

    B. Monitoring network traffic on the server for signs of compromise

    C. Determining the best time to phase in the primary server into operations

    D. Using a newer operating system with different server software

8. Your company is using an older log management system that is overwhelmed during an incident. The log management tool has stopped generating automatic alerts, so security personnel were not alerted to the incident early on. You tell your management that in the long term, the log management system and its server must be replaced. Until a new system can be implemented, which of the following compensating controls would be the best approach to remediating the situation?

    A. Manually audit the logs until the new system is implemented.

    B. Stop all auditing processes until the new system is implemented.

    C. Take the log management system offline.

    D. Configure the server to only log safe network traffic to prevent it from becoming overwhelmed.

Answers

1. D. Reverse engineering is the process of decomposing malware to understand what it does and how it works.

2. D. Additional scanning should be performed during validation, part of the eradication and recovery process, to ensure that no additional vulnerabilities exist after remediation.

3. A. The goal of containment is to prevent or reduce the spread of this incident while you strive to eradicate it.

4. B. Containment is the set of actions that attempts to deny the threat agent the ability or means to cause further damage.

5. C. Since unauthorized access of computer systems is a criminal act in many areas, it may be useful to take a snapshot of the device in its current state using forensic tools to preserve evidence.

6. B. Generally, the most effective means of disposing of an infected system is a complete reimaging of a system's storage to ensure that any malicious content was removed and to prevent reinfection.

PART III

7. **D.** The goal of the IR process is to get services back to normal operation as quickly and safely as possible. Introducing completely new and untested software may introduce significant challenges to this goal.

8. **A.** Until a new system is implemented, you should manually review audit logs since there is no guarantee security personnel will be alerted in the event of another incident.

CHAPTER 15

Post-Incident Response Activities

In this chapter you will learn:

- The activities that take place after an incident
- Incident response reporting and communication
- The importance of metrics and key performance indicators

Predicting rain doesn't count. Building arks does.

—Warren Buffett

The activities we perform during an incident are critical to keeping the organization's systems and data confidential, intact, and available to its authorized users. In the previous chapter, we discussed the incident response phases of preparation, detection and analysis, containment, and eradication and recovery. A phase just as critical as these others, post-incident activities, will be discussed in this chapter.

How you deal with the aftermath of an incident is just as important as the response itself. One of the goals of an incident response should be to help prevent the next incident, by using the results of the analysis to close the gap on controls, remediate vulnerabilities, patch and reconfigure systems, and learn from the incident. During the incident itself, as well as afterward, data is analyzed to determine the root cause so that the appropriate steps can be taken to prevent or mitigate the same circumstances from happening again. The details of the response itself, such as the effectiveness in detecting and analyzing the incident, as well as containment and eradication efforts, are examined so that any lessons learned are developed that may help the organization respond more efficiently and effectively. Finally, an incident report is generated for appropriate stakeholders to inform them of exactly what happened and how it happened. We will discuss all of these post-incident activities in this chapter.

This chapter continues our discussion on incident response and includes coverage of Objective 3.2, "Given a scenario, perform incident response activities"; Objective 3.3, "Explain the preparation and post-incident activity phases of the incident management life cycle"; and Objective 4.2, "Explain the importance of incident response reporting and communication."

Post-Incident Activities

No effective business process would be complete without some sort of introspection or opportunity to learn from and adapt to our experiences. This is the role of the post-incident phase of an incident response. It is here that we apply the lessons learned and information gained from the process to improve our posture in the future. While several of the activities we discuss are also performed at various points during the response itself, most of these activities are performed after the incident is resolved to discover more details about the incident, apply any lessons learned, and generally "clean up" after the incident.

Forensics

Digital forensics is a process normally associated with computer crime or abuse. However, there is a significant use for forensic analysis during and after an incident. Digital forensics is the process of locating and recovering digital evidence from systems, networks, applications, and digital storage. Forensics is critical in understanding the root cause of an issue as well as how an incident actually occurred and progressed over time. During a widespread incident, forensic activities are not limited to only one system; forensic processes are normally executed on any affected system, network devices, applications, and network-based storage. Forensics also often involves other processes, such as reverse engineering malware and log analysis. All these contribute to determining the causes of an incident so that those causes can be eliminated and prevent future incidents. Note that Chapter 16 discusses digital forensics in far more detail.

To Pull the Plug or Not?

In the early days of security operations and incident response, the common school of thought was that in the event of an attack, IT and security personnel should pull the plug on devices to prevent the attack from spreading. This meant not only disconnecting network cables so that the hosts were unplugged from the network, but also removing their power so they would be completely off. This school of thought remained for a few years, until the necessity of recovering critical forensic evidence about the attack became apparent. Then the paradigm shifted to one of contention, in that there had to be a balance between allowing an attack to do more damage, while evidence was actively collected, and minimizing the damage by pulling the plug on the device itself.

Fast-forward to the present, and the option of pulling the power on a device really isn't necessary anymore. Incident response has matured a great deal, and now with modern technologies and processes that are able to logically isolate and segment network devices, we really don't have a need to be powering off devices during an attack. A device can be left powered and running while valuable forensics evidence is collected, and the connection to the network can be logically or physically severed.

Sometimes, disconnection from the network or the Internet is not even necessary since traffic can be dynamically rerouted so that it does not respond to an attacker's remote commands or transfer malicious traffic to other hosts. Traffic can also be sent into a "black hole" or a "bit-bucket"; that is, it can just be discarded so that it doesn't go to other hosts or the Internet and cause any more harm. In some cases, there are even proactive security technologies that will also fool an attacker into thinking that the host is still online, but in fact it has been completely disconnected from the Internet. There are very few occasions in today's modern incident response when a box has to be completely powered down; typically, that is only necessary to prevent the active destruction of data on the host—and then as a last resort.

Root Cause Analysis

Discovering the underlying cause of an incident is critical to its analysis; in fact, this is one of the entire reasons for analyzing an event—to determine the *who, what, where, when,* and *how* of an incident. The root cause is something that must be discovered and reported so that the organization understands the factors that led up to the incident and can take steps to eliminate or mitigate those factors, thus preventing future incidents. Root cause analysis is performed using several processes, including the aforementioned forensics analysis process. Reverse engineering malware, log analysis, timeline analysis, and traffic analysis all also contribute to determining the root cause of an incident. Note that in many cases, during the root cause investigation and analysis, you will require access to a variety of sensitive information, such as log files, network architecture diagrams, workflows, and so on. Make sure you keep potentially sensitive information secure and prevent unauthorized access by anyone not directly working on the analysis.

 EXAM TIP The CySA+ exam contains simulations in which the goal is to determine a root cause. You are often presented with scenarios or data that may come from an initial helpdesk call, for example, or a log file or other artifacts. You should understand how to develop a root cause from the information given during the exam scenario.

Change Control Process

In the aftermath of an incident, the team will discuss and document important recommendations for changes. Although these changes may make perfect sense to the IR team, you must be careful about assuming that they should automatically be made. Every organization should have some sort of change control process. Oftentimes, this mechanism takes the form of a change control board (CCB), which consists of representatives of the various business units as well as other relevant stakeholders. Whether or not there is a board, the process is designed to ensure that no significant changes are made to any critical systems without careful consideration by all who may be affected.

PART III

Some of the changes that the incident response team will recommend may include policy changes, device configuration changes, the addition of new equipment or system upgrades, and even changes to business processes. These decisions may make perfect sense from an information security perspective, based on what the team determines were the causes or contributing factors to the incident, but would probably face some challenges from other departments. The formal change control process is the appropriate way to consider all perspectives and arrive at sensible and effective changes to the systems.

 EXAM TIP Change management and control processes are not specifically tested as objectives on the exam, but you may see questions list change processes as part of the answer or as a distractor. You may also see a mixture of terms, including change management, change control, and configuration management, although technically they are all three distinct processes.

Updates to the Incident Response Plan

As discussed in Chapter 14, incident management is a process. In the aftermath of an event, we take actions that enable us to prepare better for future incidents, which starts the process all over again. Regardless of whether the change control process implements any of the recommendations from the IR team, the response plan should be reviewed and, if appropriate, updated. Whereas the change control process implements organization-wide changes, the response team has much more control over the response plan. Absent sweeping changes, some decisions can be made at the IR team level and simply approved by the IR team lead or other management.

Any significant changes to the IR lifecycle, however, should also be considered from the perspectives of appropriate stakeholders. For example, if a change to the IR plan dictates that critical production systems must be taken offline under certain circumstances, this will affect business process owners who must be involved in the decision. They need to be aware that this change to the IR plan is taking place and give their input. This will ensure that the IR team is creating changes that make sense in the broader organizational context. To get stakeholders' perspectives, establishing and maintaining positive communications is paramount.

Indicator of Compromise Generation

We already mentioned the creation of IoCs as part of isolation efforts in the containment phase of the response. Now you can leverage those IoCs by incorporating them into your network monitoring plan. Most organizations would add these indicators to rules in their intrusion detection or prevention system (IDS/IPS). You can also cast a wider net by providing the IoCs to business partners or even competitors in your sector. This is where organizations such as the US-CERT and the ISACs can be helpful in keeping large groups of organizations protected against known attacks.

Monitoring

Once you have successfully responded to the incident, implemented new controls, and ran updated vulnerability scans to ensure that everything is mitigated, you must continue to monitor the incident. This is to ensure that there are no residual effects from the event that may still be lingering in the infrastructure and may still affect the organization. You should also strengthen your monitoring capabilities in general so that incidents can be detected before they occur. These are all-important preventive measures, but you still need to ensure that you improve your ability to react to a return by the same (or a similar) actor. Armed with all the information on the adversary's TTPs and new IoCs, you now need to update your monitoring plan to help you better detect similar attacks.

Incident Reporting and Communication

Communication is one of the most important aspects of an incident. Without it, the various stakeholders, such as the IR team itself, management, customers, suppliers, partners, employees, and others, are not aware of what's going on and what they should be doing to help respond to the incident. This can definitely slow things down and prevent an organization from effectively containing and eradicating an incident as well as recovering from it.

It's also worth mentioning that communication during an incident, as mentioned in Chapter 14, occurs constantly—from the very beginning of the incident, when it is first detected, triaged, and escalated, all the way to the end during the incident reporting stage. Throughout the entire incident response lifecycle, you must maintain good communications up the chain of command, downward into the trenches, and laterally across the organization, as well as with external stakeholders, as appropriate to the situation.

Stakeholder Identification and Communication

In the midst of an incident response, it is all too easy to get so focused on the technical challenges that we forget about the human element, which is arguably at least as important. Here, we focus our discussion on the various roles involved and the manner in which we must ensure that these roles are communicating effectively with one another and with those outside the organization.

The key roles required in incident responses can be determined beforehand based on established escalation thresholds. The in-house technical team will always be involved, of course, but when and how are others brought in? This depends on the analysis that your organization performed as part of developing the IR plan. Figure 15-1 shows a typical escalation model used by many organizations.

The technical team is unlikely to involve management in routine responses, such as a response to an e-mail with a malicious link or attachment that somehow gets to a user's inbox but is not clicked. You still have to respond to this and will probably notify others (such as the user, supervisor, and threat intelligence team) of the attempt, but management will not be in the loop at every step of the response. The situation is different, however, when the incident or response has a direct impact on the organization, such as when you have to reboot a production server to eradicate malware installed on it. Management needs to be closely involved in decision-making in this more serious scenario.

PART III

Figure 15-1
Typical role
escalation model

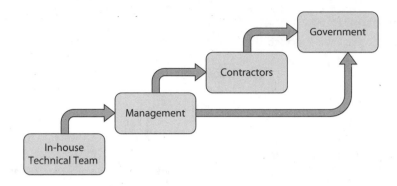

At some point, the skills and abilities of the in-house team will probably be insufficient to deal effectively with an incident; this is when the response is escalated, and you bring in contractors to augment your team or even take over aspects of the response. Obviously, this is an expensive move, so you want to consider this option carefully, and management will almost certainly be involved in that decision. Finally, some incidents require government involvement. Typically, though not always, this comes in the form of notifying and perhaps bringing in a law enforcement agency such as the FBI or Secret Service. This may happen with or without your organization calling in external contractors, but it will always involve senior leadership. Whatever the process, it's important to publish the specific escalation paths for your analysts and maintain a call list or contact information for those required to be notified or involved in case of an incident. Let's take a look at some of the issues involved with each of these roles.

 EXAM TIP For the purposes of the CySA+ exam, *IR stakeholders* are individuals and teams who are part of your organization and who have a role in helping with some aspects of an incident response. However, a broader set of stakeholders will be affected by the incident, including business partners, customers, outside agencies, and so on.

The term *stakeholder* is broad and could include a very large set of people. Each stakeholder has a critical role to play in some (maybe even most), but not all, responses. These supporting stakeholders normally will not be accustomed to executing response operations as the direct players are. You and the IR team must make extra efforts to ensure that each stakeholder knows what to do and how to do it when bad things happen.

Legal Counsel
Whenever an incident response escalates to the point of involving government agencies such as law enforcement, you will almost certainly be coordinating with your organization's legal counsel. Apart from requirements to report criminal or state-sponsored attacks on your systems, your organization may be affected by regulatory considerations. For instance, if you work in an organization covered by the Health Insurance Portability and Accountability Act (HIPAA) and you are responding to an incident

that compromised the protected health information (PHI) of 500 or more people, your organization will have some very specific reporting requirements that will have to be reviewed by your legal and/or compliance team(s).

The law is a remarkably complicated field, so even actions that may seem innocuous to many of us can have some onerous legal implications. Though some lawyers are very knowledgeable in complex technological and cybersecurity issues, most have only a cursory familiarity with them. In our experience, starting a dialogue early with the legal team and then maintaining a regular, ongoing conversation are critical to staying out of career-ending trouble.

Human Resources

The most likely involvement of human resources (HR) staff in a response occurs when the team determines that a member of the organization probably had a role in the incident. The role need not be malicious, mind you, because it could involve a failure to comply with policies (for example, connecting a thumb drive into a computer when that is not allowed) or repeated failures to apply security awareness training (for example, clicking a link in an e-mail even after a few rounds of remedial security training). Malicious, careless, or otherwise, the actions of our teammates can and do lead to serious incidents. Disciplinary action in those cases requires HR involvement.

In other situations, as well, you may need to involve HR in the response, such as when overtime is required to deal with the response, or when key people need to be called in from time off or vacation. The safest bet is to involve HR in your IR planning process, and especially in your exercises, and let them tell you what, if any, involvement they should have in various scenarios.

Public Relations

Managing communications with your customers and investors is critical to recovering from an incident successfully. What, when, to whom, and how you divulge information is of strategic importance, so you're better off leaving it to the professionals who, most likely, reside in your organization's marketing or public relations (PR) department. If your organization has a dedicated strategic communications, media, or public affairs team, it should also be involved in the response process.

 NOTE Not every aspect of the incident is appropriate for dissemination to all stakeholders. Some, like senior management, law enforcement, and regulatory agencies, as well as the incident response team, need to be aware of all the details of the incident, including sensitive information. Stakeholders such general employees, the public, customers, and even business partners don't always need to know the specific details of the incident, particularly while it is in progress. You don't want to disclose any sensitive information, such as vulnerabilities or how the attacker is compromising your network. Your public relations people, as well as senior management, should decide who gets exactly what type of sensitive information.

As with every other aspect of IR, planning and practice are the keys to success. When it comes to the PR team, this fact may be more applicable than it is with some other teams. These individuals, who are probably only vaguely aware of the intricate technical details of a compromise and incident response, will be the public face of the incident to the broad community. Their main goal is to mitigate any damage to the customers' and investors' trust in the organization. To do this, they need to have just the right amount of technical information, must be able to present it in a manner that is approachable to broad audiences, and must present information that can be dissected into effective sound bites (or "tweets"). For this, the PR team will rely heavily on members of the technical team who are able to translate "techno-speak" into something the average person can understand.

 NOTE The public relations team is the primary part of the organization that communicates directly with the general public and the media. For other external organizations, such as law enforcement and regulatory agencies, it will not necessarily be the public relations team that communicates with those agencies. Instead, the legal department or senior management may communicate directly with them.

Incident Response Team

The composition of the technical incident response team will usually depend on the incident itself. Some responses will involve a single analyst, while others may involve dozens of technical personnel from many different departments. Clearly, there is no one-size-fits-all team; you need to pull in the right people to deal with each problem. The part that should be prescribed ahead of time is the manner in which we assemble the team and, most importantly, who is calling the shots during the various stages of incident response. Note that many of the people on the incident response team may have other jobs they are required to do during normal operations, so there may be some conflict when these people are taken off of their normal duties and placed on our team, especially full time. This can cause some conflict in the organization because normal business operations will be interrupted. If you don't build this into your plan, and then periodically test how it will actually work, you will likely lose precious hours (or even days) in the "food fight" between internal departments that will likely ensue during a major incident.

One of the key issues involved with communications is actually one of decision-making. Unless the decision-making process and clear lines of authority are outlined in the incident response plan, there can be difficulties communicating the right information to the right people. At each major decision point in the process, you should ask, "Who decides?" Whatever your answer, the next question should be, "Does that person have the required authority?" If the person is lacking authority, you have to determine whether someone else should make the decision or whether that authority should be delegated in writing to the decider. These are important determinations: you don't want to be in the midst of an incident response and have to sit on your hands for a few hours while the decision is vetted up and down the corporate chain.

Contractors and External Parties

No matter how skilled or well-resourced an internal technical team is, you may have to bring in help from the outside at some point. Very few organizations, for example, are capable of responding to incidents involving nation-state offensive operators. Calling in the cavalry, however, requires a significant degree of prior coordination and communication. Apart from the obvious service contract with the IR firm, you have to plan and test exactly how they would come into your facility, what they would have access to, who would be watching and supporting them, and what (if any) parts of your system are off limits to them. These IR companies are very experienced in doing this sort of thing and can usually provide a step-by-step guide as well as templates for nondisclosure agreements (NDAs) and contracts. What they cannot do for you is train your staff (technical or otherwise) on how to deal with them once they descend upon your networks. This is where rehearsals and tests come in handy—in communicating to every stakeholder in your organization what a contractor response would look like and what each role would be.

It is possible to go too far in embedding IR contractors, however. Some organizations outsource all IR as a perceived cost-saving measure. Their rationale is that they pay only for what they need, because qualified personnel are hard to find, slow to develop in-house, and expensive. The truth of the matter, however, is that this approach is fundamentally flawed in at least two ways: First, incident response is inextricably linked with critical business processes whose nuances are difficult for third parties to grasp. This is why you will always need at least one qualified, hands-on incident responder who is part of the organization and can at least translate technical actions into business impacts. Second, IR can be at least as much about interpersonal communications and trust as it is about technical controls. External parties will have a much more difficult time dealing with the many individuals involved. One way or another, you are better off having some internal IR capability and augmenting it to a lesser or greater degree with external contractors.

Law Enforcement

A number of incidents will require you to involve a law enforcement agency (LEA). Sometimes, the laws that establish these requirements also have very specific timelines, lest you incur civil or even criminal penalties. In other cases, there may not be a requirement to involve an LEA, but it may be a very good idea to do so. If you (or your team) don't know which incidents fall into the two categories of required and recommended reporting, you may want to put that pretty high on your priority conversations list with your leadership and legal counsel.

When an LEA is involved, they will bring their own perspective on the response process. Whereas you are focused on mitigation and recovery, and management is keen on business continuity, the LEA will be driven by the need to preserve evidence (which should be, but is not always, an element of your IR plan anyway). These three sets of goals can be at odds with each other, particularly if you don't have a thorough, realistic, and rehearsed plan in place. If your first meeting with representatives from an LEA occurs during an actual incident response, you will likely struggle with it more than you would if you rehearsed this part of the plan before an incident occurs.

Senior Leadership

Incident response almost always has some level of direct impact (sometimes catastrophic) on an organization's business processes. For this reason, the IR team should include key senior leaders from every affected business unit. Their involvement is more than about providing support; it will help shape the response process to minimize disruptions, address regulatory issues, and provide an interface into the affected personnel in their units as well as to higher-level leaders within the organization. Effective incident response efforts almost always require the direct and active involvement of management as part of a multidisciplinary response team.

Integrating these business leaders into the team is not a trivial effort. Even if they are as knowledgeable and passionate about cybersecurity as you are (which is exceptionally rare in the wild), their priorities will oftentimes be at odds with yours. Consider a compromise of a server that is responsible for interfacing with your internal accounting systems and your external payment processing gateway. You know that every second you keep that compromised box on the network, you risk further compromises or massive exfiltration of customer data. Still, every second the box is off the network will cause the company significantly in terms of lost sales and revenue. If you approach the appropriate business managers for the first time when you are facing this serious situation, things will not go well for anybody. If, on the other hand, there is a process in place everyone is familiar with and supportive of, the outcome will be better, faster, and less risky.

It's not always required for senior leaders to get involved in incidents. In fact, they are unlikely to be involved in any except the most serious of incidents, but you still need their buy-in and support to ensure that you get the appropriate resources from other business areas. Keeping leaders informed of situations in which you may need their support is a balancing act—you don't want to take too much of their time (or bring them into an active role), but they need to have enough awareness of the incident that a short call to them for help will make things happen.

Another way in which members of management are stakeholders for IR is not so much in what they do but in what they don't do. Consider an incident that takes priority over some routine upgrades you were supposed to do for one of your business units. If that unit's leadership is not aware of what IR is in general, or of the importance of the ongoing response in particular, it could create unnecessary distractions at a time when you can least afford them. Effective communications with leadership can build trust and provide you with a buffer in times of need.

Incident Response Reporting

How the incident report is formatted and written depends on the needs of the organization's stakeholders, since some or all of them will be the audience reading the report. The level of detail included in the report depends on the severity and impact of the incident. However the report is written, you must consider who will read the report and what interests and concerns will shape the manner in which they interpret it. Before you even begin to write it, you should consider one question: What is the purpose of this report? If the goal is to ensure that the IR team remembers some of the technical details of the response that worked (or didn't), then you may want to write it in a way that persuades future responders to consider these lessons. If the report is intended for a more general audience, including senior management, you may want to go lighter on the technical details and provide more information on the business impact of the incident. You also may find yourself in a situation where you are writing multiple reports, depending on the audience and the level of sensitivity of the information in them. Not every stakeholder should be authorized to read the details of an incident, particularly if vulnerabilities are disclosed or sensitive information is included in the report. Sometimes the report will have to be sanitized or redacted. Other times, you may need to develop specific reports in special formats for a particular audience, such as law enforcement or regulatory agencies. Regardless of the circumstances, the key pieces of the report are discussed in the following sections.

Executive Summary

The executive summary usually appears at the beginning of a report and is exactly what its name indicates: a high-level description of the incident, the response, and the outcome. It may be a paragraph or a page, but it is designed to succinctly summarize the entire incident for the benefit of executives or other stakeholders who just need the basic facts. It is typically nontechnical in nature. The remainder of the report is usually where a greater level of detail regarding the incident is presented.

Who, What, When, Where, Why, and How

Earlier we discussed how root cause analysis is the process of *discovering* the who, what, where, when, why, and how of an incident; in the report, we must also *describe* the results of that analysis. These five questions collectively cover the entire scope of the incident and its response and resolution. The report should discuss the following:

- The actors involved in the incident, such as the threat actor, the response team, and other relevant parties (*who*)
- The details of the incident, usually in chronological order, including the detection, escalation, response, containment, eradication, and recovery actions (*what* happened)
- The timeline of the entire incident (*when*)
- The physical and logical locations of the incident, such as which geographic facility and which logical subnets and hosts were affected by the incident (*where*)
- The reason the incident took place (for example, faulty network device configuration, unpatched hosts, or user complacency)—in other words, the *cause* of the incident (*why*)
- The attack methods, techniques, and tools that were used during the incident (*how*)

Note that this information likely won't be presented in the report itself in this fashion; you will likely see it sprinkled throughout the report under the appropriate headings, such as "Scope," "Timeline," and so on.

Impact

On the surface, it's tempting to describe the impact only in terms of an attack and which systems were compromised or what data has been accessed, exfiltrated, or destroyed. However, there is much more to impact that should be discussed. This section of the report should detail not only which systems and data were affected, but also the impact on the organization's entire infrastructure, information, people, budget, customer base, reputation, and so on. When reporting the impact to the organization, think about how many lost hours in productivity were due to the incident as well as how much money, time, and other resources it took to respond and recover from the attack. Impact can be expressed in monetary terms of business impact, such as revenue lost, labor hours spent, and so on, but it also can be expressed in qualitative values. Sometimes the only way to describe certain elements of impact, such as loss of consumer confidence, may be in qualitative terms, such as very low, low, moderate, high, and very high.

Evidence

During our analysis of an incident, we are looking for evidence that shows us what exactly occurred and how it occurred during an incident. Evidence from an incident can take many forms. This includes log files, samples of malware, and other digital evidence. However, evidence can also be derived from our analysis. For example, a timeline derived from examining many different log files that reconstructs the story of when various events occurred would also be considered evidence. For the purposes of reporting, evidence is usually summarized and referenced in the report, rather than attaching pages and pages of log files, for instance. However, all the evidence should be kept in secure storage and available for examination by appropriate personnel, including technicians and managers, if needed. The report should refer to evidence as appropriate to support its assertions, such as the cause of the incident and how the infrastructure was affected by the incident. Note that we will discuss evidence collection and analysis during the digital forensics analysis process in Chapter 16.

 EXAM TIP Evidence is collected throughout the entire incident response process and stored securely with limited access. During the reporting phase of the incident, evidence is typically summarized and may be made available in the report as an attachment or to appropriate personnel separate from the report.

Recommendations

A critical portion of the report should include recommendations from the incident response team. These recommendations will likely discuss the actions necessary to prevent another incident of its type. These may include short- and long-term recommendations, such as the installation of new equipment, the addition of more trained personnel, and so on. There will almost certainly be separate conversations surrounding implementing the recommendations in the report, such as budgetary discussions, for instance.

However, the purpose of recommendations in the incident report is to tell stakeholders exactly what is needed to prevent or mitigate another incident of this type in the future. The associated political discussions over budget or feasibility of allocation of resources is not the purpose of the incident report, so the team should discuss exactly which recommendations they believe are needed, without regard to whether these recommendations will actually be implemented.

Regulatory Reporting

In addition to the report required for any internal stakeholders, external stakeholders such as regulatory agencies may become involved due to data protection laws and regulations. These agencies may require the organization to report details on the incident and its response to them. They likely will have specific reporting requirements, such as reporting time frames, format, and report content. This may be in addition to any reporting requirements that law enforcement agencies may have, as discussed earlier in the chapter.

Lessons Learned

In spite of all the planning that the incident response team and the organization can do, not everything will go smoothly during the response. This doesn't necessarily mean that the planning was poor; it just means that every situation is different, and sometimes things don't always go the way you plan, for whatever reason. The nature of the attack could be different, people and other resources that may not have been in place may have affected the plans, and the dynamic nature of incident itself may cause the incident to deviate from the planned response. In any event, there will always be lessons that can be learned from the response. These lessons are important to capture for several reasons.

First, the organization should understand what it did well and what it needs to improve upon. This could be throughout the response efforts, such as incident detection, analysis, containment, eradication, recovery, and so on. Lessons may indicate that the IR plan needs to change or that more resources need to be committed to the response effort. Lessons learned may also indicate that processes and procedures need to be updated or that people need to be trained in different aspects of incident management. In any event, these lessons can help the organization fine-tune its incident response capability.

These lessons should be captured and documented for further action. Someone in the incident response chain of command should be responsible for tracking the changes that must necessarily take place as a result of lessons learned. The lessons should also be summarized and reported in the incident response report itself.

 EXAM TIP Although the information we have just covered is common to most incident response reports, the organization will determine the exact format and headings of the report and how it is organized. For the exam, you should understand the critical elements of the report, such as executive summary, scope and impact, recommendations, lessons learned, and so on.

Metrics and Key Performance Indicators

Since incident response is a key part of security management in most organizations, it's important to know how well the incident response program and its efforts are performing. Measuring certain characteristics of the response and developing key performance indicators (KPIs) are critical in conveying to stakeholders the effectiveness of the program and what areas of improvement are needed. While there are likely several metrics and indicators that an organization could develop to measure the performance of its incident response program, there are a few that we will discuss in the upcoming sections that are the most useful. Keep in mind that many of these metrics have individual components to them and can be further decomposed, which may be reported as individual elements or in aggregate.

Mean Time to Detect

Mean time to detect is a measurement that attempts to convey the time between the beginning of an incident and the time it is detected by people or systems in the organization. The goal of this metric is to determine if there are issues with an organization's detection capabilities. The actual time an incident begins can be subjective; it may be the point in time that an intruder entered the infrastructure, or that a piece of malware was placed on the system, or when the propagation of the attack occurred. This is something the organization will have to decide, based on its measurement requirements. This starting point may be arbitrarily decided on by the organization or determined after the incident has been analyzed. Once the organization has nailed down what exactly constitutes the beginning of an incident, it can then measure how long it took for the incident to be detected. The time to detect is based on several factors, including the effectiveness of intrusion detection devices, such as IDS/IPS, logging and alerting, and so forth. In developing this metric, the organization should also factor in the possibility of false positives that may skew detection time. This performance indicator can help the organization improve its detection capabilities and its response time.

Alert Volume

Another metric that will likely tell the organization how its detection processes are working is one that measures the number of detectable indicators for an incident that alerted personnel and how many alerts were generated in a given period of time. Alert volume can indicate if an organization needs to fine-tune its detection and alerting mechanisms. If this metric seems to be too low, it may mean that the system is not effectively capturing the indicators of an incident. This may mean that the detection and alerting controls need to be adjusted. This could also be the case if the alert volume is considered too high for a given incident; this could generate a great deal of false positives. In either case, this may mean those mechanisms need to be adjusted somewhat based on the needs of the organization. In any case, once detection and alerting mechanisms are properly adjusted, the alert volume may tell stakeholders how intense an attack is and how well its detection mechanisms are working.

Mean Time to Respond

This metric tells stakeholders how long it took the organization to respond, typically from the moment the incident had any detectable indicators to the time a response was initiated. Response time could include the time it takes to formally declare that an incident has actually taken place as well as the time for any level of response to begin. If the response is initially automated, such as dropping or rerouting traffic when IDS/IPS rules detect malicious traffic, this measurement can also be important in tuning automated systems.

Mean Time to Remediate

This metric measures the majority of the incident response process. Although mean time to detect and mean time to respond are separate metrics, mean time to remediate could include overlap time between these two metrics as the time it takes to actually remediate issues related to the incident. This measurement could conceivably last from hours to days and could be measured all the way until the very last system has been remediated and the incident has been contained and eradicated, depending on how the organization chooses to measure it.

 NOTE These metrics are common for measuring the performance of an incident response. However, the organization may also develop its own unique measurement requirements based on these or other criteria.

Chapter Review

This chapter continues our discussion on incident response and details the post-incident activities that take place. Some of these activities, such as incident forensics and root cause analysis, actually start during the incident itself and become the primary focus after the organization shifts gears once the incident is contained, the cause eradicated, and recovery has concluded. Others, such as the change control process, occur after the incident itself, where formal organizational changes must be vetted and approved to help prevent future incidents. This could include changes to host configurations, infrastructure, or even the organization's business and security processes. After the incident, the incident response plan is normally updated based on information gained during the incident, such as changes in procedures and processes to make future responses more effective and efficient. These are generally gained from the lessons learned during the incident. The organization may also generate additional indicators of compromise based on knowledge gleaned from the incident and then incorporate those into its detection mechanisms. Monitoring is also critical for ensuring that an incident has truly concluded, that there are no remnant aftereffects, and that the attacker's presence has been eliminated from the organization.

Incident communication is critical with all stakeholders. Stakeholders are identified as both internal and external and receive communication updates both during the incident and afterward during the reporting phase. It is important that stakeholders only receive information for which they're cleared; sensitive information should not be shared with all stakeholders. Internal stakeholders include legal counsel, who will most certainly deal with regulatory and law enforcement agencies; human resources, who may have to deal with an internal person contributing to an incident; and public relations, who primarily deal with external stakeholders such as the public, customers, business partners, and so on. The incident response team is the core of the IR stakeholders and is concerned with the incident response itself. Senior leadership plays an important part as an internal stakeholder by making the strategic and sometimes operational decisions associated with the response. External stakeholders include contractors, business partners, customers, and even law enforcement and regulatory agencies. These stakeholders must be considered for the correct legal communications and reporting during and after the incident.

After the incident response has concluded, the reporting phase comes into play. While different organizations have different formatting and reporting requirements, the organization must ensure that it reports the right information to the right stakeholders. This may include multiple reports containing information of varying sensitivity. Normally, a report will contain critical elements such as the executive summary, which summarizes the report for nontechnical management, as well as the who, what, where, when, why, and how of an incident. The report also discusses the scope and impact of the incident and its timeline of occurrence. Evidence is summarized in the incident response report, and root cause analysis is provided, along with recommendations that will help prevent future incidents of this type. Lessons learned are also included in the report so that the organization can improve its response capability.

Another post-incident activity is to review and adjust metrics and key performance indicators, which will show how the incident actually progressed and how the response capability performed. These include key performance indicators and metrics such as mean time to detect, alert volume, mean time to respond, and mean time to remediate.

Questions

1. Which of the following processes must be considered when organization-wide alterations are required to respond to and prevent future incidents?

   A. Root cause analysis

   B. Regulatory reporting

   C. Internal communication

   D. Change control

2. Which of the following uses techniques such as log analysis, reverse engineering, and timeline correlation to determine how an incident happened?

   A. Indicator of compromise generation

   B. Triage

   C. Forensics

   D. Root cause analysis

3. Which of the following stakeholders is ultimately responsible for approving the communications that occur with external stakeholders?

   A. Senior leadership

   B. Public relations

   C. The IR team

   D. Human resources

Use the following scenario to answer Questions 4–8:

Your IR team successfully completes an incident response, effectively containing an incident, eradicating its cause, and recovering organizational assets. You must now communicate with the appropriate stakeholders about the incident and its response. You must also develop the incident response report and disseminate it to appropriate stakeholders.

4. With which of the following external agencies are you normally legally required to share specific sensitive details about the incident?

   A. Suppliers

   B. Regulatory agencies

   C. Business partners

   D. Customers

5. Which portion of an incident response report is generally nontechnical and condenses details of the incident response into an overview?

   A. Scope and impact

   B. Recommendations

   C. Executive summary

   D. Lessons learned

6. Which of the following may not necessarily be included in its entirety in a report but may be summarized in attachments or made available for appropriate stakeholders offline, separate from the report?

   A. Root cause analysis

   B. Evidence

   C. Lessons learned

   D. Recommendations

7. Which of the following is not necessarily part of the report analysis but indicates areas where the incident response capability itself should be improved, based on the quality of the response itself?

   A. Incident response plan update

   B. Change control

   C. Root cause analysis

   D. Lessons learned

PART III

8. Which of the following measures the effectiveness of the organization in discovering an incident has even occurred?

   A. Mean time to detect

   B. Mean time to respond

   C. Mean time to remediate

   D. Alert volume

Answers

1. **D.** Change control processes are necessary to implement organization-wide changes that can help respond to and prevent future incidents.

2. **D.** Root cause analysis uses all of these techniques to determine how an incident occurred, or its root cause.

3. **A.** Although public relations may actually communicate with external agencies, senior leadership is ultimately responsible for the content of the communications with external agencies, and must approve any communications, particularly those that contain sensitive information.

4. **B.** You are normally required by law and regulation to share specific sensitive details of an incident with regulatory agencies and law enforcement. You are not necessarily required to share all sensitive details of an incident with customers, business partners, or suppliers.

5. **C.** The executive summary summarizes the incident for nontechnical users and senior management and condenses it into an overview of the incident.

6. **B.** Evidence may be so voluminous that it simply cannot be included in the report. It may be summarized or included as an attachment to the report. It also may be available for offline review by appropriate stakeholders, separate from the report.

7. **D.** Lessons learned normally apply to the quality of the response itself, such as how the incident response team performed and how different processes and procedures in the incident response plan were executed. Lessons learned are used to improve the response capability itself, not necessarily to implement changes to prevent an incident.

8. **A.** Mean time to detect measures the time it takes for an organization to detect or discover that an incident has taken place. This indicator can tell an organization how effective its detection capabilities are.

Utilize Basic Digital Forensics Techniques

In this chapter you will learn:

- How digital forensics is related to incident response
- Basic techniques for conducting forensic analyses
- Familiarity with a variety of forensic utilities
- How to assemble a forensics toolkit

Condemnation without investigation is the height of ignorance.

—Albert Einstein

Digital forensics is the process of collecting and analyzing data to determine whether and how an incident occurred. The word *forensics* can be defined as an argumentative exercise, so it makes sense that a digital forensic analyst's job is to build compelling, facts-based arguments that explain an incident. The digital forensic analyst answers the questions *what, where, when,* and *how,* but not *who* or *why.* These last two questions are answered by the rest of the investigative process, of which digital forensics is only a part.

The investigation of a security incident need not end up in a courtroom, but it is almost impossible to predict whether a criminal charge is appropriate in the event of a breach. To ensure that we can bring a case to court if necessary, we should treat every digital forensic investigation as if it *will* ultimately be held to the level of scrutiny of a criminal case. We all know, however, that this is not always possible when we're trying to bring critical business processes back online or simply based on our required workload. Still, the closer we stay to the principles of legal admissibility in court, the better off we'll be in the end.

The National Institute of Justice identifies the following three principles that should guide every investigation:

- Actions taken to secure and collect digital evidence should not affect the integrity of that evidence.

- Persons conducting an examination of digital evidence should be trained for that purpose.

- Activity relating to the seizure, examination, storage, or transfer of digital evidence should be documented, preserved, and available for review.

Phases of an Investigation

Forensic investigations, like many other standardized processes, can be conducted in phases. In this case, we normally recognize four: seizure, acquisition, analysis, and reporting. *Seizure* is the process of controlling the crime scene and the state of potential evidentiary items. *Acquisition* is the preservation of evidence in a legally admissible manner. The *analysis* takes place in a controlled environment and without unduly tainting the evidence. Finally, the goal in *reporting* is to produce a report that is complete, accurate, and unbiased.

 EXAM TIP We break down digital forensics into four phases—seizure, acquisition, analysis, and reporting—though many organizations have reduced this to three phases by combining seizure and acquisition. The CySA+ exam will not cover the phases of an investigation but will focus on the techniques and technologies used throughout the process.

Evidence Seizure

The goal of seizure is to ensure that neither the perpetrators nor the investigators make any changes to the evidence. An overly simplistic, but illustrative, example of protecting evidence is putting up yellow "crime scene" tape and posting guards around the area where a murder took place so that guilty parties can't return to the scene and pick up shell casings with their fingerprints on them. Obviously, the digital crime scene is different from a physical scene, in that the invisible perpetrator may continue to make changes even as the investigators are trying to gather evidence.

Controlling the Crime Scene

Whether the crime scene is physical or digital, it is important that processes be put in place to control who comes in contact with the evidence of the crime to ensure its integrity. The following are just some of the steps that should take place to protect a crime scene:

- Allow only authorized individuals access to the scene.
- Ensure that each person involved in technical tasks is trained and certified for their role.
- Document who is present at the crime scene.
- Document who last interacted with the systems.
- If the crime scene does become contaminated, document it. The contamination may not negate the derived evidence, but it will make investigating the crime more challenging.

After you have secured and documented the environment, you can prepare to begin acquiring data. This may involve collecting evidence at the scene or, in some cases,

Figure 16-1
A sample chain
of custody form

CHAIN OF CUSTODY

Received from_____ By_____

Date_____Time_____A.M./P.M.

Received from_____ By_____

Date_____Time_____A.M./P.M.

Received from_____ By_____

Date_____Time_____A.M./P.M.

Received from_____ By_____

Date_____Time_____A.M./P.M.

WARNING: THIS IS A TAMPER-EVIDENT SECURITY PACKAGE. ONCE SEALED, ANY
ATTEMPT TO OPEN WILL RESULT IN OBVIOUS SIGNS OF TAMPERING.

unplugging electronic devices and removing them for transport to a forensics lab. It's
often a good idea to photograph the scene and individual elements before you touch or
move anything. It is also important that you properly tag, label, and inventory everything
you seize to avoid questions later on about evidence tampering or other issues. You'll
need access to disassembly and removal tools, such as antistatic bands, pliers, and screw-
drivers, with appropriate packaging such as antistatic bags and evidence bags. Also, keep
in mind that weather conditions (for example, extreme temperatures, snow, or rain) may
impose additional requirements on your packaging and transportation arrangements.

Chain of Custody

A *chain of custody* is a documented history that shows how evidence was handled, collected, transported, and preserved at every stage of the process. Because digital evidence
can be easily modified, a clearly defined chain of custody demonstrates that the evidence
has not been tampered with and is trustworthy. It is important to follow very strict and
organized procedures when collecting and tagging evidence in every single case. Furthermore, the chain of custody process should follow evidence through its entire life cycle,
beginning with identification and ending with its destruction, permanent archiving, or
return to the owner. Figure 16-1 shows a sample form that could be used for this purpose.

EXAM TIP   You will be expected to understand the basics of evidence seizure,
including the concept of chain of custody, on the exam. Be sure you're familiar
with the fact that chain of custody ensures unbroken accountability for the
evidence from the time it is seized until the conclusion of the investigation.

Evidence Acquisition

Forensic acquisition is the process of extracting digital content from seized evidence so
that it may be analyzed. This is commonly known as "taking a forensic image of a hard
drive" (or any other storage media), but it actually involves more than just that. The main
reason you extract the data is to conduct your analysis on a copy of the data evidence and
not on the original; this protects the original content from changes, to ensure that it can
be used later as evidence.

PART III

Evidence Preservation

Throughout the process, preserving the integrity of the original evidence is paramount. To acquire the original digital evidence in a manner that protects and preserves it, the following steps are generally considered best practices:

1. *Prepare the destination media/medium.* Secure any media on which you will store the digital content of your seized evidence. This destination medium may be a removable hard drive or a storage area network (SAN), for example. You must ensure that the destination is free of any content that may taint the evidence. The best way to do this securely is to wipe the medium by overwriting it with a fixed pattern of 1's and/or 0's.

2. *Prevent changes to the original.* The simple act of attaching a device to a computer or duplicator will normally cause its contents to change in small but potentially significant ways. To prevent any changes at all, you must use write-protection mechanisms such as hardware write blockers (described in the section "Write Blockers and Drive Adapters" later in this chapter). Some forensic acquisition software products enable software-based write protection, but it is almost always better to use hardware mechanisms because a physical barrier or separation could guarantee that no changes can ever be made.

3. *Hash the original evidence.* Before you copy anything, you should take a cryptographic hash of the original evidence. Most products support MD5 and SHA-1 (Secure Hash Algorithm 1) hashes. Though these protocols have been shown to be susceptible to collision attacks and are no longer recommended for general use, we have seen no pushback from the courts on their admissibility with evidence in criminal trials.

4. *Copy the evidence.* You can use a variety of applications to make a forensic copy of digital media, including the venerable dd utility in Linux systems. All these applications perform complete binary copies of the entire source medium. Merely copying the files is insufficient because you may not acquire relevant data in deleted or unallocated spaces.

5. *Verify the acquisition.* After the copy is complete, compare the cryptographic hash of the copy against the original. If they match, you can perform analyses of the copy and be assured that it is perfectly identical to the original.

6. *Safeguard the original evidence.* Because you now have a perfect copy of the evidence, you must store the original in a safe place and ensure that no one can gain access to it.

 EXAM TIP You should be familiar with the principles of evidence acquisition and preservation, remembering that evidence should be safeguarded at all times and that its integrity should never be disturbed.

Analysis

Analysis is the process of interpreting the extracted data to determine its significance to the case. Though the specific applications and commands you use for analysis may vary depending on the operating or file systems involved, the key issues are the same.

Examples of the types of analysis that may be performed include the following:

- **Time frame**   What happened and when?
- **Data hiding**   What has been intentionally concealed?
- **Applications and files**   Which applications accessed which files?
- **Ownership and possession**   Which user accounts accessed which applications and files?

One of the most important tools to a forensic analyst is the time frame, or time line, which establishes a basis for comparing the state of the system at different points in time. For example, you may suspect that a user copied sensitive files to a thumb drive last Friday, but you don't see that drive registered on the system until Monday. Without evidence of the user tampering with the data and time on the system, you can conclude that the exfiltration mechanism was not that particular thumb drive. The time frame provides a chronologically ordered list of actions taken on the system, which can be categorized as read, write, modify, and delete operations on an item of interest.

Many investigators we know keep track of time lines in a simple spreadsheet with the following columns:

- Data and time
- Time zone
- Source (for example, Windows registry or syslog)
- Item name (for example, registry key name or filename)
- Item location (full path)
- Description

 EXAM TIP   You should always regard system timestamps with a healthy dose of skepticism. Threat actors are known to modify the system clock to hide the true sequence of their actions. This practice is known as *timestomping*. Keep an eye out for inconsistencies in timestamps during the CySA+ exam incident simulations, as they may be evidence of tampering.

At every step of the process, you should take copious notes on each specific action you take, down to the command and parameters you use. If you use a forensic analysis suite such as EnCase or Forensic Toolkit (FTK), the tool will record your actions for you. Even so, it is a best practice to keep notes on your own throughout the investigation.

Legal Hold

Legal hold is an administrative process that organizations often make use of during digital forensic investigations. It entails retaining a device in a secure storage area and not allowing it to be used until an investigation has concluded. Forensic processes such as evidence acquisition and analysis are allowed to take place, but the device is not returned to the end user until after the investigation. Legal hold is imposed just in case an investigatory agency outside the organization requires the evidence, particularly if any laws have been broken, or if the device is needed for any evidentiary value for prosecution of a crime. If the investigation remains internal, often the device is released after the investigation has concluded and sanitized before it is returned to inventory or the user.

Reporting

If you have been taking notes, you have been writing parts of your report as you conduct the investigation. Once you arrive at sound conclusions based on the available evidence, you can put together narrative statements in a report that present your arguments and conclusions in a readable fashion. As with any form of communication, knowing your audience is crucial. If the report is geared toward executive leaders, for example, the document would be different from one that would be presented in a court of law. If you need help creating a report, all major commercial forensic analysis suites have a feature that will generate a draft report you can customize for your own purposes. Note that we discussed incident reporting in detail in Chapter 15; those same principles apply to a forensics investigation.

Network

Before you begin to analyze network data for its usefulness in an incident or investigation, it must be collected as completely as possible. Broadly speaking, there are two approaches to capturing packets on a network: header captures and full packet captures. The difference, as the terms imply, is whether you capture only the IP headers or the entire packets, which would include payloads. Although it may be tempting for you to jump on the full-packet bandwagon, you should keep in mind that this approach comes with significant data management as well as potential legal and privacy issues associated with collecting network traffic. It's important that any collection activity that might involve capturing employee or customer data be brought to the attention of your legal and privacy team. Capturing very large sets of packet data is useful only if you can gain actionable information from them. You may choose to keep the data for reference in case a major incident occurs, but this doesn't do away with the need to be able to handle all this data at collection time. Note that the tools used for capturing traffic for a forensics effort are tools we have already discussed in Chapter 6, such as Wireshark, TShark, tcpdump, and so on. Many solutions are available for storing and retrieving very large data stores. The point is not that it shouldn't be done but rather that it should be carefully engineered.

Network Tap

A common option for packet capture is the network tap. Using tap hardware, you may be able to capture traffic between various points on the network for follow-on analysis.

Like a phone tap, network taps can be used for diagnostic or monitoring operations. There are two types of network taps: passive and active.

A *passive tap* requires no additional power. A passive tap on copper cable will form a direct connection to wires in the cable and split the signal going across the line; power is still flowing to the destination, but enough is diverted to the tap to be used by the packet sniffer. Similarly, passive optical taps attempt to split the light beam passing though the fiber and divert a portion to a sensor. Although these taps require additional hardware, the original signal is not likely to be impacted greatly should the device fail. There are some disadvantages with this tap method, particularly on Gigabit-speed lines. Gigabit Ethernet connections are much more sensitive to power fluctuations and may experience high error rates, distortion, or failure should a passive tap be installed. For this reason, on Gigabit lines, an *active tap* (or active relay) must be used. Active taps completely terminate the signal in the tap device, sending a copy of the signal to a local interface and moving the original signal to a forwarder. That forwarder then amplifies the original signal, if necessary, and passes it to its original destination. This method works well for Gigabit lines, but at the expense of adding another electrical device in the chain. Should the active tap fail, the entire circuit may remain open, alerting the administrator that something is amiss.

 CAUTION   Tapping a network using these methods has the potential to change the transmission characteristics of the line.

Hub

An alternate method of collection is to capture the traffic directly from the intermediary device, or hub. Because hubs share traffic coming in and out of all interfaces equally, they rely on the connected hosts to be honest and listen in on only what's addressed to them. On some networks, it may be possible to place a hub at a network chokepoint and collect traffic traversing that location. Hubs are increasingly rare, even in home use, and have been replaced with the more discerning switch.

Switches

In a switched environment, data units called *frames* are forwarded only to destinations they are meant for. As each frame enters the switch, the switch compares the incoming frame's destination Media Access Control (MAC) address with its existing list of addresses and their matching physical ports on the switch. When it finds a match, the switch forwards the data to the appropriate interface and then on to the destination device. Because a device's MAC address is meant to be immutable, collecting from switches requires additional setup steps. Some switches have built-in functionality, called *port mirroring*, that directly supports packet capturing. With port mirroring enabled, the switch sends a copy of all the packets it sees to a monitored port. In some devices, this is referred to as the switched port analyzer (SPAN) port.

Endpoints

One of the most important steps you can take during a forensic investigation is to *not* power off anything you don't have to. The one universal exception to this rule is if you are pretty sure there is a running process that is deliberately destroying evidence. There are many reasons for keeping the devices running, but a key one is that memory forensics (that is, digital forensics on the primary storage units of computing devices) has dramatically evolved over the past few years. Although it is possible for a threat actor to install rootkits that hide processes, connections, or files, it is almost impossible to hide tracks in running memory. Furthermore, an increasing number of malware never touches the file system directly and lives entirely in memory. Shutting down a device without first acquiring the contents of memory could make it impossible to piece together the incident accurately.

 NOTE To acquire volatile memory, you will likely have to make some changes to the computer, which typically include connecting an external device and executing a program. As long as you document everything you do, this should not render the evidence inadmissible in court.

Another important, if seemingly mundane, step is to document the entire physical environment around a device. An easy way to do this is to take lots of photos of the scene. Regardless of whether you take pictures, you should certainly take notes describing not only the environment but also each action your team takes to seize the evidence. Specific photos you typically want to take are listed here:

- Computer desktop showing running programs (if the device is unlocked)
- Peripherals connected to the device (for example, thumb drives and external drives)
- Immediate surroundings of the device (for example, physical desktop)
- Proximate surroundings of the device (for example, the room or cubicle)

Tales from the Trenches: A Picture Is Worth...

We were once chatting with a federal law enforcement agent about best practices for photographing crime scenes. He described a case in which he raided a suspect's home and seized a large amount of evidence, including a stack of dozens of CDs. When law enforcement attempted to acquire the contents of the hard drive, they found out it was protected by strong full-disk encryption. They asked the suspect for the passphrase, but he happily informed them that he didn't know it. Incredulous, our friend asked him how that was possible. The suspect responded that he never memorized the passphrase because it was simply the first character in each CD's title. To his horror, our friend realized that he didn't take any photos that showed the stack of CDs in order, and the discs had been shuffled during handling.

Servers

Conducting a forensic analysis of a server requires addressing additional issues compared to workstations. For starters, it may not be possible to take the server offline and remove it to a safe analysis room. Instead, you may have no choice but to conduct an abbreviated analysis on-site. *Live forensics* (or live response) is the process of conducting digital forensics on a device that remains operational throughout the investigation. We already touched on a related issue earlier when we described the importance of capturing the contents of volatile memory before shutting off a device. If you cannot remove the server from a production environment, the next best thing is to capture its memory contents and files of interest (for example, log files).

 CAUTION Understand that there is a fine balance between the decision to perform a live forensic analysis on a host versus shutting it down to prevent further damage during an attack. You must weigh the value of obtaining evidence that cannot be obtained if the host is shut down versus the possibility that the host will be further compromised and that the compromise may spread from the host to the entire network.

Another consideration when dealing with servers is that they typically have significantly more storage capacity (both primary and secondary) than workstations. This is guaranteed to make the analysis process take more time, and it may also require special tools. For example, if your server uses a redundant array of inexpensive disks (RAID), you will likely need specialized tools to deal with those disks. Apart from the hardware differences, you will also have to consider the particular architectures of the software running on servers. Microsoft Exchange Server, for example, has a large number of features that help a forensic investigator, but that person will have to know their way around Exchange's complex architecture. This point also holds for database management systems (DBMS) and in-house web applications.

OS and Process Analysis

We know that an operating system (OS) manages and controls all interactions with a computer. Though clearly a variety of operating systems are in use today, they all perform the same three basic functions:

- Manage all computer resources such as memory, CPU, and disks
- Provide a user interface
- Provide services for running applications

The first of these is of particular interest to a forensic analyst, because every action that occurs on a computer system is mediated by its OS.

If you are investigating a Microsoft Windows system, two of the most important sources of information are the registry and the event log. The registry is the principal data store where Windows houses most of the systemwide settings. Though all major analysis suites include viewers for this database, you can also examine it directly on any Windows computer by launching the Registry Editor application. You can find literally hundreds of interesting artifacts in the registry, including the following:

- **Autorun locations**   This is where programs tell Windows that they should be launched during the boot process. Malware oftentimes uses this for persistence (for example, HKLM\Software\Microsoft\Windows\CurrentVersion\Run).

- **Most Recently Used lists**   Often referred to as MRUs, this is where you'll find the most recently launched applications, recently used or modified documents, and recently changed registry keys. For example, if you want to see recently used Word documents, you would look in HKEY_CURRENT_USER\Software\Microsoft\Office\16.0\Common\Open Find.

- **Wireless networks**   Every time a computer connects to a wireless network, this is recorded in the registry, which you can then examine an as investigator in HKLM\SOFTWARE\Microsoft\Windows NT\CurrentVersion\NetworkList\Profile.

Another useful source of information is the event logs, which you can access by launching the Event Viewer application in any Windows computer. There is actually a collection of logs, the number of which depends on the specific system. All Windows computers, however, will have an application log in which applications report usage, errors, and other information. The OS also maintains in a security log security-related events such as unsuccessful login attempts. Finally, every Windows system has a system log in which the OS records systemwide events.

Although Linux doesn't have the convenience of a centralized registry like Windows, it has its own rich set of sources of artifacts for a forensic investigator. For starters, a lot of relevant data can be found in plaintext files, which (unlike Windows) makes it easy to search for strings. Linux also typically includes a number of useful utilities such as dd, sha1sum, and ps, which can help you acquire evidence, hash it, and get a list of running processes (and resources associated with them), respectively. You can do all this in Windows, but you'll need to install additional tools first.

The Linux file system starts in the root directory, which is denoted by a slash. As an analyst, you need to be familiar with certain directories. We highlight a few of these here, but you should build up your own list from this start:

- **/etc**   This primary system configuration directory contains a subdirectory for most installed applications.

- **/var/log**   All well-behaved Linux applications will keep their log files in plaintext files in this directory, making it a gold mine for analysts.

- **/home/$USER**   Here, *$USER* is a variable name that you should replace with the name of a given user. All user data and configuration data are kept here.

Log Viewers

Every major OS provides the means to view the contents of its log files, and log analysis is one of the most important forensic processes an analyst can perform. The reason you may need a dedicated log viewer is that the built-in tools are meant for cursory examination and not for detailed analysis, particularly when the logs number in the thousands. Like most other features described so far, this functionality is oftentimes found in the forensic analysis suites. If you need a dedicated log viewer, there is no shortage of options, including many free ones.

A scenario in which a standalone log viewer would make sense is when you are trying to aggregate the various logs from multiple computers to develop a holistic time line of events. You would want a tool that enables you to bring in multiple files (or live systems) and filter their contents in a variety of ways. Some tools that help you do this include Splunk, Elastic Stack, Graylog, LogRhythm, QRadar, SolarWinds Event Log Consolidator/Manager, and even an older tool that is still widely used, Ipswitch's WhatsUp. Many log viewers are standalone tools that can ingest logs in many different formats; however, some of the larger logging systems also come with their own log viewer utilities.

Mobile Device Forensics

These days, it is uncommon for criminal investigations not to include mobile device forensics. Though this is somewhat less true in the corporate world, you should still be aware of the unique challenges that mobile devices present. Chief among these is that the device will continue to communicate with the network unless you power it off (which we already said may not be a good idea). This means that a perpetrator can remotely wipe the device or otherwise tamper with it. A solution to this problem is to place the device into a Faraday container that prevents it from communicating over radio waves. Faraday bags have special properties that absorb radio frequency (RF) energy and redistribute it, preventing communication between devices in the container and those outside. Obviously, you will also need a larger Faraday facility in which to analyze the device after you seize it.

Although you can do some amount of forensic analysis on a live Windows or Linux system, mobile devices require dedicated forensic tools. The exceptions to this rule are jailbroken iPhones or iPads and rooted Android devices, because both of these expose an OS that is very similar to Linux and includes some of the same tools and locations. To make things a bit more interesting, many phones require special cables, although the migration toward USB-C in recent years is simplifying this as more devices adopt this interface.

Among the challenges involved in mobile forensics is simply getting access to the data. The mobile OS is not designed to support acquisition, which means that the forensic analyst must first get the device to load an alternate OS. This usually requires a custom bootloader, which is an almost-essential feature of any mobile forensics toolkit. Another peculiarity of mobile devices is that much of their data is stored in miniature DBMSs such as SQLite. These systems require special tools to view their data properly. Their advantage, however, is that the systems almost never delete data when the user asks them to. Instead, they mark the rows in the database table as deleted and keep their entire contents intact until new data overwrites them. Even then, the underlying file system may allow recovery of this deleted information. As with the bootloader, any common analysis suite will include the means to analyze this data.

Forensic investigators face many challenges with mobile devices. Because of the highly proprietary and locked-down nature of some of these devices by their manufacturers, many of the same forensic tools will not work across platforms. Additionally, the forensic analyst has to deal with other issues inherent to mobile devices, such as hardware and software encryption and secure enclaves. And, although not within the scope of this book, mobile device issues such as device encryption, remote wipe, mobile device management, containerization, and device patching can also be factors that make forensics examinations of mobile devices problematic. Backups can also be an issue since many users of mobile devices back them up to secure cloud storage. Data privacy in cloud forensics is a subject we will touch on next.

Virtualization and the Cloud

All forensic efforts require that investigators follow specific procedures to collect evidence in a careful, verifiable, and repeatable manner. By following these procedures, if the evidence needs to be admissible in a court of law, you can be confident that you did the work to protect its integrity. Performing forensics on virtual environments has some significant benefits because the entire OS, memory contents, and in some cases networking and other infrastructure are all stored as files on a disk. When you combine this with the fact that virtualization technologies enable you to take a snapshot of the state of the OS, you can see how this could speed up a forensic analyst's workflow as it related to acquiring the data.

VMware's vSphere Hypervisor, for example, uses virtual devices such as network cards, memory, and certain peripherals. When creating a virtual machine, the hypervisor will create several important files. Among the most useful are the machine's configuration in a VMX file, virtual hard drive in a VMDK file, BIOS state in an NVRAM file, and main memory in a VMEM file. While the vSphere Hypervisor may be useful if the security team has control of the hypervisor and supporting hardware, the challenge increases in a cloud environment. In you're preparing for forensic analysis, it's critical that the identification of cloud computing occur as early as possible, because this may significantly affect the resources required to acquire that data, depending on its location.

Even with the rapid adoption of new distributed technologies, traditional forensics concepts are still generally applicable to cloud storage. As in traditional environments, cloud storage contains everything from the network and system configurations to files and user information. What gets particularly tricky is identifying and tracking data associated with virtualized devices and functionality. Because this is not normally exposed to the end user, and is often volatile and ephemeral, it will take more effort to track down and verify. Another aspect of cloud computing that complicates the forensics model is the actual location of the data in question. The physical location of data in the cloud environment may pose a challenge, particularly if the investigation extends beyond the security team and involves legal and law enforcement efforts.

Given the existing strong auditing policies in place at many cloud service providers, you may have opportunities to take advantage of those offerings to support your forensic efforts.

You may recall from our discussion of cloud technologies in Chapter 1 that many providers use the shared responsibility model when providing services to customers. Depending on your organization's agreement with the provider, both in terms of which model is used as well as outlined by any service level agreements (SLAs), your security team may be entitled to a great deal of access to the underlying hardware, or they may have none at all. Additionally, it's worth noting that in highly virtualized environments, it may be trivial to recover full snapshots of a system before, during, and after an attack. This can be incredibly useful in piecing together what occurred. It may also be the case that the same challenges that exist for auditors will exist for you, in that artifacts may sometimes not be traceable or available because of the distributed nature and rapid turnover of compute and storage resources.

 NOTE You may face some special considerations with collecting and analyzing forensic evidence in cloud situations due to issues such as jurisdiction, data privacy, data ownership, and so on. Before engaging in cloud forensics, you should do your research and make sure you understand the legal and privacy ramifications involved.

Procedures

Among the core principles of forensics is maintaining the integrity of data regardless of whether it will be presented in a courtroom or kept in the security team's archives. Security analysts, therefore, must take extra steps to document the process as completely as possible. Checklists and standard operating procedures ensure that the entire team is prepared to conduct at least a baseline level of forensics if needed.

Building Your Forensic Kit

There is no one-size-fits-all answer for what you should include in your forensic kit. It really depends on your environment and workflow processes. Still, there are some general tool types that almost everyone should have available if their work includes forensic analyses.

The jump bag is a prepackaged set of tools that is always ready to go. This is your first line of help when you are asked to drop everything you're doing and respond to an incident that may involve a forensic examination. Because you want to ensure that the bag is always ready, you'll probably want to develop a packing list that you can use to inventory the bag after each use to ensure that it is ready for the next run. You'll probably want to include each of the following items in the jump bag.

Live Response Tools

Some live response tools enable responders to collect live volatile data quickly from a system using a USB stick, optical discs, or external drive. This is a useful solution for data that may be lost forever if the system is powered down.

Write Blockers and Drive Adapters

Hardware write blockers come in many flavors and price points, but they all do essentially the same thing: they prevent modifications to a storage device while you acquire its contents. Your most important consideration is the type of interfaces they support. You should consult your asset inventory to see how many different types of storage interfaces are in use in your environment. Some tools support SCSI and ATA, but not SATA, and others may not support USB devices. As long as you have an adapter and cable for each type of storage device interface in your organization, you should be in good shape.

Cables

A good part of your jump bag will be devoted to cables of various types. A good rule of thumb is that if you've ever needed a particular cable for one investigation, you should probably keep it in your jump bag forever. Here are some ideas for cables to include:

- Ethernet cables (such as crossover, straight-through, and one-way)
- Serial cables (various flavors of USB and RS-232)
- Power cables
- Common proprietary cables (such as Lightning and Thunderbolt)

Wiped Removable Media

You may not have a few hours to wipe a hard drive before you must respond to an incident, so it pays to keep a few packed and ready. The type of interface doesn't much matter (as long as it is supported by your write blocker), but the capacity does. In general, look into your asset inventory, find the largest workstation or external drive in your organization, and pack at least twice that amount of storage in your bag. Servers tend to have significantly larger drives than workstations, so if that is a concern, you may have to invest in a portable RAID solution. Solutions like these are portable and designed to facilitate the acquisition of evidence.

A common approach in organizations that deal with fairly frequent investigations is to set up a network-attached storage (NAS) solution specifically for forensic images. As long as you have a fast network connection, you'll be able to image any workstation or server with ease. An added advantage is that the NAS can serve as an archival mechanism for past investigations that may still be pending in court. In these cases, it is important to abide by your organization's data retention policies.

Camera

A camera is an often-overlooked but critical item in your jump bag. It is important to photograph the crime or incident site, and pretty much any digital camera with a flash will do. A useful addition to your camera is a small ruler that you can include in shots whenever you need to capture a sense of distance or scale. Ideally, the ruler should have a matte surface to minimize glare.

Crime Scene Tape

This may sound like overkill, but having some means of notifying others in the area that they should not enter is critical to the seizure process. Crime scene (or other restricted area–labeled) tape does the job nicely and inexpensively.

Tamper-Proof Seals

When the amount of evidence you collect, or the distance you have to transport it, requires the assistance of others (for example, drivers), you probably want to seal the evidence containers with a tamper-resistant seal. In a pinch, you can use tape and sign your name across it. However, if you can afford them, dedicated lockable containers will be best.

Hand Tools

On the surface, it may not seem to make sense to have manual hand tools included in a forensic toolkit for a digital investigation. However, you will be surprised at the times you need a pair of pliers or a screwdriver or wire cutters. It's a good idea to incorporate these tools, possibly even in the form of a multitool, in your toolkit. You never know when you may need to disconnect something using a screwdriver or even, unfortunately, wire cutters. There also may be physical barriers to getting to systems, such as zip ties, cage locks, and so on. Having these tools handy can help you circumvent some of those barriers. Hand tools can be useful even during a digital investigation.

Mobile Hotspot

Another item that may be useful in your mobile forensic toolkit is a cellular hotspot. This may be necessary in case you need to connect your laptop or tablet to the Internet to upload files such as those acquired during an investigation if there is an urgent need to do so. You definitely do not want to depend on onsite Internet connections since you don't want to send traffic related to the investigation over the network you are investigating. You also can't necessarily rely on the security of a third-party network to ensure the confidentiality of the data you need to send. If you have a smartphone or other device that can act as a mobile hotspot, that will work as well, but as a general rule you do not want to use personal devices to provide hotspot capability for your investigation. It's better to use a company- or agency-provided smartphone or hotspot if the need arises.

Documentation and Forms

Digital forms and other documents may be required by your organization during an investigation. It is a good idea to print hard copies and keep them in your jump bag, because you never know whether you'll be able to access your corporate data store in the middle of an incident response. Following are some items most of us would keep in our bags.

Chain of Custody Form   Earlier in the chapter, Figure 16-1 showed an example of a chain of custody form, but you should tailor this to your own organization's requirements if you don't already have your own form. The important aspect is to ensure that there

PART III

are enough copies to match with each seized piece of evidence. Ideally, your evidence transport containers have a waterproof pouch on the outside into which you can slide a form for the container (individual items in it may still need their own forms).

Incident Response Plan   It is not unusual for an incident response to start off as one thing and turn into something else. Particularly when it comes to issues that may have legal implications (for example, forensic investigations), it is a good idea to have a copy of the incident response plan in your jump bag. This way, even if you are disconnected from your network, you will know what you are expected or required to do in any situation you encounter.

Incident Log   Every good investigator takes notes. When you're performing a complex investigation, as most digital forensics investigations are, it is important that you document every action you take and every hypothesis you are considering. The most important reason for this level of thoroughness is that your conclusions are only as valid as your processes are repeatable. In other words, any qualified individual with access to the same evidence you have should be able to follow your notes and get the same results that you did. Keeping a notebook and pen in your jump bag ensures that you are always ready to write down exactly what you do.

Call/Escalation List   If the conditions on the ground are not what you thought they'd be when you started your investigation, you may have to call someone to notify them of an important development or request authorization to perform some action. Though the call/escalation list should really be part of your incident response plan, it bears singling it out as an important item to carry in your jump bag.

Cryptography Tools

It is often the case that you must ensure the confidentiality of an investigation and its evidence. To accomplish this, you can turn to a variety of cryptography tools that are available for multiple platforms. Perhaps the simplest approach to encrypting files is to use the compression utilities available in most operating systems, but you must ensure that they are password protected. The advantage is that these applications are ubiquitous, and the files are mostly usable across platforms.

If you need something a little more robust, you can try any number of available encryption tools. One of the most popular and recommended open source solutions is VeraCrypt, which is based on the now defunct TrueCrypt. This tool is free and available for Windows, macOS, and Linux systems. VeraCrypt supports multiple cryptosystems, including AES, Twofish, and Serpent. It also supports the creation of hidden, encrypted volumes within other volumes.

Acquisition Utilities

The acquisition phase of a forensic investigation is perhaps the most critical point in terms of ensuring the admissibility of evidence, analysis, and conclusions in court. This is where you want to slow down, use a checklist, and ensure that you make no mistakes at all, because doing so could possibly invalidate all the work that follows.

Forensic Duplicators

Forensic duplicators are systems that copy data from a source to a destination while ensuring that not even a single bit gets altered in the process. What sets them apart from other copying utilities is that they do not rely on file system operations, which means they can recover file system artifacts such as the Master File Table (MFT) in Windows systems and the inode table in Linux. This means that a hard drive running the macOS, Windows, or Linux can be copied in the same way using the same utility. Imaging tools usually allow for the entire contents of the drive to be duplicated to a single file in a remote destination. Unlike regular file copies, forensic duplicates also include the file system's slack and free space, where the remnants of deleted files may reside.

dd Utility

Using the dd utility is just about the easiest way to make a bit-for-bit copy of a hard drive. You can find the program in nearly every Linux distribution as well as in macOS. Its primary purpose is to copy or convert files, and accordingly there are several options for block sizes and image conversion during the imaging process that may assist in follow-on analysis. Because almost everything in the extended file system (ext) used in Linux is a "file" (even network connections and peripheral devices), dd can duplicate data across files, devices, partitions, and volumes. The following command will do a bit-for-bit copy of hard drive hda to a file called case123.img using a block size of 4096 bytes, and it will fill the rest of a block with null symbols if it encounters an error:

```
dd if=/dev/hda of=case123.img bs=4k conv=noerror,sync
```

FTK Imager

FTK Imager is a free data preview and imaging tool developed by AccessData. Unlike the dd utility, this imager is a full-featured product that enables you to perform a forensically sound acquisition, verify it by generating MD5 and/or SHA-1 hashes, and even preview the files and folders in a read-only fashion. FTK Imager will also read registry keys from Windows and let you preview them and their values. It also supports compression, encryption, and multiple output formats, including EnCase evidence file format (E01) and the raw format generated by dd (001).

MacQuisition

It's definitely worth mentioning MacQuisition as an imaging tool you should consider, although it is an entire forensic suite of tools. Developed and sold by BlackBag Technologies (which was acquired by Cellebrite in early 2020), it is designed to triage and acquire Apple devices, such as Macs. It supports HPS+ file systems and HFS+, and it has the capability to retrieve data from secure enclaves.

Password Crackers

It is increasingly common to find encrypted files or drives in everything from mobile devices to back-end servers. If a suspect is unable or unwilling to provide the password, or if there is no suspect to interrogate in the first place, you may have to resort to specialized software that is designed to guess passwords and decrypt the protected resources.

PART III

A popular commercial solution in this space is Passware Kit Forensic. It can operate on its own or be integrated with EnCase. Passware Kit Forensic can decrypt more than 280 different types of protected files, including BitLocker, FileVault, iCloud, and Dropbox. Additionally, because password cracking can take a very long time, this tool can take advantage of graphics processing units (GPUs) and multiple networked computers to accelerate the process. The two most popular password-cracking tools among security professionals are John the Ripper and Hashcat. Though their feature sets are very similar, there are subtle differences with which you may want to become acquainted.

John the Ripper

John the Ripper is an open source password-cracking tool, initially developed for Unix, that now has variations for many other operating systems. Figure 16-2 shows options for usage with the command-line tool. John runs attacks with wordlists, which reference a precompiled list of possible passwords, or by brute force, which tries many possible combinations in the character space. Additionally, John supports autodetection of password hash types, the protective measure used by operation systems to prevent unauthorized viewing of the password file. The commercial version expands on the already impressive selection of hashes supported.

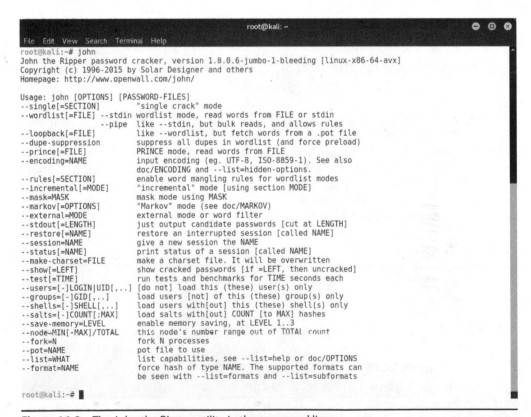

Figure 16-2   The John the Ripper utility in the command line

Hashcat and oclHashcat

Hashcat and its GPU-optimized variant, oclHashcat, are powerful password-cracking utilities that support a vast number of attack modes, such as brute force, dictionary, and rule-based. Combined with their ability to target various hash types, databases, and full-disk encryption schemes, these software products have become the go-to tools for many forensic analysts.

 NOTE Password-cracking software has been used successfully for many years, but the trend of increasingly affordable hardware has ushered in the age of hardware-accelerated password cracking. Using "rigs" composed of several GPUs, a user can brute-force passwords orders of magnitude faster than traditional CPU-only methods.

Hashing Utilities

The most popular hashing algorithms for forensic analysis are MD5 and SHA-256, and these are both supported by all the popular tools we've discussed in this chapter, although you may find older tools that use other algorithms. If you need a standalone hashing utility, these are included by default by many operating systems. For example, macOS has the md5 tool available from the command line. Linux typically has the md5 tool as well as sha1sum. Finally, Microsoft provides the File Checksum Integrity Verifier (FCIV) command-line tool as a free but unsupported download. FCIV is able to compute both MD5 and SHA-1 hashes, as shown in Figure 16-3.

Forensic Suites

Reconstructing what happened after the fact is inherently a difficult task, but we have many tools at our disposal to assist with the entire process, from documentation to reporting. *Forensic suites* include a range of tools to uncover data thought to be lost, or data that may be lost easily, such as in the case of volatile memory. Because documentation is an important part of forensics, particularly in criminal investigations, some suites automatically document the evidence analysis progression and technical tasks that have been performed by the analyst.

EnCase

The EnCase suite of tools is very popular with law enforcement and government agencies for forensic missions because of its easy-to-use GUI and chain-of-custody features. The EnCase suite includes tools for forensic acquisition, analysis, and report generation. Its evidence file format (E01) is among the most common types of forensic imaging formats, in part because of its high portability. The imaged volume's data, metadata, and hashes are all included in a single file.

FTK

AccessData Forensic Toolkit, or FTK, is a popular choice for investigators needing to create forensic images of hard drives. FTK is a favorite for forensic analysis because of its built-in logging features, which make the process of documentation easier for investigators

PART III

```
Windows PowerShell                                                        —  □  ✕

PS C:\Users\Brent\Desktop> .\fciv.exe
//
// File Checksum Integrity Verifier version 2.05.
//

Usage: fciv.exe [Commands] <Options>

Commands: ( Default -add )

        -add    <file | dir> : Compute hash and send to output (default screen).
                dir options:
                -r       : recursive.
                -type    : ex: -type *.exe.
                -exc file: list of directories that should not be computed.
                -wp      : Without full path name. ( Default store full path)
                -bp      : specify base path to remove from full path name

        -list            : List entries in the database.
        -v               : Verify hashes.
                         : Option: -bp basepath.

        -? -h -help      : Extended Help.

Options:
        -md5 | -sha1 | -both   : Specify hashtype, default md5.
        -xml db                : Specify database format and name.

To display the MD5 hash of a file, type fciv.exe filename
PS C:\Users\Brent\Desktop> .\fciv.exe .\ReadMe.txt
//
// File Checksum Integrity Verifier version 2.05.
//
79ac8d043dc8739f661c45cc33fc07ac .\readme.txt
```

Figure 16-3   The Windows File Checksum Integrity Verifier options and usage

looking to preserve details of the analysis itself. One of the more popular tools included in the FTK suite is the FTK Imager, a data preview and volume imaging tool.

Cellebrite

Cellebrite is a company that developed data transfer solutions for mobile carriers and has since moved into the mobile forensics market. Its flagship product, the Universal Forensic Extraction Device (UFED), is a handheld hardware device primarily marketed to law enforcement and military communities. With the UFED, a user can extract encrypted, deleted, or hidden data from select mobile phones. Cellebrite also provides evidence preservation using techniques such as write blocking during the data extraction procedure. As mentioned earlier, Cellebrite also owns BlackBag Technologies, the company that developed MacQuisition.

File Carving

File carving is a technique used to fully recover partially recovered files or those discovered to be damaged. Because carving techniques don't depend on the file system in use, file carving is a common method for data recovery when all else fails. The basic concept of carving is that specified file types are searched for and extracted from raw binary data by looking at file structure and content without any matching file system metadata.

```
● ● ●                    brent — brent@budgie-dev: ~ — ssh budgie — 96×32

PhotoRec 7.0, Data Recovery Utility, April 2015
Christophe GRENIER <grenier@cgsecurity.org>
http://www.cgsecurity.org

Disk /dev/sda - 128 GB / 120 GiB (RO) - VMware Virtual disk
     Partition                    Start        End    Size in sectors
  1 * Linux                   0  32 33  15664 222 46  251654144


Pass 1 - Reading sector   2272856/251654144, 1025 files found
Elapsed time 0h00m16s - Estimated time to completion 0h29m15
txt: 953 recovered
elf: 37 recovered
xz: 11 recovered
gz: 8 recovered
tx?: 5 recovered
icc: 4 recovered
a: 2 recovered
zip: 2 recovered
dat: 1 recovered
png: 1 recovered
others: 1 recovered
 Stop
```

Figure 16-4 PhotoRec command-line utility actively recovering files from a volume

A popular multiplatform carving utility, PhotoRec is among the fastest and most reliable free tools available. While originally designed to recover media files from damaged digital camera memory, the program is capable of extracting files, including system files and documents, from hard disks, optical discs, and external media. Figure 16-4 shows the progress screen from a PhotoRec recovery attempt. Notice that the utility lists the types and quantity of the recovered files. It's able to determine the file type by reading the media block by block, looking for patterns associated with certain document types. JPEG files, for example, can be identified by looking for blocks with any of the following byte sequences:

- 0xff, 0xd8, 0xff, 0xe0
- 0xff, 0xd8, 0xff, 0xe1
- 0xff, 0xd8, 0xff, 0xfe

Chapter Review

Digital forensic investigations require a very high degree of discipline and fixed adherence to established processes. A haphazard approach to these activities can mean the difference between successfully resolving an incident and watching a threat actor get away with criminal behavior. The challenge is in striking the right balance between quick responses to incidents that don't require this level of effort and identifying those that do require the effort early enough to adjust the team's approach. Because you may not know which events can escalate to forensic investigations, you should always be ready to perform investigations in a forensically sound way, even if you must conduct the investigation with little or no notice.

The CySA+ exam will require you to be familiar with the techniques associated with seizure, acquisition, analysis, and reporting in digital forensics. For example, you may see questions that present a scenario in which some part of the process has already been completed, and you are asked to decide what should be the next thing to do. This may require familiarity with the way in which you would use some of the most common tools, such as the Linux dd utility. Though you will probably not see questions that require you to issue commands with arguments, you may have to interpret the output of such tools and perform some sort of simple analysis of what may have happened.

Questions

1. In the event of a serious incident, which task is *not* a critical step to take in controlling the crime scene?

   A. Record any interactions with digital systems.

   B. Verify roles and training for individuals participating in the investigation.

   C. Remove power from currently running systems.

   D. Carefully document who enters and leaves the scene.

2. What is the practice of controlling how evidence is handled to ensure its integrity during an investigation called?

   A. Chain of control

   B. Chain of concern

   C. Chain of command

   D. Chain of custody

3. As part of the forensic analysis process, what critical activity often includes a graphical representation of process and operating system events?

   A. Registry editing

   B. Time line analysis

   C. Network mapping

   D. Write blocking

4. The practice of modifying details about a file's creation, access, and modification times is referred to as what?

   A. Timestomping

   B. Timestamping

   C. Time lining

   D. Timeshifting

Use the following command-line input to answer Questions 5–7:

```
dd if=/dev/sda of=/dev/sdc bs=2048 conv=noerror,sync status=progress
```

5. How many bits of data are read and written at a time?

    A. 2048

    B. 16384

    C. 256

    D. 512

6. What is the destination of the dd operation?

    A. noerror

    B. /dev/sda

    C. sync

    D. /dev/sdc

7. What is the purpose of the command?

    A. To copy the primary partition to an image file

    B. To restore the contents of a hard drive from an image file

    C. To copy the entire contents of the hard drive to an image file

    D. To delete the entire contents of /dev/sda

Use the following scenario to answer Questions 8–10:

You are called to the scene of a high-profile incident and asked to perform forensic acquisition of digital evidence. The primary objective is a Linux server that runs several services for a small company. The former administrator is suspected of running illicit services using company resources and is refusing to provide passwords for access to the system. Additionally, several company-owned mobile phones appear to be functioning and are sitting on the desk beside the servers.

8. What utility will enable you to make a bit-for-bit copy of the hard drive contents?

    A. MFT

    B. dd

    C. MD5

    D. GPU

9. What type of specialized software might you use to recover the credentials required to get system access?

    A. Forensic duplicator

    B. dd

    C. Password cracker

    D. MD5

10. You want to take the mobile phones back to your lab for further investigation. Which two tools could you use to maintain device integrity as you transport them?

    A. Faraday bag and a tamper-evident seal

    B. Write blocker and crime scene tape

    C. Thumb drive and crime scene tape

    D. Forensic toolkit and tamper-evident seal

Answers

1. **C.** Removing power should not be done unless it's to preserve life or limb, or for other exigent circumstances. In many cases, it's possible to recover evidence residing in running memory.

2. **D.** A chain of custody is a history that shows how evidence was collected, transported, and preserved at every stage of the investigation process.

3. **B.** Time line, or time frame, analysis is the practice of arranging extracted data from a Unix file system, the Windows registry, or a mobile device in chronological order to better understand the circumstances of a suspected incident.

4. **A.** Timestomping is a technique that attackers use to modify details about a file's creation, access, and modification times.

5. **B.** The **bs** argument indicates the number of bytes transferring during the process. Because there are 8 bits in a byte, you multiply 2048 by 8 to get 16384 bits.

6. **D.** The **of** argument indicates /dev/sdc as the *output* file, or destination, of the process.

7. **C.** This command will duplicate the contents of the entire hard drive, indicated by the argument **/dev/sda**. You should be careful to double-check the spelling of both input and output files to avoid overwriting the incorrect media.

8. **B.** dd is a common utility included in most Linux-based systems that enables you to make bit-for-bit copies of hard drive contents. It can duplicate data across files, devices, partitions, and volumes.

9. **C.** Password crackers are specialized software designed to guess passwords and decrypt the protected resources. The software can be very resource intensive since cracking usually requires a lot of processing power or storage capacity.

10. **A.** A Faraday container will prevent the devices from communicating over radio waves by absorbing and redistributing their RF energy. You should secure the bag with a tamper-evident seal to help you identify whether its contents have been interfered with during transport.

PART IV

Appendixes and Glossary

Objective Map

Exam CS0-003

Official Exam Objective	Ch #	All-in-One Coverage
1.0 SECURITY OPERATIONS		
1.1 Explain the importance of system and network architecture concepts in security operations		
Log ingestion	1	Log Ingestion
• Time synchronization	1	Time Synchronization
• Logging levels	1	Logging Levels
Operating system (OS) concepts	1	Operating System Concepts
• Windows Registry	1	Windows Registry
• System hardening	1	System Hardening
• File structure	1	File Structure
- Configuration file locations	1	Windows Registry Linux Configuration Settings
• System processes	1	System Processes
• Hardware architecture	1	Hardware Architecture
Infrastructure concepts	1	Infrastructure Concepts
• Serverless	1	Serverless Architecture
• Virtualization	1	Virtualization
• Containerization	1	Containerization
Network architecture	1	Network Architecture
• On-premises	1	On-premises Architecture
• Cloud	1	Cloud Service Models Cloud Deployment Models
• Hybrid	1	Hybrid Models
• Network segmentation	1	Network Segmentation
• Zero trust	1	Zero Trust

Official Exam Objective	Ch #	All-in-One Coverage
• Secure access secure edge (SASE)	1	Secure Access Secure Edge
• Software-defined networking (SDN)	1	Software-Defined Networking
Identity and access management	1	Identity and Access Management
• Multifactor authentication (MFA)	1	Multifactor Authentication
• Single sign-on (SSO)	1	Single Sign-On
• Federation	1	Federation
• Privileged access management (PAM)	1	Privileged Access Management
• Passwordless	1	Passwordless Authentication
• Cloud access security broker (CASB)	1	Cloud Access Security Broker
Encryption	1	Encryption
• Public key infrastructure (PKI)	1	Public Key Infrastructure
• Secure sockets layer (SSL) inspection	1	Secure Sockets Layer and Transport Layer Security Inspection
Sensitive data protection	1	Sensitive Data Protection
• Data loss prevention (DLP)	1	Data Loss Prevention
• Personally identifiable information (PII)	1	Personally Identifiable Information
• Cardholder data (CHD)	1	Cardholder Data
1.2 Given a scenario, analyze indicators of potentially malicious activity		
Network-related	4	Network-Related Indicators
• Bandwidth consumption	4	Bandwidth Consumption
• Beaconing	4	Beaconing
• Irregular peer-to-peer communication	4	Irregular Peer-to-Peer Communication
• Rogue devices on the network	4	Rogue Devices on the Network
• Scans/sweeps	4	Scans/Sweeps
• Unusual traffic spikes	4	Unusual Traffic Spikes
• Activity on unexpected ports	4	Activity on Unexpected Ports
Host-related	4	Host-Related Indicators
• Processor consumption	4	Capacity Consumption
• Memory consumption	4	Capacity Consumption
• Drive capacity consumption	4	Capacity Consumption
• Unauthorized software	4	Unauthorized Software
• Malicious processes	4	Malicious Processes
• Unauthorized changes	4	Unauthorized Changes
• Unauthorized privileges	4	Unauthorized Privileges
• Data exfiltration	4	Data Exfiltration

Official Exam Objective	Ch #	All-in-One Coverage
• Abnormal OS process behavior	4	Malicious Processes
• File system changes or anomalies	5	File Analysis
• Registry changes or anomalies	4	Registry Change or Anomaly
• Unauthorized scheduled tasks	4	Unauthorized Scheduled Task
Application-related	4	Application-Related Indicators
• Anomalous activity	4	Anomalous Activity
• Introduction of new accounts	4	Introduction of New Accounts
• Unexpected output	4	Unexpected Output
• Unexpected outbound communication	4	Unexpected Outbound Communication
• Service interruption	4	Service Interruption
• Application logs	4	Application Logs
Other	4	Other Indicators
• Social engineering attacks	4	Social Engineering
• Obfuscated links	4	Obfuscated Links

1.3 Given a scenario, use appropriate tools or techniques to determine malicious activity

Tools	5	Techniques for Malicious Activity Analysis
• Packet capture	5	Capturing Network Traffic
- Wireshark	6	Wireshark and TShark
- tcpdump	6	tcpdump
• Log analysis/correlation	5	Log Analysis and Correlation
- Security information and event management (SIEM)	5	Security Information and Event Management
- Security orchestration, automation, and response (SOAR)	5	Security Orchestration, Automation, and Response
• Endpoint security	5	Endpoint
- Endpoint detection and response (EDR)	5	Endpoint Detection and Response
• Domain name service (DNS) and Internet Protocol (IP) reputation	5	Domain Name System and Internet Protocol Reputation Analysis
- WHOIS	6	WHOIS
- AbuseIPDB	6	AbuseIPDB
• File analysis	5	File Analysis
- Strings	6	Strings
- VirusTotal	6	VirusTotal
• Sandboxing	5	Dynamic Analysis
- Joe Sandbox	6	Joe Sandbox
- Cuckoo Sandbox	6	Cuckoo Sandbox

PART IV

PART IV

Official Exam Objective	Ch #	All-in-One Coverage
1.5 Explain the importance of efficiency and process improvement in security operations		
Standardize processes	2	Process Standardization
• Identification of tasks suitable for automation	2	Identification of Tasks Suitable for Automation
- Repeatable/do not require human interaction	2	Minimizing Human Engagement
• Team coordination to manage and facilitate automation	2	Team Coordination to Manage and Facilitate Automation
Streamline operations	2	Streamlining Security Operations
• Automation and orchestration	2	Automation and Orchestration
- Security orchestration, automation, and response (SOAR)	2	Security Orchestration, Automation, and Response
• Orchestrating threat intelligence data	2	Orchestrating Threat Intelligence Data
- Data enrichment	2	Data Enrichment
- Threat feed combination	2	Orchestrating Threat Intelligence Data
• Minimize human engagement	2	Minimizing Human Engagement
Technology and tool integration	2	Technology and Tool Integration
• Application programming interface (API)	2	Application Programming Interface
• Webhooks	2	Webhooks
• Plugins	2	Plug-Ins
Single pane of glass	2	Single Pane of Glass
2.0 VULNERABILITY MANAGEMENT		
2.1 Given a scenario, implement vulnerability scanning methods and concepts		
Asset discovery	9	Asset Discovery
• Map scans	9	Asset Mapping Scans and Fingerprinting
• Device fingerprinting	9	Asset Mapping Scans and Fingerprinting
Special considerations	9	Special Considerations for Vulnerability Scans
• Scheduling	9	Schedule
• Operations	9	Operations
• Performance	9	Performance
• Sensitivity levels	9	Sensitivity Levels
• Segmentation	9	Network and Security Device Considerations
• Regulatory requirements	9	Regulatory Requirements

Official Exam Objective	Ch #	All-in-One Coverage
Internal vs. external scanning	9	Internal vs. External Scanning
Agent vs. agentless	9	Agent-Based vs. Agentless Scanning
Credentialed vs. non-credentialed	9	Noncredentialed and Credentialed Scans
Passive vs. active	9	Passive vs. Active Scanning
Static vs. dynamic	9	Software Vulnerability Assessment Tools and Techniques
• Reverse engineering	9	Reverse Engineering
• Fuzzing	9	Fuzzing
Critical infrastructure	9	Critical Infrastructure
• Operational technology (OT)	9	Operational Technology
• Industrial control systems (ICS)	9	Industrial Control Systems and Operational Technology
• Supervisory control and data acquisition (SCADA)	9	Supervisory Control and Data Acquisition Systems
Security baseline scanning	9	Security Baseline Scanning
Industry frameworks	9	Industry Frameworks
• Payment Card Industry Data Security Standard (PCI DSS)	9	Payment Card Industry Data Security Standard
• Center for Internet Security (CIS) benchmarks	9	Center for Internet Security Controls
• Open Web Application Security Project (OWASP)	9	Open Web Application Security Project
• International Organization for Standardization (ISO) 27000 series	9	ISO/IEC 27000 Series

2.2 Given a scenario, analyze output from vulnerability assessment tools

Tools	10	Network Scanning and Mapping
• Network scanning and mapping	10	Network Scanning and Mapping
- Angry IP Scanner	10	Angry IP Scanner
- Maltego	10	Maltego
• Web application scanners	10	Web Application Scanners
- Burp Suite	10	Burp Suite
- Zed Attack Proxy (ZAP)	10	OWASP Zed Attack Proxy
- Arachni	10	Arachni
- Nikto	10	Nikto
• Vulnerability scanners	10	Infrastructure Vulnerability Scanners
- Nessus	10	Nessus
- OpenVAS	10	OpenVAS

Official Exam Objective	Ch #	All-in-One Coverage
• Debuggers	10	Debuggers
- Immunity debugger	10	Immunity Debugger
- GNU debugger (GDB)	10	GDB
• Multipurpose	10	Multipurpose Tools
- Nmap	10	nmap
- Metasploit framework (MSF)	10	Metasploit Framework
- Recon-ng	10	Recon-ng
• Cloud infrastructure assessment tools	10	Cloud Infrastructure Assessment Tools
- Scout Suite	10	Scout Suite
- Prowler	10	Prowler
- Pacu	10	Pacu
2.3 Given a scenario, analyze data to prioritize vulnerabilities		
Common Vulnerability Scoring System (CVSS) interpretation	11	Common Vulnerability Scoring System
• Attack vectors	11	Attack Vector
• Attack complexity	11	Attack Complexity
• Privileges required	11	Privileges Required
• User interaction	11	User Interaction
• Scope	11	Scope
• Impact	11	Impact
- Confidentiality	11	Impact
- Integrity	11	Impact
- Availability	11	Impact
Validation	11	Validating Vulnerabilities
• True/false positives	11	True Positives False Positives
• True/false negatives	11	True Negatives False Negatives
Context awareness	11	Context Awareness
• Internal	11	Internal
• External	11	External
• Isolated	11	Isolated
Exploitability/weaponization	11	Exploitability and Weaponization
Asset value	11	Asset Value
Zero-day	11	Zero-Day

PART IV

Official Exam Objective	Ch #	All-in-One Coverage
Patching and configuration management	13	Patching and Configuration Management
• Testing	13	Testing
• Implementation	13	Implementation
• Rollback	13	Rollback
• Validation	13	Validation
Maintenance windows	13	Maintenance Windows
Exceptions	13	Exceptions
Risk management principles	13	Risk Management Principles
• Accept	13	Risk Acceptance
• Transfer	13	Risk Transference
• Avoid	13	Risk Avoidance
• Mitigate	13	Risk Mitigation
Policies, governance, and service-level objectives (SLOs)	13	Vulnerability Management Governance and Policy Service Level Objectives
Prioritization and escalation	13	Prioritization and Escalation
Attack surface management	13	Attack Surface Management
• Edge discovery	13	Edge and Passive Discovery
• Passive discovery	13	Edge and Passive Discovery
• Security controls testing	13	Security Controls Testing
• Penetration testing and adversary emulation	13	Penetration Testing and Adversary Emulation
• Bug bounty	13	Bug Bounty
• Attack surface reduction	13	Attack Surface Reduction
Secure coding best practices	13	Secure Coding Best Practices
• Input validation	13	Input Validation
• Output encoding	13	Output Encoding
• Session management	13	Session Management
• Authentication	13	Authentication
• Data protection	13	Data Protection
• Parameterized queries	13	Parameterized Queries
Secure software development life cycle (SDLC)	13	Secure Software Development Lifecycle
Threat modeling	8	Threat Modeling Methodologies

PART IV

Official Exam Objective	Ch #	All-in-One Coverage
Post-incident activity	15	Post-Incident Activities
• Forensic analysis	15	Forensics
• Root cause analysis	15	Root Cause Analysis
• Lessons learned	15	Lessons Learned
4.0 REPORTING AND COMMUNICATION		
4.1 Explain the importance of vulnerability management reporting and communication		
Vulnerability management reporting	13	Vulnerability Management Reporting and Communication
• Vulnerabilities	13	Vulnerabilities
• Affected hosts	13	Affected Hosts
• Risk score	13	Risk Score
• Mitigation	13	Mitigation
• Recurrence	13	Recurrence
• Prioritization	13	Prioritization
Compliance reports	13	Compliance Reports
Action plans	13	Action Plans
• Configuration management	13	Configuration Management
• Patching	13	Patching
• Compensating controls	13	Compensating Controls
• Awareness, education, and training	13	Awareness, Education, and Training
• Changing business requirements	13	Changing Business Requirements
Inhibitors to remediation	13	Inhibitors to Remediation
• Memorandum of understanding (MOU)	13	Memorandum of Understanding
• Service-level agreement (SLA)	13	Service Level Agreement
• Organizational governance	13	Organizational Governance
• Business process interruption	13	Business Process Interruption
• Degrading functionality	13	Degrading Functionality
• Legacy systems	13	Legacy and Proprietary Systems
• Proprietary systems	13	Legacy and Proprietary Systems
Metrics and key performance indicators (KPIs)	13	Metrics and Key Performance Indicators
• Trends	13	Trends
• Top 10	13	Top 10
• Critical vulnerabilities and zero-days	13	Critical Vulnerabilities and Zero-Days
• SLOs	13	Service Level Objectives
Stakeholder identification and communication	13	Stakeholder Identification and Communication

Official Exam Objective	Ch #	All-in-One Coverage
4.2 Explain the importance of incident response reporting and communication		
Stakeholder identification and communication	15	Stakeholder Identification and Communication
Incident declaration and escalation	14	Incident Declaration and Escalation
Incident response reporting	15	Incident Response Reporting
• Executive summary	15	Executive Summary
• Who, what, when, where, and why	15	Who, What, When, Where, Why, and How
• Recommendations	15	Recommendations
• Timeline	15	Who, What, When, Where, Why, and How
• Impact	15	Impact
• Scope	14	Incident Scope and Impact
• Evidence	15	Evidence
Communications	14	Establishing a Communication Process
• Legal	15	Legal Counsel
• Public relations	15	Public Relations
- Customer communication	15	Public Relations
- Media	15	Public Relations
• Regulatory reporting	15	Regulatory Reporting
• Law enforcement	15	Law Enforcement
Root cause analysis	15	Root Cause Analysis
Lessons learned	15	Lessons Learned
Metrics and KPIs	15	Metrics and Key Performance Indicators
• Mean time to detect	15	Mean Time to Detect
• Mean time to respond	15	Mean Time to Respond
• Mean time to remediate	15	Mean Time to Remediate
• Alert volume	15	Alert Volume

About the Online Content

This book comes complete with TotalTester Online customizable practice exam software with 170 practice exam questions.

System Requirements

The current and previous major versions of the following desktop browsers are recommended and supported: Chrome, Microsoft Edge, Firefox, and Safari. These browsers update frequently, and sometimes an update may cause compatibility issues with the TotalTester Online or other content hosted on the Training Hub. If you run into a problem using one of these browsers, please try using another until the problem is resolved.

Your Total Seminars Training Hub Account

To get access to the online content you will need to create an account on the Total Seminars Training Hub. Registration is free, and you will be able to track all your online content using your account. You may also opt in if you wish to receive marketing information from McGraw Hill or Total Seminars, but this is not required for you to gain access to the online content.

Privacy Notice

McGraw Hill values your privacy. Please be sure to read the Privacy Notice available during registration to see how the information you have provided will be used. You may view our Corporate Customer Privacy Policy by visiting the McGraw Hill Privacy Center. Visit the **mheducation.com** site and click **Privacy** at the bottom of the page.

Single User License Terms and Conditions

Online access to the digital content included with this book is governed by the McGraw Hill License Agreement outlined next. By using this digital content you agree to the terms of that license.

Access   To register and activate your Total Seminars Training Hub account, simply follow these easy steps.

1. Go to this URL: **hub.totalsem.com/mheclaim**
2. To register and create a new Training Hub account, enter your e-mail address, name, and password on the **Register** tab. No further personal information (such as credit card number) is required to create an account.

   If you already have a Total Seminars Training Hub account, enter your e-mail address and password on the **Log in** tab.
3. Enter your Product Key: `hv0z-q7hw-9h72`
4. Click to accept the user license terms.
5. For new users, click the **Register and Claim** button to create your account. For existing users, click the **Log in and Claim** button.

   You will be taken to the Training Hub and have access to the content for this book.

Duration of License   Access to your online content through the Total Seminars Training Hub will expire one year from the date the publisher declares the book out of print.

Your purchase of this McGraw Hill product, including its access code, through a retail store is subject to the refund policy of that store.

The Content is a copyrighted work of McGraw Hill, and McGraw Hill reserves all rights in and to the Content. The Work is © 2024 by McGraw Hill.

Restrictions on Transfer   The user is receiving only a limited right to use the Content for the user's own internal and personal use, dependent on purchase and continued ownership of this book. The user may not reproduce, forward, modify, create derivative works based upon, transmit, distribute, disseminate, sell, publish, or sublicense the Content or in any way commingle the Content with other third-party content without McGraw Hill's consent.

Limited Warranty   The McGraw Hill Content is provided on an "as is" basis. Neither McGraw Hill nor its licensors make any guarantees or warranties of any kind, either express or implied, including, but not limited to, implied warranties of merchantability or fitness for a particular purpose or use as to any McGraw Hill Content or the information therein or any warranties as to the accuracy, completeness, correctness, or results to be obtained from, accessing or using the McGraw Hill Content, or any material referenced in such Content or any information entered into licensee's product by users or other persons and/or any material available on or that can be accessed through the licensee's product (including via any hyperlink or otherwise) or as to non-infringement of third-party rights. Any warranties of any kind, whether express or implied, are disclaimed. Any material or data obtained through use of the McGraw Hill Content is at your own discretion and risk and user understands that it will be solely responsible for any resulting damage to its computer system or loss of data.

Neither McGraw Hill nor its licensors shall be liable to any subscriber or to any user or anyone else for any inaccuracy, delay, interruption in service, error or omission, regardless of cause, or for any damage resulting therefrom.

In no event will McGraw Hill or its licensors be liable for any indirect, special or consequential damages, including but not limited to, lost time, lost money, lost profits or good will, whether in contract, tort, strict liability or otherwise, and whether or not such damages are foreseen or unforeseen with respect to any use of the McGraw Hill Content.

TotalTester Online

TotalTester Online provides you with a simulation of the CompTIA CySA+ CS0-003 exam. Exams can be taken in Practice Mode or Exam Mode. Practice Mode provides an assistance window with hints, references to the book, explanations of the correct and incorrect answers, and the option to check your answer as you take the test. Exam Mode provides a simulation of the actual exam. The number of questions, the types of questions, and the time allowed are intended to be an accurate representation of the exam environment. The option to customize your quiz allows you to create custom exams from selected domains or chapters, and you can further customize the number of questions and time allowed.

To take a test, follow the instructions provided in the previous section to register and activate your Total Seminars Training Hub account. When you register, you will be taken to the Total Seminars Training Hub. From the Training Hub Home page, select your certification from the Study drop-down menu at the top of the page to drill down to the TotalTester for your book. You can also scroll to it from the list on the Your Topics tab of the Home page, and then click the TotalTester link to launch the TotalTester. Once you've launched your TotalTester, you can select the option to customize your quiz and begin testing yourself in Practice Mode or Exam Mode. All exams provide an overall grade and a grade broken down by domain.

Technical Support

For questions regarding the TotalTester or operation of the Training Hub, visit **www.totalsem.com** or e-mail **support@totalsem.com**.

For questions regarding book content, visit **www.mheducation.com/customerservice**.

access control list (ACL) A list of rules that control the manner in which a resource may be accessed.

active defense Adaptive measures aimed at increasing the amount of effort attackers need to exert to be successful while reducing the effort for the defenders.

address space layout randomization (ASLR) A technique used in operating systems that prevents exploitation by randomizing the locations where software components are loaded into memory, making it more difficult for an attacker to predict target addresses.

advanced persistent threat (APT) The name given to any number of stealthy and continuous computer-hacking efforts, often coordinated and executed by an organization or government with significant resources over a longer period of time.

algorithm A sequence of instructions that are defined to perform a task. This task can be anything from sorting data to encrypting or decrypting information.

allow-list A list that that permits access or privileges, typically to specific users, IP addresses, or programs.

anomaly analysis Any technique focused on measuring the deviation of some observation from some baseline and determining whether that deviation is statistically significant.

application programming interface (API) Code written to facilitate communications and data exchange between disparate applications.

artificial intelligence (AI) An interdisciplinary field of computer science dedicated to creating expert systems capable of executing tasks typically requiring human intelligence.

assessment A process that gathers information and makes determinations based on it.

asset Anything of value to an organization, whether that value is measured quantitatively or qualitatively.

asymmetric cryptography A cryptosystem that uses two different but complementary keys for encryption and decryption.

attack surface The sum of all possible attack vectors into a system, process, or organization.

attribute-based access control (ABAC) An authorization model that evaluates attributes instead of roles to determine access, protecting objects from unauthorized users based on predefined attributes defined by security policies.

audit   A systematic inspection by an independent third party to determine whether the organization is in compliance with some set of external requirements.

authentication (authN)   The process of verifying the identity of a user, device, or system.

authorization (authZ)   The process of granting or denying a user, device, or system the right to access resources, perform operations, and execute commands based on their confirmed identity.

beaconing   A periodical outbound connection between a compromised computer and an external controller.

Berkeley Packet Filter (BPF)   A construct in the Linux kernel that operates like a virtual machine. It allows safe execution of bytecode at different hook points, often providing a mechanism to interact directly with network packets, enabling monitoring, debugging, and filtering.

blue team   The group of participants who are the focus of a training event or exercise; they are usually involved with the defense of the organization's infrastructure.

broken function level authorization (BFLA)   A vulnerability where functions that should require elevated permissions can be accessed by users with inadequate privileges, due to improper or missing authorization checks.

broken object level authorization (BOLA)   A vulnerability where data or resources can be access by users with inadequate privileges, due to improper or missing authorization checks, at the application's object level.

cardholder data (CHD)   Data relating to the holder or user of a credit card, such as financial or personal information.

certificate authority (CA)   A trusted entity that issues digital certificates used to cryptographically link an entity with a public key to verify the ownership and authenticity of websites, binaries, and other digital resources.

chain of custody   A documented history that shows how evidence was handled, collected, transported, and preserved at every stage of the investigative process.

cloud access security broker (CASB)   A software system that sits between each user and each cloud service, monitoring all activity, enforcing policies, and alerting when something seems to be wrong.

cloud computing   The use of shared, remote computing devices for the purpose of providing improved efficiencies, performance, reliability, scalability, and security.

command and control (C2)   A method used by threat actors to issue commands and thereby control compromised systems.

Common Vulnerability Scoring System (CVSS)   A well-known standard for quantifying severity ratings for vulnerabilities.

compensating control   A security control that satisfies the requirements of some other control when implementing the latter is not possible or desirable.

Completely Automated Public Turing test to tell Computers and Humans Apart (CAPTCHA)   A challenge-response test designed to determine whether the user is human.

configuration management database (CMDB)   A database that stores information about hardware and software assets designed to help organizations understand the relationships between assets and configurations.

containerization   A virtualization technology that abstracts the operating system for the applications running above it, allowing for low overhead in running many applications and improved speed in deploying instances.

containment   Actions that attempt to deny the threat agent the ability or means to cause further damage.

content security policy (CSP)   A defense against cross-site scripting (XSS), clickjacking, and other code injection attacks, enforced in the browser. A CSP allows website administrators to specify which resources a browser is allowed to load.

credential stuffing   A type of brute-force attack in which credentials obtained from a data breach of one service are used to authenticate to another system in an attempt to gain access.

cross-site request forgery (CSRF)   An attack that coerces an authenticated user into unintentionally performing actions on a web application, exploiting the trust the application has for authenticated requests. The vulnerability hinges on the application's inability to discern between legitimate requests from the user and unauthorized requests made by an attacker.

cross-site scripting (XSS)   A vulnerability in a web application that provides an opportunity for malicious users to execute arbitrary client-side scripts.

cyber threat intelligence (CTI)   A discipline in cybersecurity that focuses on analyzing and gathering information about potential threats and threat actors to predict, prevent, and respond to attacks.

dynamic application security testing (DAST)   A process that examines an application during runtime to discover vulnerabilities.

data enrichment   The process of giving depth and context to an individual piece of data, such as an IP address.

Data Execution Prevention (DEP)   A security feature present in numerous operating systems that blocks specific memory areas from executing code, consequently hindering the execution of malicious code.

data loss prevention (DLP)   The actions and technologies an organization uses to prevent the loss of sensitive data to unauthorized external parties.

database firewall (DBFW)   A specialized application firewall that monitors and audits all database activity, identifying and preventing any unauthorized, suspicious, or anomalous behavior or transactions.

dereferencing   A common flaw that occurs when software attempts to access a value stored in memory that does not exist, which sometimes enables attackers to bypass security measures or learn more about how the program works by reading the exception information.

DevSecOps   A combination of the terms *development, security,* and *operations* that denotes the practice of incorporating development, security IT, and quality assurance (QA) staff into software development projects to align their incentives and enable frequent, efficient, and reliable releases of software products.

digital certificate   A file that contains information about the certificate owner, the certificate authority (CA) that issued it, the public key, its validity timeframe, and the CA's signature of the certificate itself, typically following the X.509 standard defined by the Internet Engineering Task Force (IETF) in RFC 5280.

digital signature   A short sequence of data that proves that a larger data sequence (say, an e-mail message or a file) was created by a given person and was not modified by anyone else after being signed.

distributed denial of service (DDoS)   A denial-of-service attack that leverages multiple, often compromised, systems to target a single system, service, or application.

Domain-based Message Authentication, Reporting & Conformance (DMARC)   An e-mail protocol that uses SPF (Sender Policy Framework) and DKIM (DomainKeys Identified Mail) to determine the authenticity of an e-mail message.

DomainKeys Identified Mail (DKIM)   An e-mail authentication technique that allows the receiver to check whether an e-mail was sent and authorized by the owner of that domain. This is achieved by adding a digital signature to the headers of an e-mail message, providing a mechanism to validate the authenticity and integrity of the e-mail.

domain generation algorithm (DGA)   A threat actor technique used to generate domain names rapidly using seemingly random but predictable processes. This enables malware to connect eventually with its command and control (C2) infrastructure without providing defenders the opportunity to identify and block the domains.

endpoint detection and response (EDR)   A solution that provides continuous monitoring of end-user devices, enabling the detection and response to mitigate cyber threats. Also known as *endpoint detection and threat response* (EDTR).

Entity Behavior Analytics (EBA)   A process that utilizes data analytics to identify anomalous behavior or actions by entities on a network.

event   Any occurrence that can be observed, verified, and documented.

eXtensible Markup Language (XML)   A markup language that defines a set of rules for encoding documents in a format that is both human-readable and machine-readable.

false negative   Lack of data or indication that a given condition is not present, when in fact the condition is present, as shown by additional research and data. Also referred to as a Type II error.

false positive   A piece of data or an indication that a given condition is present when in fact it is not.

federation   The use of a digital identity and assisted credentials to gain access to various services across organizations using a common credential broker.

file carving   A technique independent of the file system used to fully recover partially recovered files or those discovered to be damaged.

File Integrity Monitoring (FIM)   A security solution that continually monitors and verifies the integrity of files and directories on a system in order detect unauthorized changes.

file system   A logical structure created and maintained by the operating system for managing files on media such as a hard disk.

firewall   A device that permits the flow of authorized data through it while preventing unauthorized data flows.

firmware   Software that is stored in read-only, nonvolatile memory in a device and is executed when the device is powered on.

forensic acquisition   The process of extracting the digital contents from seized evidence so that they may be analyzed.

fuzzing   A technique used to discover flaws and vulnerabilities in software by sending large amounts of malformed, unexpected, or random data to the target program in order to trigger failures.

hardening   The process of securing information systems by reducing their vulnerabilities and functionality.

hashing function   A one-way function that takes a variable-length sequence of data such as a file and produces a fixed-length result called a "hash value." Sometimes referred to as a digital fingerprint.

Health Insurance Portability and Accountability Act (HIPAA)   A US federal law that sets standards and mandates security and privacy rules for healthcare providers, health plans, and other entities that handle health information to ensure the safeguarding of patient data.

heuristic   A "rule of thumb" or any other experience-based, imperfect approach to problem-solving.

heuristic analysis The application of heuristics to find threats in practical, if imperfect, ways.

honeynet A network of devices created for the sole purpose of luring an attacker into trying to compromise it.

host-based intrusion detection system (HIDS) An IDS that is focused on the behavior of a specific host and packets on its network interfaces.

identity and access management (IAM) A framework of policies and technologies used to manage and control user access to various resources, ensuring that individuals have the appropriate permissions to access specific data and systems, while preventing unauthorized users from gaining access.

incident One or more related events that compromise the organization's security posture.

incident response The process of negating the effects of an incident on an information system.

indicator of activity (IoA) A pattern of activities or behaviors that may indicate potential threats or malicious actions.

indicator of compromise (IoC) An artifact that indicates the possibility of an attack or compromise.

industrial control system (ICS) A cyber-physical system that enables specialized software to control the physical behaviors of some system.

Infrastructure as a Service (IaaS) A cloud computing model in which a service provider offers direct access to a cloud-based infrastructure on which customers can build and configure their own devices.

input validation An approach to protect systems from abnormal user input by testing the data provided against appropriate values.

insecure direct object reference (IDOR) A vulnerability that occurs when an application allows an attacker to access or manipulate data directly by modifying the object's identifier, usually a URL parameter, without proper authorization.

International Organization for Standardization (ISO) An independent, nongovernmental international organization that is the world's largest developer and publisher of international standards.

Internet of Things (IoT) The broad term for Internet-connected, nontraditional computing devices such as televisions and refrigerators.

intrusion detection system (IDS) A system that identifies violations of security policies and generates alerts.

intrusion prevention system (IPS)   A form of IDS that is able to stop any detected violations.

isolation   A state in which a part of an information system, such as a compromised host, is prevented from communicating with the rest of the system.

IT service management (ITSM)   The planning, delivery, and support of IT services through the coordination of people, processes, and technology. In the context of software, ITSM streamlines IT processes, such as incident management, problem resolution, change management, and service requests.

jailbreaking (iOS) and rooting (Android)   Jailbreaking and rooting are processes that elevate privileges to bypass software restrictions imposed by the operating system, typically mobile operating systems such as iOS and Android. This allows the user to access and modify system files and settings, install unauthorized apps, and customize their devices beyond what is typically allowed by the manufacturer.

legal hold   An administrative process that organizations often make use of during digital forensic investigations. A legal hold entails retaining a device in a secure storage area and not allowing it to be used until an investigation has concluded.

machine learning (ML)   A subset of artificial intelligence (AI) that involves the development of algorithms and statistical models, enabling computers to improve their performance on a specific task through experience or data input without being explicitly programmed to do so.

mean time to detect (MTTD)   A measurement that attempts to convey the time between the beginning of an incident and the time it is detected by people or systems in the organization.

mean time to remediate   Metric indicating the time it takes to remediate issues related to an incident.

mean time to respond (MTTR)   Metric that tells stakeholders how long it took the organization to respond, typically from the moment the incident had any detectable indicators to the time a response was initiated.

MITRE ATT&CK   The MITRE Corporation's Adversarial Tactics, Techniques, and Common Knowledge (ATT&CK) framework is a model that enables organizations to document and exchange attacker tactics, techniques, and procedures (TTPs).

multifactor authentication (MFA)   Authentication techniques that require multiple pieces of information to authenticate a user.

National Institute for Standards and Technology (NIST)   An organization within the U.S. Department of Commerce that is charged with promoting innovation and industrial competitiveness.

NetFlow   A network protocol designed to collect and analyzes network traffic data. It provides information about the flow of data in a network, including source address, destination address, source port, destination port, start time, end time, packet size, bytes transferred, and other important metrics.

network access control (NAC)   A solution that manages and enforces access policies for devices seeking to connect to a network by ensuring that only authorized and compliant devices can access network resources.

network-based intrusion detection system (NIDS)   An IDS that is focused on the packets traversing a network.

Network Time Protocol (NTP)   TCP protocol used to ensure time synchronization between devices.

network segmentation   The practice of separating various parts of the network into subordinate zones to thwart adversaries' efforts, improve traffic management, and prevent spillover of sensitive data.

nmap   A popular open source tool that provides the ability to map network hosts and the ports on which they are listening.

on-path attack   An attack in which an adversary intercepts communications between two endpoints to obtain illicit access to message contents and potentially alter them (previously known as a *man-in-the-middle* attack).

on-premises   Infrastructure model where all resources are hosted within the organization's own logical and physical infrastructure.

open source intelligence (OSINT)   The collection and analysis of publicly available information appearing in print or electronic form.

Open Source Security Testing Methodology Manual (OSSTMM)   A security testing framework and methodology that provides guidelines and procedures designed to assess security controls, identify weaknesses, and improve overall information security. It covers various aspects of security testing, including penetration testing, vulnerability assessments, and security audits.

Open Web Application Security Project (OWASP)   An organization that promotes web security and provides development guidelines, testing procedures, and code review steps.

OpenIOC   A framework to organize indicators of compromise (IoC) in a machine-readable format for easy sharing and automated follow-up.

operational control   Security mechanisms implemented primarily through people and procedures.

P2P (peer-to-peer)   A decentralized communication model where computers and devices in a network directly connect and communicate with each other, without the need for a central server.

packet analyzer   A tool that captures network traffic, performs some form of analysis on it, and reports the results. Also known as a network or packet sniffer.

password spraying   A type of brute-force technique in which an attacker tries a single password against a system and then iterates though multiple systems on a network using the same password.

passwordless authentication   Any method of authentication that does not use a password as an authenticator, such as multifactor authentication.

patch management   The process by which fixes to software vulnerabilities are identified, tested, applied, validated, and documented.

patching   The application of a fix to a software defect.

Payment Card Industry Data Security Standard (PCI DSS)   A global standard for protecting stored, processed, or transmitted payment card information.

penetration test   The process of simulating attacks on a network and its systems at the request of the owner or senior management for the purpose of measuring an organization's level of resistance to those attacks and to uncover any exploitable weaknesses within the environment.

personal health information (PHI)   Information that relates to an individual's past, present, or future physical or mental health condition.

personally identifiable information (PII)   Information, such as Social Security number or biometric profile, that can be used to distinguish an individual's identity.

phishing   The use of fraudulent e-mail messages to induce recipients to provide sensitive information or take actions that could compromise their information systems. Phishing is a form of social engineering.

physical control   A safeguard that deters, delays, prevents, detects, or responds to threats against physical property.

Platform as a Service (PaaS)   A cloud computing model in which a service provider offers cloud-based platforms on which customers can either use preinstalled applications or install and run their own.

playbook   An automated workflow that assists in visualizing and executing complex processes across a security infrastructure.

plug-in   A piece of code developed to provide additional functionality or enhanced functionality to an application such as a vulnerability scanner.

potentially unwanted application/potentially unwanted program (PUP/PUA) Software that might be considered unwanted or unnecessary, often exhibiting undesired behavior. These applications are not inherently malicious but may introduce security risks, consume network resources, or violate the organization's security policies.

Privileged Access Management (PAM) A critical security function that enforces the concept of least privilege, using technical controls and periodic reviews.

proxy An intermediary device or software that acts as a gateway between a user's device, an application, and the Internet. When a user requests a resource from the Internet, the request is first sent to the proxy, which then forwards it to the target server. The response from the target server is sent back to the proxy, which then relays it to the user's device or application.

public key infrastructure (PKI) A framework of programs, procedures, communication protocols, and public key cryptography that enables a diverse group of individuals to communicate securely.

purple team A collaborative approach that combines the "red team" and "blue team." The red team attempts to breach the organization's defenses, while the blue team responds to the simulated attacks from the red team.

red team A group that acts as the adversary during a security assessment or exercise.

regression testing The formal process by which code that has been modified is tested to ensure that no features and security characteristics were compromised by the modifications.

regulatory environment An environment in which the way an organization exists or operates is controlled by laws, rules, or regulations put in place by a formal body.

remediation The application of security controls to a known vulnerability to reduce its risk to an acceptable level.

remote code execution (RCE) A security vulnerability that enables attackers to remotely execute arbitrary code on a target system or application.

remote file inclusion (RFI) A web application vulnerability that allows an attacker to remotely include and execute external files on a web server.

representational state transfer (REST) A software architectural style that defines a set of constraints to be used for creating web services.

reverse engineering The process of deconstructing something in order to discover its features and constituents.

risk The possibility of damage to or loss of any information system asset, as well as the ramifications should this occur.

risk acceptance   The decision that the potential loss from a risk is not severe enough to warrant spending resources to avoid it.

risk appetite   The overall amount of risk that senior executives are willing to assume for the organization.

risk avoidance   One of the ways organizations respond to risk by simply avoiding the activities that incur unacceptable risk.

risk mitigation   One of the ways of responding to risk in which risk is reduced to an acceptable level through security controls.

risk tolerance   The amount of risk deviation that senior managers are willing to accept from the organizational risk appetite level for a specific business venture.

risk transference   The risk response method that involves sharing risk with another organization such as an insurance company or other third party.

role-based access control (RBAC)   An access control model that restricts system access based on roles, or "groups," assigned to individual accounts.

rootkit   A typically malicious software application that interferes with the normal reporting of an operating system, often by hiding specific resources such as files, processes, and network connections.

Runtime Application Self-Protection (RASP)   A security technology that is embedded directly into an application's runtime environment, designed to monitor and protect applications while they are running by detecting and blocking potential attacks in real time.

sandbox   A type of control that isolates processes from the operating system to prevent security violations.

sanitization   The process by which access to data on a given medium is made infeasible for a given level of effort.

Secure Access Secure Edge (SASE)   A security model that combines the concepts of software-defined wide area networking and zero trust, with services delivered through cloud-based deployments.

Secure/Multipurpose internet Mail Extensions (S/MIME)   A cryptographic e-mail security standard that enables digitally signed and encrypted e-mail to verify sender authenticity and protect sensitive information during transit.

Secure Shell (SSH)   A cryptographic network protocol similar to telnet, providing secure remote access to networked devices and servers over an unsecured network.

Secure Sockets Layer (SSL)   A now obsolete cryptographic protocol, superseded by TLS, that was used to establish a secure and encrypted connection between a web server and a user's web browser, ensuring the confidentiality and integrity of data during transmission.

Security Assertion Markup Language (SAML) An open standard for exchanging authentication and authorization data between parties, specifically between an identity provider and a service provider.

Security Content Automation Protocol (SCAP) A protocol developed by NIST for the assessment and reporting of vulnerabilities in the information systems of an organization.

security information and event management (SIEM) A software product that collects, aggregates, analyzes, reports, and stores security information.

security orchestration, automation, and response (SOAR) An integration of security tools that allows organizations to collect security data and perform complex security tasks.

security policy An overall general statement produced by senior management (or a selected policy board or committee) that dictates what role security plays within the organization or that dictates mandatory requirements for a given aspect of security.

Sender Policy Framework (SPF) An e-mail authentication technique that helps prevent e-mail spoofing by allowing domain owners to specify which mail servers are authorized to send e-mails on their behalf.

server-side request forgery (SSRF) An exploit where an attacker abuses a server's functionality to access or manipulate information that is usually not directly accessible to them within the server's realm. By exploiting vulnerable server parameters, an attacker can potentially interact with internal systems, scan the network, and retrieve sensitive information.

serverless architecture Architecture model using the concepts of virtualization and containerization to deliver services to users without a server infrastructure.

service-oriented architecture (SOA) A set of interconnected but self-contained software components that communicate with each other and with their clients through standardized protocols called application program interfaces (APIs).

session hijacking A class of attacks by which an attacker takes advantage of valid session information, often by stealing and replaying it.

Simple API for XML (SAX) A streaming XML API that provides an efficient method for reading and parsing large XML files, without requiring the entire document to be loaded into memory.

Simple Object Access Protocol (SOAP) An SOA messaging protocol that uses XML over HTTP to enable clients to invoke processes on a remote host in a platform-agnostic way.

single pane of glass (SPOG) A concept of security operations that consolidates the various data feeds and sources of security information flowing into an organization so they can be parsed, correlated, and analyzed to a certain degree before the user even sees them.

single sign-on (SSO)   An authentication mechanism that enables a user to log in once with a single set of credentials and gain access to multiple related but separate systems.

social engineering   The manipulation of people with the intent of deceiving or persuading them to take actions that they otherwise wouldn't take—and that typically involve a violation of a security policy or procedures.

Software as a Service (SaaS)   A software distribution model in which a service provider hosts applications for customers and makes them available to customers via the Internet.

software composition analysis (SCA)   An engineering practice that involves identifying and assessing the open source components and third-party libraries used in software applications. SCA tools analyze these components for known vulnerabilities and licensing issues.

software-defined networking (SDN)   A network architecture in which software applications are responsible for deciding how best to route data (the control layer) and then for actually moving those packets around (the data layer).

spear phishing   Phishing attempts directed at a specific individual or group.

static application security testing (SAST)   A security testing methodology that scans the source code of an application to identify potential vulnerabilities and security weaknesses.

static code analysis   A technique that is meant to help identify software defects or security policy violations and is carried out by examining the code without executing the program.

stress test   A test that places extreme demands that are well beyond the planning thresholds of the software in an effort to determine how robust it is.

Structured Query Language injection (SQLi)   An attack that exploits vulnerabilities in a web application's input fields to insert malicious SQL statements.

Structured Threat Information eXpression (STIX)   A standardized language for conveying data about cybersecurity threats in a way that can be easily understood by humans and security technologies.

supervisory control and data acquisition (SCADA) system   A system for remotely monitoring and controlling physical systems such as power and manufacturing plants over large geographic regions.

symmetric cryptography   A cryptosystem that uses the same shared secret key for both encryption and decryption.

syslog   A popular protocol used to communicate event messages.

PART IV

tactics, techniques, procedures (TTPs)   A framework used to categorize and analyze threats and attacks. *Tactics* are the high-level objectives of attackers. *Techniques* are the specific methods used to achieve the tactics. *Procedures* outline the processes followed by attackers to execute their techniques successfully.

technical control   A software or hardware tool used to restrict access to objects. Also known as a logical control.

threat hunting   The proactive process of thoroughly examining the infrastructure for potential threats based on intelligence.

threat intelligence   Raw threat data given context and meaning in a usable manner.

time-of-check to time-of-use (TOCTOU)   A vulnerability that arises when a program checks a resource at one point in time (time-of-check) and then uses the resource at a later point in time (time-of-use). The time gap between the check and the use can be exploited by an attacker to modify the resource's state, leading to undesired behavior or unauthorized access.

Transport Layer Security (TLS)   A cryptographic protocol that provides a secure channel over a computer network, ensuring the confidentiality, integrity, and authenticity of data transmitted between two systems.

trend analysis   The study of patterns over time in order to determine how, when, and why they change.

true negative   Data proving that a specific condition is in fact not present.

true positive   Data indicating that a given condition is in fact present.

Trusted Automated eXchange of Indicator Information (TAXII)   An application protocol that defines how cyber threat intelligence, specifically that formatted in accordance with the STIX standard, may be shared among participating partners.

User Behavior Analytics (UBA)   A process that utilizes data analytics to identify anomalous behavior or actions by users on a network.

virtual desktop infrastructure (VDI)   A virtualization technology that separates the physical devices the users are touching from the systems hosting the desktops, applications, and data, typically resulting in a thin-client environment.

virtual private network (VPN)   A system that connects two or more devices that are physically part of separate networks and enables them to exchange data as if they were connected to the same local area network.

vulnerability   A flaw in an information system that can enable an adversary to compromise the security of that system.

web application firewall (WAF)   An application layer firewall that inspects, filters, and potentially blocks HTTP requests and responses. WAFs are designed to protect web applications from a variety of attacks, including SQL injection (SQLi), cross-site scripting (XSS), and other application layer attacks.

webhook   Simple code written to automatically transfer messages and data back and forth between web-based applications.

whaling   Spear phishing aimed at high-profile targets such as executives.

white team (white cell)   The group of people who plan, document, assess, or moderate a training exercise.

Windows registry   A proprietary database containing all configuration settings for the Windows operating system.

write blocker   A device that prevents modifications to a storage device while its contents are being acquired.

XML external entity (XXE) attack   An XML-based exploit that occurs when an XML input with a reference to an external entity is handled by a poorly configured XML parser, potentially leading to the disclosure of confidential data, denial of service (DoS), server-side request forgery (SSRF), and other system impacts.

zero-day   A vulnerability or exploit that is unknown to the broader community of software developers and security professionals.

zero trust   A security model characterized by the belief that no entity should inherently trust another entity on the network and that trust must be periodically reestablished and verified.

PART IV

INDEX